Harwich Submarines in the Great War

The First Submarine Campaign of the Royal Navy in 1914

Mark Harris

Helion & Company Limited

To the memory of my father, Raymond G.H. Harris and my mother, Ellen Harris, whose stories of service in the Second World War inspired me to write military history.

Helion & Company Limited
Unit 8 Amherst Business Centre
Budbrooke Road
Warwick
CV34 5WE
England
Tel. 01926 499 619
Email: info@helion.co.uk
Website: www.helion.co.uk
Twitter: @helionbooks
Visit our blog at blog.helion.co.uk

Published by Helion & Company 2021
Designed and typeset by Mary Woolley (www.battlefield-design.co.uk)
Cover designed by Paul Hewitt, Battlefield Design (www.battlefield-design.co.uk)

Text © Mark Harris 2021
Images © as individually credited
Maps © Mark Harris 2021

ISBN 978-1-914059-97-1

British Library Cataloguing-in-Publication Data.
A catalogue record for this book is available from the British Library.

For details of other military history titles published by Helion & Company Limited contact the above address or visit our website: http://www.helion.co.uk.

We always welcome receiving book proposals from prospective authors.

Contents

Foreword

The entire history of the Royal Navy submarine service is marked by stories of human and technical endeavour. Whether it be the early pioneers who first operated in the hostile underwater environment or those today exploiting the cutting edge of technology to contribute to the safety and security of our nation. What is common to both is the fact that being underwater in a submarine is, and always has been, a hazardous activity. To keep safe and be an effective and deadly fighting capability certainly requires a technological superiority, but it needs more than that; it needs a certain type of person willing to master the risks, environment and hardships and exploit them to achieve the upper hand on an adversary.

The significant contribution made by submariners in the Great War is often overlooked. Prominent in most people minds would be their exploits during the Second World War and maybe more recently the Cold War and subsequent operations. However, as this book accurately captures and comprehensively describes submariners made a real campaign winning contribution during the Great War and perhaps none more so than those of the 8th Submarine Flotilla operating out of Harwich and in the backyard of the German High Sea Fleet. This dramatic story is a critically important part of the embryonic development of Royal Navy submarine service and, until publication of this comprehensive account has not been widely acknowledged.

I recollect being told stories of how my Grandfather made an early version of a float flood alarm from a tin can, a 2.5v battery, cork and torch lamp. The story may not have been entirely accurate (most submariners would be familiar with the adage don't spoil a good "dit" with the truth), but it certainly left me with the impression of just how basic submarines were in my Grandfather's day; he served from 1919 until 1935 and then again after being recalled for further service in submarines from 1939 until 1943. When I joined my first diesel submarine, I must admit I was surprised to be told about "Cobwebs Day" where we dived in area Keyhole south of the Isle of White to see "where we leaked"; maybe not too great a different experience from that of my Grandfathers. I went on to command a nuclear submarine, head up the submarine training organisation and command the Devonport and Faslane Flotillas. Throughout my time in submarines, I was constantly amazed by the dedication and professionalism of all those I served alongside and was fortunate enough to command; some things have not changed.

In this well researched and presented book Mark Harris brings to life just what the 8th Submarine Flotilla contributed to the war effort. It provides colour and detail to allow the reader to appreciate the skill and daring of the men involved in this very important first campaign of the young Royal Navy submarine service. It highlights the lessons learned and experience gained; many of which have helped develop where the service is today and provides an important reference that any military historian or naval enthusiast will find immensely valuable.

Rear Admiral Jonathan Westbrook CBE
Chairman of The Society of Friends of the Royal Navy Submarine Museum, Cornwall
7 May 2021

Acknowledgements

My thanks go first to the Committee of the Friends of the Royal Navy Submarine Museum (RNSM) and the Submarine Service community for their support and encouragement for the project. In particular to Rear Admiral Jonathan Westbrook CBE for his foreword.

Thanks are due to those individuals who have generously permitted the use of material in the book:

Mal Blenkinsop and RN Subs, Website of the Barrow Submariners Association, <http://rnsubs.co.uk/> for reference material on submarine design. Darren Brown for making available a number of rarely seen images from his collection and his background research used in captioning them. Michael H. Clemmesen for use of material from his article 'E11s Problemer – HAVMANDENS lykke', published in *Marinehistorisk Tidsskrift* and for assistance with Danish translation. Alex Franke, webmaster of <http://www.thefrankes.com>, for the use of images from the family's historical archive. Keith Hiscock for information and use of material in relation to *D.2* and his grandfather, Petty Officer LTO Arthur Hiscock DSM. Michael Lowrey for help with material from *U-Boat Kriegstagebuchen*. Bryan Williamson CD for the use of the image from his collection.

Numerous other relatives, friends and acquaintances are also to be thanked for their support or encouragement, including John Spence, grandson of Commander F.H.H. Goodhart.

Thanks are due to the following bodies for their kind permissions for the use of quotations, information and images:

Forsvarsgalleriet of the Danish Forsvaret for the use of the image from their archive. Naval History and Heritage Command (NH) of the U.S. Navy for the use of images from their archive. The Imperial War Museum for quotations from the private papers of Captain O.E. Hallifax, Commander F.H.H. Goodhart and Vice Admiral Sir Cecil Talbot. The Trustees of the National Museum of the Royal Navy for the use of images from the RNSM photographic archive and quotations from the Memoir of Commander R.R. Turner. The National Records of Scotland (NRS) for the use of images from their photographic archive. The Navy Records Society for quotations from The Keyes Papers. The Swedish Sjöhistoriska Museet for use of an image from their archive.

The research to complete the book would not have been possible without the work of the staff of the various archives that have made their material accessible and especially those of the UK National Archives over numerous visits.

Most of all my thanks go to my wife Mandy for her sound advice and enduring the ups and downs of the writing process with me over the three years it took to complete the work.

Glossary & Notes

Airship: Any lighter than air aircraft using hydrogen for buoyancy. Includes non-rigid types operated by all combatants and the rigid types operated by Germany.

Destroyer: sea-going fast torpedo craft also carrying significant gun armament. The term is contemporary, but also applies to the British Torpedo Boat Destroyer, or TBD and the German Grosse-Torpedoboot or Hochsee-Torpedoboot.

Drop Keel: On a submarine a heavy part of the keel, which forms the lower part of the hull. This could be detached, forcing the submarine to the surface in an emergency.

Knot: one nautical mile per hour. Approximately 1.15 land miles per hour, or 1.85 kilometres per hour.

Mile: A nautical mile, the international measure of distance at sea. Traditionally one minute of latitude; about 2,025 yards or 1,852 metres.

Torpedo Boat: small coastal torpedo craft, with limited range and sea-going abilities.

Zeppelin: A large, long range airship with rigid construction, named after its inventor.

All military ranks and place names are contemporary spellings in the relevant language. There are a few exceptions for place names where there are widely accepted English language equivalents, such as Heligoland, rather than Helgoland.

All translations of quoted passages into English are by the author.

All times are in Greenwich Mean Time, which is one hour behind the Central European Time used in German sources.

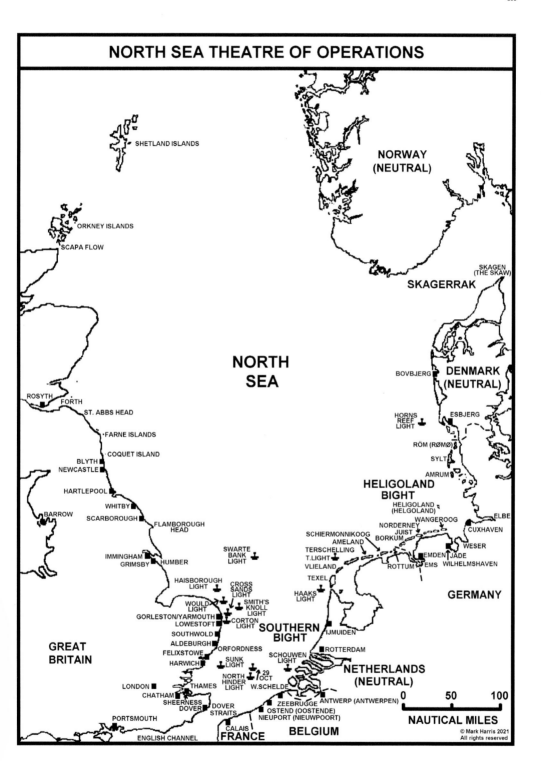

NORTH SEA THEATRE OF OPERATIONS

SHETLAND ISLANDS

NORWAY
(NEUTRAL)

ORKNEY ISLANDS

SCAPA FLOW

SKAGEN
(THE SKAW)

SKAGERRAK

NORTH
SEA

BOVBJERG

DENMARK
(NEUTRAL)

ROSYTH
FORTH

ST. ABBS HEAD

HORNS
REEF
LIGHT

ESBJERG

FARNE ISLANDS

RÖM (RØMØ)

COQUET ISLAND

SYLT

BLYTH
NEWCASTLE

AMRUM

HARTLEPOOL

HELIGOLAND
BIGHT

WHITBY

BARROW

SCARBOROUGH

FLAMBOROUGH
HEAD

HELIGOLAND
(HELGOLAND)

WANGEROOG

ELBE

NORDERNEY
JUIST

CUXHAVEN

SCHIERMONNIKOOG
AMELAND
BORKUM

WESER

SWARTE
BANK
LIGHT

TERSCHELLING
T.LIGHT

EMDEN JADE

IMMINGHAM
GRIMSBY

HUMBER

VLIELAND

ROTTUM EMS

WILHELMSHAVEN

HAISBOROUGH
LIGHT

TEXEL

GERMANY

CROSS
SANDS
LIGHT

HAAKS
LIGHT

WOULD
LIGHT

SMITH'S
KNOLL
LIGHT

GORLESTON/YARMOUTH
LOWESTOFT

CORTON
LIGHT

SOUTHWOLD

SOUTHERN
BIGHT

IJMUIDEN

ALDEBURGH

GREAT
BRITAIN

ORFORDNESS

FELIXSTOWE

SCHOUWEN
LIGHT

ROTTERDAM

HARWICH

SUNK
LIGHT

29
OCT

NORTH
HINDER
LIGHT

W.SCHELDE

NETHERLANDS
(NEUTRAL)

LONDON

THAMES

CHATHAM

ANTWERP (ANTWERPEN)

SHEERNESS
DOVER

ZEEBRUGGE

OSTEND (OOSTENDE)

0   50   100

PORTSMOUTH

DOVER
STRAITS

NIEUPORT (NIEUWPOORT)

NAUTICAL MILES

CALAIS

ENGLISH CHANNEL

FRANCE

BELGIUM

1

The boats and their crews

'The submarine has entirely altered the conditions in our operational base in the German Bight, bringing constant danger and surveillance to this confined area, which we have no means of avoiding. In favourable weather conditions the German Fleet will be literally blockaded in the estuaries by enemy submarines unless it is prepared to expose itself to the risk of significant losses.'[1] So wrote the commander of the German Fleet, Admiral von Ingehohl, in September 1914. The 8th Submarine Flotilla was the enemy causing Ingenohl's problems. This is the story of the dramatic impact their boats and crews created in the first campaign of the Royal Navy's Submarine Service.

The Submarine Service was only 13 years old when it first went to war. Technical developments were revolutionising naval warfare at the beginning of the twentieth century. Torpedoes were becoming an ever greater threat. A single torpedo hit could sink a ship. Then came the submarine, able to deliver torpedo attack from the unseen depths, in which it was almost invulnerable to attack. The threat of torpedo attack by swarms of torpedo boats and submarines meant the end of the traditional naval tactics of blockading the enemy fleet in port, leaving its ships relatively free to come and go from their own harbours.

At first submarines had only a short range, with limited sea-keeping abilities. The Royal Navy regarded them as a cheap substitute for static minefields, able to shield the ports where they were based and the nearby coastline from attack.

As designs improved, the newest submarines were able to operate at longer range in the open sea. Submarines now offered the opportunity to lie in wait off enemy ports and coasts, to both monitor and attack ships as they came in and out.

By 1914 Britain had the largest submarine force in the world; a total of 68 boats, mostly intended for coastal defence. The 17 bigger and more seaworthy boats of the latest D and E classes were intended for offensive operations and were known as overseas boats. *D.1* had commissioned in September 1909 and quickly made her mark in the 1910 manoeuvres, 'torpedoing' two cruisers off the 'enemy' fleet base. She had been followed by seven more of her class. The improved E class began entering service in May 1913 and nine of these boats were in service by July 1914, with seven more on the way in various stages of construction. Another two were ordered as soon

---

1   Otto Groos, *Der Krieg zur See 1914–1918 – Der Krieg in der Nordsee Band 2* (Berlin: Mittler & Sohn, 1922), p.24, correspondence with Chief of Naval Staff.

as war broke out. A number of experimental boats and boats trialling foreign designs were also in various stages of construction.[2]

As first the Ds, then the Es were completed, they were formed into the 8th (Overseas) Submarine Flotilla. In order to understand how the Flotilla operated, it is necessary to understand the capabilities of the submarines and their crews.

The E class was the backbone of the offensive submarine force of the Royal Navy in the Great War. They carried a crew of 29–30. This included three officers; the commander and two junior officers to share watches, 15 in the engineering department, four seamen, three torpedo specialists, two coxswains to steer the boat, a telegrapher for the wireless if there was one, a signaller and a cook. There was a smaller crew of 25 in the earlier D class. Their twin diesel engines could propel them at a top speed of 15 knots, and enough fuel was carried to cruise for 2,600 miles, but they could only be used on the surface. When submerged they relied on their electric motors. These were powered by batteries, which took up a large amount of the hull space. They could propel the boat at a top speed of around 10 knots when submerged, but this speed would quickly drain the batteries. *D.1* was typical of the early boats, with an endurance of just one hour at nine knots, or four hours at seven knots. This meant that most warships could quickly escape from the position of a submerged submarine once detected. Battery life could be extended if a boat stopped its motors and lay on the bottom. As the boats were only certified to dive to 100 feet (30m), this could only be done in shallow water. A flat battery would force the submarine to surface to re-charge by running the diesels, exposing it to whatever dangers were there. It took several hours to build up a full charge.

The striking power of the submarines was provided by their torpedo armament. Guns were not carried, with the exception of an experimental mounting in *D.4*. The first eight E boats had four 18-inch (45cm) torpedo tubes. These were in a compartment at the bow, firing directly ahead, a compartment at the stern, firing directly aft and a beam tube compartment amidships, with one tube firing to starboard and one to port at 90 degrees to the boat's hull.[3] A total of eight torpedoes were carried, one in each tube and one reload for each. From *E.9* onwards the bow armament was increased to a pair of tubes side by side, bringing the total torpedoes carried to ten. The earlier D boats had only three tubes (two at the bow, one above the other and one at the stern) and six torpedoes. Their 18-inch torpedoes delivered an explosive warhead of 200–210lb (90–95kg) of wet guncotton, enough to sink a small warship with one hit.[4]

The success of a boat on patrol depended on its crew. Whilst in port they would work in the boat during the day, but live and eat ashore or in a depot ship. At sea submarine crews faced unique dangers. Frequent long distance patrols in war conditions were extremely exacting. Some crewmen would prove unequal to the task. Machinery and weaponry largely filled the hull, so creature comforts were almost entirely absent. At sea, food in the boats was dull and monotonous. There was only enough fresh produce for two to three days, as it would quickly spoil in the atmosphere of the boat. After this corned beef, tinned fish, soup and ships biscuits were

2   The National Archives (TNA) ADM137/2067: Commodore (S) War Records, Volume I, Reports of proceedings of submarines attached to HMS Maidstone, 1914, p.673. Two E boats were also in the Royal Australian Navy.
3   The beam is the direction directly to the side of a ship.
4   TNA ADM186/15: War Vessels and Aircraft (British and Foreign) Quarterly Return, Oct 1915, p.29; For further details of submarine classes see Appendix I.

E.12 undergoing maintenance on the floating dock. The chequered band and pendant number 92 on the conning tower suggests a date around December 1914. The two sets of horizontal rudders used to control depth, known as hydroplanes, are visible forward and aft. The bulge on the side houses the ballast tanks outside the pressure hull, assisting stability; it was known as a saddle tank. The opening for the port beam torpedo tube can be seen in the middle of it. The closed outer shutters for the port forward and stern torpedo tubes can also be seen. (NRS AAA03469 & AAA03443)

the staples. Food often had to be eaten cold. The boats had hot plates and an electric oven, but these frequently could not be used when the boat was submerged. Using any appliance drained battery power. As a result using power for something as simple as boiling a kettle required the permission of the boat's commander. Water was in short supply and was rationed during a patrol – there was barely enough for drinking, let alone washing. Sleeping arrangements for the crew were almost non-existent and generally consisted of finding a spot on the deck. Only officers had access to a bunk, or a mattress in a drawer that pulled out on the deck. The overseas boats did have toilets, but these could only be flushed on the surface or at periscope depth. The backup was a bucket partly filled with oil. Most crew tried to avoid having to use either, simply going over the side when surfaced. The atmosphere on board a dived boat became unpleasant in the extreme. It was hot, humid and smelly – $E.6$ recorded a temperature of 26½ centigrade on a patrol at the end of October. Condensation dripped from the hull overhead and crew would even sleep in their oilskins to keep dry. The air became charged with carbon dioxide after a time. The boat carried a battery of high pressure air bottles, which were needed for the torpedoes and to blow the water from the ballast tanks when surfacing. These could be used to refresh the air from time to time by releasing stored air from one bottle, whilst running the air compressor to draw the stale air into an empty bottle. The barometer had to be used to keep the air pressure stable! High levels of carbon dioxide impair consciousness. When a boat finally surfaced and aired the crew could feel a sense of dizziness and euphoria as the air returned to normal. The lives of the crew depended on a myriad of contraptions all working correctly and a mistake in drill whilst diving or surfacing could be the last one a crewman ever made. Six coastal boat crews had been lost with almost all hands in peacetime accidents.

Despite the hardships there were compensations that attracted men to the boats. All ranks received 'hard lying' money to compensate for the hardships of life on-board. This greatly boosted the pay of the lower ranks; a cause of envy for their ship-bound comrades. It also gave a much needed boost to the pay of officers of more limited means who had to rely on their pay. Formal discipline had a more pragmatic focus than that on a bigger ship. The small crew lived and worked in close proximity. There was no distance between officers and men and certainly no room for spit and polish, but high standards of performance were vital. Submarines gave the opportunity for independent command to junior officers away from the rigid hierarchy of a larger ship. The technological novelty and risk were also an attraction. It was no co-incidence that many officers were keen motor-cycle racers and amongst the few who had taken up flying.[5]

With such a small crew the commander was vital to the effectiveness of a boat. Any lack of confidence or knowledge would be quickly apparent, with a dramatic effect on morale and efficiency. Over familiarity in the confines of the boat risked lax discipline. The success in any attack was also almost entirely dependent on the skill of the commander. There was no access to sophisticated devices to calculate a firing solution. There were tables of courses, speed and target angles that could be referred to, but most commanders relied on experience to gauge the course and speed of the target, then steer to reach the sweet spot around 500 yards (450m) away to its side. However, if the commander made a mistake and got closer than about 200 yards (180m) the torpedo would miss under the target, as after firing torpedoes dived deep until they picked

5   Imperial War Museum (IWM) Sound_721: William Halter – Oral History. A rare insight from the lower ranks into life in the Flotilla.

up speed, then gradually came up to the set depth. The torpedo could also dive to the bottom and never come up if the boat was not level when fired. The quality of the commander and crew were critical, but issues with armament and technology also affected the way the boats carried out their attacks and patrols.

The doctrine of short range torpedo attack meant that relatively unsophisticated torpedoes were carried. The overseas submarines had been re-armed in 1912 with 18-inch (45cm) Mark V* torpedoes, supplemented by the more recent Mark VI, both of which were cold torpedoes. This type of torpedo simply relied on the expansion of compressed air to drive its engines. Various settings could be chosen, with ranges from 1,000 to 4,000 yards (910–3,660m) and speeds from 35 to 18½ knots. Long ranges required low speed settings. This meant more time to target, amplifying the impact of any errors in estimating course or speed. It also gave the target longer to spot and evade the torpedo, which left a trail of bubbles in its wake. Fast settings were therefore preferred with the doctrine of short range attacks, but it was not possible to adjust the selected setting at short notice. Indeed it was extremely difficult to change it at all whilst at sea to attack a target at longer range.[6]

Submarines could attack from a distance in the general direction of a large group of ships, or at a high value target that the submarine was not fast enough to close – referred to as browning shots. To enable this it had been decided in 1913 that longer range heater torpedoes should be supplied to replace cold torpedoes in the forward tubes of all overseas submarines.[7] It took time for these torpedoes to become available and submarine logs reveal that two were finally issued to each boat from September to December 1914. Heater torpedoes got their name from a jet of burning fuel used to heat the compressed air that drove the torpedo engine, massively improving range or speed. Those issued were mainly the very latest Mark VII**, with ranges of 3,000 yards (2,750m) at 41 knots and an alternative slow setting giving 7,000 yards (6,400m) at 29 knots. With a bit of notice, the pre-set fast or slow setting could also be selected at sea on these heater torpedoes.[8] Another consideration for the commander was that all torpedoes had to be adjusted to run at the right depth to suit the target, and this also required some notice to change. A torpedo set to hit a battleship would run underneath a destroyer, whilst a torpedo set to hit a destroyer would risk hitting the side armour of a battleship, greatly reducing damage. As a result depth was pre-set for the most likely target.

However, attack at longer range required more than a long range torpedo. Each overseas boat carried two retractable periscopes, which were used for underwater observation and attack respectively. The attack periscope was the only way for the commander to identify the target and its course and speed whilst submerged. This was difficult at the best of times, especially if the sea was rough, but at long range it required very good optics. Unfortunately, British periscopes had a miserable reputation for quality that had resulted from a monopoly being given to an indifferent supplier, Howard Grubb. Visits arranged to overseas navies (Germany, France and Italy) had revealed that all had far better periscopes, in terms of both their optics and their mechanics. Six periscopes were obtained from Germany and one from France. *S.1*, shortly to be completed

6   TNA ADM189/33: Torpedo School Annual Report 1913, p.12; TNA ADM189/31: Torpedo School Annual Report 1911, pp.13, 51.
7   TNA ADM189/32: Torpedo School Annual Report 1912, p.38.
8   TNA ADM189/35: Torpedo School Annual Report 1915, pp.31–2; Details of torpedoes used in submarines are in Appendix II.

The control room of *E.50* looking aft. In the centre is the forward periscope, with the ladder up to the conning tower behind it. The two beam torpedo tubes can be seen at floor level behind the ladder. To port is the steering wheel and the edge of the chart table. The large wheel to starboard controls the angle of the aft hydroplanes, with the gyrocompass behind it. Another wheel just out of shot controlled the forward hydroplanes. (NRS AAA03496)

to an Italian design, was to receive Italian periscopes made under licence. The lessons learned from foreign designs and the threat of competition had resulted in improvements by Grubb in the latest periscopes, but the position was still not fully satisfactory. The effect on attacks is hard to quantify, but it was a handicap their German opposite numbers did not have to deal with.

Assuming the commander had correctly identified the target, got a torpedo with the right settings and had managed to work out how to reach an attack position correctly, when he got there, the chosen torpedo tube also had to be pointed at the spot ahead of the target where the torpedo would cross its track. German submarines avoided this problem by making extensive use of angled gyroscopes, allowing torpedoes to turn onto a new course after leaving the tube, meaning that it was unimportant what direction the submarine was facing when it fired. However, there was no provision for angled firing in British submarines. Beam tubes were introduced in the E class to allow fire in one of four fixed directions instead. War experience would prove whether this was a good design decision.[9]

Long patrols out of sight of land meant good navigation skills were required of the officers. However, traditional compasses were particularly unreliable in a submarine. If positions could not be checked by the sun and stars big errors could build up. Electrically powered Sperry gyrocompasses and Forbes Logs to measure the distance travelled helped overcome this problem, but these were still being fitted to submarines when war broke out and had not yet had a chance to bed in. Reported positions of submarines out of sight of land therefore often became increasingly approximate on patrols.

Another bugbear for the commander were the temperamental diesel engines and electric motors. Diesels were capable of powering submarines over long distances, but the first diesel engine had only been produced in 1897. The strain of frequent war patrols put heavy demands on the new technology and the engineering hands responsible for it, with breakdown being an ever-present concern. The design used in the D boats was a particular cause for concern, especially the prototype engine in *D.1*.[10]

The final issue was that not all boats had been fitted with wireless by the time war broke out. Wireless was vital to enable communication beyond the limit of visibility. The overseas boats began being fitted with a wireless rig specially designed for submarines, the Type XI, from late 1913. Using this meant raising a 35 foot (11m) wireless mast and it could only be used on the surface. In practice it was found that the sending range of this wireless was only about 50 miles, which meant that it could not be used to report from patrols near to German bases without a nearby ship to pass on the messages, reducing the timeliness of any intelligence gathered. German submarines in contrast possessed a wireless capable of sending over long ranges.[11]

Issues with equipment aside, the Submarine Service took pride in its professionalism and expertise, reflected in its navy nickname, The Trade, which had originally been meant as a disparaging label by their surface brethren. The officers and crews were well trained for their tasks and were in no doubt that they would quickly triumph against anyone foolish enough to challenge the might of the Royal Navy. The effectiveness of both them and their submarines was about to be tested.

9   TNA ADM189/34: Torpedo School Annual Report 1914, p.46. From 1914 tubes in new boats were to be fitted for angled firing to enable potential future use. Mark VIII heater torpedoes being developed for submarines were to be fitted with blanks to permit easy upgrade for angled fire but were not yet available.
10   TNA ADM137/2067: pp.675–679, Keyes report 'Development of British Submarines', 6 April 1914.
11   TNA ADM189/33: Wireless Supplement pp.17–18. Wireless allocation to specific submarines particulars are reproduced in Appendix I

A view inside a D Class. The picture is taken looking aft from just in front of the twin diesel engines, past the electric motors, which are almost out of sight in the lower part of the hull, to the stern torpedo tube at the far end of the submarine. There were no internal bulkheads in this class. (Darren Brown Collection)

2

Preparing for war

The commander of the Royal Navy Submarine Service was Commodore Roger J.B. Keyes, who had been in post since 1910. He was aged 42 and was a gregarious, but intransigent character, with a desire to be at the heart of the action. Whilst he had no previous experience of the Submarine Service, his abundance of energy and ideas meant that he threw himself into his duties with gusto. To say that he spoke his mind to those high and low is an understatement. All of this led to his nickname in the Flotilla, 'The Arch Instigator'. A ditty was penned to describe him in the flotilla rag, the *Maidstone Muckrag* (later renamed *The Maidstone Magazine*): 'O where, O where is the Commodore gone, O where, O where can he be? With his manner blunt, and his head full of stunt, O where, O where can he be?' Keyes could also clearly take a joke or this would never have been printed. No technical expert, and knowing his limitations in this area, he assembled a Submarine Committee of experts to steer the way forward for the service. This committee had carried out an evaluation of foreign submarine designs and driven action on periscopes and gyrocompasses. Admiral de Robeck had recently evaluated him as: 'One of the best officers I have ever met. It is impossible for me to speak too highly of him. The work he has done as Commodore (S) is above praise.' [1]

The 8th Flotilla itself was commanded by Captain Arthur Kipling Waistell. He was aged 41 and had only recently moved to the Submarine Service, having been appointed in September 1913. He was a torpedo specialist and well regarded as a destroyer commander. Captain Culme-Seymour had evaluated him in 1907: 'Extremely clever & a good organiser – carries out as well as devises schemes.' Keyes thought highly of him, as just prior to the outbreak of war he recommended that Waistell should be given direction of overseas submarine operations if anything should happen to him as: '[I] am convinced that their direction could not be in better hands.' His pen portrait in *Maidstone Magazine* is that of a diligent administrator, bearing his 'anxieties and troubles' with 'courage, patience, and endurance', whilst also being fond of relaxing with an eclectic mix of 'cricket, football, jig-saws, tennis, badmington [sic] and chess'. [2]

---

1   Stopford C. Douglas (ed.), *The Maidstone Magazine – Volume 1–1915* (London: Strangeways and Sons, 1916), p.19; TNA ADM196/88/90 Officer's Service Records: Summaries of Confidential Reports, Roger John Brownlow Keyes.
2   TNA ADM137/2067: p.610; Douglas, *Maidstone Magazine*, pp.224–5; TNA ADM196/89/97 Arthur Kipling Waistell

Whilst Waistell looked after the day to day running of the Flotilla, when war came Keyes devoted most of his time to frontline command of the overseas force, the defensive routine of the numerous Local Defence Flotillas being little to his taste.

Keyes and Waistell had worked hard to prepare the Flotilla for war, which had become an increasingly likely prospect in the years leading up to 1914, as Germany built up a fleet to challenge the Royal Navy. In the event of war with Germany, Keyes understanding was that the 8th Flotilla was to be employed in offensive operations from Harwich, although the War Plans did not actually specify a location. Harwich was conveniently close to the German coastal ports where their fleet was based. The Flotilla's task was confirmed in the War Orders issued on 28 July as: 'offensive operations on the German Coasts, on the lookout for outgoing and incoming ships. It is the intention to employ the submarines initially in the Heligoland Bight, but it may be desirable to send some of these vessels to operate in the Skagerrak also.'[3]

These were the orders, but Keyes was not entirely happy with them. He had written a report on the lessons of the fleet manoeuvers of August 1913. Whilst accepting that the overseas boats could be used to watch the approaches to enemy bases, Keyes had reservations with the approach: 'The losses on such a service are certain to be heavy, for, apart from the risk the submarines would run of being caught on the surface in hazy weather … they would also run some risk of being stalked and torpedoed … by an opposing submarine.' He proposed that the overseas submarines should be used in conjunction with the fleet cruisers to attack the enemy fleet. He believed they should only later be used in the Bight when numbers had increased to the point where heavy losses could be sustained and that four flotillas would be needed to do this. The unreliability of the engines on the D class was also a concern, as they were 'liable to break down and are inaccessible to repair.' He proposed that they should be withdrawn to coastal patrol as soon as sufficient E class boats were available.[4]

The 8th Flotilla shared Harwich with the 1st and 3rd Destroyer Flotillas, which were under the orders of the senior officer of the fleet destroyer forces, Commodore Reginald Y. Tyrwhitt. Keyes and Tyrwhitt both came under the command of the Commander in Chief Home Fleet, Admiral Callaghan, who had directed that they co-operate in their missions, with the destroyers providing escort for the submarines when required. Indeed, the Flotillas had exercised together recently. However, Tyrwhitt's primary mission was patrolling the southern area of the North Sea, keeping it clear of the enemy. In 1907 Admiral Montgomery had assessed him as: 'a most excellent & valuable officer in every respect, possessed of dash, judg[emen]t & tact. The whole of his service has been in sea service.' In Tyrwhitt, Keyes found a like mind and a co-conspirator. A forceful, resolute and strong-minded character, Tyrwhitt was determined to get to sea and come to grips with the enemy.

Keyes wrote to his wife that '[Tyrwhitt] is a splendid fellow and we are such very good friends'. This was clearly reciprocated, as on the very same day Tyrwhitt wrote after a meeting with Keyes: 'Roger and I get on well and he is a great comfort to me, as he approves of my

3   TNA ADM137/818: War Plans and War Orders, Home Fleets and Detached Squadrons, October 1913 to July 1914: pp. 154, 399.
4   TNA ADM137/1926: Grand Fleet Secret Packs Volume XLVI – Number 22, Part B – Submarine Committee, pp.428-430.

arrangements and I of his. Perhaps we are a mutual admiration society,' adding: 'Roger has the *entrée* practically everywhere at the Admiralty. I sometimes wish I had it too.'[5]

The Admiralty was the nerve centre of the naval war and Keyes had an office there. Here he could influence operational planning to keep the overseas submarines at the forefront of the action. Winston Churchill, the First Lord of the Admiralty and political master of the Navy, was a key ally in this. Churchill was a warrior at heart, a kindred spirit to Keyes and a champion of all the latest technical innovations, including submarines. He had a hand in all aspects of naval strategy and operations and wrote that decision making in the war quickly focused round a group of three men in the Admiralty including himself. The others were Vice-Admiral Sturdee, Chief of the War Staff, responsible for the overall direction of operations, intelligence and planning for the Royal Navy and Admiral Battenberg, the First Sea Lord, the military head of the Navy. Keyes relationship with Churchill would be a lifeline in the coming months when his views and actions met with disapproval from Sturdee and the First Sea Lord.[6]

The full blown crisis that led to the Great War began with the mobilisation of Serbia and Austria-Hungary on 27 July, with Austria-Hungary declaring war on Serbia the day after. Britain's alliances meant that it was likely to quickly be drawn in to war.

As a result, Battenberg authorised Sturdee, who had just been appointed to his post, to issue the mobilisation War Orders for the Fleet on the 28th, sending all ships to their war stations. As a result of 'some misunderstanding' in the staff work, 8th Submarine Flotilla was ordered to concentrate at Immingham in the Humber, not at Harwich. Telegrams went out to those on leave ordering them to re-join the Flotilla at Immingham on the following afternoon.

Keyes was annoyed when he discovered that the Flotilla had been sent to the Humber. He had 'a horror of being mined in there'. If he had been German he could imagine nothing he would like more than to 'lead a destroyer attack in to the place'. The Royal Navy had been impressed by the spectacular surprise attack that Japan had launched on the Russian Fleet at Port Arthur prior to their declaration of war in 1905. Many expected their German opponents to do the same given the long, easily accessible coast and harbours on the east coast of Britain.

Keyes quickly obtained Sturdee's approval to move the Flotilla to Harwich, as long as Keyes commander, Admiral Callaghan, concurred. Ironically, Keyes had spent that morning with Callaghan, with whom he enjoyed a good relationship, going back to their days in China during the Boxer Rebellion. During this conversation Keyes was told 'pretty straight' that he was not to go to sea in the early stages of the war, which he was keen to do. He later laments to his wife that it is 'awful to think of sitting here while others are at sea'.

At 10pm Keyes finally managed to get back in touch with Callaghan about the change of base and was given 'an absolutely free hand to do whatever I like with the "overseas" [submarines].'

Keyes rushed to get the last train to Grimsby, arriving at 5am on the 30th. He jumped on the workmen's train to Immingham Dock. There he boarded the Flotilla's Depot Ship, *Maidstone*, which had only arrived at 5:30pm the previous afternoon with Waistell and the eight immediately available submarines from the peacetime base of the Flotilla in Portsmouth.[7]

5   A. Temple Patterson, *Tyrwhitt of the Harwich Force* (London: MacDonald, 1973), pp.43, 298; TNA ADM196/89/41 Reginald Yorke Tyrwhitt.
6   Winston S. Churchill, *The World Crisis 1911–1918 – Volume 1* (London: Odhams Press, 1938), pp.195-6.
7   *E.2, E.3, E.4, E.6, E.8, E.9, D.3* and *D.5.*

Maidstone with *D.3* and *D.5* alongside off Harwich. (Darren Brown Collection)

They were busy loading their full complement of torpedoes and war stores. *Maidstone* provided everything the Flotilla needed on a day to day basis and had been purpose built for the role, entering service in 1912. She carried no armament but served as an administrative hub and home for up to 12 submarines and their crews when they were not on patrol. She carried the reserve torpedoes of the Flotilla and the crew ensured that all of the 'mouldies' (as torpedoes were referred to in the Submarine Service) were maintained in good running order. A torpedo that was not regularly maintained was a torpedo that would probably not run properly when fired – if it ran at all. Her workshops and the spares she carried were also capable of fixing all but the most complex running problems the submarines would encounter. The Flotilla had a second, much smaller purpose built depot ship, *Adamant,* which had also entered service in 1912. This could support up to three submarines at a second base if required. She had arrived in the Humber at 8:30pm on the 29th with a ninth submarine, *E.7,* which had been delayed at Portsmouth by repairs.[8]

The Flotilla headed back the way they had come to Harwich at daylight on the 30th. Keyes used the voyage south to arrange with Waistell for getting the Flotilla ready for action on arrival. Practice torpedo attacks on the depot ships were carried out. *E.7* made dummy attacks

8   Roger J. B. Keyes, *The Naval Memoirs of Admiral of the Fleet Sir Roger Keyes – The Narrow Seas to the Dardanelles 1910–1915* (London: Thornton Butterworth, 1934), p.44, 60; Navy Records Society, *The Keyes Papers – Volume 1 – 1914–1918* (London: William Clowes & Sons Ltd., 1972), pp.7–9, letter to his wife 1 August 1914.

on *Maidstone* as she left the Humber. The force anchored off the Suffolk coast for the night. *E.7* fired two torpedoes in practice attacks on *Adamant* before heading in to Harwich on the following afternoon.[9] The dash from Portsmouth to Immingham and straight back to Harwich, whilst also getting the submarine and torpedoes ready for war, had put a strain on the crew of *E.7*. Much of the work had to be completed at sea on the way down from Immingham. Lieutenant Hallifax, the second in command, recorded in his diary that '[the men] were pretty well tired out after 4 nights & days hard work'.

The crews now settled into their new home, a welcome respite after the frenetic activity getting to Harwich. Lack of space on *Maidstone* and *Adamant* meant that some of the crews had to be accommodated on *Thames*. This was the depot ship for the small 5th Submarine Flotilla, made up of coastal boats responsible for local defence of the Thames Estuary. The number of officers grew with the addition of a third officer to each boat. These were allocated from training classes and reservists. Rooms were later used in the Parkeston Quay Great Eastern Hotel for officers who did not have cabins on the depot ships. A cross channel ferry, the *SS Vienna*, was moored astern of *Maidstone* from 27 August and was used as additional accommodation for both third officers and engineer crew.[10]

All 17 overseas submarines had been allocated to the Flotilla in the war plans, but not all of these were immediately ready for service, with some in dockyard hands for routine refits and repairs. The *E.3* and *E.9* had only completed their trials and joined the Flotilla on 25 July. Keyes had the oldest boat, *D.1*, re-assigned to Dover local defence as he was concerned that her engine was not reliable enough for overseas service, leaving 16 boats allocated to 8th Flotilla. The nine boats arriving with Keyes from Immingham were joined by *D.7* at Harwich. *D.2* and *D.8* arrived in the next few days as the clock ticked down to war. On 2 August *Adamant* had to make a trip to fill in gaps in her submarine stores from the Dover Flotilla depot ship *Arrogant*.

Keyes was keen to reduce his reliance on Tyrwhitt for destroyer co-operation, not to mention giving himself the option to go to sea. He had gone to the Admiralty on 31 July to ask for the allocation of two destroyers to the Flotilla.

On the morning of the 3rd he was informed that two I class 'specials', *Lurcher* and *Firedrake*, were being transferred from Dover. Both were modern destroyers, completed in 1912 by one of the world's leading destroyer builders, Yarrow, and were capable of an impressive 32 knots maximum speed with their oil fired turbine engines. They were armed with two 4-inch (10.2cm) and two 12-pdr (76mm) guns, as well as two 21-inch (53.3cm) torpedo tubes and were more than a match for most German destroyers. *Lurcher* was out on patrol when she received the new orders and broke away to head for Harwich at 8:40pm. The war was now spreading fast through Europe and the crew cleared for action as she steamed through the night, throwing encumbering spare peacetime gear over the side lest they encounter a German ambush on the way. *Lurcher* arrived at Harwich at 1:30am on the 4th and immediately topped up her oil tanks. *Firedrake* left Dover at 9:30pm on the 3rd and anchored for the night off Harwich, then headed

---

9   Torpedoes fired in practice attacks were fitted with an inert collision head and set to float for recovery at the end of their runs.
10   TNA ADM53: HM Ship Logs, *Adamant*, 28–29 July 1914; IWM:Documents.2175: Private Papers of Commander F H H Goodhart, letter to wife 20 August; IWM:Documents.20134: Private Papers of Vice Admiral Sir Cecil Talbot, 1914 Daily Diary 15 August; IWM: Documents.1003: Private Papers of Captain O E Hallifax, 1914 Daily Diary 28–31 July.

"H.M SUBMARINE. D.7"

The crew of *D.7* soon after war broke out. Their commander is absent. The officers seated in the centre are believed to be the second in command, Lieutenant Robin B. Martin and to his left, the Third Hand, Acting Lieutenant Thomas Godman RNR. (RNSM Neg. 10508)

in at first light. Unfortunately, they had both got a little caught up in the drama and had left their spare torpedoes at Dover. *Firedrake* was quickly despatched to pick them up and returned that evening![11]

Keyes adopted *Lurcher*, whilst Waistell normally used *Firedrake* when he went to sea. As well as shepherding the submarines to sea, the destroyers could act as targets for practice attacks. They also provided a way to get in touch with submarines at sea using both wireless and direct signalling. In 1913 trials had successfully been carried out with small explosive charges to communicate with submerged submarines. A pattern of charges could be thrown overboard at set intervals and the sound carried well underwater. Specially designed bells had also been fitted to two of the E boats to trial communication underwater from the boats themselves. However, underwater communication was in its infancy, so *Firedrake* and *Lurcher* carried a large black ball, which they hoisted to their foremast as a signal that they wanted submerged submarines to surface for communication.[12]

11   TNA ADM53: *Firedrake, Lurcher*, 3–4 August 1914.
12   TNA ADM189/33: p.122; TNA ADM137/2067: p.609.

Lurcher at speed. The black paintwork was typical of British and German destroyers in the North Sea throughout 1914. (NH 59911)

With the Flotilla now gathered and ready for action, on the morning of the 4th things came to a head as Britain issued an ultimatum to Germany to withdraw from their unprovoked attack on Belgium, of whose neutrality Britain was a guarantor. War would be declared unless a satisfactory answer was received by midnight. Keyes addressed the assembled crews that evening packed onto the quarterdeck of *Maidstone*. After outlining why he thought that Germany had engineered the path to war, he finished his talk with the words: 'you must go into this seeing red, that's the only way'. Half a dozen different voices now struck up half a dozen different tunes. Just as 'Rule Britannia' was getting the upper hand, Keyes stopped them, saying: 'That will do; better keep that for the end', then wished them all luck and goodnight. The officers were then briefed on his initial plans in his cabin.[13]

---

13   TNA ADM53: *Maidstone*, 29 July 1914; IWM:Documents.1003: 4 August. For the composition of 8th Flotilla see Appendix III.

3

Commence hostilities

Britain's ultimatum to Germany expired at 11pm (midnight German time) on 4 August. Wireless stations immediately sent the message: 'Commence hostilities against Germany' to all Royal Navy ships and establishments.

Keyes had plans in place for an offensive operation, involving two boats, and a defensive operation covering the approaches to the Dover Straits, involving another four. The rest of the flotilla was held in reserve. He told his wife that all of his commanders were 'splendid gallant fellows' and that those not selected for the first patrol were going about with long faces, particularly Lieutenant-Commander Ernest W. Leir, the Senior Submarine Officer. He was unable to lead the first patrol as his boat, *E.4*, had to dock for repairs after losing a propeller blade on the journey from Immingham to Harwich.[1] With Leir ruled out, on 31 July Keyes had selected his second most senior commander, Lieutenant-Commander Cecil P. Talbot of *E.6*, to lead the first offensive sortie against the enemy, with Lieutenant-Commander Francis H.H. Goodhart of *E.8*.

Talbot was 29 years old and was the son of an Indian Army Major. Keyes describes him as 'your gallant little knight' in a letter to his wife. An incident from 1901 when he was serving on the Yangtze River in China as a Midshipman during the Boxer Rebellion illustrates this. Whilst ferrying sailors back and forth, an Able Seaman was swept away in the powerful current whilst getting into Talbot's boat. He jumped over the side, grabbed first his man, then an anchor chain as they were swept past. He clung on grimly until they could be fished out. He won a medal for saving life from the Royal Humane Society, an engraved sword from the Admiral and the thanks of the Admiralty. Talbot achieved first class passes in all of his Lieutenant's examinations and joined the Submarine Service in 1905. In 1908 Captain Brandt had assessed him as: 'Very hardworking, plenty of sound sense & judgement ... Good manner with men. Strong, active & bold in handling his vessel.' He returned to submarine command after a dalliance with the Naval Air Service in which he survived the destruction of the airship *Mayfly*, again being commended for getting some of the crew out. Talbot was appointed to *E.6* as she neared completion in March 1913.[2]

---

1   TNA ADM173: HM Submarine Logs, *E.4*, 29 July–1 August 1914.
2   TNA ADM196/143/371 & 196/49/127: Cecil Ponsonby Talbot; Life of Cecil Talbot by his son, <http://www.maritimequest.com/misc_pages/cecil_p_talbot/vadm_sir_cecil_p_talbot_his_life_

E.6 underway on the diesel engines shortly before the war. (NH 54964)

Goodhart was 30 years old and was the son of a clergyman. He achieved very good results in his Lieutenant's examinations and joined the submarine service in 1905. Early commands in coastal submarines were followed by *D.3* in 1912. In 1913 Captain Brandt evaluated him as: 'Very capable, reliable & sound. Skilful S/M [submarine] captain.' He transferred to *E.8* as she neared completion in February 1914. Goodhart seems to have had a character true to his surname and writes some touching sentiments to his wife in his letters.[3] Both Talbot and Goodhart also had in common the fact that they kept detailed diaries of their experiences.

E.6 and *E.8* were to be towed to the starting point for their patrol by the Harwich Destroyer Flotillas, on the way out to their own first war patrol. This would allow the crews to rest ahead of the patrol, but also reduce wear on the engines and avoid the possibility of mistaken identity. The submarines would slip their tows in the vicinity of the Terschelling Light Vessel at nightfall and proceed independently into the Heligoland Bight. Other British vessels would keep west of a line joining the Terschelling and Horns Reef Light Vessels, unless chasing the enemy. The submarines would keep to the east of this line to avoid friendly vessels. It was left to the two commanders to agree how they would divide up the patrol area. They were to return to Harwich via a stop-over in Yarmouth or Lowestoft, ensuring their arrival in daylight. The original orders left it to the discretion of the commander as to when to return, as long as they were back within six days of departure. On 1 August the orders were amended. They were now not to remain

above_and_below_the_waves.htm> (accessed 6 April 2018)
3   TNA ADM:196/49/70 & 196/143/303: Francis Herbert Heaveningham Goodhart.

more than three days and unless 'well placed for offensive operations', they were not to remain more than two. The aim was now to get information quickly on what the situation was in the Bight.

Keyes gave the commanders a degree of freedom to make their own decisions. Fostering an independent spirit of command was something that he consistently encouraged. Waistell and Talbot saw Tyrwhitt to make the necessary arrangements. Goodhart and Talbot then perfected their plans in Talbot's cabin on *Maidstone*. They divided the Bight into two operating areas, with Talbot to take the southwest part and Goodhart the northeast. Talbot took the crew ashore for a walk along the north bank of the Stour on the 3rd to give them a break from preparations. Both commanders took their submarines out for diving exercises on the 4th and Goodhart made a dummy attack on *Adamant*. A letter from Goodhart to his wife gives a candid description of this first patrol. He tells her that: 'we weren't to get in too close to Heligoland & were mainly there to see what the conditions were like & also intercept any of the enemies ships that might come in & out'. Heligoland was a heavily fortified island used as the base for German light forces defending the Bight.[4]

Keyes wrote a memorandum to Callaghan on 31 July in which he describes this first patrol as 'a hazardous experiment'. This echoed the concerns he had expressed after the 1913 manoeuvres. He only proposed to send two more boats if the first two came back with a favourable report and felt that the rest were better used defensively in the early stages of the war. This was partly because 'their engines are still somewhat unreliable for long surface cruises'.[5]

From the perspective of a hundred years in which submarine capabilities have been well established, it is worth remembering that although the commanders were experienced submariners, no one knew how long a submarine could stay out on patrol in hostile waters. Only so much could be learned from peacetime exercises. The real task for Talbot and Goodhart was to start to find out how submarines would perform in war.

Early on the morning of 5 August, the Harwich force slipped out of harbour. Crowds of boys from the training ship *Ganges* cheered themselves hoarse as each of the 38 vessels passed, joined by the crews of the other depot ships in the harbour. In contrast *E.6* and *E.8* had been seen off without fanfare before dawn by Keyes and Waistell. They waited for the departing ships outside the harbour and were taken in tow behind Tyrwhitt's own cruiser *Amethyst* and the 1st Flotilla destroyer *Ariel*.

At noon firing was heard from ahead. The force turned towards the sound of the guns. They arrived in time for Talbot to see the German minelayer *Königin Luise* sinking in a 'column of smoke and steam.' She had been intercepted and sunk after a short gun action with 3rd Flotilla. The crew of *E.6* were brought up to the bridge and 'gave a great cheer for first blood.' The previous course was resumed. A sharp lookout was kept between rain showers and *Ariel* twice had to pick up the tow to *E.8* when the line parted. *Amethyst* passed on information that German light vessels had been removed and the Heligoland light had been extinguished. The boats also were warned of the position of mines that the sunken minelayer had laid off the coast. Before darkness fell Tyrwhitt signalled the two submarines: 'We wish you every success and a safe return from your hazardous undertaking. Your gallant efforts will never be forgotten.' An

4   TNA ADM137/2067: pp.16–18; IWM:Documents.2175: letter to wife 20 August 1914.
5   TNA ADM137/2067: p.603.

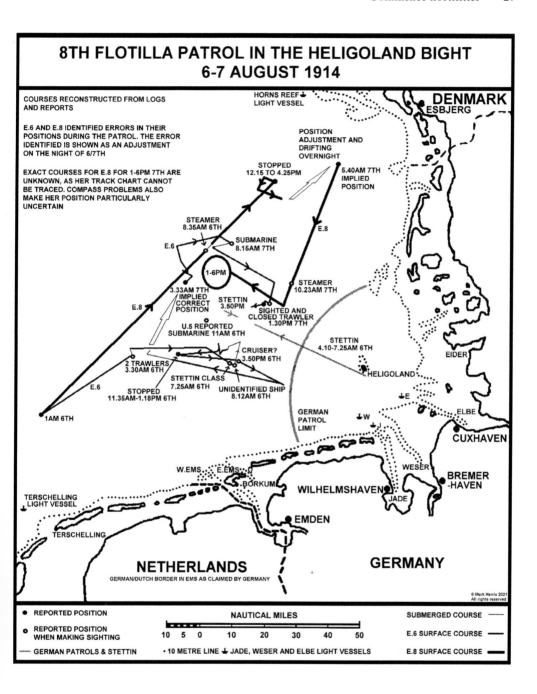

8TH FLOTILLA PATROL IN THE HELIGOLAND BIGHT
6-7 AUGUST 1914

COURSES RECONSTRUCTED FROM LOGS AND REPORTS

E.6 AND E.8 IDENTIFIED ERRORS IN THEIR POSITIONS DURING THE PATROL. THE ERROR IDENTIFIED IS SHOWN AS AN ADJUSTMENT ON THE NIGHT OF 6/7TH

EXACT COURSES FOR E.8 FOR 1-6PM 7TH ARE UNKNOWN, AS HER TRACK CHART CANNOT BE TRACED. COMPASS PROBLEMS ALSO MAKE HER POSITION PARTICULARLY UNCERTAIN

HORNS REEF
LIGHT VESSEL

DENMARK
ESBJERG

POSITION ADJUSTMENT AND DRIFTING OVERNIGHT

STOPPED 12.15 TO 4.25PM

5.40AM 7TH IMPLIED POSITION

STEAMER 8.35AM 6TH

E.8

E.6

SUBMARINE 8.15AM 7TH

1-6PM

3.33AM 7TH IMPLIED CORRECT POSITION

STETTIN 3.50PM

STEAMER 10.23AM 7TH

E.8

SIGHTED AND CLOSED TRAWLER 1.30PM 7TH

U.5 REPORTED SUBMARINE 11AM 6TH

STETTIN 4.10-7.25AM 6TH

EIDER

CRUISER? 3.50PM 6TH

HELIGOLAND

2 TRAWLERS 3.30AM 6TH

STETTIN CLASS 7.25AM 6TH

UNIDENTIFIED SHIP 8.12AM 6TH

E.6

STOPPED 11.35AM-1.18PM 6TH

E

ELBE

W

GERMAN PATROL LIMIT

CUXHAVEN

1AM 6TH

WESER

W.EMS

E.EMS

BREMER-HAVEN

BORKUM

WILHELMSHAVEN

TERSCHELLING LIGHT VESSEL

JADE

EMDEN

TERSCHELLING

NETHERLANDS

GERMANY

GERMAN/DUTCH BORDER IN EMS AS CLAIMED BY GERMANY

● REPORTED POSITION	NAUTICAL MILES	SUBMERGED COURSE
○ REPORTED POSITION WHEN MAKING SIGHTING	10 5 0 10 20 30 40 50	E.6 SURFACE COURSE
— GERMAN PATROLS & STETTIN	• 10 METRE LINE ⬇ JADE, WESER AND ELBE LIGHT VESSELS	E.8 SURFACE COURSE

unimpressed Goodhart described the message as 'hot air', but Talbot enthused: 'Sensation!' *E.6* and *E.8* slipped their tows from *Amethyst* and *Ariel* in darkness at 1am on the 6th, and were given their estimated position, 30 miles north-northeast of the Terschelling Light Vessel. They started their diesel engines and departed on slightly diverging courses to the northeast at their cruising speed of 12 knots.

Talbot dived *E.6* at 3am to check her trim. The crew had to pump water ballast backwards or forwards to ensure the submarine was dead level whilst submerged, a vital task at the start of every patrol. As dawn broke, two trawlers were spotted four or five miles away to the south when she surfaced. Talbot dived the boat and headed north for a while to avoid them.[6] *E.6* surfaced at 4:15am and headed off towards Heligoland, spotting *E.8* four miles away as she did so. Visibility would remain good all day, punctuated by occasional showers. Tension rose when a German cruiser of the *Stettin* class was identified on the horizon to the east-northeast at 7:25am. The position was recorded and a sketch of the distinctive funnel layout was made in the log, capturing this first glimpse of the enemy. Talbot dived for 40 minutes to avoid being seen, as the cruiser was too far off to attack. When *E.6* surfaced a trail of smoke was sighted six miles to the northwest. Talbot dived and gave chase at maximum speed to intercept. The target, which turned out to be a ship with a yellow funnel, was apparently doing about 25 knots. After 40 minutes he had to abandon the chase, having only closed to three miles. As he did so a trawler passed directly overhead. Talbot remained dived for almost an hour to let it move off, in case this had been deliberate. He then surfaced and headed west to charge the badly depleted batteries, later stopping to use both diesels to charge more quickly.

Talbot headed back east after nearly two hours stationary. *E.6* dived to avoid another trawler on reaching the area of the previous sightings. Talbot was frustrated again when a small cruiser or large destroyer was sighted on surfacing around 4pm, 10 miles to the north, heading east at speed, again too far away to attack. *E.6* reached a position reckoned to be 23 miles from Heligoland at 5:45pm. This was 10 miles inside the reported German patrol line, but there was nothing in sight except numerous trawlers. Talbot turned round, heading 'against a nasty sea' to be well offshore before nightfall. *E.6* dived at 9:30pm, in the middle of a trawler fleet. After organising watches on the control wheels, Talbot turned in for some sleep and *E.6* kept underway at 50 feet (15m) until the next morning, moving dead slow to maintain depth. Rest inevitably came at the expense of accurate position keeping.

By 3:15am the next morning it was light enough for *E.6* to surface and resume the patrol. Talbot wanted to make for where he had seen the warships but was forced to work round to the north of the trawler fleet, trying not to be seen. He eventually decided that this was impossible, merely ensuring he kept at least a mile away from them. Most of the trawlers were sailing boats and many were Dutch. Talbot sighted a German submarine, four or five miles to starboard, apparently stopped, at 8:15am. *E.6* dived and turned to attack, but Talbot could not spot her in the periscope and initially assumed she had also dived. He spotted her on the surface half an hour later, heading west, and gave chase. Once again *E.6* could not keep up. On surfacing at 9:35am the target was nowhere to be seen. Talbot submerged and went on for another 45

---

6   Merchant vessels were protected by international law and were not targets, unless proven to be carrying contraband cargo destined for the enemy. Confirming this required examination of their papers, which was usually impractical for a submarine in enemy waters. The exception was if the vessel was obviously engaging in war activity, such as troop transport.

minutes, hoping that the German might stop. *E.6* then surfaced and headed back towards Heligoland. A position sight could finally be taken when the weather cleared and revealed that she was north of her intended position, so *E.6* altered course to south around 1pm. This was unsurprising after two and half days without an exact position fix. Talbot now became suspicious of a trawler. *E.6* had stopped briefly at noon, allowing the trawler to pass well ahead. She had been in sight for an hour and a half and seemed to be tailing him. Talbot decided to steer directly at her, signalling by international flag codes for her to show her colours and stop. She showed a German merchant ensign. Talbot passed ahead of her, fearing she might be dropping mines. He noted that she seemed to be fitted for wireless, then headed off at high speed. The trawler headed off towards the Ems River, roughly the direction in which *E.6* had previously been heading. It was now 1:45pm and feeling there was no reason to remain longer, Talbot set course for home, avoiding the patrol area of the Harwich destroyers.

Swarte Bank Light Vessel was sighted at 6:30am on the 8th. Talbot was pleased that after the entire patrol his dead reckoning was only 10 miles out. He headed to Lowestoft, where he signalled the coastguard station to report his return. Talbot was unable to go ashore in a boat to report by phone as planned, as the sea was too rough. He continued on to Harwich but was forced to reduce speed to 10 knots at 3:45pm after the port propeller lost a blade. *E.6* was then signalled by the coastguard station at Aldeburgh, which passed on orders to return to Yarmouth for the night. Talbot asked them to report his loss of the propeller blade to *Maidstone* so that a replacement would be ready when *E.6* returned to Harwich. Lowestoft coastguard also repeated the new orders as he passed, accompanied by the firing of rockets to get his attention! *E.6* secured for the night at Gorleston (Yarmouth's Harbour) at 8pm. The urgent recall had been made to give Talbot details of the swept channel through the German minefield laid off the coast three days earlier. *Firedrake*, *E.4*, *E.9* and *D.5* were all in harbour at Yarmouth.

Captain Waistell arrived by train at 1am the next morning. Talbot turned out to give him a report. All the boats except *E.4* then left at 2:30am in company with Waistell in *Firedrake*, as they were required back at Harwich. Talbot soon received a wireless signal from Keyes with good wishes, inquiring about the patrol. He replied: 'Very many thanks, regret I have nothing to show for it, enemy very wild and very scarce'. He records in his diary that he was 'very sick at coming back without firing a torpedo, I had not considered the possibility of seeing nothing.' *E.6* was back alongside *Maidstone* by 9am. When Talbot shoved off to head in to the floating dock for repair that afternoon, *E.6* was caught by the strong tide. Her manoeuvrability was compromised by having only one propeller working; the rudder struck the aft hydroplanes of *E.8* and jammed *E.6*'s steering gear at the angle for a hard turn. Talbot got no help from the harbourmaster, but his own attempts to direct launches to nudge him into the dock were also unsuccessful. There were no tugs available in Harwich. It took until the next morning to dock and the propeller blade took the whole day to replace. The steering gear took until 1pm on the 11th to fix. By now Talbot had started a beard, as he couldn't afford to waste precious time shaving![7]

Meanwhile, *E.8* had an uneventful journey to Goodhart's patrol billet after dropping her tow at 1am on the 6th, sighting large numbers of trawlers on the way. He felt certain that the

7   TNA ADM137/2067: pp.19–20; TNA ADM173: *E.6*, 5-11 August 1914; IWM:Documents.20134: 31 July-11 August.

trawlers would report *E.8* as soon as they returned to port. *E.8* was dived for almost an hour before dawn as a precaution against being surprised in the growing light. Goodhart dived again a few hours later to avoid being seen by a steamer until she was out of sight. At 12:15pm *E.8* reached her patrol billet in the northern part of the Bight. Goodhart stopped the engines and remained on the surface, expecting the enemy to show up and 'always on the strain to see them'. He restarted the engines at 4:35pm and patrolled the area at low speed. Nothing was seen other than the numerous trawlers. *E.8* stopped at 7:15pm and Goodhart decided to remain in place on the surface for the night, with everything prepared to dive quickly. He tells his wife that: 'I had meant to sit on the bottom & have a nights rest, however I funked it a bit,[8] as it was rather uneven & there was a good tide there'. Goodhart split the watch with his second in command, Lieutenant Alexander Greig, and managed to grab a bit of sleep when he was off watch in the conning tower, despite the sea being a bit rough.

   E.8 got underway at 5:30am on the 7th for a point 30 miles from Heligoland, inside a patrol line rumoured to extend 50 miles from the Elbe. Nothing was seen in the six hours it took to get there, except numerous sailing trawlers and a solitary cargo steamer. Goodhart now headed out to a new position farther out to sea and spent the afternoon cruising around this area hoping to catch any warship that had been driven in by the Harwich destroyer patrol. *E.8* altered course for home at 6:30pm having seen nothing; like Talbot he felt that there was no justification for remaining an extra day. Goodhart once again stopped on the surface for the night at 9pm, as 'I had an idea that it would be better to be stopped as it would be easier to see things before they saw you'. Given the limited bridge facilities of an E class submarine this was a questionable idea. He got underway again after carrying out a dive 'for practice' at 4:30am next morning. Goodhart later got an accurate position fix using the sun as the weather cleared and deduced that his compass was 'a lot out'. The sea roughened with a strong wind from the south and Goodhart 'got a bit lost in my bearings'. He eventually found the Swarte Bank Light Vessel, fixing his position. *E.8* anchored off Yarmouth at 11pm, as it was too late to go into harbour. Goodhart headed for Harwich the next morning, the 9th, arriving at noon 'past the *Amethyst* & other ships … all … cheering us. I felt very wretched then as I had convinced myself by that time that we ought to have gone further in.' On finding out that Talbot had also not made an attack, or pressed in closer, he 'felt I had been right after all'. *E.8* spent the rest of the day carrying out a repair to the starboard motor, whilst Goodhart grabbed a much needed bath and some rest on *Maidstone*.[9]

   A meagre intelligence haul, so what of the elusive enemy?

   Germany expected the British Fleet to sortie as soon as war was declared and impose a close blockade of the North Sea coast. This would be opposed by destroyers and submarines, which would chip away at the blockading force. The arrangements on 6 August were that one flotilla of 11 destroyers was in place on an arc 35 miles from the Elbe Light Vessel, with two more flotillas six and 12 miles behind them during daylight. Submarines and patrol cruisers were held back in reserve. Talbot got close to the outer line on the 6th but did not spot the patrols. As Goodhart had feared, *E.8* was always too far out to do so.

---

8   Feeling nervousness or lacking in confidence.
9   TNA ADM137/2067: p.21; TNA ADM173: *E.8*, 6 August 1914; IWM:Documents.2175: letter to wife 20 August 1914.

The submarine sighted by Talbot on the 7th cannot be identified. No German submarines were in the area. Both boats had trouble fixing their positions early in the patrol and *E.8* also had a faulty compass. There is a good chance Talbot was actually chasing *E.8*.

However, *E.6* had almost certainly sighted, and been sighted by, the first offensive sortie by the German submarine force on the 6th, although this is not apparent from Talbot's report. Ten submarines left Heligoland from 3:30am, fanning out to the west. Two light cruisers, *Hamburg* and *Stettin*, were scouting 10 or more miles ahead of them, with two destroyer leader boats following. These surface ships turned round and headed back to Heligoland once the force was out of the Bight. The U-boats turned north to seek out the British Fleet. The position Talbot gives for the cruisers seen in both the morning and afternoon roughly correspond to the actual courses and positions of *Stettin* on both occasions. During the long submerged chase of what appears to have been a cargo steamer, the German submarines, steaming in line abreast to his north, would have approached from the east. Talbot had then surfaced and headed unknowingly at a similar speed across their path. Around 11am, *U.5*, the southernmost German submarine, reported 'probable enemy submarines' after catching sight of an enemy submarine conning tower. This was lost sight of and was assumed to have dived. The German submarines left *E.6* behind when Talbot stopped to charge.

The commander of 1st U-Bootsflottille concluded that *U.5*'s report was probably false, as patrols had seen nothing and no attacks had been recorded. The report was also mixed in with submarine sightings by commercial trawlers well out into the North Sea and an unlikely claim by the cruiser *Stralsund* that she had two torpedoes fired at her whilst anchored in shallow water at the mouth of the Elbe. Fleet Command concluded that there were no submarines operating within 100 miles of Heligoland.[10]

It is clear from both commander's reports that the British were already aware of the approximate position of the German patrol line. The estimate of 50 miles from the Elbe was not far wrong and had no doubt been observed and reported by steamers, as it had been in place since 1 August. However, the outer patrol line was actually about 10–15 miles closer to the Elbe. The warships sighted by Talbot appeared to confirm the rumour, but this was roughly the right conclusion for the wrong reasons.

Both commanders, and Goodhart in particular, took significant risks remaining stopped on the surface, even in daylight. The fact that *E.6* may have been sighted by *U.5* without being aware of her presence illustrates the danger. At the same time both commanders suffered from what could be termed first patrol paranoia. The sinking of the disguised minelayer, *Königin Luise*, put the whole Royal Navy on the lookout for covert warships everywhere for months and must have had an impact on the thinking of Talbot and Goodhart as they went out on their first patrol. They saw sinister motives and a non-existent elaborate surveillance web in the actions of what were in reality uninterested trawlers and steamers going about their work. Over-elaborate precautions were taken to avoid being seen. Diving to avoid being seen by trawlers reduced their own chance of seeing the enemy. The German trawler stopped by *E.6* appears to have made no report and the skipper perhaps concluded that he had been flagged down by a German

10   Otto Groos, *Der Krieg zur See 1914–1918 – Der Krieg in der Nordsee Band 1* (Berlin: Mittler und Sohn, 1920), pp.74–6, 128–9, 132–3, 251–2, Karten 7, 9; Bundesarchiv (BA) RM92: Schwere und mittlere Kampfschiffe der Preußischen und Kaiserlichen Marine, *Stettin* Kriegstagebuch/Skizze, 6 August 1914.

submarine, a common enough sight exercising in the area in which they were based. Talbot had also taken the precaution of painting out the tell-tale '86' pendant number on the conning tower. It goes without saying that fishermen were unlikely to have any idea of the difference between a British and German submarine. The only reports that were received from trawlers were misleading sightings far out to sea in positions where there were no submarines, British or otherwise. Accurate navigation had also been a major challenge for both boats, made worse by an apparently inaccurate starting position from *Amethyst*. This was an inauspicious start to the campaign. The flawed deductions drawn by both British and German command shows how hard it was going to be to turn scattered observations into useful intelligence.

Keyes reported on the patrol to the Admiralty on the evening of 8 August. It was such a bucket of cold water that Sturdee queried it, forcing Waistell to confirm the message in full the next morning, Keyes being at sea at the time. He says neither Talbot nor Goodhart 'at present recommend any further operations in the Heligoland Bight', as it is 'full of trawlers fitted with wireless telegraphy'. These were deemed to have warned the submarine and two cruisers sighted by Talbot to return to base. Trawlers were stated to have forced them to 'dive all day' and 'there is no doubt that our submarines were seen'. These statements exaggerate the facts and draw spurious conclusions. Talbot had spent a significant, but by no means excessive amount of time dived; seven hours on the 6th and just under five on the 7th. His report states that only one trawler was suspected of having wireless. Goodhart had only submerged for one hour on the 6th and none at all on the 7th. As has been related, Keyes was lukewarm about patrols in the Bight at this point and was keen to deploy his force in other ways. Waistell, Talbot and Goodhart dutifully supported this position and clearly saw nothing in the apparently meagre pickings on offer in the Bight to question it. Keyes closes by recommending a drive to clear away the trawlers once the Army had been transferred to France.[11]

11   TNA ADM137/2067: pp.59, 614; TNA ADM186/610: Naval Staff Monographs, Vol. III Monograph 6 – Passage of the BEF, August 1914, p.31.

4

Defensive patrols

Keyes had planned another operation whilst the clock counted down for war. This supported the defensive arrangements in the Southern Bight, the area of the North Sea between the British and Dutch coasts. Any German force seeking to penetrate to the Thames or the Channel had to pass through here. Defending it was a key task of Tyrwhitt's Flotillas, but Keyes was anxious for the submarines to play their part.

Keyes was also keen to put into practice his ideas concerning co-operation between cruisers and submarines. His report after the 1913 fleet manoeuvres concluded that 'it is perfectly feasible for E class submarines to accompany a fleet to sea'. In proposing that submarines should work with observing cruiser squadrons, he was keen to see if the enemy could be induced or forced to alter course toward submarines accompanying the fleet. In the report he credits the cruising speed of the E class as 13 knots. This is a little optimistic, especially in rough water, but even so a battle fleet was likely to be going several knots faster.[1]

On 1 August Keyes passed a memorandum to Callaghan outlining a proposal to backstop Tyrwhitt's Flotillas and report any vessels heading southwards. He proposed placing one pair of boats on a patrol line 14 miles northwest from the North Hinder Light Vessel and another 14 miles southeast from the Outer Gabbard Light Vessel. At least one of each pair would have wireless. Tyrwhitt agreed to provide two destroyers from his force to scout for the submarines if required. Keyes also confirmed that he would confer with Rear-Admiral Campbell, the commander of the 7th Cruiser Squadron, to arrange co-operation as soon as they arrived to patrol the Southern Bight. Campbell's Squadron was made up of four large armoured cruisers of the 1900 *Cressy* class. Since these were not modern vessels, most of their crew were reservists, so it would take time for them to be mobilised.

On the 2nd, Leir's *E.4*, which was now repaired, was assigned with *E.9* to the North Hinder patrol. *D.3* and *D.5* were assigned the Outer Gabbard patrol. The boats in each pair were to remain in sight of each other and no more than five miles apart during the day. At night they would patrol independently on likely approaches near the local light vessels. The boats would sortie when war was declared and remain in place until relieved, probably after three days.

Keyes heard that Campbell had arrived at Chatham on the evening of the 2nd. He immediately went up to London to discuss his plans for cruiser co-operation with Sturdee, then early the

---

1   TNA ADM137/1926: pp.431–2.

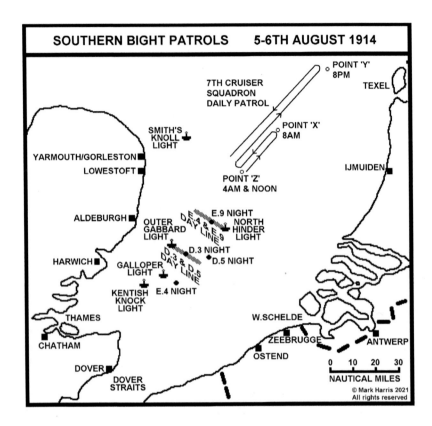

following morning met Campbell and his four captains on board the *Cressy* in Chatham. He was delighted to find that one of his good friends was the Admiral's Chief of Staff. Keyes proposed that each of the patrolling cruisers should tow a submarine. This would help the submarine by saving its engine and allow the cruisers to fall back behind the submarines in the event that they encountered a superior force. Keyes returned to the Admiralty to outline the plans he had agreed to Sturdee and Battenberg.

The details were fleshed out in memorandums issued by Campbell and Keyes on 4 August. The new arrangements would supersede the Light Vessel patrol as soon as 7th Cruiser Squadron was available. The cruisers were to patrol behind the Harwich Flotillas. Each day, starting at 4am they would repeat a patrol pattern backwards and forwards between three points, 'X, 'Y' and 'Z'. The cruisers would steam in line abreast, normally two miles apart and the exact position of the points would be varied by up to 15 miles each day.

Each morning four Submarines would leave Smith's Knoll, accompanied by *Lurcher* or *Firedrake*, to rendezvous with the cruisers at point 'Z'. The submarines would each be towed by one of the armoured cruisers, which were to be supplied with specially made towing hawsers. The tow would be slipped at point 'Y' and the submarines would then return to Smith's Knoll followed by *Lurcher* or *Firedrake* 10 miles astern of them. If the cruisers met the enemy with the submarines in tow, they were to slip the tow and dive. The forward pair of submarines would head toward the enemy and the other pair would follow the cruisers, which would steer a course to lead the enemy past the waiting submarines and then turn to engage once they had done so.

Keyes also wanted to attach a submarine to Tyrwhitt's cruiser, *Amethyst*. He was concerned that it was weakly armed and too slow to evade a modern enemy cruiser, but Tyrwhitt was apparently 'unperturbed'. Tyrwhitt was pushing hard to get a faster cruiser, but no doubt felt that towing around a submarine at a maximum speed of 12 knots whilst leading his Flotillas was not going to improve things in the meantime! Keyes intended to go out himself for the first 24 hours 'to ensure arrangements are satisfactorily completed' and also pushed for the allocation of a third destroyer to 8th Flotilla, although one was not forthcoming.

The four assigned submarines took up the Light Vessel Patrol with the outbreak of hostilities on the 5th, as Campbell's cruisers were not ready. They followed the Harwich Flotillas out in the early morning light, followed later that morning by Keyes in *Lurcher*. He had arranged for Commander Wilfred Tomkinson to be given command of *Lurcher*. Tomkinson had been with Keyes as his second in command in the destroyer *Fame* in China and had 'been in some tight places with me'.

Keyes headed off to rendezvous at the Kentish Knock Light vessel with Campbell's Squadron and boarded his Flagship, the *Bacchante*, to make the final arrangements to commence the new cruiser patrol the next day. Campbell had only three Cruisers in company as the fourth, *Cressy*, was not yet ready. Whilst Keyes was aboard a message was taken in, 'Third Flotilla engaging Scout Cruisers'. He quickly boarded *Lurcher* and tore off at high speed intending to gather his boats and take them forward to attack, an idea quickly abandoned when it turned out to be just the solitary minelayer, *Königin Luise*. After spending some time cruising on the submarine line to communicate the arrangements agreed with Campbell, *Lurcher* returned to Harwich at dusk, just as the destroyer *Lance* was landing 22 wounded enemy survivors.[2]

The submarines on the Light Vessel patrol had spent the day cruising about on the surface. *E.4* briefly dived on sighting *Lurcher* around 3pm, but quickly surfaced again after identifying her as friendly. Keyes ordered *D.5*, *E.4* and *E.9* to meet up before dusk at the North Hinder Light vessel. They were to depart from there shortly before midnight for rendezvous point 'Z'. They duly met up with Campbell in the early light at 4am next day and Waistell also turned up at the same time in *Firedrake*, having left Harwich at midnight to steam through the night. Keyes had ordered *D.3* back into Harwich on the previous evening as there were only three cruisers. The Light Vessel patrol had been superseded before the night patrol positions had even been occupied.

Each cruiser took one of the submarines in tow at 5am. As senior officer Leir in *E.4* was towed by the flagship, *Bacchante*; *Euryalus* towed *E.9* and *Aboukir* towed *D.5*. The cruisers headed for point 'Y' at a sedate 4 knots in line abreast, one mile apart. After halting for 40 minutes at 2pm, they resumed their course at 5-6 knots. *Firedrake* was sent to investigate a Norwegian steamer and a couple of trawlers during the advance. Waistell went ahead to a lookout position at 7:30pm, the cruisers stopped again and the submarines dropped their tows. The three submarines then started their engines and returned to the vicinity of Yarmouth Roads in company with *Firedrake* at 12 knots, their maximum cruising speed. They anchored offshore at 5:30am next morning. The cruisers headed back the way they had come at 6 knots.

2   Keyes, *Memoirs*, pp.61–2, 68; TNA ADM137/2067: pp.23–52.

The joint cruiser patrol was now cancelled as new priorities intervened. *Firedrake* and her submarines were ordered to remain on stand-by at Yarmouth Harbour during the 7th for new orders. Waistell returned by train to Harwich. *Firedrake* was ordered to carry out a patrol on the night of the 7/8th off Yarmouth on the lookout for suspicious vessels. She investigated what turned out to be a French sailing ship and a Spanish steamer. The *Königin Luise* had generated a considerable scare in relation to disguised minelayers.

Campbell's cruisers were withdrawn to the Channel on the 8th. The submarines left Yarmouth to join *Firedrake* at anchor offshore that afternoon, but *E.4* damaged the threads of her steering gear. She had to go alongside the local yard in Gorleston for repairs. Waistell returned to *Firedrake* and in the murky light at 3am on the 9th led *D.5* and *E.9*, together with the recently returned *E.6*, back to Harwich through the newly swept and marked mine free channel. *E.4* completed repairs at 3:15am on the 10th and left to join them. More problems were encountered on the way when an exhaust valve became stuck. Fortunately the engine room hands were able to fix this whilst *E.4* proceeded on one engine.[3]

This patrol was uneventful and short-lived but was the first of many wartime attempts at close co-operation between surface vessels and submarines by the Royal Navy. It also demonstrated Keyes energy and persuasive powers in proposing and agreeing the whole scheme with the senior officers involved. He also quickly got the specialised hawsers made up to enable the tows. However, the patrol was naïve in conception. Cruisers towing submarines at four to six knots was an absurdly easy target for an enemy submarine lying in ambush. Limited surface speed was an insurmountable barrier to joint patrols of the kind Keyes had been so keen to try. The reduction in engine wear on the submarines was certainly not worth the risk. Campbell's cruisers had used up some of their luck, but there were no German warships or submarines near the Southern Bight at the time.

Keyes did also send out two boats to backstop Tyrwhitt's patrol, despite his being 'unperturbed'! Details are scanty, but *E.2* and *D.3* were sent out at 9pm on the 6th to take up a patrol line at dawn on the 7th near the North Hinder Light. *Lurcher* went out to scout for them, but nothing was sighted apart from a Dutch steamship and 1st Destroyer Flotilla returning from their patrol. They were recalled on the evening of the 7th and arrived back in Harwich next morning, after detouring round the suspected mined area off the coast. *E.2* developed an engine fault which was not repaired until late on the 9th.[4]

3   TNA ADM173: *E.4*, 5–10 August 1914; TNA ADM53: *Euryalus, Firedrake*, 5–10 August 1914
4   IWM: Documents.1003: 6–9 August; TNA ADM173: *D.3*, 6–8 August 1914; TNA ADM53: *Maidstone, Lurcher*, 6–9 August 1914; TNA ADM186/610, BEF, pp.11, 30–31.

5

Protecting the Army

E.5 had broken-off a refit in Portsmouth as a result of the declaration of war.[1] She reached Harwich on the evening of 5 August; it was a port expecting attack. Sure enough, the alarm was raised shortly after midday on the 6th. The Nore Defence Flotilla reported destroyers firing off the harbour entrance near the Sunk Light Vessel. Three submarines ready for sea were immediately ordered out to buoys off Felixstowe. Keyes boarded *Lurcher* and headed out to cheers as he passed *Maidstone*. The other submarines in harbour scrambled to get themselves ready for sea. The whole thing was very quickly revealed as a false alarm. A cross-channel steamer, the *SS St Petersburg*, had been taking the German Ambassador and his legation back home via Holland. Destroyers of the 3rd Flotilla returning from patrol fired shots across her bows after seeing her flying the German merchant ensign. *Lurcher* and the three submarines returned to harbour.

Rumours about a surprise attack persisted. That night Keyes had all the available submarines in harbour readied for action and placed at buoys in the approaches. *D.2*, *E.3* and *E.7* were off Felixstowe with torpedoes loaded in all tubes and ready for firing. The remaining boats were at buoys near *Maidstone*. Lieutenant Hallifax of *E.7* thought an attack unlikely as there was a full moon. He slept fully clothed anyway, with a sentry posted on watch on the bridge, but got little sleep in the cold boat. In the morning the submarines returned to harbour.[2]

News had also come in on the 6th that mines laid by *Königin Luise* had sunk the 3rd Flotilla Leader, the light cruiser *Amphion*, on her return to Harwich. Keyes recorded in his diary that the loss of *Amphion* in the trade track had convinced him that the Germans intended to wage a ruthless war. His visit to the *Bacchante* had also convinced him that the 7th Cruiser Squadron should be pulled back to receive a proper shake down before facing the enemy. He was increasingly concerned that Tyrwhitt's Flotillas were too spread out and could be attacked in detail. The impending passage of the British Army's Expeditionary Force (BEF) to France struck him as the best opportunity the Germans would have to strike a blow with their Fleet. The need to get his Flotilla into action to prevent this now occupied his attention. Keyes says that his concerns were 'shared by Tyrwhitt'.

---

1   TNA ADM173: E.5, 20 July-5 August 1914.
2   IWM:Documents.1003: 6-7 August.

Keyes headed up to his office in the Admiralty and arrived at 10pm to find 'service channels ... blocked.' It appears he was rebuffed by Sturdee, who should have been his first point of contact. Sturdee could be difficult. Rear-Admiral Oliver, Director of Naval Intelligence, described him as: 'A pompous man who would never listen to anyone else's opinion. I could not stick him.'[3] Keyes therefore took his concerns 'very forcibly' straight to the top – the Board of the Admiralty, who all had offices in the building. Winston Churchill, Admiral Battenberg, Vice-Admiral Hamilton (the Second Sea Lord) and Rear-Admiral Lambert (the Fourth Sea Lord) all received a visit over the next three hours.

Keyes says that he obtained agreement to restrict the over-extended patrol area of Tyrwhitt's Flotilla's and get the 7th Cruiser Squadron pulled back to the Channel approaches – both did happen. He certainly obtained permission to use all available boats of 8th Flotilla to form a barrier across the entrance to the Channel during the passage of the Army to France. Keyes was pushing hard at service protocol. He was senior in date of commission to Tyrwhitt and hence was the ranking officer at Harwich, but he was inferior in rank to Campbell and had no direct authority over either. Unlike Keyes, the Board members did not think that the German surface fleet would attack the troop transports, but it was necessary to plan on the basis that they might. They were certainly concerned that the Germans might seek to interrupt the crossing with either a raid on the East Coast (possibly including a troop landing), a massed submarine attack on the transports, or a surface raid by light forces into the Dover Straits.[4]

It is impossible to know how much Keyes intervention influenced existing plans. The whole might of the Navy in home waters, including the Grand Fleet[5], the Channel Fleet, detached Cruiser Squadrons and the Local Defence Forces at Rosyth, the Tyne, the Humber, Dover, Sheerness and Portsmouth, not to mention the French naval force in the Channel (2e Escadre Légère), were all involved. The aim was to ensure that any raiding force would never get back to Germany and that the BEF was able to cross unmolested to France. The Harwich forces were a small part of this formidable armada but were likely to make first contact with the enemy. The BEF would begin crossing on the 9th.

The submarines in the flotilla were told on the 7th to ensure that they had provisions for one week on board. The rumour mill already had the news, as Hallifax observed in his diary: 'I believe the Expeditionary Force is to sail on Sunday [9th] & we are to keep their route clear'.[6] At midnight Keyes informed Sturdee that he proposed postponing offensive operations to concentrate all available submarines 'in area arranged'. Keyes forwarded details of the detailed disposition to Sturdee next day, prefaced by what verges on a lecture about the strategic position. He stated, 'I propose to act on the supposition ... that orders will be given to the High Sea Fleet to prevent reinforcements being given to France at all costs', whereas an attack on the East Coast by them (considered more likely by the Admiralty) could 'achieve nothing of vital importance'.

3   Arthur J. Marder, *From the Dreadnought to Scapa Flow: Volume II – The War years to the Eve of Jutland 1914-1916* (London: Oxford University Press, 1965), p.92.
4   TNA ADM137/2067: p.615; Churchill, *World Crisis*, pp.210-213; Keyes, *Memoirs*, pp.70-71.
5   The main battle fleet composed of the most modern warships.
6   IWM:Documents.1003: 7 August 1914.

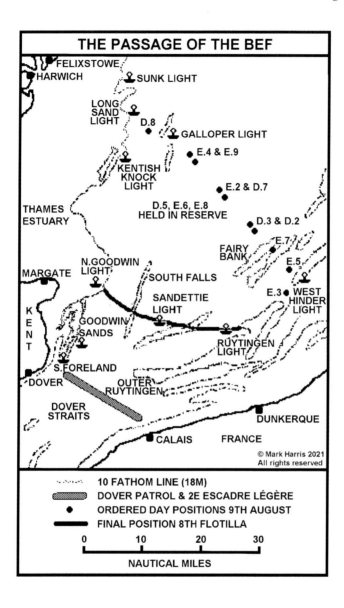

THE PASSAGE OF THE BEF

FELIXSTOWE
HARWICH
SUNK LIGHT
LONG SAND LIGHT
D.8
GALLOPER LIGHT
E.4 & E.9
KENTISH KNOCK LIGHT
E.2 & D.7
THAMES ESTUARY
D.5, E.6, E.8 HELD IN RESERVE
D.3 & D.2
FAIRY BANK
E.7
E.5
N.GOODWIN LIGHT
MARGATE
SOUTH FALLS
SANDETTIE LIGHT
E.3 WEST HINDER LIGHT
KENT
GOODWIN SANDS
RUYTINGEN LIGHT
S.FORELAND
DOVER
OUTER RUYTINGEN
DOVER STRAITS
DUNKERQUE
CALAIS
FRANCE

10 FATHOM LINE (18M)
DOVER PATROL & 2E ESCADRE LÉGÈRE
ORDERED DAY POSITIONS 9TH AUGUST
FINAL POSITION 8TH FLOTILLA

0   10   20   30
NAUTICAL MILES

Thirteen submarines would take up a 40 mile line from near the Long Sand Light Vessel to the West Hinder Light Vessel, starting at daylight on the 9th. This covered the entire deep water approach to Dover and the Thames. Keyes and Waistell would scout five miles north east of the submarines to signal the approach of the enemy in *Lurcher* and *Firedrake*. Arrangements were to be made for placing buoys on the line and for signal rockets to be issued to the destroyers. The rockets would be used to signal the approach of either capital ships or light forces by day or night. The submarines would close in to the light vessels at the ends of the line during the night, taking up station again each morning.[7] Keyes also requested that the destroyers *Lennox* and *Legion* were detached from Tyrwhitt as additional scouts for 8th Flotilla, but the request had to be rescinded as they were 'required by [Tyrwhitt]'. It seems that he had drawn a line in the sand with Keyes over the requisitioning of his boats. Tyrwhitt's Flotillas would be scouting well to the north of the submarine line. Sturdee eventually sent his agreement to the arrangements at 11pm and confirmed that the passage of the BEF would be completed by the 27th.[8]

Six submarines were either detached to Yarmouth or fixing defects, so *Lurcher* could only lead the seven available submarines out of Harwich at 3:45am on the 9th. They took up their billets between 6:30am and 9:30am. *D.2*, *D.7* and *D.8* alone had to be spread over the northern half of the line, as *E.2*, *E.4*, *E.9* and the three boats allocated as reserves were absent. *E.9* and *D.5* arrived at 11:30am to fill all but one of the gaps in the line. Meanwhile, *Lurcher* steamed down the patrol line to the West Hinder. Keyes decided the boats would be unable to keep in touch except in perfect visibility. He also felt that his two destroyers were insufficient to scout for the extended line. He signalled Sturdee via *Maidstone*, proposing a shorter line to the south covering the immediate approach to the Dover Straits. He began steaming back up the line at 10:30am to order the nine submarines to rendezvous at the Ruytingen, Sandettie and North Goodwin Lightships and await further orders, assuming that approval would be received. *Lurcher* reached the other end of the line at 1:30pm, then headed for the Sandettie and North Goodwin Lights to assign new patrol positions to the submarines. Meanwhile, *Firedrake* had refuelled at Harwich and arrived with Waistell to assign patrol positions at the Ruytingen at 6:30pm. The patrol line was only briefly established before all submarines anchored for the night near the three light vessels. *E.7* was ordered to 'keep quiet & sink if anyone approached'.

The message came in during the night that Sturdee had not approved the new positions. Keyes and Waistell ordered the submarines to return to their original patrol line at dawn on the 10th. Keyes repeated his objections to Sturdee and stated that he would keep the reserve boats at Sandettie. The Trinity House vessel *Alert* arrived on the original line to buoy the designated positions.

Meanwhile, *E.8* and *E.2* had completed their repairs and left Harwich just before midnight, forming a reserve off Sandettie at 5:30am. *E.4* arrived at Sandettie from Yarmouth at 1pm. Goodhart was disappointed to discover that a looming target in the half-light on the way turned out to be a British steamer. *Lurcher* soon arrived and Goodhart boarded with his chart to give Keyes a personal report on his patrol in the Heligoland Bight. *E.8*'s dodgy motor decided to pack up completely whilst he was aboard. Keyes ordered Goodhart back to Harwich for repairs, '& sleep which he said I looked as if I needed & I did.' The tension of the first patrol had clearly exacted its toll. The starboard motor was repaired with help from *Maidstone*. Goodhart obtained reliefs for two of his engine room hands and got a sound night's sleep in the borrowed cabin of *E.3*'s commander, Cholmley.

Keyes finally obtained Sturdee's permission to take up the line to the south around 1pm and had to once again work down the line to pass on the new orders over the next few hours. The submarines were sent to a set of parallel echeloned lines between the Light Vessels on the North

---

7   At night *E.4* and *E.9* to Long Sand, *E.2* and *D.7* to Galloper, *D.8* to Kentish Knock, *E.5*, *E.7* and *E.3* to West Hinder, *D.2* and *D.3* to Ruytingen. Until the buoys were placed *E.4*/*E.9*, *E.2*/*D.7* and *D.2*/*D.3* were to operate within 1½ miles of each other to ensure they kept in touch.

8   TNA ADM186/610: BEF p.30; TNA ADM137/2067: pp.55–62, 615.

Goodwin, Sandettie and Ruytingen Shoals, stationed in pairs.[9] In this way, Keyes hoped at least seven boats would be able to deliver an attack whatever route the Germans used. Sturdee told him that the patrol would be needed for up to two weeks and that he should arrange for submarines to cover the line in reliefs, keeping a strong force in place for at least two days until German intentions clarified.

This somewhat farcical episode of submarines going backwards and forwards demonstrates a downside of the new era of wireless communication. Senior officers behind a desk were able to micro-manage detailed dispositions which were actually better left to officers aware of the situation on the spot, stifling tactical initiative.

Both *E.6* and *E.8* completed their repairs and left Harwich to bolster the reserve at the Sandettie Light Vessel at 1pm on the 11th. Talbot spotted a drifting British seaplane about six miles away on the water with a broken down engine on the way. *E.6* gave it a tow, handing over to *Firedrake* when they arrived at the Sandettie around 7:30pm. All 13 submarines were now on the patrol line. *Firedrake* towed the seaplane back to Margate and then returned.

The submarines left the light ships each morning and usually anchored on the surface at their billets against the strong currents in the area, often trimmed down with only the conning tower out of the water. The weather remained good, although the boats got damp at night and Talbot says that the sea was quite agitated for much of the time. Goodhart observed that the coastal steamer traffic seemed to be returning to normal during the stay and did not share Keyes optimism about a German attack developing. Hallifax took the opportunity to bathe in the sea on the 11th, finding it 'very refreshing', but only Engine Room Artificer (ERA) Williams and Leading Torpedo Operator (LTO) Sims saw the need to join him! *E.7's* crew were in good spirits, at one point enjoying a 'sing-song down below'. Patrolling British seaplanes or airships passed overhead occasionally – the airships were short range non-rigid types. *Lurcher* and *Firedrake* visited from time to time with fresh provisions, newspapers and mails. They patrolled to the north and made runs through the submarine line to test their response. At night the boats returned to the lightships and anchored or tied up to them, with the boat partially submerged and ready to dive immediately if approached. The French crew of the Sandettie Light Vessel were unaware that war had been declared, so *E.6's* French speakers helpfully wrote them out a summary of events and threw it aboard in a tobacco tin 'much to their delight'.

The routine was occasionally interrupted. The commander of *E.7*, Feilmann, came hurtling down the ladder from the bridge with orders to dive at 2am on the 11th. Hallifax writes that apparently 'a steamer's lights were coming straight at us'. After this experience Feilmann chose to spend the rest of the night and the next night resting on the shallow bottom in around 65 feet (20m). *E.7* had also sheered bolts on her starboard flywheel on the 10th, which was not repaired until *Firedrake* picked up some new bolts from Dover on the 12th. The danger inherent in hanging about on the surface near to the Dover Straits Patrol was demonstrated to *D.7* on the morning of the 11th. The destroyer *Mohawk* had spotted a submarine, went to action stations and turned to attack. She hoisted the challenge. *D.7* raised the reply. A minute later *Mohawk* fired a gun, a fact her log does not mention. This was assumed by *D.7* to be fired to miss – perhaps it was. Fortunately, *D.7's* pendant was then recognised!

---

9   Logs and diaries show *D.7* and *D.8* occupied South Falls/North Goodwin Light, *E.4* Sandettie Light, *E.5* and *E.7* west of Ruytingen/Ruytingen Light, *D.2* and *D.3* Ruytingen Light. The remainder are unclear.

D.7 underway before the war. (NH 54958)

Keyes reported to Sturdee on the 12th that temporary buoys had been laid to mark the new patrol lines. They were to be replaced with permanent buoys. The signal rockets had also been issued to *Lurcher* and *Firedrake*. Keyes planned to keep all the boats out until the 15th. After this he had arranged to start sending three boats at a time in to rest for a few hours at nearby Dover, unless the Germans showed up. *Adamant* had relocated to Dover to support this on the morning of the 11th.[10]

The main body of the Army was due to cross from the 12th to the 17th. The Admiralty believed that this was the period of greatest risk of a German intervention. Intelligence now confirmed the concentration of the German High Sea Fleet at Cuxhaven in the Elbe. The Admiralty responded by ordering the Grand Fleet into the North Sea, with a view to arranging cruiser sweeps towards the Heligoland Bight as soon as possible. Keyes was told to stand down the level of patrol effort in the Channel on the evening of the 12th. Half of the boats were to be withdrawn to Harwich, refuelled and held in readiness. Two Es were to be sent immediately to Yarmouth to cover against a potential raid on the Norfolk coast. This was considered to be the most likely enemy action by the Admiralty.

Waistell detached *E.5* and *E.7* from the patrol at 3am next morning. They arrived at noon to cheers from a crowd at Gorleston pier. An impromptu sing-song by the combined crews on the

---

10   TNA ADM137/2067: pp.63–64, 615; Keyes, *Memoirs*, pp.71–72; TNA ADM53: *Mohawk*, 11 August 1914.

decks of the boats that evening met with applause from a large patriotic crowd that had gathered on the jetty. When the crowd then decided to join in the noise was deafening, so the crews were piped down for the night. Both submarines had problems with tipsy crewmen returning after being granted two hours leave ashore the next day. The locals had enthusiastically provided free drinks![11]

D.2, D.3, D.7 and *D.8* had left the patrol for Harwich at 4am on the 13th. Keyes informed Sturdee that he planned for them to return to relieve *E.3, E.4. E.6, E.8* and *E.9* on the 15th. This group would then go in to Harwich to rest and prepare for offensive operations. *D.5* and *E.2* would be sent in to Dover on the 15th for rest and maintenance work by *Adamant* as they had developed defective clutches on the propeller shafts; the first sign of what would become a major issue. Once repaired they would act as a reserve for the patrol. Keyes assumed it would continue until the BEF had finished crossing.

Lurcher and *Firedrake* had taken turns to quickly top up with fuel at Dover on the 12th, where they had also picked up provisions for the submarines on the patrol, but with only two watches available for the engine room, the stokers were exhausted after six days almost constantly underway. Keyes got agreement to send *Firedrake* in to Harwich for 24 hours rest and she left at 7:30pm on the 13th.

When *Firedrake* returned Keyes planned to take *Lurcher* in to Harwich for a rest while he headed up to London to discuss offensive operations at the Admiralty. Meanwhile, on the 13th he once again pushed the idea of a drive into the Heligoland Bight to clear out the German fishing fleet, or at least any boats carrying wireless or carrier pigeons, once the BEF had crossed to France. He believed this would force the Germans to protect them and place warship pickets, which would then fall 'easy prey' to submarines operating out of Yarmouth as a forward base. Keyes proposed that if a closer watch was kept on the Heligoland Bight the submarines could co-operate inshore to attack enemy vessels coming out to engage the watch. He wanted to visit the C-in-C to discuss these plans. His enthusiasm for the defensive patrol had evaporated, as he conceded that it now appeared that the High Sea Fleet had no intention of attacking the BEF transports. He had effectively done an about face to begin advocating early offensive operations in German waters.

The Fleet was about to be ordered to push cruiser sweeps right into the Heligoland Bight and Keyes was duly summoned to the Admiralty early on the 14th. Before leaving Keyes had Talbot brought on-board *Lurcher* by boat and spent an hour in discussion with him to get a first-hand impression of conditions off the German coast. *Lurcher* then headed in to nearby Dover. Keyes disembarked at 8:15am to get the train up to London and *Lurcher* was sent back to the patrol line. The switch to offensive operations in support of the fleet was approved. Keyes was directed to withdraw the defensive patrol next morning. *Adamant, Lurcher* and the remaining submarines got underway at 4am on the 15th and were all back in Harwich by 11am.[12]

11   TNA ADM186/619: Naval Staff Monographs Volume X – Home Waters from the outbreak of War to 27 Aug 1914, pp.80–81; TNA ADM186/610: BEF, p. 36; IWM:Documents.1003: 13 August.
12   TNA ADM137/2067: pp.65–68; Keyes, *Memoirs*, p. 73; TNA ADM173: *D.3, D.7, E.4, E.5, E.6, E.7, E.8,* 9–15 August 1914; TNA ADM53: *Adamant, Lurcher, Firedrake* 8–15 August 1914; IWM:Documents.2175: letter to wife 20 August; IWM:Documents.20134: 8–15 August; IWM:Documents.1003: 8-15 August

The defensive patrol arrangements had not been tested. The German Army never seriously considered landing troops in England since they would be cut off with overwhelming force by the Royal Navy and inevitably destroyed. When the Germans received intelligence that the BEF had begun crossing, their Army High Command told the Navy that they would prefer to destroy the BEF in France rather than have them in England. In a mirror image of British concerns, they feared that they might be landed on the German coast. An attack on the transports by the Fleet was ruled out in the war plan. Nevertheless, the Kaiser did authorise attacks on the transports by torpedo and mine armed vessels, especially submarines. A half-hearted probe by just four available submarines did not get any farther south than Rotterdam.[13]

13   Groos, *Nordsee 1*, pp.78-86.

6

The first attack

Keyes was briefed on important changes in the command structure when he arrived at the Admiralty late on 14 August. He was already aware that his commander, Admiral Callaghan, had been replaced by Admiral Jellicoe on the 5th. Three days later, Jellicoe had asked the Admiralty to take over direction of the Harwich Flotillas and 7th Cruiser Squadron. He had found it impossible to exercise effective control as his Grand Fleet was based in northern waters and was almost continuously at sea.

The Admiralty had therefore decided to combine Tyrwhitt's Destroyer Flotillas, the 8th Submarine Flotilla and the 7th Cruiser Squadron into a new command called Southern Force. Rear-Admiral Arthur H. Christian had been appointed on the 13th to the command. Christian was aged 50 and his recent career had alternated sea commands with several periods of study on specialised gunnery, signals, torpedo and War College courses. In his latest spell at the Naval War College in 1912 he came second out of five flag officers in his class and was judged to be 'very zealous, careful and sound.'[1]

Keyes was informed that both the Grand Fleet and Tyrwhitt's Flotillas would sweep into the Heligoland Bight on the 16th as part of the new advanced covering position for the BEF. The role of the Harwich Flotillas had been agreed by Churchill, Battenberg, Sturdee and Tyrwhitt at a meeting at the Admiralty earlier that day. Tyrwhitt wrote that Churchill was 'very much on the warpath and seeing red'.[2] Keyes was therefore playing catch-up, but this was exactly the sort of operation he had already advocated. He proposed that four of his submarines should proceed at once to watch the exits from the key German bases on the North Sea coast. He also sent a proposal to Christian that a continuous presence of three submarines should be maintained in the Heligoland Bight, in line with his new found enthusiasm for offensive operations.[3]

Firedrake, with *Druid* of Tyrwhitt's 1st Flotilla, was directed to proceed to Yarmouth at 3:30am next morning, the 15th, then tow *E.5* and *E.7* to the Bight. A telegram was sent to *E.5* ordering the boats out into Yarmouth Roads next morning to meet their tows and receive their orders. The submarines were to slip their tows at nightfall off the Dutch coast and proceed to

1 The Dreadnought Project, <http://www.dreadnoughtproject.org/tfs/index.php/Arthur_Henry_Christian> (accessed 6 April 2018); TNA ADM196/42/157: Arthur Henry Christian.
2 Patterson, *Tyrwhitt*, p.50.
3 Churchill, *World Crisis*, pp.210–213, TNA ADM137/2067: p.616.

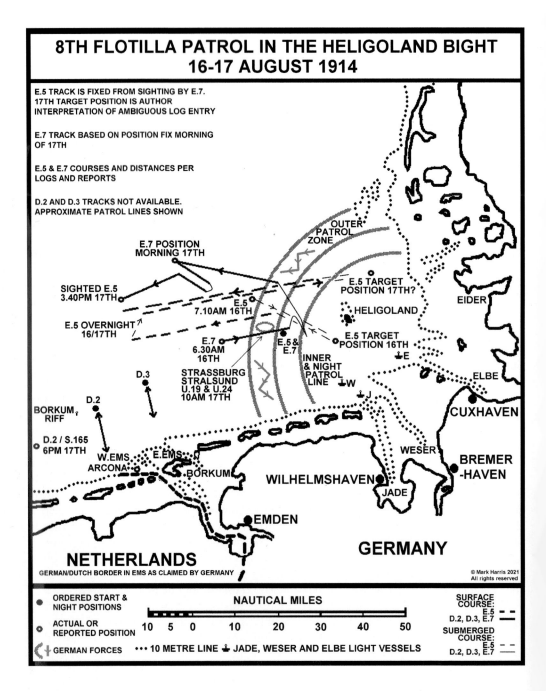

8TH FLOTILLA PATROL IN THE HELIGOLAND BIGHT 16-17 AUGUST 1914

E.5 TRACK IS FIXED FROM SIGHTING BY E.7.
17TH TARGET POSITION IS AUTHOR
INTERPRETATION OF AMBIGUOUS LOG ENTRY

E.7 TRACK BASED ON POSITION FIX MORNING
OF 17TH

E.5 & E.7 COURSES AND DISTANCES PER
LOGS AND REPORTS

D.2 AND D.3 TRACKS NOT AVAILABLE.
APPROXIMATE PATROL LINES SHOWN

OUTER PATROL ZONE

E.7 POSITION MORNING 17TH

SIGHTED E.5 3.40PM 17TH

E.5 TARGET POSITION 17TH?

E.5 7.10AM 16TH

HELIGOLAND

EIDER

E.5 OVERNIGHT 16/17TH

E.7 6.30AM 16TH

E.5 & E.7

E.5 TARGET POSITION 16TH

E

D.3

INNER & NIGHT PATROL LINE

W

ELBE

STRASSBURG STRALSUND U.19 & U.24 10AM 17TH

D.2

CUXHAVEN

BORKUM, RIFF

J

D.2 / S.165 6PM 17TH

WESER

BREMER-HAVEN

W.EMS ARCONA

E.EMS

BORKUM

WILHELMSHAVEN

JADE

© Mark Harris 2021
All rights reserved

EMDEN

GERMANY

NETHERLANDS

GERMAN/DUTCH BORDER IN EMS AS CLAIMED BY GERMANY

ORDERED START & NIGHT POSITIONS

NAUTICAL MILES

SURFACE COURSE:
E.5
D.2, D.3, E.7

ACTUAL OR REPORTED POSITION

10 5 0   10   20   30   40   50

SUBMERGED COURSE:
E.5
D.2, D.3, E.7

GERMAN FORCES   ••• 10 METRE LINE   JADE, WESER AND ELBE LIGHT VESSELS

a position 15 miles west of Heligoland. They were to close the mouth of the Elbe and Weser respectively each day, returning to their start position at night. On the afternoon of the 17th they were to return to Harwich via Lowestoft. *Ferret* and *Forester*, also of 1st Flotilla, were to take *D.2* and *D.3* in tow at Harwich at 7am and follow the same routine. These submarines were to head to a position 15 miles north of the Ems, closing in to the Western and Eastern exits during the day. Commander Palmer of *Thames* was to go in *Ferret* and Waistell would go in *Firedrake*. A late addendum to the orders confirmed that the Fleet battle cruisers and cruisers would be carrying out a drive from the northwest towards the Bight on the morning of the 16th. The Harwich Destroyer Flotillas and 7th Cruiser Squadron would also be operating off the Dutch coast between Terschelling and Borkum Riff off the Western Ems.[4]

E.5 was commanded by Lieutenant-Commander Charles S. Benning. He was 29 years old and had joined the Submarine Service in 1905. After commanding a number of coastal submarines he was assessed by Captain Willis in 1913: 'Most zealous & capable. Rec[ommende]d for c[omman]d of E class S/M.' That September he took command of the new *E.5*. Benning also had an inventive streak and received the thanks of the Admiralty for designing the collapsible wireless mast being fitted to submarines in the Flotilla. The author Rudyard Kipling described him as 'one of the most charming men I had ever met' after a visit to the Flotilla.[5]

E.7 was commanded by Lieutenant-Commander Ferdinand E.B. Feilmann, or 'Ferdi' to his fellow officers. He was to be 31 years old on the 19th. Feilmann had joined the Submarine Service in 1904. He had commanded a succession of coastal submarines, but he was also an accomplished swordsman. Feilmann was the British Sabre Champion in 1907 and was in the Sabre Team at the 1912 Olympics. The assessments on his record are all remarkably bland, 'Capable & zealous' being typical. He had been appointed to *E.7* in November 1913 as she neared completion. *The Maidstone Magazine* implies that his love of hearty meals led to jokes at the expense of his weight. Feilmann had a reputation for being difficult to serve with; he had a recurring deeply troubled relationship with alcohol, evidenced in his later record, but there may have been more behind his bouts of challenging behaviour. Whatever the underlying reason, the stresses of wartime patrolling certainly had an immediate and serious negative impact. Feilmann had been genial whilst the boat was out on the Channel patrol, but there had been an awkward journey up to Yarmouth with Hallifax writing that he had been; 'barking orders like a lunatic' at the crew.[6]

Firedrake and *Druid* met *E.5* and *E.7* off Yarmouth at 7am on the 15th. Waistell sent their orders across in a boat, along with a third officer for *E.7*, Sub-Lieutenant Cunard. The destroyers took up their tows and headed out to sea. *E.5*'s tow from *Firedrake* broke twice, so she eventually proceeded under her own power. *Firedrake* gave them their position at dusk. Waistell signalled: 'I wish you best of luck and a good bag' and the destroyers returned to Harwich. The submarines headed off together for their billets at 7:30pm.

4   TNA ADM137/2067: pp.82–3.
5   TNA ADM196/49/192: Charles Stuart Benning; National Maritime Museum: Personal Collection, Leslie Cope Cornford, letter from Kipling 26 November 1915
6   TNA ADM:196/143/149 & 196/48/98 & 196/126/153: Ferdinand Eric Bertram Feilmann; IWM:Documents.1003: 13 August; Douglas, *Maidstone Magazine*, pp.3, 7, 15; *International Olympic Committee*<https://stillmed.olympic.org/Documents/Reports/Official%20Past%20Games%20Reports/Summer/1912/ENG/1912-RO-S-Stockholm_VIII.pdf>

E.5 underway before the war. (NH 54963)

Both Benning and Feilmann now sighted a merchant ship, which steamed parallel to them, and both were suspicious of it. Benning identified a Danish flag, but Feilmann couldn't make a flag out. Benning felt that she might have reported their course and position, since 'as subsequent events seemed to show, we were expected.' After three hours the submarines lost sight of each other.

Benning approached the Bight next morning. He sighted smoke from shipping to the east at 4am, then three hours later spotted what appeared to be buoy markers. As he got closer these were identified to be destroyers, moving in different directions on the horizon. He had initially been fooled by the recognition triangles carried at the top of their foremasts, which he only learnt of after the patrol. Benning now began his approach to the Elbe. *E.5* was dived to 50 feet (15m) and turned towards a position six miles southwest of Heligoland, moving at five knots to prolong the battery life. Benning came up to periscope depth at 10 minute intervals. He reports that: 'On raising periscope at 9.30 I saw a Destroyer right ahead; as sea was very calm Destroyer saw wake of my periscope and turned to Starboard, firing a torpedo. I dived immediately to 50 feet and torpedo missed.' After this several destroyers turned up and steamed on different courses and speeds around *E.5*. They were 'passing and re-passing over me … continually … obviously trying to keep me down and so expend battery'. He only dared to raise the periscope when their propeller sounds receded. Benning had noticed ship traffic inshore to the east of Heligoland during this time. He speculated in his report that: 'from way traffic was together, it might point to a minefield being laid between this channel and the sea'.

After three hours of this cat and mouse game only one destroyer was within four miles and Benning decided to use her tactics against her. *E.5* surfaced and Benning: 'opened conning tower hatch to attract her'. He no doubt felt there was little risk from her guns at this range. After some time she altered course in his direction at high speed. Benning dived at once and commenced an attack run working out to her starboard beam so that he could fire at the target side on, maximising the chance of a hit. The crew had prepared the bow torpedo for firing and set it to run at six feet depth (1.8m), to ensure that it did not run under the shallow draught destroyer. The outer shutter protecting the torpedo tube was opened and the tube was brought to the ready by flooding it with water from an internal tank. Benning brought *E.5* into the ideal attack position 500 yards (450m), about 80 degrees off the destroyer's bow, in other words off to the side and a little ahead. The outer tube door was opened. He lined up on the spot that he estimated his torpedo would cross her track. At this range the torpedo would take less than a minute to reach the target. Benning gave the order to fire. A blast of compressed air into the tube launched the torpedo. The engine was started by the firing lever as it left the tube, quickly accelerating it to full speed. The target now 'just avoided the torpedo by putting her helm hard to port', having apparently spotted the torpedo. During the entire patrol the weather throughout the Bight was good, with little wind and high visibility. The lack of waves made it easier to spot a torpedo wake in the water. Thus, Benning and his crew had delivered the Royal Navy's first ever wartime torpedo attack.

It was now 1pm. The crew reloaded the bow tube. Benning continued on his submerged course towards the Elbe for another three hours. There were no big ships in sight, so *E.5* reversed course to head back out to sea. Benning wanted to surface to charge the batteries, but a destroyer was close by, so he pressed on. The battery was completely exhausted by 7pm after almost 10 hours underway. Benning had to surface. Fortunately, it was clear up above. The crew started the diesels and *E.5* headed west for three hours, by which time the battery 'was charged sufficiently'. Benning chose to dive to 50 feet at 11pm, moving very slowly to the northeast to maintain depth all night, as 'the Destroyers would in all probability be trying to catch submarines on the surface at night'.

E.5 surfaced at dawn on the 17th. Benning headed back the way he had come to the east charging his batteries, with nothing in sight, either aiming for, or eventually reaching, a position 12 miles northeast of Heligoland. Unfortunately, the log and his report are ambiguous about this and also have contradictory timings. Sometime around 9am he: 'suddenly saw a German periscope 100 yards on my Starboard beam. I immediately put helm hard to starboard and dived to 50 feet, the torpedo fired by submarine passing under my stern.' The steep emergency dive had lifted the stern up. The attacker was not seen again. Half an hour later he sighted what looked like three British four funnelled cruisers heading west, on the horizon to the southwest. He remained submerged and kept heading east until about 10am. There was now nothing in sight. *E.5* reversed course and Benning surfaced at around noon to return to Harwich.[7]

E.7 approached her billet on the 16th after diving to check trim. The newly arrived Cunard was detailed to get a position sight, which Lieutenant Hallifax then worked out. This ended up in recriminations as: 'I [Hallifax] say he took it wrong, and he says I worked it out wrong; he cannot work it out as I have the old pattern Inman tables & he does not understand them'. After taking a best guess at their position *E.7* headed towards her billet. At 7:34am Feilmann sighted a ship on the horizon and dived to attack, but she quickly disappeared and *E.7* returned

---

7   TNA ADM137/2067: pp.85–6.

to the surface. An hour later a destroyer was spotted approaching. *E.7* dived and headed at high speed to cut her off. The target continually altered course away. Speed had to be reduced to save battery power and she disappeared. Feilmann pressed on. Each time the periscope was raised, at least one destroyer was sighted moving at high speed, altering course frequently. This made both attack and returning to the surface impossible. Hallifax deduced that the patrol position was behind several lines of destroyers, so *E.7* would also have a hard time getting clear after an attack. Feilmann believed that it was useless running down the battery attempting to approach the destroyers and hoped that one would happen to get close, as the calm water made attack at anything other than very close range a waste of time.

At 10am *E.7* altered to southeast to close the Elbe. At noon Hallifax spotted a town and chimneys in the periscope. Feilmann was sceptical, but on closing it was clearly Heligoland, which was much closer than expected. He headed north to get clear of the island. By 3:50pm Hallifax writes that: 'things began to look a bit serious for the battery was down ... and we did not know how many more lines [of destroyers] we had to pass through', added to which 'the engines were shaking like anything'. There was not enough charge left to get clear and a destroyer was still in sight. Power was reduced to an absolute minimum in the hope that *E.7* would coast clear, but instead she sank. An attempt to blow a ballast tank failed, so the motors were put full ahead. This had no effect. *E.7* touched the bottom in 95 feet (29m) of water. The motors were quickly stopped. A depth of at least 120 feet (37m) had been feared, beyond the certified diving depth of 100 feet (30m).[8]

Feilmann in his report glosses over the accidental bottoming, but in any case sensibly decided to stay put until after dark. Hallifax writes that: 'lights were cut down to a minimum ... dinner was biscuits when we thought about it, but it was so fuggy that one did not want to eat ... the boat got clammy & chilly & when I got to sleep I woke again fairly soon, wondering, I think, if [darkness] had yet come.' Nothing was heard above. Ballast tanks were blown at 8:55pm. *E.7* surfaced: 'the hatch was opened the air rushed out ... the atmosphere in the boat was visible! It formed a blue mist!'[9] *E.7* had been submerged for 12 hours. Feilmann got underway out to sea charging the battery, with only two sentries on the bridge and everyone else at diving stations in case an enemy was encountered. *E.7* stopped at 11:30pm to speed up charging, seeming well clear of the patrol. The charge was finally completed at 4:30am.

The officers had held a council of war during the night and 'decided unanimously against piercing the screens again today but being determined to sink someone ... decided to attack the outer line of destroyers.' It was intended to close the enemy line around midday to ensure enough time to escape submerged after the attack. *E.7* even anchored in place for nearly two hours, a risky decision in daylight. Two sights were obtained at intervals to fix her position. At 11:30am Feilmann got underway for the position west of Heligoland. Smoke was soon spotted to the south, suggesting the enemy screen had been extended westwards. Half an hour later, as Hallifax was taking another sight, the signalman spotted more smoke ahead, which soon turned out to be a destroyer. *E.7* dived and all tubes were readied for firing, but the destroyer moved out of sight. At 1pm Feilmann decided to partially surface for a better look around. Hallifax climbed up on the periscope stand. At first he saw nothing, but then quickly jumped

---

8   In practice E-boats proved capable of diving to over 200 feet during the war (60m).
9   Air leaked from the high pressure systems whilst a boat was dived, gradually increasing the pressure inside.

down when a black shape with no mast, set against the sun, came into focus only two miles away. Hallifax suspected a submarine and *E.7* dived. Feilmann quickly lost sight of her through the periscope and Hallifax wondered if it could have been *E.5*.

An hour later there was still nothing around. Feilmann decided to end the patrol. *E.7* surfaced and immediately headed off west at full speed on the motors until the diesels could be started, in case the submarine was lurking. At 3:40pm *E.5* was spotted ahead, but the port engine now stopped. It took an hour to trace the problem to water that had got into the fuel. *E.7* now caught up and joined astern as Benning was Senior Officer. The boats exchanged news.[10]

Despite appearances the Germans were not expecting Benning and Feilmann. The suspicious steamer sighted on the night of the 15th was just plying its route. However, various bogus reports had convinced the Germans that submarines were operating northwest of Heligoland and west of the Ems. On the night of the 15/16th sweeps by around 20 destroyers supported by two cruisers out to sea from Heligoland were made to catch them on the surface, but at this point there was nothing for them to find. It was smoke from this large force that had been spotted in the distance as they returned on the morning of the 16th.

The routine day patrol took up position in the Bight from 4am on the 16th. The 8th Torpedoboots-Flottille was spread across the outer zone, steaming backwards and forwards between its inner and outer edges. This had 11 boats at full strength. An inner line was patrolled by the torpedo boats of 3rd Minensuchdivision (Mine Sweeping Division), with a strength of up to 13 boats. These had swapped their torpedo tubes for sweeping gear. The destroyers drew back to the inner line at 6pm, whilst the torpedo boats withdrew to Heligoland Harbour. The constant course alterations by these boats were intended to make them hard for submarines to attack and ensure that they were unable to surface in the patrol zone during daylight. The tactics were successful, as both *E.5* and *E.7* exhausted their batteries and failed in the only attack. Feilmann was deterred from even trying to break through the next day. However, none of the patrol boats reported enemy submarines. Benning's attack and torpedo were not seen by his target, which must have simply turned away roughly when he fired. Whatever he saw 'fired' at *E.5*, it was not a torpedo.

Next morning the 8th Torpedoboots-Flottille were relieved on patrol by the rather threadbare 7th Torpedoboots-Flottille, which could muster only seven boats, with another two borrowed from the 8th. 3rd Minensuchdivision were ordered to steam round the Inner Bight during the morning as an anti-submarine precaution instead of taking up their patrol line, since the battle cruisers of the German 1st Aufklärungsgruppe (Scouting Group) were coming out in the late morning for gunnery practice. The battleships of the 1st Geschwader were also swapping the Jade for the Elbe with 2nd Geschwader. The result was the unusually sparse patrol line that *E.5* and *E.7* encountered on the 17th, down from over 20 boats to nine.

Ironically, having failed to spot either *E.5* or *E.7* during their patrol, reports of three submerged submarines off the Weser and Jade entrances later that afternoon caused a frenzied response. These were soon identified to be a false alarm, encouraging the Fleet Command to schedule more exercises!

German submarines no longer patrolled in the Bight. It is impossible to say what Benning mistook for an attack by one on the morning of the 17th. Many things could be mistaken for

---

10   TNA ADM137/2067: pp.8790; IWM: Documents.1003: 15-17 August 1914.

periscope wash, not least surfacing porpoises. Identifying a sighting on watch in all weathers is not easy. An acquaintance once dived his modern submarine whilst on watch in the South Atlantic to avoid a boat that turned out to be a penguin on raising the periscope. Benning was better off diving rather than waiting around to get a good look.[11]

The cruisers seen by Benning on the 17th could not have been British. The fleet was much farther out to sea. However the light cruisers *Strassburg* and *Stralsund*, accompanied by *U.19* and *U.24*, left Heligoland at 7:40am, steering zig-zag courses west for a reconnaissance raid on the British patrols in the Southern Bight. The cruisers were similar to a British Town class. *E.7* had missed a chance to attack them by remaining out at sea most of the morning and had seen their smoke to the south. Benning almost certainly also saw them based on their bearing from *E.5* and her implied position. It is difficult to account for the fact that Benning saw no patrolling destroyers at all on the 17th and his position was vaguely reported as 'in between Heligoland and the mainland', but Hallifax probably also saw *E.5* in the afternoon.

E.5 and *E.7* returned together, heading through the night towards the Smiths Knoll Lightship to fix their position on the way into Lowestoft. At 4:30am next morning, the 18th, Benning sighted first a smoke cloud, then later a four funnel cruiser on the horizon ahead. Benning decided it was a *Cressy* class after consulting his ship recognition guide, Janes. The 7th Cruiser Squadron patrolling this area were all of this class. They closed on roughly opposite but parallel courses over the next hour. Benning still had the bridge screen rigged and his wireless mast up and in his report says he still had no doubts about his identification. He now raised the challenge flag signal to confirm her identity and note it in the log. Benning saw a flag raised in response. This was followed by ripples of light from the ship and the arrival some seconds later of what he took to be 6-inch (15cm) shells! He immediately ordered a crash dive to 80 feet (24m), but before the boat went down several salvoes had fallen round it. Benning then observed the cruiser appear to turn to starboard and make off to the northeast. In the rush to dive there had been a casualty. An unnamed Stoker caught his arm in the counter gear at the stern, tearing it to the bone from his wrist almost to his elbow.

Goodhart wrote in a letter to his wife that Benning did have doubts about his identification and should have dived before now. Hallifax writes: 'I was furious at *E.5*'s criminal stupidity in hoisting a demand to a man of war.' Previous mess discussions had agreed that it was always prudent to dive for a ship closing ahead. This would allow an attack if an enemy and avoid being mistakenly fired on if a friend. Correct identification from ahead was difficult.

E.7 was 400 yards to starboard of *E.5* and had the ship itself in sight for 20 minutes. Cunard was on watch at the time. He had tentatively identified the vessel as a four funnelled *Argyll* class cruiser. These ships were part of the Grand Fleet. Cunard was a new hand and it would not be expected they would be this far south, but Feilmann did not come to the bridge, a fact omitted from his report. He was in his bunk and simply sent up the recognition signal. Cunard said that Benning's demand flag went unanswered for 10 minutes, by which time the cruiser was passing two or three miles away. When the salvo arrived the alarm bell was rung rapidly to signal a crash dive and everybody cleared down as fast as possible. Hallifax was woken by the din: 'I heard

---

11   BArch:RM92: *Von der Tann* Kriegstagebuch 15-17 August 1914, Übungen Befehl 91, Tagsicherung 15-16 August 1914, Befehlen 86, 89, 92; *Cöln* Kriegstagebuch 15-16 August 1914, Nachtsicherung und Vorstoss 15 August 1914; Groos, *Nordsee 1*, pp.104, 137 incorrectly gives 16th as date of gunnery practice.

Strassburg steaming at high speed. (Sjöhistoriska Museet Fo195701)

Feilmann's agitated voice shouting "One of our own? Argyll?" Cunard replied "looks like her, but she fired at us; the shot fell about 30 yards off" … I ran like a stag amidships, opening vents … People were falling down the hatch like flies, Feilmann was shouting "Full speed ahead, dive to 40 feet", the 2 Cox was screaming for his foremost hydroplane to be unlocked … I was pleased with the … crew's behaviour. Osborne who was steering turned the boat bows on to the cruiser directly she fired so as to present as small a target as possible, without orders. The signalman [Sidney C. Johnson], usually such a fool, had the sense to secure my telescope as he came down.' Further salvos fell around with an unnerving sound like rifle bullets striking the hull. However, a stool, a sou'wester and a set of hand flags were left behind and never seen again.[12] The wireless aerial also broke free. *E.7* stayed down for 15 minutes by which time nothing was in sight except smoke. Feilmann had claimed he could see nothing through the periscope as it was fogged and Hallifax implies he had been drinking.

The cause of the commotion was *Strassburg* under the command of Fregattenkapitän Retzmann. The raiding group that had left Heligoland had split up. Retzmann had advanced to within 35 miles of Lowestoft and was now on the return leg, steaming at 25 knots. *Strassburg* was a fast, modern light cruiser and carried an armament of 12x10.5cm (4.1-inch) guns that could range to 12.2km (6.6 miles), with a six gun broadside. At 5:15am she sighted three submarines 12km (6½ miles) ahead and to port. She identified them as being of the British D class and one appeared to dive. Retzmann immediately turned a little to starboard to bring his full port battery into action. Rangefinders confirmed the range, then three minutes later *Strassburg* opened salvo fire at 10.5km (5.7 miles), spotting down to 8.5km (4.6 miles) as the targets disappeared. Retzmann

---

12 Johnson, aged 21, from Southsea, had three years of service and a superior rating for his signalling ability. See TNA ADM 188/662/7867.

reported a probable hit on the rear boat with the second straddling salvo, but was actually seeing the spray thrown up from *E.7*'s emergency flooding of the tanks as she went down steeply, lifting her stern out of the water. Nevertheless this was good shooting. For the British, the difficulty in gauging range by eye was demonstrated as the range was reported as 3,000 yards (2.7km) and the inexperienced Cunard even estimated 1,200 yards (1.1km).[13]

The apparent inactivity of the German Fleet had perhaps caused complacency and a disaster could have been the result. Another opportunity to attack *Strassburg* had also been missed, this time by both submarines.

E.5 had lost most of her charts in the crash dive, so *E.7* took the lead. The boats diverted to Yarmouth, arriving at 10am. Benning wanted to get his Stoker treated quickly, as he was in considerable pain. A doctor was summoned but failed to materialise, so he went alongside and landed him for treatment at Yarmouth Hospital. The submarines arrived back in Harwich at 5pm. Keyes was waiting for Benning on arrival. He used his charm to spin a tale that painted him as the hero of the piece, whilst not concealing the facts about coming under fire, then repeated the performance in the mess. Goodhart writes that: 'Feilmann was very sick with Benning who got some Kudos when he made his report to the Commodore... [Feilmann said that] the submarine reported by Benning was probably either himself or Boyle, & that Benning hadn't been near his proper position at all'. Goodhart records that not everything Feilmann said was to be believed, but that there was 'apparently something in it'. It is undeniable that it is hard to make sense of where *E.5* was. The two attacks reported on *E.5* do also suggest that Benning's imagination got the better of him during the patrol.

Keyes commended Benning's 'gallant persistence' in his own report and considered him 'unlucky not to have achieved success', but also writes that the 'narrow escape of *E.5* and *E.7* impressed on the officers of the flotilla the folly of remaining on the surface within gunfire of a possible enemy.' Just how narrow was confirmed when Hallifax found that *E.7* had lost some of her paintwork as a result of a near miss. Keyes says nothing about Feilmann. He was perhaps unimpressed that he did not push forward as ordered on the morning of the 17th.[14]

E.7's crew traced the cause of the engine noise on the patrol to the starboard engine flywheel. It needed major work and the repair was only completed on the 22nd. It turned out that Chatham Dockyard had done a bodged job at the last refit and it was hanging on with only two badly fitted bolts. *E.5* also spent a couple of days on the Harwich floating dock. She had broken off a refit to join the Flotilla at the outbreak of war and needed to paint her bottom.[15]

D.2 and *D.3* had left Harwich as planned on the 15th, towed by *Ferret* and *Forester* respectively. They slipped their tows as darkness fell and headed for their billets.

D.3 was commanded by Lieutenant-Commander Edward C. Boyle, aged 31. He had achieved good results in his Lieutenant's examinations and excelled at both drawing and French. Boyle joined the Submarine Service in 1904. Captain Johnson assessed him in 1911 when he graduated from coastal submarine command to *D.2*: 'Kept his S/M in excellent order. Makes V[ery]G[ood] attacks.' In 1914 Captain Fisher of the *St. Vincent* was less impressed during his mandatory service on a surface ship: 'Quiet nice disposition. Somewhat lacking in

13   Groos, *Nordsee 1*, pp.102–5; BArch:RM92: *Strassburg* Kriegstagebuch 17-18 August 1914.
14   TNA ADM137/2067: p.81; IWM:Documents.2175: letter to wife 25 August 1914.
15   TNA ADM173: *E.5*, *E.7* 15–21 August 1914; IWM:Documents.2175: letter to wife 25 August 1914; IWM:Documents.1003: 18 August 1914.

authority & confidence. Not at present sufficient enthusiasm nor leadership.' He was appointed to command *D.3* in March 1914. His fellow officer Nasmith found him: 'lanky, loose-jointed and always carefully dressed, courteous though distant and elusive with strangers, but very ready to sympathise.'[16]

Boyle arrived at his position off the Eastern Ems at 8:10am on the 16th. On the first day of the patrol *D.3* cruised back and forth to within seven miles of the entrance and saw nothing. At dusk Boyle headed out to a position 18 miles to the north and remained there on the surface till 4am. He returned to his patrol area the next morning, but only saw a large sailing trawler that might have been acting as a lookout. At 2pm *D.3* got underway for return to Harwich. Whilst passing the Western Ems 45 minutes later, Boyle sighted a destroyer up ahead. *D.3* dived and started an attack, but could not get closer than 2½ miles, at which point the destroyer headed off to the west. Boyle surfaced and followed her smoke until darkness intervened, then headed for home. *D.3* arrived back at Harwich at 4pm on the 18th.[17]

Lieutenant-Commander Arthur G. Jameson was 30 years old. His family owned the famous Dublin Whiskey Distillery, but his father was a church minister. Jameson joined the Submarine Service in 1905, commanding *C.2* for nearly three years. He was picked to train for the Naval War Staff in 1912. He showed exceptional ability on the courses and Captain Webb assessed him as having a: 'Special aptitude for operations. Tactful solid quiet. Very dependable & zealous. Broad & clear thinker.' Rear-Admiral Madden added: 'An officer of exceptional ability.' He was recommended for early promotion by Rear-Admiral Pakenham. On completing the courses he had taken command of *D.2* in March.[18]

D.2 arrived 20 miles north of the Western Ems at 5:45am on the 16th and proceeded slowly south towards the estuary. Jameson sighted four destroyers approaching from the west at 11am and dived to attack. As they got closer, he recognised that they were the expected British forces from Harwich. In order to avoid any problems, Jameson did not surface until after they began retiring westwards at noon.[19] A protected cruiser, either the *Fürst Bismarck* or a *Hertha* class, was identified after arriving off the Ems, moored inside the Huibert Gat entrance. This was in waters claimed by both Germany and the Netherlands.[20] *D.2* dived to make an attack run at 4:30pm, but spent the next two hours failing to find an approach route through the very shallow water. Jameson retired north, back out to sea. As the light began to wane at 7pm he sighted a patrol of eight small destroyers and trawlers coming out of the Western Ems. The destroyers spread out fan wise about five miles from the entrance and the trawlers remained on patrol just outside. *D.2* spent the night charging the batteries on the surface 20 to 25 miles north of the Ems.

Daylight came at 4:15am and Jameson closed the main entrance to the Western Ems. The patrol began disappearing into it at 4:30am. By 5am they were all gone. In order to avoid a

16   TNA ADM196/143/142: Edward Courtney Boyle; Peter Shankland & Anthony Hunter, *Dardanelles Patrol* (London: Collins, 1964), p.21.
17   TNA ADM137/2067: p.94; TNA ADM173: *D.3* 15–18 August 1914
18   TNA ADM196/143/309: Arthur George Jameson; <http://www.famousjamesons.com> (accessed 18 October 2020).
19   TNA ADM186/619: p.83.
20   Admiral von Pohl (Chief of the Naval Staff) intervened to prevent the Foreign Office acceding to a Dutch demand that Germany desist from using the Huibert Gat for offensive war operations on 8 August.

D.2 and crew prior to the war. (NH 54942)

pilot vessel, Jameson was forced to remain dived from 9 to 11:40am. He now headed round to the more southerly Huibert Gat entrance to try and get at the cruiser seen the day before. He found a trawler patrolling where the Light Vessel at the entrance used to be. He closed in to half a mile and examined it through the periscope, concluding that it was unarmed and without wireless. The cruiser was spotted in the same place as the day before, but once again shallow water frustrated his approach, so he decided to return to Harwich.

At 5:55pm *D.2* was about 20 miles from the Ems, cruising northwest at 12 knots. Suddenly, a German destroyer of the S type was spotted closing rapidly from the west, coming out of the glitter of the late afternoon sun and close enough to make out a flag at the mainmast! Jameson quickly ordered full speed and turned away to starboard to get end on in order to create a harder target. He then ordered the engines stopped and dived. Jameson does not report how close the destroyer was. Hallifax, after hearing the story in the mess, writes that she was a few hundred yards off, whilst Talbot states 1,500 yards (1,400m). As *D.2* dived Jameson reported that the 'port muffler box refused to close, and port engine and after bilges rapidly flooded'. The exhaust system for the diesel engine was effectively open to the sea. The use of diesels to the last moment and rush to dive may have been part of the problem. The boat lost buoyancy before the valve could be isolated. *D.2* began to sink uncontrollably. Jameson ordered full speed ahead to generate more lift on the hydroplanes. This bought the 20 minutes it took for the pumps to get on top of the flooding and restore buoyancy. Apparently unperturbed by the narrow escape from disaster, Jameson 'proceeded to attack German Destroyer which was steering irregular courses at moderate speed in vicinity of our original dive'. *D.2* closed to 3,000 yards (2,750m).

The destroyer then retired to the east and the attack had to be broken off. Jameson returned to Harwich via Lowestoft without further incident. *D.2* was the last boat to return at 5:45pm on the 18th. Keyes writes in his own report that '[Jameson's] coolness and presence of mind when … [*D.2*] flooded, undoubtedly saved her.'[21]

Although *D.2* and *D.3* were not expected, the 11 destroyers of the 3rd Torpedoboots-Flottille had carried out an overnight sweep from the Ems to Terschelling on the night of the 15/16th. This was part of the operation to ambush British submarines believed to be lurking off the Dutch coast. It was like looking for needles in haystacks and they saw nothing of the inbound submarines in the darkness. The destroyers returned to coal at Emden next morning.

The German routine patrol off the Ems was provided by the Local Defence Flotilla. This was a scanty force of three old destroyers, recently reinforced by four armed trawlers. At night only an armed trawler remained in the Western and Eastern exits. There was also a force of trawlers used as auxiliary minesweepers. They were supported during the day by the old light cruiser *Arcona*, moored in the Huibert Gat, a smaller cruiser than that reported by Jameson. At night, from the 16th onwards, the 3rd Torpedoboots-Flottille and the light cruiser *Kolberg* took position in the Huibert Gat entrance. Three of the destroyers took up an outpost position four miles outside. The entire force headed back up river to Borkum Island each morning. It was this force that Jameson saw coming out on the evening of the 16th and returning next morning.

On the afternoon of the 17th, the Trawler Minesweepers were ordered to sweep off the Ems as a precaution, as strange lights and loud British wireless had been intercepted the night before. *S.165* of 3rd Torpedoboots-Flottille preceded them at 12:30pm, scouting to the west to ensure they were not ambushed. Jameson was focussed on *Arcona* at the time.

S.165 was on her way back to the Ems at the end of her patrol, when a conning tower was spotted ahead. It was unlike that of a German submarine. She turned towards it, just as it dived. *S.165* promptly wirelessed: 'submerged enemy submarine' and her position at 6:06pm. A few minutes later she reported that she was hunting the boat and zig-zagged around the area at high speed for the next half hour. She then stopped for 15 minutes before returning to the Ems! The flooding had robbed *D.2* of a chance to attack a sitting duck. The hunt had been cancelled since *U.19* and *U.24* were known to be heading out, casting doubt on the identification until later in the day. The destroyer hunted that afternoon by Boyle was probably from the Local Defence Flotilla.[22]

The position taken up by the British Fleet to defend against a German sortie had proved unnecessary. The Germans were unaware of the huge force, getting only a few random reports of isolated ships. Nevertheless, the positions chosen by Keyes for the submarines meant that useful intelligence was obtained. Jameson and Boyle had identified the pattern of defence off the Ems, including the change times of the day and night watch. Benning and Feilmann had discovered the scope of the defence cordon of destroyers around Heligoland and their tactics. The gloom about all pervasive trawler harassment also evaporated, as Keyes highlights the lack of any problems with trawlers in his report, whilst noting that some are now supporting the

---

21   TNA ADM137/2067: pp.91–3; TNA ADM53: *Adamant* 18 August 1914.
22   BArch:RM92: *Kolberg* Kriegstagebuch 16-17 August 1914; TNA ADM223/808: Admiralty Monthly Intelligence Reports – 1920, April – Translation of the Correspondence of Admiral von Pohl p.46; Groos, *Nordsee 1*, p. 130.

patrols. However, Benning's speculation about a potential minefield protecting a channel east of Heligoland was a false conclusion. The Germans had laid no mines in the Bight at this point.

With the exception of *D.2* all of the submarines had evaded detection, despite Benning believing that he had twice been attacked with torpedoes. They had certainly experienced how hard it was to successfully attack patrolling destroyers.

The last word at this point should go to the crews. Two days after the patrol Hallifax pinned a signal of congratulations to the Flotilla from the Admiralty for the recent patrols onto the notice board of *E.7*. He read it out to the crew nearby, at which point LTO Sims enquired: 'And what is it for, Sir?' When Keyes read it out the next day to the assembled crews it was received 'without enthusiasm.' Apparently, it would take more than missing a destroyer with a torpedo for the crews to feel they had earned some praise.

7

A near miss

Keyes acted on the intelligence gained by his four submarines as soon as they reported back on 18 August. He notified Sturdee that he would go out himself at 4am on the 19th with *Lurcher*, *Firedrake*, *D.5*, *E.4* and *E.9* of his own Flotilla, plus the 4th Division of 1st Destroyer Flotilla (*Ferret*, *Druid*, *Forester* and *Defender*), which Tyrwhitt had placed under his orders. He also 'submitted' to Admiral Christian to meet him in the vicinity of Smith's Knoll with his cruisers, to convoy the submarines to a position 10 miles north of Terschelling Light. The substantial escort was a precaution against a repeat of the German cruiser raid.

The submarines would slip their destroyer tows off Terschelling and proceed deep into the Bight. Keyes focussed on the supposed inshore channel north of Heligoland reported by Benning. Two submarines would operate north of Heligoland and one south of it. Keyes concluded that there was 'very little going on in the vicinity of Emden', but pushed for a future destroyer attack descending just before dawn to cut off and destroy the patrol there, supported by a submarine to attack the cruiser reported by Jameson.

At noon on the 19th Keyes found Christian's six cruisers waiting at Smith's Knoll owing to a 'badly worded signal'. He had expected to meet them 20 to 30 miles to the south. Christian got into a covering position with his five armoured cruisers,[1] while his light cruiser, *Sapphire*, moved off to scout ahead of the destroyers. The whole force then advanced at a sedate nine knots. At around 7pm the submarines proceeded to their patrol from a position around 30 miles off the Texel, somewhat closer to home than had been planned.

Keyes was expecting the cruisers to withdraw well to the south, as he believed that he had made his point at the Admiralty that they were in too exposed a position. He had dropped his tow of *E.4* early to go alongside *Euryalus*, in order to ask Christian's permission to station some submarines across the entrance to the Southern Bight should the enemy cruisers return. Christian proved less amenable than Campbell had been. He had no intention of leaving the area and denied permission on the grounds that the submarines might restrict the movements of his own cruisers. The stationing of three submarines between Swarte Bank and Smith's Knoll Light Vessels was approved instead, covering the approach to Yarmouth, which his cruisers would avoid.

---

1   Christian's flagship, *Euryalus*, plus 7th Cruiser Squadron under Campbell: *Bacchante*, *Cressy*, *Aboukir* and *Hogue*.

Tyrwhitt's destroyers headed back to Harwich. Keyes wirelessed *Maidstone*, ordering *E.2*, *E.3* and *D.7* to meet *Lurcher* and *Firedrake* off Southwold for orders next morning. The submarines left Harwich before dawn on the 20th and arrived at 6:45am. Keyes sent their orders across in one of *Lurcher*'s boats, whilst *Firedrake* was sent to warn the local patrol destroyers of the presence of the new submarine patrol in their area. The submarines were to spread out on the billet agreed with Christian and patrol on the surface. They would then rendezvous at Smith's Knoll at 5pm next day, returning to Yarmouth by nightfall. This would ensure there were no incidents with the submarines returning from the Bight. *Lurcher* and *Firedrake* returned to Harwich.

The submarine patrol off Yarmouth was uneventful as the German raid had been a one off. *D.7* dived for an hour at 3:30pm later that day to approach some smoke, only to discover that it was two harmless steamers. The submarines tied up at Gorleston at 8pm on the 21st as planned. They returned to Harwich the next day, exchanging recognition signals with the battle cruiser *Invincible* as she passed them, heading to her new war station on the Humber. *E.2* now had to go to Chatham for dockyard repair as major problems had developed in her engine clutches. She did not return to Harwich until 27 September. Keyes had evidently been right to be concerned about engine reliability.

On his return to Harwich Keyes vented his growing frustrations in a private letter to a good friend, Rear-Admiral Leveson, the Director of Operations in the War Staff, one of Sturdee's key subordinates. Keyes felt 'sick and sore'. His posed the question: 'When are we going to make … the Germans realise that whenever they come out … they will be fallen on and attacked?' Of his submarines he writes: 'that they are ready for war … is proved by the fact that when those four came back [from the recent patrol to the Bight]… they got no sympathy – the others made it clear that they had made a mess of it, and that they all ought to have done better – and they are spoiling to go back and try again.' As for Christian's cruisers: 'they are untrained and can't shoot … For Heaven's sake take [them] away!' He had also raised this issue on the 15th to Jellicoe, with whom he wishes he was in touch and: 'not in this stagnant backwater … What I wouldn't give for a Command … of a few light cruisers, destroyers and submarines … supported at a distance by cruisers.' His bellicosity was not entirely shared in the Flotilla. After *E.7*'s difficult patrol, Hallifax wrote that: 'going over by Heligoland … [is] not worth the risk, for an E boat is of much greater value to us than the loss of 2 German destroyers.'[2]

Meantime, the submarines on the latest patrol had headed to their billets off Heligoland over the night of the 19/20th.

E.4 was commanded by Lieutenant-Commander Ernest W. Leir, the 31 year old Senior Officer of the Flotilla and the son of a church minister from Somerset. Leir was a pioneer member of the Submarine Service in 1903. In 1907 Captain Hall assessed him as: 'A splendid S/M commander. Plenty of Dash at the right time. Most enduring.' After commanding a number of early coastal boats, Leir went out to Malta to command the Submarine Flotilla there in 1911. He returned to take command of *E.4* in October 1913. Leir was known in the Flotilla as the 'Arch Thief'. *The Maidstone Magazine* is full of tales celebrating his ability to profit from a range of items at the expense of the Admiralty and his messmates, from lead ballast and coal to

2   TNA ADM137/2067: pp.70-1, 96; TNA ADM173: *D.7* 20 August 1914; TNA ADM53: *Firedrake, Lurcher, Euryalus, Sapphire* 19–20 August 1914, *Adamant* 27 September 1914; IWM:Documents.2175: letter to wife 25 August 1914; IWM:Documents.1003: 19 August 1914; Keyes, *Memoirs*, pp.74-78.

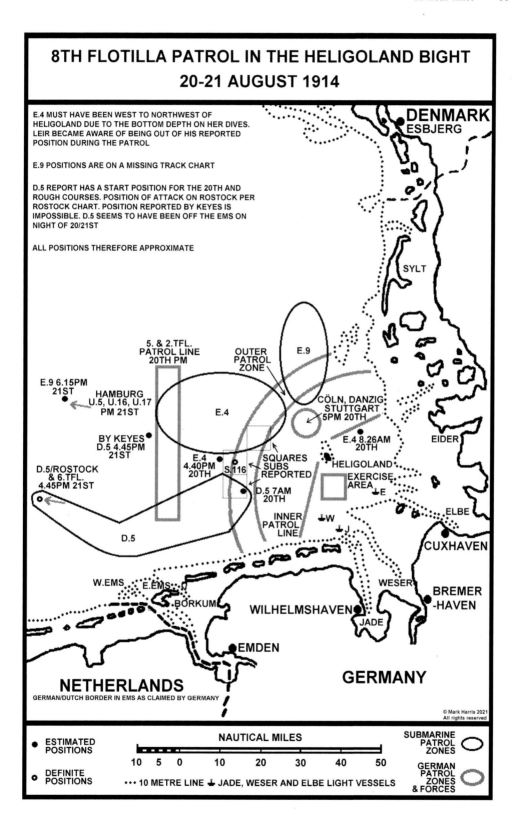

8TH FLOTILLA PATROL IN THE HELIGOLAND BIGHT
20-21 AUGUST 1914

E.4 MUST HAVE BEEN WEST TO NORTHWEST OF
HELIGOLAND DUE TO THE BOTTOM DEPTH ON HER DIVES.
LEIR BECAME AWARE OF BEING OUT OF HIS REPORTED
POSITION DURING THE PATROL

E.9 POSITIONS ARE ON A MISSING TRACK CHART

D.5 REPORT HAS A START POSITION FOR THE 20TH AND
ROUGH COURSES. POSITION OF ATTACK ON ROSTOCK PER
ROSTOCK CHART. POSITION REPORTED BY KEYES IS
IMPOSSIBLE. D.5 SEEMS TO HAVE BEEN OFF THE EMS ON
NIGHT OF 20/21ST

ALL POSITIONS THEREFORE APPROXIMATE

DENMARK
ESBJERG

SYLT

5. & 2.TFL.
PATROL LINE
20TH PM

OUTER
PATROL
ZONE

E.9

E.9 6.15PM
21ST

HAMBURG
U.5, U.16, U.17
PM 21ST

E.4

CÖLN, DANZIG,
STUTTGART
5PM 20TH

EIDER

BY KEYES
D.5 4.45PM
21ST

E.4 8.26AM
20TH

D.5/ROSTOCK
& 6.TFL.
4.45PM 21ST

E.4
4.40PM
20TH

S.116

SQUARES
SUBS
REPORTED

HELIGOLAND

EXERCISE
AREA
E

D.5 7AM
20TH

ELBE

D.5

INNER
PATROL
LINE

W

J

CUXHAVEN

W.EMS
E.EMS

BORKUM

WESER

BREMER
-HAVEN

WILHELMSHAVEN

JADE

EMDEN

GERMANY

NETHERLANDS
GERMAN/DUTCH BORDER IN EMS AS CLAIMED BY GERMANY

ESTIMATED
POSITIONS

DEFINITE
POSITIONS

NAUTICAL MILES

10 5 0   10   20   30   40   50

••• 10 METRE LINE ⚓ JADE, WESER AND ELBE LIGHT VESSELS

SUBMARINE
PATROL
ZONES

GERMAN
PATROL
ZONES
& FORCES

cigarettes and apples. When Leir later left 8th Flotilla, Waistell wrote that: 'his work has been most ably carried out & his resourcefulness, coolness & keenness … have afforded a splendid example to all in the Flotilla.'[3]

Leir began his patrol with a brief dive at first light on the 20th, then surfaced and headed east. Times of subsequent events vary significantly between his report, which is also selective about events, and the log. It was a fine day with only a breath of wind creating a very slight swell. An hour later he spotted a submarine only 1½ miles ahead of *E.4*. It was end on, making recognition difficult, so *E.4* dived. There was nothing to be seen through the periscope. As a precaution, Leir altered his course for three miles to get clear, then surfaced with nothing in sight.

At 8:26am *E.4* was thought to be 10 miles east-northeast of Heligoland based on her plotted course, roughly where she had been ordered to patrol, but Talbot writes that Leir was actually 10–15 miles northwest of Heligoland and Goodhart confirms that *E.4* never reached the billet. Leir sighted a steamer 10 miles ahead steering north, then a few minutes later a destroyer five miles to the east heading in his direction. *E.4* dived and more destroyers 'of the latest type' appeared. Leir gives a detailed description of their tactics, after a number of failed attack runs:

> owing to their frequent alteration of course, it was not advisable to continue … [they] did not keep in any apparent formation, but about 3 or 4 miles apart and appeared to steam in a triangular area, each side about 1½ miles; speed about 15 knots; when getting to a corner they stopped or went dead slow for a few minutes, then off again on new leg; remaining in same place did not bring one near, so apparently the triangle advanced.

The second officer, Lieutenant Lockhart, related his own recollections of the patrol to Hallifax. Around midday, *E.4* partially surfaced, with just the conning tower out of the water: 'Lockhart opened the lid & put his head out; the first thing he saw was a T.B.D. [destroyer] rushing at him, so he did not waste much time & down they went.' Leir also reports being seen by a destroyer, around 2pm. This was probably also when a gun was fired at *E.4*, but his report only mentions this in a note at the end. Circumstances point to this being part of one event.

Soon afterwards Leir sighted a submarine on the surface, steering east. Leir later described this as resembling *U.1* in the mess, but there is no identification in his report. *E.4* got into position for a bow shot after manoeuvring for 12 minutes. Leir fired a Mark V* torpedo at a distance of 1,200 yards (1,100m) as he 'could not get closer.' A destroyer now appeared to signal the target by flashing light; it is unclear whether this was the destroyer that had apparently seen him. A few seconds after the torpedo was fired the target turned away. The range of over 1,000 yards meant that the torpedo must have been pre-set for long range firing, with a speed of no more than 22 knots. This meant over two minutes to reach an extremely small target and would have run very wide if it turned away when fired. The elaborate explanation for the miss may indicate an attempt to rationalise a shot made more in frustration than with a realistic expectation of getting a hit.

3   TNA ADM196/48/21: Ernest William Leir; Douglas, *Maidstone Magazine*, pp.31, 37–9, 56, 65, 188–9.

For the rest of the day *E.4* was 'harassed by destroyers', all steaming at around 20 knots on an almost unruffled sea. Leir could not get into a firing position on any of them. At 7:40pm he was finally able to surface and get on deck in the gloom. A destroyer was then seen half a mile away. Leir reports that it 'charged at me'. After a hasty dive he tried again at 9pm. This time Hallifax writes that: 'Lockhart got his body out of the hatch when in the darkness he saw a black shape & then a flash & down he dropped & they dived again.'

Leir took *E.4* to the bottom for the night in 112 feet of water (34m), somewhat beyond the authorised diving depth. There were no leaks, although a few glands had to be tightened up. Leir also reported that beyond 75 feet the rudder would not move! Lockhart said that: 'all the time they were on the bottom they could hear the [destroyers] constantly passing over them, & could hear the propellers so distinctly & so loud that it prevented them sleeping. ... they could hear the rattle of the helm being put over, & at first thought it was a chain sweep, which was not a comforting thought!'[4]

At 4:30am the next morning Leir came up to periscope depth for a look around. Lockhart told Hallifax that a destroyer was waiting. Leir headed northeast at slow speed until 7:45am. By this time there were 15 destroyers surrounding *E.4*. At 8am Leir went back to the bottom, which was 125 feet deep (38m). He constantly heard destroyer propellers for the next four and a half hours, some of them quite close. On coming up to periscope depth at 2pm, three destroyers were still in sight to seaward, so he headed out to sea at slow speed with the battery low on charge. After four hours and about 10 miles, *E.4* finally passed beyond the patrol line, but the battery was now almost exhausted. Leir increased speed to use the last of the charge. *E.4* had now been without a change of air for 24 hours. Leir reported that he was breathing at twice the normal rate, indicating the onset of hypoxia, but he experienced 'no discomfort at all'. Since this can be another symptom of hypoxia it was not necessarily a good sign! *E.4* finally surfaced at 7pm, started the diesels and headed for home. She had spent 35½ hours submerged on the two days of the patrol. Leir had to dive briefly during the night to avoid a suspected destroyer. On the final approach to Yarmouth *E.4* ran aground on the Scroby Sand Bank. She was stuck for an hour but got off with no apparent damage and anchored for the night off Gorleston Pier. Next morning, the 23rd, *E.4* headed back to Harwich, but lost a blade off the starboard propeller on the way. She spent the 25th in the dock, exchanging both propellers for spares and getting her hull scraped whilst the work was done. Heavy marine growth would slow the boat and may help explain why she was farther west than expected on the 21st.[5]

Lieutenant-Commander Max K. Horton was aged 30. He was an early pioneer of the Submarine Service, joining in 1904. An assessment in 1907 was: '*Good* at his boat and *bad* socially ... A boxer and footballer – desperate motor-cyclist. Troublesome in the mess – insubordinate to First Lieutenant. Bad language – but extremely intelligent.' He progressed through coastal submarine commands to *D.6* in 1912. Horton demonstrated his skill and daring by taking her submerged for 40 miles up the Firth of Forth during manoeuvres, then 'torpedoed' the Flotilla's depot ship at anchor off Rosyth. His assessments are full of superlatives. Captain Hall

---

4   Minesweeping chains could be modified to carry explosive charges as a rudimentary anti-submarine device.
5   TNA ADM137/2067: pp.76–7; TNA ADM173: *E.4*, 20–25 August 1914; IWM: Documents.1003: 23 August; IWM:Documents.20134: 23 August; IWM:Documents.2175: letter to wife 25 August 1914.

writes in 1910: 'Makes the most brilliant attacks in his submarine.' Captain Brandt in 1912–13: 'Exceptionally able. Fearless of responsibility … Has a very steady nerve & good eye.' Keyes added: 'Most determined & should prove invaluable in War. Sound judgement.' Horton was known for being a showman; a poker player, intensely competitive, ruthless and ambitious. His reputation for dalliances with women was the source of humorous jibes in *The Maidstone Magazine*. Much later Horton was a pivotal figure in delivering the allied victory in the North Atlantic in the Second World War as C-in-C, Western Approaches. One of his officers at this time, Commander Rayner, wrote that: 'Horton's own staff regarded him as something less than God, but more than Man. If they had not done so they would have found themselves relieved [of their job]. He had more personal charm than any man I ever met but could be unbelievably cruel to those who fell by the wayside.' Horton had assumed command of *E.9* in March 1914 at Vickers shipyard as she neared completion. No-one was better placed to make use of the newest and best armed submarine in the flotilla.[6]

Max Horton, photographed in 1915. (Author's collection)

6   TNA ADM196/49/335 & 196/143/253; D.A. Rayner, *Escort: the Battle of the Atlantic* (London, William Kimber & Sons Ltd., 1955), p.128; Keyes, *Memoirs*, p.102; Douglas, *Maidstone Magazine*, pp.4, 247; W.S. Chalmers, *Max Horton and the Western Approaches* (London, Hodder & Stoughton, 1954), p.4.

Horton arrived at his assigned billet, off the island of Sylt, about 20-40 miles north of Heligoland, at 8am on the 20th.[7] He sighted masts and funnels and turned towards what was apparently a light cruiser. On getting closer it proved to be a destroyer patrolling backwards and forwards on an east to west line. Horton had been fooled by a mirage effect on the calm sea. *E.9* dived to attack. After two hours chasing backwards and forwards Horton had to give up, having never got closer than 5,000 yards (4,600m). *E.9* surfaced and moved on. At 4:32pm Horton sighted a light cruiser to the south, heading north towards *E.9*. He dived, but 40 minutes later she changed course and was lost to sight. Half an hour later Leir sighted another light cruiser to the southeast. This was also heading north with destroyers astern. Over the next 20 minutes *E.9* headed closer to intercept. She had reached 6,000 yards (5,500m) when six destroyers broke away from the cruiser and headed west in pairs at high speed, whereupon the cruiser came about and headed south. Horton broke off, surfaced an hour later at 7pm and then headed to the 10 fathom line (18m) to dive to the bottom for the night.

At 4 am Horton surfaced with nothing in sight in a glassy calm, with a crystal clear horizon; very bad news for submarine attacks. He returned to patrol and dived on sighting a destroyer at 8:15am. This disappeared, so *E.9* surfaced and headed south. At noon three destroyers were sighted ahead. Horton saw them disappear to the west after diving. *E.9* surfaced, but only occasional smoke was seen to the west and southwest. At 3pm Horton headed out to sea to begin the return to Harwich. Three columns of smoke were sighted soon afterwards. They were suspected to be from the paraffin engines of German submarines and disappeared northwest.

By 6:15pm *E.9* was about 50 miles north of the Ems. Horton observed the masts of a *Roon* class armoured cruiser and much smoke to the southwest, heading northwest. The cruiser altered course to port and was out of sight by 7:15pm. Fifteen minutes later, as darkness closed in, dense smoke approached rapidly from the southwest. After diving Horton could not see a ship but remained deep for one and a half hours as a precaution. He then resumed his course. *E.9* was the first boat back to Harwich at 5:30pm on the 22nd.[8]

D.5 was the boat of Lieutenant-Commander Godfrey Herbert, or 'Bertie' to his messmates. He shared a love of motorcycle racing and a lifelong friendship with Horton. Herbert was aged 30 and was the son of a solicitor from Coventry. He joined the Submarine Service in 1905, commanding a succession of C class boats. He was one of three commanders who had taken their submarines on the long journey to establish a Flotilla at Hong Kong. Here he had earned himself a reputation as 'the swimming devil' amongst the Chinese merchantmen for stunts hanging on to the periscope stands whilst the boat was underway submerged. Captain Johnson rated him a: 'V[ery] G[ood] Comm[anding] Off[ice]r of S/M. Bold & ready in action.' Keyes concurred, but whilst considering him 'a gallant Capt[ain]', rather prophetically thought that he was 'unstable & at present rather lacking in judgement.' One of his more risky habits was proceeding trimmed right down with only the very top of the conning tower out of the water to enable a fast dive. With the hatch open this also left the boat open to potentially being swamped. This tactic had caused some raised eyebrows when it was observed by other

---

7   Locations in his report rely on a missing track tracing, but the area is confirmed by Talbot, Goodhart and Hallifax.
8   TNA ADM137/2067: p.78; IWM:Documents.2175: letter to wife 25 August 1914; IWM: Documents.1003: 22 August; IWM:Documents.20134: 22 August 1914.

Lieutenant Herbert early in his career. (Author's collection)

commanders whilst covering the BEF. Keyes concerns had not prevented Herbert from taking command of *D.5* in November 1913.[9]

Herbert had been assigned the southernmost billet to the south and west of Heligoland. He sighted enemy destroyers to the east at 7am on the 20th and dived to approach them. He reports that: 'Owing to the apparent high speed and continually altering courses it seemed futile … to single out any one in particular for attack. I therefore kept on slowly [east] in hopes of one coming my way.' After two hours he was finally in a position to fire, but the destroyer: 'observed me owing to the flat calm; she steamed straight towards me and I endeavoured to turn towards her … but did not swing very far. She evidently saw the manoeuvre … allowed for my greater speed … [and] passed 50 yards clear of my bow, and I am convinced fired a torpedo at me, as my periscope passed through what must have been the wake.' Herbert decided to keep down deep as he could continually hear the noise of propellers overhead. Eventually things died down and he was able to attack another destroyer on coming back to periscope depth at 3pm. He lined up for a bow shot, but she altered course and steamed past no more than 100 yards (90m) from his stern: 'She was travelling very fast and I could distinctly see a look-out man call attention to

9   TNA ADM196/49/45 & 196/143/298: Godfrey Herbert; Douglas, *Maidstone Magazine*, p.184; Keble Chatterton, *Amazing Adventure – A Thrilling Naval Biography* (London, Hurst & Blackett Ltd., 1935), pp.63, 78-9.

my periscope. It was useless my firing my stern tube, the torpedo being set for 12 feet (3½m).[10] He again went down deep and moved off slowly out to sea, occasionally putting the periscope up, but 'as I was being constantly harassed … and the sea being flat calm, I decided to remain down until dark.' Herbert was finally able to surface to charge the battery and get some air in the darkness at 9pm. *D.5* had been dived for 14 hours. After two and a half hours charging Herbert went to the bottom for the night.

D.5 surfaced at 3am and headed slowly to the west for an hour until full daylight. Herbert then stopped on the calm surface, with nothing in sight. At 9am he dived on seeing smoke. Four destroyers passed in formation, apparently heading roughly northwest. An hour later Herbert surfaced *D.5* and slowly followed, hoping to meet them coming back. He stopped after five hours to fix his position, with a clear horizon. At 4pm Herbert spotted six columns of smoke to the eastward and dived. He stayed put, as he soon realised that he was in the centre of their line of approach. As they closed he made out a *Roon* class armoured cruiser with three destroyers off each bow screening her, the nearest 1,500 yards (1,400m) from her. *D.5* went ahead dead slow on one motor to attack the cruiser: 'I … had very little distance to proceed before coming within 500 or 600 yards immediately before her starboard beam. I fired both bow tubes … She appeared to have sighted me only a few seconds before I fired, … as shots were falling round me immediately after the first torpedo had left, I fired the second at once but am of opinion that as they were only set to five feet [1½m] and the sea was very calm, she must have been able to avoid them. The cruiser was not going more than 10 knots, but I had allowed for 14.' Hallifax and Goodhart were impressed that Herbert had managed to get into the perfect attack position in difficult conditions without being spotted. *D.5* headed west for three miles whilst the crew reloaded the bow tubes, then went to the bottom. Herbert came up to periscope depth after two hours and saw a destroyer two miles astern, apparently looking for him. He went back to the bottom until darkness at 120 feet (37m). Lieutenant Douglas, her stand-in third officer, told Hallifax: 'When it was dark, they rose, got underway on the engines & went as hard as they could; … they were so tired that they could not see properly & imagined searchlights, flashes of guns, & dark shapes, every minute, so after they had gone about 12 miles they went to the bottom and remained there all night.'

D.5 surfaced before dawn at 2:30am next morning and headed for Yarmouth. She arrived at sunset and asked a patrolling destroyer to report her to Harwich, then anchored for the night. The report was delayed and Talbot records concern about her safety as she was overdue. *D.5* was the last boat back to Harwich at 9:30am on the 23rd.[11]

Herbert had attacked the 6,200t (6,100 long tons) light cruiser *Rostock*, commanded by Fregattenkapitän Thilo von Trotha, flagship of the Second Leader of the High Sea Fleet Destroyers, Kommodore Hartog. She should have been five miles behind six destroyers of 6th Torpedoboots-Flottille scouting ahead. They were one half of a force heading out from the Jade for a raid against the British fishing fleet on the Dogger Bank. At 4:45pm, *Rostock* was about 70 miles west of Heligoland steaming at 14 knots. The destroyers had passed *D.5* and seen nothing.

---

10   German destroyers had a maximum draught of 3.3m (11 feet) or less depending on type.
11   TNA ADM137/2067: pp.79-80.

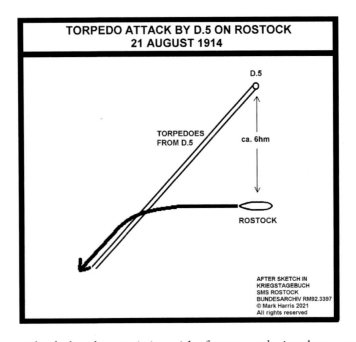

TORPEDO ATTACK BY D.5 ON ROSTOCK 21 AUGUST 1914

D.5

TORPEDOES FROM D.5

ca. 6hm

ROSTOCK

Trotha then sighted the characteristic swirl of water and air when a torpedo is fired underwater, about 600m (650 yards) directly to starboard. A periscope and the upper edge of a conning tower came out the water. Evidently *D.5* had lost trim when she fired. Trotha ordered the helm to be put hard to port and called for maximum speed. An agonising wait ensued for those on the bridge as they waited for the rudder to take effect. The two torpedo tracks closed straight for *Rostock*, about 10m (30 feet) apart. She had turned about 30 degrees when the torpedoes crossed her path. They were judged to have missed ahead at an angle of about 70 degrees, but the bubbles came to the surface as they cut through their trail on both sides of the bridge. Trotha ordered the helmsman to stop the turn to keep parallel to the torpedoes and avoid re-crossing their track. Three of *Rostock*'s guns had spotted *D.5* and immediately opened fire, getting off nine rounds before she disappeared. *Rostock* had 6x10.5cm (4.1-inch) guns on each broadside and Trotha recommended that in future all guns should open a protective fire whether they could see the target or not. Despite his self-recriminations Herbert had judged the speed and course of the target perfectly, although it does not speak highly of *D.5*'s periscope optics that *Rostock* was identified as a *Roon* class at such close range. Although both had four funnels, Roons were large armoured cruisers, with prominent turrets fore and aft. The fast response of Trotha and *Rostock*'s gunners had just saved their ship. A petty officer working below decks forward had even heard the whirring of the torpedo propellers as they rushed past. The destroyer *V.157* was left behind to keep the attacker down, as Hartog was concerned that the advance might be reported by wireless, but also to attempt to ambush her attacker when darkness fell. The remaining destroyers were belatedly ordered to form a close submarine screen and *Rostock* commenced zig-zagging behind them.[12]

---

12   BArch:RM92: *Rostock* Kriegstagebuch 21 August 1914; Erich Gröner, *German Warships 1815–1945 Vol. I: Major Surface Vessels* (London: Conway Maritime Press, 1990), p.109; Groos, *Nordsee 1*, pp. 115–6.

Keyes report to Sturdee on recent operations says that there is no possible excuse for missing the target. He writes that Herbert admitted the target was a 'gift' and had acted contrary to orders in firing both of his torpedoes simultaneously. He adds that he is a very gallant and determined officer and will do better next time. Keyes wrote later that Herbert had told him that he should be dis-rated for missing such an easy target. Goodhart tells his wife that: '[Herbert] was awfully sick about missing naturally but the Commodore hardly considered the difficulty when he blamed him severely.' Goodhart also felt that the standing order to refrain from firing the second torpedo until the effect of the first had been observed was practically impossible; something which Keyes did not appreciate. Goodhart was right; a delay in firing would have meant that *Rostock* would have been stern on to the second torpedo. Submariners soon realised that it was better to fire as many torpedoes as possible when they had good targets in their sights to maximise the chance of hitting.

Suspicion also fell on potential torpedo depth keeping problems. Before the war torpedoes had been adjusted using practice collision heads which were 40lb lighter than the explosive warhead. On 10 September Goodhart took *E.8* out into Harwich harbour for a depth keeping test, losing a torpedo in the mud. Investigations found that Mark VI and newer torpedoes did not have any problems when adjusted correctly, but Mark V* and older torpedoes experienced an excessive initial dive if fired on a high speed setting. The cause was traced to old pattern hydrostatic glands. The Flotilla moved quickly and new hydrostatic glands and instructions for torpedo adjustment were issued. *E.8* received hers on 18 September. Trials continued to fine tune adjustments. *E.2* lost a heater torpedo in the harbour in a test on 7 October. Waistell and Talbot attended a conference at the Admiralty on 31 December where it was agreed that the latest valve patterns should be fitted for all submarine torpedoes. By the end of 1915 this had been completed for even the oldest coastal submarines. Torpedoes were now found to reach their correct depth after 300 yards (275m).[13]

Even if there was an issue with accurate depth keeping, 600 yards should still have been enough to approach the selected depth in the attack on *Rostock*. The torpedoes had also been fired at a much shallower setting than that required to hit. Bubbles surfacing level with the bridge indicate a near miss ahead at a hitting depth rather than running under.[14] One superstitious member of the crew had a simpler explanation. He decided that *D.5*'s mascot, a teddy-bear, was to blame. Whilst muttering the words: 'I'll teach you to be a good joss [lucky charm],' Herbert saw him cut the bear's throat and pour out the stuffing.[15]

The encounter with *Rostock* was part of a wider operation planned by the German Fleet over the period of the patrol. On the 20th the 4th Torpedoboots-Flottille had the day watch on the outer patrol line in the Bight. The inner line had been moved farther back around Heligoland Island and was now occupied during the day by 12 armed trawlers. The 2nd Minensuchdivision was sweeping off the Jade ahead of firing practice later that day by two battleships of 3rd

---

and Karte 14.
13 TNA ADM137/2067: p.75; IWM: Documents.2175: letters to wife 25 August & 18 September 1914; IWM: Documents.1003: 7 October; TNA ADM189/34: pp. 24–5; IWM:Documents.20134: 31 December; TNA ADM189/35: pp. 43–4; Keyes, *Memoirs*, p.79.
14 TNA ADM189/32: p.24. Bubbles took 4.5 seconds to reach the surface from eight feet and 9.6 seconds from 20 feet.
15 Chatterton, *Amazing Adventure*, pp.88-9

Geschwader. The impending raid on the British fishing fleet was to be preceded by a major overnight reconnaissance sweep on the 20/21st for a distance of 120 miles in the sector west-northwest to north of Heligoland, by the light cruisers *Cöln*, *Stuttgart* and *Danzig*, with the 2nd and 5th Torpedoboots-Flottillen. Five destroyers of the 3rd Torpedoboots-Flottille were also to reconnoitre along the Dutch coast to a distance of 80 miles west of the Ems, on the lookout for submarines, but there was nothing to find here. Three destroyers had swept 60 miles out from the Ems the night before but had not spotted any of the inbound British submarines.

The patrols apparently reported no sightings of submarines in the Bight during the morning of the 20th, so Herbert mistook random course changes for having been seen at this time. A comparison of observations back at Harwich revealed that the first submarine seen by Leir was *E.9*. It is impossible to say what Leir later fired his torpedo at. *U.1* was in the Baltic, but a destroyer might have been mistaken for a submarine at a distance. Horton had reported mirage effects nearby. *Hamburg* was exercising with submarines of 4th U-Boots-Halbflottille at the time, but apparently east of Heligoland. No German warship reported being attacked but given the range and the target's early turn away this is unsurprising.

Around 1pm, *S.116* spotted a periscope only 20m (65 feet) away, fired her 5cm (2-inch) guns at it and reported the 'tactical square' in which she had sighted it, 20 miles west of Heligoland. This was around the time that Leir believed *E.4* was spotted. 1st Torpedoboots-Flottille was ordered out from Heligoland to search the area. Around 3:40pm a destroyer from this flotilla reported a submerged enemy submarine in the 'tactical square' to the south of the first sighting. This ties up with *D.5*'s report of being spotted at close range.

The result of this second sighting robbed Horton of his two cruiser targets. The second of these was certainly in the departing force led by *Cöln*, which had just passed Heligoland heading north, although the first may have been *Hamburg*. At 4:30pm 5th Torpedoboots-Flottille was ordered to break away from the cruisers and join the submarine search to the west. Half an hour later the 2nd Torpedoboots-Flottille was ordered to join them in an overnight 30 mile outpost line west of Heligoland and north of Borkum. At the same time *Cöln*, *Stuttgart* and *Danzig* were ordered to double back to the safety of the river estuaries. This meant that by late afternoon around 40 destroyers were hunting submarines in the area in which *E.4* and *D.5* were patrolling!

A final report of a surfaced enemy submarine was made by a destroyer of 5th Torpedoboots-Flottille at 6:49pm in the square northeast of the first sighting. This would have been when Leir was caught on deck.

The multiple submarine sightings meant that searches continued on the 21st. Two destroyer Flotillas and two aircraft were sent to the area in addition to the routine patrol mounted by 5th Torpedoboots-Flottille, but nothing more was seen. The destroyers Herbert had seen in the morning were probably those patrolling north of the Ems.

As the patrols saw nothing that morning, the cruiser raid was allowed to proceed as planned, but support from the heavy cruisers *Seydlitz*, *Moltke* and *Blücher* was cancelled as a precaution. *Rostock*'s raiding group was accompanied to starboard by *Strassburg* with the other five destroyers of 6th Torpedoboots-Flottille. Apparently Herbert did not see them, although *Strassburg* was certainly close as she was signalled by signal-light by *Rostock* about the attack.

Hamburg sailed from Heligoland with three submarines (*U.5*, *U.16* and *U.17*) at 1pm on the 21st, heading west to support the raid. Horton narrowly missed a chance to attack as he was steaming a roughly parallel course leaving the Bight. He first sighted the distinctive white smoke from their paraffin fuelled engines, then later that evening *Hamburg* as she crossed his track.[16]

Despite the frustrations of missed torpedoes and many abortive attacks, this operation had confirmed the day patrol location and tactics in the outer screen off Heligoland seen on the previous patrol. On both days their search had concentrated in *E.4*'s patrol area. The tactics had succeeded in keeping *E.4* submerged for 24 hours, but Leir had still escaped thanks to his ability to save his batteries on the bottom. Keyes highlights this learning in his own report and singles him out for praise. The British submarines had also been kept on the outer patrol lines, well away from the battleships exercising south of Heligoland. The alarm raised by the destroyers had robbed the submarines of better targets, but had also stripped the raiding forces of reconnaissance preparation and support. However, there were no British forces in position to exploit this.

Keyes deduced that at around 5–6pm enemy light cruisers led destroyers out to the night patrol positions, which fanned out and then returned at daylight. It is easy to see why this might have been concluded, but is incorrect, as the cruisers spotted by *E.9* were heading out on a specific mission, which happened to be recalled as Horton attacked. Night hunting by the destroyers was also not routine but was a response to the sighting of the British submarines.

Keyes was now concerned that the meagre pickings in the patrolled zones were not worth the risk to the submarines, just as Hallifax had felt after *E.7*'s patrol. He therefore proposed in his report that the forays into the patrol zone should be limited to one day. He highlighted that it would be better for the submarines to be able to communicate sightings to a supporting cruiser. Information was currently being delayed until return to port. *D.5* and *E.9* had made important sightings of enemy sorties on the 21st but had been unable to report them. Keyes felt that submarines outside of the patrolled zones would be in a good position to attack and report future sorties.

A destroyer drive commencing inshore was once again proposed by Keyes to catch the returning night patrols. Submarines lying on the bottom off the enemy ports could also attack enemy cruisers coming out in response. He thought that the destroyers patrolling off the Ems could be sunk with little risk, but detailed planning was needed to ensure success. Keyes now focussed on making just such an operation happen.

16   Groos, *Nordsee 1*, pp.113–5, 265–7; BArch:RM92: *Hamburg, Cöln , Danzig, Kolberg, Nassau, Stuttgart* Kriegstagebuch 19-20 August 1914.

8

The Battle of Heligoland

The crews in Harwich were beginning to chafe at their inactivity, as they were not allowed outside the military area around Parkeston Quay for recreation. Goodhart writes to his wife that they 'spend the time loafing when we haven't anything else to do in the boat.' He took *E.8* out for test dives in the harbour on the morning of 21 August 'to keep our hands in'. The papers were scanned for news of what was happening on the various fronts of the war. Heated rumours were rife; a party of Canadians being repatriated from Germany brought the false news that mobs in Berlin were shooting any Frenchman or Briton they could find and that they had heard the same was happening to Germans in England.

Feilmann and Talbot improvised a tennis court in an empty warehouse on the Quay and used it to while away time in the evening playing games of doubles with other officers. Football, rounders and boxing matches provided another outlet for pent up energy. A shed was equipped with a cooking range to allow all the crews in harbour to mess together when in port. Route marches in to the countryside were organised to provide some relief for the crews from the boredom of the Quay. Talbot had a serious problem with his Chief ERA, Stevens, who came back to the boat drunk after a trip to buy provisions for his mess. Talbot wrote that he was 'a most excellent man and will be an enormous loss to the boat.' After discussion with Waistell he stayed but lost a good conduct badge and the associated pay.

In a sign of the approach to war hardening, on the 23rd orders came through that any German trawler equipped with wireless could now be sunk. The Flotilla also received its first reinforcement in the form of the previously spurned *D.1*, which made fast alongside *Adamant* that afternoon. She had been relieved at Dover by the newly completed *S.1*. The concerns about the reliability of her engines had been put aside. With her came *D.4*, which had been refitting her battery at Portsmouth since war broke out. She was followed on the 27th by the brand new *E.10*, fresh from working up after completion at the Vickers Yard in Barrow on the 10th. She made fast alongside *Maidstone* at 4:40pm to find a good part of the Flotilla absent. Keyes had got what he had been agitating for and a major operation was underway.[1]

---

1 TNA ADM173: *D.4* 3-23 August 1914; IWM:Documents.20134: 16-19 August; IWM:Documents.1003: 20–25 August; IWM:Documents.2175: letters to wife 20 and 25 August 1914; TNA ADM188/431/269451: Royal Navy Registers of Seamen's Services, Ernest Edward Stevens

Keyes had fleshed out the idea for a destroyer drive against the patrols in the Bight in collaboration with Tyrwhitt, whom he says fully concurred in the proposal. He took it up to the Admiralty on the afternoon of 23 August to 'pilot it through the proper channels', accompanied by Leir. The crews of *E.6*, *E.8* and *D.8*, which had been expecting to head out to the Bight for the next routine patrol, were told to stand by pending the result of the trip. Finding the Naval War Staff – in other words Sturdee – too busy with 'daily matters', he used his network and dropped some heavy hints to Churchill's Naval Secretary, Rear-Admiral Hood, to the effect that he was in the Admiralty if Churchill wished to see him. Churchill did and was promptly 'fired' by Keyes animated presentation of his proposal. Tyrwhitt, who in the meantime had gone out to sea on patrol, was ordered to come back and attend a meeting on the following afternoon at the Admiralty.

The meeting took place as soon as Tyrwhitt arrived at 5pm the next day, chaired by Churchill and also attended by Battenberg, Sturdee and Keyes. It was agreed that Tyrwhitt's Flotillas would push in to Heligoland in the early morning to get behind the German patrols. They would then sweep westward from 8am, destroying any patrol vessels that they encountered. The timing would ensure that they struck at the point that the day patrol were already out at sea on station, rather than attacking the returning night patrol, as Keyes had originally proposed. Submarines would be used to attract and draw out as many patrol vessels as possible before the attack commenced, turning their tactics against them.

Battenberg approved the plan, which was to be carried out as soon as possible. The raid was to be supported by Christian's cruisers as well as the battle cruisers *Invincible* and *New Zealand* of the newly created Cruiser Force K, under Rear-Admiral Sir Archibald Moore, which was based in the Humber. Keyes suggested that if the German battle cruisers came out in strength this was too weak a force. He proposed that the more formidable Grand Fleet Battle Cruiser Squadron and Light Cruiser Squadron be added to the support force. Sturdee said that they were not available.[2]

Whilst the attack was being organised, Keyes ordered out another patrol. Four submarines were to leave Harwich at 4am on the 25th. The patrol positions were aimed at ambushing cruisers exiting the Heligoland Bight, given the number of these that had been recently encountered. *D.2* alone was to press in close to confirm whether the cruiser was still in the Huibert Gat and confirm that it was not Dutch. From daylight on the 26th a line would be occupied from the mouth of the Western Ems to a point 50 miles to the north, in the order *D.2*, *D.7*, *D.3* and *E.3*. One torpedo in the bow was to be set for five feet (1½m) depth, suitable for attacks on shallow draught vessels, with all the other torpedoes set for 12 feet (3½m) depth, ideal for attacking cruisers. Submarines were to remain on station until the afternoon of the 26th, then return to Gorleston harbour and await further orders. The boats were to be escorted out by *Lurcher* and *Firedrake*, which would also tow *D.3* and *D.2* to Smith's Knoll. The destroyers would then scout ahead of the submarines to Terschelling until the light failed. In the event of poor visibility all were to make for Smith's Knoll and await new orders.

The force headed out up the east coast on an almost windless day, into thick mist and fog patches. They pressed on in the hope that the weather would clear and turned out to sea towards Terschelling as planned, with *D.3* slipping her tow early to form a patrol line with *D.7* and

2   Keyes, *Memoirs*, p.81, Patterson, *Tyrwhitt*, pp.52-4.

E.3 behind the destroyers. By 2pm the weather was no better and the decision was taken to turn back with the exception of *D.2*. Jameson dropped his tow and pressed on in the hope that he could scout the Ems entrance. *Lurcher* took *D.7* in tow, *Firedrake* picked up *E.3* and they returned with *D.3* to Gorleston Harbour.

Next day the weather had improved. With the raid imminent, *Lurcher* and *Firedrake* were ordered to carry out target firing practice that morning in Yarmouth Roads, then return to Harwich. *Lurcher* encountered problems during the shoot and had to replace a gun cradle on arrival. The three submarines were ordered to carry out a short patrol towards Terschelling in a line at three mile intervals. They headed out at 11:45am, turning to head back at 3:15pm. The sweep was uneventful, with nothing to report. The submarines anchored for the night in Yarmouth Roads and headed back to Harwich next morning, the 27th.

D.2 returned to Yarmouth later that day. Jameson reported by telephone to Keyes. The poor weather had prevented him from confirming that the cruiser in the Huibert Gat was definitely German. In the absence of proof, a plan to attack it during the raid with three seaplanes launched from a carrier, using bombs and a torpedo, was cancelled.

German cruisers had been out to cover a minelaying sortie off the Tyne and Humber on the night of the 25/26th. *Mainz* returned to the Ems at midday on the 26th, but there is no evidence Jameson saw her as visibility off the German coast was only two to three miles in the misty haze. No written report can be traced.[3]

As he finalised the orders for the attack Keyes found out that suspicion of reporting submarine movements had fallen on the owner of the Victoria Hotel in Dovercourt. Stoker Petty Officer Cook, of the destroyer *Leonidas*, had seen a pigeon rise from the hotel and head eastwards as the submarine patrol had left on the 25th. The owner was identified to him by another crewman as 'Fritz', a fellow pigeon-fancier of German heritage. Keyes remembered that he had been asked some months earlier by Sir Graham Greene, the Cabinet Secretary at the Admiralty, if the Flotilla had any concerns, as the man in question was a suspected German agent. He immediately asked the Harwich Base Commander, Captain Cayley, to have the police arrest the man. If he encountered any problems he was ordered to take an armed party from *Maidstone* and do so himself! The man ended up on remand in Ipswich jail for a week, but it is unclear what happened to him after that – was he a really a spy, or a victim of anti-German hysteria? Keyes did have some grounds for suspicion, but anti-German sentiment was running very high and would ultimately contribute to the removal of Battenberg because of his German name and heritage. Keyes took the matter up with Sturdee as he did not understand how a suspected agent had been allowed to remain in place.[4] Just how seriously the issue of pigeons was being taken is evidenced by the fact that the otherwise utterly uneventful log of *Maidstone* notes that on the 16th she had sent an officer in a boat with an armed guard to investigate a suspicious pigeon seen flying towards Harwich at 3:30am![5]

3   TNA ADM137/2067: pp.99, 109; TNA ADM173: *D.3, D.7* 25–27 August 1914; TNA ADM53: *Firedrake, Lurcher* 25–26 August 1914; IWM:Documents.20134: diary 25 August 1914; TNA ADM186/610: Naval Staff Monographs Vol. III: Monograph 11 – Battle of the Heligoland Bight, August 28th, 1914, p.150; BArch:RM92: *Frauenlob* Kriegstagebuch 26 August 1914, *Mainz* Tätigkeite des kleinen Kreuzers "Mainz".
4   TNA ADM137/2067: pp.621–2.
5   TNA ADM53: *Maidstone* 16 August 1914.

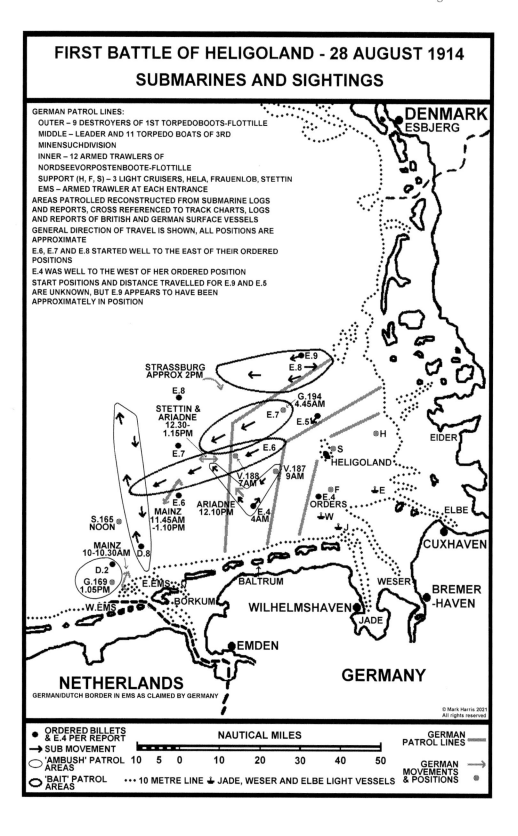

FIRST BATTLE OF HELIGOLAND - 28 AUGUST 1914
SUBMARINES AND SIGHTINGS

GERMAN PATROL LINES:
 OUTER – 9 DESTROYERS OF 1ST TORPEDOBOOTS-FLOTTILLE
 MIDDLE – LEADER AND 11 TORPEDO BOATS OF 3RD
 MINENSUCHDIVISION
 INNER – 12 ARMED TRAWLERS OF
 NORDSEEVORPOSTENBOOTE-FLOTTILLE
 SUPPORT (H, F, S) – 3 LIGHT CRUISERS, HELA, FRAUENLOB, STETTIN
 EMS – ARMED TRAWLER AT EACH ENTRANCE
AREAS PATROLLED RECONSTRUCTED FROM SUBMARINE LOGS
AND REPORTS, CROSS REFERENCED TO TRACK CHARTS, LOGS
AND REPORTS OF BRITISH AND GERMAN SURFACE VESSELS
GENERAL DIRECTION OF TRAVEL IS SHOWN, ALL POSITIONS ARE
APPROXIMATE
E.6, E.7 AND E.8 STARTED WELL TO THE EAST OF THEIR ORDERED
POSITIONS
E.4 WAS WELL TO THE WEST OF HER ORDERED POSITION
START POSITIONS AND DISTANCE TRAVELLED FOR E.9 AND E.5
ARE UNKNOWN, BUT E.9 APPEARS TO HAVE BEEN
APPROXIMATELY IN POSITION

DENMARK
ESBJERG

STRASSBURG
APPROX 2PM

E.9
E.8

E.8

STETTIN &
ARIADNE
12.30-
1.15PM

G.194
4.45AM

E.7

E.5

H

EIDER

E.7

E.6

S

HELIGOLAND

V.188
7AM

V.187
9AM

E.6

ARIADNE
12.10PM

MAINZ
11.45AM
-1.10PM

E.4
4AM

F
E.4
ORDERS

E

W

J

ELBE

S.165
NOON

CUXHAVEN

MAINZ
10-10.30AM   D.8

D.2
G.169
1.05PM

E.EMS

BALTRUM

WESER

BREMER
-HAVEN

BORKUM

W.EMS

WILHELMSHAVEN

JADE

EMDEN

NETHERLANDS
GERMAN/DUTCH BORDER IN EMS AS CLAIMED BY GERMANY

GERMANY

ORDERED BILLETS
& E.4 PER REPORT
SUB MOVEMENT
'AMBUSH' PATROL
AREAS
'BAIT' PATROL
AREAS

NAUTICAL MILES

10   5   0   10   20   30   40   50

••• 10 METRE LINE ⚓ JADE, WESER AND ELBE LIGHT VESSELS

GERMAN
PATROL LINES

GERMAN
MOVEMENTS
& POSITIONS

Final orders for the sweep into the Bight were issued on the 26th, following a meeting of all of the participating commanders of submarines and destroyers with Keyes on *Maidstone* in the morning. The news of the audacious raid was well received, Talbot writing: 'At last, thank heaven!' in his diary after describing the plan. An extra submarine off the Ems was added as a result of the information brought back by *D.2* from her patrol, but there is no clue what this information was. An amendment was also slipped in confirming that Keyes would go to sea himself in *Lurcher*. The submarines were divided into two groups.

The first group, led by *Firedrake*, with *E.4*, *E.5* and *E.9* were to leave Harwich at 10:30pm. They would form an inner 'ambush' line of submarines tasked with attacking enemy cruisers that sortied as a result of the raid. They were to remain unseen until Tyrwhitt commenced his westward drive at 8am.

The second group, led by *Lurcher*, with *E.6*, *E.7*, *E.8*, *D.8* and *D.2* would leave Harwich two hours later. The three E boats would form an outer 'bait' line tasked with attracting the enemy destroyers out to sea away from Heligoland in order to set them up for destruction by Tyrwhitt's attack. They were to move to the east on the surface at dawn until they were seen but were not to go farther east than the attack line of the British destroyers, which would pass over them heading west during the attack. The two D boats were placed off the Western and Eastern Ems entrances to attack enemy forces heading in or out of the river. The two groups would rendezvous at sea and keep well clear of the other forces heading in to the Bight, with the two destroyers keeping lookout ahead for the submarines until nightfall. All submarines were to ensure they kept battery power in hand to submerge during the period when British forces passed their positions. They could use their discretion as to when they left the area and were to return directly to Harwich via a corridor kept free of other vessels for this purpose.

The submarines were to be in position by 4am on the 28th. After parting from the submarines off Terschelling at dusk, *Lurcher* and *Firedrake* would spend the night patrolling to the south of the final position of Moore's battle cruisers. They would warn Moore by wireless if any submarines were spotted approaching this position, 50 miles north of the Ems, which he would reach at 8:30am. Moore would then retire, leaving *Lurcher* and *Firedrake* conveniently free of orders. Christian with his cruiser force would patrol off Terschelling to cover Tyrwhitt's withdrawal.[6]

The staff-work now went horribly wrong. Jellicoe found out about the raid when it was mentioned almost as an afterthought in a signal about the situation at Ostend. He was alarmed and 'made urgent representations' to the effect that the raid needed proper support from battle cruisers. It was eventually agreed early on the 27th that he could send his 1st Battle Cruiser Squadron (1st BCS), under Acting Vice-Admiral Beatty, with the 1st Light Cruiser Squadron (1st LCS) to rendezvous with Moore, as Keyes had proposed. All five battle cruisers in home waters would now be supporting the raid, with Beatty, as senior officer, taking command of the support force. Jellicoe asked the Admiralty to inform the raiding force of the revised support forces.[7]

6   TNA ADM137/2067: pp.101–9.
7   John R. Jellicoe, *The Grand Fleet 1914–1916 Its Creation, Development and Work* (London: Cassell & Company Ltd., 1919), p.109; TNA ADM137/1943: Grand Fleet Secret Packs – Pack 0022 Operations – Section O – Miscellaneous Operations and Battles, p.8.

The signal informing Keyes and Tyrwhitt about the changes was sent after they had sailed. By then both were out of range of the destroyer wireless band used. A telegram informing Keyes of the change was finally received via Felixstowe at 3am on the 29th, after his return to Harwich![8] This would have been bad in any event, but after the recent recognition problems, Keyes had impressed on his commanders that there were only two British light cruisers going in to the Bight; *Fearless* – the leader of 1st Flotilla – and *Arethusa* – Tyrwhitt's brand new cruiser to replace the ageing *Amethyst*. That meant any light cruiser in the Bight with *two* masts and *four* funnels *must* be the enemy.[9] All six of the 1st LCS 'Town' type cruisers joining the raid had two masts and four funnels.

The force left Harwich according to plan. *Lurcher*'s group stopped at Smith's Knoll on the morning of the 27th to meet *D.2* from Yarmouth. Whilst they waited Talbot took the opportunity to swing his boat off *Lurcher* to adjust his compass, which had been found to be out of true on the journey up the coast. As they crossed over to Terschelling both *Lurcher* and *Firedrake* investigated a number of trawlers and a sailing vessel that they encountered, but all proved harmless. The submarines headed off through the night to their patrol positions.

The weather on the day of the raid was a major factor in the way the action developed. There was almost no wind. A low blanket of cloud and mist reduced visibility to around three to four miles. A confused melee was the inevitable result. The sea was almost a completely smooth calm. Getting position fixes was impossible, making it difficult to reconcile where vessels were in relation to one another.

On the 26th the German day patrol arrangements had been altered to a new system of three lines, with three light cruisers in direct support. The changes were intended to increase the area being patrolled, after a submarine torpedo attack was reported by *G.111* off Heligoland on the 25th, although no British submarines were in the Bight that day. Unless an attempt was being made to block the entrances to the German ports with blockships, patrols were to fall back if attacked by superior forces. They therefore fell back when Tyrwhitt's force appeared. Light cruisers rushed out from the German ports in support, just as Keyes and Tyrwhitt had hoped.[10]

E.7 was in the middle of the outer 'bait' line. She dived to adjust trim on being dropped off by *Lurcher* on the evening of the 27th. This turned into a roller coaster ride, with the boat initially sinking stern first. Hallifax says that the corrective action made her 'sink like a stone from 10–90 feet, nose down'. It took 45 minutes to get things sorted out and *E.7* then headed off to her patrol billet.

Feilmann passed his start position at 3am and continued heading east. An hour later, in the half light of dawn, Hallifax was on watch. He sighted what he at first took to be a sailing vessel. It was soon apparent that it was heading straight for them and now looked like a cruiser. *E.7* dived. Feilmann asked Hallifax his opinion of the target through the periscope and he identified a *V.186* class destroyer going at about 10 knots. He rushed forward to flood the bow tube for firing, which already had a torpedo set for firing at a destroyer, but while it was filling Cunard

8   TNA ADM137/2067: pp.114–5.
9   Keyes, *Memoirs*, p.82.
10 Julian Corbett, *History of the Great War based on official documents – Naval Operations – Volume 1* (London: Longmans, Green & Co., 1920), Enclosure Map 5; Groos, *Nordsee 1*, p.270 and Karte 19. Square 150ε quoted in orders is a typographical error and should read 150β. Most maps of the battle incorrectly show patrol lines ordered on 18 August. Karte 19 shows the correct positions.

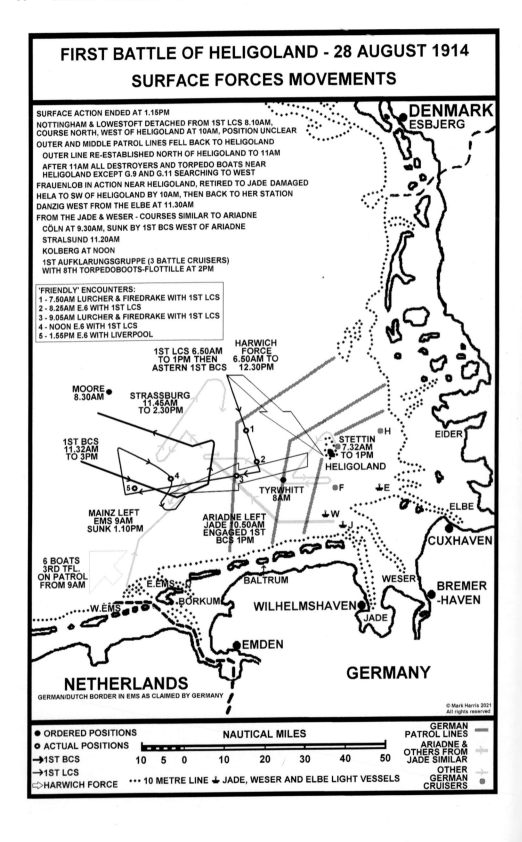

FIRST BATTLE OF HELIGOLAND - 28 AUGUST 1914

SURFACE FORCES MOVEMENTS

SURFACE ACTION ENDED AT 1.15PM

NOTTINGHAM & LOWESTOFT DETACHED FROM 1ST LCS 8.10AM,
COURSE NORTH, WEST OF HELIGOLAND AT 10AM, POSITION UNCLEAR

OUTER AND MIDDLE PATROL LINES FELL BACK TO HELIGOLAND

OUTER LINE RE-ESTABLISHED NORTH OF HELIGOLAND TO 11AM

AFTER 11AM ALL DESTROYERS AND TORPEDO BOATS NEAR
HELIGOLAND EXCEPT G.9 AND G.11 SEARCHING TO WEST

FRAUENLOB IN ACTION NEAR HELIGOLAND, RETIRED TO JADE DAMAGED

HELA TO SW OF HELIGOLAND BY 10AM, THEN BACK TO HER STATION

DANZIG WEST FROM THE ELBE AT 11.30AM

FROM THE JADE & WESER - COURSES SIMILAR TO ARIADNE

CÖLN AT 9.30AM, SUNK BY 1ST BCS WEST OF ARIADNE

STRALSUND 11.20AM

KOLBERG AT NOON

1ST AUFKLARUNGSGRUPPE (3 BATTLE CRUISERS)
WITH 8TH TORPEDOBOOTS-FLOTTILLE AT 2PM

'FRIENDLY' ENCOUNTERS:
1 - 7.50AM LURCHER & FIREDRAKE WITH 1ST LCS
2 - 8.25AM E.6 WITH 1ST LCS
3 - 9.05AM LURCHER & FIREDRAKE WITH 1ST LCS
4 - NOON E.6 WITH 1ST LCS
5 - 1.55PM E.6 WITH LIVERPOOL

DENMARK
ESBJERG

HARWICH FORCE
6.50AM TO
12.30PM

1ST LCS 6.50AM
TO 1PM THEN
ASTERN 1ST BCS

MOORE
8.30AM

STRASSBURG
11.45AM
TO 2.30PM

1ST BCS
11.32AM
TO 3PM

STETTIN
7.32AM
TO 1PM

HELIGOLAND

H

EIDER

TYRWHITT
8AM

F

E

MAINZ LEFT
EMS 9AM
SUNK 1.10PM

ARIADNE LEFT
JADE 10.50AM
ENGAGED 1ST
BCS 1PM

W

ELBE

CUXHAVEN

6 BOATS
3RD TFL.
ON PATROL
FROM 9AM

E.EMS.

BALTRUM

WESER

BREMER
-HAVEN

W.EMS.

BORKUM

WILHELMSHAVEN

JADE

EMDEN

GERMANY

NETHERLANDS

GERMAN/DUTCH BORDER IN EMS AS CLAIMED BY GERMANY

● ORDERED POSITIONS
○ ACTUAL POSITIONS
→1ST BCS
→1ST LCS
⇨HARWICH FORCE

NAUTICAL MILES

10 5 0   10   20   30   40   50

••• 10 METRE LINE ⚓ JADE, WESER AND ELBE LIGHT VESSELS

GERMAN
PATROL LINES

ARIADNE &
OTHERS FROM
JADE SIMILAR

OTHER
GERMAN
CRUISERS

shouted, 'Too late!' The destroyer disappeared. The resulting gloom lifted when Feilmann spotted her returning at high speed in the opposite direction 20 minutes later. He ordered a burst of high speed to get into an attacking position. *E.7* ended up 150 yards ahead of her starboard bow. Feilmann ordered Hallifax to fire the bow tube. For Hallifax: 'a lifetime seemed to pass & then I realised it must have missed; it was really rather laughable seeing everyone's expressions; all tense, mouths open, & then slowly the latter closed & a gloom settled on their faces.' When the torpedo was fired the destroyer was seen to turn towards *E.7*. Feilmann ordered: 'Take her down 40 feet' and dived under her. His report says that the track of the torpedo was seen to pass under the stern of the target. Hallifax: 'went into the fore compartment to console [Able Seaman J. R.] Smith ... a minute later there was a rushing, rattling noise ... so close did it seem that I instinctively ducked my head; on going to the gauge we were at 70 feet [20m]!' The destroyer passed over their position twice in the next 10 minutes. Feilmann believed she may have been towing a sweep, but the destroyer soon headed off. At 5:15am, half an hour after the attack, *E.7* surfaced with nothing in sight. She remained stationary, running one engine to charge the batteries. They had not done so the previous night, as charging affected the compass.

The target had been correctly identified and was the *G.194*. She was one of nine boats of the 1st Torpedoboots-Flottille on the outer patrol line. The patrol spread out to the day positions at 4:30am and then commenced the usual zig-zag patrol pattern. At 5am *G.194* spotted two submarine periscopes just 50m (55 yards) to starboard, which then disappeared and were replaced by the swirl of water and air that marked the firing of a torpedo. Two tracks were seen to pass under her hull. *G.194* turned to ram, failed to make contact, but made out *E.7* heading off submerged. She then wirelessed: 'At 6 a.m. [German time] I was fired at by a submerged submarine, square 142ε centre, two torpedoes, no hits. Have sighted periscope. Distance 50m. This is not a false alarm. Enemy submarine is on a north-westerly course.' *E.7* was significantly farther east than her plotted position. It had not been possible to get a position fix from the stars during the night.

The Mark VI torpedo that was fired needed about 250 yards to recover to its set depth. It would certainly have run underneath the shallow draught destroyer whether the range was 150 yards or 50m. The second 'track' spotted may have been air escaping from the tube immediately after firing. Although this was a wasted torpedo, it had exactly the desired effect on the German defence. At 6:10am the 10 destroyers of the 5th Torpedoboots-Flottille, on stand-by at Heligoland, were ordered out to hunt for the submarine. The position of *E.7*'s attack drew them directly towards Tyrwhitt's approaching force of two light cruisers and 31 considerably more powerful destroyers. Aeroplane reconnaissance was also requested.

At 7am Feilmann heard gunfire to the north, dived and headed towards it. Within half an hour the cruiser *Fearless* with her 1st Destroyer Flotilla was sighted steaming in towards Heligoland. The nearest boats passed directly over *E.7*. Once nothing was in sight Feilmann surfaced. The firing was now to the south, drawing westwards. *E.7* remained in place apart from a short run to close a few miles nearer to Heligoland.

The 5th Flottille reversed course ahead of Tyrwhitt and escaped back to Heligoland, although *V.1* was significantly damaged by two shell hits, losing one man killed and two wounded, a result that can be indirectly credited to *E.7*.[11]

---

11   Groos, *Nordsee 1*, pp.140, 147-8, 206 and Karte 1.

At 10:03am four cruisers, all with four funnels, were sighted to the northwest apparently steering south. Feilmann dived and headed west to intercept, but they soon went out of sight in the haze. They were thought to be German at the time, but later it was thought that they were British Town class. The only warships nearby to the west were *Nottingham* and *Lowestoft*, retiring to the north.[12] *E.7* surfaced at 10:25am. The firing moved round from south to southwest over the next 45 minutes. Feilmann finally moved off to the south, then west. All eyes were straining to spot ships. At noon 'someone looked up and saw a seaplane coming over'. Fearing a bombing attack, Feilmann dived to 60 feet (18m) and remained down for 20 minutes. The seaplane had not been heading directly for them and made no report.

Soon after surfacing Feilmann sighted a three funnelled cruiser to the south, apparently steering southwest. *E.7* dived and altered course to attack. Hallifax and Cunard thought it could be a *Deutschland* class battleship, but no battleships were present. It was either *Stettin*, coming from Heligoland, or the two funnelled *Ariadne*, coming from the Jade, heading to attack the retreating British Flotillas. The cruiser was lost sight of through the periscope and *E.7* surfaced at 12:50pm. When Hallifax went up to the bridge he heard very heavy firing in the direction she had last been seen. After a while gun flashes could be made out and the enormous splashes of at least 12-inch (30.5cm) shells hitting the water. *E.7* continued south for 10 minutes until ricochets started to land nearby, then dived to 70 feet (21m). Feilmann turned west, hoping to cut the cruiser off if she happened to be driven his way. After another 10 minutes of 'continuous banging' as the shells hit the water, the firing ceased. At 1:15pm *E.7* came up to periscope depth and saw the unmistakable, but unexpected, silhouettes of two British *Lion* class battle cruisers, together with *New Zealand* and *Invincible*. Beatty had brought them into the Bight to support the hard pressed Tyrwhitt. They had just ceased fire as their target, *Ariadne*, fled out of sight. *E.7* went back down to 70 feet to avoid a collision as they passed by. At 2:05pm Feilmann sighted two Town class cruisers of 1st LCS heading northwest with the four destroyers assigned to the battle cruisers in company, as the last British forces left the Bight.

Both *Ariadne* and *Stettin* had fled past the deeply submerged *E.7* to escape the battle cruisers. *Ariadne* was stopped very nearby with fatal damage inflicted by the 13.5-inch (34.3cm) and 12-inch (30.5cm) shells of the battle cruisers. The light cruisers *Danzig* and *Stralsund* stopped to rescue the crew of the sinking ship. They would have all been sitting ducks for submarine attack if sighted.[13]

At 2:20pm *E.7* surfaced with nothing in sight and headed southwest for home. She soon spotted what turned out to be *E.4* ahead. Feilmann increased to full speed to close up astern by 6pm and exchanged news. Fifteen minutes later in the failing light, *E.7* was challenged by the Harwich destroyer division screening ahead of the two Humber battle cruisers, on their way back to port. The submarines stopped and had some anxious moments as they returned the challenge. Leir had acquired some passengers, which he transferred to a boat from the destroyer *Sandfly*. The battle cruisers swept majestically past only 100 yards (90m) away, passing the news that two German light cruisers had been sunk. After this both submarines continued in company through the night to Yarmouth, until thick fog caused Feilmann to doubt what *E.7* was following and break off. Hallifax wrote that 'the truth is our eyes were so tired that one sees

---

12   The British chart reproduced in the official histories notes the sighting as being of the main body of 1st LCS at 9:03am, but the time is at odds with *E.7s* log, Feilmann's report and Hallifax's diary.

13   Groos, *Nordsee 1*, pp.181–8.

all sorts of things that don't exist, & don't see some which <u>do</u> exist!' Around 3am, her flywheel sheered its newly replaced bolts and the starboard engine had to be stopped. Two hours later, whilst Hallifax was sleeping off watch he was 'woken by that bell ringing madly, & down we dived; a T.B.D. [destroyer] had shot out of the fog, about 300 yards off.' Feilmann later came across a trawler that gave the course for the Smith's Knoll Light Vessel. *E.7* moored at the Yarmouth jetty at 3:40pm, not Harwich, as ordered. Feilmann asked Hallifax to report to Keyes by phone, an unusual action for a commander. Afterwards Hallifax wrote Feilmann's report. Cunard was sent off to Harwich by train with it. *E.7* returned to Harwich next morning, the 30th, arriving at 3:30pm. The next four days were spent fixing the flywheel, with a day on the floating dock to deal with some leaks, then scrape and paint the hull, removing weed that was slowing the boat.[14]

Leir's *E.4* reached a position to the north of Baltrum at 11:30pm on the 27th. She rested on the bottom until 4am. There is no explanation why this was well to the west of the position ordered. Leir came up to periscope depth and crept northeast at very slow speed – 2½ knots. At 8:20am a German destroyer was spotted with eight British destroyers chasing it, west of Heligoland. Leir watched the action unfold over the next 40 minutes. *V.187*, leader of 1st Torpedoboots-Flottille, had steered to support her outpost boats to the north. She was surrounded by British forces, cutting off her line of retreat. A close range gun action ensued and she was sunk by the 3rd and 5th Divisions of the British 1st Flotilla. Suddenly, a three funnelled cruiser appeared from the east and opened fire on the British destroyers, which quickly made off to the southwest.

This was the opportunity that Leir had been waiting for. He began an attack on the cruiser, but she quickly made off to the north and disappeared. *Stettin* had steamed to the support of the outpost line from Heligoland. She had no idea that *V.187* had been sunk, but her salvos interrupted rescue work by the British destroyers. *Defender*, which had stopped and lowered boats to pick up survivors, was forced to abandon them. *Stettin*'s commander was concerned that she would be torpedoed if he followed the numerous destroyers and temporarily turned back to Heligoland.

Leir steered back to the south to cover the retreating destroyers. He sighted some small boats when *E.4* surfaced at 9:28am. Lieutenant Richardson, with three boats and nine crew of the *Defender*, had collected his boats and the German survivors together. The British sailors stripped their uniforms to the waist and tore them up to make bandages for the German wounded. Leir now approached and took on board the crew from the *Defender* and three of the unwounded Germans, which he later described to Keyes as 'a sample'. They were Oberleutnant zur See Friedrich Braune, the senior unwounded officer and an unnamed senior petty officer and stoker. Leir counted 30 to 40 other survivors, but could take no more in *E.4*, as: 'I considered it would impair … efficiency'. He provided a box of ships biscuits and fresh water, made sure the boat had a compass and asked Braune to instruct his men what course to steer for home. Those taken on board received an issue of rum.

Differing bogus accounts have multiplied about what happened to the survivors, including one that they were never found. The 44 survivors were rescued a couple of hours later by the

---

14   TNA ADM137/2067: pp.127–9; IWM:Documents.1003: 27–30 August; TNA ADM173: *E.7* 28 August-3 September 1914.

destroyers *G.9* and *G.11*, which had been sent out to search for damaged boats and survivors. A number of the severely wounded had died in the meantime.[15]

At 10:10am Leir headed southwest. He heard heavy firing ahead. Two hours later *E.4* intercepted a German cruiser heading westwards. This was identified as *Hela*. Leir dived to begin an attack but could not manage to get close enough to fire before it passed out of sight in the poor visibility. Braune had never been on a submarine before, as they were off limits to non-submarine officers. He was therefore very interested in its workings. Leir, playing the good host, allowed him to stay in the control room. On breaking off the attack he turned to him and said: 'I nearly got one of your cruisers then', to which Braune replied 'yes, I heard you ready the torpedo'.[16] Leir followed at a slow speed hoping she would turn back. The cruiser was the old *Ariadne*, with a similar profile to *Hela*. She was heading out from the Jade at her best speed of around 21 knots. *Ariadne* sighted a submarine on her port beam at this time, which immediately dived and was seen to attempt to manoeuvre to attack.[17]

Leir sighted her coming back eastwards an hour later, along with a *Stettin* class cruiser, three miles to the north. They were under fire from unseen ships. This was *Ariadne* and *Stettin* fleeing from Beatty. Leir was too far away to attack. At 2pm heavy firing was heard to the southwest. *E.4* headed off to investigate, but found nothing, even when the haze lifted. At 3pm Leir began the journey back to Harwich, which he reached at 1pm next day.

Leir had continued to use his charm to pump his prisoners for information whilst on-board. Braune would not confirm the name of his destroyer as Leir leafed through *E.4*'s copy of Janes, pointing at the boats. The petty officer was looking over his shoulder and said 'ja' when Leir got to what may have been the right one, receiving a swipe round the head from Braune for his trouble. This earned Braune a reprimand from Leir. Someone let slip that a patrol line in an arc 30 miles from Heligoland was patrolled day and night. This was approximately correct, but not new information. Other random snippets were noted, including the fact that British submarines were thought to come from Hull and remain off the German coast for a week at a time.[18]

Horton's *E.9* was the farthest north on the 'ambush' line. He arrived at his billet around 1am on the 28th and remained on the bottom out of sight until 5:40am. Just over an hour after surfacing Horton spotted a destroyer and dived to attack, but she promptly disappeared to the south. This was probably *G.193*, at the end of the German patrol line. Horton surfaced and from 8am heard firing in the distance to the south and later the southwest. He worked his way west during the day, no doubt aiming to catch any German vessels fleeing to the north but saw nothing. *E.9* set course for Harwich at 4pm and arrived 24 hours later.[19]

Benning's *E.5* was on the 'ambush' line north of Heligoland, just outside the line patrolled by the German torpedo boats. She had arrived at her position at 1:45am on the 28th and remained on the bottom until 7am. Visibility was three miles when she surfaced, with nothing in sight. Benning heard firing to the southwest at 8am. *E.5* dived to periscope depth and headed towards it. Two hours later the firing was loud enough to hear through the water, but Benning could

15   William G. Carr, *By Guess and by God – The Story of the British Submarines in the Great War* (London: Hutchinson & Co., 1930), p.146; Groos, *Nordsee 1*, pp.166–8.
16   Keyes, *Memoirs*, p.94.
17   Groos, *Nordsee 1*, p.184 and Map 19.
18   TNA ADM137/2067: pp.122–3; TNA ADM173: *E.4*, 28 August 1914.
19   TNA ADM137/2067: p.131.

see nothing. A destroyer was finally spotted two miles to the south at 1pm. Benning altered towards her, but she disappeared to the southwest. It was probably a boat of 2nd Torpedoboots-Halbflottille which abandoned a temporary outpost line off Heligoland at this time. Nothing more was observed, but heavy firing was later heard to the southwest. *E.5* surfaced to return to Harwich at 3pm and arrived at 1:15pm on the 29th.[20]

Talbot's *E.6* was at the southern end of the 'bait' line. She submerged and crept in slowly on the last leg of her approach at 3am on the 28th. Talbot explains that: 'I always dive from the start of dawn to daylight, as it is such a dangerous time … due to the visibility changing so rapidly'. He surfaced in position at 4am. A German destroyer was spotted when he reached the bridge, apparently stopped one mile to the east. At this time the destroyers were still on the night patrol line, where the torpedo boats patrolled during the day. *E.6* sat on the surface 'hoping to be observed', but after 15 minutes the destroyer made off to the northeast. Talbot dived to attract attention but failed to do so. *E.6* crept farther east for half an hour then stopped and surfaced with nothing in sight. A German destroyer soon appeared. She stopped three miles away and signalled a total of three times in his direction. After half an hour 'looking at each other', the destroyer got underway towards *E.6*. Talbot had done his best to act suspiciously and be reported. He now dived towards her, and the destroyer headed off. After once again creeping farther east for 15 minutes, *E.6* again surfaced. Two destroyers quickly came into sight north and south of her heading out in a westerly direction. Talbot dived in the same direction 'with much fuss and splashing' hoping to draw them after him, but they turned away and were lost to sight. Talbot now surfaced, started the diesels and headed west for 25 minutes, making as much smoke as possible and charging his batteries. Regardless of whether they had seen *E.6*, none of the destroyers had reported an enemy submarine. A submarine in poor visibility is hard to spot and even harder to identify.

At 7:05am *E.6* turned round and headed east. Talbot soon 'sighted a destroyer steaming at me at full speed, about 4 miles distant'. *E.6* dived to attack:

> [H]e was within 3000 yards [2,750m] when I got under and firing at me … he was going so fast … that I could not get anywhere but right ahead of him. At the last moment I put the helm hard over to give him the stern tube, when within 150 yards [45m] saw he had ported his helm to ram me and I was forced to dive steeply to 60 feet [18m]; he passed over my bridge & must have missed the periscope … by inches only.

The affair had only taken eight minutes. The destroyer now passed overhead again, causing alarm when a crewman claimed that he had heard a chain being dragged across the boat. *E.6* had finally attracted some attention!

The destroyer was *V.188* of 1st Torpedoboots-Flottille. She was clearly keeping a good lookout and sighted *E.6* at a range of 8,000m (8,750 yards). Her commander, Kapitänleutnant Callisen, called for full speed ahead and made straight for her. *V.188*'s stokers shovelled coal for all they were worth to get her up to 33½ knots. The recognition challenge went unanswered. Callisen ordered the bow 8.8cm (3.5-inch) gun to open fire at 6,000m (6,500 yards). *E.6* had almost disappeared by the time the second round was fired. The periscope was spotted twice as

20   TNA ADM137/2067: p.124; Groos, *Nordsee 1*, p.165.

V.188 criss-crossed the area, aiming to keep her submerged. Callisen was unable to get a report through! *V.188*'s wireless sending gear proved defective. Talbot had picked the wrong boat to get the attention of. The hunt was given up when reports of British surface forces came in. *V.188* retired to Heligoland.[21]

Talbot headed west at low speed. *E.6* stopped and surfaced with nothing in sight and mist hanging about in the almost still air at 8:27am. Nothing happened for the next hour when: 'Suddenly out of the mist under the sun, in a cloud of smoke, loomed the hulls of two big cruisers beam on, 2 to 3 miles off & steering south.' *E.6* dived on a parallel course to get a closer look: 'When I found them in the periscope a few minutes later, very misty, they had altered course to WxS and were so close that I had no room to do anything but go under them … nationality thought to be British'. The lead vessel had four funnels. After passing under them at 60 feet (18m), *E.6* turned to follow and raised the periscope. Talbot saw the two cruisers receding ahead of him. Two more cruisers, or possibly destroyers, were seen indistinctly two miles to port of them heading in the same direction.

E.6 had encountered the main body of 1st LCS, just as it made a turn to head west. Beatty had sent them in with Tyrwhitt to give him a powerful supporting squadron close at hand. These cruisers were at risk of attack as a result of Keyes instructions. Commodore Goodenough was leading 1st LCS from the bridge of the *Southampton*. Goodenough reported that he 'sighted and attempted to sink a submarine; subsequent events tend to indicate that this was a British submarine', later adding: 'Fortunately I missed her' in ink! The *Birmingham* was astern. Either could have sunk or seriously damaged *E.6* at periscope depth. Goodenough was aware that British submarines were in the area somewhere, but he was hardly going to take any chances. It was fortunate that Talbot went out of his way to confirm identity before attacking. A four funnelled cruiser could have been the *Fearless* and he needed to confirm the number of masts to be sure. The second pair of vessels was probably the cruisers *Falmouth* and *Liverpool*.[22]

E.6 slowly followed for an hour, then stopped and surfaced with nothing in sight. Another hour passed. A German armoured cruiser, resembling *Kaiserin Augusta*, now emerged from the mist to the south-southwest, pursuing British destroyers and heading towards *E.6*. It was now 11:45am.

This was actually the light cruiser *Mainz*, which had come out from the Ems to cut off Tyrwhitt's retiring forces. She was engaged in a gunnery duel at about 7,000 yards (6,400m) with 11 destroyers of the 2nd, 3rd and 5th Divisions of the 1st Flotilla, which were heading north to draw her away from the badly damaged *Arethusa*. *E.6* dived. Talbot could not see any ships in the periscope, but soon two lines of smoke approached either side of *E.6* and heavy firing was heard through the water. Talbot made for the nearest smoke approaching from the north, which was then made out to be three German four funnel cruisers. Talbot made an attack run on the rear ship. The cruisers came into firing range when they altered course towards him, presenting an ideal target angle: 'At the last moments I had doubts as to their nationality, as shot were falling all round me from the cruiser I knew to be German, and I could find nothing else which these three ships could be firing at'. The sound of each shell striking the water nearby 'sounded as if it had struck the casing & the noise was almost deafening'. Talbot continued

21   Groos, *Nordsee 1*, p.163.
22   TNA ADM137/1943: p.17.

closing to well within 400 yards (370m) to make sure of the target. He glimpsed red in the ensign. The ship had to be British. He realised it was a Town class cruiser. He was too close to avoid her and for the second time that day went down to 60 feet (18m) to pass beneath a British cruiser! Talbot writes that 'that this was a very severe trial of my self-restraint ... I was so close that I could not possibly have missed.'

His target was again 1st LCS, which Beatty had ordered back in to the Bight to assist the hard pressed Tyrwhitt. Goodenough advanced in line abreast and his fourth cruiser was not spotted. *Mainz* was totally outgunned by 1st LCS. She turned to escape and the gun action swept on to the south. On coming back to periscope depth British destroyers were spotted heading at speed the same way. This was seven boats of the 2nd and 3rd Divisions of 1st Flotilla which had swung out wide to the north after *Mainz* had broken off, heading to re-join their Flotilla. Talbot decided to continue heading to the west.

At 1:45pm *E.6* came to the surface. Talbot made out *Fearless* with a Flotilla to the southwest, heading west. A large cruiser was coming up from astern, apparently chasing them, and closing fast in a cloud of smoke. Talbot headed south to intercept. He passed along her port side at a range of 300 yards (275m) to confirm the colour of her ensign. He once again saw the tell-tale red and identified her as a Town class, 'which are the most German looking ships we have.' This was the *Liverpool*, which Goodenough had detached to pick up survivors from the sunken *Mainz*. She was now heading for home.

E.6 had completed a hat-trick of aborted attacks on 1st LCS! Talbot concludes that: 'It will be a wonderful thing if I get two more such opportunities for a certain hit'. There is no evidence that *E.6* was spotted in the last two attacks.

Talbot surfaced at 2:20pm, three miles astern of *Liverpool*. *Fearless* and six boats of 3rd Flotilla were approaching. The destroyer *Lysander* closed and exchanged recognition signals with *E.6*. At 3pm the crew started the diesels to head back to Harwich.

E.6 encountered two of Christian's armoured cruisers in their position off Terschelling at 6:30pm. Talbot got a position fix after exchanging recognition signals and was 'glad I met them before dark'. Three hours later it was pitch dark. Three destroyers loomed out of the fog and *E.6* sheered away to avoid them. Talbot says they were 'most probably British returning home, but at night just as dangerous as Germans.' A stationary ship later appeared less than half a mile away when the fog parted and switched on her navigation lights. *E.6* stopped. Talbot had just blown his whistle in a particularly dense fog patch. He immediately regretted it, fearing attack, but it proved to be a merchantman. *E.6* got back underway and worked round her. Talbot grabbed a couple of hours 'well earned' sleep whilst underway submerged during his usual dive around dawn. At 6am *E.6* came across the returning destroyer *Landrail* and Talbot was relieved to follow her in to Smith's Knoll in heavy fog after swapping position fixes. He was even more pleased when it turned out that his position fix was right and hers wasn't but got some hot ash from her funnel smoke in his eye which left him in agony for the rest of the day! *E.6* parted company to head towards Yarmouth but had to stop at the Cross Sands Light Vessel as the fog was too dense to risk going on with her 'unreliable compass'. The light vessel crew were allowed to have a peek round the submarine and Talbot returned the visit. The fog cleared at noon and *E.8* came past, hopefully with a reliable compass. *E.6* followed her to Harwich, arriving at 4:25pm.

Much to Talbot's relief, *Adamant*'s doctor was finally able to remove the cinder from his eye that evening. On the 31st he had the new navigator of *Maidstone*, Lieutenant-Commander

Collings, swing *E.6* to correct the compass. *E.7* did the same on 1 September. Hallifax says that 'we had not much faith in our last [swing]'. Collings replaced Lieutenant Ventris, whom Talbot said, 'had been thrown out for general incompetence.' The patrols to date had been consistently dogged by serious position errors. On the 4th work began on fitting a gyrocompass to *E.6*.[23]

The most northerly boat on the outer 'bait' line was Goodhart's *E.8*. He submerged whilst still heading to his billet in the hours around dawn on the 28th. An E class was sighted on surfacing at 4:20am. This was assumed at the time to be the neighbouring *E.7*. After the patrol Goodhart discovered that it had been *E.9*, meaning he was already too far east. Goodhart thought he was 10 miles short of his billet and continued cruising east. He slowed down on 'arriving' at 5am. At 6:20am a destroyer was spotted in the distance to starboard. *E.8* stopped, but it was soon lost sight of in the mist. Goodhart got underway again. Another destroyer was soon spotted 5,000 yards (4,500m) to the south. *E.8* dived to attack, but the target kept altering course and after 40 minutes headed off to the south. Goodhart tells his wife that 'we have found it practically useless to attack destroyers as owing to their speed and good lookout they can avoid the torpedo fairly easily.' Neither of these destroyers from 1st Torpedoboots-Flottille reported a submarine. At 7:44am Goodhart heard a considerable volume of gunfire from small calibre guns to the south when *E.8* surfaced. He began to move slowly west. The firing ceased after half an hour, then started up again to the southwest. At 9:35am *E.8* altered course towards the firing. An hour later a German destroyer was spotted crossing his track ahead, steering northeast. Goodhart dived, but could not locate the target in the periscope and surfaced again. This was probably a boat of 2nd Torpedoboots-Halbflottille, which had re-established the outpost line north of Heligoland.

Goodhart sighted a submarine at noon, off to starboard. He assumed at the time that it was German, but told his wife later that it was *E.9* again. It made off and could not have been German. *E.8* continued for an hour and a half without incident. Suddenly, Goodhart: 'saw an aeroplane fairly close to us, & dived quickly for him. When I got to 50 ft I thought it was rather useless being there & decided to come up again and have a go at him with revolvers & rifles!' The plane was nowhere to be seen on surfacing and made no report. It had been about one mile away at only 150 feet (45m).

Goodhart continues: 'The next excitement was a lump of smoke coming straight for us, we dived & got down all right, but … we broke surface when turning to attack. The ship (a light cruiser) saw us & sheared off. She was going very fast & I only got about 1½ miles off her.' She had been about three miles away to port and ahead when sighted at 1:53pm. Goodhart identified her as a four funnelled *Rostock* class light cruiser. She was almost certainly the very similar *Strassburg*, which was making 25 knots in a wide detour north to avoid Beatty's forces. She did not spot *E.8*. The series of course alterations to starboard at this time were made to join up with the ships to the south of her. Goodhart was later concerned it might have been *Southampton* and could not make out the ensign at the time, but 1st LCS were not in the area.

At 2:40pm *E.8* surfaced, started the diesels and headed for home. At dusk the lookout sighted dense smoke ahead. *E.8* dived as a precaution, inconveniencing Goodhart in the middle of

23   TNA ADM137/2067: pp.125-6; TNA ADM173: *E.6*, 28–29 August 1914; IWM: Documents.20134: 28 August–4 September 1914.

popping a painful blister that had developed on his foot. A painful end to a frustrating day! Once out of sight she surfaced and headed off for her subsequent encounter with *E.6*.[24]

D.8 had the billet off the eastern exit of the Ems. This was her first offensive patrol, under Lieutenant-Commander Theodore S. Brodie, aged 30. He had been especially recommended for the Submarine Service in 1908; later in his career than many of his contemporaries. His twin brother was also in submarines. Navy humour led to his nickname of 'Dummy Head', whilst his twin was 'War Head'.[25] However, the epithet was ironic as Theodore scored highly in his examinations. Both were deeply religious. He would gather the crew to offer prayers to the Almighty for success before making practice attacks pre-war. Such ostentatious religious tendencies were likely to make his ratings uncomfortable. It seems his crew regarded Brodie as a bad 'joss', a view that can easily be self-fulfilling. He had commanded a number of C class boats before being appointed to *D.8* as she neared completion in November 1911. In 1912 Captain Brandt rated him: 'Capable & reliable', to which Keyes added: 'Skilful & trust[worth]y'. Brodie was also a musician and played the violin. He was normally quiet and diffident, but popular in the wardroom. Once he warmed up a little he would challenge all comers to anything from board games to billiards to wrestling.[26]

D.8 arrived off the Eastern Ems at 2:08am on the 28th and dived an hour later in the pre-dawn glow. Visibility was somewhat better off the coast than it was out to sea when she surfaced at 4:38am. A three funnelled cruiser could be seen inside the river, three miles west of the Borkum Light House. This was *Mainz*. *D.8* headed five miles out to sea as visibility increased to avoid being spotted by a trawler off the eastern entrance. Soon afterwards two signal rockets were fired by ships in the river.

However, the hours passed with nothing happening. At last a Taube biplane was spotted two miles away heading towards *D.8* from Borkum at 9:58am. Brodie trimmed the boat down so that only the conning tower remained above water and let the plane pass just ahead of *D.8* to the north-northwest. It was scouting ahead of *Mainz* and saw nothing. After a few minutes he followed its lead, dived and headed northwest, no doubt intending to intercept any German vessels following the now retiring Harwich Force, but losing an opportunity to attack *Mainz* as a result. Over the next hour he got a few glimpses of smoke, then surfaced with nothing in sight. A destroyer was finally sighted approaching from the south-southwest at noon. Brodie dived in her direction, but the boat went out of sight and he surfaced. A destroyer was soon seen again steaming on various courses to the southwest. This was probably *S.165* of 6th Torpedoboots-Halbflottille, which was scouting north out of the Ems.

Brodie appears to have returned to his northwest course. He then sighted a number of destroyers heading west and dived to intercept them at 1:37pm. As he closed they were identified to be British. This was the Harwich Force retiring out of the Bight. Brodie altered course back to northwest intending to attack anything following them. After a short time *D.8* popped up to the surface for a look round and spotted another group of destroyers. Brodie dived and headed east to intercept. At 2:46pm *D.8* surfaced again and sighted three battle cruisers to

24 TNA ADM137/2067: p.130; TNA ADM173: *E.8*, 28 August 1914; IWM:Documents.2175: letter to wife 10 September 1914; BArch:RM92: *Strassburg* Kriegstagebuch 28 August 1914.
25 The two types of torpedo heads.
26 TNA ADM 196/49/3: Theodore Stuart Brodie; Richard Compton-Hall, *Submarines and the War at Sea 1914–18* (London: Macmillan, 1991), pp.125, 164; Shankland & Hunter, *Dardanelles Patrol*, p.21.

the southeast. Brodie dived and headed in their direction, then turned east, hoping to intercept them if they turned northeast – presumably the destroyers he could see were in this direction. However, they continued west, as it was Beatty's battle cruisers retiring from the Bight. An hour later he surfaced with nothing in sight. It was now 3:56pm. Brodie retraced his track back to Borkum. He finally started the diesels and headed back to Harwich at 7:30pm, arriving at 3:30pm on the 29th.[27]

At 4:20am on the 28th Jameson's *D.2* was heading for her billet off the Western Ems, south of the Borkum Riff. Smoke was spotted aft, off westwards. A four funnelled ship came into sight. *D.2* dived and headed slowly in to the Ems on an intercept course, but within 20 minutes the target had disappeared westward. The three funnelled cruiser *Mainz* had been patrolling back and forth during the night, returning to anchor in the Ems at dawn. *D.2* came to the surface and headed to her billet, seven miles north of the entrance to the river. At 6:30am what looked like a large trawler was seen patrolling the entrance and beyond it masts and smoke, assumed to be the cruiser seen previously in the Huibert Gat.

At 10am a *Kolberg* class light cruiser was seen coming out of the river, steering northwest at a moderate speed. *D.2* dived and began an attack run. Suddenly, 15 minutes later, the cruiser turned east and made off along the coast at high speed. This was *Mainz* coming out to attack the Harwich Force.

The cruiser was followed out by about five destroyers, identified as early S types. These patrolled around the entrance on the usual constantly varying courses and speeds. Jameson pursued one of them and made two failed attack runs. On the third attempt he managed to get into the ideal attack position. He reports: 'Fired one Torpedo at her at 1.5 p.m. at 500 yards [460m] abeam [side-on] in a smooth sea. Destroyer appeared to stop and go astern shortly after Torpedo was fired, and it passed about 20 yards [18m] ahead of her.' Jameson had apparently kept the periscope up to observe the torpedo run. *D.2* had broken the surface and he probably realised that she had been seen. The impact of three shells hitting the water was heard after diving.

The destroyer was *G.169*, commanded by Kapitänleutnant Lemelsen of 6th Torpedoboots-Halbflottille, a more modern boat than Jameson identified. She was one of six boats from her Flotilla ready for action in the Ems that morning. Their commander had asked permission to accompany *Mainz* when she sortied but was ordered to patrol off the Ems entrance to defend it from attack. *G.169*'s crew had spotted a periscope several times around 12:30pm. She was off the entrance to the river channel when *D.2* was spotted firing her torpedo at 1:17pm. Part of the conning tower had broken the surface. *G.169* opened fire with her 8.8cm (3.5-inch) gun battery. She carried two guns, one forward and one aft, but claimed no hits. Despite the warning there was little time to react and the torpedo passed just 15m (50 feet) ahead of the bow, as Jameson reported.

Three destroyers now began hunting *D.2*, zig-zagging at high speed round the area. Jameson was finally able to surface at 5:30pm, five miles west of the attack position. The German destroyers had not seen anything after the attack. He was now able to fix the position of the cruiser seen earlier in the Huibert Gat. The doubt over her nationality was still not dispelled. Jameson saw two funnels and two masts, resembling a Dutch *Holland* class. It was *Arcona*,

27   TNA ADM137/2067: p.121; Groos, *Nordsee 1*, 1920, p.175.

The lucky destroyer *G.169*, typical of the boats in the High Sea Fleet Flotillas in 1914. (NH 45586)

similar in profile and size to these Dutch cruisers. Suddenly, a German monoplane appeared, approaching rapidly from the east. Jameson ordered *D.2* to dive. The plane had got within half a mile at a height of 600 feet (180m) as she submerged but made no report. Jameson kept going west deep out of sight until after dark. He surfaced at 7:40pm and headed back for Harwich, arriving at 7pm on the 29th.[28]

Lurcher and *Firedrake* scouted south of Cruiser Force K on the morning of the 28th. At 7am *Lurcher* intercepted a wireless signal indicating that Tyrwhitt was in action northwest of Heligoland. Keyes decided to head 'towards Heligoland … with the object of inducing the enemy to chase … to the westward.' *Firedrake* followed astern. Visibility dropped as they headed east. Suddenly, two four funnelled cruisers 'loomed up' about three miles away coming up from astern on the port side, heading roughly towards the Jade River. Keyes says that: 'It was impossible to make out details in the mist, but their general outline … closely resembled the "ROSTOCK" class … I took them to be enemy and kept them in sight.' Their four funnels and two masts had ruled out Tyrwhitt's cruisers. It was now 7:50am. *Lurcher* was thought to be about 30 miles west of Heligoland. Keyes reported the two enemy cruisers by wireless, with his position, repeating the message periodically as he shadowed them. He does not say why he did not manoeuvre to attack with torpedoes if he thought that the cruisers were German.

28   TNA ADM137/2067: pp.119-20; Groos, *Nordsee 1*, pp.175, 180; BArch:RM92: *Mainz* Tätigkeite des kleinen Kreuzers "Mainz".

The signal was taken in by Goodenough at 8:15am in the *Southampton*. He soon turned west for the reported position to give assistance with the four cruisers he had in company, encountering *E.6*. *Lurcher* had lost sight of the cruisers by 8:40am. Keyes believed that they must have altered course to northeast, and *Lurcher* doubled back to follow. Heavy firing was then heard to the east, so Keyes altered towards it. At 9:05am two cruisers appeared ahead steering across his bow apparently heading south-easterly. Two more were dimly made out. Keyes ordered *Lurcher* to turn northwest, aiming to lead the cruisers towards Moore's *Invincible* and *New Zealand*. The cruisers seemed to follow. Unaware that Beatty was present, he sent a wireless message to Moore informing him that he was being chased by four cruisers and was leading them to him. *Arethusa* also received part of this signal at 10am, without the position, as repeated by *Firedrake*. Tyrwhitt did not hesitate to offer support. Assuming Keyes was in contact with the enemy to the east he 'ordered all ships to turn 16 points [turning directly round] at once and called up "FIREDRAKE" for her position without result.'

This time Keyes must have had doubts as to the identity of the cruisers he was in touch with. At 9:15am *New Zealand* intercepted a signal from him to Tyrwhitt asking whether British light cruisers had come into the area. No reply was logged. Visibility gradually improved. It became clear to Keyes that the four following cruisers all had four funnels and two masts and looked like British Town class. At 9:50am *Lurcher* made the recognition challenge by light. Goodenough's *Southampton* answered. She had *Birmingham*, *Falmouth* and *Liverpool* following astern. Keyes explains that he had not wished to challenge earlier as this would have given the code group away to vessels that he was certain were not British. Goodenough signalled back the news that the 1st BCS were also in the area. The situation gave Keyes great concern, as his instructions put the 'Town' type cruisers in particular at high risk of attack from his own submarines. He signalled Goodenough: 'I was not informed you were coming into this area; you run great risk from our submarines ... Your unexpected appearance has upset all our plans. There are submarines off Ems.' Goodenough was alarmed at the news. He must have immediately realised that the submarine seen attacking earlier was British. He signalled Beatty at 10:10am: 'Commodores S [Keyes] and T [Tyrwhitt] have no knowledge of 1st L.C.S. taking part. I consider we should withdraw at once. Submarines are closing us.'

Based on track charts the first sighting must have been a glimpse of the four cruisers in the main body of 1st LCS and possibly also *Lowestoft* and *Nottingham*, which had been temporarily detached. *Falmouth* logged two following destroyers in sight at 8:20am, but her commander was obviously unconcerned about British destroyers. *Lurcher*'s navigator had placed her too far to the west, which generated major confusion. A situation resembling a theatre farce had developed with Goodenough altering course to support the very destroyers that were shadowing and reporting his own cruisers. This also diverted him from supporting Tyrwhitt, who had himself altered back to the east for 30 minutes to try and give assistance, when in fact Keyes was west of him. This could have had serious consequences as the speed of *Arethusa* was considerably reduced by damage.[29]

At 10:30am Goodenough altered course to the north, with Keyes astern. Around 11am *Lurcher* and *Firedrake* broke away from 1st LCS. Keyes attempted to locate and join the Harwich Force, having become concerned that Tyrwhitt was not answering signals, but his movements

---

29   TNA ADM186/610: Battle of Heligoland, p.126, 151–2.

are unclear. At noon: 'a great grey shape loomed up in the mist … followed by other phantom-looking ships, steaming at high speed towards the Jade … For some moments I felt sure they must be enemy battle cruisers, but as they were sufficiently close to blow us out of the water and they refrained, our anxiety was brief.' Beatty had decided to bring his five battle cruisers into the Bight to extract the beleaguered Tyrwhitt. New light grey paintwork, with a dark panel representing a smaller ship alongside had caused the confusion. Keyes altered course and increased speed to 30 knots to get ahead of Beatty in order to try and warn his submarines, although this seemed a hopeless task in the visibility. Heavy firing broke out ahead. Keyes ordered 32 knots and turned towards it. The 1st LCS came into sight at 12:37pm and were engaging a German light cruiser. Keyes turned to close, but by 12:50pm the enemy cruiser was stopped, on fire and had struck her colours. He altered course towards a new bout of heavy firing in the distance to the northeast. This took him through a number of the crew of the German cruiser who had already abandoned ship and were around a mile astern of her in the water. Keyes ordered *Lurcher* and *Firedrake* to stop. Each lowered a boat to pick the men up. The *Liverpool* had been detailed by Goodenough to pick up survivors and had also lowered her boats. Keyes thought that the cruiser seemed to be on an even keel and to have full buoyancy: 'For a few moments … I had thoughts of boarding and, if possible, towing her home!' Keyes ordered that *Lurcher* be taken alongside, whilst *Firedrake* was left to pick up survivors in the water.

Once within 100 yards (90m) the cruiser was identified as *Mainz*. Her crew realised that *Lurcher* intended to come alongside. Some ran aft and trained a gun on *Lurcher*'s bridge. An officer aft, fearing that the British intended to board to seize confidential papers, ordered the crew to prepare to repel boarders. Several got hold of rifles, but most of these had been damaged in the action. By now it was obvious to Keyes that *Mainz* was rapidly sinking by the bows. At least 200 men could be seen still on board, many of whom were badly wounded. On the bridge of *Lurcher* Commander Tomkinson quietly said: 'They are going to fire on us.' Keyes grabbed a megaphone and shouted: 'Don't fire, damn you, I am coming alongside to save life. Get your fenders out at once.' Fortunately, the Germans understood and complied. One of the surviving Petty Officers, Willi Klein, reported that the gun, which was the only one still in action, had in fact fired all of its available ammunition, so it may be lack of means that prevailed.[30] Tomkinson brought *Lurcher* alongside the starboard side aft. Three boats from *Liverpool* had already taken away one load of wounded, but were now ordered away by her commander, Captain Reeves, as he feared *Mainz* would explode.[31] Some of the wounded had been lashed to hammocks and other crew were attempting to swim with them to reach the boats. Keyes now accused the commander of *Liverpool*'s cutter of being a coward for refusing repeated appeals from him to close in and pick up the survivors. Meanwhile, the crew of *Mainz* carried their wounded over to *Lurcher*. The unwounded crew then clambered across as she began to list to port. Keyes could see her starboard propeller had moved under *Lurcher* and feared being struck by it if *Mainz* capsized.

The evacuation had taken about five minutes. Only three crew appeared to still be on-board apart from the dead and dying. This included the officer on the stern who had organised the evacuation, one man cut off aloft by the fires and another officer on the bridge, who later

---

30   Groos, *Nordsee 1*, p.179.
31   *Keyes Papers*, p.21, Letter from Captain Reeves to Keyes 14 September 1914.

transpired to be the son of Großadmiral von Tirpitz, the head of the German Navy. The Paymaster, unseen by Keyes, was vainly trying to persuade him to leave. Keyes had left *Lurcher's* bridge to help organise the evacuation. He told the officer on *Mainz's* stern that he had done splendidly, but there was nothing more to be done and held out his hand to help him on-board. He replied: 'Thank you, no'. *Mainz* then lurched to port and rapidly went down by the bow around 1:10pm, as *Lurcher* backed away with full astern power. The propellers narrowly missed her as the stern leapt up out of the water. Honour satisfied, the officer on the poop, unseen by Keyes, ran to the starboard rail and jumped into the sea. He, Tirpitz and one of the wounded who had been lashed to a raft were picked up by a boat from *Liverpool*.[32]

The unwounded German captives had been seated under armed guard on *Lurcher's* forecastle forward. They stood to give three cheers for the Kaiser and their ship as she sank and had to be told to sit down. The 70 crew of *Lurcher* were heavily outnumbered by the 224 prisoners, causing some concern to Keyes. The crowded decks would have made it almost impossible to fight the guns. *Firedrake* had rescued 33 men from the water. *Lurcher* had taken in a signal from Beatty ordering a general withdrawal. It took around half an hour to pick up the last men in the water and hoist the boats back aboard. *Lurcher* then headed west at 25 knots in company with *Firedrake*. She was unable to steam any faster as the condenser inlets had been choked by scum that had come to the surface after *Mainz* sank. The crew tore up sheets and shirts to make bandages for the 60 or so wounded, some of whom had dreadful shrapnel injuries. A destroyer had very limited medical facilities and no medical officer, but fortunately the prisoners included the unwounded doctor and sick berth attendant of *Mainz*. At 2:30pm Keyes came upon two of Tyrwhitt's damaged destroyers, *Laurel* and *Liberty*. They were limping along at 16 knots, so he slowed down to remain with them.

Keyes felt 'considerable relief' when at 4:15pm Admiral Christian's cruisers came into sight. *Lurcher* transferred 165 unwounded and walking wounded prisoners to the *Cressy*. Keyes brought back the surgeon and a sick berth attendant to help with the more seriously wounded cases on *Lurcher*. *Firedrake* transferred her small number of wounded prisoners to the *Bacchante* and *Cressy*. Both then got back underway, with the damaged *Liberty* still in company. *Laurel* was handed over for a tow by the *Amethyst*, which was now attached to Christian's force.

Lurcher halted briefly at 8:30pm to hold a committal for 12 of the most seriously wounded who had since died. As night fell she proceeded as fast as she could to get the wounded back to Harwich quickly, leaving *Firedrake* to accompany the *Liberty* back at her best speed. *Lurcher* arrived at Harwich at 3am on the 29th, by which time two more of the wounded had died. She landed the 45 surviving wounded prisoners with their doctor and sick berth attendant. *Firedrake* arrived four hours later.

Keyes reported that several of the wounded had 'bullet wounds' in the back and noted that a German officer had been seen firing at the men abandoning ship. This has often been repeated. A German report states that a wounded officer, Kuhlman, had been taking pot-shots at *Liverpool* from the conning tower with his pistol until he passed out. This misunderstanding is perhaps the origin of the accusation. Keyes report includes remarks from some of the petty officers and engine room staff of *Mainz* who had spoken very freely to those helping them. Most are things

---

32   Hugo von Waldeyer-Hartz, (Translated F.A. Holt) *Admiral von Hipper* (London: Rich & Cowan 1933), pp.116-7, quoting unnamed German officer's account.

those who are grateful to be rescued would say, such as: 'It was a very unnecessary war'. They did give some details about the proceedings and loss of their ship. Their officers said nothing.[33]

Heligoland was hailed as a decisive victory, but Keyes and the Flotilla had little to celebrate. Goodenough wrote to Keyes a week later. He wrote that the officer on the *Liverpool*'s cutter was terribly upset at 'someone on board one of the destroyers' calling him a coward. He felt that 'it is necessary at this moment to be v[er]y careful that no word among ourselves c[oul]d possibly create any discussion', in reference to their mutual entanglement in the action. Keyes replied that: 'I ought not to have used the word "coward"'. He asked for forgiveness from Goodenough and Reeves but hoped that the officer in question had learned a lesson. In respect of the recent action he writes that: 'I think an absurd fuss was made over that small affair … It makes me sick and disgusted to think what a complete success it might have been but for, I won't say dual, but – multiple control. We begged for light cruisers … but were told none were available.' The lack of success in attacks so far was on his mind, as he predicts that: 'loss inflicted by submarines will not amount to much on either side during the war. The North Sea is a big place – so is the Heligoland Bight – once located a submarine danger area is so small – and can easily be avoided particularly with high speed at command'.[34]

Keyes frustration is understandable. Critique of the role of 8th Flotilla in the action tends to focus on the farcical and potentially disastrous events that occurred as a result of Keyes and his submarine commanders having no inkling of the inclusion of 1st LCS in the operation. The blame for the bungled staff work, initially inadequate arrangements for support and muddled command structure sits primarily with Sturdee and his staff. Jellicoe's insistence on adding Grand Fleet forces and Beatty's risky decision to head in to support Tyrwhitt delivered a decisive victory, both tactically and strategically, with three German light cruisers sunk for no loss.

Despite Keyes frustration, he did partially achieve his objectives. The execution of the bold plan conceived by Keyes and Tyrwhitt had a salutary impact, increasing risk aversion in the German Fleet Command as a result of the one sided result and causing a rethink about strategy and patrol tactics. At a tactical level the 5th Torpedoboots-Flottille were drawn out to sea by the attack on *G.194* and would otherwise not have been engaged by Tyrwhitt. An opportunity to attack *G.169* was created when she sortied in response to the raid. Better visibility and a less calm sea may have created additional opportunities and increased the chance of torpedo hits, but the action would have developed in a different way, potentially negating this.

In his report to Christian, Keyes does highlight the low visibility and very calm water as contributory factors in the lack of success, whilst emphasising that destroyers are already very hard targets. Talbot is praised for not attacking 1st LCS, when he had every reason to do so, together with both his and Feilmann's daring in attracting enemy attention on the day. Leir's 'altogether admirable' rescue of the crew of the *Defender* and 'gallant optimism and extraordinary confidence' as Senior Officer is highlighted. Tomkinson is recognised for his skill handling *Lurcher* whilst rescuing the crew of *Mainz*. Benning, Horton, Herbert and Jameson are picked out for their work in earlier reconnaissance.

33   Keyes, *Memoirs*, pp.82–92; TNA ADM137/2067: pp.110-114; TNA ADM53: *Firedrake, Lurcher, Euryalus*, 27-29 August 1914; TNA ADM137/1943: pp.13, 43-45; BArch:RM92: *Mainz* Kriegstagebuch, Berichte 28. August 1914.
34   *Keyes Papers*, pp.17-22, correspondence between Goodenough, Keyes and Reeves.

Keyes direct participation had a negative impact on events. A lot of this was bad luck, or predictable dead reckoning errors by *Lurcher's* navigator, but it was stretching his role beyond the limits to be charging round a battlefield. The successful outcome deflected scrutiny. Given the glaring errors in staff work this is unsurprising, as there was plenty of blame to go round. However, for precisely this reason, Keyes repeated protests about the staff muddle were not appreciated. In a letter to his friend and mentor, Rear-Admiral de Robeck, he writes: 'They – particularly W.C. [Winston Churchill] – were awfully annoyed with me for making such a protest about it'.[35] He got a ticking off from Jellicoe in a communique on the 31st for omitting his course and speed when making signals. Keyes responded that other signals made shortly before or after the offending examples had given this information and that with so many changes of course and speed after 24 hours of dead reckoning, his position was also likely to be inaccurate.[36]

Whether Keyes should have gone to such lengths in risking *Lurcher* and *Firedrake* to rescue the crew of *Mainz* in the middle of a battle is a debatable point. The disasters that overtook vessels stopping to pick up survivors were in the future. The axiom that once out of action, the enemy became fellow sailors to be rescued ran deep. However, Goodenough wrote in his letter that he did not intend to do so again. Keyes actions certainly saved many lives.

A number of flaws in the plan and tactics had a limiting effect on the scope for success. Having submarines amongst the surface action was counter-productive. Ships in action were usually moving at high speed and changing course frequently, making them very difficult targets to attack, whilst forcing submarines deep to avoid ramming. It was difficult to identify friend from foe in these circumstances, even allowing for the similarity between 'Towns' and German cruisers. The tendency to 'chase firing', rather than remaining on reinforcement and retirement routes, often meant arriving after action had moved elsewhere.

The fact that vessels would exit the main harbours in response to the raid was anticipated. More submarines placed nearer these choke points may have increased the chance of success, with targets steering straight courses and with no doubt as to identity. The placement of *E.5*, *E.8* and *E.9* to the north of Heligoland was poor. They were not in a position to intercept ships leaving harbour or ships fleeing the raid. They predictably saw little.

All the E class left as soon as the raiding ships withdrew and there was no sweep for damaged vessels. It took the Germans time to assess the operational situation and organise a response. Many ships, including the German battle cruisers, were still steaming out into the Bight, as it was not obvious that the British had retired. The early departure meant that additional opportunities for attacks were almost certainly lost.

35   *Keyes Papers*, p.31, letter to De Robeck 29 September 1914.
36   TNA ADM137/2067: pp.116–8, 134–6.

9

Back on patrol

Arethusa had to go into the dockyard for repair after the Heligoland battle. Whilst waiting for a temporary replacement Tyrwhitt used a cabin aboard *Maidstone* for a couple of nights. This gave Keyes the opportunity to plot their next steps together. They were both keen to repeat an attack on the Bight as soon as possible but were concerned that the Germans would vary their patrol arrangements as a result of the battle.

Keyes ordered seven submarines to depart Harwich on 1 September to confirm the situation in the Bight.[1] Each was to be towed by a destroyer from 1st Flotilla as far as Terschelling. The force would first rendezvous at Smith's Knoll, then proceed with *Lurcher* and *Firedrake* scouting ahead. They were to reach Terschelling at 7pm as night fell. The nine destroyers would then return to Harwich and the submarines proceed onwards to their billets. *E.5*, *E.8* and *E.9* departed Harwich at 3:30am and would form an inner patrol line north of Juist. Captain Waistell, with *Firedrake* and *Lurcher*, followed at 4:45am. Finally, *D.3*, *D.4*, *D.5* and *E.3* left at 5:30am and would form an outer patrol line north of Terschelling. This would be the first trip to the Bight for *E.3* and the first operation for *D.4*. Both had spent the previous day making practice attack runs on *Adamant* off the Cork Light Vessel along with *D.3*, *D.5*, *D.7* and *E.10*.[2]

The submarines would remain on patrol until the evening of the 3rd. They were to return to Harwich via Yarmouth.[3] Sturdee had ordered that patrols were to be farther out from shore than previously in the hope of catching enemy vessels heading in and out of the North Sea ports. There was an expectation that the Germans might well react with an offensive operation of their own in response to the recent raid.

Herbert's *D.5* had an uneventful journey to her billet on the 1st after dropping her tow from *Badger*. She arrived at 5am next morning but saw nothing all day. The 3rd was little better. Herbert shifted his position at least three times. The boredom was relieved when the crew sank a large wooden buoy with rifle fire in the morning, suspecting it might be a marker for enemy patrols. At noon smoke was spotted from a possible destroyer, but it turned back before it could

---

1   Keyes, *Memoirs*, p.98.
2   TNA ADM53: *Adamant*, 31 August 1914.
3   TNA ADM137/2067: p.150.

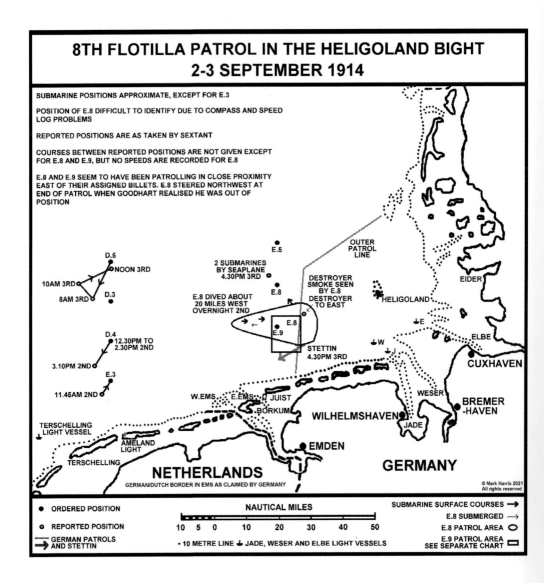

**8TH FLOTILLA PATROL IN THE HELIGOLAND BIGHT
2-3 SEPTEMBER 1914**

SUBMARINE POSITIONS APPROXIMATE, EXCEPT FOR E.3

POSITION OF E.8 DIFFICULT TO IDENTIFY DUE TO COMPASS AND SPEED LOG PROBLEMS

REPORTED POSITIONS ARE AS TAKEN BY SEXTANT

COURSES BETWEEN REPORTED POSITIONS ARE NOT GIVEN EXCEPT FOR E.8 AND E.9, BUT NO SPEEDS ARE RECORDED FOR E.8

E.8 AND E.9 SEEM TO HAVE BEEN PATROLLING IN CLOSE PROXIMITY EAST OF THEIR ASSIGNED BILLETS. E.8 STEERED NORTHWEST AT END OF PATROL WHEN GOODHART REALISED HE WAS OUT OF POSITION

be identified. *D.5* left for Yarmouth at 6pm and arrived there at 2pm next day. She returned to Harwich on the morning of the 5th.[4]

Boyle's *D.3* was next to the south in the outer line. Her Mark VI torpedoes had all been adjusted for their 4,000 yards (3,650m) long range and 10 foot (3m) depth at the leisurely speed of 22 knots, perhaps a precaution against premature diving. She got underway after slipping her tow from *Sandfly* and headed for her billet. Boyle observed lights from a vessel coming up astern at 11pm. *D.3* stopped and trimmed down to reduce her silhouette, ready to attack. It was a false alarm. A steamer passed by and *D.3* got back underway. As *D.3* dived at dawn next

4   TNA ADM137/2067: pp.155, 164.

morning, Boyle spotted a submarine nearby. He suspected that it was *D.5*, but remained down for an hour anyway. Nothing was seen for the rest of the day after arriving at the billet. The 3rd was almost equally uneventful. Finally, at 3:45pm, Boyle dived when a large steamer was seen approaching. She passed about 400 yards (375m) away, showing no flag. No doubt suspecting a disguised minelayer, Boyle reports that: 'I showed my conning tower when she was close, but as she did not fire I let her go.' *D.3* surfaced after she had gone, then headed for home at 6pm. Ships loomed up ahead at 1:35am. They were showing no lights and looked like destroyers. *D.3* stopped and trimmed down. Eventually trawlers were made out and *D.3* got back underway. Boyle passed Yarmouth, went straight on to Harwich and arrived at 5:10pm on the 4th.[5]

The third boat in the outer line was *D.4*, under Lieutenant-Commander Kenneth M. Bruce, aged 31. He was the son of a doctor. Bruce joined the Submarine Service in 1906 and Captain Brandt rated him as: 'Capable & reliable – Sound & steady' in 1911. He had taken command of *D.4* in August 1912. *The Maidstone Magazine* alludes to his fondness for gambling and Bruce was apparently a keen poker player with his fellow officers. This would be his first and only patrol in *D.4*, as he was slated for command of *E.12*, nearing completion at Chatham.[6]

After dropping his tow from *Jackal*, Bruce seems to have had trouble navigating to his billet and did not arrive until just after noon on the 2nd. He halted on the surface. It was now 2:10pm. Bruce left the bridge to get a drink, leaving his Signalman, William Halter, alone on watch. He says it was 'a beautiful day', but he felt petrified. Halter spotted a torpedo running on the surface at the end of its run, then sink, about 150 yards (140m) away to port. He immediately rang the alarm bell. Bruce came up and ordered the boat to crash dive. He was sceptical about the torpedo, telling Halter that he should not have left him alone on the bridge with his nerves. Nevertheless, after later surfacing, *D.4* moved 10 miles to the southwest. Halter says that his accurate description of a German torpedo to the Flotilla's Torpedo Officer on return to base increased the credibility of his story. Bruce does not share his doubts or his absence from the bridge in his report, writing that he 'thought a German submarine must be in the vicinity'. After the incident *D.4* periodically dived to periscope depth for the rest of the patrol. The night was spent on the bottom.

There was a brief glimpse of smoke next morning, but nothing else until 5pm. A steamer was sighted coming from the direction of Heligoland. *D.4* submerged. Bruce reports: 'Attacked her and observed her to alter course five times in about 10 miles. She passed within 400 yards [350m], but I could observe nothing out of the ordinary, so did not fire a torpedo at her.' Apart from a Dutch merchant ensign his description tallies with that of Boyle, including her deck cargo of wood. He followed after surfacing at 7:10pm, as it was time to leave the patrol, but she did nothing suspicious. Bruce returned to Harwich at 1:30pm on the 4th. Since paranoia about disguised minelayers was at its height, the steamer had been at some risk of attack from both submarines. Despite the recent refit, *D.4* went into the dockyard at Sheerness on the 7th for more work on her machinery and battery, not returning to Harwich until the 17th.[7]

The southernmost boat on the outer line was *E.3*, under Lieutenant-Commander George F. Cholmley, who was 32 on the 1st. He had received early promotion for submarine work in the pioneering days of 1903. After commanding a number of coastal boats, in 1911 Captain

5   TNA ADM137/2067: p.153; TNA ADM173: *D.3* 1-4 September 1914.
6   TNA ADM196/143/146: Kenneth Mervyn Bruce; Douglas, *Maidstone Magazine*, p.248.
7   TNA ADM137/2067: p.154; TNA ADM173: *D.4* 1-4 September 1914; IWM:Sound_721.

Johnson rated him as: 'Sound & reliable. V[ery]G[ood] organiser. Reliable man for a responsible position.' Command of the new depot ship *Alecto*, as a senior officer of 7th Flotilla followed. Keyes recently rated him: 'Zealous, cool and collected. Handles his ship well.' He took command of *E.3* at the builders in January 1914.[8]

Cholmley arrived at his billet at 6am on the 2nd. *E.3* dived to avoid being spotted by a patrolling aircraft soon afterwards. A two funnelled cruiser appeared on the horizon to the south at 11:45am. Cholmley dived and began an attack, but she disappeared to the southwest. He reports that: 'about half the funnels came above the horizon. She looked like one of the "Hansa" class'. The shore was now in sight and Cholmley was able to get an exact position fix from some tall features. *E.3* shifted position, as she was five miles southwest of her assigned billet.

Nothing more was seen until 4:30am the next morning. A submarine was sighted. *E.3* dived and crept closer on one motor. Cholmley now realised that it was actually the fuselage of a capsized seaplane. Sitting on the floats were her pilot, Oberleutnant Hans Andler and his crewman, Oberheizer der Reserve Otto Bauer, who were no doubt mightily surprised when *E.3* surfaced alongside. Cholmley took them aboard and made an attempt to salvage the seaplane's engine. This proved too difficult to lift out of the water, as the seaplane was upside down and largely submerged. Holes were bashed in the floats and the aircraft went to the bottom. This was the first material damage the Flotilla had done to the enemy! Cholmley told Goodhart that Andler was 'a very cheery fellow'. He proved to be a mine of information and the verifiable parts were accurate. Cholmley provided a detailed report; mainly Andler's views on the progress of the war. He had seen a salvaged British torpedo recently and stated that Dutch warships did not use the Ems. Andler did not carry bombs in order to increase the amount of fuel that could be carried. He thought it was almost impossible to hit anything with them. It was his plane Cholmley had sighted the previous day heading out on patrol from Borkum. He had not seen *E.3* but had examined a patch of oil in the area where they had dived. Not long after this his engine failed and the plane had turned a somersault on landing. It had been drifting for 20 hours and was not expected to float much longer.[9]

During the proceedings *D.4* had been seen approaching, but neither Bruce nor her log mention this. A destroyer was sighted around three miles away heading in the direction of Terschelling at 7am. Cholmley lost sight of her after diving. *E.3* dived again on sighting two steamers an hour and a half later, but these turned and headed in to Terschelling. At 7pm she left for home, reaching Harwich at 11am on the 4th, where Andler and Bauer were handed over to the Army.[10]

The most northerly of the boats on the inner line was Benning's *E.5*. She headed for her billet after dropping her tow from *Phoenix*, arriving at 7am on the 2nd. *E.5* patrolled on the surface, diving three times for short periods. Nothing was seen all day, despite high visibility. Benning submerged for the night at 8pm. One motor was left running, turning *E.5* in a circle at 55 feet (17m), just fast enough to maintain depth. Benning surfaced at 5am next day and repeated his patrol pattern, but again saw nothing, with visibility down to five miles. He left the billet at

8   TNA ADM196/143/67: George Francis Cholmley.
9   *Geheime Marine Verlustliste 7*, p.41.
10   TNA ADM137/2067: pp.156-8

5pm, passing a merchant steamer on his way back a couple of hours later – the only thing seen on the entire patrol. *E.5* reached Harwich at 2pm on the 4th.[11]

The middle boat on the inner line was Goodhart's *E.8*. The towing experience was 'pretty rotten' and Goodhart complains that it limited progress to just eight knots. The tow from *Lapwing* had parted after just two hours. It had taken an hour to clear the trailing cable before *E.8* could proceed on her engines. She picked up the tow again at Smith's Knoll. It parted again at 5:20pm. Goodhart ditched the towing cables. *E.8* arrived at her billet at 10:15am on the 2nd, sounding the water depth and sampling the seabed to help confirm the position. Goodhart tells his wife that he was: 'hazy as to my whereabouts as my patent log [measuring distance travelled] was hopeless & the compass a bit out too. However, we got sights [using the sextant], although I fear Burrowes[12] [the Third Officer] isnt a great hand at them somehow, as they dont always correspond.' Whilst the sight was being taken whoever was emptying the urinal bucket managed to lose it overboard.

Goodhart welcomed the clear calm weather, with gently agitated water, making for ideal attacking conditions, but nothing came along. He got underway at 2:29pm and kept moving for the rest of the day, first to the northwest, then looping back. He was concerned that enemy submarines could be around. Nothing was seen until dusk at 5:30pm. Goodhart sighted a submarine. *E.8* dived and stayed down for 40 minutes. The other submarine seemed to have also dived. Goodhart was unsure if it was *E.9*, *E.5* or an enemy. Searchlights were seen to the south at 7:30pm, but it was time to submerge for the night. This was spent heading west: 'at 60 feet diving ahead slow & got some good sleep. The boat didn't get fuggy at all really, & we only had to correct our trim once owing to a slight leak in the after compartment.'

E.8 surfaced at 4:30am on the 3rd and went back to her patrol position charging the batteries. Goodhart sighted a German submarine ahead of him on arriving at 7:30am. He dived to attack but could not catch up and returned to his position. It was a little misty, with nothing in sight. Goodhart surfaced at 8:40am: 'On looking round I saw a destroyer as large as life about 2 miles off, so down I went, & took a bearing of him intending to watch him.' The destroyer had re-appeared from the direction the supposed submarine had vanished and Goodhart concluded they were one and the same. He saw her make various course alterations and decided to go to 50 feet (15m) and head west in case she altered towards him. The sea was 'an oily calm' and the standing orders were not to waste torpedoes on destroyers. They had avoided them previously in these conditions. After 15 minutes: 'he came right over us going full speed … by the sound, whether it was a fluke or not I don't know but I kept down for a couple of hours.' Goodhart surfaced at 11:20am. The weather had cleared. Smoke from destroyers could be made out behind to both left and right, so *E.8* kept going west to get clear. At noon Goodhart spotted *E.9* ahead and altered course to northwest until 2pm, realising he was out of position. He was now able to get some clear views to calculate by sextant that the destroyer smoke was 20 miles north of Norderney Island. *E.8* got underway to return to Harwich at 4:50pm.

Goodhart spotted a steamer coming out of the Ems at 7pm. He submerged for 12 minutes to get a good look. As she went past the Norwegian ensign made her appear 'harmless enough … one can never say without going on board … thats hopeless from our point of view.' Shortly after

---

11   TNA ADM137/2067:, p.159; ADM173: *E.5* 1-4 September 1914.
12   Not traced, possibly Acting Sub-Lieutenant John G. Barrow, borrowed from *Lurcher*, who was appointed Third Officer of *E.3* on 14 September.

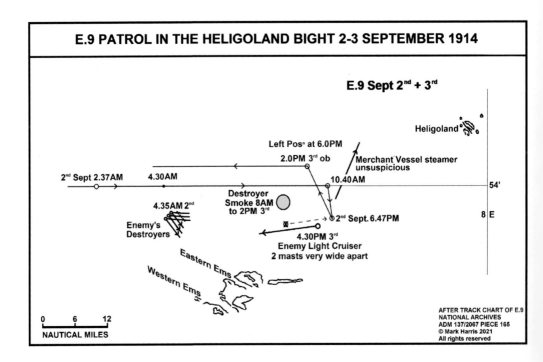

E.9 PATROL IN THE HELIGOLAND BIGHT 2-3 SEPTEMBER 1914

E.9 Sept 2nd + 3rd

Heligoland

Left Pos^{n} at 6.0PM

2.0PM 3rd ob

Merchant Vessel steamer unsuspicious

2nd Sept 2.37AM   4.30AM

10.40AM

54'

Destroyer Smoke 8AM to 2PM 3rd

4.35AM 2nd

2nd Sept. 6.47PM

8 E

Enemy's Destroyers

4.30PM 3rd
Enemy Light Cruiser
2 masts very wide apart

Eastern Ems

Western Ems

0   6   12
NAUTICAL MILES

getting back underway a submarine was sighted. This gave the correct response to the challenge and was presumably *E.9*. Goodhart arrived at Harwich at 3:30pm on the 4th. Next day *E.8* went on to the floating dock for two days work painting the bottom and fixing her leak.[13]

Horton's *E.9* had the beat closest inshore. Only track traces and some details given by Keyes have survived. A destroyer patrol was sighted off the Ems whilst heading to the billet on the 2nd. The patrol turned towards the estuary at 4:35am, eight to 10 miles to the south of *E.9*. Horton saw nothing of importance after reaching his billet. On the 3rd, destroyer smoke was seen to the west for most of the day and a sight taken in the afternoon seems to have revealed that he was 8 miles further east than thought. Horton sighted the masts of a cruiser, apparently steaming from Heligoland to Emden, 13 miles to the south of him at 4:30pm. Frustratingly, he had been in the perfect position to intercept it at 6:47pm the previous day! *E.9* left the patrol at 6pm, but was delayed overnight at Yarmouth by minor repairs, from where Horton reported by telephone. *E.9* arrived at Harwich at 9:25am on the 5th.[14]

Keyes concluded from the reports of *E.8* and *E.9* that the Heligoland and Ems destroyer patrols were being maintained. The information provided by Andler was taken as proof that the cruiser in the disputed waters of the Ems was German.

13   TNA ADM137/2067: p.161; TNA ADM173: *E.8* 1-6 September 1914; IWM:Documents.2175: letter to wife 5 September 1914; TNA ADM196/145/960 John Gerald Barrow.
14   TNA ADM137/2067: pp.160, 165; TNA ADM53: *Adamant* 5 September 1914; The British Library (BL):AddMS82461: Keyes Papers. Volume lxxxix. Submarines: reports by Commodore (S) 31 July–29 October 1914, p.109.

The German Fleet Command had concluded that the British submarines sighted before the recent raid had identified their patrol patterns. The outer destroyer patrols were now withdrawn at night or in bad visibility to avoid being ambushed. Anti-submarine patrolling within the inner patrol zone by armed trawlers was stepped up and joined by destroyers at night. Horton spotted a one off patrol by 4th Torpedoboots-Flottille out of the Ems on the 2nd. From the 5th onwards this flotilla permanently replaced the day patrol by the few ageing local defence destroyers in the Ems, so the sighting was fortuitous.

Horton spotted *Stettin* on the 3rd, heading from the Jade to the Ems via Heligoland, but the warships seen by Cholmley off the Dutch coast were Dutch neutrality patrols. The torpedo seen by Halter was possibly drifting after being fired during the battle a few days earlier. A very large number were fired. Whilst set to sink at the end of their run during an action, sinking mechanisms did malfunction. Three German submarines, *U.20*, *U.21* and *U.22*, did pass through *E.5*'s billet, probably after sunset on the 2nd, but none were anywhere near *D.4*.

At 10:50am on the 2nd Andler's AGO Pusher, Seaplane '65', had been reported two hours overdue. Four boats of 4th Torpedoboots-Flottille had been sent out of the Ems. They had searched the coast for 10 miles out to sea as far as Ameland Lighthouse, just short of the outer line of submarine billets, but found nothing.

The only enemy submarine sighting by the Germans was a report of two submarines 35 miles west of Heligoland at 4:30pm on the 3rd by a seaplane patrol. One was submerged and the other dived five minutes after sighting. This could have been *E.5*, and just maybe *E.9*. The report arrived too late in the day for action to be taken.

Keyes was satisfied that German day patrol arrangements had been confirmed, but Sturdee's direction to place most of the submarines so far offshore had meant they had seen nothing of value. The important, but not very visible change in night patrolling had not been identified. In his report to Sturdee, Keyes pointed out that in a large area out to sea it was pure luck whether a target came close enough to attack, citing Horton's experience. Placing the submarines closer to the ports of entry and exit would have increased the chance of interception; a large force had moved unobserved from the Jade to the Elbe on the 3rd.[15]

The information that the German patrol routine was apparently unaltered was what Keyes and Tyrwhitt needed. They went up to the Admiralty on the 4th to recommend another raid on the Bight. An overall plan had already been drafted and circulated by the War Staff under the codename Plan IV. Sturdee saw another raid as a chance to draw out the German battleships. Jellicoe had been asked to confirm the earliest date that he could support the operation with the Grand Fleet.

Battenberg now approved the plan in principle. A meeting followed to discuss it in detail with both Battenberg and Sturdee in Churchill's rooms. Keyes and Tyrwhitt went through the proposed arrangements and were told to draft the detailed orders for their Flotillas to put the plan into effect. Keyes asked to be given a light cruiser, but was declined, so he proposed that after seeing the submarines to their stations, *Lurcher* and *Firedrake* should form a screen for Goodenough's light cruisers, which were to support Tyrwhitt. He left under the impression his participation had been agreed.

---

15   Groos, *Nordsee 2*, pp.1-2; TNA ADM137/2067: pp.151-2; BArch:RM92: *Stettin* Kriegstagebuch 3 September 1914, *Kolberg* Kriegstagebuch 2-4 September 1914, *Stralsund*, *Nassau* Kriegstagebuch 2 September 1914

The vessels involved were to depart Harwich in the days prior to the attack, to ensure enemy agents were thrown off the scent. A sealed copy of the draft Plan IV and detailed orders for each boat had already been left by Keyes with Leir in anticipation of approval. He contacted Harwich after the meeting and ordered that *D.2*, *D.8*, *E.4*, *E.6* and *E.7* proceed. They were ordered to complete with stores and Leir put about that they were going to the Humber. The submarine commanders revealed the true destination once at sea. They departed Harwich for Yarmouth from 2pm and would wait there for word to open the orders. A few hours later Jellicoe requested some changes to the plan. The Fleet needed to coal after the sweep that was underway, so the Admiralty's proposed date of the 8th was put back to the 10th.

Keyes was back at the Admiralty on the 6th to agree 8th Flotilla's orders under the plan. Sturdee objected to his 'barging about in the Bight' and to *Lurcher* and *Firedrake* having any close participation in the raid. Keyes was told to remain ashore. He protested. Sturdee left and returned with the Flotilla's orders, to which Battenberg had added: 'The Commodore is not to go in a destroyer', before signing. Sturdee told him that he could go wherever he needed to advise on submarine tactics and procedure but was not to go to sea. Goodenough's advice to not draw attention to his part in the recent action had come too late.[16]

Meanwhile, another patrol had left Harwich on the 5th. Three submarines were to take up a 25 mile long watch line off the western end of Terschelling Island. They were permitted to proceed slowly eastwards each day during daylight. The patrol was a chance to break in the newly arrived *D.1* and *E.10*, whilst the third boat, *D.7*, had not yet been on any offensive patrols. They left Harwich at noon and proceeded together to Smith's Knoll, then headed off independently to their billets at 7pm. Their orders informed them that Christian's cruisers would pass through their billets in the early part of the night. They were to remain on patrol until the evening of the 7th.[17]

There were no leisurely tows for the submarines this time and *D.1* was placed close inshore, just outside Dutch territorial waters. She was the boat of Lieutenant-Commander Archibald D. Cochrane, the son of Baron Cochrane of Cults; a renowned Scottish family of soldiers, sailors and diplomats. He was aged 29 and only recently promoted. Cochrane had joined the Submarine Service in 1906 and had commanded various coastal boats. He took on the notoriously unreliable *D.1* in August 1912. In 1913 Captain Brandt rated him: 'Capable, sound & reliable', Keyes adding that he had 'done exceedingly well in a very trying vessel.' He later rated him exceptional for ability, but an underwhelming 'satisfactory' for attitude. Hallifax knew him as a good skipper, but also a bit of an enigma, being reserved and untalkative, but very calm in a crisis. He had been 'rather frightened' of him when serving with him in *Defence* in 1911, as he 'never quite knew how to take him'. *The Maidstone Magazine* includes him in the inner circle of Flotilla poker players. Cochrane was known for his lucky green hat that was worn whenever he went out on patrol.[18]

16   Keyes, *Memoirs*, pp.98-99; BL:AddMS82461: p.58; TNA ADM186/620: Naval Staff Monographs Volume XI: Home Waters – Part II September and October 1914, pp.30–31, 154; IWM: Documents.1003: 4 September
17   TNA ADM137/2067: pp.167–8
18   TNA ADM 96/49/237: Archibald Douglas Cochrane; IWM:Documents.1003: 22-23 November, 22 December; Douglas, *Maidstone Magazine*, p.248.

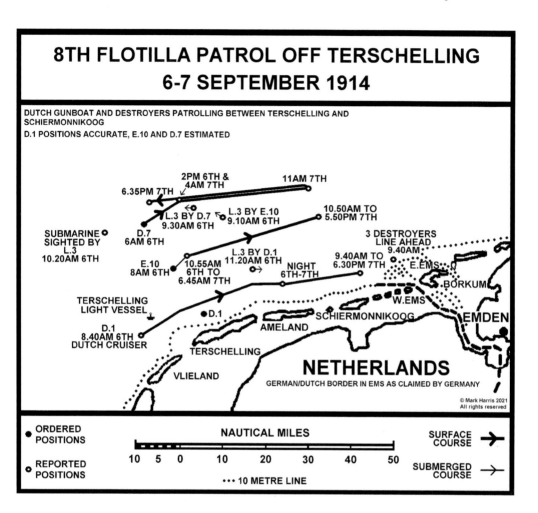

**8TH FLOTILLA PATROL OFF TERSCHELLING
6-7 SEPTEMBER 1914**

DUTCH GUNBOAT AND DESTROYERS PATROLLING BETWEEN TERSCHELLING AND SCHIERMONNIKOOG
D.1 POSITIONS ACCURATE, E.10 AND D.7 ESTIMATED

2PM 6TH & 4AM 7TH
11AM 7TH
6.35PM 7TH
L.3 BY D.7 9.30AM 6TH
L.3 BY E.10 9.10AM 6TH
10.50AM TO 5.50PM 7TH
SUBMARINE SIGHTED BY L.3 10.20AM 6TH
D.7 6AM 6TH
3 DESTROYERS LINE AHEAD 9.40AM
E.10 8AM 6TH
10.55AM 6TH TO 6.45AM 7TH
L.3 BY D.1 11.20AM 6TH
NIGHT 6TH-7TH
9.40AM TO 6.30PM 7TH
E.EMS
BORKUM
TERSCHELLING LIGHT VESSEL
D.1 8.40AM 6TH DUTCH CRUISER
D.1
W.EMS
SCHIERMONNIKOOG
EMDEN
AMELAND
TERSCHELLING
NETHERLANDS
VLIELAND
GERMAN/DUTCH BORDER IN EMS AS CLAIMED BY GERMANY

ORDERED POSITIONS
NAUTICAL MILES
SURFACE COURSE

REPORTED POSITIONS
10   5   0   10   20   30   40   50
SUBMERGED COURSE

••• 10 METRE LINE

Cochrane was approaching his billet when he spotted a cruiser off Vlieland Island at 8:40am on the 6th. She was coming up from astern. He dived to attack and worked into a good position 600 yards (550m) off the port bow. He now spotted a Dutch naval ensign and identified her as a *Holland* class protected cruiser. *D.1* surfaced and was greeted by the cruiser's officers cheering and waving their caps. Cochrane worked slowly eastwards six miles off the Dutch coast. He encountered the Dutch fishery protection ship *Dolfijn* and four Dutch destroyers patrolling in pairs up to 30 miles east of Terschelling. The latter closely resembled German types. A zeppelin was also spotted on patrol 10 miles east of his position at 11:20am. The night was spent on the bottom off Ameland Island.

Cochrane surfaced at 4:30am the next morning and headed east for the mouth of the Ems. Three destroyers were sighted in formation eight miles ahead as he passed Schiermonnikoog Island at 9:40am. *D.1* dived. As the day progressed up to six destroyers were made out at times. However, salt water had got into a few cells of the battery. Cochrane reports that: 'The necessity of dealing with the chlorine gas generated prevented "D.1" from watching any movements of ships.' This was a little understated, as if the problem got any worse, the crew would either

Lieutenant-Commander Cochrane.
(Friends of the RNSM)

suffocate or be forced to the surface and have to stay there. It took most of the day to fix the problem. *D.1* surfaced at 5:20pm, with nothing in sight. Two large ships, apparently armoured cruisers, soon loomed out of the dusk to the east screened by four to six destroyers. Cochrane dived to attack, but with darkness closing in the ships could not be spotted through the periscope. *D.1* surfaced at 6:30pm and returned to Harwich.[19]

E.10 was in the middle of the line. She was commanded by Lieutenant-Commander William St. John Fraser, who was the son of a noted Professor of Medicine at Edinburgh University and aged 30. He had joined the Submarine Service in 1904. Captain Hall assessed him in 1907 as: 'A very good officer but rather slow.' He progressed from coastal submarine command to *D.7* in 1912. Captain Brandt had a more upbeat view of Fraser in 1913: 'Cannot speak too highly of him. Steady, resolute, and patient.' He had been appointed to command *E.10* as she neared completion in June 1914.[20]

Fraser began cautiously by diving at dawn on the 6th. *E.10* proceeded submerged for nearly three hours, then surfaced and reached the billet at 8am. He soon sighted the Dutch *Hollana*

19   TNA ADM137/2067: p.171.
20   TNA ADM196/48/72: William St John Fraser.

class cruiser heading northeast. A large airship came in sight heading northwest at 9:10am, far off at high altitude. Fraser dived to avoid being seen. It was seen to turn round and head towards Borkum. *E.10* surfaced and it went out of sight at 11:30am. Nothing more was seen until the Dutch cruiser returned going south at 5:30pm. Fraser stayed on the surface until well after dark, submerging at 11:30pm and keeping underway steering in a circle at two knots for the rest of the night. Next morning *E.10* surfaced and headed east to a point 25 miles northwest of Borkum Island. Nothing was seen all day and Fraser headed back to Harwich at 5:50pm, arriving at noon on the 8th.[21]

The outer boat on the line was *D.7*. She was commanded by Lieutenant-Commander George C. Street, aged 30. His examination results and early record are good. Street joined the Submarine Service in 1905 and had commanded a number of coastal boats. He suffered a fractured skull in a riding accident in 1909 but continued to receive good reports. Street was blamed for a fatal coaling accident in *Hibernia* in 1911 and her Captain rated him: 'Zealous, attentive but occasionally seems to lose his judgement.' He took over *D.7* from Fraser in June. His final commander, Captain Prowse, rated him average and: 'Painstaking & hardworking rather slow and lacking in initiative'. These were attributes that were ill suited to a submarine commander patrolling enemy waters in time of war.[22]

Street dived at dawn on the 2nd and proceeded submerged for 90 minutes. He then surfaced and arrived at his billet at around 6am. *D.7* briefly dived three times during the day, heading northeast whilst submerged. Something was spotted each time on surfacing; twice unremarkable trawlers and once a cargo steamer. Street also sighted an airship passing west, seven miles off and 2,000 feet (600m) high at 9:30am. *D.7* submerged for over an hour until it was out of sight. Street remained on the surface overnight, steering one hour legs backwards and forwards at five knots. After diving to avoid the dawn, he surfaced and slowly headed east in the full light, turning back at 11am. Nothing was seen all day. *D.7* left for Harwich at 6:35pm and arrived at 10:30am on the 8th.[23]

Zeppelins now regularly patrolled along the Dutch coast and could be effective in spotting or forcing submarines to dive to avoid detection. *L.3* was out on the 6th and reported a surfaced enemy submarine off Terschelling at 10:20am. This was probably *D.7*, or possibly *E.10*. The Ems had been busy on the 7th. The destroyer *S.122* had escorted *U.8*, *U.9* and *U.10* from Heligoland to their new base there. This was probably the first sighting by Cochrane. *U.28* and *U.24* arrived later. *Stettin* was at the entrance in support of the routine patrol by about six destroyers of 4th Torpedoboots-Flottille. It seems Cochrane spotted both her and the destroyer patrol when they headed in to the river at 6pm, perhaps distorted by the setting sun against the light haze *Stettin* recorded.[24] The battery problems had perhaps robbed Cochrane of an attack opportunity, but the other submarines had again been placed too far from likely transit points. They returned to find that the last of the Es under refit when war broke out, *E.1*, had arrived at Harwich on the 6th.[25]

21   TNA ADM137/2067: p.170; TNA ADM173: *E.10* 5–8 September 1914.
22   TNA ADM196/243/255: George Campbell Street.
23   TNA ADM137/2067: p.172; TNA ADM173: *D.7* 6-8 September 1914.
24   BArch:RM92: *Stettin* Kriegstagebuch 6-7 September 1914, *Nassau* Kriegstagebuch 6 September 1914.
25   TNA ADM53: *Maidstone* 6 September 1914..

10

An empty net

The crews at Yarmouth were awaiting orders to proceed with Plan IV, having arrived on 4 September. Next morning Signalman Johnson of *E.7* spotted two men apparently sketching the submarines on the opposite bank of the River Yare. Talbot and Jameson armed themselves with revolvers. A 'spy hunt' followed, with Hallifax, Cunard and a boat from the destroyer *Lively* under her commander, Lieutenant Baillie-Grohman. The suspected spies were surrounded, rounded up, interrogated and then handed over to the police. They admitted taking photographs, but Talbot says he did not believe they meant any harm.

Spy hunting aside, Yarmouth was an agreeable place to wait in the glorious weather of late summer 1914, although Talbot was bored. Several officers spent their free time bathing and listening to a band in deck chairs on the beach. Hallifax felt 'back in civilisation' after the dour surroundings of Parkeston Quay at Harwich.

Leir had been ordered to burn his sealed orders as a result of the changes requested by Jellicoe. Lieutenant Meynell of *Maidstone* finally arrived by motorcar with revised orders at noon on the 8th. The commanders read them, but to maintain secrecy the content was kept from the rest of the crews until after they had gone below for the night.

The objective of the raid was 'to tempt the larger ships of the enemy, and possibly their main fleet, to come out and protect the vessels attacked.' The three E class would leave Yarmouth to rendezvous with Waistell, who would arrive with *Firedrake* and *Lurcher* off Smith's Knoll at 4:30am next morning.[1] The destroyers would scout five miles ahead of the submarines to Terschelling. They would then screen Admiral Christian's cruisers, which would arrive there at dawn to support the raid. There would also be support by the Grand Fleet, from northwest of Heligoland.

E.4 would take position north of Heligoland, with *E.6* and *E.7* to the south. *D.2* and *D.8* were to follow two hours later and take position off the Ems. All submarines were to be at their billets by 2:30am on the 10th. They would remain on the bottom until 6am. The intention was to allow the submarines to attack heavy ships that came out in response to the raid. Wireless was not to be used except in the event of a breakdown. The time of return seems to have been left to the discretion of each commander.

---

1   Waistell's presence is assumed. *Lurcher* was astern of *Firedrake* during the operation, indicating that *Firedrake* had an officer senior to Tomkinson aboard.

RAID ON THE HELIGOLAND BIGHT
10-11 SEPTEMBER 1914

GERMAN PATROL LINES:

INNER LINE OFF HELIGOLAND - ARMED TRAWLERS

MIDDLE LINE NORTH OF HELIGOLAND - 7 DESTROYERS OF 3RD TORPEDOBOOTS-FLOTTILLE FROM 4AM TO 4PM

GROUP OF DESTROYERS OFF NORDERNEY

OUTER LINE - 7 SUBMARINES FROM 6AM TO 3PM

ABOUT 4 DESTROYERS OF 8TH TORPEDOBOOTS-HALBFLOTTILLE AND LIGHT CRUISER ARCONA OFF THE EMS

4 LIGHT CRUISERS OFF THE WESER

SUBMARINE POSITIONS ARE AS PER REPORTS OR GERMAN SIGHTINGS. THEY ARE APPROXIMATELY CORRECT, DESPITE THIS E.6 AND E.7 POSITIONS FOR WRECK BUOY DIFFER BY 5 MILES.

E.4, E.6 AND E.7 PATROLLED WITHIN ZONES SHOWN. FULL DETAILS FOR E.6 ONLY. SEE SEPARATE CHART

D.8 COURSES BETWEEN OBSERVED POSITIONS NOT KNOWN

TIMES FOR 10TH UNLESS STATED OTHERWISE

MINEFIELD IS AS PER FINAL GERMAN MINE CHARTS. IT WAS PLANNED TO HAVE BEEN LAID TO A POINT FURTHER NORTHEAST

SEE DETAILED CHARTS FOR ATTACK ON U.25 AND SIGHTINGS BY U.23 OF E.4

DENMARK
ESBJERG

RÖM

SYLT

SUBMARINE BY U.25 6.3AM BY U.23 9.25AM, 10.45AM & 1PM

OUTER

SUBMARINE BY U.23 & U.25 3.20PM

MIDDLE

E.4

LOWESTOFT & 3RD DF TURNED WEST 3.45AM

HELIGOLAND

EIDER

INNER

SUBMARINE REPORTED 2PM 11TH

E.6

FEARLESS & 1ST DF TURNED BACK 5AM

E

8.30PM   U.28 3.50PM

E.7

W

ELBE

U.22 4.56PM   D.8   G.111 7.25 & 7.40AM

D.2

J

CUXHAVEN

ARIADNE CLASS 4 DESTROYERS 5 SWEEPERS BY D.8

E.EMS

LANGEOOG

NORDERNEY

WESER

BREMER-HAVEN

BORKUM

WILHELMSHAVEN

W.EMS

JADE

AMELAND

EMDEN

GERMANY

NETHERLANDS

GERMAN/DUTCH BORDER IN EMS AS CLAIMED BY GERMANY

ORDERED POSITIONS

REPORTED POSITIONS

MINEFIELD

BUOY REPORTED

HARWICH FORCE

NAUTICAL MILES

10 5 0   10   20   30   40   50

GERMAN PATROLS

PATROL ZONES:

E.4 & E.7

E.6

10 METRE LINE   JADE, WESER AND ELBE LIGHT VESSELS

D.2 & D.8 MOVEMENTS

Tyrwhitt's 1st and 3rd Flotillas would sweep in to attack the enemy night patrol off the Ems and Heligoland respectively, prior to its relief by the day patrol. They would then fall back on Christian and the Grand Fleet cruisers in the support positions. The submarines were kept away from British surface ships to avoid a repeat of the near misses on the previous raid. The ships were therefore ordered to regard all submarines as hostile. The raiders would all to be retiring before sunrise at 5am. Both Jellicoe and Tyrwhitt were in favour of a later arrival time, but there was no change. Keyes is silent about the timing but had originally wanted to attack the night patrol in the previous raid. Talbot wrote on reading his orders: 'to me it seems too early in the day, as the 3rd Flotilla turn to the westward at 3.45am.' More hopefully Hallifax recorded: 'Great Scott, if only it is successful.'[2]

The E class were due to leave Yarmouth at 2:15am on the 9th. However, *E.7* was unable to get underway. Leir ordered Jameson to take *D.2* to the important billet closest to the German estuaries in place of *E.7*. This meant an earlier departure. The crew rushed to ready the boat and got underway half an hour later. Off Yarmouth a steamer and a destroyer failed to answer *D.2*'s challenge. Concerned that they might be German raiders, Jameson dived to avoid them. The delay meant that Waistell and the other submarines had left Smith's Knoll by the time *D.2* arrived. Jameson therefore proceeded alone, keeping close to the Dutch coast and sighting a *Holland* class cruiser and two Dutch destroyers near Terschelling. *D.8* then came into sight and *D.2* fell in with her until darkness. Jameson used a buoy off Langeoog Island to fix his position at 2:30am, then steered for the Weser and went to the bottom.

D.2 surfaced at 6am. Jameson remained in position with only the conning tower out of the water all day. Visibility was good and he was able to see the exits from both the Weser and Jade estuaries. Eventually a small single funnelled steamer was spotted moving in the entrance to the Jade at 4pm. After sitting off the main German Fleet bases all day with no useful target, *D.2* headed back to Harwich as darkness closed in at 6:55pm. Jameson encountered bad weather on the return and diverted to stop in Yarmouth Roads on the night of the 11/12th. *D.2* arrived back in Harwich at 10:30am on the 12th.[3]

After parting company with *D.2*, Brodie's *D.8* headed to her billet off the eastern entrance of the Ems. She arrived at 11:45pm on the 9th and went to the bottom for the night. Brodie rose off the bottom for a look round at 6:15am. There were only two small vessels sweeping. An hour later he surfaced and immediately sighted an *Ariadne* class cruiser steering backwards and forwards in the distance two miles off the Western Ems entrance. She was signalling four patrolling destroyers or torpedo boats and five small boats which were sweeping in a line, accompanied by a steamer. Twenty minutes went by. One of the destroyers evidently spotted *D.8* in the growing light, turned towards her and opened fire. Brodie dived. He returned to periscope depth five times during the morning, each time sighting one or two destroyers, but never in a position to attack. At 12:40pm the sweepers headed back into the Ems. Brodie eventually got clear and surfaced.

A submarine was spotted approaching end on from the northwest at 3:30pm. Brodie thought that it was *D.2* out of her position. As it closed it was identified as a German submarine of the *U.8* type. *D.8* dived, but the German boat had now disappeared as well. About an hour later Brodie

2   TNA ADM137/2067: p.174; TNA ADM186/620: p.34, 214–218; IWM: Documents.20134: 4–8 September; IWM: Documents.1003: 4–8 September.
3   TNA ADM137/2067: p.178.

re-surfaced, only to spot the German boat doing the same! *D.8* dived again immediately. Brodie began an attack run, as the German boat was still on the surface. However, she disappeared in a south-easterly direction within half an hour. Brodie later remarked to Keyes: 'neither knew what to do with the other'.

D.8 left for Harwich when the light failed. During the night Brodie reported a light, thought to be a submarine on a westerly course, which remained in sight for 20 minutes. A possible submarine was also sighted at 7am the next morning heading west between rain squalls approaching Smith's Knoll. *D.8* arrived back at Harwich late on the 11th.[4]

When *E.7* shoved off to leave harbour at 1:40am on the 9th, her steering gear jammed hard to starboard. After being told to get out of the way by Leir, so that he and Talbot could leave, then to switch places with *D.2*, Hallifax writes that 'F[eilmann] was very upset, talking about being court martialled.' The helm had been pushed over too hard, causing the teeth of the mechanism to bind up. By the time the problem was fixed *D.2* had a 15 minute head start. Brodie was ranking officer on the spot and now told Feilmann to catch Jameson and send him back to Yarmouth in order to leave with *D.8* for the Ems.

Feilmann never saw *D.2* to deliver the message. He was baffled to reach Waistell first at Smith's Knoll. He now simply complied with his original orders, as instructed by Brodie. *E.7* must have passed *D.2* whilst she was submerged. Brodie did nothing to clear things up when he later came across *D.2*. The result was that there was nothing in place to attack the targets seen by Brodie off the Western Ems!

E.7 reached her billet off the Weser and went to the bottom at 1am. The crew's hope of rest was ruined, as they were continually woken up in the night by an infestation of flies. Feilmann surfaced at 6:45am, keeping trimmed down with the conning tower out of the water. In the next two hours only two patrolling trawlers were seen on the horizon. *E.7* dived and crept north, occasionally coming to periscope depth for a look around. She surfaced two hours later, trimmed down again, but dived away west when two trawlers headed towards her at 3pm. After half an hour Feilmann surfaced and spotted *E.6*. Talbot closed and signalled: 'I suppose you have seen nothing', then confirmed that he too had only seen patrolling trawlers. As the two trawlers were again closing, both submarines dived and *E.7* headed farther west, surfacing at 5pm with only one trawler still in sight on the horizon. Feilmann stopped for the crew to take pot-shots with rifles at a 'navigational hazard.' They gave up after realising that the supposed floating trunk was actually an open topped wooden case! *E.7* turned south and passed *E.6*. Talbot signalled that he was staying until 2pm the next day. Feilmann stopped to charge the batteries at 6:30pm. Not long afterwards, lights were spotted approaching from the direction of Heligoland, possibly from destroyers. *E.7* went to the bottom to avoid a night encounter. She surfaced for half an hour at midnight to ventilate the stale air. The annoying flies had been wiped out during the day.

On the 11th Feilmann surfaced at 6:15am to patchy mist. Wind was making the water choppy. *E.7* headed north after charging stationary for an hour. Feilmann later stopped to sink a suspiciously new looking wreck buoy with rifle fire, believing it might be a marker for patrols or mines. *E.6* was again in sight patrolling two or three miles to the north. When an attempt was made to start the starboard engine, yet again a bolt sheared on the flywheel. It took the crew over five hours to replace it. Meanwhile, *E.7* got going on the port engine to the southeast.

4   TNA ADM137/2067: p.176, 179.

Heligoland loomed out of the mist only eight miles to the northeast at 10:55am. *E.7* turned away to the southwest. Soon afterwards two enemy submarines appeared from behind and off to port on a parallel course. *E.7* was in a good position to attack. Feilmann dived to manoeuvre for the shot. The targets turned right round as they were almost in position for firing. *E.7* surfaced an hour later and headed west with only a trawler in sight, the third seen that morning. At 1:20pm two enemy submarines again came into view. *E.7* dived, but the targets had apparently turned round and disappeared. After waiting for over an hour Feilmann surfaced to return to Harwich. The diesels now refused to start. They had flooded when a stiff valve had taken too long to close on the previous dive. *E.7* got underway on one engine fifteen minutes later, but it took another half an hour before the port engine could be started.

E.7 stopped at 5:25pm off the Ems. Feilmann had spotted a body floating in the water near wreckage. It turned out to be face down, wearing only a lifebelt and presumed to be a German sailor. A grim reminder of the action two weeks earlier. Night fell. Hallifax now tells us that: 'The sea got up steadily & it came on to rain like nothing on earth ... one was blinded. ... We were going 12 knots & practically underwater all the time.' Feilmann reduced speed to 10 knots when the bridge screens carried away. Cunard took the next watch and they carried away again. Two men were almost washed overboard. He reduced speed to six knots. After *E.7* turned southwest the sea moderated a bit and Feilmann increased speed, causing her to roll badly. Hallifax, who was off watch, had an uncomfortable time in his 'bunk'. This was a mattress in a cabinet drawer which opened at deck level – it kept closing and opening, pinching his anatomy!

At 8:30am next morning *Lurcher* and *Firedrake* were sighted leading out the next patrol. *E.7*'s news that enemy submarines were patrolling in pairs was exchanged for a position fix. Shortly afterwards two more bolts of the starboard engine flywheel sheared and she had to proceed on one engine. It was now impossible to reach Harwich before dark. *E.7* secured at Yarmouth Quay at 3:30pm. Hallifax telephoned Harwich and reported to Keyes. *E.7* left at 11:30am next morning, the 13th, after replacing some of the sheared bolts. This was just as well as the port circulating pump shifted loose, causing the engine to keep cutting out! *E.7* finally reached Harwich at 4:30pm.

As a result of the recurring problems the senior engineers of *Maidstone*, Engineer Lieutenant-Commander Ham and Engineer-Lieutenant Simpson, examined the offending flywheel. It was decided to send *E.7* to Chatham for repairs. She left next morning. Simpson went with them to ensure the work was done properly. When the engine was opened up further problems were identified with the crank shafts. The crew had 48 hours leave by turn while the engine was repaired. ERA Page failed to return and a warrant was issued for his arrest. Hallifax writes that Page had 'a bad attack of cold feet ... & has tried to get out of the boat in various ways', including feigning deafness. He now appeared in plain clothes at Chatham Barrack Gate claiming to have lost his memory, but thought he was a submariner there. Feilmann put him on the sick list for observation. The sick bay steward told him that he was being packed off to a mental asylum where he would probably spend the rest of his life. He was actually being transferred to hospital. Page immediately recovered his memory and wanted to return to *E.7*. The repairs were completed on the 28th and *E.7* returned to Harwich, but without Page.[5]

5   TNA ADM137/2067: p.184; TNA ADM173: *E.7* 9-28 September 1914, IWM: Documents.1003: 9-28 September

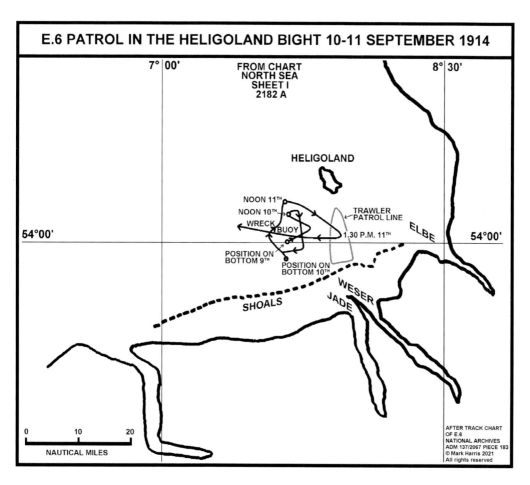

E.6 PATROL IN THE HELIGOLAND BIGHT 10-11 SEPTEMBER 1914

FROM CHART
NORTH SEA
SHEET I
2182 A

7° 00'   8° 30'

HELIGOLAND

NOON 11TH
NOON 10TH   TRAWLER
WRECK   PATROL LINE
BUOY   ELBE
54°00'   1.30 P.M. 11TH   54°00'
POSITION ON
BOTTOM 9TH
        POSITION ON
        BOTTOM 10TH
                        WESER
                  JADE
        SHOALS

0   10   20
NAUTICAL MILES

Talbot's *E.6* arrived at her billet, about six miles north of *E.7*, at 1:30am on the 10th. Talbot lay on the bottom, 'comfortably … swinging to the tide'. A ship passed over. Five more followed when Tyrwhitt was expected to pass by at 3:45am. At 6am Talbot came off the bottom and headed east to avoid any ships hanging around the busy spot. He had a look round through the periscope and surfaced in very misty weather. Several patrolling trawlers were sighted coming in and out of the mist several miles to the east over the next few hours. Twice Talbot dived to attack but was unable to get close without exhausting the battery. He wrote that 'they are not worth chasing, and a torpedo would almost certainly pass underneath them.' At 9:45am *E.6* dived to the west, then surfaced in place to charge her depleted batteries for three and a half hours. At 3:10pm Talbot headed back east until Heligoland came into sight, then turned south with occasional trawlers visible in the distance. A submarine looking like *E.7* had been spotted three times and avoided during the morning. Talbot soon saw *E.7* again. He closed her and had the exchange detailed above, with only half the conning tower out of the water. Talbot then headed west to avoid the trawlers which kept approaching. At 6:30pm *E.6* went to the bottom for the night. Talbot surfaced at midnight for fresh air and to let the crew stretch their legs on deck for an hour, then went back to the bottom.

E.6 surfaced at 6:05am on the 11th. The weather was very misty with sporadic rain squalls. Talbot thought there was worse to come. He headed north, spotting the buoy later sunk by *E.7.* He charged in place for two and a half hours from 7:30am. A full charge was needed for his plan. Talbot headed towards Heligoland to fix his position. It was sighted at 11:30am. He then submerged and headed east, 'with the object of getting beyond the patrol and seeing if they were protecting anything.' After a 10 mile run Talbot came as close to the surface as he dare, with the bridge just out of the water to get a clearer view through the periscope. There were three trawlers within one mile! He was only eight miles from the entrance to the Elbe. Luckily, the weather had cleared. Visibility was six to seven miles, but he could see nothing beyond the patrol. *E.6* headed back under the patrol line. On surfacing at 2:40pm visibility was good, but the sea was very bad. Six or seven trawlers were still in sight astern, so Talbot dived. None too soon, as a destroyer then appeared out of a rain squall and passed close to the stern. *E.6* surfaced with nothing in sight at 3:50pm and headed for Yarmouth, avoiding a probing light off the Ems and ship's lights off Terschelling. The sea forced Talbot to reduce to seven knots in the middle of the night. *E.6* arrived at Gorleston Quay at 6pm on the 12th. Talbot telephoned to report to Keyes, who gave him the news that his wife, 'Dillie', was arriving at Harwich later. *E.6* returned to Harwich at 10am next morning. Talbot had a much needed bath and stayed the next few days with his wife at the Hotel, enjoying walks and an evening out in Dovercourt, whilst the actual installation of *E.6*'s new gyrocompass commenced.[6]

U.25 as completed in 1914, prior to the fitting of her deck gun. All the early German diesel boats were of similar design. (Frankes.com Collection)

6   TNA ADM137/2067: pp.181-3; TNA ADM173: *E.6* 10-12 September 1914; IWM: Documents.20134 10-17 September 1914.

Leir's *E.4* arrived at the billet north of Heligoland at 2:35am on the 10th and went to the bottom. At 6:08am he reports: 'Rose to Surface. Observed German submarine "U.25" 150 yards [140m] abeam steaming about 10 knots.' *E.4* had just been breaking the surface and Leir took her back down while the German boat headed off. The morning was spent submerged, surfacing briefly at intervals. A Norwegian steamer passed south between Heligoland and the mainland and at least one destroyer was in sight every time he surfaced from 8am onwards. A German submarine was spotted at 11:30am three miles away, heading northwest. Leir went in pursuit immediately on the surface, using the motors to avoid delay. He was forced to dive when a destroyer approached 15 minutes later and lost sight of the submarine. At 1pm Leir surfaced. He spotted a submarine surfacing about 1½ miles away. *E.4* began an attack, but the target got underway before he could get into range.

Leir dived and followed her. She was seen returning at 3:20pm. As Leir passed he fired a Mark V* torpedo from his port beam tube at only 150 yards (140m). Once again he was close enough to read her number; *U.23*. He reports that 'it went under her – judging by the gesticulations of those on her bridge.' At such short range the torpedo would almost certainly not have recovered to the set depth, so this was presumably the best Leir could do in the circumstances. He continues: 'Seeing one of her crew semaphoring, I found that another submarine was following her. I fired a torpedo at the second submarine at 100 yards [90m] set to run on the surface – which it did, missing however, probably ahead. The submarine was swinging under helm and fired a few rounds from her gun, obscuring my view with [water from] bursting shell.' The torpedo, another Mark V*, was fired from the starboard beam tube of *E.4*. The surface run was possibly set up in a rush, as this was an unusual setting. Both targets made off at high speed. Several destroyers now approached. Leir remained in the vicinity in the hope of being able to make another attack.

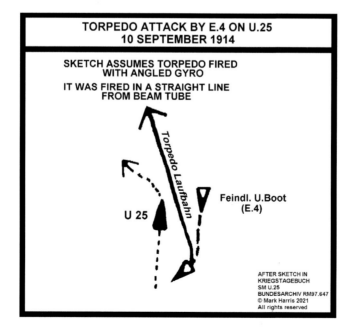

TORPEDO ATTACK BY E.4 ON U.25
10 SEPTEMBER 1914

SKETCH ASSUMES TORPEDO FIRED WITH ANGLED GYRO

IT WAS FIRED IN A STRAIGHT LINE FROM BEAM TUBE

Torpedo Laufbahn

U 25

Feindl. U.Boot (E.4)

AFTER SKETCH IN
KRIEGSTAGEBUCH
SM U.25
BUNDESARCHIV RM97.647
© Mark Harris 2021
All rights reserved

U.23 and *U.25* has been returning to Heligoland at the end of their patrol for the day. *U.23* suddenly spotted the swirl of a torpedo being fired, only 75m (80 yards) away to port at 3:32pm. The helm was put hard to starboard. The bubbles ran directly under the boat before the rudder took effect. The periscope disappeared aft. *U.25* was zig-zagging 1,000m (1,100 yards) behind *U.23*, saw her fire a red flare and turn off course. A few minutes later she spotted a periscope 150m (160 yards) to starboard. Her recently installed 8.8cm (3.5-inch) gun was ready. The crew opened fire, getting off three rounds before the periscope disappeared aft; two shells burst long and one short. As the periscope passed aft a torpedo surfaced about 30–40m from it, on an intercept course for *U.25*. The helm was put hard to port. The torpedo passed to starboard, leaving a track for 3,000m (3,250 yards) in the distance. It must have been set for the long range speed of 22 knots, helping to avoid an initial dive, but not much faster than *U.25*. The attack angle from aft was fatal at this speed. Leir had perhaps been thrown off in his approach by zig-zagging in both attacks.

E.4 went to the bottom for the night at 5:35pm, with a 20 minute break for air around midnight. Leir came up to periscope depth at 5:50am next morning and cruised around, but found nothing in sight, even after surfacing at 10:30am. *E.4* had been submerged without charging for a marathon 32 hours 15 minutes, with only 90 minutes of short breaks to change the air. Leir set course for Harwich at 2pm, arriving at 4:35pm on the 12th.[7]

After dropping off the submarines *Lurcher* and *Firedrake* had steamed to rendezvous with Christian off Terschelling. They had screened eastwards ahead of the armoured cruisers to Ameland. At 7am on the 10th they turned to cover the retirement. After later breaking away to return to Harwich, *Lurcher* took the opportunity to carry out a practice shoot at a target that afternoon.[8]

The Germans had been at an increased level of alert prior to the attack. They had received warnings from agents in Britain from 8 September onwards. On the 9th a defensive minefield was laid in the Bight between the buoy marking the vacated position of Norderney Light Vessel and Heligoland.[9] This protected the approaches to the estuaries and reduced the demands on the overstretched patrol force. A single row of 689 mines was laid, about one every 70 yards/m, 2½m (8 feet) below low water level. The aim was to snare larger warships. The draught of an E class was less than 4m (13 feet), so they would only be dangerous to submarines on the surface around the time of low water. Special arrangements were made during daylight to meet an attack. Seven destroyers of 3rd Torpedoboots-Flottille were stationed from the minefield east to the coast from 4am, with a picket of seven submarines from Heligoland spread out beyond them from 6am. More destroyers were posted in the gap off Norderney. The 8th Torpedoboots-Halbflottille was off the Ems, with six submarines from the Ems and the light cruiser *Arcona* ready off the estuary at dawn. Armed trawlers continued to patrol the innermost patrol line. Minesweepers swept off the estuaries each morning. Four Light Cruisers would cruise off the Weser from 7am and the Fleet was placed at short notice for sea.

7   TNA ADM137/2067: p.180; TNA ADM173: *E.4* 10–12 September 1914; BArch:RM97: Unterseeboote der Kaiserlichen Marine: *U.23* and *U.25* Kriegstagebuch.
8   TNA ADM53: *Firedrake, Lurcher* 9-10 September 1914.
9   Illustrations show the minefield as per the chart of the minelayer *Nautilus* and war diary of the covering cruiser *Roon*. Maps in Krieg zur See confuse true and magnetic bearings and show a gap made by removal of part of the minefield at a later date.

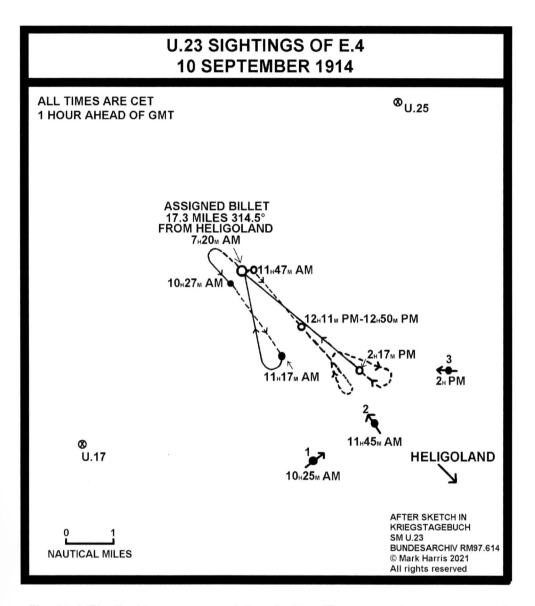

U.23 SIGHTINGS OF E.4
10 SEPTEMBER 1914

ALL TIMES ARE CET
1 HOUR AHEAD OF GMT

⊗ U.25

ASSIGNED BILLET
17.3 MILES 314.5°
FROM HELIGOLAND
7ₕ20ₘ AM

○●11ₕ47ₘ AM

10ₕ27ₘ AM

12ₕ11ₘ PM-12ₕ50ₘ PM

2ₕ17ₘ PM

3
←●
2ₕ PM

11ₕ17ₘ AM

2
11ₕ45ₘ AM

⊗
U.17

1
10ₕ25ₘ AM

HELIGOLAND

0   1
NAUTICAL MILES

Tyrwhitt's Flotillas hit empty sea in their early drive. There was no longer an outer night patrol. *S.129* spotted the 1st Destroyer Flotilla off the Ems after they had turned at the end of their sweep at 5:45am. Nearer the coast visibility was fairly good and a seaplane patrol spotted both 1st Flotilla and Christian's cruisers off Ameland. The commander of the submarines off the Ems ordered his boats into a line to the north, then west to attack. In contrast, out to sea visibility varied from two to five miles and the seaplane patrols never sighted the rest of the retiring raiding force. The German Fleet command were not even aware a 'raid' had taken place!

U.25 encountered *E.4* as she was heading for her patrol billet at 6:03am. It was an extremely lucky escape. A periscope appeared 100m (110 yards) to port, then the upper edge of the conning tower. It had the look of a British boat. The deck gun was trained on the target, but *E.4* moved close astern, out of the gun's arc and disappeared. *U.25* wirelessed the sighting as soon as she was clear.

D.8 was sighted surfacing at 7:20am off the Ems and the destroyer *G.111* spotted her diving at 7:45am. *G.111* opened fire with one or two 5cm (2-inch) guns but claimed no hits.

The two submarine alarms and decreasing visibility resulted in the immediate recall of cruisers into harbour. The destroyers were pulled back to near Heligoland and the Ems.

E.4's conning tower was spotted at a distance of three to four miles by *U.23* on one of Leir's brief trips to the surface at 9:25am. This sighting triggered a search in the area. *U.23* and *U.25* were joined at 11am from Heligoland by *U.18*, *U.14*, their destroyer leader, *S.122*, and several destroyers from 3rd Torpedoboots-Flottille. Leir was spotted again by *U.23* at 10:45am and 1pm. Each time *U.23* dived to attack, but lost sight of *E.4*. It seems Leir was not spotted when he closed *U.23* at 11:30am. She had briefly surfaced to make a wireless report. *U.23* gave up searching, surfaced and went back to her patrol station at 1:17pm. She did not see Leir closing in.

Following Leir's later torpedo attacks on *U.23* and *U.25*, the Light Cruiser *Hamburg*, with the Leader of Submarines aboard, rashly sortied from Heligoland to join the hunt. She was not sighted by *E.4* but did come close to being attacked by *U.27*!

Meantime, the Ems based submarines were also returning from their unsuccessful chase after Christian. *U.28* spotted a submarine whilst heading into the Ems at 3:50pm. A number of men were clearly seen on the bridge, but the target dived before an attack could be delivered. *U.22* also sighted a submarine at 4:56pm, which dived four minutes after being sighted. Brodie had sighted his attackers on both occasions, but it was two different boats that he had seen. *U.28* had got dangerously close before being recognised.

On the 11th only routine patrols were out, except for the six Ems submarines, which were deployed in a patrol line off Terschelling. Heligoland relayed the sighting of a submarine diving east of the new minefield at 2pm, which was almost certainly *E.7*, but details are lacking. The two pairs of submarines that Feilmann twice made attack runs on cannot be identified. One possible candidate is *U.19*, on a routine move from Heligoland to the Ems.

The numerous submarine sightings and the obvious attacks got the attention of the German Fleet commander, Admiral von Ingenohl. His report notes the activity of the British submarines:

> Enemy submarines continue to operate chiefly off the Ems estuary and in the area northwest of Heligoland, where they feel safe from mines. The "Sailing Directions" published in the beginning of August designate a point 10 miles northwest of Heligoland as a point of approach for merchant vessels. The enemy is thereby informed of a safe route into the German Bight.

The reasoning is a little obtuse as no minefields had been announced. Hints of their existence were not an effective deterrent. The conclusion about where most of the British submarines were lurking was false, as three had been south of Heligoland in an area now scantily patrolled behind the minefield.

Ingenohl was understandably less clear about the objective of recent activity:

It is not obvious what the intention of our opponent was on the morning of 10 September. He may have intended an operation against either the Ems or the German Bight, which for unknown reasons – perhaps because of the bad visibility or observation by our aircraft – was abandoned, or he may also have hoped to lure out German light forces.[10]

Keyes report began by confirming that the day patrol had not been the target of the raid. He writes that it had come out from the Ems and Heligoland: 'as usual – too late, as was anticipated, to be engaged by our destroyer sweep.' He continues that there was no night patrol, but that one had 'undoubtedly been seen on several occasions since the operations of the 28th August.' In fact there are no warship night contacts in any of the recent reports filed as there was nothing to see. The defensive tone about the timing for the attack indicates that Keyes had supported and even proposed it.

Despite the lack of tangible results, the armed trawler patrol line between Heligoland and the Jade had finally been identified for the first time. Brodie had delivered a very accurate report on the Ems patrol, even correctly identifying the cruiser class and gathering further proof that it was not Dutch – apparently an Admiralty fixation. Keyes conclusion that pairs of submarines had joined the outer patrol line was understandable, but the picket line was a one off precaution against an expected attack. It is odd that Jameson did not see more going on. He may have been farther west than he thought but would have had better target opportunities in the vacant billet off the Western Ems.

The use of a channel between Heligoland and the mainland by the Norwegian steamer and the destroyer patrol ended the idea that this area had been mined – a false conclusion since the report by Benning in August. However, the new German minefield farther west had not been detected. It is likely that the sunken buoy was a marker at the northern end. *E.6* and *E.7* had both crossed it at least twice when arriving and leaving the patrol. Tyrwhitt's 3rd Flotilla had also passed very close to or even over it on their sweep.

British submarine commander's tactics remained uneven. Only Leir and Brodie had been under pressure to stay submerged by the defensive arrangements. Leir's caution in remaining submerged as much as possible had kept him safe from an intensive hunt and even created attack opportunities, although his earlier failure to spot *U.25* close by could have been disastrous. The submarines had generally remained in place after the advance this time, increasing the chances of attacking any response. However, a dangerous complacency about stopping on the surface remained in evidence for some commanders.

Keyes report emphasises that the submarine seen by *D.8* at 7:30am on the 11th was definitely not British, but there were no German submarines in this area. Brodie makes it clear in his report that it was not clearly identified. The apparent enemy submarine sightings close to home certainly alarmed Christian. He wrote to Keyes on the 19th wanting to know why Brodie's report was not passed on immediately. His cruisers were patrolling in the area at the time. An uncanny foreboding of the eventual fate of his Squadron.[11]

---

10   Groos, *Nordsee 2*, pp.18-23, Karte 2; BArch:RM92: *Roon, Stralsund, Stettin, Danzig, Nautilus, Nassau,* Kriegstagebuch 9-11 September 1914, *Nautilus* Befehl und Skizze GB.604 22 December 1914.
11   TNA ADM137/2067: pp.175–7, 186–7.

Placing the submarines farther in to the Bight had not paid off this time, as the bait for the trap had gone largely unnoticed. *Hamburg* was the only major unit that came out of the estuaries that day. However, it left the Jade for Heligoland too early to be spotted.

As an example of the random fortunes of war, if the operation had taken place a day earlier, the submarines would have been amongst a multitude of good targets, laying the new minefield and covering the minelayers.

11

The Jolly Roger

Keyes must have been encouraged by the lack of harassment experienced in the inner Bight on the last patrol. For the next he decided that most of the submarines would push right into the Bight to reconnoitre enemy deployments. This meant higher stakes for the crews and he ordered that confidential books were to be left behind. As the inner Bight was very shallow, a lost boat might be recovered by the enemy. Signal challenges and responses for the length of the patrol only were allowed, written on a slip of paper.

Five submarines would leave Harwich at 11am on 11 September. After an overnight stop at Yarmouth they would leave for their patrol positions on the 12th. *Lurcher* and *Firedrake* would, as usual, escort them on the first leg of their trip.

E.1 would be inshore from the mouth of the Ems as far east as Langeoog. *D.3* would be offshore north of *E.1* and west of Heligoland, on the outer edge of the German patrols. She alone would be in deeper water and was allowed her confidential books.

D.5 and *E.9* were to patrol in the Inner Bight, to the south and east of Heligoland, whilst *E.8* would push into the area between Heligoland and Sylt Island. Keyes placed no restrictions on these three boats movements, so the level of risk they took was left to their own judgement.

The patrol would be maintained from dawn on the 13th until the evening of the 14th unless bad weather intervened. The three inner boats were also given discretion to remain until the evening of the 17th but were warned that another patrol would be entering on the 16th and 17th.

Harwich was buzzing with an attack alarm on the morning of departure. The boats scrambled to move up their departure time to 8:30am. Goodhart's crew worked flat out to replace the torpedo lost in the depth keeping test the day before. The panic subsided when it turned out that the alarm had been raised as a result of destroyers doing target practice off Margate! Departing as planned at 11am, the boats endured awful weather on the journey up the coast to Yarmouth, with a heavy following sea, wind and rain, but duly arrived about 5pm. *Lurcher* towed *D.5* and *Firedrake* towed *E.9*, allowing their crews some respite. Horton, Herbert and Goodhart shared a meal at a hotel ashore before turning in early, with departure scheduled for 3am.

The boats assembled outside the harbour in the darkness. The crews had the recent news of the sinking of the cruiser *Pathfinder* by *U.21* on their minds and were determined to level the score. However, they had to hang around for an hour, as it was too dark to safely get underway. All shore lights in Yarmouth had been extinguished – a new precaution to hinder potential minelayers. When they got underway *Firedrake* attempted to tow *E.9*, but the hawser parted under the strain of the rough seas soon after getting out of the lee of the coast. The destroyer

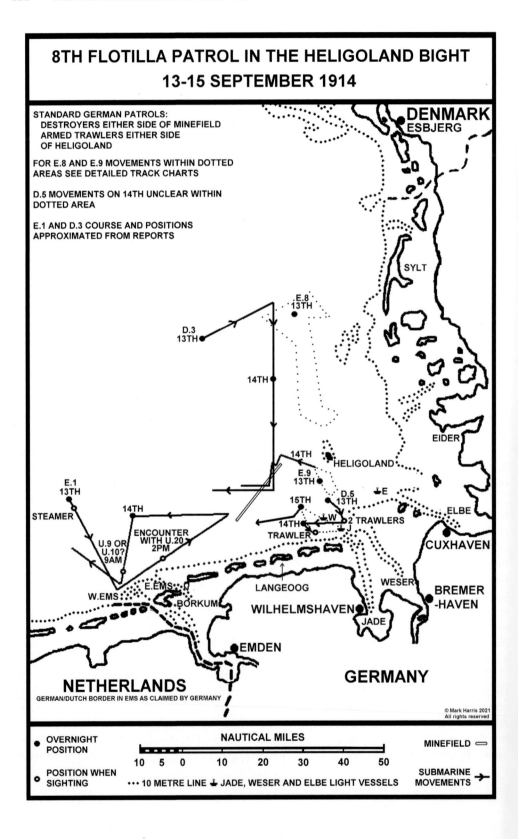

8TH FLOTILLA PATROL IN THE HELIGOLAND BIGHT
13-15 SEPTEMBER 1914

STANDARD GERMAN PATROLS:
DESTROYERS EITHER SIDE OF MINEFIELD
ARMED TRAWLERS EITHER SIDE
OF HELIGOLAND

FOR E.8 AND E.9 MOVEMENTS WITHIN DOTTED
AREAS SEE DETAILED TRACK CHARTS

D.5 MOVEMENTS ON 14TH UNCLEAR WITHIN
DOTTED AREA

E.1 AND D.3 COURSE AND POSITIONS
APPROXIMATED FROM REPORTS

DENMARK
ESBJERG

SYLT

E.8
13TH

D.3
13TH

14TH

EIDER

14TH
HELIGOLAND

E.9
13TH

D.5
13TH

E

15TH

ELBE

E.1
13TH

STEAMER

14TH

ENCOUNTER
WITH U.20
2PM

2 TRAWLERS

14TH
TRAWLER

W

J

CUXHAVEN

U.9 OR
U.10?
9AM

E.EMS

BORKUM

LANGEOOG

WESER

BREMER
-HAVEN

W.EMS

WILHELMSHAVEN

JADE

EMDEN

NETHERLANDS
GERMAN/DUTCH BORDER IN EMS AS CLAIMED BY GERMANY

GERMANY

© Mark Harris 2021
All rights reserved

OVERNIGHT
POSITION

NAUTICAL MILES

MINEFIELD

10 5 0   10   20   30   40   50

POSITION WHEN
SIGHTING

SUBMARINE
MOVEMENTS

••• 10 METRE LINE ⚓ JADE, WESER AND ELBE LIGHT VESSELS

escort turned back at noon, anchored for the night off Southwold, then headed back to Harwich next morning.[1]

D.5 approached her patrol billet in the small hours of the 13th, deep in the Bight off the Weser, after crossing the undetected German minefield. Suddenly, at 1:45am a destroyer shape loomed out of the gloom directly ahead. Herbert dived quickly and completed the approach submerged, arriving at 2:30am. The rough sea forced him to the bottom for the rest of the night. He had planned to remain surfaced, trimmed down to show only his conning tower.

In the morning Herbert sounded his way in to the Weser submerged. He popped up at 8am and sighted Heligoland 12 miles away but could only make out some smoke. A heavy rain squall then shut down visibility, so Herbert decided to sit it out on the bottom. *D.5* came up to periscope depth later that morning after vessels were heard passing overhead, but only two trawlers were sighted. The weather was too bad to go farther into the Weser. Nothing else was seen that day, apart from several distant destroyers in the late afternoon, apparently coming out of the Elbe. Herbert headed out to sea to charge the batteries and spend the night on the bottom.

On the 14th the weather deteriorated. Herbert headed inshore, but the only thing sighted all morning was a trawler. He cruised around this in the hope that something better would turn up. He again headed out to charge in the afternoon and spend another night on the bottom.

Herbert surfaced three times at intervals on the morning of the 15th. Each time he found a steadily worsening westerly gale making it 'impossible to attack anything'. Back on the bottom at 100 feet (30m) the boat rolled heavily in the swell. He gave up at 10am as it was 'altogether too unfavourable for any work near the surface.' Herbert headed for home, remaining submerged to avoid the weather. *D.5* surfaced at 5:30pm, as the sea had moderated, and crept into the turbulent seas at five knots to charge the depleted battery. Herbert passed the Ems submerged during the night, avoiding some probing searchlights. Surfacing again at first light, he gradually picked up speed as the gale blew itself out and arrived back at Yarmouth at 7:30pm on the 16th, returning to Harwich next morning. His was the only boat to try and extend the patrol in the weather on the 15th. The frustration Herbert must have felt after sitting just off the main anchorage of the German Fleet for two and a half days and seeing next to nothing can only be imagined.[2]

D.3 had an utterly uneventful patrol northwest and west of Heligoland. The crew did not see a single ship on either day of her patrol but did get away with crossing the undetected minefield on the afternoon of the 14th. However, the weather gave *D.3* a real beating on the way back to Harwich on the 15th, heading into heavy seas and a south-westerly gale. Boyle battled forward at dead slow ahead on his motors, switching to a diesel engine when the battery was drained. The propeller would race alarmingly as it came out of the water if a higher speed was tried. The boat covered only 40 miles that day. Boyle returned to port when the weather moderated on the 16th and he finally reached Harwich at 4:40pm. His rather skimpy report concludes: 'The foremost hydroplanes were damaged, but otherwise the boat was all right'. In reality the boat was heavily damaged. *D.3* went to Sheerness to be docked for repairs on the 17th, not returning until the 25th. The hydroplanes were beyond repair and new ones had to be fitted. All of the

1   TNA ADM137/2067: pp.190–1; Keyes, *Memoirs*, p.101; TNA ADM53: *Lurcher, Firedrake* 11-13 September 1914
2   TNA ADM137/2067: pp.203-5.

bridge rails, bridge screens and damaged plating in the superstructure over the hatches also had to be replaced. *D.3* could not have dived with damaged hydroplanes as they were used to control depth. Boyle's judgement in trying to proceed whilst surfaced in such heavy weather is questionable and contrasts sharply with Herbert, who kept his identical boat submerged as much as possible in the bad weather and avoided damage.[3]

Lieutenant-Commander Noel Frank Laurence was leading *E.1* out for its first patrol. He was the son of a wholesale grocer from Maidstone, Kent, aged 31. He had achieved excellent results with firsts in all of his Lieutenant's examinations. Laurence joined the Submarine Service in 1904. After commanding a succession of coastal boats, he became the commander of *D.1* on its notable debut in the 1910 manoeuvres, following which Captain Hall rated him: 'Invaluable as Capt[ain] of S/M. Excellent nerve'. He quickly moved on to *D.2* when she commissioned. Keyes also chose him as one of the six members of his advisory Submarine Committee. He took command of *E.1* in 1912, whilst she was under construction. Keyes assessed him in 1913 as: 'Most skilful & determined ... Inspires confidence.' He was also described as 'serious, reserved and rather imposing.' He famously fell out with Horton. His manner could cause friction and Goodhart describes him as having 'no tact & does very rotten things sometimes'.[4]

E.1 arrived off the Ems at 7pm on the 12th and spent the night on the bottom. Laurence surfaced at first light and spotted a small steamer apparently steering erratic courses. The steamer then seemed to spot *E.1* and head straight for Borkum. Laurence headed toward the Western Ems entrance after charging the batteries, making out a warship in the mouth of the river, but it was too far in to the shallows to attack. He headed off to the northeast at noon. Two hours later, Laurence spotted a German submarine, 12 miles offshore, heading for the Eastern Ems entrance. He dived to attack, but 'was unable to obtain a position of less than 1,000 yards range, so did not fire'. No impetuous waste of torpedoes by this commander! Laurence surfaced and continued east. This had been *U.20* on the way from Wilhelmshaven to the Ems; she reported sighting an enemy submarine heading west. He turned short of his patrol limit, Langeoog, in the late afternoon and went back to a position 20 miles north of Borkum to spend the night on the bottom.

Next morning Laurence slowly headed south into the Ems on the surface. Alarmingly, a German submarine was spotted in an attack position at 9am, which immediately dived. Laurence quickly dived to avoid being attacked. He stayed down for 90 minutes to play safe and nothing was in sight on surfacing. The submarine was either *U.9* or *U.10*, on their way from the Ems to Heligoland that morning. Neither seems to have made a sighting report. Laurence headed back out of the Ems as visibility was now poor and nothing more was seen before setting course for home that evening. He experienced the same awful weather as Boyle on the way back but does not even mention it in his report. *E.1* arrived late in the evening of the 15th at Gorleston, having averaged only eight knots and returned to Harwich the next morning. The 'suspicious' steamer is the only evidence of over-elevated first patrol caution in his report. Laurence seems to have taken both the anxieties and the awful weather calmly in his stride.[5]

3   TNA ADM137/2067: p.201; TNA ADM173: *D.3* 12-25 September 1914.
4   TNA ADM 196/143/207 & 196/48/176: Noel Frank Laurence; Compton-Hall, *Submarines 1914–18*, p.137; IWM:Documents.2175: diary 30 October 1915.
5   TNA ADM137/2067: p.194

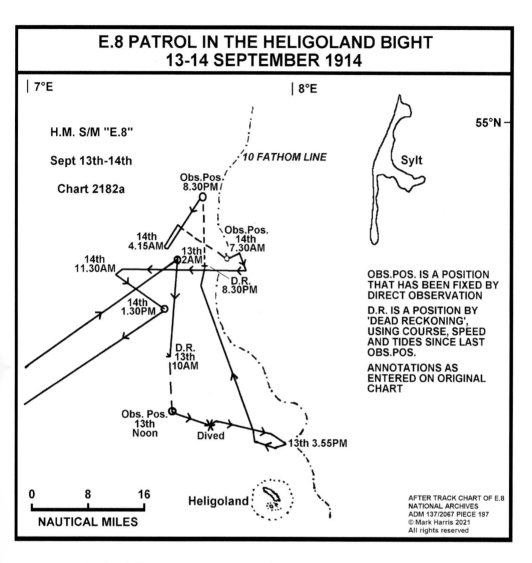

**E.8 PATROL IN THE HELIGOLAND BIGHT
13-14 SEPTEMBER 1914**

| 7°E

H.M. S/M "E.8"

Sept 13th-14th

Chart 2182a

| 8°E

10 FATHOM LINE

55°N —

Sylt

Obs.Pos.
8.30PM

14th
4.15AM

14th
11.30AM

13th
2AM

Obs.Pos.
14th
7.30AM

D.R.
8.30PM

14th
1.30PM

OBS.POS. IS A POSITION
THAT HAS BEEN FIXED BY
DIRECT OBSERVATION

D.R. IS A POSITION BY
'DEAD RECKONING',
USING COURSE, SPEED
AND TIDES SINCE LAST
OBS.POS.

ANNOTATIONS AS
ENTERED ON ORIGINAL
CHART

D.R.
13th
10AM

Obs. Pos.
13th
Noon

Dived

13th 3.55PM

0   8   16

NAUTICAL MILES

Heligoland

E.8 arrived at her billet at 2am on the 13th. Goodhart had navigation problems on the way over as his patent log had again been playing up, making speed uncertain. This resulted in a number of corrections when positions could later be verified, as evidenced by his track chart. *E.8* spent the rest of the night on the bottom off Sylt. Goodhart soon shifted position, as the boat was bumping in the swell, after which: 'we were easier & only rolled. It was nice getting a quiet sleep until 7am.'

Goodhart surfaced in the morning and 'went off to the Southward my intention being to keep close to the 10 fathom line [18m] & go straight towards Heligoland'. He sighted smoke approaching twice during the morning, apparently from destroyers patrolling east and west. Each time Goodhart dived, hoping that a target would get near, but each time he was disappointed. A large quantity of smoke was sighted to the southeast just after noon. This time he closed on the surface. He identified four or five ships in line, which went out of sight to the east. *E.8* followed and an hour later they came back into sight. Goodhart was 'awfully bucked up at the idea of having a big ship in sight at last after seeing destroyers only & we got all the tubes ready.' He closed as much as he dare before diving and commencing an attack. The attack continued for three frustrating hours, 'but all I could find was destroyers 3 or 4 of them.' Goodhart could not work into an attack position on any of them and was getting into ever shallower water. The heavy swell and frequent showers had concealed his periscope, but one of the destroyers now turned in his direction. *E.8* touched the bottom in 10½ fathoms (19m) whilst avoiding her as she passed almost overhead. Goodhart did not think he had been seen but was forced to give up and head out to sea, as there was insufficient depth to be able to escape after an attack. He surfaced at 5:35pm, just making out the destroyers retiring to Heligoland. It had been 2nd Torpedoboots-Halbflottille on outpost patrol that day; they spotted nothing. Goodhart decided to return to his start point for the night, charging the batteries as he went, rather deflated as 'the sea was getting worse and we had a cheerless time going north against it'.

Goodhart dived to the bottom at 8:30pm. He tried two spots, but the boat was bumping about in the heavy seas and tide. After an hour of this he decided to proceed submerged at 50 feet (15m) to seaward, at slow speed, reversing course at 4:15am. He says that this: 'adds complications to ones navigation as ones speed is so very doubtful. However it meant a night's rest & so is always worth it.'

Next morning there was a moderate sea, but an ominous heavy blow from the west. Goodhart headed south after getting a position fix and charging the batteries but was soon forced to dive to avoid an approaching steamer. *E.8*'s after hydroplanes now jammed. This was dangerous, as the crew could barely control the boat with the forward hydroplanes in the choppy seas. *E.8* surfaced and headed west whilst making repairs. Goodhart concluded that the coastal channel must be a regular commercial supply route after a second laden steamer was spotted off Sylt. The crew freed up the mechanism after three hours of toil at midday, but the underlying cause was not discovered until after the patrol. Goodhart headed back towards Heligoland after a satisfactory test dive, but the weather worsened, strengthening to a south-westerly gale, with visibility dropping to one mile. As 'one couldn't expect to see anything in time to get under', he soon decided to abandon the patrol early and head for home. Goodhart admits to his wife that he could have stayed an extra day: 'but as I'd hardly been dry since leaving Yarmouth & all were in the same condition, I didn't feel like doing it'. A huge wave hit at 10pm that night and carried away the port stanchion, wrecking the bridge screen. The metal rod hit Goodhart on the back and the coxswain was almost washed overboard. Goodhart quickly ordered slow ahead on the engine telegraphs and got Greig up on the bridge to replace him, as he was 'pretty well knocked out'. It was fortunate that Greig was 'a man … you can trust', as one of the forward hydroplane guards also started a nasty leak into the boat through loose rivets. *E.8* pushed on at eight knots against the weather, but finally, as they neared the coast at 4pm on the 15th, the sea moderated. Two steam trawlers were hailed to confirm their position, but neither proved very accurate and *E.8* had to anchor for the night off Lowestoft. Goodhart was thankful that Greig and Burrows had been up to standing all the watches after his accident and told his wife: 'they did awfully well.' He had tried to get back to the bridge twice but had only succeeded in aggravating his injuries.

E.8 returned to Harwich on the morning of the 16th after fixing her position. Goodhart saw his doctor, who confirmed that no bones were broken. *E.8* was not as badly damaged as *D.3*. She went into the floating dock at Harwich the next day for two days of repairs to the hydroplane

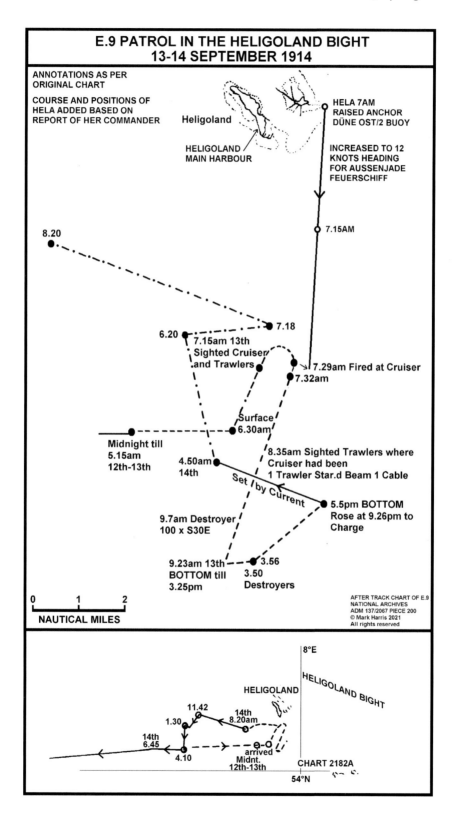

E.9 PATROL IN THE HELIGOLAND BIGHT
13-14 SEPTEMBER 1914

ANNOTATIONS AS PER
ORIGINAL CHART

COURSE AND POSITIONS OF
HELA ADDED BASED ON
REPORT OF HER COMMANDER

Heligoland

HELA 7AM
RAISED ANCHOR
DÜNE OST/2 BUOY

HELIGOLAND
MAIN HARBOUR

INCREASED TO 12
KNOTS HEADING
FOR AUSSENJADE
FEUERSCHIFF

7.15AM

8.20

7.18

6.20

7.15am 13th
Sighted Cruiser
and Trawlers

7.29am Fired at Cruiser
7.32am

Surface
6.30am

8.35am Sighted Trawlers where
Cruiser had been
1 Trawler Star.d Beam 1 Cable

Midnight till
5.15am
12th-13th

4.50am
14th

Set / by Current

5.5pm BOTTOM
Rose at 9.26pm to
Charge

9.7am Destroyer
100 x S30E

9.23am 13th
BOTTOM till
3.25pm

3.56
3.50
Destroyers

0   1   2

NAUTICAL MILES

8°E

HELIGOLAND BIGHT

HELIGOLAND

11.42

14th
8.20am

1.30

14th
6.45

4.10

arrived
Midnt.
12th-13th

CHART 2182A

54°N

guard. Goodhart had learned his lesson and tells his wife: 'next time I shall clear the bridge quite early in such weather & look out through the periscopes ... I can't really think why I didn't do it this time'.[6]

E.9 arrived six miles south-southwest of Heligoland at midnight on the 12th, after crossing the undetected minefield. Horton spent the night deep on the bottom at 120 feet (37m). He came up to periscope depth on the morning of the 13th and headed east, surfacing for only a couple of minutes to ventilate the boat in heavy rain, low visibility and a slight swell. He then dived to 70 feet (21m) and headed towards Heligoland, popping back up to periscope depth 45 minutes later. The weather had cleared and Heligoland was five miles away. Horton spotted a cruiser, heading in his general direction, about 1½–2 miles away, with wisps of smoke and trawlers visible in various directions. He attacked, gradually turning to starboard to get into position ahead of the cruiser for a bow shot to make the most of the twin tubes forward. Horton raised the periscope 13 minutes after beginning his attack run and confirmed that he was within 600 yards (550m) on the starboard beam of the cruiser, which had two funnels. He confirmed to the crew that they were attacking. Quickly lowering the periscope, Horton ordered the motors stopped and counted down the seconds until he estimated the cruiser would be in position, with the crew standing silently at their action stations. After checking the clock, the depth gauge and the compass he ordered 'Raise Periscope'. Timing the shot was awkward, as the submarine was, in his words, 'very lively' in the swell. He came up with the periscope, crouching down almost on his knees and as soon as he saw that the cruiser was where he expected ordered 'Stop Periscope', followed quickly by 'Fire One' and 15 seconds later 'Fire Two'.

Horton immediately took *E.9* down to 70 feet and turned to the same course as the cruiser. The seconds ticked by. A loud explosion slammed the boat, at the point that the second torpedo was expected to reach the target (also heard by *D.5* many miles away). Horton describes what happened a few minutes later: 'Rose to 28 feet observed cruiser between waves; appeared to have stopped and to have list to starboard. Splashes from shot on our port side and ahead of cruiser. Turned periscope to see where shot were coming from, but submarine was very deep and only observed wisps of smoke and mast very close.' With no opportunity for a further attack, Horton was also concerned about breaking surface under fire. He went down to 70 feet to trim the boat to compensate for the two torpedoes he had fired, proceeding very slowly. Horton observed about four or five trawlers in a cluster where the cruiser had been, presumably rescuing survivors, when he came back to periscope depth an hour after the attack. He had to immediately go back down to 70 feet as a trawler was only one cable away (180m). He tried again 30 minutes later, but destroyers were only 100 yards away (90m). Horton decided to rest on the bottom as things were too hot above to make another attack.

His target was the 2,082t (2,050 long tons) Scout Cruiser *Hela*, under the command of Fregattenkapitän Paul Wolfram. She was the oldest small cruiser in the Fleet and as part of the 4th Aufklärungsgruppe (Scouting Group) was regularly used for outpost duty behind the inner patrol line.[7] It is hard to understand why she was ever employed on this duty, as

6   TNA ADM137/2067: pp.195–6; TNA ADM173: *E.8* 12-19 September 1914; IWM: Documents.2175: Letter to wife 18 September 1914.
7   *Hela* was 105m (345 feet) long, 11m (36 feet) wide, maximum draught 4.64m (15 feet). Armament was 3x8.8cm (3.5-inch), 6x5cm (2-inch) guns and 3x45cm (17.7-inch) torpedo tubes. Speed 20 knots. Completed in 1895, modernised in 1910.

Hela after her reconstruction in 1910. She would have looked like this when sunk, apart from an additional 8.8cm gun added at the stern. (Author's Collection)

her weak gun armament and low speed gave her little chance of survival or escape if attacked by surface vessels. *Hela* got underway at 7am from east of Heligoland, heading for the Fleet anchorage in the Jade after five days working on the outpost line. She was steaming at her cruising speed, a leisurely 12 knots, rolling heavily in the choppy sea. Wolfram's report does not state that she was zig-zagging, implying she was not, but *Hela* had employed this anti-submarine tactic before. Lookouts aft spotted the two torpedo tracks only 30m (100 feet) away. It was too late. Seconds later the first passed astern. The second then struck the propeller shaft tunnel compartment immediately aft of the starboard engine room, blowing holes in nearby bulkheads and in the armour deck above. One man who was above the explosion in his office was never seen again. Three crewmen on the deck above suffered leg breaks, with many others injured by being thrown against bulkheads. Electric power failed immediately, putting all lights out below and neither wireless nor signal lights would function. The aft part of *Hela* almost immediately took up a list to starboard and the starboard engine room began filling with water. Flags were raised requesting assistance, accompanied by blasts of the horn and firing of the guns (the splashes seen by Horton). The engines were stopped and the engine rooms quickly had to be abandoned. It was impossible to stop the water spreading. Leutnant Dahlmann found the ladders to the deck above destroyed and had to get out through the hole in the deck. After only 20 minutes it was clear that the ship would soon sink. Wolfram gave the order to abandon ship. OberMatrose (Leading Seaman) der Reserve Willy Kittner had two broken legs. Doctor Slauck and Vizesteuermann (Acting Warrant Officer) der Reserve Kohnert quickly tied him to a mattress to keep him afloat and pushed it over the side. The crew managed to launch one of the boats, but most had to jump. The doctor ran out of time to help another crewman with a broken leg, who was swept under as the ship foundered. *Hela* began to settle stern first, the funnels collapsed and she broke in two, disappearing in a cloud of coal dust. She went down to three cheers and a chorus of 'Deutschland über alles' from her crew in the water, 25 minutes after being hit, at about 8am. *E.9* was not spotted at any point.

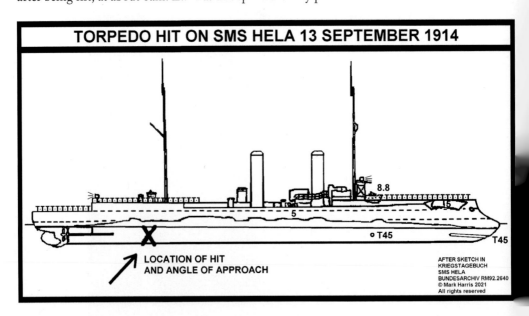

TORPEDO HIT ON SMS HELA 13 SEPTEMBER 1914

LOCATION OF HIT
AND ANGLE OF APPROACH

The tug *Beowulf* quickly came along, following the same route. *U.18* was exercising nearby and raised the alarm by wireless at 8:30am. They rescued almost all the men in the water, assisted by numerous other nearby outpost boats and later destroyers from Heligoland. Only four of the 243 crew were lost, despite the cold, choppy seas, although 16 men developed pneumonia. Kittner was pulled out of the water still alive by an outpost trawler. *Hela* was a difficult target in the swell, being small and shallow in draught, but the swell had also made the periscope and torpedoes hard to spot. The *Beowulf* did claim to have sighted a submarine during the rescue. The attack stirred up a hornet's nest of response. The 8th Torpedoboots-Flottille was ordered out of Heligoland and the 4th Torpedoboots-Flottille out of the Ems to search for the assailant. The forces on patrol and their reinforcements were at least successful in keeping *E.9* down and preventing her from making a further attack, or interfering with rescue work, but they were without means to harm her whilst submerged. The area had recently been swept by minesweepers, but the attack illustrates that unless the vessel itself was being screened this was largely worthless.[8]

Horton periodically came off the bottom during the afternoon for a look round, but the destroyers were relentless and the thump of their propellers kept on criss-crossing overhead. More were heard arriving at noon from the direction of the Weser. Eventually the noises subsided after dark. *E.9* was finally able to surface with nothing in sight, air the boat and run the engine to charge the depleted batteries at 9:26pm, having been submerged for all but two minutes since midnight. The air must have been dangerously depleted of oxygen after 15 hours continuously submerged. After 14 hours submerged neither cigarettes nor matches would burn.[9] The ability to conserve the batteries by resting on the bottom had been vital. Horton would have been forced to surface if his batteries were exhausted, even if the air was still good. At 11:10pm *E.9* went back to the bottom for the night.

E.9 rose to periscope depth on the morning of the 14th but could see nothing except patrolling trawlers. Horton headed in towards Heligoland submerged. He had Heligoland in sight for over an hour from 6am, as well as the outer anchorages, but there was nothing visible except trawlers. Horton therefore headed west, intending to ambush any submarines patrolling the outpost line, based on the information from *E.7*. He surfaced mid-morning and headed south to charge for a couple of hours, then submerged and continued to search west until dusk. The visibility had constantly varied up and down between clear horizons and one mile, with intermittent heavy rain. Horton surfaced near the line of the undetected minefield and headed for home at 6:45pm, with the seas turning very heavy. After the bridge fittings were bent by the heavy seas

8   BArch:RM92: *Hela* Kriegstagebuch 1–31 August 1914, Wolfram – Bericht über den Untergang *S.M.S.* „Hela" 14 September 1914, Erfahrung über die Wirkung des englischen Torpedos u.s.w. auf *S.M.S.* „Hela" 26 September 1914; Gröner, *German Warships*, p.99, gives wreck position as 54°3'N, 7°55'E, two miles south of the position on Horton's chart, omits two missing later presumed dead; Groos, *Nordsee 2*, pp.23–4; *Verlustliste 7*, p.61; *Verlustliste 9*, p.2. Those lost were: OberVerwaltungsschreiber-Maat (Chief Petty Officer Writer) Alfred Fischer – missing at scene of explosion, SchiffsBarbier (Ships Barber) Georg Winkler – died of heart attack in the water, Matrose (Seaman) Franz Szulczewski and OberHeizer (Leading Stoker) Hugo Voß – reported missing, so presumed drowned. One crewman suffered a broken ankle, OberMatrose Walter Thurow.

9   J.G. Klaxon, *The Story of our Submarines* (Edinburgh & London: William Blackwood & Sons, 1919), p.48

he decided to rest on the bottom, but at 120 feet (37m) the boat was still bumping, even with full ballast tanks. He therefore resumed course submerged for the rest of the night.

Horton surfaced at 5am next morning, but it was impossible to remain on the bridge, so he trimmed down and proceeded on his diesels, with the conning tower closed up and only the conning tower ventilator open to provide air for the engines. He steered the boat by using the periscopes. Around 2pm the sea finally calmed enough for *E.9* to surface. On his return to Harwich at noon the next day, Horton decided to put on a show. His signalman was instructed to use the boat's supply of signal flags to make the skull and crossbones of a Jolly Roger flag – one traditionally flown by pirates. The yellow flag was embellished with a black skull and crossbones, which the boat proudly displayed from its periscope. Goodhart spotted it still flying when he later came in. This was a joke at the expense of former First Sea Lord Admiral Wilson who is reputed to have said that submarines were: 'underhand, unfair and damned un-English … They'll never be any use in war and I'll tell you why. I'm going to get the First Lord to announce that we intend to treat all submarines as pirate vessels in wartime and that we'll hang all the crews.' It is worth adding that there is actually no hard evidence that he actually said any of this and he had actually been an early proponent of submarine use! The Admiralty were very unhappy with Horton's stunt, but despite official attempts to stamp out the practice, the use of a Jolly Roger on return to port after a successful attack by a submarine gradually caught on in the Royal Navy and is now a firmly embedded tradition that continues to this day.[10]

The news had preceded him, as the German Admiralty officially announced the loss of *Hela* on the 14th: 'On the morning of September 13th, His Majesty's Light Cruiser "Hela" was torpedoed and sunk by an enemy submarine. Almost the entire crew has been saved.' News quickly got to Keyes, who wrote to his wife on the 15th from Harwich: 'You will have seen the German announcement that the *Hela* has been sunk by a British submarine. I am very anxious to know where it was and who did it.' Later, whilst travelling to a conference with Admiral Jellicoe, he wrote that: 'I was rather anxious about *D.3* which was 2 days late – but the weather was so awful I only saw Laurence and Horton before I left, the others hadn't got back … Horton, *E.9*, is the man who dived 40 miles up the Firth of Forth. A splendid fellow.'[11] Keyes commended Horton in his report to the Admiralty as 'a skilful and most enterprising submarine officer, and I beg to submit his name for favourable consideration of their Lordships.' Horton wrote his name in the history books with a flourish, but his report and the way he handled the boat exude professional detachment and control. The Admiralty announced on the 17th: 'Submarine E 9 (Lieutenant-Commander Max K. Horton) has returned safely after having torpedoed a German vessel believed to be the *Hela*, six miles south of Heligoland.'[12]

Keyes decision to push up the perceived risk level and send the submarines deep into the Bight had paid off, encountering the cruisers supporting the patrol line for the first time. The weather had been both a friend and an enemy on the patrol, helping to conceal the boats, but also causing damage and an early end to the patrol. There is no evidence that any of the submarines on patrol were detected other than the report by *Beowulf*. Fortune had also been

---

10   TNA ADM137/2067: pp.198-200; Carr, *Guess and by God*, pp. 89-92; IWM:Documents.2175: Letter to wife 18 September 1914.

11   *Keyes Papers*, pp.24-25; *Amtliche Kriegs-Depeschen nach Berichten des Wolff'schen Telegr.-Bureaus-Band 1*, (Berlin: Nationaler Verlag, 1915), p.96; *Official Naval Despatches*, (London: The Graphic, 1914), p.8.

12   TNA ADM137/2067: p.206.

with them, as the new minefield had been crossed at least three times. After seven attacks and 10 torpedoes fired, the 8th Flotilla had at last scored the first successful attack by a Royal Navy submarine, and payback for the *Pathfinder*.

Horton was lucky to be in the right place at the right time to catch *Hela* in transit. However, he had seen *Stettin* in transit from Heligoland on his last patrol and this may have influenced his choice of location. The *Maidstone Muckrag* gleefully reported that Horton only spotted *Hela* as a result of a need to surface to clear the air, after his Lieutenant, Chapman, had taken some laxatives. The story probably has a grain of truth. Goodhart tells his wife, immediately after the events, that Horton was underway and had 'very luckily' sighted *Hela* after coming up to periscope depth at that specific moment in order to pump out the heads.[13] In contrast, Herbert was unlucky that no Flotilla sortied from the Jade or the Weser to counter Horton's attack. The weather perhaps prevented Laurence seeing the destroyer flotilla leave the Ems. It appeared that patrol cordons of both destroyers and submarines off Heligoland and the Ems were still in place, but the submarines sighted had been on routine transits and there was no regular patrol by them. The area *D.3* was patrolling was too far out for routine patrols.

The fame brought by Horton's successes and lack of images of his new boat resulted in many doctored images of other boats being produced for sale, which proliferate to this day. This rarity really is *E.9* at Barrow heading out for trials around June 1914, with a large number of yard workers aboard. The battleships *Emperor of India* and *Reşadiye* can be seen fitting out in the background. (Darren Brown Collection)

13 Compton-Hall is sceptical but does not seem to be aware of Goodhart's letter, which dovetails with Horton's report and a Hallifax diary entry. It seems some versions of the story later outgrew the facts, requiring Horton to surface to air the boat, which cannot be reconciled with his report.

Hela was not a great loss to the High Sea Fleet, and the official German History emphasises her low value, but it could just as easily have been a much more valuable ship. Admiral von Ingenohl summed up his increasing concerns about the Fleet being potentially blockaded in harbour in memoranda dated 13th and 18th September:

> We know of no means of keeping out submarines. Our forces in the outer and inner German Bight are constantly exposed to enemy submarine attacks.
>
> The only security measures that can be adopted, which are of questionable value, are: day and night patrolling by destroyers, ships steering high speed zig-zag courses; proceeding to sea at night through shallow water and screened by destroyers.
>
> These measures may easily be adopted by small groups of fast ships (cruisers), but they are not adequate for battleship formations. ... it is dangerous for formations to proceed to sea in the daytime even with those security measures which are possible and leaving harbour repeatedly at night is also of concern.

As a result:

> If the despatch of the Fleet or a particular formation to undertake military operations is contemplated, the submarine danger must be accepted. ... Conversely, serious damage or losses suffered by leaving harbour solely for the purpose of exercises cannot be justified. ...
>
> War experience has shown that the German Bight is unsuitable for exercises, leaving only the Baltic for this. ... There are obvious reasons why it is not feasible to strip the North Sea of Battle Squadrons.
>
> Consequently, we can only despatch single Battle Squadrons to the Baltic for 8 or 10 days at a time.
>
> ... Before despatching a Battle Squadron, it must be remembered that its recall, allowing for coaling etc. will take at least two days. During this time any thought of taking decisive action must be rejected, even if the British Fleet enters the German Bight.[14]

By forcing the fleet to use the Baltic for exercising, 8th Flotilla had severely curtailed their ability to respond tactically in the North Sea. The Kaiser approved the new arrangements on 24 September.

---

14   Groos, *Nordsee 2*, pp.24-5, quoted in Ingehohl's memoranda.

12

Gales and a farcical rumour

Keyes issued orders for the next patrol before he left for his conference with Jellicoe on 15 September. The submarines left Harwich at 11am that day and stopped at Yarmouth. They departed for the patrol around midnight. *D.1* was assigned the billet off the Ems as far east as Juist. *E.3* was assigned a neighbouring coastal billet from Juist eastwards. *D.8* was to the north of her, covering the area west and south of Heligoland. *D.7* would patrol a new billet off the Lister Deep between the islands of Sylt and Röm. Finally, *E.10* would patrol inshore between Heligoland and Vortrapp Deep off Amrum Island. The boats therefore covered the coastal entry and exit points all the way round the German coast, with *D.8* covering the seaward approaches to Heligoland. They would patrol until the evening of the 18th, weather permitting. Discretion was granted to remain an extra day, with the caution that the next patrol would be entering the Bight on the 19th or 20th. Return to either Yarmouth or Harwich was permitted to give maximum flexibility in timing departure.[1]

However, this patrol was to be dominated by the westerly gale that continued to sweep the Heligoland Bight. The shallow nature of the Bight whips it into high, steep sided waves in these conditions, making patrolling in a submarine at best extremely difficult and at worst dangerous.

Cochrane's *D.1* arrived off the Western Ems at 10:30pm on the 16th and spent the night on the bottom. He surfaced at 5:30am and spent the day cruising slowly along his billet and back, five to 10 miles offshore, 'the sea being too much for the boat to dive close inshore.' Cochrane went to the bottom for the night in 15 fathoms (27m) off the Eastern Ems in near gale force winds at 5:30pm. He reports: 'There was a good deal of noise from sand and small stones being thrown against the hull by the sea. By 2:30 a.m. … the boat was rolling and bumping on the bottom.' Cochrane found deteriorating weather on a trip to the surface at 3am and returned to the bottom. By 1pm the rolling and bumping got too much. *D.1* surfaced and steered northwest into the gale on the diesel engines. Cochrane reduced speed to slow ahead on one engine to hold position overnight. Next morning, the 19th, he headed for Yarmouth and anchored off Lowestoft at midnight. *D.1* arrived at Harwich at noon the next day. The crew then had to clear away a lot of fine sand, which had found its way into ventilators, periscope and steering gear bearings.[2]

1 TNA ADM137/2067: p.208.
2 TNA ADM137/2067: p.212.

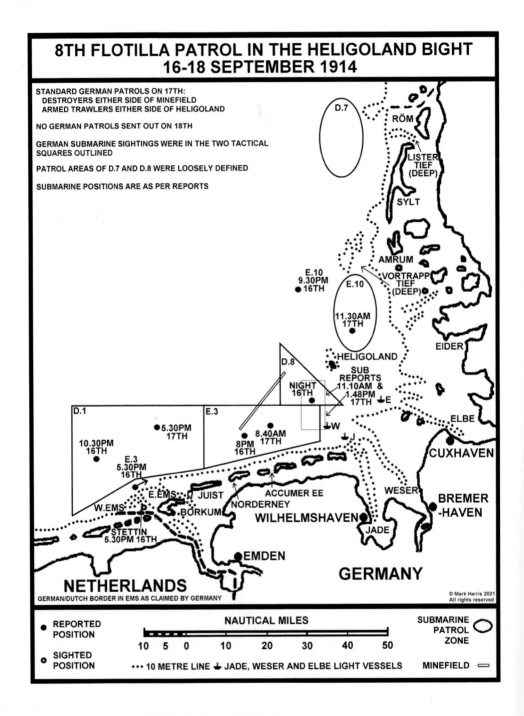

8TH FLOTILLA PATROL IN THE HELIGOLAND BIGHT
16-18 SEPTEMBER 1914

STANDARD GERMAN PATROLS ON 17TH:
  DESTROYERS EITHER SIDE OF MINEFIELD
  ARMED TRAWLERS EITHER SIDE OF HELIGOLAND

NO GERMAN PATROLS SENT OUT ON 18TH

GERMAN SUBMARINE SIGHTINGS WERE IN THE TWO TACTICAL
SQUARES OUTLINED

PATROL AREAS OF D.7 AND D.8 WERE LOOSELY DEFINED

SUBMARINE POSITIONS ARE AS PER REPORTS

D.7

RÖM

LISTER
TIEF
(DEEP)

SYLT

AMRUM

E.10
9.30PM
16TH

E.10

VORTRAPP
TIEF
(DEEP)

11.30AM
17TH

EIDER

HELIGOLAND

D.8

SUB
REPORTS
11.10AM &
1.48PM
17TH

NIGHT
16TH

E

D.1

E.3

ELBE

5.30PM
17TH

8.40AM
17TH

W

10.30PM
16TH

E.3
5.30PM
16TH

8PM
16TH

J

CUXHAVEN

E.EMS   JUIST

ACCUMER EE

NORDERNEY

WESER

BREMER
-HAVEN

W.EMS

BORKUM

WILHELMSHAVEN

STETTIN
5.30PM 16TH

JADE

EMDEN

GERMANY

NETHERLANDS

GERMAN/DUTCH BORDER IN EMS AS CLAIMED BY GERMANY

NAUTICAL MILES

• REPORTED
  POSITION

SUBMARINE
PATROL
ZONE

10 5 0   10   20   30   40   50

○ SIGHTED
  POSITION

••• 10 METRE LINE ⚓ JADE, WESER AND ELBE LIGHT VESSELS   MINEFIELD

Cholmley's *E.3* was to the east of Cochrane. He passed the now familiar Dutch cruiser and two destroyers on the morning of the 16th. The equally familiar, tantalising German cruiser was sighted getting underway and heading up the Western Ems as *E.3* passed the estuary at 5:30pm. Cholmley identified a *Stettin* class. *Stettin* had been taking her turn anchored on watch at the estuary mouth that day. *E.3* reached her billet at 8pm and went to the bottom for the night. At 5:45am next morning Cholmley surfaced and fixed his position using Norderney Lighthouse. Two trawlers came out from Norderney and the Accumer Ee channel. Cholmley thought the second had seen him and half an hour later a destroyer arrived. He moved off east and at 8:40am two trawlers came towards his position in line abreast at five knots. He passed one of them just 100 yards (90m) away to get a good look through the periscope. There was neither ensign nor wireless aerials, but there was a small gun mounted forward, resembling a British 3-pdr. He could even see a man cleaning the gun, apparently not in uniform! A patrolling armed trawler would have been a legitimate, but very difficult target for a torpedo. Torpedoes also had a limited supply and a trawler was of doubtful value as an exchange for one. Cholmley would not have been expected to attack it. The trawler off Norderney was still patrolling at 1pm, but he reports that it was: 'Too rough for submarine work.' *E.3* went to the bottom at 6pm, but 'before midnight the boat began to bump badly and I had to dive about for the remainder of the night.'

On surfacing at daylight on the 18th there was: 'a strong North Westerly gale and very heavy sea, and visibility about 200 yards [180m], it was quite impossible to do any submarine work. To avoid being sent on to the shoals at the entrance of the Elbe, … I opened a ventilator and ran one engine dead slow, making about 4 knots, steaming straight [into the wind] and continually pumping out the water which came through the ventilator.' Finally, at 6am on the 19th the seas had eased somewhat. Cholmley opened the conning tower hatch for the first time in 36 hours and headed for Harwich. He arrived at 7pm that night.[3]

Brodie's *D.8* had the billet north of Cholmley. He passed the patrolling Dutch cruiser and torpedo boats off the Texel on the afternoon of the 16th. Soon afterwards, a submarine was sighted four miles to starboard, which appeared to turn and dive towards him. It is possible that this was *U.24*, which was heading out for a reconnaissance of British patrols off the Dutch coast at this time, but she made no sighting report.[4] *D.8* crossed the minefield and reached her patrol billet off Heligoland at midnight. During the next morning she sighted only two trawlers. Brodie dived when a submarine was sighted at Noon. Heligoland came into sight at 2:40pm. *D.8* went to the bottom for the night at 6pm.

At 2:10am Brodie reports: 'Rose as submarine was rolling and bumping heavily, and then found that short, steep sea rendered it impossible to keep conning tower hatch or ventilators open and the gas engine stopped for lack of air.' Brodie therefore dived the boat and headed northwest for five hours. Another attempt to start the diesels then failed. Brodie dived, going down beyond certified diving depth to reach bottom in 22 fathoms (40m). The boat was still rolling heavily! *D.8* remained there all day. Brodie surfaced at 6:40pm. The wind had moderated a little. He was able to run one engine slowly, with a couple of ventilators open to re-charge the batteries and top up the depleted air reserves until daylight. By 5:15am the next morning, the

---

3   TNA ADM137/2067: pp.215–6; BArch:RM92: *Stettin* Kriegstagebuch, 16 September 1914.
4   Groos, *Nordsee 2*, p.48.

19th, Brodie was able to open the conning tower hatch and return to Harwich, almost certainly re-crossing the minefield on the way. *D.8* arrived at 11:30am on the 20th.[5]

Fraser's *E.10* sighted a homeward bound British submarine off the Texel at 10:30am on the 16th. *D.5* was definitely passing at the time, but Herbert does not mention it. Fraser arrived near his billet in the midst of a thunderstorm, rain and heavy seas at 9:30pm. He spent the night rolling on the bottom, but it was 'quite comfortable.' *E.10* rose at 7am next morning in a heavy rain squall with 400 yards (365m) visibility. Fraser dived and headed slowly towards his billet. He had to switch to the magnetic compass as the gyrocompass became defective. Fraser surfaced when the visibility improved somewhat, but the gale was still blowing and he continued southeast, charging the battery. Five destroyers came into view, closing gradually at a range of about 2½ miles at 11:15am. Ten minutes later Heligoland was sighted to the southwest about eight miles away. *E.10* dived and Fraser settled down to observe the destroyers, which were apparently patrolling inshore. He began an attack on the closest at 2pm, but suddenly they all turned and headed south. An hour later *E.10* surfaced and headed north to charge the batteries into a strengthening gale. Fraser had to dive before the charge completed as it was too rough. When he next surfaced at 8:30pm, hoping to finish, he 'had to close down could not keep conning tower hatch open.' The log records: 'Sea now enormous. Heavy thunderstorm.' Fraser dived to the bottom, but it was only 65 feet (20m). After enduring five hours of bumping and rolling, he eventually got underway submerged at low speed in a circle, 'pumping [up and down] 15–20 feet [4.5–6m], rolling considerably.'

Fraser surfaced at 7am on the 18th. The log records: 'Sea breaking. Very heavy swell. Wind 8–9 N.W. [a severe gale with winds up to 47 knots] Lookout almost impossible.' *E.10* was forced to close up and steer southeast with a following wind on one engine to complete her charge, with just one ventilator open for air. Fraser turned west once charged to get into deeper water, then set course for Yarmouth. He was finally able to open the conning tower hatch at 2am. He arrived at 6:40pm, then proceeded to Harwich next morning, the 20th, arriving at 1:30pm. The crew spent the next three days repairing the hydroplanes, upper deck casing and bridge gear, but it wasn't necessary to go into the dock.[6]

Street's *D.7* went to the bottom for the night after arriving off Lister Deep on the 16th. She bumped around too badly in the swell to remain there. At 3pm next day Street saw a submarine with her mast up, one mile away to the east in gale force winds. *D.7* was well placed and dived to attack. However, Street was unable to see anything through either periscope, as water had got into them whilst on the bottom! When *D.7* surfaced two hours later the wind had risen to a severe gale. Street dived to the bottom for the night at 6:30pm. Even at 85 feet (26m), *D.7* was bumping and rolling heavily. Street got underway, heading slowly out to sea at 50 feet (15m).

D.7 surfaced at 11:30pm. Before the crew could lock down the forward hydroplanes they were hit by a big wave which fractured the mechanism. The crew now got the locking bolt in, but another wave broke the bolt, leaving the hydroplanes twisting and turning as each wave hit. This meant *D.7* would be unable to dive, as she would be impossible to control underwater. The hydroplanes were also acting like sails, driving her backwards as each wave hit. Street headed slowly west. By midnight the wind was storm force; enough to flatten trees on land. The

5   TNA ADM137/2067: p.214.
6   TNA ADM137/2067: p.217; TNA ADM173: *E.10*, 15-23 September 1914.

The bridge of *D.7*, showing how exposed to the weather it was. (NH 54984)

sea was coming right over the bridge. All Street reports for the next 33 hours is: 'Proceeding to Westward'. The details are filled in by Acting Lieutenant Thomas Godman RNR, the Third Officer. First the interior compass stopped working. A man now had to be lashed to the bridge to steer from there. *D.7* was steered farther north than usual, to reduce the chance of encountering a German warship, prolonging the journey. Sea water got into the battery. The crew were choking on chlorine fumes as a result. *D.7* pressed on, but Godman told Hallifax that they did not expect to make it back. At last a patrolling cruiser was sighted at 9:30am on the 19th. They simply had to hope that it was British. By now *D.7*'s mast had broken. The challenge was held over the side of the bridge by hand. *D.7* closed to within half a mile over the next 20 minutes. Finally the challenge was answered. It was Rear-Admiral Christian's flagship, *Euryalus*, with her sister ships *Aboukir*, *Hogue* and *Cressy*. In fact Christian had *D.7* in sight for over an hour before she was recognised as British. He had increased speed and concentrated his cruisers round her until she was identified. This was a rash action. The cruisers now formed up to provide an escort. *Euryalus* screened the worst of the seas from *D.7*. The *Hogue* was soon detached to continue screening *D.7* all the way to Smith's Knoll. Good deed complete, *Hogue* left to re-join her squadron, wishing *D.7* good luck. Her own luck was about to run out. Street brought *D.7* in to Gorleston at 10:30pm and returned to Harwich at 4:15pm the next day. She left on the 21st for major repairs in Chatham Dockyard and did not return until 25 October.[7]

Cholmley, Brodie and Fraser had encountered the standard German patrols on the 17th. The submarine sighted by Brodie at noon was in the area used for exercising off Heligoland. *D.8* was also seen, as a surfacing enemy submarine was reported at 11:10am in the tactical square he was patrolling in. A patrolling trawler also reported an enemy submarine in the neighbouring square to the south at 1:48pm. *E.3* does not seem to have been reported. The submarine reported by Street cannot be identified.

Keyes writes in his report of the 'strain and hardship' endured by the crews on the patrol. He continues: 'their position … was undoubtedly precarious, and it was creditable that they should have maintained their position in the hope that the weather would moderate.' However, he gave orders that in future the submarines were to return when severe westerly weather threatened. In his opinion, the almost certain damage and serious risks run could not be balanced by any likely success. Keyes was right that it would be almost impossible to attack successfully, even if a target appeared. The Flotilla had learnt the limitations that North Sea weather imposed the hard way and it had been a close call for *D.7*. Talbot notes that all four submarines had some damage to their hydroplanes.[8]

Whilst his submarines were being battered by the weather, Keyes had attended an important conference held on-board the Grand Fleet flagship, *Iron Duke*, at the remote, secret, temporary anchorage of the Fleet at Loch Ewe on the west coast of Scotland. Keyes travelled from London with Tyrwhitt, Churchill and the senior members of the Admiralty, including Sturdee, first by train and then by car. Keyes and Tyrwhitt shared the back seat of a car with Churchill. He clearly enjoyed their company and conversation. On the way back a bizarre armed expedition was led by Churchill to eliminate a searchlight Tyrwhitt had spotted on a remote Scottish country house. Wild speculation had transformed it into a device to communicate the presence of the Fleet to Zeppelins. More seriously, Keyes and Tyrwhitt once again raised the issue of Christian's old cruisers, referring to them as the 'live bait squadron'. Churchill heard their arguments and acted on his return to London, sending a note to Battenberg: 'The Bacchantes ought not to continue on this beat. The risk to such ships is not justified by any services they can render.' Battenberg agreed and directed Sturdee to move them, but time had run out.

Jellicoe and all his senior commanders attended the conference. Keyes was there as one of the agenda items – or perhaps more accurately his agenda item – was the future employment of submarines in the war. The main purpose was to discuss a direct attack on Heligoland, which was firmly rejected by the Admirals. The possibility of a fleet operation in the Baltic was now discussed and again rejected. However, Vice-Admiral Bayly, commander of the 1st Battle Squadron, proposed that Kiel should be attacked by light cruisers and destroyers. Tyrwhitt, whose force was the one indicated, had to dispose of the idea, writing to his wife later that day that: 'I was not going to agree to murdering half my command.' Keyes now saw an opportunity to push instead for an expedition into the Baltic by submarines, as it would provide a wider and potentially more profitable location for getting at the enemy than the narrow, shallow waters of

7   TNA ADM137/2067: p.213; TNA ADM53: *Euryalus* 19 September 1914; IWM:Documents.1003: 20-26 September and 25 October; details related to Hallifax by Godman and Lieutenant Nuthall of *Euryalus*.

8   TNA ADM137/2067: pp.210–11.

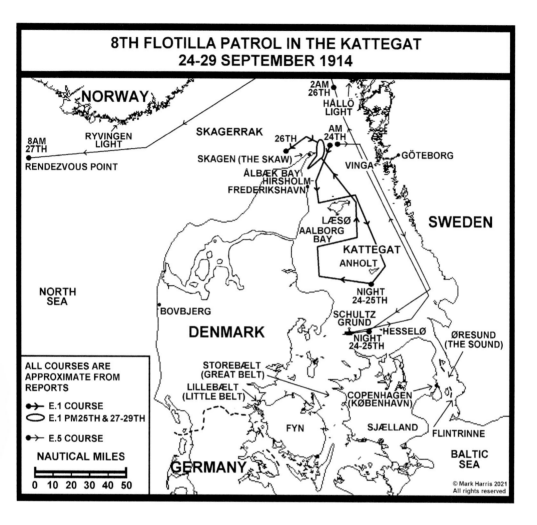

**8TH FLOTILLA PATROL IN THE KATTEGAT
24-29 SEPTEMBER 1914**

the Heligoland Bight. Crucially, Jellicoe offered his support. Perhaps he seized on the idea to close the discussion on a positive note of action. It was resolved that enquiries would be made about basing submarines in Russian Baltic ports and in the meantime two submarines would be sent to scout the approach to the Baltic in the Kattegat.[9]

Orders were issued on the 19th. *E.1* and *E.5* were chosen. They were to leave Harwich that day and spend the night at Gorleston. At 5am on the 20th, Waistell, with *Firedrake* and *Lurcher*, would meet them at the Corton Light Vessel and tow them until dark to conserve fuel. They were then to proceed in company and arrive at Skagen – the northernmost tip of Denmark – at daylight on the 22nd. From there they were to proceed independently into the Kattegat, examining Aalborg Bay and Ålbæk Bay for any signs that they were being used clandestinely

9   Keyes, *Memoirs*, pp.102–6; Churchill, *World Crisis*, p.276; Jellicoe. *Grand Fleet*, pp.128-30; Patterson, *Tyrwhitt*, pp.67-71.

by German forces. They were then to examine the channels leading into the Baltic. Finally, they were to rendezvous at 8am on the 24th at the entrance to the Skagerrak with cruisers and escorting destroyers of the Grand Fleet. After communicating the results of their reconnaissance to them, they were to return together to Harwich. This was a round trip of over 1,000 miles, although well within the radius of action of the boats.[10]

The submarines left for Gorleston as planned. However, the appalling weather meant that departure from there was delayed until 4:30am on the 22nd. The return rendezvous was revised to the 27th, allowing an extra day for reconnaissance.

Waistell met the submarines on the 22nd, as planned. *Firedrake* took *E.1* in tow and *E.5* was taken in tow by *Lurcher*. However, the destroyers slipped the tows early and turned back just after midday, having been recalled by Keyes. The two submarines proceeded together on their diesels at their 12 knot cruising speed. They parted company in the darkness and continued separately on their way from 11pm. Benning spotted a zeppelin as the light came up at 5am, on patrol 10 miles to the east. *E.5* dived for 10 minutes until it was out of sight heading northeast. A zeppelin was also sighted by Laurence at 1:35pm off the Danish coast at Bovbjerg, heading south. *E.1* dived until it was out of sight. The *L.3* had been out scouting to cover a sortie by German surface minelayers and did not report any sightings.[11] Both submarines arrived off Skagen at around 4am the next day, the 24th. They both waited briefly on the surface for the sun to come up before proceeding on their reconnaissance.

E.1 proceeded down the Danish Coast past Hirsholm Island. An accident in the engine room now resulted in Leading Stoker Arnold F. Batchelor severely crushing two of his fingers. He needed better medical attention than the crew of *E.1* could provide. At 10:50am Laurence stopped to ask the skipper of a Danish fishing boat if he could take Batchelor in to a hospital. He agreed to take him in to nearby Frederikshavn. The skipper's command of English was very limited, but Laurence understood him to have seen German warships both anchored and patrolling north of Skagen recently. After examining the channel west of Læsø, then the island itself, *E.1* headed to Anholt Island. Laurence stopped for the night five miles south of the lighthouse at 6pm. The next day he decided not to examine the entrances to the Baltic through the Storebælt and Lillebælt as planned. Instead he got underway at 5am to examine Aalborg Bay, planning to devote his last day to searching for the German patrol described by the fisherman. *E.1* spent the night on the bottom off Skagen Lighthouse.

Laurence searched along the coast west from Skagen for the German patrol on the 26th but found nothing. A leak had developed in the crank case in the bilges which could not be stopped. A great deal of lubricating oil was being lost when *E.1* rolled in the increasingly heavy seas. The westerly wind was increasing and Laurence noticed that the Skagen Lighthouse had hoisted a storm warning. It would be unwise to try and make the rendezvous, since *E.1* would run out of lubricating oil before getting back home. Laurence decided to remain in the Kattegat until the weather moderated. He took *E.1* into the shelter of the Danish east coast to ride out the storm. *E.1* stayed there watching the steamer routes for the next two days. There was a lot of neutral steamer traffic up and down the Danish coast, plus some steamers rounding Anholt going both to and from The Sound, the main entrance to the Baltic between Denmark and

---

10   TNA ADM137/2067: p.220.
11   Groos, *Nordsee 2*, Karte 5.

Sweden. Laurence sighted two vessels sweeping the horizon with searchlights 15 miles to the east for several hours from 11pm on the 28th. As soon as it was light he headed out to investigate but found nothing; it was later realised to have been Göteborg harbour lights. The weather had calmed, so the leak was now under control. Laurence headed back to Gorleston, arriving at 10pm on the 30th. *E.1* returned to Harwich at noon the next day.

Batchelor was interned on a depot ship in Copenhagen Harbour after being treated. Diplomatic efforts finally got him released on 29 November 1915 and repatriated back to Britain, where he returned to submarine service.[12]

E.5 had submerged for the last hour of her journey to Skagen on the 24th to avoid a fleet of suspicious trawlers. Benning then got underway, crossed the Kattegat and headed down the Swedish coast as far as the approach to The Sound. One unusual problem was that: 'Many small islands along this coast much resembled torpedo craft, at a distance of 7 or 8 miles.' He crossed back over the Kattegat and stopped at 3pm, seven miles west of Hesselø Light, off the main Danish Island of Sjælland, then anchored for the night. Benning had seen little commercial traffic all day. The next day visibility was an excellent 14 miles. He examined the approach to the only other entrances to the Baltic, the Storebælt and Lillebælt, from Schultz Grund Light Vessel, but saw nothing. *E.5* headed back towards the Swedish coast. Benning decided to dive and close in to examine a large steamer, but on surfacing one mile away from her she hoisted the Danish flag. He headed back up the Swedish coast in the afternoon. In the evening there was considerable commercial traffic heading down the coast between Skagen and The Sound. *E.5* passed Hållö Lighthouse at 2am, then five hours later turned southwest to head for the rendezvous in the Skagerrak. Benning met several steamers on the southern Norwegian coast, then headed out into a heavy sea off Ryvingen Light.

E.5 arrived at the rendezvous co-ordinates at 8am on the 27th. The light cruiser *Nottingham* was soon sighted three miles away to the north, followed by the armoured cruiser *Drake*. Jellicoe had despatched *Drake*, along with two destroyers of 4th Flotilla, to meet the submarines and offer a tow if required. An elaborate routine was put in place to reduce the risk of mistaken identity. A destroyer was first to show her silhouette to any submarine sighted, then confirm her identity before the cruiser closed. The Battle Cruiser Squadron and Light Cruiser Squadron were later ordered to the same area to intercept a feared breakout by the German liner *SS Prinz Friedrich Wilhelm* from internment in Bergen. As a result *Nottingham* was ordered to take over escort duty for the submarines from *Drake*.[13]

E.5 therefore had an impressive reception committee as the battle cruisers also came into sight. Benning made his report for onwards transmission by the powerful wireless of *Drake*. After waiting in vain for Laurence until 11:40am, *E.5* got underway with *Nottingham* and the destroyer *Cockatrice*. They headed to make landfall off the Farne Islands on the Northumberland coast, at an easy seven knots into the heavy weather. The direction would minimise the chance of encountering German vessels. If separated they were to rendezvous 10 miles off St Abbs Head. It was too rough for a tow. At 6pm *E.5* took position behind *Cockatrice*. Benning lost sight of her at around 1am next morning, after vainly signalling for her to reduce speed in the worsening seas. At 11am the wind started blowing from the northwest and *E.5* was forced off course to steer into it. Nearer land the sea was calmer. *E.5* was able to get back on course and increase speed, arriving off Coquet Island, well to the south of her intended position, at 11am. A destroyer of the coastal patrol soon closed in. Benning asked her to signal *Nottingham* to report her arrival. *E.5* secured safely alongside in Blyth harbour at 1:30pm.

That evening Benning telephoned ahead to ask the Captain of 7th Destroyer Flotilla at Newcastle to inform the coastal patrols that he was heading for Grimsby next day, the 30th. *E.5* rounded Flamborough Head at 1:05pm. Out of the blue, the Grimsby armed trawler *Ariadne* fired a gun at *E.5*. Benning stopped and dived. Although *Ariadne* only had a small 3-pdr (47mm) gun, this could still have caused serious damage. Fortunately no harm was done. Benning blew his tanks to re-surface within five minutes. He does not mention how the mistaken identity was sorted out. *E.5* may not have actually completed the dive before *Ariadne*'s crew realised their mistake. Her apologetic skipper then came aboard. He had been told there were no British submarines in the area and had prepared his explosive sweep for dropping before firing the gun. This was a crude early anti-submarine device – essentially a looped line rigged with explosive charges that could be fired if a submarine was 'caught' with it. Benning ordered *Ariadne* to proceed ahead of him. At 5pm he reached the Humber. Fog was obscuring the war signal station, so he stopped at the Spurn Light Vessel and sent in *Ariadne* to get permission to enter. She returned at 7:50pm and *E.5* followed her in to anchor for the night off Grimsby.

The following day, 1 October, Benning arranged for an escort for the rest of the journey. He left at 8pm with one of the Humber based destroyers. He was then handed from destroyer to destroyer down the coast as he passed through each patrol beat. *E.5* finally secured alongside *Maidstone* at 9:15pm on the 2nd. She had left Harwich on the 19th with 10,700 gallons of diesel. After 1,660 miles she had used 6,550 gallons. The Es had certainly proved they could undertake a long range mission.[14]

Keyes reported to Sturdee that the reconnaissance had shown there were no German forces patrolling the Kattegat, unless they were in Swedish or Norwegian ports at the time, which was unlikely. This was true, as German patrols did not extend beyond the southern exit from the Sound in the Baltic. Keyes commends Benning for bringing his boat through three days of heavy weather without damage and Laurence for good judgement in delaying his return to ensure he got his leaky boat back. His failure to make the rendezvous off the Skagerrak had caused some anxiety about the fate of *E.1*.[15] The patrol also shows the problem of boats showing up in waters where they were not expected. Patrol vessels were likely to shoot first and ask questions later when dealing with submarines they were not familiar with. It would have been better to avoid the coast altogether as Laurence did.

It also has to be said that there were better ways to collect intelligence in this area. Anyone with a pair of binoculars could monitor the shipping movements through The Sound as Sweden and Denmark were both neutral. The presence of German Naval forces patrolling in the Kattegat would quickly have been reported. This is exactly what had happened to the two British submarines in the busy shipping lanes. The patrol blew the element of surprise for the proposed breakthrough to the Baltic and could easily have resulted in the closure of the only

---

14   TNA ADM137/2067: pp.226–8, TNA ADM173: *E.5* 19 September-2 October 1914.
15   TNA ADM137/2067: pp.221–2.

remaining passage to get there. Denmark had already been forced by German demands to close all passages into the Baltic through her waters with minefields.

Submarine sightings in the Skagerrak and off Vinga on the 23rd and 24th were combined with the sighting of Beatty's battle cruisers at the entrance to the Skagerrak and turned by the rumour mill into reports of an attack by the British Fleet. This force was said to have penetrated into the Baltic via the Storebælt between the main Danish islands of Fyn and Sjælland! The report caused Prinz Heinrich, commander of the German Baltic Naval Forces, to call off a major operation on the Russian Coast and scramble to get his ships back to the other end of the Baltic. The High Sea Fleet began preparations to move through the Kiel Canal into the Baltic. The rumour apparently originated with a report by a Swedish soldier, which was misheard by a German agent and passed up through the consular staff in Sweden to the German High Command! This misinformation was identified within 24 hours as a false alarm, but once the wheat was sorted from the chaff, the submarines had been well and truly spotted. A German Foreign Office note to Sweden of 30 September confirmed the sightings: 'Five British battle cruisers, each with a submarine, sighted in the Skagerrak on September 23 or 24. On the 24th off Vinga a submarine. On the 25th a British submarine stopped a Swedish fishing boat between Läsö and Anholt. On the 24th a British submarine landed a sick sailor at Hirsholm, then headed towards Läsö. On the 25th a British submarine was sighted off Hesselö.' Whilst the exact details were a little off, the results read like a show the flag cruise. The sighting off Vinga of *E.5* even correctly identified the submarine as an E class.

The direct result was that Germany renewed pressure on Sweden to block the only remaining entry and exit point into the Baltic; the Flintrinne channel, which passed through Swedish territorial waters in The Sound. Sweden was better placed to ignore German sabre-rattling than Denmark. The diplomatic push failed to get the Flintrinne closed, but an additional mine barrier was laid by the Germans to close the approaches to Kiel and the watch off the southern exit from The Sound was reinforced. Four submarines were despatched to search the Skagerrak and northern Kattegat on the 30th, but Laurence and Benning had gone.[16]

---

16   Rudolph Firle, *Der Krieg zur See 1914–1918 – Der Krieg in der Ostsee Band 1* (Berlin: Mittler und Sohn, 1921), pp.150-2, 168–9, 174-5.

13

A lucky escape

The weather had delayed orders for the next patrol into the Bight until 21 September. The billets were loosely defined. *D.2* was to patrol off the Ems, with *D.4* cruising 25 miles to the northeast. *E.4* was to cruise between Horns Reef and Heligoland, whilst *E.6* cruised to the south and west of Heligoland. Submarines were to depart next morning and return on the evening of the 25th, with discretion to stay an extra day. The orders included the new instruction to return if severe westerly weather threatened.[1]

The successful work of the Flotilla in difficult conditions was also getting noticed. Churchill had asked Keyes to inform both Leir and Talbot before they left for the patrol that they were to receive early promotion. Talbot's reaction was modest surprise: 'It seems extraordinary, and very hard luck on all the people senior to me.'[2]

The boats left together from Harwich at 9:40am on the 22nd. They expected new orders at Lowestoft. News had come in that *Hogue* and *Aboukir* were sinking off the Dutch coast, probably as a result of a submarine attack. However, Orfordness Coastguard Station signalled a message to Leir to execute their original orders as they passed by. They split up at 4pm off Smith's Knoll to head to their billets.

Jameson's *D.2* arrived off the Ems to a calm sea and good visibility on the morning of the 23rd. At 10am he met the German patrols. Eight destroyers were sighted, covering all of the buoyed channels into the Western Ems, patrolling from two to six miles outside. All but two of them were working in pairs, steering at high speed on unpredictable courses. They were of the relatively old *S.114* and *S.82* classes. Jameson dived under the patrol to approach the main entrance. He was unable to see anything inside except a column of smoke in the distance, as a haze had developed. The direction was consistent with the previously reported cruiser position. He dived out to the north in the afternoon and saw the smoke move upriver at sunset. *D.2* spent the night on the bottom. The next morning there was flat calm with only moderate visibility. Jameson spent the day off the Eastern Ems entrance with Borkum and Juist in sight. Having seen nothing patrolling, he moved out to sea in a fog at 4pm and decided to spend the night on the surface. The next morning, the 25th, visibility had improved somewhat. Jameson closed the

---

1   TNA ADM137/2067: p.231. These orders specify return on the 23rd! Apparently an incorrect draft. It is unnumbered and presumably amended on issue.
2   IWM: Documents.20134: 20 September 1914.

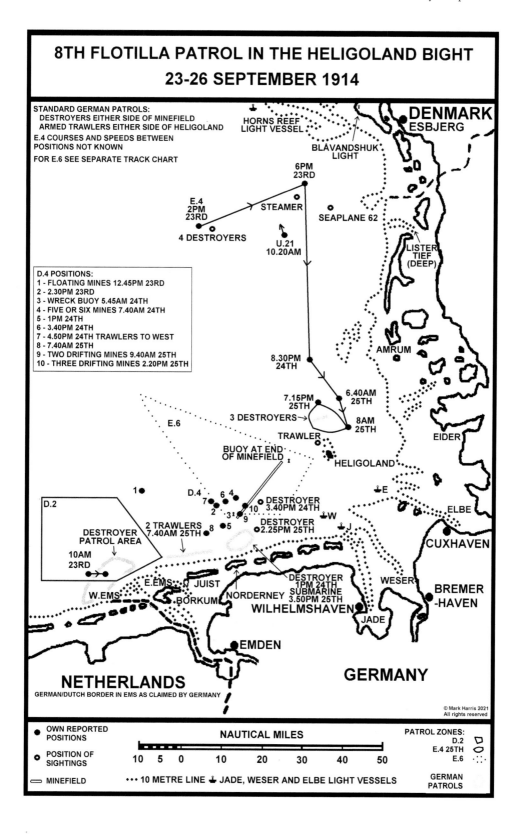

8TH FLOTILLA PATROL IN THE HELIGOLAND BIGHT
23-26 SEPTEMBER 1914

STANDARD GERMAN PATROLS:
DESTROYERS EITHER SIDE OF MINEFIELD
ARMED TRAWLERS EITHER SIDE OF HELIGOLAND
E.4 COURSES AND SPEEDS BETWEEN
POSITIONS NOT KNOWN

FOR E.6 SEE SEPARATE TRACK CHART

HORNS REEF
LIGHT VESSEL

DENMARK
ESBJERG

BLÅVANDSHUK
LIGHT

6PM
23RD

E.4
2PM
23RD

STEAMER

SEAPLANE 62

4 DESTROYERS

U.21
10.20AM

LISTER
TIEF
(DEEP)

D.4 POSITIONS:
1 - FLOATING MINES 12.45PM 23RD
2 - 2.30PM 23RD
3 - WRECK BUOY 5.45AM 24TH
4 - FIVE OR SIX MINES 7.40AM 24TH
5 - 1PM 24TH
6 - 3.40PM 24TH
7 - 4.50PM 24TH TRAWLERS TO WEST
8 - 7.40AM 25TH
9 - TWO DRIFTING MINES 9.40AM 25TH
10 - THREE DRIFTING MINES 2.20PM 25TH

AMRUM

8.30PM
24TH

6.40AM
25TH

7.15PM
25TH

3 DESTROYERS →

8AM
25TH

EIDER

TRAWLER

E.6

BUOY AT END
OF MINEFIELD

HELIGOLAND

1

D.4

6 4

E

D.2

7
2   3 10 DESTROYER
3.40PM 24TH

ELBE

DESTROYER
PATROL AREA

2 TRAWLERS
7.40AM 25TH

8   5

9

W

DESTROYER
2.25PM 25TH

CUXHAVEN

10AM
23RD

E.EMS   JUIST

W.EMS

BORKUM

NORDERNEY

DESTROYER
1PM 24TH
SUBMARINE
3.50PM 25TH
WILHELMSHAVEN

WESER

JADE

BREMER
-HAVEN

EMDEN

NETHERLANDS

GERMANY

GERMAN/DUTCH BORDER IN EMS AS CLAIMED BY GERMANY

● OWN REPORTED
  POSITIONS

NAUTICAL MILES

PATROL ZONES:
D.2
E.4 25TH
E.6

○ POSITION OF
  SIGHTINGS

10 5 0   10   20   30   40   50

⬭ MINEFIELD

••• 10 METRE LINE ⚓ JADE, WESER AND ELBE LIGHT VESSELS

GERMAN
PATROLS

Western Ems entrance. He met the patrol at 8:30am. There were only four destroyers working separately. Once again he dived under them to observe the entrance. He stayed until 1:40pm, by which time it was getting hazy and the destroyers were becoming 'very irritating'. He retired to the northwest to spend the night on the surface in the murk. On the 26th, his fourth day on patrol, the wind had strengthened and visibility was only moderate. He patrolled up and down outside the destroyer patrol but sighted nothing all morning. With mist again closing in he headed back to Harwich at 4pm, arriving the next morning. Jameson's report of German patrol arrangements was extremely accurate, right down to the destroyer types. He draws attention to the fact that at night no patrol vessels were encountered. Various moored wooden buoys and floats positioned off the Ems were reported, which turned out to be solid when shot at with rifles.[3]

D.4 had a new commander on his first war patrol, Lieutenant-Commander John R.G. Moncreiffe, aged 30. He was the son of Baronet Moncreiffe and later inherited the title. The evaluation: 'No special defects or high qualifications' sums up his early service. He had joined the Submarine Service in 1906 but had suffered a string of health issues commanding a succession of coastal boats. He had only: 'made some good attacks' according to Captain Johnson. In 1911 Keyes had evaluated him as: 'Not physically strong. Unless his health improves he is not likely to be fit to stand life in a [submarine].' After a leave of absence he had returned in 1913 to command C.9 in the 6th Flotilla based in the Humber. He relieved Bruce in command of D.4 on 7 September.[4]

Moncreiffe had E.6 in sight for most of the morning as he approached his billet on the morning of the 23rd. D.4 passed about six objects in the water shortly after noon. They resembled mines, but rifle fire had no apparent effect. Moncreiffe arrived at his billet at 2:30pm. It was a few miles west of the southern end of the German minefield. He patrolled all afternoon, but only sighted a single trawler to the east. D.4 went to the bottom for the night at 7:45pm.

When D.4 surfaced at 5:45am an uncharted black wreck buoy was spotted nearby. Norderney Lighthouse was in sight, allowing a good position fix. The buoy was at the southern end of the unknown mine line! Moncreiffe headed north for a few miles charging, then east, which brought him across the mine line at 7:40am. D.4 passed five or six objects which looked like mines. The closest two resembled Leon mines. This was a British fixation early in the war; it was a drifting mine that oscillated in depth. The German Navy had purchased a small number, but they were unserviceable and never used. However, the mines were real enough. They were of the standard German moored spherical horned type. The storms over the previous week caused some of them to break free, or surface after dragging into shallower water. Smoke was now spotted ahead. D.4 dived to periscope depth. A submarine, apparently E.6, was spotted diving at 10am. Moncreiffe surfaced an hour later and headed back to the west, passing occasional wooden wreckage and a dead body. He spent the afternoon patrolling, apart from an hour stopped to charge the battery. Occasionally vessels were sighted in the distance, including two destroyers, a group of sailing drifters and a group of steam trawlers. D.4 dived each time, but nothing approached. Moncreiffe went to the bottom at dusk, returning to the surface for an hour to finish charging the battery during the night.

3   TNA ADM137/2067: pp.234–5.
4   TNA ADM196/143/407: John Robert Guy Moncreiffe.

The next morning, the 25th, *D.4* surfaced at 6:30am and headed inshore. Moncreiffe soon sighted two trawlers: 'steering zig zag courses passing about five miles inshore of me' and dived to observe them. They met, then returned the way they had come. Moncreiffe surfaced and saw two more drifting mines whilst patrolling near the black buoy, then headed out west to halt for a couple of hours to charge. On returning at 2:25pm three mines were sighted drifting to the south, thought to be those first seen in the morning. A few minutes later a destroyer was sighted near the coast, heading rapidly to the east. Moncreiffe dived to observe until it went out of sight. A submarine was sighted in the distance to the south when *D.4* surfaced at 3:50pm. Moncreiffe closed, deliberately passing the mines seen earlier! A rifle was used to attempt to sink them at a range of 150 yards (140m). Despite 11 hits on one mine, no effect was observed. German mines exploded only when one of their horns was broken.

Moncreiffe finally retired west and dived to the bottom for the night at 6:20pm. He surfaced 12 hours later to a slight haze and a threatening sky, with the wind and sea increasing. After sitting to charge the batteries, *D.4* headed west into increasingly heavy seas. Nothing was seen all day and Moncreiffe altered course for Harwich at 4:36pm, arriving at 3pm the next day, the 27th.[5]

On the 23rd *E.4* was 50 miles west of the Lister Deep, heading for her patrol billet in good visibility. At 2pm Leir spotted two destroyers ahead and smoke from two more to the south. He reports that: 'One destroyer signalled to me on searchlight and steamed round me with flag and shape signal flying.' *E.4* dived and it took an hour for the destroyers to go out of sight to the south. Leir left it another hour before he surfaced. He finally arrived off the Danish coast at 6pm, fixing his position by the light of Blåvandshuk Lighthouse. *E.4* went to the bottom at nightfall.

Next morning Leir surfaced at 5:30am to a clear sky and sighted a small steamer heading south, apparently making for a German port. This was the only commercial steamer seen on the entire patrol. Leir headed slowly south, keeping in about 10 fathoms (18m) of water to give himself space to dive safely. A patrolling aeroplane passed four miles away. Leir then spotted a German submarine of the latest type coming into sight from the south at 10:20am. *E.4* dived and began an attack run. Leir was unable to get closer than one mile: 'When she had passed came to surface; followed in her wake course North (true), to clear Horn Reef.' Leir lost sight of her after an hour and resumed his cruise to the south. Nothing more was seen that day and *E.4* went to the bottom for the night off Amrum Island at 8:30pm.

There were clear skies and a smooth sea on surfacing at 5:30am next morning, the 25th. Leir resumed his southerly course. Heligoland came into sight an hour later, 13 miles away. *E.4* dived and closed to within seven miles. Leir surfaced for a look around at 8am: 'No large vessels appeared to be anchored East of Heligoland. An armed trawler was patrolling to the West and North of Island.' *E.4* dived and spent the rest of the day patrolling back and forth to east and west, coming up to look round for half an hour every two hours. Leir saw nothing else and went to the bottom for the night at 7:15pm. Next morning *E.4* surfaced at 5:30am and headed south, but visibility was now only about four miles and the wind had caused a swell. Two destroyers soon passed in the opposite direction off the coast to the east. *E.4* dived until they were out of sight. Suddenly a torpedo boat came out of the sun at 8am. Leir dived to avoid it, but thought he

5   TNA ADM137/2067: pp.236–7; TNA ADM173: *D.4* 22-27 September 1914.

had been seen. He surfaced again when it was out of sight and resumed course, in deteriorating weather. At 11:30am he broke off the patrol to return to Harwich, arriving at 1:45pm on the 27th. Like Jameson, Leir draws attention to the absence of any sounds of patrolling at night.[6]

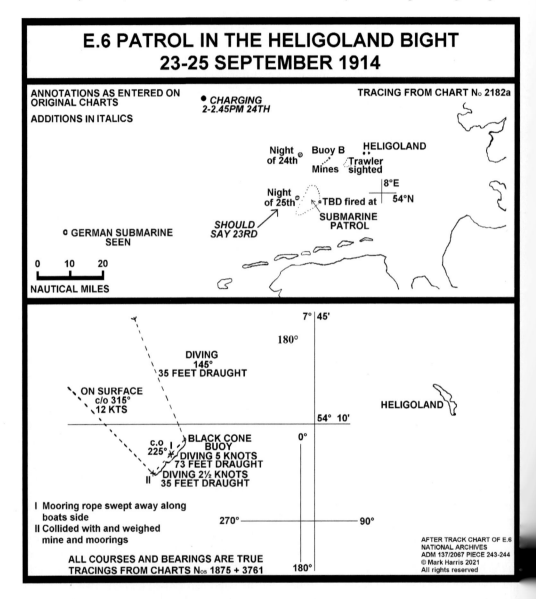

E.6 PATROL IN THE HELIGOLAND BIGHT
23-25 SEPTEMBER 1914

ANNOTATIONS AS ENTERED ON ORIGINAL CHARTS

ADDITIONS IN ITALICS

● *CHARGING*
2-2.45PM 24TH

TRACING FROM CHART No 2182a

Night of 24th   Buoy B   HELIGOLAND

Mines   Trawler sighted

Night of 25th   ●TBD fired at   8°E   54°N

SUBMARINE PATROL

SHOULD SAY 23RD

○ GERMAN SUBMARINE SEEN

0   10   20

NAUTICAL MILES

7° | 45'

180°

DIVING
145°
35 FEET DRAUGHT

ON SURFACE
c/o 315°
12 KTS

HELIGOLAND

54° 10'

c.o 225°   BLACK CONE BUOY   0°
DIVING 5 KNOTS
73 FEET DRAUGHT
II   DIVING 2½ KNOTS
35 FEET DRAUGHT

I Mooring rope swept away along boats side
II Collided with and weighed mine and moorings

270° ———————— 90°

ALL COURSES AND BEARINGS ARE TRUE
TRACINGS FROM CHARTS Nos 1875 + 3761

180°

6   TNA ADM137/2067: pp.238–9; TNA ADM173: *E.4*, 22-27 September 1914.

Talbot's *E.6* was following the same route as Moncreiffe on the 22nd. It was an exceptionally clear night. Talbot saw gun flashes or searchlights to the southeast as he crossed the Southern Bight. He altered course to investigate. After 10 minutes he realised it was the supposedly extinguished IJmuiden Lighthouse, around 50 miles away! Thus proving that even an officer with good sea experience can be deceived by weather phenomena. Talbot resumed course, frequently being forced to avoid trawlers during the night. He dived as the sky grew light and surfaced a couple of hours later off Terschelling at 6:37am. A Swedish timber carrier was passing by heading south. A few minutes later a German submarine surfaced only a mile away to the north. She seemed to react to the presence of *E.6* and dived. Talbot followed suit, turned north for three miles to get clear, then surfaced to resume the journey. He later stopped when another submarine was sighted, but it turned out to only be sailing vessels. At noon *E.6* apparently passed the same objects seen by *D.4* but logs several moored fishing 'P buoys' and a metal buoy, not potential mines. *D.4* was recognised ahead an hour later. In contrast *E.6* had been in sight from *D.4* almost all morning. Perhaps a result of *E.6*'s lookouts facing the sun. Talbot's billet was beyond *D.4*. He worked round and *D.4* disappeared astern.

E.6 reached her billet at 3pm and stopped. A large amount of smoke was soon sighted from a trawler patrol to the east. Talbot dived and half an hour later: 'Sighted two German submarines on the surface, with their funnels up and belching forth smoke', apparently patrolling.[7] He steered to intercept. They turned away 15 minutes later. Talbot followed to what he thought was their patrol line. At some point he had crossed the unknown German minefield. *E.6* surfaced at 5:10pm. Talbot immediately: 'Sighted hostile submarine on surface, proceeding on gas [diesel] engine.' He dived to attack. The sun set. He now saw the new moon through the periscope, 'which would have horrified Dill.' His wife obviously subscribed to the superstition that it was bad luck seeing a new moon through glass! Talbot continued the attack for half an hour, keeping his night vision by wrapping his head in a black cloth he had made especially for the purpose. The attack was abandoned when the target turned away into the growing darkness. *E.6* went to the bottom for the night at 6pm. The estimated position was near the middle of the German minefield! Talbot surfaced at 7:30pm to charge the batteries. Forty-five minutes later: 'Two bright white lights, horizontal, showed about 400 yards [375m] away for about 10 seconds, followed by a single green light.' It was assumed to be a German destroyer showing recognition lights, *E.6*: 'Returned hurriedly to the bottom.'

Talbot rose to periscope depth at 6:20am next morning, the 24th. A German submarine was sighted in the periscope, but quickly disappeared southward. *E.6* surfaced and headed east. An hour later smoke was sighted approaching from the direction of Heligoland. Talbot dived and began an attack run, expecting another submarine. He reached the ideal attack position 500 yards (450m) from the target twenty minutes later at 8:13am. It was a destroyer. He confides to his diary that he 'could not resist the temptation of a shot.' The sea was a glassy calm; standing orders discouraged shots at destroyers in these conditions. Talbot ordered the bow tube to fire. The torpedo had been set to run shallow at five feet (1½m). It was apparently a Mark V* cold torpedo set for 3,000 yards (2,750m) long range, an unimpressive 22 knots. This had presumably been chosen for reliable depth keeping but left more time for the destroyer to react. Changing it would have taken far too long. The destroyer 'must have seen the burst of air on firing, circled

---

7   The first 18 German U–Boats employed funnels for their paraffin engines on the surface.

round, and opened fire on me from about 200 yards [175m] range, I having shown my periscope standards.' Talbot later added a note in his diary that the torpedo had probably run under. This could have been the case if the destroyer crossed the track at such short range. Talbot took *E.6* down to a safe depth of 50 feet (15m) and steered west. The propellers of the destroyer thrashed overhead several times. He slowed to just two knots to conserve the battery.

Talbot had fired at *G.193* of 2nd Torpedoboots-Halbflottille, which immediately wirelessed sighting a submerged submarine, later adding that a torpedo had missed her. The tactical square reported corresponds with Talbot's chart. Such reports had become a regular occurrence. The recent sinking of *Hela* appears to have made lookouts in the Bight very edgy. The minelayer *Kaiser* reported being chased by a submarine and having two torpedoes fired at her east of Heligoland later that morning; a complete fantasy. Two submarines were despatched from Heligoland to investigate the reports and more went out next morning to search off Heligoland to both north and south but reported nothing.[8]

Meantime, Talbot rose to periscope depth at 9:50am for a look around, saw nothing and surfaced 10 minutes later. He was preparing to get underway when 5 feet [2m] of periscope was spotted less than a mile away. *E.6* quickly dived and headed farther west for an hour. Unknown to Talbot, it was *D.4* and Moncreiffe had recognised *E.6*. Talbot tells his wife that he: 'Rose to the surface, my battery getting low and I being determined to get out and charge up.' Once again a periscope was spotted, ¾ of a mile away, moving fast through the water. Talbot immediately got going on the starboard motor while the port diesel engine was started. Once this was done he stopped the motor to get the starboard diesel started. Meanwhile a submarine, presumed to be German, had surfaced and begun following *E.6* three miles astern. Talbot was safe from torpedoes. He 'did not worry about her, as though they carry a gun we are pretty hard to hit.' As soon as the second diesel was started Talbot ordered maximum speed – 15 knots – and turned northwest out to sea. The following submarine, actually *D.4*, apparently stopped after half an hour. This illustrates both how easy it was to spot a periscope in calm water and how difficult it was to identify even a familiar submarine end on!

Talbot once again crossed the minefield. He reduced speed to 12 knots and began charging the battery. Once far out to sea he stopped to complete the charge at 2pm. After 45 minutes *E.6* headed back to her billet. Talbot spotted a large amount of smoke ahead in increasingly heavy mist 18 miles west of Heligoland at 5pm. He dived, then broke surface, trimmed down with only the conning tower showing to observe. *E.6* soon went to the bottom when the light faded. Three vessels were heard to pass overhead at 10pm.

E.6 came off the bottom, then, remaining submerged, headed east towards Heligoland at 6:10am on the 25th. Talbot continued on the surface once it was full daylight. There was a mist with the sun shining above it, no sign of the German submarine patrol that he had expected and just a glimpse of some smoke. Heligoland came into view seven miles away at 9:16am. Talbot stopped and trimmed down to keep watch. Some masts were spotted above the mist heading west half an hour later. *E.6* dived and steered to intercept, but the mist prevented anything being seen through the periscope. Talbot was disappointed to find a patrolling trawler on surfacing. He headed southwest and sighted what looked like a trimmed down submarine at

8   The British Naval Staff Monograph incorrectly assumes that *Kaiser* saw *E.4*, but she was not anywhere near her. The writer also assumes she was the steamer sighted by Leir, but *Kaiser* was 50 miles away at the time and already making a panicked return to base.

11:25am. *E.6* dived and began an attack run, but it turned out to be a large black conical buoy. Its calculated position was roughly at the northeast end of the unsuspected minefield. Talbot half surfaced near it to keep watch.

After a short time: 'It got very clear indeed, and as I was in sight from Heligoland I decided to move further out.' *E.6* dived and headed southwest at 73 feet (22m) at five knots. This was the worst possible course, following the exact line of the minefield! The ominous sound of a mooring cable clattered along the entire length of the boat ten minutes later but cleared aft. *E.6* rose to periscope depth, but nothing could be seen. Talbot got underway again at 35 feet (11m) and 2½ knots. *E.6* hit another mooring cable ten minutes later. This time it sounded like it had got fouled forward and was being towed along. Talbot surfaced. On reaching the bridge he saw the alarming sight of a red painted, three foot (1m) diameter horned contact mine, rolling around on the port forward hydroplane. He reports that: 'The end of the hydroplane guard had got between the two chain legs from the lower part of the mine to its mooring rope; the mine and its mooring being weighed [lifted] as the boat rose.' Fortunately the detonator horns were pointing outwards. Talbot put the motors into reverse to stop *E.6* moving forward, then slowly pumped out enough ballast water from the tanks to bring the mine to the surface. Talbot sent his second in command, Lieutenant Frederick A. P. Williams-Freeman, together with Able Seaman Ernest R. Cremer forward with a boat-hook to see what they could do. They were well chosen. Several times the mine was almost off, then rolled back, forcing them to cling to it with the boat hook. A broken horn would have meant certain death for both of them and the end of *E.6*. After half an hour of this, the mine was finally pushed clear with a big kick from both of them, as they pushed the top of it outwards. The mooring cable pulled it back into the sea. It then bobbed back up with a horn just out of the water! Talbot went full speed astern and *E.6* just cleared the mine. He made a very detailed sketch and description of it in his report! Talbot concluded that the buoy seen earlier almost certainly marked the northern end of a mine line running southwest. He tells his wife that: 'Freeman was for coming out diving deep, but as it was nearly high water, I chose the surface.' The ballast tanks were emptied to reduce draught to the minimum. *E.6* then headed northwest at right angles to the supposed mine line for half an hour. Talbot headed straight back to Harwich to report the discovery of the minefield, arriving at 1pm the next day.[9]

The Germans had planned a raiding sortie by their battle cruisers on the 23rd. Three submarines took up a line at dawn west of Lister Deep, with four more in a line north of Terschelling to cover their departure and return. Otherwise the standard destroyer and trawler patrols were out over the four days. *E.4* passed the patrol line at Lister Deep and these could have been the supposed destroyers seen in the distance, but the circling destroyer is unidentified. The submarine seen off Terschelling by Talbot was either *U.28* at the end of the patrol line or *U.9*, which surfaced here at the time reported after a night on the bottom. She was on her way back from her attack on Christian's cruisers, so Talbot may have missed a chance to avenge them. The pair of submarines he stalked that afternoon and the one stalked as darkness fell cannot be identified, but the latter could have been *D.4*, which was close by. Heligoland did report a British submarine to the southwest at 8:36pm, so Talbot may have been seen, or it could

9   TNA ADM137/2067: pp.240-4, TNA ADM173: *E.6*, 22-26 September 1914, IWM: Documents.20134: 22-26 September; IWM: Documents.1003: 28 September 1914.

The crew of *E.6*, probably taken in October 1914. Talbot is seated at the centre with Williams-Freeman to his left. Acting Lieutenant Douglas G. Jeffrey RNR is to Talbot's right and Chief ERA Stevens is next right. Cremer is in the back row fourth in from the left hand end. Stoker 1c John J. Watts, the original owner of the card, is directly in front of Stevens near the right hand end of the front line. (Darren Brown Collection)

be a false report. Coloured recognition light signals were used by German warships. There was no outer patrol line at night, but destroyers still roamed within the Inner Bight off the estuary approaches on anti-submarine patrols. The 16th Torpedoboots-Halbflottille was despatched to investigate the area but found nothing. The only definite sighting of British submarines during the patrol was by the destroyer attacked by Talbot.

The battle cruiser sortie was cancelled because of reports that the British Fleet was at sea. The seven German outpost submarines returned to harbour on the 24th without sighting the British submarines. It was not these, but *U.21* that Leir had stalked that morning, as she headed out for a patrol to the Moray Firth. *E.4* was not reported at any point on her patrol.[10]

Eighth Flotilla had at last identified the German minefield, although *E.6* was lucky to survive her encounter. Keyes gives Freeman and Cremer a mention in his report to the Admiralty. However, he draws the obtuse conclusion that the large number of mines sighted by *D.4* in one place, together with the drifting wreckage seen, were evidence that a mine carrier could have sunk in the vicinity, rather than the obvious conclusion that *D.4* was in a minefield. Talbot was correct that the buoys encountered by *D.4* and *E.6* marked the ends of the minefield, as orders to the minelayer *Nautilus* refer to this 'black buoy' as an end marker. Keyes attributes only the buoy sighted by *E.6* to this purpose in a letter of the 29th to de Robeck. Moncreiffe's judgement in deliberately returning to a mined area seems poor, but Keyes says nothing.

The allocation of overlapping patrol zones had caused problems and was potentially dangerous. One result was that Keyes identifies six German submarine sightings between Norderney and Heligoland. One of these was probably *D.4* and Keyes might have realised that another was definitely *D.4* if Moncreiffe hadn't left his sighting of *E.6* out of his report. None of the other four correspond to known German submarine positions. The reports make it clear that British commanders expected to see submarines on the patrol line and were looking for them. They may have simply seen what they expected to see when spotting small destroyers and trawlers in the distance. The reports gave a false impression of the level of routine submarine patrolling in the Bight, but submarines were being increasingly used to respond to sighting reports. Keyes told de Robeck that he was pushing to have the spot where they patrolled south of Heligoland mined as it is 'an unhealthy spot'. The lack of good targets caused by being near the minefield, combined with apparently high levels of submarine patrolling had created a false impression of both risk and reward in the wider area. The lack of night patrolling outside the Inner Bight was becoming apparent, but Keyes does not yet draw attention to it. His report dismisses the groups of moorings sighted on the patrol as probably fishing buoys. In fact German orders direct that patrol positions are to be marked with inconspicuous mooring buoys.[11]

Back in Harwich the sinking by *U.9* of three of Christian's cruisers, the *Hogue*, *Aboukir* and *Cressy*, in a single attack on the 22nd caused consternation. Keyes and Tyrwhitt had warned repeatedly of the danger. In a bitterly ironic twist Keyes had been awakened at 2am that morning with news that the Director of Mobilisation was acting on his suggestion to exchange married reservists on the ships for young men from the depot ships. He was inquiring as to the numbers available.

---

10   Groos, *Nordsee 2*, p.75–7, Karten 4, 5; BArch:RM92: *Nassau, Nautilus* Kriegstagebuch 23-24 September 1914, *Nautilus* Befehl GB.604 22 December 1914; TNA ADM137/2018 p.273.

11   TNA ADM137/2067: pp.232-3; BArch: RM97: *U.7* Kriegstagebuch, Befehl Führer der U-Boote 9 September 1914.

Keyes reacted immediately to the news of the sinking, received at 7am on the 22nd. Tyrwhitt was at sea with his 3rd Flotilla. *Lurcher* and *Firedrake* were towing *E.1* and *E.5* on their journey to the Kattegat. Keyes 'was feeling very bloody minded and went on board the *Fearless* ... boiling with rage.' He ordered Captain Blunt, commander of 1st Destroyer Flotilla, to raise steam immediately. At 11:05am a signal was received from Tyrwhitt addressed to Keyes, Blunt and Cayley. It confirmed that a submarine was responsible for the attack and asked for destroyers to be sent to cut it off before it could escape back to the Bight. Keyes rang the Admiralty at once and informed the Director of Operations, Rear-Admiral Leveson, of Tyrwhitt's signal, adding that: 'I was going out as a passenger with Blunt ... to hunt the submarines.' Leveson was opposed until he assured him that: 'Blunt was quite agreeable' – who knows whether he really was – and that there was 'no one better qualified than the Commodore of Submarines to hunt submarines.' Keyes knew perfectly well that there was 'no such thing as hunting submarines in the open sea' with existing methods. He told Blunt that his real plan was to strike an immediate counter-blow. This would 'mop up' the Ems destroyer patrol using the detailed information his submarines had accumulated over the last two months. Keyes made a signal to Jellicoe that he was proceeding to sea with *Fearless* and 17 destroyers and would arrive off Terschelling at 6pm. 1st Flotilla set off at a brisk 23 knots at 11:30am.

Waistell was ordered to meet Keyes off Terschelling with *Lurcher* and *Firedrake* to bolster the attacking force. Once underway he again signalled Jellicoe, outlining his proposal for an attack on the night patrol off the Ems at dawn the next morning. He asked if any Grand Fleet forces were in the vicinity, hoping for support. Leir was signalled the news and asked to inform *D.2*, which was still in company, of the impending attack on the Ems, as Jameson would find himself in the area of the attack. Further signals followed between Jellicoe and Keyes. After a hesitant initial response, Jellicoe confirmed at 5pm that two armoured cruisers of 2nd Cruiser Squadron led by the *Achilles* would be 30 miles north of Terschelling to offer support from 5am. He warned that the destroyers should retire at daylight in view of the weak support available. Waistell had dropped his tows, raced off at 30 knots and confirmed that he would be at the rendezvous for 6:30pm.

Keyes told Blunt that 'directly we met *Lurcher* and *Firedrake*, I would hoist my broad pennant on board the former and take him under my command.' Blunt acquiesced as long as Keyes took full responsibility. Since Keyes was senior it is hard to see what else he could have done. *Firedrake* and *Lurcher* arrived and took station astern of *Fearless*. Keyes mini armada was now assembled and heading for the Ems, when just before 7pm a signal came in from the Admiralty to *Fearless*: 'If no submarines seen before dark return to Harwich with flotilla.' Keyes writes that: 'I could not pretend I had not received it'. The message had already been acknowledged. The force was back in Harwich by 7am next morning.

The War Staff had seen his communications with Jellicoe. He was ordered to 'report myself at the Admiralty at once.' Keyes revealed the details in his letter to de Robeck. Sturdee refused to see him. The reprimand was delivered by the First Sea Lord, Admiral Battenberg, who told him that he had exposed his force to attack by the two cruisers in the Ems, adding that 'it was monstrous that I should have taken direction of a flotilla with which I [was] in no way connected.' Keyes was unrepentant. His defence was that he was only there to 'advise' and that the cruisers would have been sunk by the numerous destroyers if they had come out. He implies that Battenberg's heart was not in the reprimand and says he was forgiven by both Battenberg and Sturdee. His mood had been influenced by travel up to London on a train packed with survivors from the sinkings. He had learnt that one of his recent flotilla commanders, Captain Johnson of the *Cressy*, had gone down with his ship. In view of the amount of egg on the face of all concerned with the deployment of the cruisers, the matter appears to have been quietly dropped. In defence of Keyes, it is hard to see that any significant risk was being run, as German heavy units could not have reacted quickly enough to intervene, although there was no night patrol off the Ems anymore! Keyes had not communicated directly with Tyrwhitt about his plans on the day, writing that he was 'fully occupied out of reach' and 'would not mind my borrowing a part of his command for such a purpose'. Tyrwhitt does not appear to have recorded his own view. The whole episode is quintessential Keyes.[12]

Sturdee asked Keyes to submit his views on submarines taking over the patrol beat of the sunken cruisers in the Southern Bight. Keyes responded quickly on the 23rd to pour cold water on the idea. Whilst they could patrol there he considered that 'the few oversea submarines we possess might be very much better employed elsewhere'. He thought that the chance of attack on transiting warships was small in such a wide area and that submarines were unsuitable to report warships promptly, as they had to dive, delaying any report. Keyes suggests the use of trawlers with wireless if the area has to be watched. Since the French appeared keen to send submarines to the North Sea, their coastal types could be assigned to work with them, although their chance of making an attack would be slim. Keyes drew Sturdee's attention to his observation that after the Heligoland Battle 'the enemy's large submarines were undoubtedly kept in their ports.' They were now venturing out to attack again. He proposed that frequent incursions into the Bight would prevent this.[13]

As a result of the cruiser sinkings Southern Force and 7th Cruiser Squadron were dissolved. Christian departed on 1 October. There had been little active engagement between Keyes and Christian. He had even needed to be reminded by Christian to keep him informed about developments. Keyes had also continued to directly copy his orders and reports to his former commander, Jellicoe. His chain of command now reverted back directly to the Admiralty.

---

12 Keyes, *Memoirs*, pp.106-8; TNA ADM137/2067: pp.633-4; TNA ADM186/620: p.162; *Keyes Papers*, pp.31-5, letter to de Robeck 29 September 1914; TNA ADM53: *Lurcher, Firedrake* 22-23 September 1914.
13 TNA ADM137/2067: pp.328-32.

14

Gales and mines

Sturdee did not follow Keyes suggestions about the Broad Fourteens Patrol. Tyrwhitt's destroyers took the place of Christian's cruisers on 24 September and Keyes was to co-operate with them. The orders for the next patrol were also heavily influenced by another German submarine attack. The scout cruiser *Attentive* was narrowly missed by a torpedo in an attack by *U.18* in the Straits of Dover on the afternoon of the 27th. The orders issued later that day called for three submarines to leave at 5pm. *D.3* was to patrol five miles off the buoy near the western end of Terschelling Island, with *E.3* three miles to the North. *E.9* would patrol off the entrance to the Western Ems. They were all to keep a careful watch for German submarines returning from the Straits of Dover. The patrol was to return on the evening of the 30th. They were to make use of their wireless to warn Tyrwhitt's destroyers in the event that a cruiser coming out of the Heligoland Bight got past their position. However, the return of westerly gales to the North Sea would dominate the patrols over the next week.[1]

There is only a file note for Cholmley's *E.3*: 'nothing to report.' However, Keyes reported that *E.3* strained her hydroplanes in the heavy seas off Terschelling and had to abort the patrol early. She was the first to return and secured alongside at Harwich at 7pm on the 29th. She must have patrolled on the 28th and left her billet off Terschelling first thing the next morning. The hydroplanes were quickly back in order.[2]

Boyle's *D.3* arrived at her billet just off Terschelling at 8am on the 28th. The sea was very rough and visibility was only four miles. Boyle ran at slow speed to the northwest. At 5am the next morning: 'Thinking the weather was easing up I proceeded slowly back to my position.' The weather failed to improve and nothing had been seen apart from one trawler. At 11am he abandoned the patrol and headed back to Harwich. It was too late to enter, so at 10:30pm *D.3* anchored outside until morning. Boyle lists his damage as: 'One bridge rail broken and both hydroplanes damaged.' These had only recently been replaced! He reports that the hydroplane damage had only been spotted on the way back, so it was just as well that *D.3* had not needed to dive. It might have been the last thing she ever did. Later that day Boyle took her to Sheerness,

---

1   TNA ADM137/2067: p.246; TNA ADM186/620: pp.66-9.
2   TNA ADM137/2067: p.248; TNA ADM53: *Adamant* 29 September 1914.

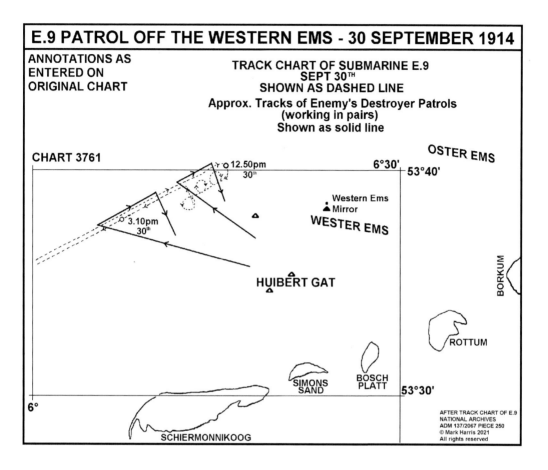

E.9 PATROL OFF THE WESTERN EMS - 30 SEPTEMBER 1914

ANNOTATIONS AS ENTERED ON ORIGINAL CHART

TRACK CHART OF SUBMARINE E.9
SEPT 30TH
SHOWN AS DASHED LINE
Approx. Tracks of Enemy's Destroyer Patrols
(working in pairs)
Shown as solid line

CHART 3761

OSTER EMS

12.50pm 30th

6°30'   53°40'

Western Ems
Mirror

WESTER EMS

3.10pm 30th

HUIBERT GAT

BORKUM

ROTTUM

SIMONS SAND   BOSCH PLATT   53°30'

6°

SCHIERMONNIKOOG

where she was docked and the hydroplanes were removed for repair. The bridge rails were also repaired, along with a faulty periscope motor. *D.3* did not return to Harwich until 7 October.[3]

Horton's *E.9* was passing Terschelling at 9:55am on the 28th in a rough sea and big waves. He sighted a suspicious vessel and dived. It turned out to be just a trawler. However, Horton realised that it would be impossible to make a submerged torpedo attack. An attack on the surface would be possible, but the hydroplanes were being too badly strained by the big waves to return there. Horton decided to go to the bottom to wait out the weather. Even on a soft patch at 116 feet (35m) the submarine was still rolling. He popped up at 3pm, but the weather was 'very bad'. *E.9* went back to the bottom. Horton surfaced at 6am next morning, but the weather was still too bad to navigate from the bridge. He closed the hatch, opened the engine ventilator, started a diesel engine and charged the battery for the next 90 minutes. *E.9* then went back to the bottom again. The weather had started to moderate when she next surfaced at 1:45pm. Cholmley and Boyle had both given up before now. Horton and his crew had spent 28 hours

---

3   TNA ADM137/2067: p.247; TNA ADM173: *D.3* 27 September–7 October 1914.

almost continuously rolling around at the bottom of the North Sea, in stale air, to ensure that *E.9* avoided damage. He now got underway for the Ems. *E.9* went to the bottom again when it got dark at 6:30pm and spent the night, in Horton's words: 'rolling; but bumping very slightly.'

E.9 was back underway again at 5:30am on the 30th. Horton sighted smoke from destroyers off the Ems and dived at 8:12am. *E.9* closed in over the next three hours. There were now four destroyers in sight patrolling in pairs, continually altering their courses and speeds. Horton steered back and forth in their path over the next five hours and made numerous attack runs. He reports that: 'from 11.0 a.m. until 4.0 p.m. ... several snapshots could have been fired. Owing to orders that I was not to fire unless in a very favourable position and a hit fairly certain, no torpedoes were fired. ... The "favourable position" was interpreted to mean between 400 – 500 yards [350–450m] on enemy's beam with both bow tubes bearing and enemy on steady course.' The restrictions imposed to conserve torpedoes had perhaps gone too far. It must have been deeply frustrating after the determined effort to reach the billet. Horton headed back to Harwich that evening as per orders, arriving at 11am on 1 October. It had been another challenging patrol for the crew, but his carefully recorded observations of the destroyer patrol patterns, which are evident from his track chart, would pay dividends on his next visit.[4] The only other German activity was *U.18* returning from the Channel to Heligoland on the 30th. She passed the Ems unseen that afternoon. Horton was not spotted by the Ems patrol.[5]

Keyes commended Horton's determination to stay on station in the prevailing weather in his report on the patrol to Sturdee. He again pushed for Tyrwhitt to be given permission for a raid on the Ems patrol, using the information from his recent reports. He suggests using a flotilla cruiser and about 10 destroyers, striking the day patrol in low visibility for an effective ambush, with the remainder of Harwich Force in support. The Ems cruiser could be ambushed by two or three suitably positioned submarines if she came out. The day chosen should be at Tyrwhitt and Keyes discretion to ensure that the weather was right. Keyes thought a similar plan would work against the destroyer patrol reported by Leir off the Danish coast – he would make a close reconnaissance to confirm the feasibility as part of the next patrol. Keyes also draws attention to the recent lack of night patrols. Their absence had at last become obvious.[6]

The orders for the patrol to the northern Heligoland Bight called for three submarines to leave at 1pm on the 29th. *E.10* was to patrol off the Danish coast between Horns Reef and Lister Deep. On the 26th Germany had directed all merchant shipping entering the Heligoland Bight to enter via Lister Deep Buoy. *E.10* was to occasionally close the Danish port of Esbjerg to confirm whether German warships were interfering with trade there. *E.8* was to patrol in a billet to her southwest, with *D.5* in a billet even farther southwest, well out to sea. They were to keep at least 25 miles clear of Terschelling on the way out to avoid the submarines already on patrol there. All were to return on the evening of 3 October, or at their discretion if fog or heavy weather intervened.[7]

4   TNA ADM137/2067: pp.249–50; TNA ADM53: *Adamant* 1 October 1914.
5   BArch:RM92: *Nassau* Kriegstagebuch 30 September 1914.
6   TNA ADM137/2067: pp.251-3.
7   TNA ADM137/2067: p.257; *Department of State: Diplomatic Correspondence with Belligerent Governments Relating to Neutral Rights and Duties*, (Washington: Government Printing Office, 1916), p.220, Nachrichten für Seefahrer, 26 September 1914.

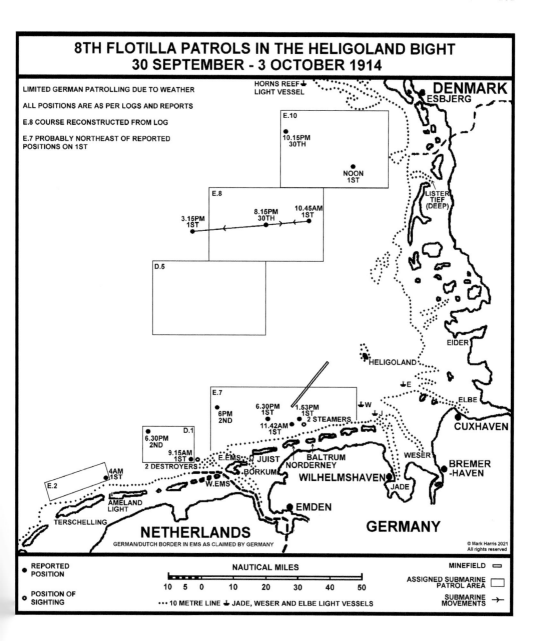

8TH FLOTILLA PATROLS IN THE HELIGOLAND BIGHT
30 SEPTEMBER - 3 OCTOBER 1914

The three submarines left Harwich together and split up off Smith's Knoll. Fraser's *E.10* crossed largely empty sea, seeing only a solitary Norwegian steamer. He arrived off the Danish coast at 10:30pm on the 30th and spent the night on the bottom. *E.10* surfaced at 7am next morning with nothing in sight. The wind was blowing hard and big waves were rolling in from the west. Fraser headed inshore. By noon visibility was down to two miles in heavy rain and steadily worsening seas, made worse by the shallower water. He turned and headed northwest at low speed into deeper water. By 11pm the wind was gale force. He abandoned the patrol. *E.10* reached shelter off Lowestoft at 9pm on the 2nd. The local drifters were already back out working. Fraser anchored for the night and arrived in Harwich at 8am the next morning.[8]

Goodhart's *E.8* arrived in the centre of his patrol billet at 8:15pm on the 30th. There was already a moderate wind blowing. He sounded the depth, dived and after proceeding a bit farther east, settled deep on the bottom for the night in 19 fathoms (35m). Despite the depth, from 3am the boat started to bump on the bottom as the weather worsened above. *E.8* surfaced at 7:30am and headed at six knots to the eastern end of the patrol area. Goodhart then turned back to the west at 10:45am, but had to abandon the bridge and close the hatch, continuing with the ventilators open. Visibility dropped to two miles. The forward hydroplane guards began to work loose in the heavy sea and cause a considerable leak in the boat. The wind increased to a full gale with heavy seas and looked set to get worse. Nothing had been seen. Goodhart decided to return to Yarmouth at 3:20pm, arriving in the harbour at 5:16pm next day, the 2nd. *E.8* returned to Harwich the following morning. She went in to Harwich Dry Dock for repairs to the hydroplanes on the 9th and took the opportunity to do some other maintenance whilst there, including a refit of the troublesome compass and a new coat of paint. *E.8* undocked on the 15th.[9]

Herbert had 'nothing to report' about *D.5*'s patrol but experienced the same weather. He returned to Harwich at 10am on 5 October, implying he remained at his billet for the entire patrol.[10]

Orders for the next patrol to the southern part of the Heligoland Bight were issued on 30 September. Three submarines were to leave Harwich at 11am. *D.1* was to take the billet off the Western Ems and *E.2* a new billet off Terschelling Island. The minefield discovery resulted in only *E.7* being sent to the inner Bight, in a billet between the Weser and Eastern Ems. She was to keep south of the 54th parallel. A hand-written note on the orders by Keyes states that enemy submarines are patrolling on the billet and that it is south of the mines spotted by *E.6*. This was a failure to properly analyse the reports and information from the previous patrol to the area. *D.4* had spotted mines well to the south of the parallel, but Keyes had obviously gone with his sunken minelayer theory to explain this. On hearing the news Hallifax wrote: 'Our billet for the next 3 days is that blooming Heligoland Bight! We all thought that health resort was closed for a season, but a bright thought suggested our presence there.' Keyes told Feilmann to move to another area if he encountered mines! The submarines were to return on the evening of 3 October.

The new patrol pattern meant that submarines in the southern area overlapped the time of their patrols with those in the northern area, so that there would always be submarines off the enemy coast. The southern patrol was timed to ensure that *D.1* relieved *E.9*, ensuring that the Western Ems would be watched without a break.[11]

Following lengthy repairs, this was the first offensive patrol for *E.2*. She was commanded by Lieutenant-Commander David de Beauvoir Stocks, aged 30. He was apparently something of a prankster and a spinner of colourful yarns, associated with a catchphrase of: 'Believe me

8   TNA ADM137/2067: p.260.
9   TNA ADM137/2067: p.259; TNA ADM173: *E.8* 30 September-15 October 1914.
10   TNA ADM137/2067: p.258; TNA ADM53: *Adamant* 5 October 1914.
11   TNA ADM137/2067: pp.262-3.

or believe me not'. Stocks featured regularly in *The Maidstone Magazine*, which refers to him as 'The Baron'. He received first class passes in all of his Lieutenant's examinations and joined the Submarine Service in 1905. After command of various coastal boats Stocks had succeeded Laurence as commander of *D.1*. In 1910 Captain Hall assessed him as: 'Perfectly imperturbable. A past master in a S/M attack, seldom if ever missing his enemy ... most valuable in training younger officers.' He took command of the newly completed *E.2* in February 1913 and soon after Keyes rated him as 'very cool and determined.'[12]

E.2 arrived off Ameland Lighthouse at 4am on the 1st. The sea was rough, which persisted for the next three days. Stocks patrolled between Ameland and Terschelling each day from 6am until 6:30pm from close inshore to 10 miles out, going to the bottom each night. The only thing he reported was four Dutch destroyers off Terschelling on the 2nd. Visibility deteriorated constantly during the patrol. By the 3rd it was never more than 1½ miles, frequently dropping to 500 yards (450m) as a result of mist. *E.2* spent most of the day dived, with only five hours on the surface when visibility improved. Stocks left his billet at 6pm, arriving in Harwich at 9:55am on the 5th, after an overnight stop at Yarmouth.[13]

Cochrane's *D.1* approached the Western Ems cautiously, diving until full light on the morning of the 1st and sounding for depth as the visibility was poor. He suddenly spotted the buoy marking the entrance just two miles ahead at 9:15am. *D.1* stopped. Five minutes later two destroyers came into sight coming out of the entrance, one after the other. Cochrane dived to attack. They were not to be seen through the periscope and had disappeared in the murk. The visibility was too bad to remain inshore. *D.1* spent the day diving at slow speed or resting on the bottom three to five miles offshore until 5:30pm. The night was spent on the bottom. The next day there was a rough sea and a strong northerly wind. *D.1* rose to periscope depth and headed out to patrol on the surface in deeper, calmer water 10 to 15 miles offshore until 6:30pm. Cochrane dived whenever he was not charging the battery. *D.1* again spent the night deep on the bottom, in 21 fathoms (38m). Cochrane surfaced at 6:30am on the 3rd and headed to the Western Ems entrance in a blustery wind. It began raining and within an hour visibility dropped to two or three miles. Cochrane dived to wait for the weather to clear. He gave up at 11am and headed straight back to Harwich, arriving at 2:40pm on the 4th.[14]

Feilmann's *E.7* set off in good weather on the 30th. Hallifax describes the contrast as they approached their billet: 'Very hazy with a nasty steep sea from all directions, the wind rising was from astern. Sometimes a sea would rise up to the level of the bridge and go with us for some moments, the whole boat submerged except for the bow and the top of the bridge!' By 11:42am on the 1st *E.7* was estimated to be north of Norderney. Suddenly, Hallifax saw a large steamer heading directly towards them four miles ahead. He spotted a small steamer following the first as he went below. *E.7* dived and began an attack run. Within a few minutes the lead steamer reversed course, followed round by the other and both disappeared in the mist. *E.7* surfaced 45 minutes later. Feilmann followed their presumed course east at low speed past a buoy, which was apparently marking a channel they were following. There was also a line of spar buoys visible off to the south. Half an hour later Hallifax spotted what he at first took to be a black buoy a

12 TNA ADM196/143/300 & 196/49/62: David de Beauvoir Stocks; Douglas, *Maidstone Magazine*, pp.15, 49, 226, 248.
13 TNA ADM137/2067: p.264.
14 TNA ADM137/2067: p.265; TNA ADM53: *Adamant*, 4 October 1914.

little ahead to starboard. As it came closer mine horns were spotted. Hallifax ordered *E.7* to stop. By the time she came to a halt the mine had been passed, but another was in sight ahead to port. It was moored at the surface, coming into sight between waves. Rifles were brought up to the bridge and fire opened from 100 yards (90m). After some time, the cook, Able Seaman Matthews, who was a marksman, came up to have a go. After he and Leading Seaman Osborne fired together the mine detonated, throwing a column of water and smoke 250 feet (75m) into the air. *E.7* got underway again, turning to the west at low speed, only to encounter another moored mine, about 200 yards (180m) directly ahead. It disappeared in the heavy swell and Feilmann gave the spot a wide berth. *E.7* had predictably encountered the southern end of the minefield. Either she was farther offshore than thought, or some mines had dragged southeast into shallower water in the heavy seas; probably a bit of both.

    E.7 patrolled to the west, sighting Baltrum, then Norderney as the haze cleared. Feilmann headed farther out to sea as the light failed, seeking deeper water to go to the bottom in the rough sea. The steering gear jammed as they were about to dive. Some cotton waste had got into the bottom of the steering compartment. It took an hour to free it, but they went to the bottom at 6:30pm. *E.7* bumped and pitched a little in the swell. There was a faint whiff of chlorine during the night from some water that had got in through the battery ventilators during the day.

    The next morning *E.7* surfaced at 5:54am. She had drifted five miles whilst bumping in the night and the seas were still rough. Feilmann and Hallifax had agreed that pushing east into the mined area was dangerous and pointless. *E.7* patrolled west at very low speed instead, prepared at any moment to stop quickly using the motors. The weather was beginning to moderate and Feilmann decided to remain on patrol, rather than leave early. He turned round with Borkum Island in sight at 11am. The watch passed to Cunard. He caused a stir when he stopped *E.7* and reported 'a big ship ahead.' It was actually a clump of houses on Juist Island, although Hallifax conceded that it looked like a ship without masts! Half an hour later there was a scream of 'stop!' from the bridge, followed by 'full astern port.' Hallifax rushed up with a rifle and Cunard reported having just missed a mine. The lookouts insisted it was a porpoise. Feilmann had also come up and now spotted a seal. Cunard admitted that he had simply spotted a black object in the water which had given him 'the shock of a lifetime.' They had got quite close to Juist, so in the afternoon *E.7* headed northwest into deeper water for the night, with the sea becoming calmer. Feilmann stopped at 4:45pm to make soundings and went to the bottom an hour later. The crew got a rest that night, rolling gently to and fro.

    Feilmann surfaced at 6am on the 3rd to hazy weather and a fairly calm sea. *E.7* returned to a point only five miles off the eastern end of Juist, then turned west to patrol at low speed. The weather was now deteriorating with rain and mist reducing visibility drastically, making patrolling almost impossible. *E.7* increased speed to 10 knots to begin the return journey at 11:30am. In the afternoon she was hit by three big waves in succession, bending the bridge rails, damaging the bridge screen and dumping water down the hatch. *E.7* got back underway at lower speed. The seas moderated after they passed Terschelling. Feilmann insisted on stopping at Yarmouth, arriving at noon on the 4th. As usual he sent Hallifax to report by phone. *E.7* returned to Harwich next morning. Waistell was unhappy that Feilmann had delayed his return at Yarmouth and Keyes wanted to know why he had not reported the minefield immediately himself.[15]

Keyes report speculates whether the two steamers were minelaying, the reason Feilmann gave for starting an attack run. In fact the German Navy had largely suspended patrolling during the high seas and poor visibility of the last week. The steamers were just that and not laying mines.

However, Keyes did now report to Sturdee on the 5th that the Germans had laid a minefield from the marker buoy 10 miles west of Heligoland to Norderney, covering the approach to the Jade, Weser and Elbe. This had already been obvious to Talbot and Hallifax in their diary entries. Keyes concluded that the shallow depth indicated that the mines had been laid to catch destroyers and submarines, but this was a result of some mines being shifted by the storms. It is unfortunate that the patrols since the sinking of *Hela* had gone like moths to a flame to the mined area southwest of Heligoland, ignoring the traffic lanes between the estuaries and Heligoland where she was sunk. Keyes also felt that the buoyed channel which apparently existed to the south of the minefield was 'unsuitable for Submarine work', as they would be unable to dive under enemy vessels. He suggested that seaplanes determine the exact limits of the field, after which submarines could be stationed to watch the exits. Until then Keyes proposed that nothing should be sent to the area east of Juist, and south of a position just north of Heligoland. This seems obtuse, when his submarines themselves could have identified the channels by observing ship movements from safe positions once the weather cleared. Submarines could also easily enter from the north into the area behind the minefield.

Nevertheless, confirmation of the minefield position was vital intelligence for planning future operations. It would restrict the scope of any future raid into the Bight. The Admiralty agreed to the proposal to avoid the area on 7 October.[16]

Whilst the submarines on patrol had been taking their beating from the weather, the Flotilla had been reinforced by the arrival of the brand new *E.11* on the afternoon of 2 October. She had been working up off Barrow, following her completion at the Vickers Yard on 19 September, then headed round the south coast to join the Flotilla. The local golf course was now available for the officers, easing the boredom of hanging around at the Quay. *Firedrake* began to vary the monotony of the crew's staple exercise of route marches by releasing watches to play football ashore. With winter looming gifts of warm clothing were also arriving from family members. Talbot was particularly pleased with a thermos flask and muffler from a distant cousin he had never heard of. The Navy League sent bundles of clothes, food treats and even a gramophone for use in each submarine.[17]

15   TNA ADM137/2067: pp.266-7; IWM:Documents.1003: 30 September-5 October; TNA ADM173: *E.7* 30 September–5 October 1914.
16   TNA ADM137/2067: pp.268–71. The writer of the Naval Staff Monograph incorrectly identifies the presence of numerous trawlers as the reason for abandoning patrolling in the Inner Bight.
17   IWM: Documents.20134: 29 September, 2 October; TNA ADM53: *Adamant, Firedrake*, 2, 8 October 1914.

15

Horton strikes again

The raid that Keyes had been promoting on the Ems day patrol was now to go ahead under the codename Plan V. The orders were finalised by Tyrwhitt. *Arethusa* and *Fearless*, with the fast destroyers of 3rd Flotilla, would make the attack. *Lurcher* and *Firedrake* were lent by Keyes to 3rd Flotilla to boost the destroyer numbers to 16. Half of the destroyers would sweep west from off the Eastern Ems at high speed, cutting off the German day patrol and driving it towards the waiting cruisers and the rest of the destroyers. It was hoped that the two cruisers in the Ems would be drawn out to support the patrol, so that they could be ambushed by submarines lying in wait. One submarine would act as a trigger, showing herself to draw the patrol out to seaward prior to Tyrwhitt's arrival. The plan made good use of the intelligence gathered and had every chance of success if the weather was right.

The submarines needed to depart from Harwich at 8:30am on 3 October, in order to get into position. On the day of the raid, the 4th, *E.9* would patrol off the Western Ems main entrance and *D.2* off the Huibert Gat entrance. *E.6* was the bait, six miles northwest of the Western Ems. The submarines would remain on patrol after the raid, relieving the previous patrol in the southern billets; *E.6* replacing *E.2* off Terschelling and *D.2* replacing *D.1* off the Western Ems. Since *E.7* had not yet returned and had no wireless sending apparatus to report the mines in her billet, *E.9* was sent to replace her between the Eastern Ems and the Weser. The three submarines would patrol until the evening of the 6th unless weather or the need to report important information intervened.

On the morning of the 3rd the bad weather made the attack a non-starter. The submarines were held back. With no sign of improvement, Tyrwhitt informed the Admiralty at 11am that the attack could not go ahead. It was delayed to the 5th, or failing that the 6th, in the hope that the weather would improve.[1]

The submarines were therefore ordered to get underway to relieve the existing patrols and then take up their positions off the Ems on the morning of the 5th. If the raid did not arrive that day, they would again be in position on the 6th. *E.3* replaced *D.2* at the last minute, as she

---

1   TNA ADM137/2067: pp.273; TNA ADM137/2081: Harwich Force: war records of the rear admiral commanding Harwich force (styled Commodore (T)) during the period 1914–1917, Vol. IV, Pack 36 pp.250–2, 257; IWM:Documents.20134: 3 October 1914.

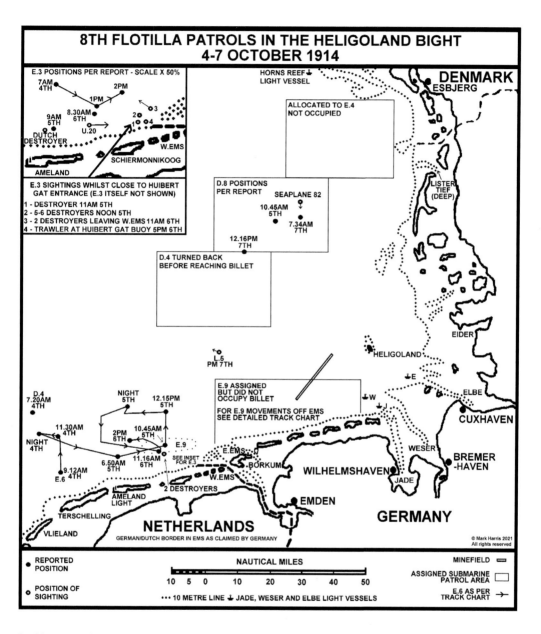

**8TH FLOTILLA PATROLS IN THE HELIGOLAND BIGHT
4-7 OCTOBER 1914**

E.3 POSITIONS PER REPORT - SCALE X 50%

7AM 4TH
2PM
1PM
9AM 5TH
8.30AM 6TH
U.20
3
2
4
DUTCH DESTROYER
W.EMS
SCHIERMONNIKOOG
AMELAND

E.3 SIGHTINGS WHILST CLOSE TO HUIBERT GAT ENTRANCE (E.3 ITSELF NOT SHOWN)
1 - DESTROYER 11AM 5TH
2 - 5-6 DESTROYERS NOON 5TH
3 - 2 DESTROYERS LEAVING W.EMS 11AM 6TH
4 - TRAWLER AT HUIBERT GAT BUOY 5PM 6TH

HORNS REEF LIGHT VESSEL
DENMARK
ESBJERG

ALLOCATED TO E.4 NOT OCCUPIED

D.8 POSITIONS PER REPORT   SEAPLANE 82
10.45AM 5TH
7.34AM 7TH
12.16PM 7TH

D.4 TURNED BACK BEFORE REACHING BILLET

LISTER TIEF (DEEP)

EIDER

L.5 PM 7TH

HELIGOLAND

E.9 ASSIGNED BUT DID NOT OCCUPY BILLET
FOR E.9 MOVEMENTS OFF EMS SEE DETAILED TRACK CHART

E
ELBE
W
J
CUXHAVEN

D.4 7.20AM 4TH
NIGHT 5TH
12.15PM 5TH
11.30AM 4TH
2PM 6TH
10.45AM 5TH
NIGHT 4TH
6.50AM 5TH
11.16AM 6TH
9.12AM 4TH
E.6
E.9
SEE INSET FOR E.3
E.EMS
BORKUM
W.EMS
2 DESTROYERS
AMELAND LIGHT
TERSCHELLING
VLIELAND

WILHELMSHAVEN
WESER
BREMER -HAVEN
JADE
EMDEN
GERMANY

NETHERLANDS
GERMAN/DUTCH BORDER IN EMS AS CLAIMED BY GERMANY

REPORTED POSITION
POSITION OF SIGHTING

NAUTICAL MILES
10 5 0   10   20   30   40   50
••• 10 METRE LINE ⚓ JADE, WESER AND ELBE LIGHT VESSELS

MINEFIELD ▭
ASSIGNED SUBMARINE PATROL AREA ▭
E.6 AS PER TRACK CHART →

had become the latest victim of a faulty clutch. *D.2* left Harwich for repairs and did not return until the 20th.[2]

The three submarines left Harwich at noon. Cholmley, the Senior Officer, ordered them to use different speeds to stagger their arrival at dawn off Terschelling. They split up to head to

2   TNA ADM137/2067: p.334. *D.2* identified as needing clutch repairs by process of elimination.

their billets off the Corton Light Vessel at 4:20pm. As they did so, Cholmley signalled Talbot that he would be off Ameland at 7am each day flying a white ensign over an eight pendant if he had an urgent message to send. He would have to send it using *E.6*'s wireless as *E.3* was not equipped to do so herself; hardly satisfactory for picket duties![3]

The weather failed to improve. Tyrwhitt had to cancel Plan V at 2:45pm on the 4th. It was too late to notify the submarines already on patrol, as they were well out of wireless reception range. They were therefore still assuming that the raid would happen on the 5th or 6th.[4]

Freeman had the watch on *E.6* at 5am on the 4th. After passing through a fishing fleet, he was convinced that he had spotted a German destroyer showing trawler lights in the bright moonlight. Talbot dived and altered course for an hour. However, he did not include the sighting in his report. A trawler was only a mile away when *E.6* came up to periscope depth. Talbot kept going until he was clear, surfacing 40 minutes later. He sighted the west end of his billet, Terschelling, eight miles away at 9:12am. A near gale was blowing from the northwest, with occasional rain showers passing by. *E.6* patrolled north, but only spotted a passing Swedish steamer and a few trawlers. Talbot writes that: 'There was a very nasty sea … my hydroplanes were having a rotten time.' *E.6* was taken to the bottom where she bumped and rolled 10 degrees each way in the turbulent water. Having had enough of this, Talbot surfaced at 4:30pm to 'a vile sea.' *E.6* headed northwest for deeper water, dead slow ahead on one engine with the hatch closed. Talbot took her to the bottom for the night in 'a nice patch of mud & clay' in 17 fathoms (31m), still rolling, but at least not bumping!

E.6 surfaced and headed to rendezvous with *E.3* off Ameland at 4am. The sea and wind had moderated somewhat, but it was now overcast with drizzling rain and mist. Talbot exchanged signals with Cholmley off Ameland Lighthouse at 6:50am, but he had nothing to communicate. *E.6* got underway for the Ems to attempt to bait the patrols, although Talbot did not expect the raid due to the weather. He had to dive a couple of hours later when a destroyer loomed up astern. She went out of sight to the south and was presumed to be Dutch. *E.6* surfaced and arrived off the Western Ems at 10:45am. Talbot patrolled up the planned route of the raiding destroyers in steady rain, 'so as to meet our ships if they came.' He saw nothing. By 1:30pm the mist became too thick to see anything. Talbot dived deep and headed slowly west. After surfacing to charge the battery in very thick mist and rain a couple of hours later, he went to the bottom for the night at 5:40pm. Talbot shifted position after once again bumping around. He found 'a good spot' where *E.6* was only rolling gently.

Talbot surfaced at 6:03am on the 6th and worked back to the Ems via Ameland. *E.3* was not sighted. The wind had shifted northeast and the sea was settling down. *E.6* approached Huibert Gat at 11:16am. Smoke and masts were spotted ahead. Talbot thought that it was too late for the raiding force to turn up. He therefore dived and began an attack run on two patrolling German destroyers. They were constantly altering course. He writes that: 'I was within about 1500 yards [1,400m] of them when they turned away.' Talbot steered out west to get clear. He did not want to surface and risk drawing the German patrol out to sea away from *E.3* and *E.9* in their inshore ambush positions. Soon after this Talbot heard what sounded like a gunshot through the water but saw nothing through the periscope. *E.6* surfaced at 2pm to return to Harwich, dodging through a large fleet of Dutch trawlers around Terschelling as the seas calmed. Talbot slowed to 10 knots in order to arrive off Yarmouth next morning. He had to fall back on the magnetic compass when the newly installed gyrocompass broke down at 7:20pm.

At 5:35am next morning Talbot spotted a Dutch drifter near Smith's Knoll, the *Cosmopolite*. Under new regulations the area was prohibited to neutral flagged fishing boats.[5] Talbot stopped and sent Freeman on board her to issue a warning. This paid dividends; the chastened Dutch crew 'provided us with a lot of fish.' *E.6* reached Harwich at 1pm. Talbot's new baby had been seriously ill, so Waistell granted him a 48 hour leave. He went up to London to see his family at his mother's home. He was relieved to find the baby on the mend, with his mother organising parcels of warm clothing for the 47th Sikhs at the front in France.[6]

Cholmley's *E.3* passed a row of curious black buoys off Ameland at 7am on the 4th. He then dived to pass a grey painted trawler arriving from the east. He was no doubt concerned that it was an armed patrol watching a mine line. *E.3* arrived off the Huibert Gat at 1pm to rough seas and a high wind, but good visibility of 15 miles. He then checked the Western Ems entrance. There was nothing to be seen, even inside the river. He remained on the surface overnight, as *E.3* bumped too much on the bottom.

Next morning rain and mist reduced the visibility at times to less than 100 yards (90m). After the rendezvous with *E.6*, a destroyer suddenly appeared astern at 9am. The ensign was not visible, but she resembled a German D type destroyer and was no doubt the same one seen by Talbot. Cholmley dived until she disappeared inshore. He closed to within 5½ miles of the Huibert Gat entrance, expecting the raid. At 11am he spotted a destroyer, two miles from the entrance buoy. Cholmley dived, but lost sight of it and surfaced. An hour later he was only four miles from the entrance. Visibility was one to two miles. He now spotted a flotilla of five or six destroyers in two groups to the east of him. He dived again. They did not approach and were assumed to have returned to harbour. At 5pm Cholmley headed out northwest to spend the night on the bottom.

At 8:30am on the 6th *E.3* was 11 miles off the Huibert Gat entrance. The wind and sea had calmed and visibility had greatly improved. *E.6* was spotted approaching from the west. As she got nearer, the silhouette became clearer; a German submarine of the U.8–12 type! Cholmley dived and steered to intercept. He was too late. She passed three miles south of him, heading into Huibert Gat. Cholmley had spotted *U.20*. She was heading out on patrol when her periscope was damaged in the heavy seas off Schiermonnikoog. *U.20* headed into the Ems for repairs and did not report seeing *E.3*. *U.28* left the Ems around the same time heading west, but *E.3* did not spot her.

Cholmley trailed *U.20* and closed to three miles off the Huibert Gat entrance. Two destroyers came out of the Western Ems entrance at 11am. The closest, a *G.132* class, was only three miles away. He altered course to position himself off this entrance, hoping that more would follow. Nothing more came out. He eventually headed out west and surfaced. He cruised in on the diesels to the Huibert Gat for the last time at 5pm. Two miles off the entrance he saw a trawler, which had previously not been noticed. She fired off two white rockets. Otherwise, only

---

5   TNA ADM186/620: pp.28-9. Neutral fishing boats were to be treated as suspected minelayers from 1 October. After receiving warnings during a grace period, they were subject to seizure.

6   TNA ADM137/2067: pp.276–9; TNA ADM173: *E.6* 4–7 October 1914; IWM:Documents.20134: 4–9 October 1914.

smoke could be seen upriver. *E.3* had been seen and even identified as an E class. The Ems was already in a state of alarm and she caused quite a stir, getting magnified into two submarines. Cholmley's habit of closing the shore on the surface had tipped off his presence and was risky behaviour. The 8th Torpedoboots-Halbflottille was ordered to raise steam to reinforce the watch at the entrance. The submarine panic continued next day; a lookout on *Stettin* even reported a periscope in the river off Borkum! Leaving the growing hue and cry behind, Cholmley headed for Harwich, arriving at 11am on the 7th. He reported a Dutch trawler spotted near Smith's Knoll, the *Catherina*.[7]

Horton's *E.9* was on her way to the Dutch coast at 10:30pm on the 3rd. A suspicious vessel was sighted, which appeared to suddenly begin closing rapidly, without any lights. Horton dived, but the vessel had disappeared. He proceeded submerged until 3:30am next morning. *E.9* surfaced in a lively sea with a strong wind. Horton reached Ameland at noon, but did not proceed to his billet. He reports: 'Did not take up position between Weser and Ems, owing to the fact of not arriving there till nightfall.' *E.9* went to the bottom instead until next morning. Horton perhaps also thought patrolling that day was a waste of time in the prevailing weather. All he had seen was more suspicious buoys off Terschelling.

Horton surfaced at 6:30am on the 5th and headed for the ambush position off the Western Ems entrance. He submerged at 8am. Ninety minutes later he sighted destroyer smoke, in an arc to the south. He reached his position off the entrance at 10:30am, but heavy rain squalls blew in and reduced visibility to only 1½ miles. Horton saw nothing more. At 3:30pm he headed off to the west. *E.9* surfaced at 5pm and continued west for two hours charging the battery, then went to the bottom for the night.

Horton surfaced at 5:30am on the 6th and headed east charging. He sighted and exchanged signals with *E.3* on the way. *E.9* dived at 8:35am, arriving in position off the Ems entrance two hours later. He sighted two lots of destroyer smoke to the southeast. The waves were a bit choppy, which would make the boat a little lively, but also offer concealment for his periscope. Two destroyers closed his position at 11am, but he refrained from attacking as: 'I was awaiting arrival of our destroyers'. They failed to show up. Horton ordered the bow torpedoes reset to run at five feet (2m) instead of the deeper setting required for the cruiser ambush. *E.9* commenced an attack on the two destroyers at 11:55am. Just as he got in position to fire they altered course to port. Horton came about and once again got into position to fire after they altered course again to come east. The patrol was following the same pattern as on his last visit. Once again his attack was frustrated when he checked again with the periscope. They turned sharply to starboard at 12:17pm. Horton quickly turned to port to intercept. Two minutes later he raised the periscope again. *E.9* had: 'Arrived in a favourable position 500 yards [450m], 7 points on bow [slightly ahead and to the side] of No.2 Destroyer.' Horton waited for one minute and then: 'Fired both bow tubes; one at her bow and one at her stern.' A shot aimed to intercept the stern would have a better chance to hit if the destroyer made an evasive turn. He quickly took the boat down to 36 feet (11m) and turned away to starboard. Another minute later there was a very loud explosion – the 'gunshot' heard by *E.6*. Horton left it eight minutes, then rose to periscope depth. The first destroyer was 500 yards away coming straight for his position. The only trace of the second

7   TNA ADM137/2067: pp.274–5; Groos, *Nordsee 2*, p.144; BArch:RM92: *Frithjof* Kriegstagebuch 6 Oktober 1914.

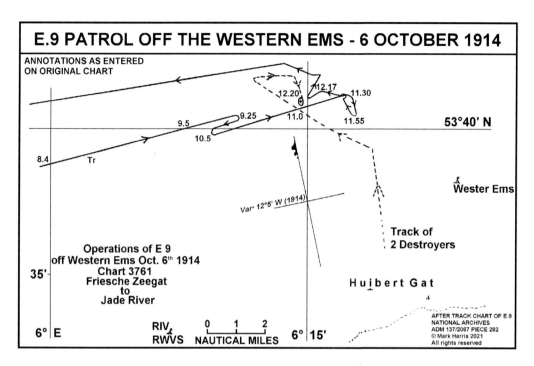

E.9 PATROL OFF THE WESTERN EMS - 6 OCTOBER 1914

ANNOTATIONS AS ENTERED
ON ORIGINAL CHART

12.20   12.17   11.30

9.5   9.25   11.0   11.55

10.5

53°40' N

8.4   Tr

Var" 12°5' W (1914)

Wester Ems

Track of
2 Destroyers

Operations of E 9
off Western Ems Oct. 6ᵗʰ 1914
Chart 3761
Friesche Zeegat
to
Jade River

35'-

Huibert Gat

6° E

RIV,
RWVS

0   1   2
NAUTICAL MILES

6° 15'

was about 15 feet (5m) of her bow sticking out of the water. He had to break off as the surviving destroyer kept up rapid manoeuvers at a distance from the wreck on constantly varying courses at high speed. At 12:45pm another pair of destroyers arrived and began a systematic search. Horton considered them to be too alert to attack and retired to the west at 50 feet (15m). At 3:45pm *E.9* surfaced with nothing in sight and headed back to Harwich, arriving at 10:30am on the 7th.[8]

Horton had attacked *S.116*. She was following astern of *S.117*, the temporary leader boat of 7th Torpedoboots-Halbflottille, commanded by Korvettenkapitän Thiele, which had just relieved the patrol off the Western Ems entrance that day. His own boat, *S.119*, was in dock. They were amongst the oldest of the destroyers in the High Sea Fleet flotillas, with 415t (408 long tons) displacement.[9] These small destroyers were a difficult target and had been taking elaborate precautions against submarine torpedo attack. They had been making major changes in their course, speed and their formation relative to one another every five or six minutes. *E.9*'s torpedoes had to reach the shallow depth that had been set in order to have a chance of hitting. Thiele reports that: '*S.116* was steaming 13 knots and was about 500m [550 yards] on the starboard quarter of *S.117*.'[10] Two approaching torpedo tracks were spotted from the bridge of *S.116*. The helmsman was ordered to turn her out of their path. There was relief as the rudder took effect and they both seemed to have passed ahead. Then a supposed third torpedo, but

---

8   TNA ADM137/2067: pp.280-2; TNA ADM53: *Adamant*, 7 October 1914.
9   63m (207 feet) long, 7m (23 feet) wide, maximum draught 2.69m (9 feet), maximum speed 28 knots. Armament of 3x5cm (2-inch) guns and 3x45cm (17.7-inch) torpedo tubes. Completed in 1903.
10 Behind and off to starboard.

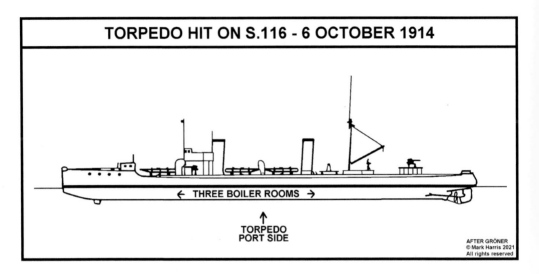

TORPEDO HIT ON S.116 - 6 OCTOBER 1914

← THREE BOILER ROOMS →

↑
TORPEDO
PORT SIDE

actually Horton's second, exploded amidships, between the funnels. The powerful explosion blew a huge hole in the hull. A wall of water slammed into the adjacent boiler room. The cold water hit the red hot coal fires and the boiler exploded. *S.116* was enveloped in steam and the explosions broke her back. The survivors rushed to don their life-jackets. Over the next three minutes, the hull continued to buckle and break at the site of the hit as the water spread. *S.116* then broke in half as the crew jumped overboard. The flooded ends of each half hit the shallow bottom, which was only about 23m (75 feet) deep. The bow remained macabrely sticking several metres out of the water. Her 28 year old commander from Strassburg, Kapitänleutnant Kurt, Freiherr (Baron) von Ziegesar and 12 other missing crew were presumed to have been killed in the explosions. Nine were from the engineering department, no doubt on duty near the site of the torpedo hit.

Thiele immediately ordered *S.117* to turn about and headed back to the site of the wreck at full speed. Her small dinghy was launched and life-jackets thrown to those without them. In return the men in the water shouted warnings that torpedo tracks had been seen. This ruled out a mine as the cause, but after grabbing those nearby, Thiele had no choice but to get back underway and zig-zag around the area at maximum speed, lest *S.117* become the next victim. *S.115* was summoned from her patrol billet off the Eastern Ems, followed by *S.118* patrolling off the Huibert Gat. The three boats thrashed around the area for the next 90 minutes, with *S.117* grabbing groups of survivors when opportunity offered. Nine men were also picked up by *S.118*. Eventually all 56 survivors were rescued and were then taken back to Borkum, leaving *S.115* on patrol. Bootsmannsmaat der Reserve (Reserve Petty Officer) Karl Sternenberg died later that afternoon.[11] Attempts to revive him by the medical staff of the cruiser *Stettin* were unsuccessful.

---

11   *Verlustliste 9*, p.2 gives casualties as: Killed – Sternenberg. Missing, presumed dead – Ziegesar, Torpedo-MaschinistenMaat (Engineering Petty Officer) Fritz Bethge, Torpedo-ObermaschinistenMaat (Engineering Chief Petty Officer) Heinrich Kaiser, Torpedo-MaschinistenAnwärter (ERA) Walter Jung, Torpedo-Oberheizer (Leading Stokers) Johann Heinrich, Heinrich Lößner, Torpedo-Oberheizer der Reserve (Reserve Leading Stoker) Peter Backes, Torpedo-Heizer (Stokers) Peter Arenz, Karl

S.116 with the crew at work on a torpedo before the war. (Author's collection)

He had been in the cold water too long, but the very effective German life-jackets had saved the rest of the crew. The other survivors transferred to *S.118*, which took them back to Emden.[12]

Horton celebrated his victory as he came alongside at Harwich. A white Jolly Roger flying above the yellow one for *Hela* was hoisted at *E.9*'s yardarm, once again constructed from the stock of signal flags. Waistell reported to the Admiralty that the sunken destroyer was probably of the *S.138* type, based on Horton's description. That evening the Admiralty announced that: 'Submarine E.9 (Lieutenant-Commander Max K. Horton) has returned safely after having torpedoed and sunk a German torpedo-boat destroyer off the Ems River'. On the 8th news of the sinking of *S.116* was confirmed via the semi-official Wolff's Bureau in Berlin by: 'a torpedo from a British submarine ... almost the entire crew was saved.'[13]

Was Horton just lucky, or was he better than his colleagues who had yet to hit anything? After the attack he himself wrote to a friend: 'To hit a destroyer always requires maximum luck.' The evidence from both world wars is that a small number of submarine commanders sunk most of the ships. Horton combined skill, careful preparation, cool headed aggression and tenacity with good tactical instincts. He did not just make the most of opportunities, he had the knack of creating them by thinking ahead about where the enemy would be and what they were likely to do next. His success created both admiration and a somewhat jealous rivalry with his fellow officers. *The Maidstone Magazine* gleefully reported that: 'SUBMARINE D3 succeeded in beating submarine E9 at football, by 3 goals to 2.'[14]

Two boats had also been despatched for relief of the patrol in the northern part of the Bight, leaving together at 1pm on the 3rd. *D.4* had the billet farthest out to sea, with *D.8* in the central billet. The billet off the Danish coast was left unoccupied, but *E.4* was possibly to be despatched later. Leir had to stay at Harwich for the present as she was the only boat left to respond to an emergency. The patrol was to return on the afternoon of the 7th.[15]

Moncreiffe's *D.4* passed a large amount of cargo timber near the Corton Light Vessel on the afternoon of the 3rd. It was a bad omen and he wondered if it was a wreck. Next morning Moncreiffe sighted smoke and dived. *D.4* was well out to sea north of Vlieland in high wind and waves. A Dutch steamer came into sight at 7:20am. He surfaced after it had passed, but *D.4*'s course was side on to the heavy seas, causing her to roll and dive into every wave. He kept going at low speed. At 9:40am *D.4* reversed course and soon stopped, but this is omitted from Moncreiffe's report. A particularly large wave then dumped a huge amount of water into the boat. The hatch was now closed. Half an hour later choking chlorine fumes appeared. The salt water had got into the battery. His report says that he decided to abandon the patrol at 11:50am

Joachimi, Karl Klotz, Oberfeuerwerks-Maat (Ordnance Petty Officer) Anton Backemeyer, Torpedo-Matrosen (Seamen) Otto Kahle, Karl Sieger. Groos and Gröner state nine casualties.

12   BArch:RM64/3: Kriegstagebuch des Ältesten Seebefehlshabers auf der Ems: Abhandlungen und Gefechtsberichte: Auszug aus dem Kriegstagebuch VII. Halbflottille, 6.X.1914; Groos, *Nordsee 2*, p.143; BArch:RM92: *Stettin, Nassau* Kriegstagebuch 6 Oktober 1914; Gröner, *German Warships*, pp.170–1 records the wreck at 53°42'N, 6°9'E, a little farther north and west than Horton's chart.

13   TNA ADM137/2067: p.283; IWM:Documents.1003: 7 October; Chalmers, *Horton*, p.12; *Official Naval Despatches*, p.15; *Amtliche Kriegs-Depeschen*, p.142. Reuters picked the announcement up but misidentified the destroyer as *S.126*. English language newspapers and Admiralty documents repeated the error.

14   Douglas, *Maidstone Magazine*, p.6

15   TNA ADM137/2067: p.285.

and return to Harwich. The log suggests he got underway again at 1:25pm. The gyrocompass became erratic and Moncreiffe had to use the magnetic compass to navigate back through very heavy seas and gale force winds. *D.4*'s propellers then fouled two nets in the middle of the fishing fleet off Lowestoft at 5am next morning, the 5th. It took 40 minutes to disentangle them. Moncreiffe got an unsympathetic reception when he reached Harwich at noon. He was told to be ready for sea again the next day. The crew worked well into the evening getting the salt water out of the boat, all of them suffering from the aftereffects of chlorine gas.[16]

D.8 had a new captain, Lieutenant-Commander William J. Foster, aged 30. He had transferred from *C.13* of 6th Flotilla in the Humber. Foster had joined the Submarine Service in 1905. In 1909 Captain Hall evaluated him as: 'A sound, capable officer.' Captain Addison added a year later that he was: 'Not very energetic.' His Lieutenant, Colin Mayers, remarked to Hallifax that he was 'all right, but <u>very</u> excitable and "<u>undignified</u>" during an attack'.[17] *D.8*'s previous commander, Brodie, had gone to Barrow to take command of *E.15* as she neared completion.

Foster's report does not mention the awful weather, but *D.8* averaged less than seven knots getting to her billet. She arrived at 10:45am on the 5th. Foster saw nothing until 7:35am on the 7th. A biplane was spotted five miles away heading towards *D.8*. He dived and remained down for an hour to try and avoid detection. *D.8* had been seen. Seaplane Number '82' reported an enemy submarine in this position on a routine reconnaissance flight. Just after noon Foster sighted an airship to the south heading out to sea, which was in sight for about an hour. He remained on the surface this time, end-on and trimmed down with only the conning tower out of the water. This was the *L.5*, one of three zeppelins carrying out reconnaissance that day. It was up to 30 miles away and unsurprisingly did not sight him. However, air patrols were beginning to demonstrate their effectiveness in submarine detection and in constraining submarine movements. Foster had seen no surface vessels to report. He left the patrol area at 3pm and reached Harwich at 5pm on the 8th.[18]

German routine destroyer and trawler patrols only came out of the estuaries during the recent patrols in the Bight when the sea briefly calmed and visibility improved. The various suspicious objects and vessels seen off the Dutch coast and in the Southern Bight were all harmless. However, the combination of mines and suspected minelayers was clearly looming large in the minds of British submarine commanders since Talbot's experience. After two attempts there was little evidence one way or the other of German patrolling in the northern part of the Heligoland Bight.

Whilst the patrols were underway, the temporary cancellation of the destroyer raid had become permanent as a result of developments in Belgium on the 5th. At 4pm Tyrwhitt and Keyes were informed that the 7th Infantry Division and 3rd Cavalry Division were to be transported to the Belgian port of Zeebrugge over the next two nights. They would reinforce the increasingly desperate defence of Antwerp by the Belgian Army. Keyes and Tyrwhitt were asked to provide a covering force in the event that the German Navy attempted to intervene.

16   TNA ADM137/2067: p.286; TNA ADM173: *D.4* 3–5 October 1914; IWM:Documents.1003: 5 October 1914.
17   TNA ADM196/49/10: William John Foster; IWM:Documents.1003: 29 October 1914.
18   TNA ADM137/2067: p.287; Groos, *Nordsee 2*, Karte 9; BArch:RM92: *Nassau* Kriegstagebuch 7 Oktober 1914.

After discussions with Tyrwhitt, Keyes telegraphed the Admiralty at 11:30pm and suggested that he take *Lurcher* across to Zeebrugge with the two submarines he had immediately available. This was *E.4* and the recently arrived *E.11*. They could provide local defence in the event of an attempted bombardment of the port, although Keyes had reservations about the shallow water off Zeebrugge. However, he thought it unwise to place submarines farther north, where Tyrwhitt would be patrolling. A confusion of identity could easily result. Since Tyrwhitt would warn of the enemy approach, the submarines would be held in the harbour and sortie as required.

Keyes heard nothing back. After another telegraph the next morning he was told that the plan had been rejected. Keyes telephoned the Admiralty. The staff officer he spoke to was unmoved, pointing out that not only was the water too shallow, but mines had also been laid west of the port to prevent German submarines entering the Channel. Keyes already knew all this but insisted that a submarine could torpedo or drive off any cruiser that appeared. After further discussion at the other end the officer returned to confirm that Sturdee had approved the plan.

Keyes moved quickly. He left in *Lurcher* to scout Zeebrugge at 11am on the 6th, as it was unclear whether submarines could tie up alongside there. If all was well, he would return at 10am next day to the North Hinder Light Vessel and rendezvous with *E.4* and *E.11* to escort them across. *Lurcher* would act as the communication link with Tyrwhitt. In the event of German attack the submarines would sortie to the north of the port to cut off the enemy line of retreat.

Everything went as planned. *E.4* and *E.11* were safely secured at the piers where the Brugge Canal entered Zeebrugge harbour by 1pm on the 7th. Keyes greatly enjoyed his time at Zeebrugge watching the Army land, especially the fine Household Cavalry mounts, as he was a keen hunt follower. He met a number of friends coming ashore there. The reconnaissance proved useful when he later planned the famous raid on Zeebrugge in 1918. Keyes hoped that some Germans would get near enough to shoot at and the experience made him 'long to be a soldier'. When reports were received of a German reconnaissance plane approaching, the crew of *Lurcher* were quickly issued rifles, but to Keyes disappointment it never got near them.

At 8:20pm on the 8th, the Admiralty notified Keyes that the transport operation was successfully completed. The last of the cavalry had crossed the previous night, so the submarines could return to Harwich next morning. They left at 5:30am. *Lurcher* went on ahead, arriving in Harwich at 10am, followed in by the two submarines at 1pm.

Green crews, poor weather and the resulting damage – such as that to *U.20* – had prevented German submarines from even reaching the transports. This was the only response the German Navy attempted to the landings. *U.28* arrived too late on the evening the 9th. There were a number of false alarms about German submarine attacks reported during the crossing.[19]

Keyes was delighted to learn of Horton's success on his return to Harwich, recording a characteristic country sports analogy in a letter to his wife: 'To get one of those wriggling destroyers is like shooting snipe with a rifle. Horton has spent several hours at a time stalking them, but this was the first torpedo he has fired. The enemy's submarines have fired 11 torpedoes at our destroyers in the past week without success, and ours don't trouble to be half as elusive as theirs.'[20]

19   Groos, *Nordsee 2*, p.152, Karte 8.
20   TNA ADM137/2067: pp. 290-2; TNA ADM186/620: pp.76, 170–173; Keyes, *Memoirs*, pp.112-5; *Keyes Papers*, pp.36–39, letter to wife of 9 October 1914; TNA ADM173: *E.4* 7-9 October 1914; TNA ADM53: *Lurcher* 6–9 October 1914

In his first public despatch issued by the Admiralty on 17 October, Keyes heaped praise on Horton: 'The enemy's Torpedo Craft pursue tactics, which, in connection with their shallow draft, make them exceedingly difficult to attack with torpedo ... Horton's success was the result of much patient and skilful zeal. He is a most enterprising submarine officer ... Lieutenant Charles M.S. Chapman, the Second in Command of "E.9," is also deserving of credit.'[21]

Cholmley and Horton between them had made it appear that the Ems was virtually under siege by British submarines, with even the most elaborate precautions failing to prevent the loss of *S.116*. This deepened the convictions of the German High Command about the submarine danger to the fleet. Admiral von Pohl, the Naval Chief of Staff, wrote in his diary: 'S.116 was sunk off the Ems by an enemy submarine. And Tirpitz [Secretary of State for the Navy] still wants to send the Fleet out into the North Sea! The man becomes more incomprehensible every day. He is always trotting out his theory of risking the Fleet.'[22]

Keyes had grounds for satisfaction. Eighth Flotilla had a growing list of successes after two months at war: an enemy cruiser and a destroyer sunk; no losses of men or material; a key defensive minefield had been located; the enemy's defensive patrol arrangements had been identified and the enemy's freedom to manoeuvre and exercise in the Bight had been severely curtailed.

21   *Third Supplement to the London Gazette of Tuesday, the 20th October, 1914* (London: HMSO, 1914), p.8500.
22   TNA ADM223/808: July Bulletin p.51, Pohl diary translation.

16

Elusive prey

Waistell issued orders for the next patrol to the southern half of the Heligoland Bight on 6 October. The patrol area between the Ems and the Weser was dropped as a result of *E.7*'s report of the minefield. The reliefs for the other patrol areas were to leave at 1pm. *E.10* was allocated the Western Ems billet. *D.4* had the billet off the Dutch coast, which was shifted east, to the north of Ameland. The patrol was to return on the evening of the 9th. The route to be used both ways was also prescribed, via Smith's Knoll. This would give confidence to vessels on patrol elsewhere that submarines encountered were not British and could be attacked.[1]

The submarines left together as planned. They passed through a large fishing fleet off Smith's Knoll that had come out as seas calmed that evening, the wind having almost completely dropped. There was good weather and reasonable visibility in the North Sea for the next few days.

Moncreiffe's *D.4* lost touch with *E.10* during the night. Soon after reaching Terschelling next morning he dived to observe a Dutch steamer ahead of him. After proceeding submerged for nearly three hours, Moncreiffe surfaced to continue heading to his billet and spotted *E.10*. She remained in sight one mile to port. At 10:30am Moncreiffe sighted a German submarine about six miles ahead of *E.10*. The enemy submarine dived. He followed suit and reversed course to the west, whilst *E.10* was seen to circle round to northward. After half an hour Moncreiffe doubled back east to search for the enemy submarine, hoping that she had surfaced in the meantime. There was nothing to be seen. He proceeded submerged, arriving at his billet off Ameland at noon. *D.4* surfaced at 2:10pm and headed north. Moncreiffe soon sighted a zeppelin a long way off to the northwest, but it was only in sight between clouds for about a minute. *D.4* dived for half an hour. It was not in sight on surfacing. Moncreiffe patrolled east, then headed back inshore to spend the night on the bottom.

Next morning, the 8th, *D.4* surfaced to charge and resumed patrolling. Smoke was sighted towards the land at 9:15am. Moncreiffe headed south to investigate. After 15 minutes a mast and two funnels came into sight to the southeast. *D.4* steered to intercept. By 10am Moncreiffe had closed to six miles. It was a steamer prominently marked as a hospital ship; white with a green band round the hull and flying the Red Cross flag. However, five minutes later she appeared to haul this down, increase speed and turn east. Moncreiffe also increased speed and

---

1   TNA ADM137/2067: p.294.

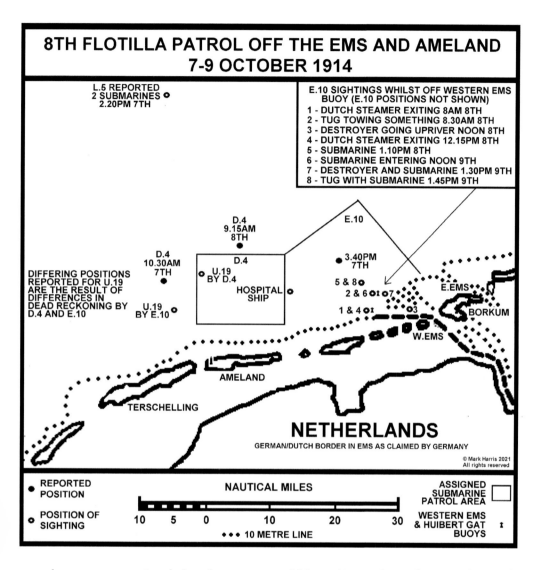

8TH FLOTILLA PATROL OFF THE EMS AND AMELAND 7-9 OCTOBER 1914

L.5 REPORTED
2 SUBMARINES
2.20PM 7TH

E.10 SIGHTINGS WHILST OFF WESTERN EMS
BUOY (E.10 POSITIONS NOT SHOWN)
1 - DUTCH STEAMER EXITING 8AM 8TH
2 - TUG TOWING SOMETHING 8.30AM 8TH
3 - DESTROYER GOING UPRIVER NOON 8TH
4 - DUTCH STEAMER EXITING 12.15PM 8TH
5 - SUBMARINE 1.10PM 8TH
6 - SUBMARINE ENTERING NOON 9TH
7 - DESTROYER AND SUBMARINE 1.30PM 9TH
8 - TUG WITH SUBMARINE 1.45PM 9TH

D.4
9.15AM
8TH

E.10

D.4
10.30AM
7TH

D.4

3.40PM
7TH

DIFFERING POSITIONS
REPORTED FOR U.19
ARE THE RESULT OF
DIFFERENCES IN
DEAD RECKONING BY
D.4 AND E.10

U.19
BY D.4

HOSPITAL
SHIP

5 & 8

2 & 6   7   E.EMS

U.19
BY E.10

1 & 4   3   BORKUM

W.EMS

AMELAND

TERSCHELLING

NETHERLANDS

GERMAN/DUTCH BORDER IN EMS AS CLAIMED BY GERMANY

REPORTED
POSITION

NAUTICAL MILES

ASSIGNED
SUBMARINE
PATROL AREA

POSITION OF
SIGHTING

10   5   0   10   20   30

WESTERN EMS
& HUIBERT GAT
BUOYS

10 METRE LINE

turned to pursue, convinced that the steamer could be a disguised minelayer. *D.4*'s 12-pdr (76mm) gun was brought up from the casing and readied for action. After 25 minutes he had to give up the chase. The steamer appeared to head in to the Western Ems and Moncreiffe returned to patrol his billet. *D.4* broke off to spend a couple of hours on the bottom at midday and returned there for the night. Moncreiffe resumed patrolling next day, then left for Harwich at 4:45pm. Whilst passing through a fishing fleet at 1:30am next morning, the 10th, those on watch had some anxious moments. A vessel that looked like a destroyer in the moonlight passed close to *D.4*'s stern. She arrived at Harwich at 11:15am.[2]

---

2   TNA ADM137/2067: pp.295–6; TNA ADM173: *D.4* 6-10 October 1914; IWM: Documents.1003: 10 October 1914.

The 12-pdr gun readied for action on *D.4* prior to the war. This was the only gun mounted on a British submarine in 1914. (Author's collection)

On the 7th Fraser's *E.10* had dived to await the dawn off Terschelling. He spotted *D.4* on surfacing to proceed to the Ems. Around 10am Fraser sighted the same German submarine as Moncreiffe. She was in the act of diving. He decided to give the German a wide berth to the north and continue on the surface, seeing *D.4* double back as he did so. At 12:30pm a zeppelin was spotted passing five miles to the northeast, heading out to sea. As *E.10* approached her billet it returned in her direction and Fraser dived at 2:30pm. When he surfaced an hour later there was nothing in sight. *E.10* briefly closed the entrance, then headed out to the north and stopped at 5pm. Fraser saw nothing that evening other than some intermittent coloured lights flashing in the Ems. He went to the bottom for the night at 9pm.

Fraser surfaced at 7am on the 8th and headed towards the Western Ems entrance. He spent most of the day on the surface, near the entrance buoy. He dived twice to investigate what turned out to be Dutch steamers coming out of the Huibert Gat and again for a tug towing something, which he quickly lost sight of. The only warship that had been seen was a destroyer glimpsed going upriver. Finally at 1:10pm a submarine was spotted three miles to the northwest. Fraser dived to attack, but lost sight of her. He headed north out to sea at 4pm to surface and charge, stopping a couple of hours later. *E.10* dived to the bottom for the night at 9:30pm.

Fraser surfaced next morning, returned to the entrance buoy and dived to keep watch at 9am. At noon Fraser was looking round through the periscope. A submarine suddenly broke surface aft, a mere 50 yards (45m) away! *E.10* was too close to fire, so Fraser turned away to try and increase the range and the crew started getting the stern tube ready. The German got underway into the Ems. Fraser had to go deep to let her pass overhead. At 1:15pm a destroyer and a submarine came out of the river. *E.10* started an attack run on the destroyer, only to see her head back into the river 15 minutes later. Fraser turned to attack the submarine, but it was too far away and soon went out of sight. Shortly afterwards a tug was sighted towing a submarine to the northwest. *E.10* turned once more to attack, but the tug headed back up the river and the submarine dived. Nothing more was seen and Fraser briefly came to the surface for a better look around at 3pm. He soon dived again and headed out to sea. Fraser surfaced two hours later and departed for Harwich as the light failed, arriving at 3pm the next day, the 10th. *E.10* had developed clutch problems on the patrol and left for repair on the 14th, not returning until the 29th.[3]

The submarine sighted on the 7th by Moncreiffe and Fraser was *U.19*, which was on her way to attack the transports off Zeebrugge. She reported avoiding an attack by two British submarines off Ameland. *U.28*, heading for the same destination, also reported briefly sighting a submarine near Terschelling. *L.5* was the patrolling zeppelin seen by *D.4* and *E.10* and had already been seen by *D.8*. She reported sighting two submarines at 2:20pm, but the position she reported is too far northwest, so evidently her navigation was off. The lights seen in the Ems had been lit on the evening of the 7th to guide in *U.29* and *U.30* arriving late from Heligoland.

The hospital ship observed on the 8th was not a disguised minelayer, despite Keyes suggestion in his report that she behaved 'in an extraordinary manner'. The ship had been searching the area where *S.116* had been sunk 48 hours earlier, looking for the missing crew.

On the 9th there was an alarm in the Ems. Gunfire was reported off Borkum at 11:20am. As a result *U.27*, *U.29* and *U.30* were ordered out of the Western Ems entrance. *Stettin* was following until the outpost trawler at the entrance signalled her at noon by light that no gunfire had been heard. Realising it was a false alarm, the entire force was recalled. *U.19* also arrived in the early afternoon, having broken off her patrol early as a result of damage. She reported briefly sighting and making an abortive attack on a British submarine off the Ems, perhaps when *E.10* briefly surfaced around 3pm. It is impossible to unscramble which submarines *E.10* saw as they exited, then returned, but the false alarm had almost put *Stettin* in Fraser's sights.

More ominously, newly commissioned submarines and those not on long distance patrol were now to be posted where British submarines had been sighted. *U.10* left the Ems to take up an ambush position north of Borkum on the afternoon of the 9th. Other warships were to avoid the ambush areas. This change in tactics spelt danger for any British submarine sitting on the surface, as *E.10* had been doing.[4]

In his report to the Admiralty on the 10th, Keyes highlighted both the absence of the Ems destroyer patrol since *S.116* was sunk and the close watch being kept by submarines. The submarine sorties as a result of the false alarm had focussed attention on them. The increasing role of auxiliaries like tugs in the defence of the exits was also apparent.[5]

On the 8th Waistell issued orders to relieve the patrol in the northern Bight. The weather had frustrated previous efforts to identify German patrol patterns in the area and determine whether trade was being intercepted off Esbjerg. The billets were reduced to two and focussed inshore. *E.5* was in the northern half of the area. *D.3*, which had just returned from her repairs, was to the south. The submarines would leave that day and return on the afternoon of the 12th.[6]

The patrol left at noon. They stopped at Gorleston Pier at 4pm and spent the night there. Boyle's *D.3* left Gorleston at 4:55am next morning, the 9th. She had to stop briefly to make

3   TNA ADM137/2067: pp.297-8, 334; IWM: Documents.1003: 10 October; TNA ADM53: *Adamant* 14, 29 October 1914.
4   Groos, *Nordsee 2*, pp.145, 152, 154, 252–3, Karte 9; BArch: RM92: *Stettin, Nassau, Kolberg* Kriegstagebuch 7-12 October 1914
5   TNA ADM137/2067: p.299.
6   TNA ADM137/2067: p.301.

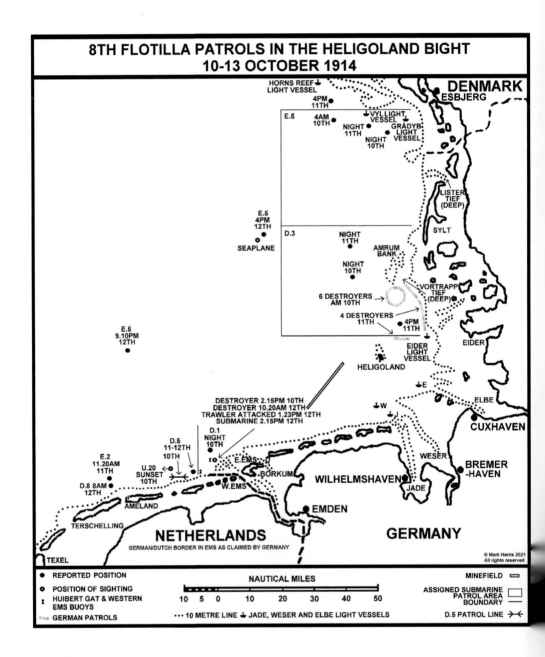

**8TH FLOTILLA PATROLS IN THE HELIGOLAND BIGHT
10-13 OCTOBER 1914**

repairs to the steering wheel late that night. Boyle spotted destroyer smoke south of Amrum Bank next morning. He closed in and dived at 10am to attack. The destroyers were close inshore around the five fathom line (9m), only occasionally coming into deeper water. At this depth *D.3* would be vulnerable to being rammed. At 11:15am Boyle: 'Sighted land with trees on it, and shortly after that the destroyers must have seen me, as six of them surrounded me, and although they did not seem to try and run me down, they kept on steering at me and then sheering off from all directions.' There was a rough sea running in the shallow water, limiting visibility through the periscope. He was unable to fire at the destroyers, which were apparently of the *G.169* class and usually too close for a torpedo when seen. After an hour of this Boyle was in only seven fathoms (13m) of water, off Vortrapp Deep, with the shallows of the Amrum Bank close by. He 'thought it better to clear out' and headed northwest. Once clear Boyle surfaced at 2:10pm to charge his battery and headed west out to sea, later returning to spend the night on the bottom.

Next morning, the 11th, Boyle surfaced at 7am. He headed out to sea to complete his charge for the battery, then headed back to investigate smoke seen earlier to the east-southeast. By 10:25am destroyers could be made out. Boyle altered course to close them and dived an hour later. He worked down the coast, only surfacing for an hour around noon, but could not get close enough to attack, as the destroyers seemed to pass by in ever more shallow water as the day went on. The four destroyers, working in two groups, appeared to go backwards and forwards from northeast of Heligoland, out of sight round the Eider Light Vessel, then up to a point inside Amrum Bank. Boyle headed back out to sea at 4pm and soon surfaced to charge. *D.3* spent the night on the bottom.

Boyle surfaced at 7:10am on the 12th. He spent the morning investigating the area west of Sylt Island, diving in towards the shore until he sighted land. There was no sign of any patrol there, just smoke to the south in the Vortrapp Deep. He headed back out to sea, surfaced at 2pm and set course for Harwich. *D.3* secured alongside *Adamant* at 5:50pm on the 13th.[7]

Benning's *E.5* left Gorleston at 4:30am on the 9th. He arrived off the Danish coast near the Vyl Light Vessel at 4am on the 10th. Benning spent the next two days patrolling back and forth in good visibility between the Horns Reef Light Vessel and Lister Deep. Most of the time during the day was spent on the surface and the nights on the bottom. The only things sighted were small fishing craft off Esbjerg.

Next morning, the 12th, Benning surfaced at 5:30am and closed the Vyl Light Vessel. Her captain was induced to come alongside in a boat with the offer of some tins of soup. He happily informed Benning that no German ships had been seen and that there had been no traffic out of Esbjerg in the last two days. At 7:40am a vessel was spotted on the horizon ahead. *E.5* dived, but a Norwegian sailing ship finally came into sight. Benning surfaced and headed for the Grådyb Light Vessel at 9am. More soup elicited the information that no German steamers had used Esbjerg since war broke out. The only regular sailing was a steamer that went to Liverpool every Tuesday. Her captain certainly had a good memory, as he also told Benning that four German warships had passed south on 17 August, but none had been seen since. This was accurate, if outdated information; the light cruiser *Mainz* and a group of destroyers from 8th Torpedoboots-Flottille had scouted Esbjerg that day. Despite being neutral, Danes were generally ill-disposed

---

7   TNA ADM137/2067: pp.306-7; TNA ADM173: *D.3* 8-13 October 1914.

towards the German Empire and would have required little encouragement to talk. *E.5* headed back out to sea at 10:36am, but with nothing in sight Benning increased speed and set course for Harwich two hours later.

At 4pm a German seaplane emerged from a thick cloud, 2½ miles ahead, heading directly for *E.5*. Benning dived to 40 feet (12m) but was certain he had been seen. An hour later *E.5* surfaced and proceeded. Assuming the sighting would be reported, he estimated that any German destroyers sent to intercept *E.5* would do so at about 9pm. A small light was sighted half a mile ahead at the expected time. Benning dived. The log records: 'enemy TBDs [destroyers] ahead'. His submarine sound signalling apparatus then picked up a signal, apparently being transmitted by siren. He surfaced at 10:30pm, but dived again almost immediately, as visibility was poor and it was raining. A few minutes later a ship passed overhead, which sounded like a destroyer. Benning proceeded submerged until just after midnight to be on the safe side. He was worried about a light two miles off to starboard until it disappeared half an hour later. A good story, but Benning's imagination was getting the upper hand again and connecting the dots on random encounters. *E.5* had to stop her engines as she approached Yarmouth at noon on the 13th. The fuel pumping system had broken down. It took the engineering hands a couple of hours to get it working again. *E.5* reached Gorleston Wharf at 3pm. Benning returned to Harwich at 2pm the next day.[8]

No German sighting reports of *D.3* or *E.5* on this patrol have been identified. If the seaplane made a report, it cannot be traced. One of the periodic destroyer sweeps northwest from Heligoland had gone out on the night of the 9/10th but seems to have headed back in just ahead of *D.3*'s arrival at her billet. No German warships got anywhere near *E.5*.[9] However, Benning and Boyle had finally delivered a detailed view of German patrol arrangements in the northern area. The destroyer patrol in the shallow waters northeast of Heligoland gave little scope for successful raiding or submarine attack.

On the 9th, Waistell issued orders for the relief of the patrol in the southern part of the Heligoland Bight. The submarines focussed entirely on the Western Ems as a result of Horton's recent success. *D.1* was off the entrance, with *D.5* west of the Huibert Gat. They were to leave at 11am and return on the evening of the 12th.[10]

Cochrane's *D.1* submerged off Terschelling at 5am on the 10th. At daylight she got underway and arrived off the Ems at 2:15pm. Cochrane sighted a destroyer outside the Eastern Ems entrance, heading for the Western entrance. He dived and began an attack run. Before *D.1* could get within a mile she disappeared into the Western Ems. Only patrolling trawlers were seen for the rest of the day, off the shallows. *D.1* went to the bottom for the night four miles west of the entrance.

Next morning Cochrane headed in to the Western Ems submerged at 5:20am. Three trawlers and two small tugs were spotted sweeping the channel as far as the entrance four hours later. Cochrane sighted smoke approaching from the north at 1:35pm. *D.1* headed off to intercept. An hour later the periscope revealed only a Danish steamer loaded with timber. During the day destroyers and trawlers had been sighted constantly moving inside the Ems, but nothing had come out.

8   TNA ADM137/2067: pp.308–9; TNA ADM173: *E.5* 9-14 October 1914.
9   Groos, *Nordsee 2*, Karte 10.
10   TNA ADM137/2067: p.302.

D.1 during testing of the prototype submarine wireless rig in 1910. (NH 54934)

On the 12th Cochrane headed in submerged towards the buoy at the Western Ems entrance at 5am. The trawlers again swept the channel. One trawler then anchored close to the outer buoy at 8:30am. Cochrane surfaced to get an accurate position fix a couple of hours later. He realised that the main marker buoy had been moved about half a mile northwest of the chart position. A destroyer now came down the channel. Cochrane decided to remain surfaced to make sure he was seen, hoping to lure her out. He reports: 'did not dive until till she was within 5,000 yards [4,500m], but immediately after doing so the destroyer stopped, & turned back although there was a flat calm at the time.' If the destroyer would not risk exiting in such poor conditions for torpedo attack it was never likely to. The patrol time was running out and Cochrane apparently became exasperated at the lack of targets. He began an attack on the trawler anchored near the outer buoy at 12:50pm. Over the next 30 minutes *D.1* crept to within 600 yards (550m). Cochrane could get no closer as there was a bank with only three fathoms (5.5m) of water between *D.1* and the trawler. He fired a single torpedo. To his mortification it missed five yards/m ahead of the target. He had failed to make enough allowance for the effect of the tide. A trawler was obviously a very small, difficult target, even anchored. After wasting one valuable torpedo, Cochrane clearly felt he could not justify firing another. *D.1* moved off to the north. An hour later a German submarine was spotted, stopped at the entrance. Cochrane started an attack. *D.1* had got to within 1,500 yards (1,400m) and was turning to line up for the final approach, but the target disappeared. Cochrane thought that his periscope had been spotted and the submarine had dived. At 5pm he headed back for Harwich, arriving at 4:30pm on the 13th. Every day three to six destroyers and trawlers had been sighted continually underway in the inner channels of the estuary. There had been a trawler anchored at the entrance to each, but no sight whatsoever of anything larger.[11]

Herbert's *D.5* patrolled west of the Huibert Gat entrance on the 10th. Nothing was seen until sunset. Herbert had just surfaced to charge the battery. A German submarine was spotted, heading west, three miles to the north. Herbert dived and headed northwest to try and cut her off but lost her in the failing light. Concluding she had come out of the entrance in daylight, he moved his patrol position for the next two days. *D.5* was never more than three to four miles from the Huibert Gat entrance. Herbert saw nothing other than a trawler anchored at the entrance buoy. He arrived back at Harwich just after noon on the 13th.[12]

The submarine Herbert attacked was almost certainly *U.20*, heading out for a patrol in the Channel. She had attacked a half-submerged British submarine near Ameland, but had lost sight of her before firing. It appears that *D.5* and *U.20* began attacks on each other at more or less the same time. The 8th Torpedoboots-Halbflottille had the watch in the Ems. *T.111* reported an enemy submarine on the surface north of the entrance at 6:50am on the 12th. Cochrane was seen again by *S.129*, which reported an enemy submarine going out of sight off Borkum at 11:11am. No trace can be made of any report of an attack on the outpost trawler; perhaps they were simply not paying attention!

The submarine Cochrane spotted late in the afternoon was almost certainly *U.10* returning at the end of her patrol. In accordance with the new tactics she had been lying in ambush off the Ems since the 9th but had not seen *D.1*. Cochrane had prudently kept submerged as much as possible during his patrol. Escalating concerns about the British submarines also led the Naval High Command to order the existing minefield to be extended around the Norderney wreck buoy on the night of the 11/12th. The mooring depth was chosen to sink submarines, as it was thought that the buoy was being used to fix their positions when entering the Bight. They were obviously unaware that the Flotilla had located and were now avoiding the minefield.[13]

On 9 October, Belgian and British forces withdrew from Antwerp. The German Army entered the city the next day. The port facilities were abandoned intact. There were reports of increased German forces in the Ems, including two coastal battleships. Keyes was concerned that they might intend to move to Antwerp, which had access to the southern part of the North Sea, through Dutch waters in the Western Schelde. He thought it was prudent to cover the possibility, as 'it cannot do much harm elsewhere'.

Keyes discussed the development with Tyrwhitt. They made a joint proposal to block the approaches to the Schelde, which was agreed by the Admiralty on the morning of the 10th. Keyes would send *E.2* and *E.4* to the eastern end of Terschelling, back-stopping the existing patrol off the Ems. They were to keep watch on the surface night and day for any vessels heading to the south or west. Details of sightings were to be sent immediately by wireless to Tyrwhitt's

11   TNA ADM137/2067: pp.304-5.
12   TNA ADM137/2067: p.310; IWM: Documents.1003: 13 October 1914.
13   Groos, *Nordsee 2*, pp.153, 161, 251-2; BArch:RM92: *Nassau* Kriegstagebuch 12 October 1914; TNA ADM137/2018, p.274.

Destroyer Flotilla patrolling between Terschelling and the Schelde. Waistell would take *Firedrake*, *E.1* and *E.11* to Zeebrugge. As before the submarines would remain at readiness at the canal entrance. They would sortie to attack anything entering the Schelde or heading towards Ostend. *Firedrake* would act as the wireless link with Tyrwhitt to the north. The force was to depart Harwich at 2pm that day. *E.2* and *E.4* would return at 5pm on the 13th, but no return date was set for the force at Zeebrugge. *Lurcher* and five other submarines would be kept ready at short notice at Harwich.

The Terschelling outpost plan was badly received by several officers in the Flotilla, due to the need to stay on the surface the whole time. As the submarines were preparing to shove off, *E.10* returned with Fraser reporting his multiple sightings of submarines off the Ems. Hallifax recorded that: 'everyone feels they have every chance of being scuppered by a German submarine … Several of the skippers … were of the opinion that this is a T.B.D.'s [destroyer's] job & not for us.' The poor view from a submarine bridge made it a bad scout. The Flotilla had been operating at full stretch recently. Some felt that the boats were being worn out by patrols in all weathers, in increasingly dangerous areas with little prospect of successful attacks. This was something Keyes had said he would not do when war broke out.[14]

E.2 and *E.4* were late leaving for Terschelling at 3:30pm, but the orders were not changed in response to Fraser's news. However, Leir's *E.4* did not get very far. She had to stop first her starboard engine and then the port engine off Southwold as a result of defects in the piston assemblies around 6pm. Although the crew got the port engine going again, Leir anchored for the night. With the starboard engine still out of action, he signalled at first light that he was returning to Harwich and arrived at 11am. The engines needed repair and were not reported correct until the 20th. Another boat with wireless sending apparatus, *D.8*, had been sent out to replace *E.4* at 5:45am on the 11th.[15]

E.2 was approaching Terschelling soon after dawn on the 11th. Stocks dived to commence attacks twice. The targets turned out to be a Dutch steamer and two Dutch trawlers approaching from the Texel. After passing another Dutch steamer he arrived at his billet, five miles off the shallows at the eastern end of Terschelling, at 11:20am. He patrolled for the next three days. *E.2* dived to make an attack on a ship that quickly disappeared to the northeast at 6:40am on the 12th. Shortly afterwards Stocks spotted *D.8* arriving and exchanged news with Foster. The 13th was a hazy day with visibility of only four miles. He dived to attack two destroyers that morning, but they turned out to be Dutch and headed back west. Stocks left for Harwich at 5pm, arriving at 10:15am next morning.[16]

Foster's *D.8* encountered three destroyers heading southwards, as he neared his billet off Terschelling, shortly after dawn on the 12th. They must have been Dutch. *D.8* reached the patrol billet, three miles south of *E.2*, at 8am. Foster aborted an attack run on the same destroyers as Stocks the next morning. *D.8* arrived back in Harwich at noon on the 14th. Foster reported that the navigation buoy that *E.2* and *D.8* had been ordered to use for their position reference had been removed.[17]

---

14   TNA ADM137/2067: pp.303, 322-6; IWM:Documents.1003: 10 October 1914.
15   TNA ADM173: *E.4* 10-20 October 1914; TNA ADM53: *Adamant,* 10 October 1914.
16   TNA ADM137/2067: p.311.
17   TNA ADM137/2067: p.312.

Firedrake, *E.1* and *E.11* had reached Zeebrugge at 9:30pm on the 10th. Waistell took *Firedrake* out next morning to patrol to the north off the Schouwen Light Vessel. In a sign of trouble to come, she stopped on the way out to sink a drifting British mine with rifle fire. It was from the British minefield recently laid to block the entrance to the Channel to the west. On her return at 1pm, *Firedrake* remained at 15 minutes notice to get underway again.

It was now determined that Zeebrugge and Ostend could not be defended. The British Army began evacuating the base at Zeebrugge on the 12th. The crews there must have had a despondent time watching the withdrawal and listening to the increasingly gloomy news coming from the front. Some of the hands were allowed ashore for exercise in the afternoon. Keyes received orders to withdraw at 4:20pm. *Firedrake* and the submarines left three hours later, arriving in Harwich at 2:55am next morning.

The Germans had no plans for anything other than submarine patrols off the Belgian ports. *U.8* attacked the destroyer *Ferret*, off Schouwen Light Vessel, close to where *Firedrake* was patrolling on the morning of the 11th. No German forces passed the submarine patrol off Terschelling whilst it was in place. The coastal battleships in the Ems were there for local defence. Basing warships at Antwerp was never a realistic option as the exits were entirely through neutral Dutch territorial waters. The Dutch Navy quickly blocked them with mines.[18]

Keyes reviewed the situation in the Heligoland Bight in a report to Sturdee on 14 October. German destroyers seemed increasingly reluctant to leave shallow water in daytime. They apparently limited patrolling to routes that they wished to keep clear for access in and out of the Bight, including the entrances to the Ems and the channel east of Heligoland. This indicated that these areas were free of mines. Keyes presumed that destroyers patrolled farther out to sea at night, but as the submarines now routinely spent the night on the bottom, evidence was lacking. Keyes highlighted that Cochrane and Boyle 'deserve credit' for obtaining this information by pushing forward into water of only seven fathoms (13m).

Keyes had heard of proposals to lay large minefields in the Bight and was alarmed about 'those waters being fouled for the submarines by indiscriminate minelaying.' To get ahead of this idea he himself suggested that it was time for targeted mining of the German exit channels, including those patrolled by the destroyers and the exits at either end of the German minefield. This would hinder the growing threat from enemy submarines as they entered and exited their bases. They were presumed to be bringing back valuable intelligence on British patrol patterns. He again pressed for an aerial reconnaissance of the minefield before any minelaying. The Ems could not be completely closed because of Dutch territorial waters, but he conjectured that the movement of the buoys that Cochrane had identified was to deceive minelayers. If it was not possible to mine Dutch waters, he considered that the Ems should be permanently watched by submarines during daytime and visited by destroyers at night.

He even suggested that *Lurcher* and *Firedrake* should be adapted to carry out the necessary minelaying, following a small destroyer raid to drive away the small craft watching the Ems. He also sent a personal letter to Sturdee. Keyes writes: 'I beg you will recommend that I may be allowed to lead them ... [and] that *Lurcher* and *Firedrake* may be fitted as minelayers.' In his memoirs Keyes reflects that: 'I am afraid I was very insistent and rather a nuisance in those days, and I think most of my offensive efforts remained pigeon-holed.' Offensive mining

---

18   TNA ADM186/620: pp.96-9, 174–5; TNA ADM53: *Firedrake* 10-13 October 1914.

never happened in 1914. Jellicoe, initially an advocate, blocked the idea, pointing out that the Germans would just sweep channels through large minefields in their own waters, as the British had done. However, small short term 'ambush' minefields could have been laid by destroyers in the way Keyes proposed and were used in this way later.[19]

19 TNA ADM137/2067: pp.313-8; Keyes, *Memoirs*, p.120; TNA ADM186/620: pp.70, 166.

17

Baltic excursion

Admiral Jellicoe had contacted Keyes on 6 October. He wanted suggestions for operations by any submarines that were not required for operations in the Heligoland Bight. Jellicoe may have been wondering why there had been no further action after the recent reconnaissance of the Kattegat. On the 10th Keyes responded, copying Sturdee.

Keyes began with an overview of submarine availability. There were two big problems. Firstly, the recent heavy weather had shown up weaknesses in the hydroplane shafting and hydroplane guards. These defects had resulted in submarines needing dock repairs, in two cases involving major work. The guards were being removed if they caused problems and replaced with a wire running the length of the boat. Keyes hoped that this would also prevent snagging of mine moorings, as had happened to *E.6*. Secondly, engine clutches were giving a great deal of trouble. Those submarines affected had to be taken out of service. An engineering firm in Ipswich was working around the clock, but it took two weeks to overhaul each boat.

Of the 19 D and E class boats in commission five were unavailable: two were laid up for clutch replacement; two for hydroplane defects; one for a long annual refit – *D.6*, since before war broke out. Of the 14 ready for service: six were at sea on patrol; two were temporarily at Zeebrugge on short notice; five were on short notice at Harwich; one was resting after returning from patrol.

In order to maintain five or six submarines continually in the Bight, Keyes felt that 12–15 were needed. Two or three could therefore probably be released for service elsewhere within a few days.

The most obvious way to use the submarines was to attack the German patrol guarding the entrance to the Baltic, south of The Sound. A recent intelligence briefing reported that the two cruisers patrolling there had been joined by eight torpedo boats, which Keyes assumed to be a response to the recent reconnaissance. However, there was concern at the Admiralty that a sortie into the Baltic would compromise Danish neutrality and provoke a German invasion. Keyes pointed out that Denmark could not be held responsible for the unaided passage of a British submarine through The Sound.

His second suggestion was also prompted by a recent intelligence briefing. This reported that the reconnaissance had resulted in the closure of the port of Lübeck for 24 hours. Keyes suggested further visits to occupy the Kattegat to disrupt trade, perhaps accompanied by destroyers. Two submarines could also be stationed off Horns Reef to warn of any attempt to cut the destroyers off by German forces from the Heligoland Bight. Since they would be beyond the short range of submarine wireless transmissions, a cruiser or destroyer would have to be within 50 miles of the submarines at specific times of day and night to pass on reports. Irrepressible as ever, Keyes suggested that he could do this with *Lurcher* and *Firedrake*. There were two issues to consider. Firstly, submarines might have to wait until nightfall to rig their wireless masts on the surface, delaying reports. Secondly, destroyers would need oil replenishment at sea for an extended patrol. Keyes believed that the submarines themselves could remain at sea for at least 14 days before needing to return.

His final suggestion was that if the Germans responded to the British blockade by coming out of the Heligoland Bight in force, Keyes should take all of the available submarines to wait off the German ports, then ambush them on their return. The timing of Keyes response was ideal, as Jellicoe had just telegraphed the Admiralty to ask that a submarine sortie into the Baltic should be considered.

Keyes was summoned to the Admiralty for discussions with Sturdee. He fleshed out his Baltic plan on the 12th, proposing implementation when a period of fair weather was expected. To conserve fuel, two submarines would start from Yarmouth and be towed by destroyers for the first day, with an escort of two destroyers as lookouts. The submarines would proceed independently at nightfall, aiming to arrive off The Sound unseen. They would each follow a neutral merchant ship through to attack the German Fleet in the Baltic. The latest intelligence indicated that it was carrying out gunnery practice there. Keyes would impress on the commanders the need to avoid any action which might compromise Denmark. At the time of their return, seven days after leaving Yarmouth, he suggested that his proposed raid on the Kattegat was launched to occupy it with friendly forces.

Following a further discussion with Sturdee, Keyes agreed on the 13th that he would order three boats into the Baltic for an extended patrol of several weeks. Once their fuel got low they were to head for the Russian port of Libava (now Liepāja in Latvia) for further orders. This change was Keyes own suggestion.

He executed the plan immediately. The submarines were ordered to depart at noon for Gorleston, where they were to top up with diesel. At 6am they would meet their tows and escorts off the Corton Light Vessel. They would head to The Sound and if possible pass at night. After avoiding the patrols to the south they would attack the German Fleet exercising off Kiel. Libava was to be approached firing red rockets and flying both the white ensign and union jack. They were given a recognition signal to use should their return to the Kattegat take place after 1 November, since British destroyers could be encountered there from 31 October. Details of German patrols and defensive minefields in the Baltic were appended to the orders.

The selection of Libava was a potentially catastrophic decision. The port was close to the German border. It was evacuated under the 1912 Russian Baltic Fleet Mobilisation Plan before war was declared. Only a handful of Russian military personnel remained. The entrances were partially closed with block-ships. The Germans added mine barriers in the approaches on the first day of the war, unaware that the Russian forces they hoped to trap had already left. The laying of the minefield was even reported by official press releases, apparently unnoticed in London. It seems incredible that both Russian plans and the most basic information about the naval situation in the Baltic were not known in the Admiralty. The proposal to send submarines to the Baltic had been raised almost a month previously, but nothing had been done to confirm the situation there. The orders to the submarines say that 'they will be expected' at Libava. The

British Embassy in St. Petersburg were apparently simply informed that the submarines would be arriving there.

Keyes now discovered that Jellicoe had prompted Sturdee to send submarines to the Baltic. He wrote in his diary: 'A regular case of mental telepathy. I had a most successful day at the Admiralty and carried my point. Laurence, Horton and Nasmith will have an opportunity of winning imperishable fame.' Jellicoe was informed by Keyes that the three submarines were leaving 'full of buoyancy and confidence.' He replied: 'wish it all success from me'.[1]

Keyes had chosen three of his most highly regarded commanders. Horton was an obvious choice after his recent victories. *E.9* was new and had been relatively trouble free. Laurence and Nasmith had done little so far, but they were pre-eminent submarine commanders and had served on Keyes Submarine Committee. In Laurence's case the problem was *E.1*. He had only been out on two patrols and had experienced mechanical problems on the second. Despite her recent major refit, *E.1* was a questionable choice for the mission. Nasmith was an experienced commander, but this would be his first war patrol. *E.11* was a new boat, with a new crew. First patrols had been steep learning curves for most of the Flotilla's commanders and crews.

Lieutenant-Commander Martin E. Nasmith was 31 in 1914. He had joined the Submarine Service in 1904. Nasmith had a gifted mind and received the Admiralty's thanks for two of his inventions early in his career. He had been court-martialled over the sinking of *A.4* in 1905. The verdict noted his 'coolness and presence of mind', as the boat filled with water on the bottom of the Solent in pitch darkness. *A.4* was brought to the surface and the crew was saved. Nasmith went on to command several C class, then *D.4*. Captain Brandt's assessment in 1911 is typical: 'Most capable. Thoroughly reliable. Careful & good seaman. G[ood] manner with men.' In 1912 Nasmith took command of the Training Flotilla at Portsmouth, where he revolutionised teaching and developed innovative attack training devices. He assumed command of *E.11* at the builders on the day war broke out. He put success above pleasure, vowing to abstain from smoking and drinking until he had sunk an enemy warship.[2]

Things started to go wrong not long after the submarines left Harwich at 2:20pm on the 13th. A defect arose in the starboard engine of *E.11*. Once at Gorleston it was found that one of the engine cylinders and liners would have to be replaced and work began immediately. Departure for all three boats was postponed. *Lurcher* seems to have been sent with the parts for the repair. She left Harwich at 3am on the 14th, anchored for an hour off Yarmouth at 6:45am, and was back in Harwich at noon. The parts presumably went ashore in a boat. The crew of *E.11* worked all day.

During the day Keyes forwarded additional information received by the Admiralty from Copenhagen. This identified that the Danish side of The Sound was closed by Danish mines. The channel on the Swedish side was clear and navigation lights were lit at night. The German patrols south of The Sound were identified, but crucially, it was also stated that German destroyers and submarines were 'patrolling the Kattegat'. In forwarding this to the three commanders Keyes also penned a note to Laurence, the senior officer, emphasising that it was important that all

1   TNA ADM137/2067, pp.333-47; Keyes, *Memoirs*, pp.116-8; N. B. Pavlovich (Translated C. M. Rao), *The Fleet in the First World War (Flot v Pervoi Mirovoi Voine) Vol. 1: Operations of the Russian Fleet* (New Delhi: Amerind Publishing Co. Pvt. Ltd., 1979), pp.33, 71–5.

2   TNA ADM196/48/179: Martin Eric Nasmith; Shankland & Hunter, *Dardanelles Patrol*, p.12, 21; Chatterton, *Amazing Adventure*, pp.37-43.

of the submarines get through The Sound before any of them made any attacks in the Baltic. Jellicoe's best wishes were also passed on.

That evening it was anticipated that the repair would be complete by 5am the next morning, the 15th. Laurence notified Keyes that he intended to depart at this time and Keyes agreed. There were now more changes of plan. The tows and destroyer escort were dropped. Keyes ordered that the boats depart together, then enter The Sound at two hour intervals, minimising the opportunity for enemy reaction.

At 5am it was estimated that the repairs would take another four hours. Laurence left as planned with *E.1* and *E.9*, leaving orders for Nasmith to follow as soon as possible. If the estimate was right, *E.11* should pass The Sound behind them at roughly the right time. *E.1* and *E.9* proceeded into the Baltic, never to return.[3]

For Nasmith the mechanical problems multiplied. More defects surfaced during the repair. *E.11* only finally got underway at 3pm. Even then only her port engine was working. Work on the starboard engine was finally completed two hours later. Both engines then had to be stopped at 7:30pm as defects developed in the cooling water circulation. This took another hour and a half to resolve. The problems continued when one engine had to be shut down later for another two hours work! *E.11* had now fallen far behind.

For the next two days the engines behaved themselves. Nasmith was careful to avoid being seen and dived three times to avoid 'suspicious craft'. On the afternoon of the 17th *E.11* entered the Kattegat and proceeded down the Swedish coast. If all had gone to plan Laurence and Horton would enter the Baltic that night.

Nasmith had to dive four more times as he headed down the busy Swedish coast next morning. He arrived at the northern entrance to The Sound in the afternoon and dived to await darkness. He was a little spooked by four merchant ships that passed in line abreast. Nasmith steered *E.11* around them, fearing they might be sweeping. He surfaced after dark amidst considerable merchant traffic. Nasmith decided to bluff his way through with his navigation lights on, as a craft without them would look suspicious and would still be silhouetted against the lights onshore. Soon after getting underway a vessel showing navigation lights approached. A collision seemed imminent. It was a destroyer! Nasmith ordered a sharp turn away, cut the lights and ordered full speed ahead. Once clear, he turned back into the channel and tagged along behind another vessel. This stopped and again turned out to be a destroyer! Nasmith submerged and headed for the Höganäs Road Light Vessel, off the Swedish coast near the entrance to The Sound, where he surfaced. He now tried again, heading up the channel on the electric motors, allowing him to dive more quickly if required. Four vessels were patrolling nearby and two others took station on either side of him. At 3am a vessel approached rapidly, shining a light ahead. Nasmith dived and the propellers churned overhead as *E.11* passed 35 feet (11m). He decided to spend the rest of the night on the bottom. Nasmith reported that: 'Although in neutral waters these vessels were undoubtedly hostile destroyers, who, although refraining from firing, attempted to sink us by ramming, which if successful would have been easily accounted an accident.' They were using a system of green lights for challenge.

Next morning, the 19th, Nasmith decided that he would make his next attempt by daylight. He first needed to find a quiet spot to surface and charge his batteries. *E.11* headed out of The

---

3   *E.1* and *E.9* remained part of 8th Flotilla for administrative purposes, but on detached service.

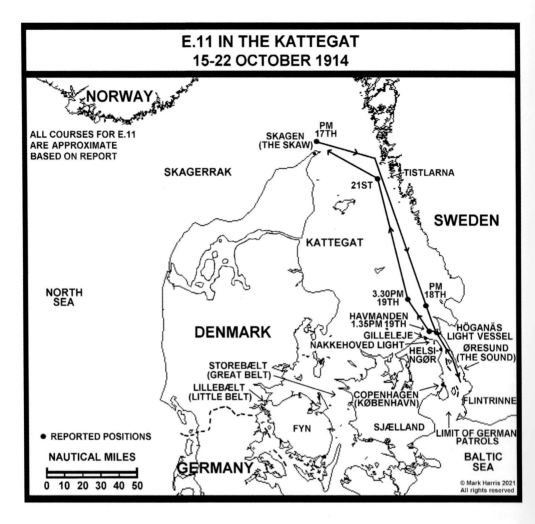

E.11 IN THE KATTEGAT
15-22 OCTOBER 1914

NORWAY

ALL COURSES FOR E.11
ARE APPROXIMATE
BASED ON REPORT

SKAGERRAK

SKAGEN
(THE SKAW)

PM
17TH

21ST

TISTLARNA

SWEDEN

KATTEGAT

NORTH
SEA

3.30PM
19TH

PM
18TH

DENMARK

HAVMANDEN
1.35PM 19TH
GILLELEJE
NAKKEHOVED LIGHT

HÖGANÄS
LIGHT VESSEL

ØRESUND
(THE SOUND)

HELSI-
NGØR

STOREBÆLT
(GREAT BELT)

LILLEBÆLT
(LITTLE BELT)

COPENHAGEN
(KØBENHAVN)

FLINTRINNE

• REPORTED POSITIONS

FYN

SJÆLLAND

LIMIT OF GERMAN
PATROLS

NAUTICAL MILES

GERMANY

BALTIC
SEA

0 10 20 30 40 50

Sound, keeping just north of Danish territorial waters. Nasmith spotted a submarine through the periscope about a mile ahead. She was apparently stopped on the surface. He altered course to close. She briefly moved off to the northwest, then quickly stopped again. Nasmith closed in and identified her as the German *U.3*. He was able to make out a '3' on the top corner of her conning tower. She matched the profile in his target book, right down to her twin masts and was not flying a visible ensign. He called his second in command, Lieutenant Henry D. Gill, to take a look to confirm his identification. Nasmith fixed his position. He was in international waters 4½ miles north of Gilleleje Harbour. Although ordered to make no attacks until south of The Sound, Nasmith was convinced that he had been seen the previous day and had nothing to lose. It was now 12:30pm. Having closed to 600 yards (550m) he fired a heater torpedo from his starboard bow tube. It would have taken less than a minute to reach the target, but nothing happened. The submarine did not move and had presumably not seen the torpedo. Nasmith carefully manoeuvred to pass close by on his port side, moving at slow speed to avoid breaking the calm surface. From 200 yards (180m) he clearly made out the '3' on the conning tower preceded by a letter that looked like 'U'. A crewman was seen to run forward. Twenty-five minutes after firing the first torpedo, Nasmith now fired a Mark V* cold torpedo from his port beam tube. Again nothing happened! When he put up the periscope a few minutes later the submarine had moved off, heading towards The Sound. Nasmith presumed the torpedo had run under because of the short range.

Batteries were now very low. Nasmith moved clear of the coast. He surfaced at 2:30pm and headed north to charge. After 40 minutes he altered course northeast to avoid 'suspicious sails' ahead to port. For obscure reasons to do with the way the sails hung, he thought they were attached to submarines, or a small boat working with them. The track of a heater torpedo now crossed ahead of *E.11*. The torpedo jumped out of the water at the end of its run a few hundred yards/m away. Nasmith dived. To avoid further attacks, *E.11* remained on the bottom all night.

Next morning, the 20th, Nasmith remained submerged and patrolled the area, hunting for German submarines. He saw nothing and surfaced at 1pm to head for the Swedish coast, charging his batteries. Nasmith had to dive at 3pm to avoid a low-flying aeroplane coming from the southwest and stayed submerged until it was dark. *E.11* surfaced to resume charging, only to get into another cat and mouse game with patrolling destroyers, showing their green recognition signals. Nasmith submerged for the rest of the night.

At dawn on the 21st *E.11* surfaced with nothing in sight and headed north charging. Nasmith had clearly given up on The Sound for now and continued past Tistlarna Island. A possible torpedo was spotted passing astern, but the sea was choppy, making it hard to be certain. A destroyer now came out from the coast and *E.11* submerged. At dusk, two different vessels approached in succession, but no ensigns could be made out, so no attacks were begun. Nasmith spent the night submerged, intending to attack in the morning.

There was nothing to be seen when *E.11* surfaced on the 22nd. Nasmith decided to return to Harwich, resupply and make another attempt to pass The Sound later. The return was uneventful and *E.11* arrived at 4:40pm on the 24th.

Unfortunately, Nasmith never reached the narrow part of The Sound, the Flintrinne, and therefore never got near any German warships. Their patrols had strict orders to remain south of The Sound, outside Danish and Swedish territorial waters. There had been a sortie by four submarines to the Skagerrak from Heligoland at the beginning of October. Just two of the submarines briefly entered the upper part of the Kattegat from the north, prompted by the reports about *E.1* and *E.5*. No German surface warships had entered the Kattegat since war was declared. The Germans were alerted to the breakthrough when Laurence attacked the cruiser *Victoria Louise* in the Baltic on the morning of the 18th. Patrols were reinforced, but still kept south of The Sound. The reason why any actual warships Nasmith might have encountered were burning navigation lights and did not ram or fire is that they could only have been Danish or Swedish. However, any clear identification would have been virtually impossible in the dark. The steamers and sailing vessels sighted were ordinary merchant vessels going about their business. As this channel was now the only way in and out of the Baltic, they were numerous. However, the Admiralty briefing was responsible for Nasmith believing that both German destroyers and submarines were in the area. The attack by Laurence could only make things worse, putting all of the naval forces in the area on the alert, including neutrals. The torpedoes fired at *E.11* did not exist. The first sighting was perhaps a porpoise, which were regularly mistaken for torpedoes even by experienced seamen, especially those who expected to be attacked. A couple of patrols before this attempt could have acclimatised Nasmith and his crew, before attempting a difficult night passage. The attribution of sinister motives to every sighting would probably have been avoided.[4]

Failure to get through the Sound was bad enough, but the submarine that Nasmith had attacked was the Danish *Havmanden*. She was a small coastal submarine of 38.8m (127 feet) commanded by Kaptajn Cai Baron Schaffalitzky de Muckadell and was part of a small flotilla based in nearby Helsingør. *Havmanden* had left Gilleleje that morning for exercises with her wireless and a seaplane, alternately sitting on the surface and moving at low speed. The first torpedo had not been seen when it was fired by *E.11*. It had probably misfired and possibly had a gyroscope failure. The two torpedoes were later spotted in quick succession. Muckadell reports:

> Premierløjtnant Scheibel observed a Torpedo about 400m [450 yards] to port of *Havmanden*, whilst heading approximately towards Höganas, speed about 5 Knots. The wireless antenna kite was aloft. Shortly afterwards, surging air bubbles as from an underwater torpedo shot and then the torpedo wake itself was seen ahead about 400m to port. This went just below *Havmanden*'s bow. Løjtnant Scheibel clearly observed the torpedo itself, the Chief and 2 of the crew the wake.

The first torpedo got close enough for a detailed description and was still venting air and petrol spray, whilst beginning to sink at an angle of 45 degrees to the surface. It should not have still been nearby. Two crewman reported that they had felt the second torpedo glance off the bottom of *Havmanden*! She had a maximum draught of 2.3m (7½ feet), decreasing towards her rounded bow. British torpedoes would glance off without detonating with a contact angle of less than 15 degrees.[5] Muckadell reports that her Danish swallow tailed ensign had wrapped itself around the flagstaff, making its distinctive shape impossible to identify. *Havmanden* turned to head for Danish waters, increased to 10 knots, raised two additional Danish ensigns and reported the attack by wireless. The next morning a torpedo exploded on the beach at nearby Nakkehoved Lighthouse.

After *E.11*'s attack on *Havmanden* the Danish Navy went to a higher state of alert, all coastal lights in The Sound were extinguished and orders given to prevent any attempt by belligerent warships of any nation to pass through The Sound via Danish territorial waters. Sweden also extinguished their navigation lights. On the 20th the Danish press reported the attack and Denmark issued diplomatic notes to Britain, Germany and Russia. The Danish Ambassador in London wrote to Sir Edward Grey, the British Foreign Minister, requesting that if the submarine in question was British, that 'the officer in command may be instructed to pay more attention in future.'[6]

Keyes reported to Sturdee on the 25th. He was critical of Laurence's decision to leave without Nasmith, as it left too much to chance. Departure could have been delayed for another day until *E.11* was ready. Keyes writes that Nasmith was: 'fearless and enterprising ... I feel sure he acted with good judgment.' He makes a lengthy defence, accepting at face value the assumed

---

4   Firle, *Ostsee 1*, p.207; Groos, *Nordsee 2*, Karte 9.
5   TNA ADM186/366: Addenda (1911) to Torpedo Manual, Vol. III, 1909, p.16.
6   Michael H. Clemmesen, 'E11s problemer – HAVMANDENS lykke', Tom Wismann (ed.), *Marinehistorisk Tidsskrift, 50 årgang, Nr. 3 – August 2017* (Marinehistorisk Selskab/Orlogsmuseetsvenner, 2017), pp.3–41.

Havmanden - pendant number 3 in centre - on exercise off København in June 1914 with three of her sister ships. (Forsvarsgalleriet)

belligerence of virtually every sighting on the patrol. Nasmith had added a note to his own report insisting that he had fired at *U.3*, noting the number, absence of a flag and the two prominent masts. The photograph of *Havmanden* he had seen showed only one. Keyes dismissed the denials of an attack by the German Ambassador to Denmark. He asked that the Danish, Norwegian and Swedish governments be informed that any vessel patrolling outside territorial waters was in danger of being attacked. A similar warning had already been issued to the Dutch government after the frequent sightings of their neutrality patrol. Keyes concluded that due to the level of opposition and disregard for Danish and Swedish neutrality by Germany, Nasmith was right to return. He did not think another attempt was advisable. Keyes also proposed that due to the heavy opposition to the passage of The Sound, it would now be advisable to keep *E.1* and *E.9* in the Baltic over the winter. He sought approval to liaise with the Russian Naval Attaché in London for torpedoes and spare parts to be despatched through the port of Archangel in the Arctic. Since Libava was an ice-free port, Keyes assumed they would be able to operate throughout the winter months. He was still unaware that it had been abandoned. The foray into the Baltic had become open ended.

Unfortunately, the conclusions reached about the difficulty of passing The Sound were flawed. There had been no violation of Swedish and Danish neutrality. Even now, the route was unobstructed, although unlit at night. It was still only watched by German warships at the southern exit, albeit more of them. Nasmith's report and the uncritical acceptance of it by Keyes distorted British perceptions of the probability of successfully getting submarines through The Sound. Intelligence failings litter the story of the operation. The most glaring was that it was not difficult for a trained eye to confirm what was going on in The Sound by direct observations from the shore. If details of the patterns of the neutrality watch had been given in the intelligence briefings it might well have mitigated Nasmith's concerns. There were significant failings in obtaining and verifying intelligence, with too much reliance placed on collecting casual observations by steamship captains. The foray into the Baltic was strategically sound, met with great success over time and gave valuable support to the Russian Navy, but this was in spite of the planning and intelligence, not because of it. Both *E.1* and *E.9* could have hit mines on arrival at Libava and were lucky not to.

Next day Sturdee requested further detail of the attack on *Havmanden* from Nasmith, which was provided with a supporting note from Keyes. On 4 November the Danish government sent a note giving details of the markings on parts salvaged from the torpedo that exploded on the beach. These were in English. A check of the torpedo register confirmed that they were from the specific Mark V* torpedo that *E.11* had fired from her beam tube. This torpedo should have sunk at the end of its run. Despite this overwhelming evidence Keyes continued to strenuously deny that the attack Nasmith made was on *Havmanden*. He insisted that *U.3* or some other submarine must have made the attack and suggested that Nasmith's report be shared with the Danes. Their Director of the Ministry of Marine was eventually shown Nasmith's report by a British diplomat in Copenhagen on 31 December. He quickly pointed out that *Havmanden* carried the pendant number '3' on her conning tower, was in the position stated at the time and met the description of the boat with two masts made by Nasmith. A man had even been sent forward just before the attack as described in his report. Her Danish ensign had been clinging to the staff as there was no wind and was 'old and dirty'.

Faced with this evidence Keyes conceded blame on 7 January, pointing out that he had been previously unaware the boat carried the number '3' or that she had been fitted with a wireless mast. He offered the Danish authorities 'an expression of deep regret for an error which so nearly resulted in the destruction of one of their vessels.' The Danish minister had already indicated that he would be satisfied with an apology and the incident ended there.[7]

Keyes had made two other suggestions for operations. Jellicoe ruled out a commerce raid in the Kattegat in a response on 15 October. Commerce was being very effectively intercepted off the Orkneys and Shetlands. It was too difficult to carry out stop and search in the Kattegat. It was far from the destroyer bases and there was also risk of submarine attack. Keyes replied the next day that he could no longer spare boats for an operation in the Kattegat, but still thought a destroyer raid would be valuable to disrupt trade, which he could cover from the Bight. He also writes: 'Am strongly urging that patrol submarines should be sparingly employed; they will be of vital importance later; request independent support.' This implies that the high level of patrolling was being pushed on Keyes by Sturdee. Jellicoe had already suggested to Keyes that patrols off the Schelde would be better done by C class 'coastal' submarines. Jellicoe politely re-iterated his reasoning against operations in the Kattegat in a reply on the 25th, whilst praising 'the valuable work carried out in the Heligoland Bight' by the Flotilla. That was the end of the idea. Jellicoe did endorse Keyes final idea to ambush the returning German Fleet with every available submarine in the event of a fleet sortie.[8]

7   TNA ADM137/2067: pp.350-71.
8   TNA ADM137/2067: pp.348-9; *Keyes Papers*, pp.40-41.

18

The enemy strike

Whilst Nasmith was away the orders for the next relief of the Ems and Terschelling patrols had been issued. The submarines were to leave Harwich at 3pm on 13 October. *E.6* was the only submarine sent to patrol the Ems, covering the main entrance and Huibert Gat. *E.7* and *E.3* were to relieve *E.2* and *D.8* on the new 24 hour surface wireless picket off Terschelling. When Feilmann and Cholmley pointed out to Waistell that they did not yet have sending gear to report enemy movements, *D.4* was substituted for *E.3*. Feilmann was told to track down *D.4* if he had anything to report! The recent discussions with Jellicoe, selection of two boats without wireless and the issue of orders only an hour before departure, all suggest that Keyes had been hoping to send *E.7* and *E.3* to offensive patrol billets in the Bight and had been overruled by Sturdee in the meeting he had earlier that day. Each submarine left as soon as it was ready. All three were to return at 5pm on the 16th.[1]

Feilmann's *E.7* left Harwich at 3:25pm for her billet five miles off Terschelling shallows. After leaving the Suffolk coast, Cunard tried to avoid a huge fleet of trawlers fishing by lights in the pitch darkness. He headed wide to the north. Hallifax had the next watch and pushed through them as there seemed no way round. At one point he had to quickly change course and increase speed to cut across the bows of a steamer heading directly for *E.7*.

It was very misty next morning. At 10:30am Feilmann turned south and slowly closed the Dutch coast. *E.7* stopped at noon to sound the water depth when land was sighted through the mist. The officers were looking for landmarks and discussing where they might be, when Signalman Johnson spotted the side silhouette of a submarine, apparently stopped, two miles astern. The binoculars revealed it to be German. Feilmann dived and headed north to attack but could not locate the target. After 45 minutes *E.7* turned back. At 1:20pm Feilmann surfaced and spotted Ameland Lighthouse six miles away. They had arrived at the billet. Shortly afterwards Hallifax spotted smoke from a ship looming up from the west. *E.7* dived towards her to attack. As they closed, the target was identified as a couple of Dutch torpedo boats. The wind dropped to a calm and the mist thickened. At 2:45pm Hallifax says that Feilmann decided to go to the bottom, as it was inviting attack to remain surfaced in the mist and he 'did not feel inclined to roam about submerged.' The gramophone was used to while away the time, although the log says: 'Courses as requisite for patrolling.' *E.7* came up to charge for nearly five hours after dark.

---

1   TNA ADM137/2067, p.373.

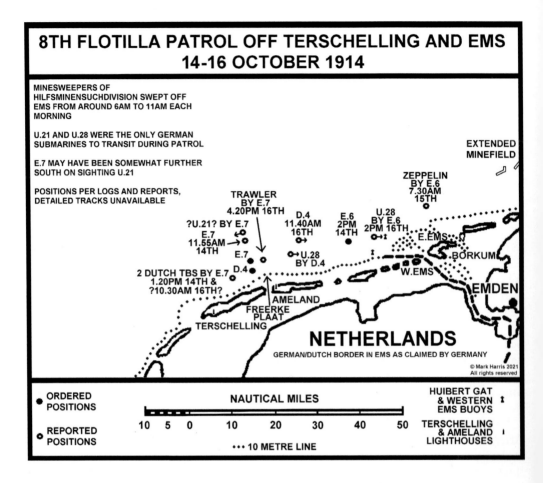

8TH FLOTILLA PATROL OFF TERSCHELLING AND EMS
14-16 OCTOBER 1914

MINESWEEPERS OF
HILFSMINENSUCHDIVISION SWEPT OFF
EMS FROM AROUND 6AM TO 11AM EACH
MORNING

U.21 AND U.28 WERE THE ONLY GERMAN
SUBMARINES TO TRANSIT DURING PATROL

E.7 MAY HAVE BEEN SOMEWHAT FURTHER
SOUTH ON SIGHTING U.21

POSITIONS PER LOGS AND REPORTS,
DETAILED TRACKS UNAVAILABLE

EXTENDED
MINEFIELD

ZEPPELIN
BY E.6
7.30AM
15TH

TRAWLER
BY E.7
4.20PM 16TH

?U.21? BY E.7
E.7
11.55AM
14TH

D.4
11.40AM
16TH

E.6
2PM
14TH

U.28
BY E.6
2PM 16TH

E.EMS

BORKUM

E.7

U.28
BY D.4

W.EMS

2 DUTCH TBS BY E.7
1.20PM 14TH &
?10.30AM 16TH?

D.4

EMDEN

AMELAND

FREERKE
PLAAT

TERSCHELLING

NETHERLANDS

GERMAN/DUTCH BORDER IN EMS AS CLAIMED BY GERMANY

ORDERED
POSITIONS

REPORTED
POSITIONS

NAUTICAL MILES

10 5 0   10   20   30   40   50

••• 10 METRE LINE

HUIBERT GAT
& WESTERN
EMS BUOYS

TERSCHELLING
& AMELAND
LIGHTHOUSES

Hallifax wrote that it was too dark to see anything, so *E.7* went back to the bottom at 11pm. She surfaced again after moonrise, but quickly went back to the bottom when the sky clouded over. Not exactly round the clock surface patrolling.

Feilmann surfaced at 7am on the 15th to fine, but misty weather. *E.7* was thought to have drifted while charging and headed inshore to fix her position on a landmark. She was actually off Terschelling Lighthouse, but this was mistaken for Ameland Lighthouse. The error was later realised and she arrived back at her correct billet at 5:25pm. Nothing was sighted all day. *E.7* went to the bottom for 'a quiet dinner'. She surfaced at 10pm to a starlit night with good visibility. At 3:30am, Feilmann decided to go to the bottom for the rest of the night as 'the men must have some rest'. In good visibility this was a clear breach of orders and neither log nor report mention it.

E.7 surfaced at 8am on the 16th to a dull, but clear day. She headed slowly southwest. Feilmann dived mid-morning for two vessels glimpsed inshore. They were presumed to be Dutch torpedo boats and disappeared. Feilmann surfaced and headed east to try and find *D.4*, to confirm whether she had also seen them. He was unable to locate her and only spotted three trawlers. At 1:45pm Feilmann decided to stop, remaining surfaced. At 4pm a trawler was spotted nearby. *E.7* soon started her diesels and got underway, as she had drifted somewhat east of her billet. Hallifax wrote: 'the bell now rang like blazes,' Feilmann rapidly descended, together with the stool he had been sitting on. The trawler had apparently 'rushed' directly towards *E.7* as soon as she moved. The bridge screen was still rigged, so the boat had difficulty submerging. The trawler seemed to be trying to follow. It was feared that she was equipped with an explosive sweep or mines. Hallifax examined her through the periscope, but there was nothing to suggest any armament. An hour later, with the trawler out of sight, *E.7* surfaced and headed for Harwich. Full speed was maintained for three hours, as a precaution against any destroyers that the trawler had summoned. At 11pm Feilmann spotted a steamer or large trawler close by. She turned towards *E.7* as they passed. Feilmann went full speed ahead and only just avoided collision. The steamer seemed to follow them for some time.

Neither of the trawler incidents are in the log. Feilmann told Hallifax to leave them out of the report, since: 'it only means the Commodore will send for me and ask me a lot of questions about them.' He exasperated Hallifax by striking matches on the bridge to light his pipe whilst on watch in the darkness. *E.7* had to constantly alter course to avoid trawlers. Hallifax later had to turn hard to starboard to avoid a collision when he found his path blocked by three trawlers close together. His alarm increased when he saw a torpedo track pass underneath the hull. It turned out to be phosphorescence, trailing a porpoise in a school riding the bow wave. *D.4* joined astern at 7am on the 17th. They arrived back in Harwich shortly after noon. The patrol is noteworthy for the level of dysfunction that had been reached at command level. Immediately afterwards Hallifax wrote: 'Every time I go out I hate it more & get more nervy; if only F[eilmann] would give me a real damning bit of evidence of criminal stupidity, or get really drunk instead of merely sozzled, I would go to the Commodore.'[2]

Moncreiffe's *D.4* left Harwich at 4pm on the 13th. Her billet was three miles south of *E.7*. She arrived at 3pm next day. Moncreiffe soon stopped the engines just offshore and anchored in place overnight. On the morning of the 15th, *D.4* dived to the bottom for a two hour break at 7am. Soon after getting back underway, she grounded on the Freerkeplaat sands between Terschelling and Ameland, in Dutch territorial waters. Fortunately, Moncreiffe was soon able to get off. Internment would have been the result if *D.4* had got stuck. Moncreiffe went to the bottom after dark, having seen nothing since arriving at the billet. The Dutch removal of local navigation buoys that had been partly responsible for running aground is in his report, but the grounding itself is not.

D.4 surfaced at 6:30am on the 16th, headed out to sea, then turned east. At 11:40am a submarine was sighted about four miles away towards the shoreline and a little behind, on a parallel course. It was 20 minutes before *D.4* dived; perhaps it was initially thought to be *E.7* closing to communicate. The time lag is only apparent from the log. Moncreiffe reports: 'Attacked but German dived five or six minutes after *D.4*. Did not see him again.' After searching at periscope depth for an hour, *D.4* took a two hour break on the bottom. Moncreiffe left for Harwich at 5:17pm.[3]

Talbot's *E.6* left Harwich at 2:45pm on the 13th. The mist that persisted throughout the patrol meant that Talbot had to use the glow of Lowestoft's lights as a cue to turn eastwards to Terschelling, dodging through the huge fleet of drifters in the darkness. He 'more or less'

2   TNA ADM137/2067: p.376; TNA ADM173: *E.7* 13-17 October 1914, IWM:Documents.1003: 13–17 October 1914.

3   TNA ADM137/2067: p.374; TNA ADM173: *D.4* 13-17 October 1914.

arrived at his billet off the Ems at 2pm on the 14th, through mist and rain, without having sighted land. Talbot writes in his diary: 'Dived all the afternoon, going dead slow, about 1½ knots; it is not worth remaining on the surface hereabouts, as they usually have some of their submarines out.' He surfaced and headed out to sea to charge the battery at 5pm, returning to spend the night on the bottom at 9:30pm. The pattern was repeated after coming off the bottom at 6am the next morning, with occasional trips to the surface for air and position fixes. A zeppelin was spotted to the east whilst surfaced at 7:30am, heading towards Borkum. Talbot dived to avoid being seen.

The routine continued on the morning of the 16th. Only a distant trawler in the entrance and a passing steamer were spotted. At 2pm, Talbot saw a submarine surfacing through the periscope. She was about 1,500 yards (1,400m) away, almost directly ahead and was quickly identified as German. This was a golden opportunity to strike before she could get underway. *E.6* immediately began an attack run. The bow torpedo had to be reset from 10 feet (3m) depth to five feet (1½m) to attack a submarine. Several hands dashed forward to help haul it back out of the tube, upsetting the trim and causing *E.6* to dive deep. By the time trim was recovered the target had got underway and was disappearing into the Western Ems, to Talbot's 'intense disgust'. Nothing more was seen. *E.6* surfaced and headed back to Harwich at 5pm.

Talbot cautiously avoided the Dutch coast, passing a slow steamer with a wide berth. Two vessels showing drifter lights were sighted at 11:30pm off Terschelling. Talbot could not lose them, despite numerous course alterations, although it seemed impossible that they could see him. They even re-appeared after he had dived for an hour. Talbot now shadowed them, intending to identify whether they were enemy destroyers in daylight, but lost them in mist at 5am next morning, the 17th. *E.6* arrived off Smiths Knoll at 10am and found three or four Dutch trawlers in the prohibited zone. A local C class destroyer was only a mile farther on. Talbot closed to ask her to examine and warn the trawlers. *E.6* replied to her challenge, but the destroyer then ignored his signals and made off despite five or six white signal lights being fired to attract attention. She later returned and challenged *E.6* again. Talbot now signalled his request again. The destroyer replied that she was heading off to investigate firing off Yarmouth.

On arriving at Harwich at 5pm, Talbot was 'so angry that I ran her in to the Commodore' and put it in writing. Keyes contacted Rear-Admiral Ballard, the Admiral of Patrols, who asked Captain Brown of the 7th Destroyer Flotilla to investigate. A bristling response came back from Commander Bowring of the *Violet*. He had investigated the trawlers earlier that day. The explosions of the rockets were mistaken for gunfire. *Violet* went to action stations and Bowring turned to engage *E.6*. Fortunately she was correctly identified just in time. A copy of the signal to *Violet* from *E.6* was included, which began: 'I have been trying to get your attention by rockets and flags for 1½ hours'. Bowring did not 'consider his signal was a correct one to make to a superior officer.' Brown thought it was 'an unfortunate misunderstanding' and Ballard concurred that 'both appeared … to some extent to blame.' The matter ended there. A storm in a tea-cup, but random chances could have ended in disaster.[4]

Poor visibility over the period meant that the only German patrol activity in the area was minesweepers working off the Ems each morning and aerial reconnaissance. It is probable that

---

4   TNA ADM137/2067: pp.375, 377–385; TNA ADM173: *E.6* 13-17 October 1914; IWM: Documents 20134: 13-17 October 1914.

E.7 sighted *U.21* on the 14th. She was passing Terschelling at the time, westbound for the Belgian coast, but *E.6* was also nearby heading east to her billet. Neither reported *E.7*, which would have been hard to spot against the land end-on. The submarine attacked by both *D.4* and *E.6* on the 16th was almost certainly *U.28*, which returned eastbound to Borkum Roads at 3:30pm from her patrol in the English Channel. She reported seeing a submarine at some point during her return and may have spotted *E.7* diving. This gave credence to bogus patrol reports of submarines on the 13th northwest of Heligoland, on the 15th east of Heligoland and on the 16th off the Eider Light Vessel. This led the Germans to deduce that British submarines were again operating in the Inner Bight after a period of absence and a destroyer sweep was ordered by two flotillas northwest of Heligoland.[5]

The torpedo boats seen by *E.7* were the Dutch neutrality patrol, as suspected. Commercial steamers and trawlers account for the numerous other sightings that caused such a navigational headache in the bad visibility. Fishing boats and steamers had been bottled up in port by the recent atrocious weather and were out in force. The hostile motives ascribed to these vessels were groundless. However, there was a consequence. Talbot described his mysterious shadow to Hallifax and asked whether *E.7* had similar problems. Hallifax described their own encounters. When Talbot asked if they had been reported, he replied: 'No, but I think we ought to have done so.' Talbot went to see Keyes to discuss it, as the information lent credibility to his own suspicions about being stalked. Talbot informed Hallifax that Keyes responded: 'E7? Then why the devil didn't they say so in their report?'

Later that day Hallifax discussed doing something about Feilmann with Lieutenant Harold V. Lyon of *E.2*. Lyon agreed with Hallifax that Leir, the Senior Officer, might dismiss it and that Talbot would be a good person to get advice from. Hallifax took a break from his worries by attending a 'good show' put on by the crew of the *Woolwich*. Next morning he screwed himself up and spoke to Talbot in his cabin. After a sympathetic hearing he was asked to play a round of golf, where discussion continued. Talbot was surprised to hear that Feilmann was drinking at sea. He did not offer specific advice beyond suggesting that Hallifax 'try to bring things to a crisis.' Talbot himself only mentions enjoying the game of golf in his diary.

Orders for the next patrol relief had been issued on the 16th. The submarines left in company at 11:45am that morning. *E.3* was to relieve *E.6* off the Western Ems. *E.8* only would relieve *D.4* and *E.7* on the 24 hour wireless picket off Terschelling. The patrol was to return at 5pm on the 19th.[6]

Goodhart's *E.8* arrived to patrol off Terschelling at 8am on the 17th in wet and gloomy weather that persisted for the first two days of the patrol. He had to dive for an hour that morning to avoid four patrolling Dutch destroyers. Goodhart stopped the engines at 2:30pm and drifted until the following morning.

At 5:50am a ship showing her lights approached from the east. *E.8* dived and steered an interception course to within firing range. She had a German mercantile ensign, but was clearly marked as a hospital ship and was immune to attack. She passed by, heading west. Once she was out of sight, *E.8* surfaced, rigged her wireless mast and attempted to call up the destroyer patrol to request that they examine her. There was no acknowledgement of the signal, despite trying

5   Groos, *Nordsee 2*, pp.164, 206, 252, Karte 10–11; BArch:RM92: *Nassau* Kriegstagebuch, 13 October 1914; *Stettin* Kriegstagebuch, 16 October 1914.
6   TNA ADM137/2067: p.387.

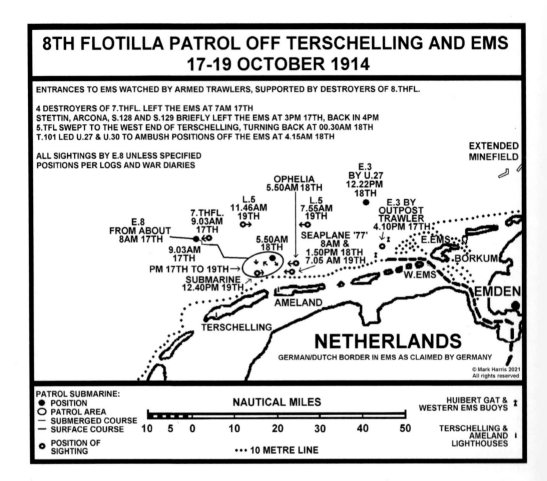

8TH FLOTILLA PATROL OFF TERSCHELLING AND EMS 17-19 OCTOBER 1914

ENTRANCES TO EMS WATCHED BY ARMED TRAWLERS, SUPPORTED BY DESTROYERS OF 8.THFL.

4 DESTROYERS OF 7.THFL. LEFT THE EMS AT 7AM 17TH
STETTIN, ARCONA, S.128 AND S.129 BRIEFLY LEFT THE EMS AT 3PM 17TH, BACK IN 4PM
5.TFL SWEPT TO THE WEST END OF TERSCHELLING, TURNING BACK AT 00.30AM 18TH
T.101 LED U.27 & U.30 TO AMBUSH POSITIONS OFF THE EMS AT 4.15AM 18TH

ALL SIGHTINGS BY E.8 UNLESS SPECIFIED
POSITIONS PER LOGS AND WAR DIARIES

EXTENDED MINEFIELD

E.3 BY U.27 12.22PM 18TH

OPHELIA 5.50AM 18TH

L.5 11.46AM 19TH   L.5 7.55AM 19TH

E.3 BY OUTPOST TRAWLER 4.10PM 17TH

7.THFL. 9.03AM 17TH

E.8 FROM ABOUT 8AM 17TH

E.EMS

5.50AM 18TH   SEAPLANE '77' 8AM & 1.50PM 18TH 7.05 AM 19TH

BORKUM

9.03AM 17TH

PM 17TH TO 19TH→

W.EMS

SUBMARINE 12.40PM 19TH

EMDEN

AMELAND

TERSCHELLING

NETHERLANDS

GERMAN/DUTCH BORDER IN EMS AS CLAIMED BY GERMANY

PATROL SUBMARINE:
● POSITION
○ PATROL AREA
− SUBMERGED COURSE
− SURFACE COURSE
◉ POSITION OF SIGHTING

NAUTICAL MILES

10 5 0   10   20   30   40   50

••• 10 METRE LINE

HUIBERT GAT & WESTERN EMS BUOYS
TERSCHELLING & AMELAND LIGHTHOUSES

for over an hour. Later a seaplane came into view to the south. Goodhart thought that *E.8* had been seen before she could submerge. He surfaced again after 20 minutes and remained in the area, occasionally patrolling legs backwards and forwards. Goodhart had to dive again later that morning for the Dutch patrol and again for a seaplane coming from the east at 1:50pm. Aeroplanes loomed large in the minds of the crew. At 11pm: 'A light was observed in the sky, travelling fast … possibly an airship.'

The 19th dawned and the clouds began to break. *E.8* soon had to dive when a seaplane approached from eastward. This was followed by a zeppelin, which was spotted through the periscope heading out to sea on the horizon. Goodhart surfaced when she went out of sight, nearly two hours after diving. He patrolled the area north of the Akkepole Gat, between Ameland and Terschelling for the next three hours. *E.8* had to dive again for an hour when the zeppelin was spotted returning in the distance. Almost immediately after surfacing at 12:35pm a submarine was spotted five miles to the south. This appeared to have also just surfaced, heading east. Goodhart dived and moved close inshore to catch her if she returned. Nothing more was seen. *E.8* headed back to Harwich at 5pm. Like Talbot on the previous patrol, Goodhart was suspicious of three steamers encountered in succession on similar courses to *E.8* in the darkness off Terschelling, which he had to alter course to avoid. Harwich was reached at 11am on the 20th.[7]

There was a minimal watch off the Ems in the misty weather at the start of the patrol. Armed trawlers were at the exits, supported inside by destroyers of 8th Torpedoboots-Halbflottille. At 7am on the 17th four destroyers of 7th Torpedoboots-Halbflottille under Korvettenkapitän Thiele left the Ems for a covert mission to lay mines in the Thames Estuary. This was the first time German destroyers were sent into British waters. They kept clear of the coast to avoid detection. Thiele, in *S.119*, sighted a British submarine at 9:03am. She altered course, intending to ram, as Thiele was desperate to prevent a wireless report. *E.8* submerged before they could reach her. *S.119* reported the sighting by wireless. The destroyers now steered into sight of the Terschelling Light, then turned east. Once out of sight they doubled back to the west. Thiele hoped that a suspected spy on the Light Vessel would see them and report them heading east. He was wasting his time, as Goodhart had identified them as the familiar Dutch patrol in the poor visibility. Large Dutch torpedo boats were similar, if a little smaller than the German *S.114* class. Ultimately it made no difference, as Thiele was heading for the cruiser *Undaunted* and a Division of 3rd Destroyer Flotilla. All four were sunk.[8] Their wireless messages requesting assistance may have given Cholmley a good target. The cruisers *Stettin* and *Arcona*, with the destroyers *S.128* and *S.129* responded and sortied from the Ems at 2:50pm but were recalled by Fleet Command to await developments at 4pm. Cholmley's *E.3* had kept in company with *E.8* until 10pm on the 16th and would have recently arrived on her billet. At 4:10pm the outpost trawler at the Huibert Gat entrance reported a British submarine in sight. This had been the first real chance to attack the Ems based cruisers since August, albeit fleeting. We do not know if Cholmley was in position to attack. The 5th Torpedoboots-Flottille was ordered to sweep along the Dutch coast to the western end of Terschelling, turning there just after midnight, but was not sighted by *E.8* in the darkness.

Next morning, the 18th, the hospital ship *Ophelia* left Heligoland to search for survivors from 7th Torpedoboots-Halbflottille. Tyrwhitt intercepted her despite Goodhart's inability to get through his report. She was sent in for examination on suspicion of spying. The previous report by *D.4* of suspicious behaviour by a hospital ship contributed to a questionable decision by the prize court to condemn her as a warship.

At 7:30am, as a result of the various submarine sighting reports, submarine leader boat *T.101* led *U.27* and *U.30* out of the Ems to dive at ambush positions in the approaches. Two seaplanes were also sent up to reconnoitre and Seaplane '77' spotted *E.8* at 8am. *U.30* was posted well to the north. *U.27* was south of her. At 10:25am, her commander, Kapitänleutnant Bernd Wegener, spotted a buoy. He soon realised it was actually a submarine conning tower. Wegener carefully manoeuvred at half speed to bring *U.27* round to attack from the side of the target, keeping the sun behind to dazzle any lookouts. The ruffled surface of the sea helped conceal the periscope, which was used sparingly to check progress every 400–500m (450–550 yards), with speed reduced to a crawl to minimise any disturbance each time it was raised. Having got within two miles, at 11:05am Wegener reduced speed to slow ahead, concerned that his engines might be picked up by underwater sound receivers. He reported that: 'Six lookouts stood in black

7   TNA ADM137/2067: pp.388–9; TNA ADM173: *E.8* 16–20 October 1914.
8   7th Halbflottille had now been annihilated. The only other destroyer in the unit had been *S.116*.

E.3 at Barrow shortly after her delayed completion in the summer of 1914. (Darren Brown Collection)

oilskins on her conning tower and were all looking in the direction of the mouth of the Ems.' The starboard bow 50cm (19.7-inch) tube was readied with a torpedo set to run shallow at 1½m (5 feet). *U.27* had been closing for 80 minutes and only now was Wegener certain that he was stalking a British submarine. Distinctive features could be made out and he turned hard about onto his final attack run at 11:45am. Wegener continues: 'my watch officer, whom I allowed to look through the periscope for a short time to confirm identification, observed a black "83" on the conning tower (*E.3*). Other than the conning tower, the boat's outlines were visible only at very close range. The boat had been charging during my attack, as faint hazy clouds were visible.' After another 40 minutes Wegener raised the periscope for the last time: 'the foe was 5° to 6° to port, in my estimation 300m [350 yards] away. I therefore ordered "full speed ahead" with the starboard engine, which had been running at low speed and turned hard to port to shoot. Fire: Midships.' *E.3* had no time to react. Only 12 seconds later a detonation was heard and a 50m (160 feet) high column of water sprang into the sky. *U.27* must have actually been about 200m (250 yards) away when she fired. The target broke in two, with the bow and stern very briefly standing out of the water. Debris rained down, one piece of which struck *U.27* on the starboard side. By the time the water had subsided no trace was left of *E.3*. Wegener reports that: 'Initially, I could not pick up four people floating in the water, because I did not want to expose my boat to attack by other enemy submarines. However, I intended to make a rescue attempt after about half an hour.' When he did so, *U.27* twice circled the scene of the sinking whilst still submerged, but apart from a few bits of cork, some loaves of bread and a wooden box, nothing was to be seen.[9]

9   BArch:RM97: *U.27* Kriegstagebuch; BArch:RM92: *Stettin, Nassau* Kriegstagebuch 17–19 October 1914; TNA ADM186/620: pp.121-2; Groos, *Nordsee 2*, pp.191-3, 198, 253-4.

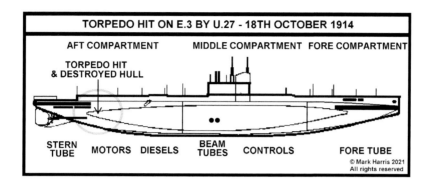

The wreck of *E.3* was located in 1994, after the stern was brought to the surface in the nets of a trawler. It is facing south in 30m (100 feet) of water. The explosion of the powerful 160kg (353lb) TNT warhead of the G/6 torpedo was devastating. It struck abreast the electric motors, destroying this part of the aft compartment. The stern, with the aft hydroplanes and stern torpedo tube, was severed. The explosion would have resulted in an overpressure inside the submerged, confined hull. This must have killed or incapacitated most of the crew instantly and certainly all those in the compartment. Those seen in the water would probably have been from the bridge.[10]

Wegener's report and the location of the wreck, at some distance from the Ems, imply that *E.3* was trimmed down charging throughout the attack, with only the conning tower above water. Her crew paid the price for sitting on the surface in an area known to be frequented by German submarines. This had been top of mind for Talbot a few days earlier. Being trimmed down made *E.3* harder to spot, but easier to hit, with her hull sitting deep in the water. All 28 crew were lost.[11] Fifteen listed wives as next of kin. Keyes paid tribute to Cholmley in his report as 'one of our most experienced and skilful Submarine Captains, and an Officer the Submarine Service could ill afford to lose.' *E.3* was both the first Royal Navy submarine lost in action and the first submarine to be sunk by another. This was only her fourth offensive patrol.

The German Admiralty announced the sinking to the press on the 19th: 'The British submarine *E 3* was destroyed on the afternoon of October 18 in the German Bight of the North Sea.'[12] They believed the cause of her loss had been concealed but utilising the number of the

---

10 The ship's bell confirmed the identity. This war grave was then plundered by trophy hunters.

11 In Command – Lieutenant-Commander George Francis Cholmley; 1st Lieutenant – Lieutenant John Stuart Binny Scott; 3rd Hand – Sub-Lieutenant John Gerald Barrow; Chief Petty Officer – George Webster MacFarlane; Petty Officer LTOs – Frederick Wallace Edroff; Herbert Joseph Harris; Leading Seamen –Stanley Vernon Coutanche; George William Taylor; John William Westrope; Able Seamen – Albert Edward Hunt; Robert Jones; William George Lowman; Peter Querotret; William Young; Signalman – Alfred Lowe Morgan; ERA 1st Class – Fred Hunt; ERA 2nd Class – Richard Saunders Hellon; ERAs 3rd Class – Charley Ellman Blake; Joseph Stothard; Acting Chief Stoker – Neil Matheson; Stoker Petty Officer – Percy George Merritt; Acting Leading Stoker – George Henry Tanner; Stokers 1st Class – William Alexander Beal; Percy Beckwith; Alfred John Douglas; Alfred Ernest House; Edgar Scott; Jesse Whittington.

12 *Amtliche Kriegs-Depeschen*, p.168.

submarine was an intelligence blunder. Keyes was aware of the report by the 21st and concluded that it pointed to an attack on the surface, most probably by a submarine getting close enough to read the pendant number. The British Admiralty announced on the 22nd that *E.3* was: 'considerably overdue, and it is feared that she has been sunk.'[13]

Keyes also assumed that the increasing sightings of German aircraft pointed to their working together with submarines, something he himself had advocated. Although sightings were followed up, communications were not yet capable of directing a submarine on to a target. The zeppelin *L.5*, spotted by Goodhart on the 19th, had been carrying out a reconnaissance towards Yarmouth to look for British warships. She reported seeing nothing, but the various aircraft sightings made it difficult for Goodhart to remain surfaced, restricting his range of vision. The submarine sighted by Goodhart on the 19th is a mystery as there were no German or British submarines recorded in this position.

The failure to get a message through highlights the poor performance of the Mark 10 wireless. Keyes reports that the destroyers were 65 miles away and hence out of range. This needed to be addressed to make the submarines effective wireless pickets.

The loss of *E.3* was the first real setback for the Flotilla. Keyes reported that submarine attack 'is a risk our Submarines are fully alive to'. However, Hallifax confided to his diary that he hoped for confirmation that it was definitely due to a submarine. This might stop Feilmann being happy to sit on the surface with bridge screens and other impedimenta, as he was dismissive of the probability of submarine attack. Hallifax writes that *E.3*'s loss was 'a sad business, Cholmley was such a nice fellow.' Talbot observed that it was 'very bad luck', but that the Flotilla had been 'extraordinarily fortunate' given the number of patrols into the Bight. Their place in the Flotilla was taken by *E.12*. Bruce returned to Harwich with his new crew on the 17th after trials off Chatham, following her completion in the Royal Dockyard there.[14]

13   *Official Naval Despatches*, p.17.
14   TNA ADM137/2067: pp.391-5; TNA ADM188 and TNA ADM196 for individual service records of crew; IWM: Documents.1003: 22 October; IWM:Documents.20134: 21 October; TNA ADM53: *Adamant*, 17 October 1914.

19

Medals all round

At the morning parade on the 18th Keyes announced to the men that medals were to be awarded for crews whose submarines had been in action. One man in each of the 10 eligible boats would receive a new award for gallantry, the Distinguished Service Medal (DSM). Keyes had resisted a request from the Admiralty for the recipients to be chosen by the commanders, as they: 'are of the opinion that it is impossible to single out individuals when all perform their duties so admirably, and in this I concur.' A ballot system was therefore to be used. After church parade the officers met and agreed an allocation by rank, weighted heavily towards senior ratings and split evenly between seamen and engineering branches. Leir drew lots to decide which group of ratings on each submarine would be eligible. The recipient was then chosen that afternoon by a ballot of those eligible in each boat, under the 'supervision and recommendation' of the commander. As E.8 and E.9 were absent, their recipients were chosen by lot.

Hallifax was relieved when the Chief Stoker, Taylor, drew the lot on E.7. There were 18 eligible crew; everyone except the Petty Officers and ERAs. They had agreed that this was the fairest approach. One dissenter had said that nobody should have it and that it should hang in the boat. Talbot felt that the medal had gone to the right man in E.6. When his Coxswain came to Talbot's cabin to draw lots for the four eligible ERAs, he informed Talbot that they had preferred to vote. They chose their Chief, the indispensable miscreant, Stevens.

The DSM recipients were: Ernest Edward Stevens, Chief ERA 1st class, E.6; Arthur Cecil Smith, Acting Chief ERA 2nd class, D.5; Edward Charles Taylor, Chief Stoker, E.7; James William Armstrong, ERA 1st class, D.3; Arthur Hiscock, Petty Officer LTO, D.2; Alfred George Antram, Petty Officer LTO, E.4; Harry Weate, Petty Officer LTO, E.5; Frederick Charles Langridge, Stoker 1st class, E.9; William Arthur McGill, Leading Seaman, D.1; Henry Hurlock, Able Seaman, E.8. The hazards of submarine service are illustrated by the fact that only four would survive the war.

E.6 and E.9 were also to receive special recognition. For sinking *Hela* and *S.116* Horton would receive the Distinguished Service Order (DSO) and be marked for early promotion. His second in command, Lieutenant Charles Manners Sutton Chapman, would receive the Distinguished Service Cross (DSC).[1] For saving E.6 from the mine Lieutenant Williams-Freeman would

---

1   The Victoria Cross was the top tier award for gallantry. The DSO and CGM were second tier awards for officers and other ranks respectively. The DSC and DSM were the third tier.

Petty Officer LTO Arthur Hiscock DSM, later lost in *D.2*. The family lived in Ilfracombe. His DSM was posthumously presented to his wife Emmalena. (Keith Hiscock)

receive the DSO and Able Seaman Cremer the Conspicuous Gallantry Medal (CGM). Talbot and Leir had their previously notified promotions to Commander confirmed. The awards were published with a despatch from Keyes in the London Gazette on the 23rd and duly celebrated in the mess![2]

Whilst the Flotilla held their ballots, the Admiralty was considering where the German destroyers sunk on the previous day had been going. The obvious target was the activity off the Belgian coast, where the Dover Patrol was now providing offshore artillery support to the Belgian Army at Nieuport. The hospital ship *Ophelia* had been captured off the Dutch coast. A decoded intercept of a wireless message to her suggested to Operations Division that a major German sortie was planned against the Harwich Force, which was covering the Dover Patrol from around the Haaks Light Vessel. As a result, at 2:35pm on the 18th, Keyes received an urgent communication: 'Reliable information. Germans are forming a line of outposts of light cruisers with armoured cruisers in support ... Send submarines at once to cruise to Terschelling and beyond to attack and intercept cruisers.'[3]

2   TNA ADM137/2068: Commodore (S) War Records, Volume II. Reports of proceedings of submarines attached to HMS Maidstone, 1915, pp.681–3; *London Gazette, 23 October 1914*, pp.8501–2; BL:AddMS82461, p.78; IWM: Documents.1003: 18 October; IWM: Documents.20134: 18 and 23 October 1914.
3   TNA ADM186/620, p.181.

Nine medal recipients from 8th Flotilla are in this group marching to Buckingham Palace for their investiture on 13 January 1915. Williams-Freeman is the officer at the front, with Stevens behind him. Cremer is in the second row of the file of men nearest to them. (Bryan Williamson Collection)

E.3 and *E.8* were still on patrol. *D.3*, *D.5* and *D.8* were ready for sea and were ordered to a line off the Noord Oost Gat at the western end of Terschelling. They were to spread into a patrol line off Lowestoft, at three to five mile intervals depending on the weather. They would then search east to the Haaks Light Vessel, *Ophelia*'s destination, then along the Dutch coast to their billets. They would maintain a 24 hour watch. The written orders were amended at the last minute. *D.3* would now proceed onwards to relieve *E.3* off the Western Ems on the morning of the 20th, with *D.5* and *D.8* remaining at billets five and 10 miles north of the shallows off Terschelling. The submarines left together at 5:20pm and were to remain on patrol until 5pm on the 21st.

D.5 received damage to her hydroplanes soon after leaving Harwich. Herbert returned at 8:45pm. Half an hour later *D.1* left to take her place. All of the other boats that were not refitting scrambled to get ready to proceed out immediately if required. This included *D.4* and *E.7*, which had only recently returned from patrol. Those on leave were recalled. *D.5*'s crew rushed to make good the damage to the hydroplane. Hallifax had to round up an ERA to finish some half completed engine maintenance on *E.7*.

Orders were issued for *E.7* and *D.5* to leave together at 1:30am. They would extend the patrol to 15 and 20 miles off the Noord Oost Gat respectively. *D.5* completed repairs and left on time, but Hallifax had to telephone the Harwich police to round up four of the senior engineering ratings who were on overnight leave in the town. *E.7* left once all were aboard at 2:20am.

The D class now lived up to their reputation for being temperamental boats. Cochrane returned to Harwich with *D.1* at 7am, having turned around well short of the billet. The reason for aborting her patrol has not been traced. As a result *D.4* was ordered to replace her and left at

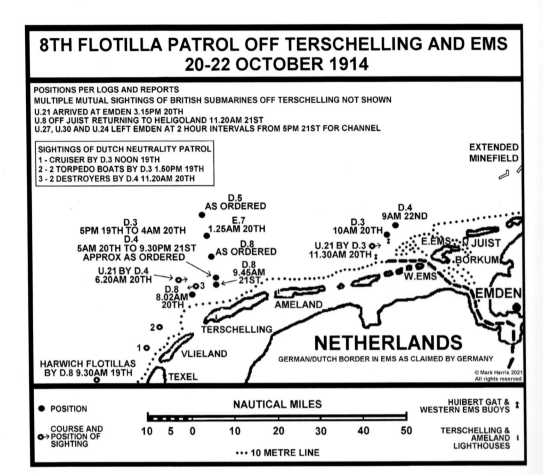

8TH FLOTILLA PATROL OFF TERSCHELLING AND EMS 20-22 OCTOBER 1914

POSITIONS PER LOGS AND REPORTS
MULTIPLE MUTUAL SIGHTINGS OF BRITISH SUBMARINES OFF TERSCHELLING NOT SHOWN
U.21 ARRIVED AT EMDEN 3.15PM 20TH
U.8 OFF JUIST RETURNING TO HELIGOLAND 11.20AM 21ST
U.27, U.30 AND U.24 LEFT EMDEN AT 2 HOUR INTERVALS FROM 5PM 21ST FOR CHANNEL

SIGHTINGS OF DUTCH NEUTRALITY PATROL
1 - CRUISER BY D.3 NOON 19TH
2 - 2 TORPEDO BOATS BY D.3 1.50PM 19TH
3 - 2 DESTROYERS BY D.4 11.20AM 20TH

EXTENDED
MINEFIELD

D.5 AS ORDERED
D.4 9AM 22ND
D.3 5PM 19TH TO 4AM 20TH
E.7 1.25AM 20TH
D.3 10AM 20TH
D.4 5AM 20TH TO 9.30PM 21ST APPROX AS ORDERED
D.8 AS ORDERED
U.21 BY D.3 11.30AM 20TH
E.EMS JUIST
BORKUM
U.21 BY D.4 6.20AM 20TH
D.8 9.45AM 21ST.
W.EMS
D.8 8.02AM 20TH
AMELAND
EMDEN
2
TERSCHELLING
NETHERLANDS
1
VLIELAND
GERMAN/DUTCH BORDER IN EMS AS CLAIMED BY GERMANY
HARWICH FLOTILLAS BY D.8 9.30AM 19TH
TEXEL

POSITION

NAUTICAL MILES

HUIBERT GAT & WESTERN EMS BUOYS

COURSE AND POSITION OF SIGHTING

10 5 0   10   20   30   40   50

TERSCHELLING & AMELAND LIGHTHOUSES

••• 10 METRE LINE

11:30am. Due to her late departure she would remain on patrol for an extra day, relieving *D.3* off the Ems on the evening of the 21st and returning to Harwich at 5pm on the 22nd.[4]

This would be Boyle's last patrol in *D.3*, as he was about to take command of the new *E.14*, shortly to complete at Barrow. Keyes had reservations about giving Boyle an E boat as 'he wants a spur all the time.'[5] He had been persuaded by 'his first class daring reconnaissance.'[6] Boyle sighted some ships without lights in the darkness of the Southern Bight on the way to his billet at 5:06am on the 19th. A light cruiser and a destroyer were soon made out heading towards *D.3*. Boyle turned away and made an emergency dive to 50 feet (15m), with the cruiser only two cables (370m) away. *D.3* had taken an agonising two minutes to dive. Boyle surfaced 15 minutes later with nothing in sight. He had escaped being rammed by Tyrwhitt's patrolling *Arethusa*, with four destroyers in company. She had spotted a submarine diving in an attack position at

4   TNA ADM137/2067: pp.394, 397–8, 406; IWM:Documents.1003: 18 October; TNA ADM53: *Adamant* 18-22 October 1914.
5   Lacked self-motivation.
6   *Keyes Papers*, p.65, letter to wife, 26 December 1914.

5:15am and had turned to ram. *D.3* was only seen as she plunged deeply, lifting her stern, but *Arethusa* apparently only narrowly missed making contact. Recognition in darkness would have been impossible.[7]

As the light grew, Boyle dived as a precaution at 6am. The *Fearless* was soon spotted passing close ahead going north with two other cruisers and about six destroyers. She had led out reinforcements for Tyrwhitt's patrol. The combined force was now sweeping towards Terschelling to intercept any potential raid. *D.3* surfaced when they were out of sight. Boyle sighted a warship when he arrived off Vlieland at noon. *D.3* dived to attack. Boyle steadily crept into firing range over the next hour. Both forward tubes were flooded and made ready to fire. The target was then recognised to be a Dutch cruiser! An hour later *D.3* went through the same routine attacking a destroyer and a torpedo boat, which eventually went in through the channel at the northern end of Vlieland. The Dutch Navy were at least providing good attack practice. Boyle reached his stopover point five miles off Terschelling at 5pm. *D.3* spent the night stopped on the surface keeping lookout, occasionally using her motors to correct drift, but nothing was seen.

At 4am next morning, the 20th, *D.3* got underway for the Western Ems. Visibility was poor on arrival. The masts and funnels of what looked like the minelaying cruiser *Albatross* was anchored inside, with a trawler nearby. Boyle dived at 10am. Ninety minutes later he spotted a German submarine approaching from the west. The weather took a hand: 'Unfortunately I lost her. It was rough with a big swell & it was very hard to see anything.' Boyle surfaced at 4:50pm to charge the battery. The sea was very rough and water was continually coming in through the ventilators. Three hours later *D.3* went to the bottom, having seen nothing else all day. After half an hour of bumping around on the bottom, Boyle got underway at 50 feet (15m) for the night with the boat rolling a stomach churning 17 degrees each way in the swell!

Boyle surfaced at 7:15am on the 21st to charge. The sea was so rough that he had to steer west into it. At 11:15am Boyle: 'Dived & attacked what I thought were destroyers, however they turned out to be Dutch trawlers.' After two hours making abortive attack runs, he surfaced. *D.3* headed slowly west, then returned to Harwich, arriving at 1:20pm the next day.[8]

Foster's *D.8* had the billet 10 miles offshore. He also encountered Tyrwhitt's force on the way to the Haaks Light on the morning of the 19th. Foster was in sight of Terschelling Lighthouse for much of the patrol and may have thought he ought to cover *D.5*'s inshore billet after she turned back. On four occasions a submarine was sighted to the northeast between 8:02am and 11:38am on the 20th. Only once was *D.8* already submerged. Each time Foster attempted to close, diving if necessary, but his report is very thin on detail. The final sighting was thought to be British. *D.8* surfaced at 2:45pm and saw nothing more that day.

At 9:55am next morning, the 21st, Foster spotted a submarine. This challenged and turned out to be *E.7*, which closed to communicate. Foster was unaware she had been sent out. Later that morning *D.8* dived for two hours after a periscope was spotted. In the afternoon yet another

---

7   Patterson, *Tyrwhitt*, p.80; TNA ADM186/620: pp.120–1; IWM:Documents.1003: 22 October 1914. The writer of the Admiralty Monograph was seemingly unaware of *D.3*'s report and speculates that *U.21* had attacked *Arethusa*. No German submarines were in the area. *U 21* was off the Western Scheldt.

8   TNA ADM137/2067: pp.399–400, 404; TNA ADM173: *D.3* 18-22 October 1914.

submarine was seen on the surface. There was one final surprise when *D.5* surfaced, just 700 yards (650m) to starboard at 3:30pm! *D.8* arrived back at Harwich at 11am next day.[9]

Feilmann's *E.7* had the billet 15 miles off Terschelling. The route there was particularly busy with warships on the 19th. By 11am *E.7* had been passed three times by groups of Harwich destroyers and challenged twice. The destroyers wanted to know where they were going to patrol. A British submarine, presumably *D.1*, was also spotted heading south. Hallifax writes that Cunard and he were largely being left to cover watches by Feilmann, with little relief. The result was that: 'Poor old Cunard is suffering badly from imagination; he sees lights & ships which don't exist … when he is up there the [alarm] bell rings incessantly.' *E.7* reached her billet at 1:25am on the 20th, sitting on the surface until a very wet and cold dawn. Feilmann headed south at 6:15am to fix position using a landmark. An hour later a D class submarine was sighted ahead. Feilmann left Cunard on the bridge with orders to close and communicate. The submarine ignored *E.7* and dived, just one mile away. The helm jammed when Cunard turned away as a precaution. *E.7* made off at full speed when it was freed. Hallifax was critical of Feilmann's lack of interest as 'there was no knowing whether she considered *us* friend or foe.' Feilmann returned to the billet at 10am after getting a fix from Terschelling Lighthouse. Once there Hallifax talked him out of sitting on the surface. He was still sceptical of the presence of enemy submarines in the area. *E.7* patrolled submerged, backwards and forwards parallel to the coast, putting the periscope up every 15 minutes for a look around. A trawler was in sight all afternoon and the conning tower of what was probably a British submarine was sighted nearby. After surfacing to charge after dark, the waves increased and rain started beating down. As it was too dark to see any ships more than 200 yards away (180m), *E.7* was taken to the bottom at 10:30pm for a 'very comfortable' rest.

Feilmann surfaced at 7:30am on the 21st to a rough sea from the northeast and headed south to get a position fix from Terschelling and Ameland Lighthouses. Soon after turning round to return Hallifax spotted a submarine to starboard and challenged. Foster answered. He confirmed that it had been *D.8* that had been repeatedly spotted by *E.7* the day before and wanted to know what she was doing there. The sea had now moderated and Feilmann returned to the billet to patrol, dead slow on the surface. Despite better visibility, the only thing seen were three small buoys lying close together during the afternoon. Feilmann thought they could be supporting a new type of submerged mine and described them in great detail in his report. He apparently hoped for some credit to redeem his recent reporting omissions. Hallifax thought they were simply buoys for lobster pots. Keyes does not mention them in his own report. All were sunk with rifle fire. *E.7* arrived back in Harwich at 11:15am on the 22nd.

During a routine harbour move on the 28th a crewman alerted Hallifax to a knocking sound from the motors of *E.7*. One of the Flotilla's senior engineers, Engineer Lieutenant Stanley Jackson, was unable to locate the problem and summoned the manufacturer's motor specialist from Chatham. On examination it was found that the armatures on both motors were full of hairline fractures. There was nothing but the wire windings holding the port one together. It could have disintegrated at any time. The problem was caused by the clutch and had already affected both *E.1* and *E.2*. Both motors would have to be completely replaced. Next day *E.7* went to Chatham for the work, towed by *Firedrake*. *E.7* would not return to Harwich until 23

---

9   TNA ADM137/2067: p.401.

November. After dropping off her tow *Firedrake* herself went in to Chatham for a much needed short refit and boiler maintenance, returning to Harwich on 7 November. Her place was then taken by *Lurcher*, which returned to Harwich on 17 November.[10]

There is no report for Herbert's *D.5* and no logs. However, she was way off her assigned position 20 miles out to sea when sighted by *D.8*. Herbert returned to Harwich at the same time as *E.7*.[11]

Moncreiffe's *D.4* arrived at her billet close inshore at 5am on the 20th, an hour after *D.3* had left. The position was her best guess, with depth confirmed by soundings. Moncreiffe dived and headed north on patrol. At 6:20am the periscope was raised. There was a German submarine, of the U.5–8 type, about 700 yards (650m) to the northwest and steering to cross *D.4*'s track. Moncreiffe turned to intercept. A bow torpedo was hauled back from the tube to set a five foot (1½m) depth setting. It was launched back in, then the tube was flooded in preparation for firing. This had taken 15 minutes and the outer door of the tube was now opened, ready for firing. *D.4* sank bow first to 45 feet (14m)! The tube had not been properly flooded. Sea water had rushed in and upset the trim.[12] It took 20 minutes for Moncreiffe to get control back and raise the periscope. The target was gone. *D.4* spent the rest of the morning patrolling, alternating between the surface and periscope depth, with a break on the bottom. At 11:20am two destroyers were seen inshore heading west. Moncreiffe dived to attack, but was 'unable to get nearer than 3 miles from them.' When *D.4* surfaced and tried to start the engine the starboard exhaust valve blew out. The afternoon and night were spent on the bottom making repairs, with a break on the surface during the night to charge the batteries.

Moncreiffe resumed patrolling at 9:25am on the 21st, but saw nothing. He departed to relieve *D.3* off the Ems at 9:30pm, arriving six hours later to spend the rest of the night on the bottom. *D.4* surfaced at 7am on the 22nd. Visibility was only about one mile. She patrolled all day, both on the surface and submerged, with a break on the bottom at noon, but sighted nothing. Moncreiffe left at 5pm and arrived back at Harwich at 1:30pm on the 23rd. *D.4* went to Sheerness for repair work on a leaking battery on the 25th, returning to Harwich on 4 November.[13]

There were no German surface forces at sea during this operation and nothing planned, so all of the warships sighted were Dutch. German patrols remained in harbour in the poor weather. As all of the British submarines closed Terschelling at one time or another, they were repeatedly sighting each other and this accounts for all but one of the sightings! Moncreiffe almost certainly attacked *U.21* on the 20th, which passed by on her way back from the Channel. *D.3* also attacked her when she entered the Ems later that morning. Unaware of her double jeopardy, she reached Emden at 3:15pm. *U.8* also returned to Heligoland past Terschelling and the Ems on the morning of the 21st, but none of the submarines saw her in the awful weather.

10 TNA ADM137/2067: pp.402–3; TNA ADM173: *E.7* 19–23 November 1914; IWM:Documents.1003: 19-29 October 1914; TNA ADM53: *Firedrake* 29 October-7 November 1914, *Lurcher* 8–17 November 1914.
11 TNA ADM53: *Adamant,* 22 October 1914.
12 To avoid upsetting the delicate trim, the tube should have already been completely flooded from a tank directly overhead.
13 TNA ADM137/2067: p.407-8; TNA ADM173: *D.4* 19-25 October 1914; IWM:Documents.1003: 23 October 1914.

D.4 and *E.7* were on the bottom at the time. Three submarines sortied from the Ems on the night of the 21/22nd for the Channel, passing *D.4* unseen as she arrived in the murk. The cruiser seen in the Ems would have been the ubiquitous *Arcona*, not an *Albatross* class.

The *Ophelia* and the isolated message to her that had caused the deployment had been imbued with unwarranted significance. The message was in the German merchant code and simply directed her where to look for survivors of the German destroyers sunk on the 17th. The scramble to get submarines into intercept positions, combined with rough seas and aborted sorties, resulted in a tangled deployment off Terschelling. Some submarines were not aware of the presence of others near their billets. Warships deployed in their path were not informed. This was very unsatisfactory and resulted in a number of encounters that could have resulted in the loss of a submarine. The high patrol frequency in increasingly difficult weather was also beginning to test the endurance of both men and machines.[14]

14   Groos, *Nordsee 2*, pp.200-1, Karten 10–11; BArch:RM92: *Nassau* Kriegstagebuch, 21 October 1914.

20

Beaten by the weather

Following the news of the loss of *E.3*, Keyes intended to avoid the Ems until he received reports from *D.3* and *D.4*. Two submarines were sent out to patrol on 21 October, but only as far as Terschelling Island. *E.5* would be eight miles north of the eastern end and *D.2* five miles north of the western end. They were to remain submerged as much as possible during the day to avoid submarine attack, but watch was still to be maintained day and night. *D.2* was to act as the wireless link to the destroyer patrol to the southwest, as *E.5* was still not equipped. They left together at 2:45pm and were to return at 5pm on the 24th.[1]

The submarines split up at 8pm off Smith's Knoll through a big fishing fleet. Jameson's *D.2* arrived at her billet at 7am next morning. The weather was ideal for the next two days. He patrolled submerged during daylight and spent the night on the surface, but only saw two Dutch destroyers off Terschelling. They appeared again at 8am on the 23rd. There was nothing else to report that day, except for a pilot boat and a passing merchant ship. Early on the 24th another merchant ship was sighted well to the west. Visibility now dropped and it began raining. Shortly after noon he was looking through the periscope. A *U.16* class submarine 'emerged suddenly from a heavy rain squall, about 2' [miles] NW of us, steering about WSW, 12 knots.' *D.2* was unable to get into attack range and surfaced to report the sighting. However, before this could be done Jameson had to dive again when a trawler approached. Once the area was clear he surfaced again at 1:45pm, but could not get the wireless message acknowledged. *D.2* departed as planned, reaching Harwich at 2:15pm on the 25th.[2]

Benning's *E.5* arrived at the eastern patrol billet at 6:30am on the 22nd. He closed the shoreline submerged during the daytime, surfacing for only a few minutes once a day to get a position fix. He surfaced at night and headed out to sea. Visibility was good on arrival, with mist inland. Benning could see clearly for about three miles through the periscope. Nothing was seen until 9:30pm on the 23rd. It had begun raining with thick mist. He reports that 'several suspicious craft were just visible.' Benning dived as a precaution. Propellers were heard several times passing overhead. *E.5* eventually surfaced again at 1:30am to finish charging. Next morning the weather had cleared, but nothing further was seen. At 5pm Benning left for Harwich. *E.5* was soon picking her way through an area where a lot of trawlers had already

---

1   TNA ADM137/2067: pp.394, 410.
2   TNA ADM137/2067: pp.411-2, 415.

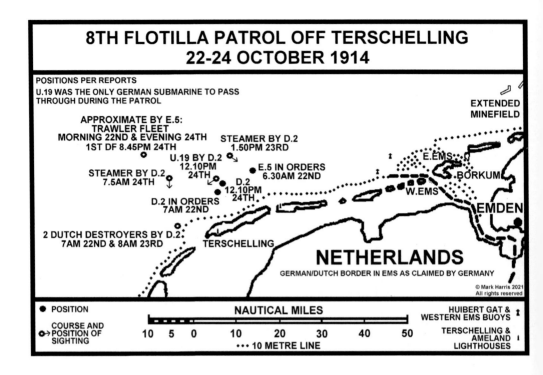

**8TH FLOTILLA PATROL OFF TERSCHELLING
22-24 OCTOBER 1914**

POSITIONS PER REPORTS
U.19 WAS THE ONLY GERMAN SUBMARINE TO PASS
THROUGH DURING THE PATROL

EXTENDED
MINEFIELD

APPROXIMATE BY E.5:
TRAWLER FLEET
MORNING 22ND & EVENING 24TH
1ST DF 8.45PM 24TH

STEAMER BY D.2
1.50PM 23RD

U.19 BY D.2
12.10PM
24TH

E.EMS.

BORKUM

STEAMER BY D.2
7.5AM 24TH

E.5 IN ORDERS
6.30AM 22ND

D.2
12.10PM
24TH

W.EMS

EMDEN

D.2 IN ORDERS
7AM 22ND

2 DUTCH DESTROYERS BY D.2.
7AM 22ND & 8AM 23RD

TERSCHELLING

NETHERLANDS

GERMAN/DUTCH BORDER IN EMS AS CLAIMED BY GERMANY

| POSITION | | | HUIBERT GAT & WESTERN EMS BUOYS |

COURSE AND
POSITION OF
SIGHTING

NAUTICAL MILES

10 5 0   10   20   30   40   50

••• 10 METRE LINE

TERSCHELLING & AMELAND LIGHTHOUSES

been seen when arriving for the patrol. Suddenly, at 8:45pm he: 'Sighted two destroyers lights, one altered course directly towards E 5.' Benning crash dived and stayed down for 1½ hours as a precaution. *E.5* returned to Harwich at noon the next day, the 25th.[3]

The submarine sighted by *D.2* was almost certainly *U.19* heading out to patrol in the Channel. Tyrwhitt had called in his Terschelling patrol due to other demands for the destroyers, so there was nobody close enough to receive *D.2*'s message. The suspicious craft encountered by *E.5* on the 23rd can only have been more of the numerous trawlers seen on the patrol. *E.5* probably ran into Tyrwhitt's 1st Destroyer Flotilla on the 24th. They made no reports of a submarine sighting at this time.[4]

The idea to launch an air attack from seaplane carriers, originally proposed as part of the August raid, had been revived. They were to be used to combat the new zeppelin menace, by bombing the airship base near Cuxhaven. Sturdee contacted Jellicoe about the idea on the 18th with a view to an attack on the 22nd, but plans had been delayed by the recent alarm about a German attack. Plans were finalised in a meeting at the Admiralty on the 22nd held by Churchill, Sturdee and Battenberg with Tyrwhitt. The air attack would launch from two carriers in a position to the north of Heligoland, escorted by Tyrwhitt with two cruisers and 16 destroyers of 3rd Flotilla. The postponed Plan V was also revamped and used as a diversion. The *Fearless* and eight destroyers of 1st Flotilla would envelop and destroy any forces patrolling

D.1 on wireless trials in 1910. The armoured cruiser *Drake* is in the background. (NH54938)

off the Ems or create a 'disturbance' to provoke a response if the Ems was undefended. Moore's two battle cruisers of the 2nd Battle Cruiser Squadron would be nearby to fall back on. Tyrwhitt tells his wife: 'I produced my little plan (or rather, Roger Keyes's plan) and got it through right away.' The force would depart at 5am next morning to deliver the attack in the small hours of the 24th, weather permitting.

Keyes was not involved in the planning meetings. Neither he nor Waistell appear to have received a copy of the orders. They only mention submarines as being 'in shore … and given strict orders not to come to the northward'. Keyes began a tour of the east coast Submarine Local Defence Flotillas in Dover on the 23rd, tasked with making recommendations to improve defences against a raid or invasion. He did not return until the 28th. In a letter to his wife he later confides to her that he was having trouble with the Admiral of Patrols, Ballard, and the C-in-C Nore, which was Admiral Callaghan's new post, as 'they don't like being advised!'[5]

5   TNA ADM137/69: p.100b; TNA ADM137/2081: pp.259-73; Patterson, *Tyrwhitt*, p.81, letter to wife 23 October 1914; TNA ADM186/620: p.136-7, 182-6; Keyes, *Memoirs*, p.127-8; *Keyes Papers*, p.41, letter to wife 31 October 1914

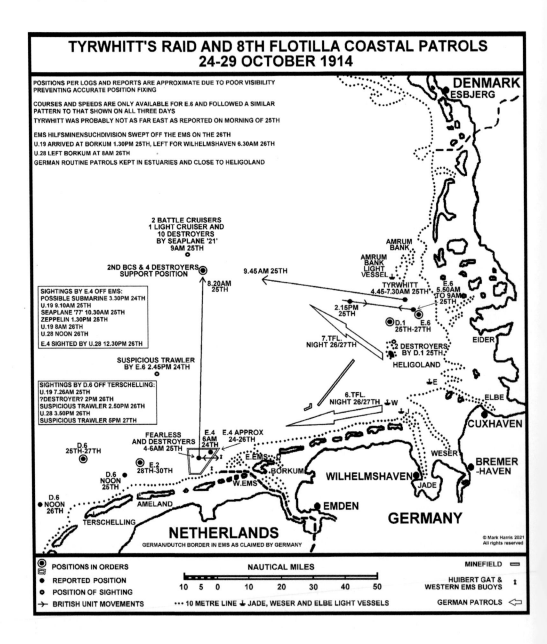

TYRWHITT'S RAID AND 8TH FLOTILLA COASTAL PATROLS
24-29 OCTOBER 1914

POSITIONS PER LOGS AND REPORTS ARE APPROXIMATE DUE TO POOR VISIBILITY
PREVENTING ACCURATE POSITION FIXING

COURSES AND SPEEDS ARE ONLY AVAILABLE FOR E.6 AND FOLLOWED A SIMILAR
PATTERN TO THAT SHOWN ON ALL THREE DAYS
TYRWHITT WAS PROBABLY NOT AS FAR EAST AS REPORTED ON MORNING OF 25TH

EMS HILFSMINENSUCHDIVISION SWEPT OFF THE EMS ON THE 26TH
U.19 ARRIVED AT BORKUM 1.30PM 25TH, LEFT FOR WILHELMSHAVEN 6.30AM 26TH
U.28 LEFT BORKUM AT 8AM 26TH
GERMAN ROUTINE PATROLS KEPT IN ESTUARIES AND CLOSE TO HELIGOLAND

DENMARK
ESBJERG

2 BATTLE CRUISERS
1 LIGHT CRUISER AND
10 DESTROYERS
BY SEAPLANE '21'
9AM 25TH

AMRUM
BANK

AMRUM
BANK
LIGHT
VESSEL

2ND BCS & 4 DESTROYERS
SUPPORT POSITION

9.45AM 25TH

8.20AM
25TH

TYRWHITT
4.45-7.30AM 25TH

E.6
5.50AM
TO 9AM
25TH

SIGHTINGS BY E.4 OFF EMS:
POSSIBLE SUBMARINE 3.30PM 24TH
U.19 9.10AM 25TH
SEAPLANE '77' 10.30AM 25TH
ZEPPELIN 1.30PM 25TH
U.19 8AM 26TH
U.28 NOON 26TH

E.4 SIGHTED BY U.28 12.30PM 26TH

2.15PM
25TH

D.1   E.6
26TH-27TH

EIDER

SUSPICIOUS TRAWLER
BY E.6 2.45PM 24TH

7.TFL.
NIGHT 26/27TH

2 DESTROYERS
BY D.1 25TH

HELIGOLAND

SIGHTINGS BY D.6 OFF TERSCHELLING:
U.19 7.26AM 25TH
?DESTROYER? 2PM 26TH
SUSPICIOUS TRAWLER 2.50PM 26TH
U.28 3.50PM 26TH
SUSPICIOUS TRAWLER 5PM 27TH

6.TFL.
NIGHT 26/27TH   W

E

ELBE

CUXHAVEN

FEARLESS
AND DESTROYERS
4-6AM 25TH

E.4   E.4 APPROX
6AM   24-26TH
24TH

D.6
25TH-27TH

E.2
28TH-30TH

E.EMS

BORKUM

WESER

WILHELMSHAVEN

BREMER
-HAVEN

D.6
NOON
25TH

W.EMS

JADE

D.6
NOON
26TH

AMELAND

EMDEN

GERMANY

TERSCHELLING

NETHERLANDS

GERMAN/DUTCH BORDER IN EMS AS CLAIMED BY GERMANY

POSITIONS IN ORDERS	NAUTICAL MILES	MINEFIELD
REPORTED POSITION	10 5 0 10 20 30 40 50	HUIBERT GAT & WESTERN EMS BUOYS
POSITION OF SIGHTING		
BRITISH UNIT MOVEMENTS	···· 10 METRE LINE ⬇ JADE, WESER AND ELBE LIGHT VESSELS	GERMAN PATROLS

Nevertheless, Waistell knew what was happening and ordered *E.4* to leave for the Ems at 2am, without waiting for *D.4* to report next day as planned. She was to be in position by 3am on the 24th, an hour before the attack. Leir was to remain off the entrance until 8am, then work slowly northwest. He was warned that 1st Flotilla could arrive any time between 4am and 6pm on that or a subsequent day. *E.4* was to return to Harwich at 5pm on the 26th.

Bad weather forced Tyrwhitt to postpone the raid by 24 hours shortly after Leir left. The delay allowed two more submarines to be sent to cover the more distant positions of the main force off Heligoland. *D.1* and *E.6* left Harwich together at 1pm. They stopped at Gorleston in case of any further weather delays until midnight, when they received confirmation to proceed with their orders. Their billets were positions 10 miles north and 15 miles northeast of Heligoland respectively. They were to be in position by 3am on the 25th and each morning afterwards until the raid happened. Tyrwhitt's force would be to the northwest of them between 4am and 7:30am, holding position until the seaplanes returned. The submarines would attack any German vessels that came out. Once the raiding force left, they were to continue their patrol northwest and south of the Amrum Bank Light Vessel respectively and return to Harwich on the afternoon of the 27th.[6]

Leir's *E.4* arrived in good time four miles off the Ems entrance at 11pm on the 23rd. She went to the bottom. Leir came up to periscope depth at 6am. Visibility was only three miles. He dived off the entrance all day, moving dead slow, only breaking surface to air the boat periodically for a few minutes. At 3:30pm he spotted a submarine coming out of the Ems and began an attack run, but lost sight of her, believing she had probably dived. Leir went to the bottom for all but one hour that night, conserving the battery.

Fearless and her destroyers arrived at 4am next morning, the 25th. Four destroyers closed the Western Ems entrance buoy and lobbed a dozen shells in the direction of Borkum, which exploded off the coast. The force remained off the Ems until 6am, hoping for a response. They then departed northwards. Leir came up to periscope depth just after they left and followed the same routine as the previous day, spending minimal time on the surface. Visibility was two to three miles. At 9:10am he sighted a German submarine out to sea heading northeast. Leir made an attack run but was unable to get within effective range. Later a seaplane, then a zeppelin passed by, heading towards Borkum. *E.4* went to the bottom as the light failed at 5pm.

On the 26th visibility was only two miles and the sea was smooth, making attack prospects poor. At 8am another German submarine passed by, heading west, out of torpedo range. At noon Leir surfaced and headed west on the diesels, as the battery had been 2½ days without a charge. He soon sighted another German submarine. He closed to 1½ miles. Four trawlers also came into view, sweeping off the entrance to the Ems. Leir dived to attack the submarine. However, he was frustrated for the fourth time, reporting that 'weather being thick, could not see it … through periscope.' He surfaced half an hour later and continued on to Harwich, arriving at 2:15pm on the 27th.

E.4's mechanical troubles soon struck again. On 2 November a bad fracture in the starboard propeller shafting was discovered by the ERAs during routine maintenance. *E.4* went into dock at Chatham where it was discovered that both shafts were cracked. This required major repairs and *E.4* was out of action in the dockyard until 14 January.[7]

Cochrane's *D.1* arrived north of Heligoland at 2:30am on the 25th. He went to the bottom after sounding to check that the water depth was correct. At 5:20am next morning *D.1* came up to periscope depth. Cochrane surfaced a couple of hours later. Nothing had been seen. Shortly afterwards the northern tip of Heligoland could be made out. *D.1* was southwest of her assigned position. Visibility was poor. At 11:20am two destroyers came out from east of the island. *D.1* dived and commenced an attack. The destroyers were about three miles from the island

6   TNA ADM137/2067: pp.417, 422
7   TNA ADM137/2067: p.418; TNA ADM173: *E.4* 23 October 1914-14 January 1915.

steering continually altering courses. Within half an hour, both bow torpedoes were adjusted for destroyer attack and ready to fire. *D.1* closed to 1,200 yards (1,100m) several times. Cochrane could not get closer and broke off the attack soon after noon. He took the boat to the bottom to conserve the battery. He came back up to periscope depth at 3pm. The two destroyers were still in sight and he once again attacked. He could not get into position before they left. Visibility was only one mile by the end of the day. *D.1* returned to the bottom at 4:30pm, returning to the surface for two hours during the night to charge the battery.

Visibility was no better when he surfaced next morning. Most of the day was spent on the bottom, coming up for a look every two hours in the forlorn hope that the weather would clear. The weather was no better on the 27th. It finally cleared around noon. Cochrane headed off on the surface at 2:15pm for his patrol position off the Amrum Bank. He found nothing and an hour later altered course for home.

At 9:55am the next morning, when about 40 miles from Yarmouth, a sailing ship was sighted. She was underway with only her topsails and had no colours. Cochrane was suspicious. As the water was calm, he decided to board. The collapsible dinghy was readied and a boarding party paddled over. She was the Norwegian *Carmel* out of Kristiania, bound for Portsmouth, and nothing suspicious was found on board. The boarding party returned and *D.1* got back underway, having been stopped for 35 minutes. She anchored off Orfordness for the night and returned to Harwich at 7am next morning, the 29th.

On the 31st Cochrane took *D.1* into Chatham. Her engine had developed major defects and she would be refitting for the rest of the year. He turned her over to Lieutenant Edward W.B. Ryan. Cochrane took over command of *D.7* from Street. She was about to complete her repairs at Chatham after the severe beating from the weather on her last patrol. Street took over the *C.3* of the 5th Flotilla based in Sheerness. This was the boat vacated by Ryan. No recorded reason for this very obvious demotion in responsibility for Street has been traced. However, he had obviously lost the confidence of Keyes and Waistell as an overseas submarine commander. He had only been on two offensive patrols, the ordeal of the last no doubt playing a part in the decision. He was to leave the Submarine Service altogether in June 1915 and went to the battle cruiser *Queen Mary*. He was lost with most of his shipmates at Jutland.[8]

In contrast Talbot was fresh from celebrating his promotion and his crew's hat trick of medals. *E.6* gave Smith's Knoll a wide berth after leaving Gorleston as drifting British mines had been reported there. The German minefield laid by *Königin Luise* had been extended by the British to shield the East Anglian coastline, but the mines were proving a hazard and breaking loose in bad weather. A trawler loomed out of the mist ahead, north of Ameland, at 2:45pm on the 24th. She was without colours, so Talbot dived. She seemed to be patrolling and he could not lose her. Eventually, Talbot followed at a distance of two miles until it was dark at 5pm. He then surfaced and resumed the journey. The mist thickened. Talbot groped through the final stretch sounding his way to check position, with lights from other vessels occasionally lighting the mist. *E.6* dived two miles from her assigned position at 11:50pm. An accident now led to the after engine compartment partially flooding. This took an hour to resolve before Talbot could dive to the bottom for the night.

---

8   TNA ADM137/2067: pp.424-5; TNA ADM173: *D.1* 23 October-31 December 1914; TNA ADM196/51/97: Edward William Blackwood Ryan; TNA ADM196/243/255.

E.6 came up to periscope depth at 5:50am. It was overcast and raining, with nothing in sight. Surfacing for a few minutes for a good look around revealed nothing. Talbot remained in position until 9am, with the weather turning misty. He then headed dead slow to the west, surfacing very briefly a couple of times for air and to take sights for position fixes. Apart from a column of smoke, glimpsed through a gap in the mist to the south and soon lost sight of, nothing was seen. At dusk he surfaced to sit charging for three hours in the mist, then headed back to where he had started to spend the night on the bottom. As the raiding force had not been seen, the same routine was followed the next day and the following morning, the 27th. Visibility was only 1½ miles in the mist and rain. Nothing was seen. Talbot surfaced at 10:34am. The sea was rising with an increasing south-westerly wind and driving rain, so he decided to leave early for Harwich and had 'a very unpleasant afternoon and evening'. Once Terschelling was passed, the seas calmed.

The 28th dawned 'a perfect sunny day.' Off Smith's Knoll Talbot spotted the Dutch sailing trawler, *KW.129*. He stopped for half an hour to send Freeman on board. He examined her and warned the skipper about being in prohibited waters. A number of other Dutch trawlers were still in the area. *E.6* arrived at Harwich at 1:15pm.

Talbot was granted 24 hours leave and got the train to London. He was pleased to find his family well and their new baby improving in health despite a recent severe cold. Sightseeing round Westminster Abbey with his wife and a shopping trip to buy a new pipe provided a welcome break from the monotony of life at Harwich. On his return *E.6* received her allocation of two heater torpedoes. On the 31st he attended a sing-song that had been arranged as entertainment for the crews in a shed on the jetty. He particularly enjoyed Benning singing some topical verses that he had set to a popular tune.[9]

Although neither Talbot nor Cochrane had realised it, the raid went ahead on the 25th. Tyrwhitt seized the opportunity of a break in the weather. However, a combination of rain soaked seaplane fabric and visibility of only half a mile, with no chance of finding the target, forced Tyrwhitt to abort the attack and withdraw in deep frustration at 7:30am. Only two seaplanes had managed to get off the water.

Submarine involvement in the operation was rushed and poorly co-ordinated. However, Tyrwhitt's haste to grab a weather window is understandable. The lack of target opportunities was a result of the lessons the Germans had learnt in the August raid. Their response was further tempered by the poor visibility, with even normal patrols largely held in harbour. The first indication that something was going on was the sight of explosions in the Ems estuary. Seaplanes and zeppelins were sortied to clarify the picture in the outer Bight and off the Ems. Increased readiness for sea was ordered. The aircraft seen by Leir off the Ems spotted nothing. Despite the poor visibility, Moore's battle cruisers, which had been joined by 1st Flotilla, were spotted by Seaplane '21'. However, they were already retiring 70 miles northwest of Heligoland. As the seaplane had no wireless, no report could be made until it landed at noon. It was too late to mount a response that day. The Fleet Command surmised that an attempt to lure out their forces into an ambush was one possible motive for the mysterious bombardment. Further aerial reconnaissance was made next morning and the minesweeping trawlers swept off the Ems to

9   TNA ADM137/2067: pp.427, 429; TNA ADM173: *E.6* 23-28 October 1914, IWM: Documents.20134: 23-31 October 1914.

ensure it had not been mined, as seen by Leir. On the night of the 26/27th another fruitless sweep was also carried out by 7th Torpedoboots-Flottille northwest of Heligoland and 6th Torpedoboots-Flottille west of the minefield.

Of the submarines spotted by Leir, the one on the 24th cannot be identified. He does not even identify nationality and it may simply have been a misidentified outpost vessel. The submarine sightings on the 25th and leaving early on the 26th were both almost certainly *U.19*. She returned to the Ems after aborting her Channel sortie for repairs after being rammed by the destroyer *Badger*, then left for repair in Wilhelmshaven next morning. The last sighting on the 26th was certainly *U.28* heading out to replace *U.19* on patrol in the Channel. She reported a British submarine on the surface by wireless off the estuary. This sighting resulted in *U.14* being sent out to lay in ambush off the Ems on the 27th and 28th.[10]

The revised German patrol strategy, relying principally on small vessels, aircraft and submarine pickets was starving the Harwich submarines of attack opportunities. Both *D.1* and *E.6* stopped to examine suspicious vessels on their return and trawlers continued to be both a navigational hazard and a source of concern. It seems that a decision had been made for the Flotilla to carry out their own stop and search following Talbot's earlier incident with the *Violet*.[11]

The last of the D class submarines, *D.6*, had finally arrived at Harwich on the afternoon of the 22nd. She had been in a major refit since 1 July at Portsmouth Dockyard. She was ordered to relieve the round the clock patrol off Terschelling on the 24th, leaving at 12:30pm and returning at 5pm on the 27th. The orders again stressed the need to remain submerged for most of the day.

D.6 was the boat of Lieutenant-Commander Robert C. Halahan, aged 29. He was outstanding as a Cadet, winning the King's Gold Medal on passing out from *Britannia*. He went on to win a prize for six first class passes in his Lieutenant's exam. After joining the Submarine Service in 1906, he commanded a number of C Class. Halahan took up flying as a hobby, obtaining a pilot's licence in 1913. He moved on to command of *D.2*, then *D.6* in March 1914. In 1913 Captain Brandt rated him: 'Capable & reliable. Vessel always in g[oo]d. order.' Keyes added: 'a very high opinion of him. V[ery] determined & capable.'[12]

D.6 arrived at her billet at 5am on the 25th and rested on the bottom until dawn. Halahan surfaced at 7:26am in a choppy sea, with overcast skies and mist. A German submarine was soon spotted. She was heading eastwards along the coast. *D.6* dived and: 'Attacked but failed to get within range.' Most of the day was spent patrolling submerged off Terschelling and despite the recent overhaul, Halahan had to switch to using the aft periscope, as the forward one sprang a leak. When it was too dark to see through the periscope, he surfaced and began charging the batteries. *D.6* soon had to dive when the lights of a 'suspicious vessel' approached. After surfacing to complete his charge it was too dark to see anything, so Halahan went to the bottom for the night. Although she was only in 95 feet of water (29m), after 3½ hours some blanks that the dockyard had installed in place of old external vents began leaking 'very badly'. Halahan had to temporarily come up to 40 feet (12m) to allow the crew to plug the leaks enough for the

10   Groos, *Nordsee 2*, pp.222, 255, Karte 11; *Nassau, Stettin* Kriegstagebuch 25-6 October 1914; TNA ADM137/2081: pp.274–8; TNA ADM53: *Invincible*, 25 October 1914.
11   TNA ADM137/2067: p.419.
12   TNA ADM196/49/322: Robert Crosby Halahan; Dulwich College <https://dulwichcollege1914-18.co.uk/fallen/halahan-rc/> (accessed 2 March 2019).

bilge pumps to be able to get the water level down. The problems did not speak well of the work by the yard.

Halahan came up to periscope depth at 7am on the 26th with nothing in sight, but both periscopes were found to have leaked badly. He had to surface to open them up and headed out to the west of Terschelling to dry them out over the next four hours. He then returned to submerged patrolling, but other than a few trawlers and three merchant steamers, none closer than five miles, nothing was seen until 2pm. Halahan surfaced and: 'Sighted what appeared to be a destroyer', heading towards *D.6* from the north at high speed. He dived immediately and commenced an attack, but the target turned round when about six miles away. Halahan was sure he was not seen by her. He surfaced to see if she was still in sight fifty minutes later. There was a trawler, five miles away. Halahan: 'Watched her for some time and had decided her movements were suspicious.' The trawler eventually came towards *D.6*, but when about a mile away at 3:45pm she turned away. As she did so the conning tower of a submarine broke the surface between them, about 1,500 yards (1,400m) away. His second in command, Lieutenant Hugh S. Hornby, told Hallifax that 'there were about 8 men on his bridge & they simply <u>fell</u> down the conning tower & they dived madly.' Hornby now realised that nobody had closed the hatch and raced back to pull it shut just as the water reached it. Although made light of in Hornby's mess tale, the lapse in drill could have been fatal. Halahan thought that the enemy submarine might have broken surface on firing a torpedo. He remained in the area for an hour in the hope of sighting her again but saw nothing. *D.6* was taken inshore to spend the night on the bottom in shallower water. Soon a vessel started passing overhead continuously for two hours, so Halahan shifted position, but their tormenter seemed to follow, as the noise started again half an hour later. Soon the leaks also started up again, forcing *D.6* to get underway and rise to 40 feet for the rest of the night.

Halahan checked to make sure there were no vessels nearby before surfacing at 6:47am on the 27th. However, he reports that: 'Periscopes now very difficult to see through.' Sure enough, there was a trawler within one mile when the crew came to the bridge and *D.6* dived again immediately. Halahan remained at 40 feet, popping up once an hour to look through the periscope, apart from a short run on the surface in the morning to top up the battery. As a result of not being able to rest on the bottom overnight the battery got too low to use the motors. At 2:15pm he therefore dropped the anchor weight and held the boat at 60 feet (18m). He was able to rise to periscope depth periodically by letting out the anchor cable. Nothing of note had been seen all day. At 5pm Halahan came up to prepare to leave. He stopped on hearing propellers at 40 feet. After 10 tense minutes Halahan began letting the cable out again, but once again thought he heard propellers and stopped. He canvassed Hornby and the three men at the controls, but only one of them thought they had heard a propeller. Halahan proceeded to the surface. On looking out of the hatch a trawler without any lights was spotted just 50 yards/m away to starboard. Halahan immediately ordered the boat to dive and went ahead to force her down quickly. The drag of the anchor weight now pulled the bow down. As *D.6* reached 40 feet the weight was dragged off the bottom. The bow shot up at an alarming angle. The spare torpedoes began to slide back out of their racks. The crew fought to hold them in place. Fortunately control was regained and disaster averted. Halahan now intended to attack the trawler 'as I had no doubt she was working with the S/m [submarine].' However, she had already made off at full speed to the southwest with her lights on. He surfaced and got underway for Harwich, arriving at 1pm next day. *D.6* was able to fix her various defects without the need for docking. She was serviceable enough to take her place as stand-by boat on 14 November.

Halahan had certainly demonstrated his determination on this patrol. It is understandable that he stuck it out after nearly four months of inactivity. However, with almost useless periscopes and a very leaky boat, he would probably have been wiser to have returned early for repairs. The attribution of sinister motives to trawlers that was often seen on a first patrol was also evident, but Talbot also had a similar experience. Keyes in his report to Sturdee also draws attention to a steamer seen patrolling off Terschelling with no colours. In reality trawlers in these positions were looking for fish, not submarines.[13]

The submarine sighted on the 25th was almost certainly *U.19* returning from her abortive patrol, also seen by Leir a couple of hours later off the Ems. *U.19* reported seeing a British destroyer with two submarines off Terschelling that morning. However, *D.6* was the only other submarine in the area. Since Halahan also saw a destroyer indistinctly later, which can only have been Dutch, *U.19* may have misidentified the Dutch coastal patrol in the poor visibility. The submarine that caused the panic on the 26th was almost certainly *U.28* (also seen by Leir) on the way out to her patrol in the channel, as she did stop for the night off Terschelling.[14]

The Ems and Terschelling patrols were certainly spotting a significant proportion of the German submarines exiting and entering the Ems. They had made 16 sightings of ten different transits in the last three weeks. There had been 17 transits during this time. Keyes correctly concluded in his report to Sturdee on *E.4*'s patrol that German submarines operating in the southern area were using Emden as a base. He hoped that before long one of the sightings would give an opportunity for a successful attack. However, turning a sighting of a small moving submarine into a successful attack was very hard. Whilst some attempts had also been made to begin to develop real time reporting of sightings these had failed so far. The limited range of British submarine wireless and the patchy provision of a suitable linking boat to relay the messages was a major obstacle. Keeping a linking vessel on the surface within 50 miles was going to be problematic anyway. Ultimately a more powerful wireless installation was required to solve this problem.

E.2 was ordered out as the next relief for the 24 hour picket. She was to leave Harwich at 12:30pm on the 27th, returning at 5pm on the 30th. The reference point for the billet was shifted again to a position 10 miles north of the Ameland Lighthouse.

Stocks report is brief. He arrived at the billet at 5:30am on the 28th. He remained submerged during the day. Three hours after arriving he began an attack on a steamer approaching from the northeast, but it turned out to be a Dutch merchantman. *E.2* patrolled and charged on the surface that night. Stocks spent the next day on submerged patrol without seeing anything. On surfacing at 5pm, he found the seas to be 'very rough' and decided to rest on the bottom. Stocks came up again to charge at 10:30pm but reported: 'Sea too rough to maintain position.' He used his discretion to end the patrol a day early and arrived back at Harwich at 5pm on the 30th.

---

13   TNA ADM137/2067: pp.423, 426, 428, 431; TNA ADM173: *D.6*, 1 July–14 November 1914; IWM Documents.1003: 30 October 1914. Hallifax incorrectly identifies Hornby's boat as *D.2*.

14   Groos, *Nordsee 2*, p.222.

E.2 was soon found to have developed the same defects as *E.7* in her motors and had to go to Chatham for repair on 3 November, returning on the morning of the 14th.[15]

The Ems patrol had been vacant since Leir left on the 26th. *E.8* was now ordered to resume the watch, leaving at 12:30pm on the 29th and returning at 5pm on 1 November. Goodhart was ordered to steer 10 miles wide of *E.2*'s billet on the way out. The need to remain submerged as much as possible by day was emphasised.

That evening *E.8* turned out to sea off the Norfolk coast. The seas that had already caused *E.2* to break off her patrol were increasing constantly. Around 11pm water breaking over the boat found its way below into the battery and traces of chlorine were detected. Goodhart decided that the weather was simply too bad and abandoned the patrol to return to Harwich. After half an hour of no water coming down the conning tower, he decided it was safe to lift the boards to inspect the battery. The North Sea now chose this moment to send an enormous breaking sea over the boat, sending a deluge of water down the conning tower hatch and straight into the exposed battery. *E.8* arrived back at Harwich at 11:55am next day, the 30th. The affected cells were pumped out as much as possible. She departed for Chatham Dockyard next morning, where her Number Three Battery was duly removed for servicing. *E.8* returned to Harwich on 5 November.[16]

The constant patrols since the opening of hostilities were taking their toll on the boats. At this point six were out of action: *E.4* refitting cracked shafts; *E.2* and *E.7* with cracked motor armatures; *E.8* renewing her battery; *D.1* with engine defects and *D.4* with leaky battery cells.[17] With both *E.2* and *E.8* unable to remain at sea, it was also clear that patrols in the North Sea could only be resumed when the weather moderated.

15   TNA ADM137/2067: pp.433-4; TNA ADM137/51–82: Home Waters Telegrams, 1914: Vol. 72 pp.476, Volume 74 pp.558.
16   TNA ADM137/2067: p.436; TNA ADM173: *E.8* 29 October-5 November 1914; IWM: Documents.1003: 30 October 1914.
17   IWM: Documents. 20134: 2 November 1914.

21

New priorities

Keyes returned to the Admiralty from his tour on 28 October. The next day he learnt of Battenberg's resignation. Anti-German sentiment in relation to his ancestry is much quoted as the reason for his departure, but the back story is that Churchill wanted a more forceful character to energise the Admiralty. This came in short order on the 31st in the return of Admiral John Arbuthnot Fisher as First Sea Lord, four years after he had last held the post. 'Jacky' Fisher was nothing short of a human phenomenon. A prodigiously talented man of vast energy, strategic vision, drive and imagination, he was also a divisive character, deeply opinionated and a famous bearer of grudges. The appointment was bad news for Keyes, who was near the top of Fisher's grudge list. He had criticised Fisher to his face about his submarine policy during his previous tenure as First Sea Lord. Keyes only hope lay in his relationship with Fisher's political master, Churchill. In a conversation that day, Churchill told him that he must 'be prevented from clashing [with Fisher] or words to that effect'. Fisher had just prevailed on Churchill to take on Captain Sydney S. Hall as 'Additional Naval Assistant to the First Sea Lord for Submarine Duties', summoning him immediately from command at sea. Hall had previously occupied the equivalent of the post now held by Keyes. He felt certain that Hall was being lined up to replace him.

In their conversation, Churchill also asked Keyes for immediate recommendations about the role submarines should take against an enemy attempting a raid or invasion. This was once again a matter of increasing concern, as few troops were left in Britain. Next day he issued a report to Sturdee, who was incidentally at the top of Fisher's grudge list. Most of the report deals with the tasks and organisation of the Coastal Flotillas. As part of this Keyes recommended that the *Adamant* and three D class submarines should be moved to Yarmouth to strengthen the coastal defences. This would also benefit submarines heading out to patrol, which could then use Yarmouth as a forward base to start and end their patrols. They were to be relieved by C class boats from Dover as soon as the situation on the Belgian coast stabilised. In the event of intelligence about a landing Keyes proposed using 8th Flotilla boats both to interdict the potential landing site and waylay the transports as they left their ports in the Bight. Meanwhile, Fisher wasted no time, summoning a conference on submarine construction for the 3rd.[1]

---

1   Keyes, *Memoirs*, pp.128-30; *Keyes Papers*, pp.41-9; TNA ADM137/2067: pp.668–9.

Keyes had ordered *D.3* and *D.5* to leave Harwich at 1pm on the 1st for the next routine patrol. They would stand by at Gorleston until the current south-easterly gale blew itself out. Both were to patrol up to 12 miles off the coast; *D.3* off Terschelling and the western end of Ameland and *D.5* off the Western Ems. They were to remain on patrol until 5pm on the third day after arrival.

D.3 was now under the recently promoted Lieutenant-Commander Robert R. Turner, aged 29. He had come to take up his new command from *C.15* of the Dover Patrol. Turner achieved top grades in his Lieutenant's examinations and had joined the Submarine Service in 1906. In 1912 Captain Johnson rated him an: 'Excellent S/M commanding officer. Makes V.[ery] G.[ood] attacks.' In 1914 Captain Bernard added: 'I hold a very high opinion of this officer... Quiet, neat, smart & popular.'[2]

Keyes had also proposed and agreed a new patrol with Sturdee. *E.10* would head for the Kattegat. She left on the same day for Gorleston, to top up with fuel and await orders for departure. Fraser was to ensure that he got to the patrol without being seen. Once there he was to attack German submarines which had been reported operating against trade in the area. Fraser was given discretion to remain as long as he wished but was to leave and communicate by wireless as soon as possible if any important intelligence was identified. Just prior to leaving the Kattegat, *E.10* was to make her presence known at the entrance to The Sound, in the hope that a report of her presence would disrupt German trade.[3]

The morning of 3 November found the three submarines at Gorleston, awaiting orders to proceed at one hour's notice. The gale was finally beginning to drop. At 7:15am the boom of gunfire grabbed everyone's attention. Out of sight from the harbour, a German raiding force had opened fire on the minesweeper *Halcyon* and the destroyers of the local patrol, then sent a few shells in the direction of Yarmouth, with some exploding on the beach. The firing went on for about 20 minutes. The Senior Officer at Yarmouth, Captain Wilmot Nicholson, ordered the three submarines to get ready for sea, clear the harbour and remain in the vicinity to await further orders. Herbert had permission to sleep ashore at a friend's house in nearby Norwich. An urgent phone call from his 1st Lieutenant, Donald F.O. Brodie, got him out of bed. He threw on his uniform, jumped into his hired car and raced the 20 miles to where *D.5* was moored at top speed. Brodie was just ready to cast off, with the motors already running. The submarines headed out into Yarmouth Roads at 7:40am. The raiding force had disappeared, heading back out to sea. Visibility was only eight miles. The submarines stopped and trimmed down with only their conning tower out of the water, awaiting orders.

Keyes was at Fisher's conference in London. Waistell received an intercepted signal from the *Halcyon* that she was under attack at 7:30am. He failed to get through to the Gorleston submarines on *Maidstone*'s wireless. Waistell eventually got hold of Nicholson's second in command, Commander Arthur J. Davies, on the telephone at Gorleston Coast Guard Station. As the submarines had by now already been ordered out into Yarmouth Roads, Waistell told him to order the submarines to carry out their existing orders. This would give them a chance to attack the raiders if they came across them on the way to their patrol positions. He also

---

2   TNA ADM137/2067: p.438; TNA ADM196/50/14, 196/143/576: Robert Ross Turner.
3   TNA ADM137/2067: p.442; TNA ADM186/621: Naval Staff Monographs Vol. XII: Home Waters Part 3 – from November 1914 to the end of January 1915, p.240.

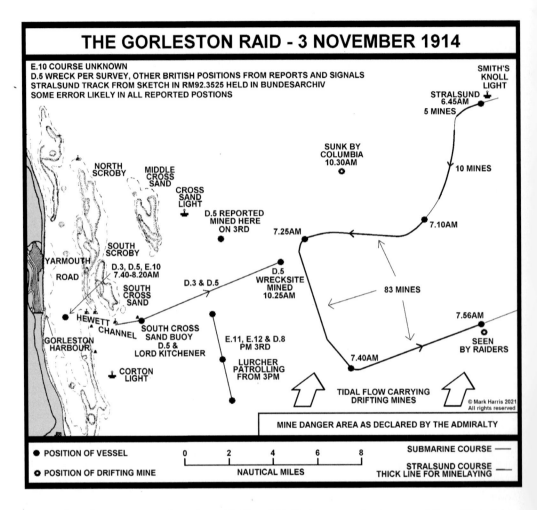

THE GORLESTON RAID - 3 NOVEMBER 1914

E.10 COURSE UNKNOWN
D.5 WRECK PER SURVEY, OTHER BRITISH POSITIONS FROM REPORTS AND SIGNALS
STRALSUND TRACK FROM SKETCH IN RM92.3525 HELD IN BUNDESARCHIV
SOME ERROR LIKELY IN ALL REPORTED POSTIONS

SMITH'S KNOLL LIGHT

STRALSUND 6.45AM
5 MINES

SUNK BY COLUMBIA 10.30AM

10 MINES

7.10AM

NORTH SCROBY
MIDDLE CROSS SAND
CROSS SAND LIGHT
D.5 REPORTED MINED HERE ON 3RD
7.25AM

SOUTH SCROBY
YARMOUTH ROAD
D.3, D.5, E.10 7.40-8.20AM
SOUTH CROSS SAND
D.3 & D.5
D.5 WRECKSITE MINED 10.25AM
83 MINES
7.56AM
SEEN BY RAIDERS
7.40AM

HEWETT CHANNEL
SOUTH CROSS SAND BUOY
D.5 & LORD KITCHENER
E.11, E.12 & D.8 PM 3RD
LURCHER PATROLLING FROM 3PM

GORLESTON HARBOUR
CORTON LIGHT

TIDAL FLOW CARRYING DRIFTING MINES

© Mark Harris 2021 All rights reserved

MINE DANGER AREA AS DECLARED BY THE ADMIRALTY

● POSITION OF VESSEL   0   2   4   6   8   SUBMARINE COURSE ——
                                                         STRALSUND COURSE ——
○ POSITION OF DRIFTING MINE   NAUTICAL MILES   THICK LINE FOR MINELAYING

gave orders for two more submarines, *E.11* and *E.12*, to get ready to proceed from Harwich to Gorleston, in order to be available to respond if raiders returned.

The submarines off Gorleston received Waistell's orders at 8:20am. Turner relates that Fraser took *E.10* north towards the Skagerrak. *D.5* set off leading *D.3* towards the Bight. About 25 minutes later they turned east through the Hewitt Channel. Shortly afterwards *D.5* was hailed by the trawler, *Lord Kitchener*, which informed Herbert that she had seen many warships in action to the eastward at 7am – this was the first concrete information he had received about enemy movements. He therefore headed for the channel leading east from Cross Sands out to Smith's Knoll at full speed ahead. As they approached the Cross Sands *D.3* was now leading *D.5* by half a mile, having presumably passed *D.5* whilst she was speaking to the *Lord Kitchener*. Turner writes: 'We met the returning fishing fleet. They were waving and sounding their horns and calling out "Mines, Mines Everywhere".'

Skipper Alfred Jenner of the drifter *Homeland*, out of Lowestoft, had been hauling in his nets that morning near Smith's Knoll. He saw the German force pass within a quarter of a mile. A battle cruiser parted one of his nets. He continues: 'After they had passed us … I noticed they were dropping something from the stern of the last ship.' Jenner headed back to Lowestoft after recovering his nets. He was following in the wake of the course steered by the raiders. He counted five mines on the way, which he reported to a patrol drifter lying near the last. The drifter asked him to go in and report them. On the way he spotted the three submarines ahead: 'I went and stopped the nearest one and told him not to go any further eastward as there were mines about … I did not understand his answer, but he sheered right around.'

Turner had heeded the warning and altered course to north. He saw *D.5* appear to follow suit, but then: 'a mine exploded aft. There was a cloud of black smoke and the boat had simply disappeared.' Jenner also: 'saw "D-5" steering towards us … He struck a mine about a quarter of a mile away … I turned round immediately and steered for the spot.'

Herbert had recently returned to the bridge after a belated breakfast, sending Brodie off to ready the torpedoes. Suddenly, at 10:25am there was a huge explosion far aft on the starboard side. The D class had no internal bulkheads. *D.5* went down stern first in less than a minute. Herbert and five or six of the crew were topside at the time. A similar number got out through the conning tower ahead of her third officer, Sub-Lieutenant Ian A.P. MacIntyre, who was last out as *D.5* slid under. The heavy sea from the recent gale made both staying afloat and rescue work difficult. Herbert recalled:

> I remember being able to kick off my seaboots (which I had always taken the precaution of wearing at least four sizes too large, in case of emergency) and, realising that I was to have a long swim, I managed to get rid of my coat and trousers, and finally had to jettison a very good pair of Zeiss glasses … I now found myself surrounded by about a dozen members of my crew. Most were obviously beginning to feel the strain of keeping afloat. It was too much for them; first one and then another would throw up his hands and go down. For some minutes I held on to one of the stokers, who was close to me, urging him to keep his head; but he got heavier and heavier till, seeing that we should both go under, I had to release my hold of him. The cold water, and the heavy clothing worn by submarine crew, were the cause of this early fatigue. … to see them perish, was terribly grim.[4]

Skipper James Collin of the *Faithful*, out of Yarmouth, had also observed the mines and had been reporting them to the armed trawler *Columbia* when he saw the explosion. He was on the scene within 15 minutes, got his boat out and threw fishing floats to the survivors to keep them afloat until they could be hauled out. Herbert, MacIntyre, Able Seaman Charles H. Sexton and Chief Petty Officer Robert A.D. Speirs, who at 40 was the oldest crew member, were pulled from the water by *Faithful* and her boat. Herbert continues: 'Spears [*sic*], my coxswain, was so dazed and nearly drowned that the drifter skipper and I tried … to bring him back to life … we were gradually succeeding and had emptied his stomachful of sea water when … with a glassy eye he gazed at me, suddenly became fully alive, and .. tried to hit me in the face with "Get out, you bloody German!"' The *Homeland* also arrived and picked up Able Seaman Albert D. Suttill from the water. Both drifters and their boats remained cruising about the area for 30–45 minutes and got the rescued survivors into dry clothing. The *Homeland* and *Faithful* then headed

4   Chatterton, *Amazing Adventure*, pp.95-6.

home, leaving three other drifters and the *Columbia* searching the area. The survivors returned to Harwich by train later that day, where Keyes granted them all three weeks leave to recover from the shock.

A candid image of the crew of *D.5* at sea. In the centre Herbert; hanging on to his right Lieutenant Brodie and below him probably CPO Speirs. To the right of Herbert with the hat and jacket is probably Acting Chief ERA Smith (Author's collection)

No more survivors were found. A total of 21 crew were lost. Ten of these had wives listed as next of kin.[5] Both drifter crews had known they were at risk from mines. The crew of *Faithful* were granted a cash reward by the Admiralty after Herbert wrote a letter praising their actions; £25 was awarded to Jenner and £8 to each of the nine crew. *Homeland*'s role in saving Suttill went unnoticed and was only highlighted months later by the Captain in Charge at Lowestoft, Alfred A. Ellison. Both Jenner and Collin were awarded the Silver Medal for Gallantry in Saving Life at Sea.

Turner states that the shock from the mine explosion unseated a master valve on the port side of *D.3*, flooding the saddle tank and giving her a dangerous list. He writes: 'As a drifter had immediately closed the position where D5 had gone down, I got all my crew on deck - less the minimum needed to operate the boat - and proceeded to clear the minefield.' The log of *D.3* shows that she stopped for 10 minutes on seeing *D.5* sunk, then about two hours later at 12:25pm secured back alongside at Gorleston. Admiralty telegrams confirm that *E.10* also returned to Gorleston at the same time as *D.3*. The Naval Staff Monograph states that the boats were ordered to return to harbour, but it is unclear whether Fraser or Turner reported to Waistell to request instructions before or after returning.

The Admiralty announced the loss that day when they reported the raid: 'The rearmost German cruiser, in retirement, threw out a number of mines, and submarine D 5 was sunk by exploding one of these. Two officers and two men who were on the bridge of the submarine, which was running on the surface, were saved.'[6] Keyes, in his report two days later, states the opinion of Nicholson that *D.5* had struck a drifting British mine and that the location of loss was nowhere near the mines which had been laid by the German raiders. This continues to be widely reported and ended up being recorded as the official cause of the loss. The original source of the confusion arises from the first signal from Lowestoft, reporting that *D.5* sank two miles southeast of 'South Cross Sands Lightship'. There was a buoy at South Cross Sands, but no lightship! The buoy ended up being recorded as the official position of the loss. It is also the last position Herbert mentions in his report, although he was underway for some time afterwards. Several other signals and a report by Commander Davies confirm the sinking as being southeast of Cross Sands Light Vessel. There were some drifting British mines spotted by both British patrols and the German raiders as they withdrew. One was destroyed by the *Columbia* nearby later that day. Six had been sunk in the area in the previous two days. They had broken free in the recent storm, and others had been dragged into swept channels.[7]

---

5   Those lost, ages in brackets: 1st Lieutenant – Lieutenant Donald Francis O'Callaghan Brodie (26); Petty Officer LTO – Frederick Drury Blunsdon (31); Leading Seamen – Wright Boardman (24), George Crimp, (30), Albert Norris (34); Able Seamen – Joseph Dunne (21), Ernest Wilcox (29); Signalman – William Richard Cass Dowsett (20); Telegraphist – George Clarence King (21), Acting Chief ERA 2c – Arthur Cecil Smith DSM (33); ERA 2nd Class – William John Copland (31); ERAs 3rd Class – Edward Houlcroft (26), John Thomas Percival Tilley (23); Stoker Petty Officer – Timothy Smith (32); Acting Leading Stokers – Frederick Bradley (29), John Robert Leake (30); Stokers 1st Class – Thomas Ingham (22), Richard Charles Penhaligon (27), Sidney Charles Stanley Simmons (24), Harry Whiting (22), Ernest Worth (23).

6   *Naval Despatches*, p.27.

7   TNA ADM137/2067: pp.449–77; TNA ADM173: *D.3* 3 November 1914; TNA ADM188 and TNA ADM196 for individual service records of crew; TNA ADM137/72: pp.397–466; Royal Navy

The location of the sinking was confirmed by the archaeology service of Historic England, who surveyed the recently discovered wreck in 2015. *D.5* is five miles ESE of the Cross Sands Light Vessel position in 1914, in 23m (75 feet) of water with her bow to the ENE and her stern buried in the sand, about eight miles from the incorrectly recorded official loss site. Apart from the conning tower, the forward part of the boat is largely intact.[8] The logs of the light cruiser *Stralsund* confirm that she was laying a continuous line of mines at 2.5–3m depth (8-10 feet) as she passed this position.[9] The evidence indicates that it is very likely that *D.5* struck one of these mines laid around three hours earlier. The occasional British mines drifting in the area were notoriously inefficient and had a very high failure rate when struck or fished up. British or German mine, the result was the same – 8th Flotilla had lost its second boat and most of the crew.

Back in Harwich, at 9am Waistell was handed a telephone message from the Admiralty ordering him to 'send all available submarines to attack Enemy's Cruisers.' He telephoned the War Staff and informed them that the three submarines at Gorleston had sortied but pointed out that submarines leaving Harwich could not arrive at Terschelling before midnight. Since the enemy were already reported to be retiring, sending additional boats to cut them off was impossible. He was told to send three submarines to patrol off the approaches to Yarmouth and three boats to do the same off Harwich, to guard against any further attack. At 9:30am Waistell ordered *E.11*, *E.12* and *D.8* to leave Harwich and establish a north-south line, two miles apart, five miles east of the Corton Light Vessel. *Lurcher* was sent to support them and arrived at the Corton Light Vessel at 3pm. The three boats ordered to positions off Harwich were 10 miles out, each covering one of the three ways in, from north to south, *E.5* in the Sledway, *D.2* in the Shipway and *D.6* southwest of the South Shipwash Buoy. All six were to remain in wireless contact and enter Gorleston or Harwich respectively at dark. *E.5* was already carrying out exercises in the harbour, but the other five boats had to get ready for sea and left at 10:20am. Nothing more was seen of the enemy. All six returned to harbour around 6pm. *Lurcher* anchored off Lowestoft until dark, then returned to Harwich, arriving at 9pm. Admiral Callaghan, Commander of the Nore Station at Sheerness, also commandeered *D.4*. She had left Sheerness at noon after having her leaking battery cells repaired. Callaghan ordered her to join four C class boats of 5th Flotilla in a diving watch off the Tongue Light Vessel at the entrance to the Thames Estuary, in case the German Raid extended south. She remained there until the next morning, then continued on to Harwich.

With five boats now in Gorleston, the *Adamant* also left Harwich at 11:15pm that night to join them, as the new disposition which Keyes had proposed in his report had been approved. By 10am next morning she was safely secured alongside Gorleston Quay to act as local depot for the boats. She shifted berth to South Quay, up the River Yare in Great Yarmouth itself on the

Submarine Museum (RNSM): Memoir of Commander Robert Ross Turner; Chatterton, *Amazing Adventure*, pp.96–97

8   *HMS D5 Off Lowestoft, Suffolk*, (Wessex Archaeology, 2016) <https://research.historicengland.org.uk> (accessed 26 January 2021). The wreck was definitively identified as a D class submarine by the unique configuration of the bow torpedo tubes.

9   BArch:RM92: *Stralsund* Kriegstagebuch und Skizze, 3 November 1914.

6th. Her crew began developing a permanent base for the submarines using the port. On-shore accommodation in the Quay's storehouses was created for use of the crews.[10]

Ironically, the terrible weather that had caused 8th Flotilla to abandon its patrols had also caused a delay in the German operation. The bombardment was carried out primarily to cover the daylight minelaying by *Stralsund*, in the vain hope that her mines would not be discovered prematurely. The main body of the High Sea Fleet had also sortied as far as Terschelling to cover the operation. The appointment of Fisher had prompted the execution of the plan, which had been in place for some time, in order to forestall the offensive that it was assumed he would immediately undertake. It was authorised by the Kaiser on the evening of 29 October and executed as soon as there was a moderation in the weather. After months of patient patrol work, the weather thus robbed 8th Flotilla of the chance to attack the High Sea Fleet as it emerged from its bases on 2 November and cruised past the Ems and Ameland. There was also no chance to give prior warning of the attack.[11]

Whilst all this was happening, Keyes, together with his technical adviser, Captain Addison, was attending the conference with Fisher, who began by delivering an ultimatum to the Director of Contracts. New submarines were to be completed within eight months and red tape was not be allowed to get in the way. A snail like delivery rate of submarines had been experienced under the current arrangements. The ultimatum was accompanied by a colourful range of threats about what would happen to the Director's family and home if the submarines did not materialise. Fisher also remarked that he would commit hara-kiri[12] if he didn't get the submarines in eight months. When Addison whispered to Keyes: 'Now we know exactly how long he has to live', he was unable to suppress a laugh. Fisher fixed him with a ferocious glare and stated: 'If anyone thwarts me, they had better commit hara-kiri too!' Not content with drawing Fisher's ire, Keyes followed up that evening by passing Fisher a paper that poured petrol on the fire. Whilst this suggested some practical steps for the immediate acceleration of overseas vessels under construction, it also needlessly explained the reasons as Keyes saw it for the current predicament – most particularly the creation of the original monopoly in construction for Vickers – a policy decision by Fisher. Keyes says that he was defending his actions in being criticised by Fisher for not building more submarines and preferred to go down with his colours flying. However, his actions seem reckless in relation to such a senior officer whose passion for vendettas was so well known. Over the next few days Fisher pushed to get Keyes out, with Churchill arguing to keep him. On the 4th Fisher did oust Sturdee as Chief of the War Staff. He was replaced by Acting Vice Admiral Henry F. Oliver, whom Keyes fortunately counted as a 'very good friend'.[13]

None of the five Gorleston boats sailed out on the 4th, as minesweepers worked to re-establish safe, swept channels out into the North Sea. Meanwhile, at 1:30pm on the 5th Brodie returned to Harwich with the brand new *E.15*. She had completed her sea trials at Portsmouth following

---

10   TNA ADM137/2067: pp.447-8, 454-5; TNA ADM137/72: pp.420, 470-670a; TNA ADM186/621: p.5; TNA ADM53: *Adamant, Lurcher* 3-6 November 1914; TNA ADM173: *D.4* 3–4 November 1914; BL:AddMS82462: Keyes Papers. Vol. XC. Submarines: reports by Commodore (S) 1 November 1914- 2 February 1915, p.28.
11   Groos, *Nordsee 2*, pp.256-60, Karten 13-14.
12   Ritual suicide of the Japanese Bushido Code.
13   Keyes, *Memoirs*, pp.130–1.

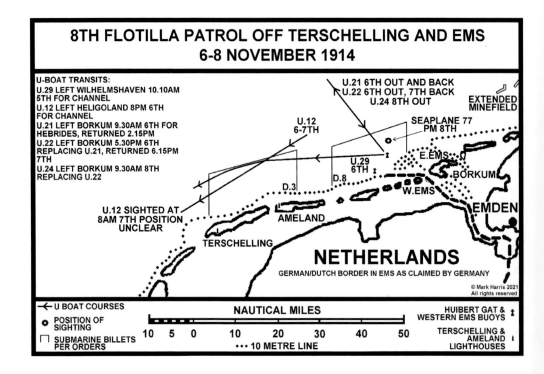

8TH FLOTILLA PATROL OFF TERSCHELLING AND EMS
6-8 NOVEMBER 1914

U-BOAT TRANSITS:
U.29 LEFT WILHELMSHAVEN 10.10AM 5TH FOR CHANNEL
U.12 LEFT HELIGOLAND 8PM 6TH FOR CHANNEL
U.21 LEFT BORKUM 9.30AM 6TH FOR HEBRIDES, RETURNED 2.15PM
U.22 LEFT BORKUM 5.30PM 6TH REPLACING U.21, RETURNED 6.15PM 7TH
U.24 LEFT BORKUM 9.30AM 8TH REPLACING U.22

U.21 6TH OUT AND BACK
U.22 6TH OUT, 7TH BACK
U.24 8TH OUT

EXTENDED MINEFIELD

SEAPLANE 77 PM 8TH

U.12 6-7TH

U.29 6TH

E.EMS

D.3

D.8

W.EMS

BORKUM

EMDEN

U.12 SIGHTED AT 8AM 7TH POSITION UNCLEAR

AMELAND

TERSCHELLING

NETHERLANDS
GERMAN/DUTCH BORDER IN EMS AS CLAIMED BY GERMANY

© Mark Harris 2021
All rights reserved

←— U BOAT COURSES
POSITION OF SIGHTING
SUBMARINE BILLETS PER ORDERS

NAUTICAL MILES
10 5 0   10   20   30   40   50
••• 10 METRE LINE

HUIBERT GAT & WESTERN EMS BUOYS
TERSCHELLING & AMELAND LIGHTHOUSES

completion in the Vickers Yards at Barrow.[14] On the 5th the weather moderated, and the coastal track up to the Haisborough Light had been swept to provide a safe passage out. The three submarines waiting at Gorleston to depart for their patrols now left, with *D.8* taking the place of *D.5*.[15]

Foster's *D.8* had the billet off the Western Ems. He reached it via the new Haisborough Light channel, passing it at 11:10am on the 5th. No report can be traced and no log is available. There was poor visibility in the Ems during her patrol. Talbot says only an aeroplane was seen. *D.8* must have remained on the billet until the time ordered, as she was reported passing Gorleston and Lowestoft on the way back on the 9th, shortly after 11am. Foster arrived at Harwich at 3:30pm. Waistell informed the Admiralty that *D.8* had nothing to report. She then proceeded in for a major refit to Chatham on the 14th and did not return to Harwich until 17 December.[16]

D.3 left Gorleston at 9:15am on the 5th. She arrived at her billet off Terschelling and Ameland at 5:40am next morning. Visibility was only four miles. Turner spent most of his time patrolling dived during the day, alternating between periscope depth and 50 feet (15m), with short spells on the surface. Nothing was seen that day apart from a solitary steam trawler and a vessel that passed close by whilst *D.3* was charging on the surface in the darkness. *D.3* was then taken to the bottom for a six hour rest.

14   TNA ADM137/72: pp.541, 891, 983.
15   TNA ADM137/2067: p.453.
16   TNA ADM137/72: p.908; TNA ADM137/73: pp.519, 520, 560, 585; TNA ADM137/74: p.565; IWM: Documents.20134: 9 November, 17 December 1914.

Turner surfaced at 7:10am next morning, with visibility much improved. At 8am he was taking a position sight when 'a submarine was observed to break surface one mile to Eastward.' *D.3* dived, but Turner could not locate her through the periscope. He headed east submerged until noon, but did not see her again. He kept up the same patrol pattern as on the first day, but saw nothing more. He left the billet at 5pm on the 8th and arrived back at Gorleston at 4:30pm on the 9th. *D.3* was now based there with *E.11* and *E.12* as part of the newly agreed arrangements covering the east coast.[17]

The submarine seen by Turner on the 7th was probably *U.12* surfacing to continue her outwards journey to her patrol in the Channel. *U.29* had passed both the Ems and Terschelling to the same destination on the 6th. *U.21* and *U.22* had left the Ems for the north of Scotland and both been quickly forced to return with mechanical problems on the 6th and 7th, followed by *U.24* on the 8th. Foster had seen none of these six transits. There were no reported sightings of the British submarines and whilst Foster saw seaplane '77' patrolling on the afternoon of the 8th, it did not see *D.8*.[18]

Fraser's *E.10* left Gorleston at 10am on the 5th for the Kattegat. She arrived off the Skaw at noon on the 7th. The sea was calm, with visibility of about six miles. Fraser spent the next four days working down the Danish coast and round the islands of Anholt and Læsø. Visibility was very variable, but only occasional coastal traffic was seen. He spent the night of the 10th off Hjelm Island. Next morning Fraser examined the entrance to the Belts, then took a look at the Swedish coast in Halmstad Bay in the afternoon. *E.10* worked her way down the Swedish coast on the morning of the 12th, arriving at the entrance to The Sound, four miles offshore, at noon. Fraser now abandoned stealth, as ordered, hoisted his colours and patrolled on the surface at six knots. He headed back to Anholt Island for the night. Fraser returned to the Sound to repeat the display next morning. However, he was not easy to spot, as visibility had only been one to two miles over the two days.

At noon *E.10* headed north, with visibility gradually dropping to just one mile. At 3:50pm a warship appeared out of the fog. Fraser dived and began an attack. The ship looked like the single funnelled Danish cruiser *Valkyrien*. Fraser lost her anyway as darkness closed in. He spent the night near the entrance to the Kattegat. On the 14th the weather was clear, but there was a gale blowing from the northwest. To advertise his presence he closed and hailed a number of fishing craft off Skagen, all of which promptly hoisted Danish colours and made off to shore. At noon *E.10* headed for home. As a precaution all east coast commands had been warned on the 11th that *E.10* would be returning to the coast during the following days. However, Fraser had an uneventful trip home, apart from the appalling North Sea weather. He made landfall at Yarmouth and arrived back at Harwich at 4pm on the 16th. The long patrol had caused some engine defects, which put her out of action from the 20th to the 23rd whilst they were attended to at the engineering works in Ipswich.[19]

To all appearances, so far as the Kattegat was concerned there was no trace of the war. German warships were still absent and remained in international waters south of the Sound. Three German submarines had been recently despatched to the Skagerrak. *U.29* and *U.10* had briefly cruised off the northern entrance to the Kattegat in October. However, they were there

17 TNA ADM137/2067: p.440; TNA ADM173: *D.3* 5-9 November 1914.
18 Groos, *Nordsee 2*, Karten 11; BArch:RM92: *Stettin* Kriegstagebuch, 6-8 November 1914.
19 TNA ADM137/2067: pp.443-5; TNA ADM137/74: p.131; TNA ADM137/75: p.884.

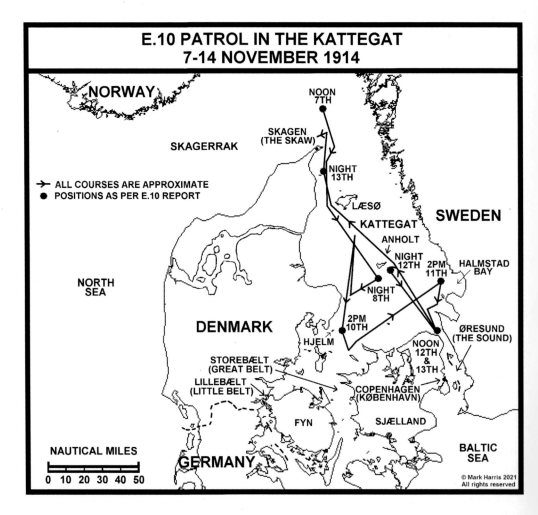

E.10 PATROL IN THE KATTEGAT
7-14 NOVEMBER 1914

NORWAY

NOON
7TH

SKAGERRAK

SKAGEN
(THE SKAW)

NIGHT
13TH

➤ ALL COURSES ARE APPROXIMATE
● POSITIONS AS PER E.10 REPORT

LÆSØ

SWEDEN

KATTEGAT

ANHOLT

NORTH
SEA

NIGHT
12TH

2PM
11TH

HALMSTAD
BAY

NIGHT
8TH

DENMARK

2PM
10TH

ØRESUND
(THE SOUND)

HJELM

NOON
12TH
&
13TH

STOREBÆLT
(GREAT BELT)

LILLEBÆLT
(LITTLE BELT)

COPENHAGEN
(KØBENHAVN)

FYN

SJÆLLAND

NAUTICAL MILES

BALTIC
SEA

0 10 20 30 40 50

GERMANY

hoping to attack warships. Their sighting and an opportunistic sinking under prize rules of the steamer *Glitra* off the Norwegian coast by *U.17* had been misinterpreted by the Admiralty as a systematic attempt to interfere with commerce. This was still seen by the German command as principally a job for surface vessels, but the debate about using submarines for commerce warfare was beginning to gather momentum. Fraser seems to have been unsuccessful in attracting attention to himself, as no reports of his presence can be traced. Whilst uneventful, the patrol of more than 11 days set a new record for the Flotilla.[20]

On the 8th Keyes had proposed a new patrol by two submarines north of Heligoland to replace the Terschelling patrol, whilst retaining a submarine off the Ems. This would place a watch at both exit points from the Bight. Oliver replied that no reliefs were to be sent for the present as 'in view of future considerations it may be inconvenient to have them there.' This is probably connected with the summoning of Tyrwhitt for meetings at the Admiralty with Oliver

---

20   Groos, *Nordsee 2*, pp.188-9.

and officers of the Air Department on the 7th and 9th. These were connected with an imminent re-run of the Cuxhaven seaplane raid. Fisher had embraced Tyrwhitt as a man of action with great enthusiasm. Jellicoe was asked whether he could support a raid on the 13th with his battle cruisers.[21]

The changes at the Admiralty had not just been in leadership. The Admiralty code breaking section, known as Room 40, began breaking German top secret naval communications from 5 November onwards, although it took time to master interpretation. It would mean greater reliance could begin to be placed on advance intelligence of major German movements, allowing pre-positioned responses. At 9pm on the 9th all the ships and submarines in Harwich were alerted to stand by at immediate readiness for full speed, as German cruisers and destroyers were thought to potentially be leaving Germany that night to attack Harwich! Talbot was 'rather doubtful' and they were soon stood down. The destination of a routine German movement had been misunderstood as a result of a decoding error!

The weather deteriorated on the 10th and the North Sea was swept by gales for the rest of the week, making any offensive action impossible, including Tyrwhitt's flotillas. A host of mines were also unleashed from British minefields. Talbot commented that 'our mines seem absolutely rotten.'

The weakening of the Grand Fleet caused by the despatch of three battle cruisers to avenge a British defeat in the Pacific at Coronel had coincided with evidence of a more aggressive German posture in the recent raid on Yarmouth. Fears of another raid or a landing during the short winter nights were once again coming to the fore. Having the maximum number of submarines on hand to counter-attack such a raid currently seemed to outweigh any advantage from offensive patrolling. Two boats were now kept on standby at all times in Harwich. All crew had to be on board and provisioned to shove off immediately from 6am to noon, dropping to 30 minutes notice for the rest of the day.

The level of alarm prevalent at the time is illustrated by an absurd incident on 13 November. Reports of German submarines in the estuary of the River Blackwater, southwest of Harwich, resulted in orders from the Admiralty to Keyes to investigate. He was dubious to say the least, given the very shallow water there. Nevertheless, at 1am the following morning Keyes took the crew of *D.7* in some launches to investigate, followed three hours later by Waistell in *Firedrake* to help blockade the estuary. Keyes also organised for the river to be swept by trawlers and a recently completed anti-submarine net was spread across the entrance to the estuary. The culprit was eventually identified that afternoon to be a flight of ducks, leaving streaks of foam in the water. A fisherman saw them after they had taken off and imagined they were periscope wakes! Keyes was not amused at the pointless waste of time and remarked that it was literally a wild goose chase. Everyone returned to Harwich.[22] Meantime, personal and professional dramas came to a head.

The impact on Keyes of Fisher's appointment continued to weigh on him. On the 8th he wrote to his wife that a friend at the Admiralty had telephoned to say that a personal letter from Fisher was on the way to him. Keyes wrote that he didn't know whether it was 'an olive branch or the other thing.' It was neither. Fisher confirmed that Hall would be progressing orders for

21   TNA ADM137/73: pp.122, 293, 467; Patterson, *Tyrwhitt*, p.83-4.
22   TNA ADM186/621: p.27, 33, 187-9; IWM:Documents.20134: 13-14 November 1914.

20 new submarines, as well as those now in progress, relieving Addison of his responsibilities in that regard. This shut Keyes out of any responsibility for submarine construction. Fisher added a pointed postscript: 'On no account imagine that I have any designs on you! ... but, I have not yet mastered on what basis our submarines harm the enemy more than themselves!' Keyes responded with a frank letter back to Fisher. He wrote: 'I am delighted to hear that you have no designs on me, for I have no illusions as to the result if you had. ... I thought your advent would mean my eclipse, but like others who may have had personal misgivings, I was glad because I felt it meant that – "we shan't be long" – in making war, ... if I am translated to another sphere, I shall ... trust to my luck to give me opportunities of engaging the enemy and proving that you were right in promoting me nine years ago.'

When Keyes returned to London on the 10th, following a visit to Ballard reviewing the new local patrol arrangements, he met Fisher in a passage at the Admiralty. He came up to him beaming, grabbed the lapels of his jacket and said: 'I got your beautiful letter!' Keyes was told to come and see him if he needed anything or wanted to tell him anything. Fisher liked a fighter and had what he wanted; at least for now. Keyes wrote to his wife the next day: 'Evidently my letter got Lord F. in the right place though I should never quite trust him.'[23]

The second part of the drama concerned Feilmann. E.7 had gone to Chatham for repairs on 29 October. Hallifax had been temporarily assigned to D.8. Her Lieutenant, Colin Mayers, had been placed on the sick list. Hallifax had been informed of a remark overheard to have been made by Leir, which encouraged him to believe he would get a favourable hearing about Feilmann. After much agonising about going outside the chain of command, on the afternoon of the following day Hallifax approached Leir with considerable trepidation. He found him difficult to speak to, but Leir heard him out, said that he had been right to speak to him and that he would look into it. He was glad that he had already spoken to Talbot, as he was the first person Leir spoke to. Talbot evidently offered his support. After tea Leir took Hallifax to see Waistell in his cabin. Waistell asked for the whole story. Hallifax rehearsed the problems caused by Feilmann drinking at sea and his lapses of judgement. Next day Waistell told Hallifax to head round to Chatham to take over the supervision of E.7's repairs, but Keyes wanted to speak directly to him first. After further reassurances from Keyes, he found himself going through the story again. Keyes told him to say nothing to Feilmann, who would not go out on patrol again until an enquiry was held.

On arriving at Chatham he found that Feilmann's suspicions had been aroused. He had stopped drinking and had enlisted Cunard to support his case. The next day Feilmann threatened Hallifax with a court martial. When this gambit failed he tried to get him to let things drop. Hallifax felt guilty and was almost persuaded, but a friend from the Majestic, which was in for refit, helped him decide to stick to his guns. On the 4th Leir arrived with E.4 for her repairs. After confirming that Hallifax wanted to proceed, he informed him that he intended to persuade Feilmann to apply to leave E.7. Things went round in circles for a while. Feilmann wrote to Keyes promising to mend his ways and insisting on staying in the boat, or if not demanding to be able to refute the charges in a court martial. Finally, on the 14th Feilmann and Leir went up to the Admiralty. Feilmann was re-assigned to command the coastal submarine

---

23   *Keyes Papers*, pp.50-1; Keyes, *Memoirs*, pp.133-4.

C.32 of the Dover Patrol. He was being given a chance to sort himself out in a relatively quiet billet and he was obviously talked out of insisting on a court-martial.

Nothing could hide the fact that moving from an E class to a C class was anything other than a big step down. Jameson was offered command of *E.7*, being first in line for an E boat, but asked to stay in *D.2* until he could have the new boat that he was scheduled for, *E.16*. Cochrane was therefore given *E.7*. He had only recently taken on *D.7* and had yet to take her on a patrol. He also brought his third officer with him from *D.1*, Acting Sub-Lieutenant Irvine M. Twyman, replacing Cunard. Lieutenant-Commander Brownlow V. Layard left *C.32* to take over *D.7*. Feilmann had become the second commander to be side-lined from the Flotilla since the war began.[24]

---

24 IWM: Documents.1003: 26 October-14 November. Feilmann would return to 8th Flotilla, but never overcame his personal demons and retired from the Navy in 1920. His problems had not been helped by a heavy drinking culture in the mess. Hallifax notes that Herbert, Bruce and Stocks were all guilty of egging him on during drinking binges.

22

The watch resumes

Warnings about another German raid had been coming into the Admiralty from the Foreign Office. Churchill writes that the state of moon and tide in the days leading up to 20 November were considered exceptionally favourable for a landing. He was personally sceptical about the possibility of German troop landings, but the invasion scare 'took a firm hold of the military and naval authorities', including Fisher.[1]

Eighth Flotilla had an important role in the defence arrangements. After discussions with Oliver, on the 16th Keyes confirmed that three or four submarines would be kept permanently at Yarmouth under *Adamant*. From the following morning onwards, at least one of the submarines stationed there was at sea in the Roads at dawn every day, normally returning around noon. The rest of the flotilla would sortie from Harwich to the site of any landing.

On the morning of the 17th the Admiralty deciphered German signal traffic, ordering one and a half flotillas of destroyers to be off Heligoland at daybreak next morning. This was thought to mean that the German battle cruisers were coming out. Tyrwhitt took *Arethusa* and *Undaunted* to Heligoland to investigate. At 1:20am on the 18th, all forces on the east coast were alerted 'to be ready to move at once'.

Keyes therefore ordered that from the 18th every submarine was to be manned and ready to go to sea from 6am, which was half an hour before dawn, until 9am. Talbot recorded the arrival of troops from the Indian Army to bolster the defences around Harwich. It was all an anti-climax when 'the Germans decided not to come today.' A welcome break came the following afternoon. Stars from the London Alhambra Theatre music hall troupe put on a free performance for the Harwich crews in one of the sheds on the Quay. Talbot took *E.6* out to make two practice attacks on *Lurcher* on the 20th, scoring a hit as she passed at 17 knots with a shot from the port beam tube.[2] The morning alert for all boats was kept up until the 26th, after which only three submarines in rotation were required to be ready for immediate departure.

On the 18th Keyes ordered *E.11* and *E.12*, which were already at Yarmouth, to take over the watch for a German sortie from Tyrwhitt's cruisers. They were to proceed first thing on the 19th, *E.12* to the Ems and *E.11* to the eastward of Heligoland. Based on previous reports these were

---

1   Churchill, *World Crisis*, pp.404-5.
2   Torpedoes were armed with inert warheads for practice attacks. These devices absorbed the impact on striking a target's hull.

The crew of *E.12*, taken at Yarmouth. Bruce is seated at the centre. On his right is Lieutenant Edward J. Price, to his left is Sub-Lieutenant Reginald J. Brooke–Booth RNR. Standing at the very back is ERA 3c Reginald J. Ballantyne. (Darren Brown Collection)

thought to be the main routes used by German warships entering and exiting the Bight. Keyes had gone to Yarmouth on the 17th to discuss the routes with Nasmith and Bruce. The details of German warship movements were too sensitive to include in written orders. Information had been leaking to the press from Harwich, much to the annoyance of the Admiralty. Keyes had recently delivered a dressing down in the wardroom on the subject. The submarines were to maintain a 24 hour watch until the 22nd. The trawler patrol in the new channel off Haisborough were to be warned of their return on the 23rd. *D.4* and *D.6* were despatched from Harwich to Yarmouth on the 19th to replace them in the permanent force there.

This was Bruce's first offensive patrol in *E.12* and only the second since the war began. He was late leaving Yarmouth, at 8:50am on the19th. Talbot records in his diary that it was a: 'Vile day, fog, very cold, and snowing when it was not raining.' *E.12* ran into dense fog before clearing the swept channel. As a result Bruce decided to return, reaching Gorleston at 12:35pm.[3]

Bruce tried again at 7am next morning, the 20th, with instructions to stay an extra day as a result of the late start. On the way across he became suspicious of a well-lit ship that appeared to follow him for half an hour near the Terschelling Light Vessel. Bruce also dived to avoid a destroyer at 3am. Land was sighted at 8:30am on the 21st. *E.12* dived and headed east to the Ems, keeping about five miles off the coast in good visibility. Nothing was seen that day apart from a balloon that Lieutenant Edward J. Price claimed to have seen to the northeast, but Bruce couldn't see anything when he reached the bridge. He headed well offshore to the north in the afternoon and surfaced to charge at 4pm. Mist closed in around 7pm and *E.12* remained on the surface during the night.

Bruce dived as the light grew next morning and surfaced a couple of hours later to get a position fix. He reported that it was 'blowing hard and getting very rough.' He dived and headed in to the Western Ems. The weather was even worse: 'Sea very rough & impossible to see very far through the periscope all day.' At 4pm *E.12* surfaced and headed slowly towards Terschelling, intending to charge. Bruce found it was impossible to remain on the bridge unless *E.12* was heading in the same direction as the very heavy sea that was running. As the weather got no better, he used the discretion in his orders to return early. The suspicious ship was seen again on the way back off Terschelling and behaved in the same way. Bruce reached Yarmouth at 2:30pm the next day, the 23rd.

German sources record no activity off the Ems whilst Bruce was on patrol. No British or German warships were off Terschelling. Suspicions that the Germans were using falsely flagged merchant vessels both as minelayers and to co-operate with submarines were looming large at this time. A German liner that had been converted to a minelayer, *Berlin*, had just been interned in Norway, so Bruce's suspicions are understandable.[4]

Nasmith was also on his second patrol. *E.11* got away ahead of the fog, leaving Yarmouth at 6:10am on the 19th. He arrived northwards of Heligoland. After diving around dawn, *E.11* surfaced and headed towards the island. Nasmith quickly spotted five columns of smoke to the west, apparently from destroyers steaming westward. By 8:15am the horizon was very clear. A zeppelin was made out 20 miles away to the south. Nasmith dived to ensure that he was not

3   TNA ADM137/2067: pp.479, 702; TNA ADM186/621: pp.49-50, 198-9; TNA ADM53: *Adamant* 17–22 November 1914, IWM:Documents.20134: 18–19 November; IWM:Documents.1003: 29 October 1914; TNA ADM137/75: pp.226, 703, 884
4   TNA ADM137/2067: p.483.

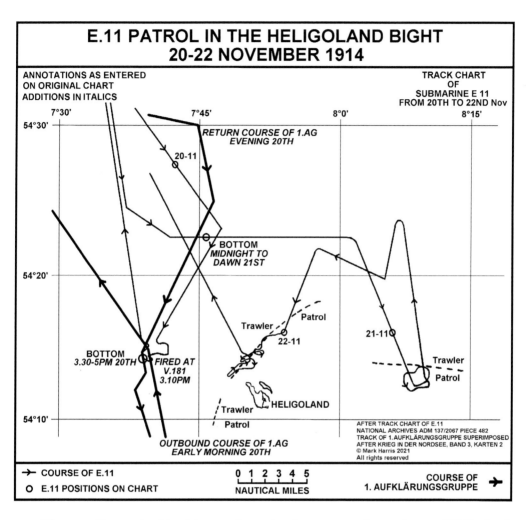

E.11 PATROL IN THE HELIGOLAND BIGHT
20-22 NOVEMBER 1914

ANNOTATIONS AS ENTERED
ON ORIGINAL CHART
ADDITIONS IN ITALICS

TRACK CHART
OF
SUBMARINE E 11
FROM 20TH TO 22ND Nov

7°30'   7°45'   8°0'   8°15'

54°30'

*RETURN COURSE OF 1.AG
EVENING 20TH*

20-11

*BOTTOM
MIDNIGHT TO
DAWN 21ST*

54°20'

Trawler   Patrol

22-11   21-11

BOTTOM
3.30-5PM 20TH   *FIRED AT
V.181
3.10PM*   Trawler

Patrol

HELIGOLAND

54°10'   Trawler

Patrol

AFTER TRACK CHART OF E.11
NATIONAL ARCHIVES ADM 137/2067 PIECE 482
TRACK OF 1.AUFKLÄRUNGSGRUPPE SUPERIMPOSED
AFTER KRIEG IN DER NORDSEE, BAND 3, KARTEN 2
© Mark Harris 2021
All rights reserved

*OUTBOUND COURSE OF 1.AG
EARLY MORNING 20TH*

✈ COURSE OF E.11

O E.11 POSITIONS ON CHART

0 1 2 3 4 5
NAUTICAL MILES

COURSE OF
1. AUFKLÄRUNGSGRUPPE ✈

seen. The zeppelin remained in sight, steering a circular course to the northwest of Heligoland. Destroyers were spotted heading in *E.11*'s direction from the east and southeast. From 9:30–11am they were patrolling around his position. At noon Heligoland was sighted about 14 miles away to the southeast and the zeppelin apparently landed there. By 1:50pm *E.11* was once again closely surrounded by patrolling destroyers. At times they were close enough for Nasmith to notice that they were not carrying the usual distinguishing symbols on their masts.

An opportunity soon presented itself. Nasmith: 'sighted several destroyers returning from various patrols and forming in single line ahead to the N.W. of the Island. Manoeuvred to attack.' There was only a slight breeze and little disturbance at the surface, which were not good conditions for an attack. Just over an hour later he managed to get into a good attack position on the last returning destroyer. Nasmith fired a two torpedo salvo from the bow tubes. The destroyer managed to avoid the torpedoes. Talbot writes in his diary that Nasmith believed that they had missed ahead. Destroyers scattered in all directions, manoeuvring at high speed. Soon after attacking *E.11* suddenly took up an alarming angle down by the stern. She was still at periscope depth. Nasmith reported that: 'An enemy's destroyer was about 250 yards [230m] on starboard beam at the moment; having shifted the crew forward and altered the trim by blowing water forward [from the aft tanks] and expelling it from aft, the boat was just manageable.' It had taken ten anxious minutes to get the boat back under control. Nasmith stopped the motors and took her to the bottom, believing he had fouled an obstruction. He remained there until 5pm. Hearing noises overhead, he now came off the bottom to investigate. *E.11* was still down aft and yet more water had to be expelled from the aft tanks to get her to answer the controls normally. After half an hour he was able to surface. There was nothing in sight in the failing light. A survey was made of the upper deck, but nothing could be seen fouling the boat, so he steered northwards charging the battery. By 11:30pm he had a full charge and went full speed astern on his motors to make sure he had got rid of any obstruction before diving. The boat now handled normally and at midnight Nasmith went to the bottom for the night about 11 miles north of Heligoland.

The following morning, the 21st, the visibility had deteriorated. Nasmith surfaced and went to examine the channel east of Heligoland. He dived at 9am on sighting destroyer smoke. The morning was spent passing through the destroyer patrol, which were manoeuvring at high speed northeast of Heligoland. At 1:30pm Nasmith reached a trawler patrol line to the northeast and east of the island. At 5pm *E.11* surfaced to charge in the darkness. She then went to the bottom for the night in thick mist.

Nasmith surfaced at 7am on the 22nd and quickly sighted the trawler patrol. He dived and steered southwest to approach close to Heligoland and the southwest channel leading to it. The trawler patrol line was in sight all day on a line from southwest to northeast of the northern side of the island. By 4:30pm *E.11* was just two miles northwest of the island with nothing in sight but small trawlers. Nasmith took a close look at them and found that each carried a small gun forward. This was as close as any British submarine had ever got to Heligoland. Once darkness fell he steered away to the northward and at 5pm surfaced and headed for home. Nasmith saw several isolated trawlers on the way to Terschelling, but none of them appeared to have any wireless. *E.11* arrived back in Yarmouth at 5:30pm the following day, the 23rd.[5]

There had been an unusual level of activity on the 20th off Heligoland, but not for a German raid. The five heavy cruisers of 1st Aufklärungsgruppe (Scouting Group) had made a cruise for exercises and torpedo practice, 80 miles north-northwest of Heligoland. They left the Jade at 2:30am and were escorted by two light cruisers and about 16 destroyers. Nasmith actually spotted the heavy cruisers smoke to the west on their way out that morning. The zeppelins *L.3* and *L.5* had gone up to scout, one on each flank of the formation and seaplane reconnaissance aircraft had flown from Borkum, Sylt and Heligoland to confirm that there were no British forces present. The airships made their presence felt, forcing Nasmith to dive and reducing his visible horizon to what he could see through the periscope. He was mistaken in believing a zeppelin landed at Heligoland. They returned to their base near Cuxhaven at the end of their cruise. The destroyers of 8th Torpedoboots-Flottille came out for the routine day patrol off Heligoland. Nasmith had attacked *V.181* of their 15th Halbflottille as it returned. She spotted and evaded two torpedo tracks in the position given by Nasmith, then reported the attack by

5   TNA ADM137/2067: pp.480-2, 484-5. The Naval Staff Monograph incorrectly states that Nasmith was east of Heligoland all day on the 20th.

wireless. Co-incidentally, in the morning the destroyer *T.99* had reported two bogus submarine attacks in the inner Bight, between Heligoland and the Jade. The successive reports were picked up by the exercising cruisers. These zig-zagged on their return, steering a somewhat round-about course, with the destroyers deployed in a submarine screen ahead of them. As a result they passed *E.11* just out of sight to the east in the dusk as she retired to charge. However, the unusually good night-time visibility and state of alert resulted in the Heligoland Mole batteries opening fire on two supposedly surfaced submarines as the formation passed by. The Germans concluded that the searchlights might have illuminated the escorting destroyers and mistaken them for submarines. No harm was done and the force was back in the Jade by 9:30pm. *E.11* was possibly sighted the next morning prior to diving, by the patrolling *S.138* of 2nd Torpedoboots-Flottille, which reported a surfaced submarine south of Amrum bank. There was another bogus submarine sighting off the Elbe at the same time. As a result surface patrols were withdrawn and replaced by submarines lying in ambush. Submarines had already been sharing the day watch with the destroyers off Heligoland since the 12th.

Random chances had robbed Nasmith of a chance to attack the German battle cruiser exercise. His very obvious torpedo attack had also added credibility to the other submarine sightings and made it seem like the Bight was suddenly infested with British submarines. This was a timely reminder of the threat they posed and reversed an entirely correct deduction of the Fleet Command that British submarines had given up coming into the Bight.

There were no mines or deliberate obstructions where *E.11* encountered her trim problems. Importantly, Nasmith had identified that this location was a well-used channel west of Heligoland and was being patrolled. Keyes had been focussed on the channel to the east of Heligoland up to this point.[6]

Meanwhile another new patrol had been initiated. Keyes had raised the prospect of using C class boats for offensive operations in the North Sea in his recent memorandum to Oliver about reorganising the flotillas. A way had been found to overcome their lack of underwater endurance, which was a fundamental barrier to their use in enemy patrolled waters. It had been found that by placing the motors in series, rather than in parallel, the underwater endurance could be almost doubled. This involved some sacrifice of underwater speed, but war experience had so far proved this to be relatively unimportant. Keyes now believed that the C class could be used for stays of up to two to three days in the Heligoland Bight in moderate weather. This could help alleviate the short term shortage of new construction. The C class were smaller and less seaworthy than an overseas boat. On the surface they were driven by a more temperamental, and potentially dangerous, petrol engine. They had a crew of 16 and two 18-inch (45cm) torpedo tubes in the bow, for which four cold torpedoes were carried.[7]

The Germans had occupied the Belgian ports of Zeebrugge and Ostend on 15 October. The short distance to Zeebrugge created an opportunity to trial a C class on a reconnaissance trip. Both ports had been left intact by the allies in the belief that they would soon be re-captured. Use had already been made of Zeebrugge by *U.12*, which arrived on 9 November. She had returned for shelter in the storms on the 12th. Decoded German signals confirmed to the

---

6   Otto Groos, *Der Krieg zur See 1914–1918 – Der Krieg in der Nordsee Band 3* (Berlin: Mittler & Sohn, 1923), pp.23-4, 47-8, Karte 2.
7   TNA ADM137/2067: pp.681-2; TNA ADM186/15: p.30. For further C class particulars, see Appendix I

C.34 leaving Portsmouth prior to the war. (Darren Brown Collection)

Admiralty that a submarine had entered on both dates. On the 14th aerial reconnaissance was ordered to find out what was happening at Zeebrugge, but the weather remained impossible for the fragile seaplanes. Decodes on the 15th indicated that a submarine would be leaving as soon as the weather moderated.[8]

Keyes was loaned one of the newest C class, *C.34*, from the 4th Flotilla of the Dover Patrol. She was commanded by Lieutenant John F. Hutchings, aged 29. He had joined the Submarine Service in 1906 and had been in command of *C.34* since November 1913. It was his third submarine command. He had an inventive mind, having been commended by the Admiralty for designing a torpedo turret for submarines, although it was not adopted. His personality had not endeared him to Captain Johnson whose assessment was: 'Handles a S/M v[ery] well & keeps her in v[ery] g[ood] order. Has a rather unpleasant manner. Requires a firm hand on him.' The picture is of a very single minded but clever individual, impatient to the point of insubordination with those who could not grasp his insights.[9]

C.34 left Dover for Harwich on the morning of the 16th but was forced to return by the northerly gale. She had better luck next day and arrived at Harwich at 4pm, but the weather then held her there for the next few days. *C.34* was finally able to leave for the reconnaissance at 9am on the 20th. Hutchings proceeded from the North Hinder Lightship to the light buoy on the Thornton Ridge by dead reckoning, however, he could not find it. He tried to fix his

---

8   Groos, *Nordsee 2*, pp.279-84, Karte 11; TNA ADM137/75: British Admiralty to Rouyer, 16 November 1914 4:05am; TNA ADM137/2067: p.499; TNA ADM186/621: p.195.
9   TNA ADM196/143/536, 196/127/5: John Fenwick Hutchings.

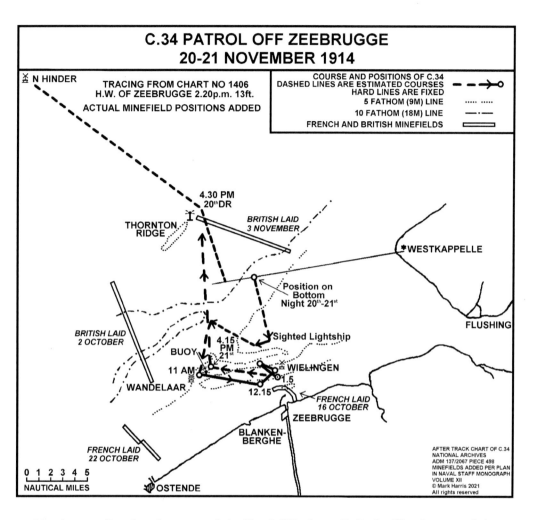

C.34 PATROL OFF ZEEBRUGGE
20-21 NOVEMBER 1914

position by sounding, but then spotted the Dutch Westkappelle Light. Hutchings used this to plot a course towards the shore. He then checked the water depth again and spent the night on the bottom.

Next morning *C.34* surfaced at 6am in a calm sea, with a haze over the land. Hutchings headed toward Zeebrugge and soon spotted the Wielingen Lightship. He was nearly three miles further east than his estimated position. He dived and headed west, but the water was found to be too shallow to fully submerge the boat. Hutchings headed into deeper water to approach the Wandelaar Lightship, which marked the western end of the channel. The lightship was gone and only the nearby light buoy was still there. Hutchings surfaced to identify it, then dived along the channel to the Wielingen Lightship, using a burst of speed to ensure he could complete the reconnaissance in the shallow water before the tide fell. He spent three hours in the early afternoon close to the lightship. There were no vessels coming in or out and no sign of activity in the harbour, but the lightship was obviously manned. Hutchings headed back out, then surfaced to get a fix from the Wandelaar Buoy. He headed back towards Thornton

Ridge, surfacing as soon as darkness fell. *C.34* continued back via the North Hinder, arriving at Harwich at dawn next morning, the 22nd.

It was an exemplary piece of reconnaissance and Hutchings observations were confirmed by a seaplane on the 20th. However, Hutchings had missed the Thornton Buoy, as the destroyer *Meteor* confirmed that it was still there at the request of the Admiralty on the morning of the 20th. There had been no submarine at Zeebrugge since *U.12* left on the 16th. Hutchings sailing instructions had kept him clear of Zeebrugge harbour, where there were French mines. However, it appears that both he and Keyes were unaware that a new line of British mines had been laid east from Thornton Ridge Buoy on 3 November, specifically to catch submarines entering from the north! This was east of the danger area previously notified to merchant shipping and the fleet. Fortunately, *C.34* crossed this line going in and out about two hours after high water, reducing the risk. In his report to Oliver, Keyes suggested that if there were to be further operations in the area, *C.34* could watch at the edge of the shallow water and ambush submarines coming in or out.[10]

10   TNA ADM137/2067: pp.496–500; TNA ADM137/75: pp.72, 209, 322, 952–3; TNA ADM186/621. Zeebrugge Approaches map, November 1914, pp. 66.

23

A cruel sea

The plans to attack the zeppelin sheds near Cuxhaven had been redrafted by Tyrwhitt after the recent meetings at the Admiralty, under the new designation of Plan X. The Harwich Destroyer Flotillas would still escort the seaplane carriers to a position north of Heligoland, but the diversionary raid on the Ems was dropped. Support was to be provided by the old *Duncan* class battleships of the Channel Fleet. Three submarines from 8th Flotilla were to be in covering positions. The carriers were ready to proceed at short notice pending a break in the weather.

The Admiralty reviewed the latest intelligence on November 20. This indicated both a big concentration of the German Fleet in the North Sea ports and a large number of submarines being despatched for patrols off the Shetlands and in the Channel. There were continued indications of preparations for a sortie. The absence of enemy submarines from the Heligoland Bight was thought to be an ideal opportunity for the Fleet to enter the North Sea and draw the German Fleet into action there. At the very least German offensive plans would be dislocated. Plan X was to be the bait. Tyrwhitt was therefore ordered at 2pm to prepare to execute the plan on the 23rd with support now promised from the Grand Fleet, rather than the Channel Fleet. Jellicoe was asked for his views and advised to coal the Fleet in preparation. This was the sort of move that the German Fleet Command had been expecting from Fisher.

Keyes was not involved in the planning or decision making but was privy to Tyrwhitt's plans and orders. He issued his own orders for 8th Flotilla later that day. *E.15*, *E.5* and *D.2* were to leave Harwich at 7:30am next morning, the 21st. They were to communicate with the signal station at Gorleston on the way past, to pick up any last minute instructions. Otherwise, they were to ensure they reached their positions before darkness on the 22nd. The submarines would take up position in an arc 10 miles northwest, north and northeast of Heligoland, five miles apart, then lie on the bottom overnight. They were to surface at daylight and were tasked with intercepting any German vessels that came out to attack the raiding force, which would be just to their north. They would also rescue any ditched pilots that Tyrwhitt's destroyers could not reach. Once the raid was over at 8:30am, *E.15* was to head for the Western Ems, but if the raid was delayed she was to patrol northwest of Heligoland. *E.5* and *D.2* were to remain in separate patrol billets north of Heligoland, with *D.2* taking the billet closest to the island. All three submarines were to resume their covering positions each morning if the raid was delayed. Whatever happened, all three were to return to Harwich on the evening of the 25th.

Keyes informed Oliver that evening that his three submarines would be departing to participate in the operation and also asked permission that he himself could 'co-operate with

8TH FLOTILLA OPERATIONS IN THE HELIGOLAND BIGHT
24-28 NOVEMBER 1914

ALL POSITIONS PER ORDERS, REPORTS AND LOGS

PATROL ZONES APPROXIMATE

PLANNED LAUNCH POSITION FOR ABORTIVE AIR ATTACK 24TH

PLANNED SUBMARINE COVERING POSITION FOR AIR ATTACK

E.15 NOON 26TH

STEAMERS ENTERING & EXITING HELIGOLAND ANCHORAGE MORNING 26 & 27TH

D.2 AS ORDERED 26-29TH

HELIGOLAND

EIDER

ELBE

D.4 POSITIONS AND SIGHTINGS:
1 - 6AM TOUCHED BOTTOM ON JUISTER RIFF
2 - 7.15AM DESTROYER SIGHTED
3 - 10AM DESTROYER SIGHTED
4 - 3.30PM MOORED OUTPOST TRAWLER

CUXHAVEN

D.4 24TH

JUISTER RIFF

D.6 24TH

E.EMS

JUIST

BORKUM

W.EMS

WESER

WILHELMSHAVEN

JADE

BREMER-HAVEN

8 TRAWLERS SWEEPING BY D.6 24TH

EMDEN

GERMANY

NETHERLANDS

GERMAN/DUTCH BORDER IN EMS AS CLAIMED BY GERMANY

	NAUTICAL MILES	MINEFIELD ⊂⊃

- ● ORDERED POSITIONS
- ○ REPORTED POSITIONS
- ▢ PATROL ZONES D.4 & D.6

10　5　0　　10　　20　　30　　40　　50

••• 10 METRE LINE ⏚ JADE, WESER AND ELBE LIGHT VESSELS

HUIBERT GAT & WESTERN EMS BUOYS

covering force.' A curt reply was quickly received: 'Submarine Boats will not take part.' Oliver pointed out that Tyrwhitt had only been warned to prepare and wait definite orders to execute the plan. There was clearly a lack of clarity between Oliver and Tyrwhitt as to what the details of the plan actually were. Fisher and Oliver were focussed at this point on retaining the maximum number of submarines at Harwich to guard against an attack on the east coast.

Jellicoe proved unenthusiastic. On the 21st he responded that he did not consider that an aerial attack was likely to bring out the German Fleet. If the plan went ahead he wanted a delay to the 24th to allow him to complete repairs that were underway, as he wanted to bring out the entire Grand Fleet, not just isolated units. Oliver agreed the 24 hours postponement. This gave Keyes the opportunity to go back to Oliver that evening. He highlighted that 10 submarines were available for patrol at Harwich and Yarmouth, with another four returning from patrol or refit in the next few days. Keyes proposed that two or three submarines should act: 'as detailed in Plan No. X; if approved suggest their waiting at Yarmouth for orders to carry on.'

Having been sent a copy of the plan, as drafted by Tyrwhitt, Oliver relented in the small hours of the 22nd. He approved the deployment of the three submarines, confirming to both Keyes and Tyrwhitt that the air attack would go ahead on the 24th. The episode demonstrates Oliver's weakness for getting over-involved in a level of operational detail better left to subordinates.

Keyes had just four hours after receiving the telegram to get the three submarines away from Harwich at 7am. They needed to get past the narrow Haisborough Channel before darkness. As *E.11* and *E.12* would now both have left their patrol billets before the attack, he proposed sending two of the Yarmouth submarines to the Ems during the raid. Since Oliver had ignored his previous hints, he also asked if he could: 'cruise off Ems Monday night [23rd] with four destroyers.'

On their way up to Yarmouth *D.2*, *E.5* and *E.15* encountered the strong easterly winds and rough seas that had caused *E.12* to end her patrol early. After a telephone conversation with Oliver, it looked like the operation could be postponed due to the bad weather, so Keyes had the Coastguard station at Gorleston signal them to head in to Yarmouth and await instructions. By 3pm all three were tied up alongside *Adamant*.

Meantime, Oliver had reviewed the midday weather report. Kingsnorth Weather Station forecast that mild calm weather currently in the northern part of the North Sea was expected to extend south later. Keyes was telegraphed the reports and told to instruct the submarines to proceed, but with discretion to return should they find the weather too bad to remain in position on the 24th. Approval was also given to send two submarines to the Ems, but only for the day of the raid. Keyes' request to take destroyers out was refused as they: 'cannot be spared'. Unfortunately, a telegram had been used when a telephone call was required. It was 3pm by the time Keyes received the new instructions. It was now too late for the submarines to get out through the Haisborough Channel before dark. Since it was impossible to safely navigate these shoals in darkness, Keyes ordered them to proceed as far as the Haisborough Channel entrance at the Would Lightship and then proceed at top speed at first light. *D.4* and *D.6* were ordered to leave Yarmouth for the Ems next morning, as they had a shorter journey; they were to return on the evening of the 24th.[1]

It was 4:40pm by the time *D.2*, *E.5* and *E.15* got underway. Keyes reports that 'it was a very dirty night and the submarines had an anxious time in the shoals.' This was an understatement. The only report that survives is that of *E.5*. By 7pm the three submarines had passed the Corton Light Vessel and were heading northeast for the Cross Sands Light. The sea was rough. Benning had already been forced to reduce speed to eight knots. He now signalled *E.15* as Brodie was the senior officer. *E.5* still had no wireless. It was now dark, so a hand signal light must have been used. Benning told Brodie that he was turning back and asked whether Brodie knew their position. He received no reply and turned round, signalling again that he was returning to the Corton Light Vessel. By 7:50pm he had reached it. Benning stopped and tried to call both *D.2* and *E.15* without success. After half an hour he took *E.5* in to Yarmouth Roads and anchored in eight fathoms (15m). Benning reports: 'During night seas broke over the conning tower,

1   TNA ADM137/75: pp.624, 919, 947, 1034, 1045; TNA ADM137/2067: pp.487-90; TNA ADM186/621: pp.51-52, 200-204.

several coming into the boat. Strong easterly wind, rough sea.' Keyes added in his report that by morning *E.5* 'was leaking badly, her hydroplane guards having torn the hull through plunging in the rough sea.' It was presumably the hydroplane damage that had caused Benning to turn back in the first place. He signalled for orders in the morning and was told by *Adamant* to return to harbour. *E.5* limped back to tie up next to her at 9:40am.

D.2 and *E.15* were still in company in the shoals off the Norfolk coast and attempted to get underway for their patrol billet at daylight on the 23rd. They found that their speed was so low in the heavy seas that they would not arrive at their patrol positions until after the raid, so Brodie used his discretion to order a return to Gorleston. *E.15* was leading *D.2* by 3 cables (550m). By 10:30am they had passed the Corton Light Vessel and turned northwards into the channel to approach Gorleston. Both of the submarines were rolling heavily as they cut across the rough seas. A particularly big swell now rolled *D.2* hard over on her starboard side. Her commander, Jameson, was slammed into the canvas bridge screen. The lashings gave way and Jameson fell overboard. Lieutenant Francis E. Oakeley was also on the bridge and he immediately ordered: 'Stop, out clutch, hard aport.'[2] As soon as the clutches were out, he ordered full ahead port, slow astern starboard to continue turning *D.2* to starboard as quickly as possible. Oakeley then made straight for Jameson's discarded clothing. Every seaman was brought up on deck with lifebuoys and lines. The church pendant was hoisted, indicating a man overboard. Brodie saw it and turned *E.15* round to join the search. A nearby steam trawler also came to assist. It was to no avail and after an hour Brodie ordered the boats into harbour. They made fast beside the battered *E.5* around 1pm.

Keyes was informed of the developments and quickly wirelessed Tyrwhitt to make him aware that the submarines would not be covering his attack next day. Keyes paid tribute to Jameson in his report as an 'enterprising officer who has carried out many daring and valuable reconnaissances, and his untimely death is a great loss to the service.' Jameson was survived by his wife and 11 month old daughter, both named Isabel. Keyes appealed to the Secretary of the Admiralty that although Jameson had not been killed in action, she should be granted the highest rate of pension, as he knew she was in 'straitened circumstances'[3]

Meanwhile, *D.4* and *D.6* had got underway together for the Ems at 7:45am on the 23rd. They encountered the same heavy seas that turned back *D.2* and *E.15*. Halahan's *D.6* had been ordered to keep in touch by wireless with *Adamant*. He reported off the Haisborough Gat that they were able to make 7½ knots, which was just enough to be able to reach the Ems in time. *E.6* kept in wireless communication until 6:30pm; after 11 hours she was still only 75 miles from Yarmouth. Halahan, therefore, arrived off the Ems with no time to spare at 6:30am on the 24th. He dived and 'proceeded into the mouth of Western Ems to investigate shipping inside.' A lightship was towed out, then taken along the coast to the northeast. Seven trawlers, supervised by another big trawler, then came out to sweep as far as the outer buoy and back. With nothing worth attacking, Halahan retired out of the channel and patrolled between the Western Ems and Huibert Gat entrances for the rest of the day but saw nothing. He surfaced at 4pm and got

---

2   Until 1934 Royal Navy helm orders referred to the direction the wheel was to turn. *D.2* went into a tight turn to starboard.

3   TNA ADM137/2067: pp.491-4; TNA ADM173: *E.5* 22 November-27 December 1914. BL:AddMS82462, pp.94–96

underway back to Yarmouth at 5:30pm. *D.6* passed the outgoing *E.15* at 8:45am next morning and tied up alongside *Adamant* at 12:35pm.[4]

Moncreiffe must have got out of his reckoning in the heavy seas on the way to the Ems. *D.4* touched the bottom on the Juister Riff shoal at the mouth of the Eastern Ems at 6am on the 24th. Fortunately no harm was done and Moncreiffe was able to get clear by going astern on the motors. This was the second time he had done this on a patrol and it is perhaps significant that he had only scraped through his navigation certificate with a 3rd! Once clear he sounded his depth, then dived to patrol. At 7:15am a destroyer was spotted to the southwest near the Eastern Ems entrance, heading east. Moncreiffe steered to intercept, but lost sight of her in a rainstorm 15 minutes later. At 10am a large destroyer was spotted to the south, heading east at 25 knots, but Moncreiffe was unable to close and she quickly went out of sight. Nothing else was seen all day. Even when *D.4* briefly surfaced for air and a look round at 3:30pm, the only thing that could be seen was a trawler anchored in the distance at the eastern end of the Ems entrance. Moncreiffe got underway for Yarmouth two hours later, arriving at 2:30pm on the 25th.[5]

Plan X had been aborted. The force was recalled when half way to Heligoland. The Admiralty believed that the slow carriers would encounter a major German sortie. Routine German signals had again been misinterpreted as evidence of a larger operation. To Tyrwhitt's frustration the weather moderated to result in ideal take off conditions with good visibility, just as the forecasters had predicted! His cruisers were still used as bait, steaming into sight of Heligoland and being fired on by the batteries there. The German Fleet Command was cautious. They wanted to clarify the picture with aerial reconnaissance, particularly after the recent spate of submarine sightings, which they had come to associate with an impending British attack. That afternoon destroyers did carry out a sweep to the northwest of Heligoland, hoping in vain to make a night attack on the retiring British forces. Nothing came out of the Ems. The vessels seen by *D.4* and *D.6* were routine sweeping and minimal patrolling in the shallows close to the entrances.[6]

Back in Harwich, the flotilla had received a welcome addition on the 23rd. The new depot ship, *SS Seti*, had arrived. She had been built for use on the Egyptian trade route in 1902, with a high level of passenger comfort. When war broke out she was being converted to a submarine depot ship for the Russian Navy on the Tyne, where Keyes had spotted her on his visit to Ballard. As there was no chance of her joining their Fleet, on his recommendation the Admiralty purchased her on 9 November. Talbot writes that she was a good ship with plentiful accommodation for the crews, but that she still needed quite a lot of money spent on her to complete her fitting as a depot ship. Junior officers were moved into her cabins and the ERAs also moved over into her and messed there. On 2 December she was renamed HMS *Pandora*.

Yarmouth now had six submarines in the harbour. *D.2* and *E.15* were to be retained as defensive cover until *D.4* and *D.6* returned. *D.2* went out on stand-by duty in Yarmouth Roads on the morning of the 24th. *E.11* and *E.12*, which had returned from their patrol the previous day, were therefore free to return to Harwich. The third boat stationed at Yarmouth, *D.3*, was due for refit. *E.5* needed repair and was also overdue for a refit since June. These four submarines got underway at 7:30am for Harwich, led by *E.5*, as Benning was the senior officer. There was

---

4   TNA ADM137/2067: p.503; TNA ADM173: *D.6, 23–25 November 1914*.
5   TNA ADM137/2067: p.502; TNA ADM173: *D.4, 23–25 November 1914*.
6   TNA ADM186/621: p.54-6; Groos, *Nordsee 3*, pp.26-31. The Naval Staff monograph incorrectly assumes that *D.4* fired a torpedo.

an altercation with some trawlers heading down the River Yare to Gorleston, resulting in *E.11* ramming *D.3* and holing her saddle tank. The Yare was notorious for its fickle currents and Turner had already been in collision with a barge on the previous afternoon! Adding to the hazards, Benning spotted a drifting mine as they approached Felixstowe and signalled *E.12* to sink it.

On arrival *E.11* was docked for examination and repair, but no trace of any obstruction to explain the mysterious loss of control off Heligoland could be found. She had only minor damage to her bow from her collision, but developed a problem requiring some repairs to her steering gear on 1 December.

On the 28th *D.3* and *E.5* left Harwich for repair and refit in Chatham Dockyard, with *D.3* sporting a collision mat over the hole in her saddle tank. *D.3* needed to renew a motor and would be out of action until well into the next year. *E.5* got a major refit with new clutches, a Forbes Log, gyrocompass and wireless gear. She was not to return to Harwich until 27 December.[7]

The next patrol destinations continued to be guided by signal intercepts. Keyes received instructions at midday on the 24th. Firstly, the Admiralty believed that a submarine was still working from Zeebrugge. Keyes was ordered to send a C class over to stalk her, as he had previously suggested. Secondly, there appeared to be considerable movement of German ships around Heligoland. Two or three submarines were to be sent there as soon as possible.

Fortunately, *C.34* was still at Harwich. Hutchings left at 4pm. He anchored on the surface off Rabs Bank at midnight. *C.34* weighed anchor and headed for Zeebrugge at 6am next morning. The sea was calm and there was a thick mist. Hutchings dived at 8am as soon as he saw the Wielingen Lightship and patrolled off the harbour until midday. He headed out down the entrance channel with the tide, but found it impossible to manoeuvre at low water, so went to the bottom in just 33 feet (10m) of water. *C.34* surfaced after dark at 4:50pm. It was a clear moonlit night. Hutchings headed out to sea, anchored to charge his batteries, then went to the bottom for the night.

C.34 surfaced at 5:30am on the 26th in thick mist, with visibility of less than a mile. Hutchings headed back inshore, sounding the depth periodically. Once the piers at Blankenberghe loomed out of the mist, *C.34* back-tracked to the Lightship. It was sighted at 7:45am, but the tide was now falling. Hutchings headed for Thornton Ridge and deeper water. With no improvement in visibility and the wind rising, he soon decided to return to Harwich and arrived at 5:30pm. He had seen no vessels on the patrol. The route over the apparently unknown British minefield had been used at the beginning and end of the patrol. It was high water on the way in, but the tide had been falling for some time on the way out. *C.34* was using up a lot of luck.

Hutchings reported that Zeebrugge was simply too shallow at low tide to make a torpedo attack. He suggested that an enemy boat was likely to go out in darkness and that more success would probably be had ambushing her in a reasonable depth of water further down the route out into the English Channel in daylight. He proposed two likely ambush positions off Ostend marked A and B on the map. Hutchings thought the northern of the two suggested routes between the minefields was the most likely.

7   TNA ADM173: *D.3* 23 November 1914–1 February 1915, *E.5* 24 November-27 December 1914; IWM:Documents.1003: 23-29 November and 1 December; TNA ADM53: *Adamant* 24 November 1914; TNA ADM137/2067: p.485; IWM: Documents.20134: 23 November and 2 December 1914.

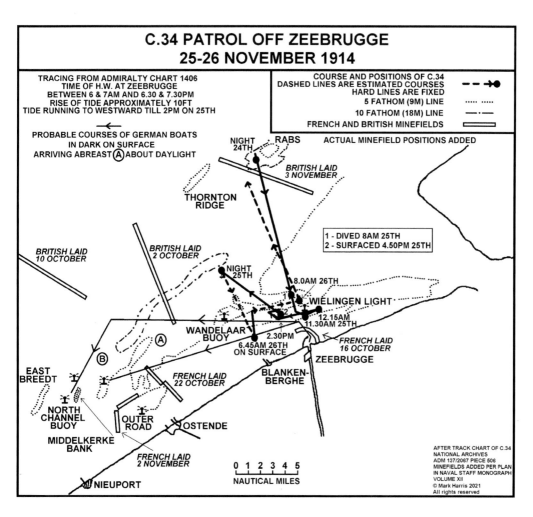

C.34 PATROL OFF ZEEBRUGGE
25-26 NOVEMBER 1914

Keyes report to Oliver on the patrol noted the unfavourable weather and tide conditions but ignored Hutchings suggestion. Instead he proposed sending *C.34* over to Zeebrugge again on 1-2 December for a couple of days, as the tidal conditions would be more favourable in daylight. Hutchings was wrong about German submarines leaving in darkness, as *U.12* had left in daylight on both occasions she had left Zeebrugge. However all four of her passages in and out had been on approximately the most likely route suggested by Hutchings and it continued in use later. The German Fleet Command had despatched *U.11* from Heligoland on the 24th in response to agent reports of an impending attack on the Flanders Coast. She arrived in Zeebrugge on the 26th, but very late in the day, after Hutchings had left. Decodes of signals about *U.11*'s movements had prompted the Admiralty orders.[8]

8 TNA ADM137/2067: pp.504-9; Groos, *Nordsee 3*, p.45; BArch:RM92: *Nassau* Kriegstagebuch, 26 November 1914.

Keyes decided to despatch *D.2* and *E.15* from Yarmouth to investigate the movements off Heligoland, since *D.4* and *D.6* were due back from patrol. They cast off from *Adamant* at 4:30am on the 25th and headed out together. Both were to leave their patrols on the afternoon of the 29th.

Brodie's *E.15* experienced another bout of the worst North Sea weather. She arrived five miles northwest of Heligoland at noon on the 26th in mist and low visibility with a strong south-westerly wind blowing. Nothing was seen that afternoon and *E.15* went to the bottom at 4:30pm. The weather was no better in the morning and the sea was now rough. Brodie quickly spotted a trawler to the east through the periscope. It went out of sight in the mist. Later that morning he observed a line of three large steamers heading out of the northern entrance to Heligoland steering west. Brodie struggled to get close enough to identify them, but believed they were Dutch. Soon afterwards another steamer headed south into the entrance. *E.15* got close enough to identify a deck cargo of timber and a probable Swedish ensign. Nothing was spotted in the afternoon and *E.15* went to the bottom for the night.

On the 28th visibility was never more than two miles all day. Two steamers were once again spotted leaving the northern entrance on a westerly heading. At 11:10am two steamers of about 1,500 tons were sighted heading south into the entrance. Brodie was closer this time. He made an attack run and got to within 200 yards (180m) of the second vessel. Their paintwork was black, with funnel markings, both typical of merchant ships. They were flying German merchant ensigns. The standing instructions from Keyes were that any suspicious merchant vessels were to be ordered to heave to. A boat would then be sent over to examine their papers. If the vessel was found to be carrying contraband, it was subject to seizure or sinking, after first making adequate provision for the safety of the passengers and crew. Brodie reports: 'boat work impossible, did not consider I was justified in torpedoing them, so remained submerged and followed in hopes of man-of-war escort meeting them.' However, he lost touch before they reached Heligoland. Nothing further was sighted.

Brodie surfaced at 1:15pm. The weather was much worse. He tried sitting it out on the bottom, but the boat was bumping badly. He now abandoned the patrol, surfaced and headed west, into the stormy seas. At 2pm disaster struck. Able Seaman George J. Morris was swept overboard by a heavy sea. Morris was aged 31. In 1910 he had purchased an early exit nine years into his 12 year enlistment. The last four years of his service had been in submarines and he had volunteered to re-join as soon as war threatened.

After 40 minutes Brodie finally succeeded in getting the bridge screen rigged, but was only able to make two knots heading west. *E.15* continued at this snail's pace next day straight into the heavy gale. She finally reached Yarmouth to tie up alongside the *Adamant* at 3:30pm on 1 December, having taken three days to cover the 240 miles from Heligoland. Brodie returned to Harwich the following day. He says little in his report, but Hallifax writes that on one of the days they had averaged just one knot and had both of the bridge screen supports knocked flat. Brodie was sporting two black eyes and his third officer another.[9]

Lieutenant-Commander Clement G.W. Head, aged 29, had recently been promoted and joined 8th Flotilla after completion of his compulsory Lieutenancy in a surface ship. Keyes

9   TNA ADM137/2067: p.510; TNA ADM188/347/200450: George Joseph Morris; IWM Documents.1003: 2 December; TNA ADM53: *Adamant* 25 November and 1 December 1914.

had sent him to Yarmouth to temporarily take command of *D.2*. He had joined the Submarine Service in 1906 and had gone on to command a number of coastal submarines in the following seven years. In 1909 Captain Hall had rated him a: 'V[ery] G[ood] off[icer] with the requisite amount of dash at the right time.' Keyes added that he had 'greatly distinguished himself' in pre-war exercises and was both zealous and capable. Head had decided to train as a pilot for the reserves in his spare time in 1912, quickly obtaining his pilot's licence. He had applied and been accepted for transfer to the Royal Flying Corps, but had withdrawn his application 'on realising sub. training would be wasted.'[10]

Head had been ordered to watch the channel to the west of Heligoland where *E.11* had observed the German trawler patrol. He was to follow any vessel making use of it. *D.2* parted company from *E.15* on the 25th to head to her billet. She was never seen or heard of again.[11] There are no clues as to the reason for her loss and the wreck has not been found. German official records make no mention of any submarine encounter on the 25th or subsequent days.[12] *D.2*'s billet was midway between Heligoland and the northern end of the German minefield. However, the position of the northern end of this mine line was accurately known. British records show 86 reports of drifting mines from 22–26 November, so it is possible that *D.2* simply struck one. She may have blundered into a minefield as a result of a mechanical problem or position error. *D.2* could also have suffered a catastrophic accident or mechanical failure. Problems with her port muffler box had almost caused her loss in August. Damage might have been caused in the heavy weather at the time of her return. Unless the wreck is one day identified and surveyed, the mystery will remain. All 26 crew were lost.[13]

Keyes reported her presumed loss on 9 December and finally confirmed it on the 14th. Churchill sent a signal to Keyes on reading his report, writing that Head was 'a good man and brilliant officer who showed skill in flying as well as in submarine piloting, and was always to be trusted where industry or daring was required.' Churchill was also an amateur flyer and presumably was well acquainted with Head. Keyes also regretted the loss of Lieutenant Oakeley,

---

10   TNA ADM196/143/479, 196/49/216: Clement Gordon Wakefield Head.
11   A news correspondent reported that at 3pm on 1 December, a British warship in a sinking condition had asked to enter the Dutch fort at Hook of Holland by wireless, which sent out three tugs. Keyes was concerned it could be *D.2*, but it was a red herring. There is some evidence that an unidentified wreck matching her dimensions and outline, lying north of Schiermonnikoog and grounded on a westerly heading could be *D.2*. If so it may suggest sinking on the way back from her billet.
12   The normally reliable Dittmar & Colledge list *D.2* as: 'Sunk 25.11.14 by Germans PB off the Ems.' This awkward sentence is ambiguous. It has been assumed by many writers that PB means 'patrol boat' but could equally be shorthand for 'probably' and apparently simply repeats this contemporary Admiralty speculation.
13   Those lost, ages in brackets: In Command – Lieutenant-Commander Clement Gordon Wakefield Head (29); 1st Lieutenant – Lieutenant Francis Eckley Oakeley (23); 3rd Hand – Lieutenant-Commander (Retired) Frederick Lewis Coplestone (32); Petty Officer – William McDonald (30); Petty Officer LTOs – Fredrick Hibbs (29); Arthur Hiscock DSM (34); Leading Seamen – Charles Henry Dawe (28); William Thomas Peters (27); Charles Burt Rolfe (27); Able Seamen – Samuel Ford Cox (23); Thomas Edward Kennett (33); Walter Henry Lock (31); Eli Pethick (23); Telegraphist – Joseph Wilkinson (20); ERA 2nd Class – George William Smith (31); ERAs 3rd Class – Charlie Edwards Kilburn (29); Joseph Lumb (26); ERA 4th Class – Edgar John Killham (21); Stoker Petty Officer – George Dalton (34); Leading Stoker – Frederick Fish (37); Stokers 1st Class – Alfred Artis (27); Alfred Barnett (30); Herbert Charles James Bird (23); George Hobson (26); Frederick James Kemp (30); William Harry Noyce (26).

The crew of *D.2*, taken shortly after war broke out. The three officers are Jameson in the centre, with Oakeley to his right and Coplestone to his left. PO Hiscock is behind Coplestone. (RNSM Neg. 6727)

whom he says was a brilliant Rugby Half-back who had played for England in 1913–14, as well as Lieutenant-Commander Coplestone, who had been invalided out in 1906 after a short time in the Submarine Service due to deafness. He had been turned down for air service in 1913 but had volunteered on war breaking out and had begged to serve in any capacity, becoming 3rd Officer, despite being more senior than his fellow officers. Typical of the concern for his men's welfare that earned him such affection in the Fleet, Jellicoe sent a message to Keyes that did not pick out the officers. However, he offered his deep regret for the loss of the 'valuable lives' of the entire crew.[14]

Keyes proposed in his report to Sturdee that since German merchant trade appeared to have resumed one or two submarines should be sent to interdict it between Horns Reef and Heligoland. One of these should be *D.4*, which was the only submarine armed with a gun, making it easier for her to force merchant vessels to stop. This is the first suggestion both of actively using submarines against enemy commerce and employing guns rather than torpedoes. The route of merchant ship comings and goings should not have been a surprise as all merchantmen had been required since 4 November to pick up a pilot at Lister Deep before heading in to the

14   TNA ADM137/78: pp.109, 127; TNA ADM137/2067: pp.513, 515-7; Keyes, *Memoirs*, p.139; TNA ADM186/621: p.77; TNA ADM188 and TNA ADM196 for individual crew service records.

inner German Bight. A mandatory pilot was also required for the journey back out. The signal decodes that had prompted the despatch of the submarines probably related to the overnight sweep by the German Destroyer Flotillas in response to Tyrwhitt's raid.[15]

The 8th Flotilla had come through the first three months of the war unscathed, whilst sinking two enemy warships. In just over a month their fortunes had changed dramatically, with three boats and 77 crew lost and almost nothing to show for it. Mindful of the impact on their families, on the 29th Waistell announced that a fund was being set up to provide relief for dependents of those who lost their lives in the Flotilla during the war. The weather was also making effective patrol work impossible. Talbot writes in his diary on 27 November that: 'Remaining in harbour for so long is getting very trying.' With the weather remaining atrocious into December, further patrols had to be put on hold and even the Harwich destroyers were kept in port. Talbot tried to keep the boredom away with golf, despite the awful weather. There were also occasional sing-songs and performances in the sheds on the Quay or the destroyer depot ship *Woolwich* in the evenings. These could be a mixed blessing, with performers drawn mainly from the crews of the Flotillas at Harwich. Another attempt to make light of their troubles was made by Lieutenant-Commander Stopford Douglas of *Maidstone*. He began producing a locally printed monthly magazine in October, initially entitled the *Maidstone Muckrag* and later *The Maidstone Magazine*, with humorous contributions from those in the Flotilla. It was clearly a hit, went on being published and was eventually reprinted in two bound editions, fronted with a poem about The Trade contributed by Rudyard Kipling. Crews were also finally able to give the boats a fresh lick of paint and iron out snags that had been building up through the intensive period of patrolling.[16]

15 TNA ADM137/2067: pp.511-2; *Diplomatic Correspondence*, p.220, Nachrichten für Seefahrer, 4 November 1914.
16 IWM: Documents.1003: 29 November; IWM:Documents.20134: 23-30 November 1914; Douglas, *Maidstone Magazine*, pp.vii–viii, 1.

24

Reinforcements and command politics

Undeterred by the two previous failures to launch an air attack on the zeppelin sheds, Plan X had been re-worked by Tyrwhitt and Keyes into a new plan, inevitably named Plan Y. The project had strong personal support from Churchill, who was a particular champion of naval aviation. The plans were finalised in a visit Keyes and Tyrwhitt paid to the Admiralty on 1 December. Furthermore, Tyrwhitt, followed by Keyes, each had separate meetings with Fisher. He probed Keyes about his relationship with Tyrwhitt and said, 'a good deal about submarines.' As Fisher was in a hurry Keyes was to 'get it from Tyrwhitt as he had told him his ideas.' This brush-off did not bode well. Tyrwhitt told Keyes afterwards that there was 'really nothing to tell.' Fisher had 'asked him about submarines – and [Tyrwhitt] had suggested that Lord F. should ask [Keyes].'[1]

Keyes had taken the opportunity to once again suggest using the coastal submarines for offensive operations in enemy waters. He came away believing Fisher was at least not opposed to this if they could be spared. He submitted a memorandum. This proposed taking four submarines from Dover, two from the Humber and three from the Forth. Keyes suggested that only the new *S.1* and later C class were used. Spare parts for early C class were not interchangeable with later boats, creating problems holding spares for both in the same flotilla.

Plan Y called for up to four C class to be used if available. Keyes already had *C.34* at Harwich. Oliver issued orders for *C.16* and *S.1* to transfer from Dover to Harwich that evening, as these were the only coastal submarines that could immediately be spared, then issued the orders for Plan Y next day. He followed up on the 6th with orders to re-constitute the 3rd Submarine Flotilla at Yarmouth, with five C class and the depot ship *Alecto*. The Flotilla was to be directly under Keyes for service as an overseas flotilla and would also take over the day patrol off Gorleston. Most of the intended boats were not yet available because of refits, so the Flotilla was only to be formed once these were completed. Meanwhile, *C.16* and *S.1* had arrived at Harwich on the afternoon of the 2nd.[2]

S.1 was the first, rather bitter fruit of Keyes attempt to bypass the Vickers submarine monopoly and assess the suitability of foreign designs. She was built to the Italian design of Fiat-San Georgio, by their British licensee, Scotts. Since commissioning on 5 August, *S.1*

---

1   *Keyes Papers*, p.53-4, letter to wife 4 December 1914; Keyes, *Memoirs*, p.152.
2   TNA ADM137/78 p.129, 260, 759, 761; BL:AddMS82462, p.101, 180; TNA ADM186/621: pp.275-7.

had been assigned to 4th Flotilla at Dover. However, she had only spent one of the last four months there. The rest of the time had been spent resolving defects. She was similar to a C class in size, with the same armament. Unlike them she had a double bottom, a high level of internal compartmentation, wireless and modern twin diesel engines. The construction method resulted in a high buoyancy reserve, taking longer to submerge when diving. She had innovative folding hydroplanes, theoretically avoiding the problems British boats had experienced in heavy weather. However, these were proving somewhat unreliable.[3]

The next day an even more unusual reinforcement was due. As early as 10 September the Navy Ministry in Paris had raised the possibility with the British Naval Attaché of the newest French submarine, *Gustave Zédé*, joining the Harwich Flotilla. This was the first French submarine designed for operations on the high seas and was in the final stages of completion. On the 18th, the French Minister of the Navy, Victor Augagneur, made a formal offer to Churchill of six or seven of the most suitable French submarines in addition to *Gustave Zédé*, to co-operate with the Harwich Flotilla.

The offer was accepted. Five of the newest submarines were identified as provisionally suitable for North Sea operations by Contre-Amiral Albert Rouyer, the commander of French forces in the Channel.[4] Capitaine de Frégate Henri T.M.J. de Cacqueray de Saint Quentin was designated for command of the French squadron and sent over to the Admiralty in London to arrange details on the 25th. Keyes told him that British experience of German anti-submarine tactics had identified three essential operational capabilities: submerge within two minutes if the enemy was encountered at night; stay submerged for up to 36 hours; ability to dive to the bottom in depths of up to 40m (130 feet). French submarines had not been designed for fast diving or extended spells of time resting on the bottom. Only *Mariotte* and *Gustave Zédé* were thought to meet the endurance requirements and *Mariotte* would need an oxygen generation system to be fitted to be able to remain submerged this long. This unwelcome news also came at a time that the French Navy found itself facing additional demands on their submarines for defensive patrols off the Belgian coast and Dover Straits.

On receipt of Cacqueray's report, The Navy Ministry concurred that crews would need further training to meet the requirements for rapid diving and extended underwater operation. Both Cacqueray and the boats at Calais were stood down on 29 September and returned to their previous duties. Keyes left it that when ready, the French would be most welcome at Harwich and *Maidstone* could act as their depot.

On 5 November Keyes wrote to Oliver that the French Naval Attaché had indicated that *Gustave Zédé* was now ready. The French government would like to repeat their offer. Keyes was in favour of acceptance. *Gustave Zédé* used steam propulsion for a high 16 knot surface speed. Valuable experience of operating a submarine of this type under war conditions could therefore be gained. The British had a similar submarine, *Swordfish*, but she was yet to become operational and the French were more experienced in operating submarines using steam power.

3   TNA ADM173: *S.1* 5 August-2 December 1914; TNA ADM137/2067: pp.676-8; see Appendix I for *S.1* particulars.
4   *Berthelot, Prairial, Archimède, Mariotte* and *Gustave Zédé*. As there were delays in the completion of *Gustave Zédé, Newton* was quickly substituted. *Archimède* and *Mariotte* were ordered from Cherbourg to join the other vessels at Calais.

Archimède underway on her electric motors off Cherbourg in 1910. The funnel is lowered. The external torpedo launchers are concealed behind the gratings below the upper deck. (Author's Collection)

On the 7th the Navy Ministry ordered Vice-Amiral Charles-Eugène Favereau, who had succeeded Rouyer, to send *Gustave Zédé* to Harwich to act under British command. He pointed out to the Ministry that she was still delayed as a result of funnel defects revealed during trials and could not be ready before the 22nd. The date came and went and she was still not ready. Favereau proposed substituting the somewhat smaller *Archimède*, which was imminently completing a refit. The Ministry accepted the proposal, whilst expressing some concerns about the condition of *Archimède*'s batteries, as well as exasperation that after three months *Gustave Zédé* was still not ready for service.

Archimède completed her refit at Brest on the 29th and returned to her base at Cherbourg the next day. She received orders to proceed to Harwich via Dover, escorted by the destroyer *Sagaie*. *Archimède* would be under Keyes orders as part of 8th Flotilla and was ordered to quickly familiarise with British operational procedures, then commence patrols. Attacks on major warships were the main objective, but discretion was given to attack destroyers if there was a good chance of success. Bad weather delayed departure until the next day, but *Archimède* finally arrived in Harwich with her escort on the afternoon of 3 December, accompanied by Cacqueray.

Observing her arrival, Talbot noted in his diary that 'she certainly does not look fit to compete with the usual North Sea weather.' He looked her over a few days later and felt that British boats compared very favourably, except for the periscopes. He also thought that the she was very dirty! The funnel must have made her hard to keep clean. Keyes was welcoming to his French allies and conducted a tour on the following day. Cacqueray was very complimentary about Keyes submarine commanders and Keyes had both he and the two senior officers of *Archimède* dine with him before Cacqueray returned to France. On the 5th *SS Newhaven* arrived from Cherbourg with spare torpedoes and stores. Waistell now went to work with *Archimède* to oversee an intensive programme of rapid diving drills off Harwich to get her ready for a patrol.[5]

Archimède had a crew of 28. She was powered on the surface by two oil fuelled boilers, driving two triple expansion steam engines, with a surface speed of 15 knots. Her batteries gave her a top submerged speed of 10 knots, with a submerged action radius of 99 miles at five knots. She was designed to take up to four minutes to submerge, since the funnel had to be stowed and secured first. Six of her seven torpedo launchers were carried externally. As they were open to the sea their reliability declined over the course of a patrol. Diving beyond 30m (100 feet) would also damage them. The only internal tube was in the bow firing directly ahead and this was the only launcher with a reload. Cold torpedoes of similar performance to British types were carried.[6]

Whilst entertaining his new guests and waiting for a break in the weather Keyes revised the detailed submarine orders for the impending seaplane raid, assisted by Talbot. As only two C class were available and were required for missions to Zeebrugge, these were dropped from the plan. Nine seaplanes would launch from three carriers to attack the zeppelin sheds, screened by Tyrwhitt's Flotillas. As the German Fleet had shown no appetite to come out on the last excursion, there would be no support from the Grand Fleet. However, *Lurcher* and *Firedrake* would lead *S.1* and nine D and E class boats out to cover the operation. They would interdict anything approaching Tyrwhitt's force, attack any German vessels leaving port and if necessary recover ditched pilots. As co-ordination with Jellicoe was no longer necessary, the date was left to Tyrwhitt and Keyes discretion based on the weather.

Once a day was settled on Keyes was to notify Oliver. The new plan was in complete contrast to the virtual afterthought given to the submarines in the previous attempt. The prominent role allocated to 8th Flotilla, even to the extent of Keyes being the one who would ultimately decide on the date of execution, suggests that Keyes had pulled rank as senior officer at Harwich. He was obviously no longer willing to remain on the side-lines.

The fallout from both of this and the interviews with Fisher was not long coming. On the 3rd Keyes received a telegram from Tyrwhitt: 'Admiralty informs me that I am appointed Commodore 1st Class from tomorrow and direct me to inform S.N.O. [Keyes].' Keyes wrote to his wife, rather unfairly, that this was: 'an outrage on him [Keyes] and the submarine service considering the size and importance of our two commands and what they have done during the war.' The whole thing left Keyes 'sick and disgusted.' The implication that Tyrwhitt had been made senior to Keyes, and the favouritism that Fisher had displayed for him, rankled. Technically, Keyes seniority on the Captain's list took precedence. The fact that nobody would see it that way was quickly proved. Keyes wrote to his wife that his friend Captain Nicholson, who now had one of Tyrwhitt's flotillas, came to see him and stated exactly that.

---

5   TNA ADM137/2067: pp.639, 680; Gérard Garier, *Sous-Marin en France – Tome 3 – 2e partie – A l'épreuve de la Grande Guerre* (Nantes: Marines Editions, 2002), pp.24-7, 30-31; Service Historique de l'État Major de la Marine: Archives de la 2ème Escadre Légère: Cartons 14, 28; Keyes, *Memoirs*, pp.139-40; *Keyes Papers*, p.55 letter to wife 5 December 1914; IWM:Documents.20134: 3-7 December 1914.

6   Gérard Garier, *Sous-Marin en France – Tome 2* (Nantes: Marines Edition, 1998), pp.154-72; See Appendices I and II for *Archimède* and her armament.

On the 5th the submarines to be involved in Plan Y had been ordered to paint up a red band around their conning towers 'as a distinguishing mark.' Crews were also required to be at 30 minutes notice to be in their boats. The reason for the orders was not yet revealed. The markings were intended to guide returning seaplanes. Hallifax was unhappy about being made easier to spot.

On the 6th Keyes sent a tersely worded signal to Tyrwhitt, setting out some additional instructions in relation to communications during Plan Y and the part to be played by Tyrwhitt's 1st Destroyer Flotilla. He added a handwritten note at the end of the signal: 'Will you be ready to carry out this operation on Wednesday the 9th if the weather promises to be favourable!' The content and wording of the signal, whether conscious or not, is frosty and seems to be more about emphasising that Keyes was in charge and senior to Tyrwhitt. It is unclear if the signal itself caused the rift with Tyrwhitt or was a consequence of it. A serious falling out resulted. Tyrwhitt wrote to his own wife on the 7th that: 'I have just written to Keyes and given him what for. I was horribly hurt at his attitude yesterday and have just given it to him in plain English.' A predictable result of Fisher's partisanship and the recent interviews.

Keyes had a discussion with Oliver. He wrote to his wife, Eva, that: 'J.F. [Fisher] had said to him [Oliver] the night before: "Why is Keyes always at the Admiralty – why doesn't he go to sea like Tyrwhitt and take command of his vessels at sea."' This was a barb that could not have been better designed to goad Keyes. He continues: 'Oliver evidently defended me nobly ... – He didn't know that I had actually been ordered not to go to sea ... [and] promised to tell him [Fisher] this.' Keyes went on to tell Eva that: 'Tyrwhitt's seniority is always in my way ... I told Oliver this, and how difficult it is for me to go sea without treading on his toes. In the early days of the war he was quite ready to serve under me, but he has had it all his own way lately and naturally would resent me being put in above him.' Keyes tried to resolve the issues with Fisher by speaking to Hall, suggesting that Hall take over responsibility for construction altogether, allowing Keyes to concentrate on leading his submarines at sea. Hall agreed to speak to Fisher and telephoned later that he had agreed to the arrangement. However, Hall had also told Keyes that he was unhappy with his 'construction job' and made it clear that Fisher had brought him back to replace Keyes entirely. Keyes was aware from his contacts that he was being frustrated from doing so by Churchill. Fisher's attitude to Keyes remained unpredictable. On the 20th, his assistant, Captain Crease, wrote to Keyes that he was to call on Fisher whenever he was up at the Admiralty and could go to his house if he was not in his office.

Keyes issued operational orders for Plan Y on the 7th. Next day the participating submarines were ordered to change the band on the conning tower into an even more prominent red and white checked pattern. Junior officers and crew were still kept in the dark about the reason.

Favourable weather reports decided Keyes to give the go ahead for the operation at 9pm on the 9th. He issued a communique to all of the 8th Flotilla vessels to be involved in the operation. After noting that the surface force would not be covered by any armoured vessels he wrote of his: 'pride that the support of this Expedition should have been confided to the Submarine Service, and I am confident that ... they will drive home their attacks, proceed to the assistance of Seaplane Pilots, or carry out any other services ... regardless of all other considerations.' Submarines were to take in provisions at 6am on the 10th for departure that night, with the air attack to be delivered on the 12th.

The weather refused to co-operate with the forecast. That night a gale blew up from the northwest. The departure was stood down; Talbot reflected that 'it is a wearying job waiting for decent weather.' Keyes signalled Oliver at 9:30am that Plan Y had been postponed. Hopefully, the wind would drop and the force could depart on the 11th. It was not to be. At 8pm Oliver signalled Keyes that Plan Y was to be postponed 'owing to other operations now contemplated.' The Harwich destroyers and submarines were required for 'another purpose.' Keyes wrote to Eva that it was 'a very great disappointment … I am very sick of this inaction!'

The delay gave time for Keyes to reflect on Tyrwhitt's letter of the 7th. Tyrwhitt wrote to his wife on the 11th that: 'I had reams from Roger yesterday, and it was full of excuses and apologies … but on the whole he was very sorry … so I have forgiven him and we've made it up. I have been for a walk with him and all is peace.' As Keyes would be heading into the Bight as part of the operation he also wrote a sealed letter to his wife on the 10th. This was only to be opened in the event of his death. Amongst the other sentiments in the letter was a request that Eva ask Tyrwhitt to be godfather to their next child which she was expecting, highlighting the day on which he had made the request when she did so. The productive partnership between Tyrwhitt and Keyes was patched up; he makes no mention of the spat in his memoirs.[7]

Whilst the command crisis simmered the gales continued; there had been little patrol activity for the submarines. On the 9th the Admiralty intercepted signals ordering a submarine to depart the Bight for Zeebrugge. Keyes was ordered to send a C boat over to Zeebrugge if the weather was suitable, to 'look out for German submarine & to scout'. The weather was too bad and the order was therefore repeated on the evening of the 10th when Plan Y was postponed.

The winds had subsided and Keyes despatched Hutchings with *C.34* at 8am on the 11th. She spent the night on the bottom off Zeebrugge. At 6am Hutchings surfaced in a calm sea and fog. He headed inwards until he saw the Wielingen Lightship, then dived out along the channel towards the Wandelaar Buoy. After only two miles the Lightship disappeared aft in the fog, so he partially surfaced and continued on the petrol engine, with just the conning tower out of the water. Hutchings remained near the buoy until noon, seeing nothing except a couple of masts sticking up above the murk off Ostend. *C.34* headed back to Thornton Ridge, reaching it at 3:30pm. There were now two buoys at the spot. Since high water had been at 6:30am, his timing was dangerous, passing the mines there well before the next high tide. *C.34* returned to Harwich at 8am next morning, the 13th. It was sixth time lucky with the mines![8]

The intelligence had been good. However, the delay for suitable weather meant that Hutchings missed the arrival of *U.5* and *U.12* on the afternoon of the 11th. The only existing submarine operating from Zeebrugge, *U.11*, had failed to return from a day patrol on the 9th, probably after running into the French minefield off Ostend. Churchill could be dismissive of operational realities at times and the lack of success against enemy submarines irked him. He wrote to Oliver on the 12th that: '[Keyes] ought really to be able to do in one of those Zeebrugge submarines with his C boats. Surely one can lie off the entrance constantly … It is high time a result was

7   *Keyes Papers*, p.53-7, 62, letters to Eva of 4–11 December 1914, Crease to Keyes 20 December 1914, Patterson, *Tyrwhitt*, pp.90-1 letters to Angela Tyrwhitt of 7 and 11 December, TNA ADM137/2067: pp.524-5; IWM: Documents.1003: 5 & 8 December; TNA ADM137/79: p.417, 549, 572; IWM: Documents.20134: 9-10 December 1914.

8   TNA ADM137/79: p.312, 572; TNA ADM137/2067: pp.514-5; IWM:Documents.1003: 11 December

The bridge of *C.34*. (NH 54980)

achieved.'[9] Throughout the operational lull Waistell had his submarines and new commanders exercising to keep then sharp.

Lieutenant-Commander Gilbert H. Kellett, aged 30, had taken command of *S.1* at the builders in November 1913. Kellett had a number of ups and downs in his career despite consistently high ratings for his ability. Captain Tudor had assessed him as 'having great capabilities for good or evil' as a Midshipman and a note was added on his record for 'improperly sending off whiskey to Gunroom Mess.' He had joined the Submarine Service in 1906 and had five years of experience commanding coastal submarines. In 1908 Captain Hall assessed him as: 'Steady & reliable. An efficient but not brilliant submarine commander.' He had hit another bump in the road when he was held to blame for damaging *C.4* in 1909 but had kept his slate clean since then.[10]

9   Groos, *Nordsee 3*, p.46; BArch:RM92: *Nassau* Kriegstagebuch 9 December 1914; Martin Gilbert, *Winston S. Churchill: Companion Vol. III, Part 1, July 1914-April 1915* (Boston: Houghton Mifflin Co., 1973), p.307
10   TNA ADM196/49/213 & 196/143/525 Gilbert Hilton Kellett.

Lieutenant-Commander Geoffrey N. Biggs, aged 29, had also been in command of *C.16* since November 1913 and had been in submarines for the same length of time as Kellett. Keyes judged him a: 'Careful & v[ery] capable S/M Captain. Makes v[ery] skilful attacks.'[11]

Kellett had taken *S.1* out every day from the 7th to the 9th for diving practice around the Sunk Light Vessel, honing her dive time as much as was possible with her high buoyancy reserve. Several other boats, including *C.16* on the 9th, had also been out for diving practice. They were joined by *Firedrake* on the 8th and *Lurcher* on the 9th for practice torpedo attacks.

Despite the gale there had been a submarine alarm at Harwich on the 10th. The examination steamer, *Daisy*, saw a periscope near the harbour entrance that morning. Cayley had the harbour swept but thought the report doubtful. However, at 8:50am next morning *Daisy* again reported sighting an enemy submarine in the harbour entrance, which was followed out to seaward. Kellett had been leaving for another practice when he was recalled to be given new orders. With Plan Y stood down, Keyes sent out *S.1* and *C.16* to stalk for enemy submarines in the approaches to Harwich.

At 11am Biggs took *C.16* out to the Sunk Light Vessel, with *S.1* heading for a billet closer to Harwich in the final approach to the harbour at the Rough Buoy. Both spent their time dodging destroyer divisions coming in and out on escort missions, not to mention assorted vessels thrashing about looking for the German submarines. Kellett only spent one hour at periscope depth, then went to the bottom until it was time to return. They were back in harbour around 4pm. It could have been a lethal situation and caused complaints in the mess on their return. Keyes was overheard to claim that he had agreed that the destroyers were supposed to have stayed in, but Tyrwhitt's destroyer movements had all been essential escort work. Nobody spotted any German submarines for the simple reason that none were anywhere near Harwich at the time. A typical 1914 submarine panic.[12]

The postponement of Plan Y was for nothing. The 'other operation' was the result of Rear-Admiral Hood, who was now the commander at Dover, then Fisher, mobilising considerable forces around an idea to re-capture Zeebrugge. This originated with Colonel Bridges, the liaison officer with the Belgian Army. It never seriously considered by either the British or French Army command. Once this was made clear, the operation was stood down. At 1:20am on the 13th Keyes was therefore once again instructed to carry out Plan Y 'as soon as the weather conditions are suitable.' The weather improved next afternoon. The air attack was scheduled for the 17th, with the submarines departing from the 15th. This time it was a Harwich entertainment featuring London stars that was postponed as a result![13]

11   TNA ADM196/143/526 Geoffrey Nepean Biggs.
12   TNA ADM137/79: pp.454, 462, 564, 614, 621, 656, 714, 723; TNA ADM173: *S.1* 7-11 December 1914; IWM: Documents.1003 and IWM: Documents.20134: 10–11 December 1914.
13   Julian Corbett, *History of the Great War based on official documents: Naval Operations, Vol. 2* (London: Longmans, Green & Co., 1921), p.19; TNA ADM137/79 p.953; IWM: Documents.1003: 14 December 1914.

25

Another interruption

Just after midnight on the morning of 15 December Keyes was again ordered to postpone Plan Y. The submarines had been due to begin leaving later that day. Another signal followed at 1:55am: 'As a preparative measure all overseas submarines which are available are to be sent to Gorleston to arrive by 1 p.m. today, Tuesday. Should they be told to carry out the plan ordered, they are to proceed to a line extending in a SSE direction from a position ... [35 miles off Terschelling] ... to ... the Dutch coast. They are to be spread on this line by daybreak Wednesday [16th], and remain on it until nightfall, when they are to return to Harwich. German vessels may be crossing this line at any time on Wednesday.' A German sortie leaving for a raid on the 16th was implied.

In fact the purpose of the deployment was to intercept the raid on the way back, should it return this way. Jellicoe and Tyrwhitt, but not Keyes, were given a more complete view of the situation, derived from decoded signals. The German battle cruisers, supported by light cruisers and three flotillas of destroyers, would shortly be setting out to an unknown destination and would be returning to port on the 16th. Jellicoe suspected this meant the entire Fleet would sortie, as in November. He wanted to respond with a full sortie by the Grand Fleet. The Admiralty directed him to sortie only part of the Fleet, which would rendezvous with Tyrwhitt's Flotillas in the North Sea. Once the target was clear, this force would block the German retirement and destroy them.

Keyes considered that it was too dangerous to attempt a sortie from Gorleston through the Haisborough Channel route with so many submarines at night. He wanted to use the route via the North Hinder, but this meant departing directly from Harwich, not Gorleston. The only alternative route from Gorleston was through the Smith's Knoll channel, which was still fouled with mines laid by *Stralsund*. He telephoned the Admiralty asking to speak urgently with Oliver. In the meantime the submarines at Harwich were told to be ready to leave at 7:30am.

Keyes had already gone aboard *Lurcher* when the Admiralty responded. With only an hour before departure Talbot took a telephone message telling Keyes to hold his submarines at Harwich ready for sea. Keyes confirmed that he had seven Es, one D, one S, two Cs and *Archimède* at Harwich. Two Ds were still at Yarmouth and Talbot's *E.6* was due to be docked for routine minor repair work at Harwich that afternoon. This could be rescinded if the need was urgent. *E.11*'s propeller had put a hole in the 'spare' ballast tank of *E.6* when shifting billets the previous day. The remaining two Es and three Ds were in repair and refit.

It may be recalled that six weeks earlier Jellicoe had agreed with Keyes that if the German Fleet put to sea, Keyes should send every available submarine to lie off the German harbours and attack them on their return. A simple, but sound plan. It was therefore not surprising that Keyes was unhappy with the deployment ordered. He protested his concerns in detail in a memorandum to Oliver.

Based on the current orders, Keyes wrote to Oliver that he planned to put 10 submarines on the line, with another two pairs held back 15 miles behind it; every available submarine. *Lurcher* and *Firedrake* would scout to the east of the line. Experience in three years of peacetime exercises had shown that submarine deployments in such a long line were 'elementary and wasteful.' Keyes knew that if his submarines were dispersed in advance it would be very difficult to contact them in order to redeploy them. At most one or two boats might get a chance to attack whatever formation crossed the line. He considered that by covering only one approach, it left nothing to cover the Humber and Thames. Keyes wrote that it was obviously necessary to intercept the enemy where he would be during daylight. Therefore: 'Since the enemy appears to leave his ports at night … No doubt the Admiralty … have good reason to think he will pass through a line … from Terschelling.' A reasonable, but false assumption. On that basis he proposed placing Tyrwhitt's full force ahead of his submarines, as his two destroyers were not enough to scout effectively. They could then wireless the course of approaching vessels to the submarines, grouped at strategic points behind the outpost line. This would allow them to move to an intercept position, dive and await their approach.

Keyes also took the opportunity to underline his view that Gorleston was no longer a good place to base his submarines. The laying of the minefield by *Stralsund* meant that they had a 60 mile passage through the constricted Haisborough Channel to negotiate, taking them 30 miles out of the direct route to their patrol billets. The additional C class submarines to form the new flotilla were still needed to free up the D class tied up at Yarmouth.

The message was despatched by motor car to the Admiralty, being too sensitive to discuss on an unsecured telephone line. At 11:15am Keyes received the message that a sortie by eight boats 'will be sufficient.' They could leave by a route of his choice but had to be in position by daybreak on the 16th on the line already ordered. The submarines were to be warned with a statement of the obvious: 'British ships will also be at sea.' Keyes acknowledged, confirmed that he would use the North Hinder route and requested details of the other British deployments. No more information was forthcoming. Keyes writes that his alternative proposal did not arrive at the Admiralty before the submarines had to leave as ordered. Whenever it was received, no-one attempted to correct Keyes assumption that the Germans would cross his line from the east. His destroyers would be looking on the wrong side of the submarine line for the enemy.

Keyes dutifully issued orders to his submarines. They would have to leave Harwich at 2:30pm. Once in position they would be five miles apart on the patrol line, with the Noord West Gat Buoy between Terschelling and Vlieland used as the inshore reference point. They left in pairs in the order of their deployment from offshore to inshore. This would reduce the chance of collisions once night came on. The submarines chosen in order were *E.2* with *E.7*, *E.8* with *E.10*, *E.11* with *E.12*, *E.15* with *Archimède*. They were to pair up again at 4pm on the 16th and return to Harwich. As usual they were also to return early if severe weather threatened. *Lurcher* and *Firedrake* would follow at 5pm and would scout to the east of the line to warn of approaching enemies. Keyes would go out in *Lurcher*, as he was now free to do so. Only *Archimède* would

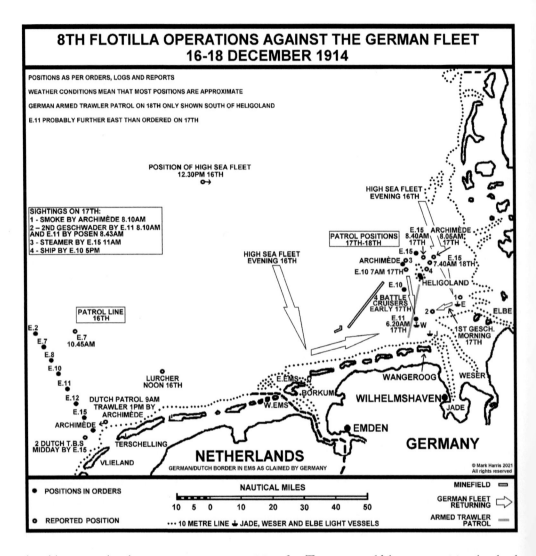

8TH FLOTILLA OPERATIONS AGAINST THE GERMAN FLEET
16-18 DECEMBER 1914

POSITIONS AS PER ORDERS, LOGS AND REPORTS

WEATHER CONDITIONS MEAN THAT MOST POSITIONS ARE APPROXIMATE

GERMAN ARMED TRAWLER PATROL ON 18TH ONLY SHOWN SOUTH OF HELIGOLAND

E.11 PROBABLY FURTHER EAST THAN ORDERED ON 17TH

SIGHTINGS ON 17TH:
1 - SMOKE BY ARCHIMÈDE 8.10AM
2 – 2ND GESCHWADER BY E.11 8.10AM AND E.11 BY POSEN 8.43AM
3 - STEAMER BY E.15 11AM
4 - SHIP BY E.10 5PM

POSITION OF HIGH SEA FLEET 12.30PM 16TH

HIGH SEA FLEET EVENING 16TH

PATROL POSITIONS 17TH-18TH

E.15 ARCHIMÈDE 8.40AM 8.05AM 17TH 17TH

E.15

ARCHIMÈDE 3
E.10 7AM 17TH

E.15 7.40AM 18TH
4

HIGH SEA FLEET EVENING 16TH

E.10

HELIGOLAND

4 BATTLE CRUISERS EARLY 17TH

E.11 6.20AM 17TH

2 E

ELBE

1ST GESCH. MORNING 17TH

PATROL LINE 16TH

E.2
E.7
E.7 10.45AM
E.8
E.10
E.11
E.12   DUTCH PATROL 9AM
TRAWLER 1PM BY
E.15   ARCHIMÈDE
ARCHIMÈDE

LURCHER NOON 16TH

E.EMS
BORKUM
W.EMS

WANGEROOG   WESER

WILHELMSHAVEN

JADE

EMDEN

2 DUTCH T.B.S MIDDAY BY E.15   TERSCHELLING

VLIELAND   NETHERLANDS

GERMAN/DUTCH BORDER IN EMS AS CLAIMED BY GERMANY

GERMANY

● POSITIONS IN ORDERS

NAUTICAL MILES

MINEFIELD ▭

10 5 0   10   20   30   40   50

GERMAN FLEET RETURNING ⇨

○ REPORTED POSITION

••• 10 METRE LINE ⚓ JADE, WESER AND ELBE LIGHT VESSELS

ARMED TRAWLER PATROL ▬

be able to see the shore to get an exact position fix. The rest would have to position by dead reckoning. Keyes knew the deployment would be flawed, with gaps and overlaps.[1]

Lurcher suffered a breakdown in her steering gear soon after leaving Harwich. She was forced to anchor whilst *Firedrake* stood by. Fortunately, the engineering hands fixed the problem after 90 minutes of frantic work. The destroyers were able to push on and make up the lost time.

The submarines headed east to the North Hinder Light on a very dark night. They then turned northeast to their billets. The weather alternated between rain, mist and the occasional snow flurry. IJmuiden Lighthouse, the only reference point on the way, was obscured by the weather. Most of the submarines lost touch with one another and were likely to be badly out of

---

1   Keyes, *Memoirs*, pp.140-1; TNA ADM137/2067 pp.562-7; TNA ADM186/621 pp.216-8; BL:AddMS82462, p.112; TNA ADM137/80 pp.21, 122.

reckoning. Even *Archimède* was out of position by five and six miles on two separate sightings by *Lurcher*.

The early morning of the 16th passed without incident. At 10:34am *Lurcher* intercepted a faint fragment of a wireless message on the destroyer wavelength from the battleship *Monarch* of the Grand Fleet's 2nd Battle Squadron, to the 4th Flotilla Destroyer *Ambuscade*, indicating that German forces were off Scarborough. As *Lurcher* was too far at sea to get a message through to shore, Keyes sent *Firedrake* off at maximum speed to get in touch with *Adamant* at Yarmouth. From here there was a direct telephone link to the Admiralty.

However, it was already obvious to Keyes that the submarines were useless where they were. If the Germans were already off the Yorkshire coast, they would not return to their ports past his position. *Lurcher* proceeded up and down the patrol line making the signal to surface for communication. The submarines contacted were ordered to meet at *Archimède*'s billet off the Noord West Gat Buoy for new instructions.

At 3:35pm Keyes received his new instructions from *Firedrake* via *Adamant*: 'High Sea Fleet is at sea and at 12:30pm was in lat. 54.38 N, long. 5.55 E. They may return after dawn tomorrow. Submarines should proceed Heligoland and intercept them; they probably pass five miles west of Heligoland steering south for Weser Light Vessel. Sent 14.10.' The position was as reported by the German flagship, *Friedrich der Grosse*, but the route of return was simply the Admiralty's best guess. As Jellicoe had anticipated, von Ingenohl had led the main body of the High Sea Fleet out to the middle of the North Sea. They covered a bombardment of Hartlepool, Scarborough and Whitby by his heavy cruisers. It was hoped that this would create an opportunity to crush any part of the British Fleet responding to the raid.

Keyes only managed to contact *Archimède*, *E.15*, and *E.10*. *Lurcher* proceeded to the rendezvous, arriving as darkness gathered at 4:10pm. *E.11* later appeared in response to searchlight signals made into the night sky. Written orders were delivered by a boat from *Lurcher*. *E.15* was to take up a position north of Heligoland so as to command the approach to the channels running both west and east of the island. The other three boats were positioned along the channel from northwest of Heligoland to the Weser entrance. Any vessel coming down this route would pass first *Archimède*, then *E.10* and finally *E.11*, which was to approach the Weser down the channel itself. They were all to be in position by 3am next morning, the 17th, remaining on the surface to attack until daylight. Keyes also warned them that British destroyers were likely to be in the area. He gave them discretion to remain on their patrol billet for an extra day until nightfall on the 18th.

Keyes now considered heading in to the Bight with *Lurcher* and *Firedrake* to launch his own torpedo attack. However, he assumed that Tyrwhitt and possibly also the destroyers of the Grand Fleet would already have been sent in to attack. He did not feel justified in cutting across these operations without further information or specific orders, particularly bearing in mind previous criticisms. *Lurcher* could not raise anyone by wireless. Keyes sent *Firedrake* west again, to make a report of the action taken and requesting further information. She was to remain in position to quickly pass any further messages from *Adamant*. Meanwhile, *Lurcher* continued trying to contact the remaining submarines, signalling by wireless and light without success. They would now have surfaced to return to Harwich. *Lurcher* got underway at 6:34pm along their return route via the North Hinder. Keyes hoped to intercept them in the morning light.

At 1:10am on the 17th *Lurcher* received a message directly from the Admiralty: 'We think Heligoland and Amrum Lights will be lighted when ships are going in. Your destroyers might get a chance to attack about 2am, or later, on the line given you. (Sent 20.12).' Keyes wrote in his memoirs that: 'Words fail me even now … to express my feelings when I received this message.' It could have been passed via *Adamant* and *Firedrake* five hours earlier. Keyes acknowledged the signal, pointing out that in the position he was now in there was no chance of making an attack in the Bight, whereas at the time the signal was drafted he was only 200 miles from Heligoland. As *Firedrake* was no longer required as a wireless link she returned to Harwich.

The message seemed even more ironic when it came to light that there had been a great deal of soul-searching by Churchill's war advisory group before it was sent. Admiral Arthur K Wilson was present and pointed out that Keyes destroyers were the only British surface ships that could reach the Bight by dawn. Tyrwhitt's destroyers had been forced to return earlier by bad weather in the north-western part of the North Sea. Wilson drafted a signal, but someone commented that sending them in meant almost certain death for the crews. Another pointed out that this was the last thing that would have concerned Keyes. Fisher nodded his assent and Oliver took it to the coding room. It was transmitted from the high power station at Ipswich on the wrong wave band. Muddled and ineffective action followed when it failed to get through. No explanation of why the message was not routed as Keyes had requested via *Adamant* was later forthcoming.

The weather deteriorated as Keyes returned. At first light he requested instructions for his other four submarines, but *Lurcher* and *Firedrake* reached Harwich at 8am without contacting them. He then received the reply that they should return to port. The Admiralty had intercepted signals confirming that the German Fleet was already back in harbour. The raiders had evaded Jellicoe's interception force. The only hope remaining was that the submarines sent in by Keyes to the Bight had been able to attack.[2]

No reports were filed by the four boats that Keyes failed to find on the 16th. Cochrane was on his first patrol in *E.7*. A steamer almost rammed her in the dark near the Galloper Light Vessel. As a result of taking avoiding action she lost touch with Stocks who was leading their pair in *E.2*. Cochrane arrived at his billet at 8:45am, with excellent visibility and bright sunshine. *E.2* was quickly spotted four miles to the northeast and *E.8* was in sight most of the morning to the south. *E.7* logged a position which had presumably been calculated by sextant at 10:45am on the 16th. If it is accurate she was well to the northeast of her billet. By implication so were *E.2* and *E.8*. Cochrane patrolled on the surface all day, but sighted nothing at all. Hallifax recorded that: 'we sat up on deck & smoked, a lovely quiet day … as clear as anything … T[wyman – the new 3rd officer] is a very amusing chap & I like him immensely.' Harmony had been restored on *E.7*. Cochrane closed *E.2* and followed her home at 4pm, but lost touch in the night as the wind rose and the rain came down hard. *E.7*'s new gyrocompass was also out of true. As a result of all this Cochrane got out of his reckoning and missed the North Hinder Light Vessel. He proceeded cautiously, sounding depths to help confirm his position. Eventually it was realised that *E.7* was too far north and had already crossed the British mine danger area! Cochrane reached Harwich at 10:45am on the 17th. *E.2* had already arrived an hour earlier. *E.8*'s log records nothing of note, but Goodhart had been forced to sound his way towards the Dutch coast to check his position before heading back, reaching Harwich at 2:15pm on the 17th.

---

2   TNA ADM137/2067: pp.568-72, 577–8, 587–8; Keyes, *Memoirs*, pp.142–9; TNA ADM53: *Lurcher Firedrake* 15-17 December 1914; Churchill, *World Crisis*, pp.421-2; TNA ADM186/621: p.218.

Bruce's *E.12* returned at the same time. Hallifax relates that she had been chased by three destroyers during the night on the way to her billet, forcing Bruce to dive repeatedly. An armed trawler had then done more of the same on the afternoon of the 16th. *E.12* ought to have been as easy for Keyes to find as *E.11* and *E.10* and may have been out of position.[3]

Fraser's *E.10* was the first submarine located by Keyes. Her patrol had been uneventful until *Lurcher* came in sight to communicate at 11am on the 16th. Fraser was apparently further east than his assigned billet to have encountered *Lurcher* so quickly after she started looking. *E.10* arrived at the rendezvous with *Lurcher* at 3:30pm. Fraser got underway after darkness fell. He headed to the northeast, well clear of the German minefield. From midnight occasional glimpses of the beam of the Heligoland Lighthouse and searchlights in the same direction helped guide him on. These ceased after a couple of hours. Heligoland was sighted four miles to the eastward at 7am. Fraser soon dived. He spent the day patrolling submerged in the channel west of the island. *E.10* surfaced to charge in the darkness at 4:30pm. A brilliantly lit ship was soon seen heading for the channel east of the island on the distant horizon. By 11:30pm it was 'very rough, with heavy rain squalls.' Fraser resumed his submerged patrol at 7am on the 18th. He had difficulty keeping the boat at periscope depth in the increasingly rough seas. *E.10* eventually had to surface at 3:30pm and quickly headed back to Harwich as night fell. No more ships were seen. The journey back through the gale and the heavy seas took two days, an average speed of under six knots. *E.10* finally reached Harwich at 3pm on the 20th.[4]

Brodie's *E.15* arrived off Terschelling at 8am on the 16th. Two Dutch torpedo boats were sighted around midday. The *Lurcher* showed up to communicate at 2:45pm. Brodie headed for the rendezvous, arriving at 3:40pm to receive his orders. He left once darkness had fallen. Unlike Fraser, Brodie only saw a single searchlight flash around 1am and had to stop to check soundings in order to feel his way in towards Heligoland. As the light grew *E.15* dived at 6:50am to complete the approach. Brodie finally spotted the island two hours later, five miles southwards. He was in almost exactly the right spot. A steamship was spotted five miles to the west at 11am, but Brodie was unable to get close enough to identify her. By 4pm the sea was already getting rough. Next morning Brodie began patrolling at periscope depth but had to surface at 7:40am. The seas were high, with a south-westerly wind approaching gale force and Heligoland was five miles southwest. *E.15* headed northwest at three knots on the diesels until 3pm, then turned west. Brodie had an even slower journey than Fraser, and diverted to Yarmouth instead of heading back via the North Hinder as ordered. He finally reached Gorleston at noon on the 20th, having averaged just over five knots on the return. *E.15* returned to Harwich the next morning.[5]

Archimède was commanded by Lieutenant de Vaisseau Émile François Marc Deville, aged 38. He had been in submarines since 1908 and had spent the last four years in command of steam powered boats, first *Pluviôse*, then the larger *Archimède* since October 1913.[6] Deville struck up a good rapport with Keyes, who had been impressed by the progress *Archimède* had made with Waistell. He had decided to use her at the first available opportunity. Herbert had returned

3   TNA ADM173: *E.7, E.8* 15-17 December 1914; IWM: Documents.1003: 15–17 December 1914; TNA ADM137/80 pp.693, 769.
4   TNA ADM137/2067: p.579.
5   TNA ADM137/2067: p.580; TNA ADM137/81: pp.297, 469, 495.
6   *Le Nouvelliste du Morbihan*, 20 Avril 1933; Garier, *Sous-Marin 2*, p.172.

from leave and was kicking his heels at Harwich. Keyes suggested that Deville take him along as a liaison officer for his first patrol.

Archimède lost contact with *E.15* in the night on the way to her billet. A defective port engine air pump also forced Deville to reduce speed. Having reached her inshore billet three vessels were sighted approaching from the east at 9am. Deville dived, but it turned out to be the Dutch patrol of two torpedo boats and a larger vessel. He surfaced after they had passed and shortly afterwards encountered *Lurcher* and *Firedrake* on the way to patrol. At 1pm a trawler was spotted five miles east heading directly towards *Archimède*. Deville dived and made for an attack position with the forward torpedoes from 400m (440 yards) away. The trawler was not armed, so *Archimède* moved slowly away and surfaced at 2:30pm. *Lurcher* arrived an hour later with *E.10* and *E.15* already in company and Deville stood by. His new orders came across a few hours later. Keyes added a personal note on the envelope: 'Je vous ai donné le place d'honneur.'[7] If the Germans used the route that the Admiralty expected Deville would be the first to engage. *Archimède* departed at 5:45pm. She began to have problems maintaining steam in the starboard boiler and was reduced to running on the port shaft. The funnel then got stuck when it was lowered to examine the boilers. Fortunately this was quickly fixed, as this would otherwise have ended the patrol. The boiler problem was traced to salt water getting into the boiler feed. Pressure was restored and *Archimède* got back underway. By 2am both engines were running and she was making her best speed without making excessive smoke, 10 knots. Nevertheless Herbert recalled that the column of smoke and cinder sparks made them 'a conspicuous object.' Searchlights were spotted five miles to starboard soon afterwards and Deville dived to continue the approach to Heligoland. Four days later a crewman mentioned that he had heard a chain scrape along the side during this dive! It is possible that *Archimède* had encountered a German mine. Deville surfaced again at 5:30am but was soon forced to dive again as the light grew.

At 8:05am Heligoland was sighted seven miles to the southwest. Four smoke clouds could be seen in the far distance to the southeast, which quickly went out of sight. *Archimède* proceeded round to her billet northwest of the island. Deville moved out of sight of the island and partially surfaced with the conning tower out of the water for better observation. Nothing more was seen. *Archimède* began heading out to sea at 2:30pm to get clear in order to charge the batteries. At 4:30pm a gale began to pick up from the west. Deville turned into the seas whilst charging. By 9pm he concluded that 'effective underwater action was impossible,' and reluctantly decided to head back to Harwich. Within two hours *Archimède* was forced to reduce speed to nine knots. A wave then smashed the control gear for the forward hydroplanes. Diving would now be problematic. Deville decided to head for Yarmouth rather than the longer route round the North Hinder. Speed was eventually reduced to six knots to lessen the impact of the seas.

At 9:45am next morning, the 18th, a trawler was spotted closing. With only the internal bow tube useable on the surface, Deville sent down for a rifle. *Archimède* increased speed and altered course to get clear. Herbert says Deville was about to open fire with the rifle when the trawler veered off. Further problems resulted from the evasive tactics. Deville reported that: 'At around 10 am, received several violent blows from the sea which snagged the funnel; tried to close it, impossible; also impossible to send men outside to free it, they would be washed away before they could do anything; we are therefore unable to dive.' *Archimède* was also being forced

7   I gave you the position of honour – roughly.

away from the direct course to Gorleston. Herbert joined the bucket brigade which had to constantly bale water out as a result of the displacement of the funnel. He amused the crew with his attempts to keep their spirits up with his schoolboy French. Quartier-Maître Mécanicien (Stoker 1st Class) Rault and Enseigne de Vaisseau (Sub-Lieutenant) de Rivoyre eventually had to go topside in the heavy seas that afternoon to cut away some debris which was threatening to get entangled in the port propeller shaft. Deville especially commended them in his report. With *Archimède* now a sitting duck, the option of heading for the Dutch coast was considered. This could have meant internment in the condition the boat was in. Deville decided in the end to press on. At 5:30pm the weather finally started to moderate and *Archimède* was able to get back on course for Gorleston and increase speed.

The 19th brought better weather. *Archimède* made the best speed she could. A lot of salt had got in to her boiler tubes as a result of the earlier problems. At 9:55am she sighted the Haisborough Light Vessel and headed down the channel, reaching Yarmouth at 4:30pm. *Adamant* supplied a change of water for the boilers overnight, but on examination the tubes were found to be heavily lined with salt. *Archimède* got underway to return to Harwich at 7:35am next morning on her electric motors. At the exit from Gorleston she was caught in a powerful current and driven into the pier. This damaged the drop keel and caused a leak, but she was able to continue and arrived back at Harwich just after midday.

Archimède was badly damaged. Apart from the smashed hydroplane gear, the most heavily salted boiler would need to be replaced and the superstructure was badly broken up. The external door to the torpedo tube had been displaced by the sea and after the altercation with the pier would not open at all. The two forward external torpedo frame mountings were out of action and the breakwater was bent back 45 degrees to port over a two metre section. The funnel panels were distorted and the funnel could not be moved. The port air pump was in a bad way and the reduced airflow was resulting in excessive water use in the boiler to maintain speed, as well as too much smoke being given off. One good thing was that the new gyrocompass had worked flawlessly! Deville ended his report of the patrol by expressing his appreciation for Herbert, finding him to be 'a perfect comrade' and of great assistance with local navigation and communication. He also praised the fulsome support he had received from *Maidstone* in maintaining *Archimède* and making repairs. For his part Herbert told Keyes that Deville remained 'calm and collected.' The crew, 'though they were disheartened, accepted the situation philosophically.' Truly Gallic sangfroid. Herbert himself would shortly take command of the redundant *SS Vienna*, transformed into a submarine decoy or 'Q Ship'. As captain of *Baralong*, another 'Q Ship', Herbert would later avenge *E.3*. In a controversial action he sank *U.27*, taking no prisoners.

Archimède could not be repaired locally. She was patched up to make her seaworthy. The destroyer *Oriflamme* arrived on the 24th to escort her back to Calais. They left at 8am on the 26th, to a rousing send off from the crews at Harwich with whom they had built such a good relationship in their short time there. *Archimède* proceeded to Cherbourg for repairs. She never returned, as in March 1915 both she and *Gustave Zédé* were ordered to join the main French Fleet in the Mediterranean. Favereau protested. *Archimède* had just completed her repairs and both submarines were finally ready to deploy together to Harwich, but his protests were to no avail. Since the remaining French submarines in the Channel were unsuitable for long distance patrol, this ended French involvement with the Harwich Flotilla.

There is no doubt that *Archimède* was unsuited to face a North Sea gale. Deville told Keyes that the seas there were a revelation to him. The funnel and external torpedo frames were particularly vulnerable to heavy seas, but those experienced were exceptionally bad. The British boats had closed up and reduced to a crawl in the heavy weather, having learnt the hard way not to proceed at speed against such seas. Steam propulsion meant that *Archimède* did not have this option, although Deville was perhaps also trying to maintain too high a speed. However, her ineffectiveness as a submarine is over-laboured in some accounts. Deville later made successful attacks in the Adriatic with *Archimède*. The lure of the high speed that steam could offer was also undiminished in the Royal Navy, which went ahead with developing its own K class boats. Steam only finally came into its own as a high speed power source for submarines with the advent of nuclear power, thus dispensing with the need for a funnel.[8]

Nasmith's *E.11* arrived off Terschelling at daybreak on the 16th. The only sightings during the day were *Lurcher* and one of the other patrolling submarines. At nightfall Nasmith got underway back to Harwich. He spotted a searchlight signalling: 'Eighth Flotilla close' in clear language into the sky. He closed to find *Lurcher* and the other three submarines. The newly pencilled orders to head for the Weser arrived by boat. Nasmith initially steered for a point five miles north of Heligoland to get a good position fix before heading into the Inner Bight. He must have set off at almost top speed. At 1:30am he: 'Sighted the island on Starboard beam; altered course to pick up channel 5 miles to the westward of it, proceeding at slow speed.' Nasmith dived when a searchlight began sweeping the channel from the southern tip of Heligoland. However, it had also allowed him to get an exact position fix, as it had silhouetted the rock outcrop at the northern end of the island. After 45 minutes, he surfaced again well south of the island and headed for the Weser.

Ostfriesland, photographed prior to the war. Main armament was 12x30.5cm (12-inch) guns.
(theFrankes.com Collection)

8   TNA ADM137/2067: p.581; AddMS82460: Keyes Papers. Vol. IXXXVIII. War orders, disposition and organisation; 1914-15, pp.86-102; Service Historique de l'État Major de la Marine: Archives de la 2ème Escadre Légère: Carton 25; Chatterton, *Amazing Adventure*, pp.110-18; Garier, *Sous-Marin 3* pp.34–5.

By 6:20am *E.11* was two miles north of the position of the Weser Light Vessel. Nasmith dived after using a searchlight on Wangeroog to help fix his position, as the Light Vessel itself was no longer there. The wind had strengthened. The sea was rolling in heavily from the northwest, causing the boat to alternate in depth between 16 and 30 feet (5 to 9m). An hour later some destroyers were sighted coming down from the north. One then fired a flare, which seemed to be a signal for them to commence a search pattern, moving at high speed in all directions. Nasmith submerged out of their way until they passed. The tension rose when at 8am two larger ships were sighted to the northeast. As they closed Nasmith identified them as *Ostfriesland* Class dreadnought battleships. They had apparently come down the channel east of Heligoland. *E.11* headed northwest to cut them off. Ten minutes later: 'Enemy altered course to the southward and proceeded to make zigzags at varying intervals, one of which put me fine on the bow of the leading ship as to render a bow tube attack impossible.' Nasmith's only option was to turn away to stop her closing, then attack with the beam tube: 'I then turned up with them and brought the starboard tube to bear, and fired at 400 yards [370m]. The track of the torpedo could not be observed, owing to the height of the sea. The boat was rolling some 6° on either side at the time.' *E.11* had happened to line up at the worst point in the roll. With the periscope having to be used intermittently to avoid being spotted, several ships of the same class altering course constantly and the boat pumping up and down and rolling in the heavy seas, Nasmith must have simply fired when he got his sights on a target at the right position for a snapshot. The seconds ticked by and there was no explosion. The torpedo was assumed to have run deep, as it seemed impossible to miss such a big target at the range.

More ships continued to approach in a long line about a mile apart and turned onto a new zig-zag leg. They did not seem to have noticed the attack. Nasmith continued: 'I turned my attention to the third ship of the line and proceeded to attack with the bow tubes, the position seeming favourable. When at a distance of 500 yards [450m] the vessel altered to bring us right under her bow.' The battleship took only a minute to reach *E.11*: 'bring[ing] her ram at right angles to my beam at a distance of about 100 yards [90m], making a collision unavoidable, except by a very rapid dive, for the accomplishment of which it was necessary to admit a considerable amount of extra water.' The battleship made *E.11* tremble as she passed below her at 70 feet (21m), with her massive propellers making so much noise that nothing else could be heard. Apparently *E.11* hit the bottom and stayed there for about a minute until the target was clear, but this is not in Nasmith's report. When the tanks were blown *E.11* came up much too quickly and also lost her trim. This, combined with the heavy swell, caused her to break surface, showing her entire conning tower. Hallifax was told that *E.11* took about 90 seconds to get back under. It was obvious that she had been seen: 'the Fleet (consisting of 9 or 10 ships) scattered and increased speed.' Those which had not already passed his position worked round to the west at long range to enter the Weser. Nasmith pushed the motors to full power to try and get into position to attack the last ship, which he thought was probably the battle cruiser *Seydlitz*. Whilst he had been submerged avoiding the destroyers, *E.11* had evidently drifted north with the tide, leaving her too far from the entrance! The target disappeared inside before he got within range.

Another destroyer flotilla following the same course as the earlier ships came over *E.11*'s position at very high speed around 2:30pm. Four of the boats passed directly overhead. A hospital ship also left the Weser and headed towards Heligoland that afternoon. *E.11*'s crew hoped that it was the result of a successful attack by *E.15*. After dark Nasmith surfaced and headed northwest to charge his battery, then went to the bottom for the night at 1:30am, between the Elbe and the Weser.

Nasmith surfaced at daybreak on the 18th. At 7:30am a number of trawlers came out sweeping the entrance to the Weser. He headed towards them to investigate. However: 'When within a few hundred yards of the channel I touched bottom at 30 feet [9m] on the depth gauge.' Believing that the shallow water lay to the south he turned to the north. The water was still getting shallower. Even worse, E.11 was being swept up the sand bank by the tide flowing into the Weser. The situation was becoming dangerous: 'The periscope was now awash in its up position when the boat was on the bottom, I therefore admitted a large quantity of water, and stopped the motors, in an attempt to keep her there.' This failed. Nasmith had only one option left: 'I therefore turned her to the westward, which appeared to be the only way out and proceeded at full speed across the line of sweepers with periscope down and the vessel bumping the bottom.' Eventually deeper water was reached and the danger was over. Nasmith had taken the risk of coming in close in the hope that the channel was being swept ahead of a major ship movement. He reported a considerable amount of commercial traffic between the Elbe and Weser during the day, as well as armed trawlers patrolling south of Heligoland during daylight, but saw nothing worth attacking. When night fell he surfaced and headed back to Harwich. The state of the sea forced Nasmith to abandon the bridge for much of the journey, with the hatch closed and the conning tower vents left open. He averaged only six to seven knots. E.11 finally reached Harwich at 11:45am on the 20th.[9]

The only German warship that got anywhere near the original line off Terschelling was a stray destroyer, S.33, which returned unseen through the area around 9:30am on the morning of the 16th. During the night of the 15/16th Tyrwhitt had two destroyers out to give warning of any enemy approaching Harwich and Yarmouth respectively, which reported nothing. These, together with Lurcher and Firedrake, were the only warships that might have been seen by Bruce that night. This was only his third patrol and he had perhaps not yet settled in. He was seeing enemies hunting him where there were none.

The German fleet spotted many floating mines on their sortie and a number of submarines were reported in the North Sea on the way back, suggesting to them that the British had a sophisticated ambush in place! There were no submarines of either navy anywhere near any of the reported positions. The sightings could well have been more floating mines, or paranoia caused by them. The last of the German Fleet to return were the heavy cruisers that had bombarded the coast. The armoured cruiser Blücher passed to the east of Heligoland heading for the Elbe only an hour or so before E.15 and Archimède arrived there. The four battle cruisers returned in two groups via the channel west of Heligoland at around 5:30–6am, heading for the Weser. They entered the river just before Nasmith arrived and must have overtaken E.11 on the surface somewhere between Heligoland and the Weser as it began to get light.

There were too many ships to safely enter the main anchorage in the Weser in darkness at once, so the eight dreadnought battleships of 1st Geschwader had anchored in the Elbe on the 16th. They got underway to return to the Jade at 6:45am next morning. It must have been their smoke that Archimède spotted in the distance. They were led by the 24,700t (24,300 long tons)

9   TNA ADM137/2067: pp.573-5; TNA ADM137/81: p.291; Shankland & Hunter, Dardanelles Patrol, pp.88–9; IWM: Documents.1003: 20 December; IWM:Documents.20134: 20 December 1914. Talbot alone names the class of the torpedo target.

Westfalen. Main armament of 12x28cm (11.1-inch) guns. (NH 45196)

Ostfriesland class of 1st Division; *Ostfriesland* – the squadron flagship of Vizeadmiral von Lans, then *Thüringen*, *Helgoland* and *Oldenburg*. Following them were the older 20,500t (20,200 long tons) *Nassau* class of 2nd Division; *Posen* – divisional flagship, then *Rheinland*, *Nassau* and lastly, *Westfalen*. All had armoured rams which would make short work of a submarine at periscope depth. The ships were steaming at 'high speed', at least 16 knots, in open order, at one mile intervals. They each began zig-zagging as soon as they left the Elbe. *E.11*'s torpedo attack, presumed to be on *Ostfriesland*, was not seen in the turbulent seas and the battleships were oblivious to her presence until Nasmith broke surface. A conning tower with two periscopes was sighted on *Posen*'s beam 800-1,000m away (900-1,100 yards). Kapitän zur See Lange himself had it clearly in sight for four seconds. Previous sightings on the sortie had been questionable, but there was no doubt about this one, despite no torpedo being spotted. He immediately ordered a hard turn to starboard and full speed ahead; 20 knots. *Posen* made off to the north, hoisting the signal: 'Surfaced enemy submarine in sight.' She gave five blasts on her horn as she turned and repeated the warning by signal light to *Ostfriesland* and her next astern. The 1st Division had already passed *E.11*; *Helgoland*, the third in line, is presumed to have inadvertently almost rammed her and certainly saved the squadron from further attack. *Rheinland* turned to port, then made off at top speed to the northwest. *Nassau* and *Westfalen* picked up the repeated warnings and followed her example. By the time the 2nd Division received permission from Lans to return to the Elbe, they had all worked round the attack point and held course into the

Weser. Nasmith's final attempt at attack must have been on *Westfalen*. Despite the miss, the attack had an impact, adding credence to the previous bogus sightings. The Crown Prince, who had been with the Fleet, told Tirpitz that 'he considered it a miracle that the capital ships had escaped damage, they had sighted so many mines and submarines.'[10]

Keyes report to Oliver inevitably focuses on Nasmith's failure. On the day of his return Keyes writes: 'That he should have missed a 1st Class Battleship, which was practically a gift, is deplorable. At the same time … I have in no way lost confidence in this Officer's skill and determination.' The verdict is somewhat harsh considering the sea conditions and the fact that the squadron was deliberately employing tactics designed to make torpedo attack as hard as possible. The nature of beam tubes meant that they were badly affected by rolling. Even a three to four degree roll would have been enough to cause the torpedo to dive deep for far too long if on the down-roll, or leap out of the water and then dive straight to the bottom on an up-roll. However, the standard British tactic of attacking at very close range also had drawbacks. The crash dive that resulted from the risk of being rammed directly resulted in *E.11* being detected. The incident also shows how effective zig-zagging at high speed was at frustrating torpedo attack. The independent movement and open order prevented Nasmith using his heater torpedoes for longer range attack against a long, tight formation. It also made it hard to gain a clear picture of courses and speeds through the periscope in the choppy sea. He did not get even get an accurate target count. The position reported by *Posen*, the fact that 2nd Division was able to get round *E.11* and the failure to spot the battlecruisers earlier strongly suggest that Nasmith may have been significantly further east than he realised. The outcome certainly deepened the cloud of gloom hanging over him.

The confinement of 8th Flotilla to harbour, ready to support an idea for an offensive on Zeebrugge that the Army never took seriously, had imposed another pause in offensive patrols. As a result there were no submarines on station in the Bight when the High Sea Fleet sailed. The Board of Admiralty were also responsible for a flawed deployment in response to the intelligence about the raid. Micro-management of the positions of individual vessels had resulted in the submarines being in the wrong place, in the wrong formation, at the wrong time. Unfortunately, Oliver had again displayed his weakness for getting too far down into the detail, rather than leaving this and a level of command discretion with subordinates. Hallifax sums up the frustration felt: 'If only the Commodore had a free hand, we should have been round outside the Heligoland Bight, but the Admiralty stepped in & put us in their well-liked line off Terschelling.' Keyes had been given a misleading situation briefing and no details of other British deployments, despite asking for them, leaving him partially in the dark about what was even intended for his deployment. Subsequent delays in transmission of messages had compounded the problem. In future Keyes requested that urgent transmissions should always be passed to *Maidstone* and the depot ship at Yarmouth by landline for onwards transmission.

---

10   TNA ADM186/621: p.216-7; BArch:RM92: *Seydlitz, Von der Tann, Blücher, Ostfriesland, Thüringen, Helgoland, Oldenburg, Posen, Rheinland, Nassau, Westfalen* Kriegstagebuch 16–17 Dezember 1914; Gröner, *German Warships*, pp.23-5; Corbett, *Naval Operations 2*, pp.45-6; Groos, *Nordsee 3*, p. 109, Karte 4 and 7; TNA ADM223/808: August Bulletin p.35, Tirpitz diary translation. Groos assumes that *Posen* was attacked, presumably as she sighted *E.11*. His account is otherwise lifted straight from Corbett, rather than German sources. The normal squadron steaming order was confirmed by the anchoring times off Wilhelmshaven and the actions of each ship recorded in her war diary.

Oliver directed that a telegraphic land line be installed directly to *Maidstone* as a result, as at the moment telegrams had to be sent via Shotley Barracks on the opposite bank of the Stour!

Nevertheless, unless more submarines had been placed between the Elbe and Weser, where they could have attacked 1st Geschwader on the 17th, they would probably have had little chance to attack. The Fleet made its approach to the harbours in darkness on the 16th, making attack difficult. Perhaps there would have been opportunities to use heater torpedoes for browning shots against large formations silhouetted by the necessary navigational illumination. Nasmith noted that Heligoland seemed ablaze with light as he passed.

Looking ahead, Keyes pointed out in his report that the absence in the inner Bight of mines and regular minesweeping there guaranteed freedom of movement. This meant that a surprise mining of the area before the return of the German Fleet might yield good results. However, he had got wind of plans to mine the Bight and was opposed to routine mining of the area. He believed that this would endanger his submarines, whilst the Germans would immediately be able to sweep channels through them. A request from Jellicoe for mining in the Bight on 16 November had already been rejected by Churchill and Fisher, specifically because the work done by 8th Flotilla had been 'of such importance' that the Admiralty did not want to restrict their ability to operate there. Keyes had felt the deployment of *E.11* had been risky. *D.2* had probably been lost in the same area and the German armoured cruiser *Yorck* had been accidentally mined in the barrier protecting the entrance to the Jade. However, he was encouraged to make repeat sorties to the area by Nasmith's report. The searchlights at Heligoland and Wangeroog had proved invaluable in assisting safe night time navigation.

The outcome of the operation revived Fisher's negative view of Keyes. Churchill continued to defend him, writing to Fisher on the 23rd that: 'I think he has done v[er]y well, & never failed us in any way … Merit, zeal & courage must not be easily overthrown by bad luck.'[11]

Meantime, there had been more reinforcements for the Flotilla at Harwich. On the 15th *E.13* arrived. She had completed her trials where she was built, at the Chatham Naval Dockyard.

Next day *C.31* of 4th Flotilla arrived from Dover to relieve *C.16*, which returned to Dover on the 17th. *C.16* was an 'early' C class and had only been attached until *C.31* completed a refit. The depot ship *Alecto* then arrived at Harwich from Dover on the 18th. The 3rd Flotilla was finally to be closed down at Dover and re-constituted with five C class at Yarmouth, relieving the 8th Flotilla outpost there. The submarines of 3rd Flotilla would also be available to co-operate on offensive missions. *Alecto* had brought all of the stores and spares for *S.1* from Dover to transfer to *Pandora*, as she was now to remain permanently with 8th Flotilla.

Alecto departed Harwich with *C.31* and *C.34* early on the 20th and arrived at Yarmouth around midday, passing *D.6* returning to Harwich on the way. *D.4* was unable to join her. She had left for the routine day patrol off Yarmouth the previous morning and quickly returned with steering problems. *Adamant* put divers over the side to examine her. They discovered that the steering gear for the rudder had broken. She was taken in tow on the morning of the 21st by *Adamant*. The armed trawler minesweeper *John Donovan* also attached a line aft to help manoeuvre the rudderless submarine. The local destroyers *Seal* and *Vixen* provided an escort. However the lines all parted off Gorleston and the attempt had to be given up for the day. Everyone anchored for the night in Corton Roads. The sea was calmer next morning. The tows

---

11   TNA ADM137/2067: pp.576, 584-6; TNA ADM137/75: p.99; Gilbert, *Churchill*, p.327.

were successfully attached and the journey to Harwich completed. *D.4* was docked for repairs on arrival and was out of action until the 28th. *Adamant* resumed her depot duties at Harwich.

C.29 was due to leave the Humber to join 3rd Flotilla on the 22nd. *C.26* and *C.27* were also to join from the Forth and had just completed their refits. These transfers would get 3rd Flotilla up and running as an overseas flotilla. In view of the recent coastal raid Keyes asked Oliver to confirm that they could go ahead. Oliver quickly replied: 'The 1st S.L. [Fisher] wants Dover Patrol to be as before now. He had forgotten all about wanting the submarines at Yarmouth … We may just as well wash out the whole thing now & tell Rosyth not to send their contribution down.' The transfer of *C.26* and *C.27* was cancelled. *C.31* and *C.34* returned to Dover next morning, the 23rd. *C.29* was allowed to proceed to Yarmouth and *Alecto* stayed there, but under the control of Ballard, the Admiral of Patrols. Fisher clearly felt that after the raid on the Yorkshire coast this was no time to weaken the coastal flotillas. Keyes plans to use the C class for offensive patrols were in tatters.[12]

12   IWM: Documents.20134: 15 December 1914; IWM: Documents.1003: 15–18 December 1914; TNA ADM173: *S.1* 18 December 1914, *D.4* 19–28 December 1914; TNA ADM137/80 p.326, 443, 668, 804; TNA ADM137/81 pp.237, 498, 715, 809, 831, 843, 846, 858, 864, 874, 887, 946, 984, 987; TNA ADM53: *Adamant* 19-22 December 1914; *Keyes Papers*, p.64, letter from Oliver to Keyes.

26

A missed recall

With the German raid over, Keyes and Tyrwhitt had been informed on 18 December that Plan Y could proceed, weather permitting. They met late on the 20th, causing speculation amongst the crews that a 'stunt' was imminent. The 21st dawned: 'A beautiful fine day, no wind, bright sun.' With surface action expected, *Lurcher* and *Firedrake* were ordered out for gunnery practice, each taking turns to tow a target for the other. Keyes met again with Tyrwhitt in the morning. At 4:15pm he notified Oliver that Plan Y would go ahead unless orders were received to the contrary by 9pm, with the raid taking place on the 23rd.

Once again it was not to be. Oliver replied two hours later: 'Postpone Plan Y and keep all your vessels in readiness for further German activities.' Talbot, Senior Officer in Leir's absence, attempted to damp down the feverish speculation. He ordered three submarines out for torpedo practice early next morning, whilst also ordering the rest to have two days provisions on board at all times. No more was heard from the Admiralty. Everyone turned in to bed.

At 9:40pm what can most charitably be described as a long and complex order was sent out by the Admiralty. A cruiser and eight destroyers from Tyrwhitt's Flotillas, plus two of Keyes submarines, accompanied by *Lurcher* or *Firedrake*, were to rendezvous at 7pm on the 22nd in a position about 45 miles off Terschelling. If orders were then received by the cruiser to proceed, the destroyers were to take up a position 10 to 15 miles north-northwest of Heligoland to intercept 'any German vessels coming out.' Two hours before sunrise, the destroyers would return to Harwich and be replaced by the submarines. The go ahead for this would be passed to *Lurcher* or *Firedrake* by the cruiser from a safe position out to sea. The submarines were to remain on watch until the evening of the 24th.

It took time for the orders to reach Keyes. *Firedrake*, *E.2* and *E.7* were chosen. Their crews then had to be roused from their slumber. Hallifax was woken thinking it was 6am only to discover that it was 12:20am! The orders were assumed by the recipients to be based on intelligence of a German Fleet sortie. The boats were ready ninety minutes later, but it was already too late to reach the rendezvous. Keyes suggested sending the two submarines directly to the position off Heligoland. Agreement was quickly received by telephone from the Admiralty. The change in orders was relayed as the submarines left Harwich at 2am on the 22nd, led by Waistell in *Firedrake*. Keyes kept all the other boats on standby to follow.

Keyes also suggested in a message to Oliver that if the cruiser remained within 50 miles, the submarines could pass details of enemy movements to her by wireless on the morning of the 23rd. If the Germans sortied, the submarines could also proceed to the river entrances, remaining there to attack them when they returned. Keyes emphasised that *Firedrake*, or Tyrwhitt in *Arethusa*, would only be in range to pass orders to the submarines until 7pm. The time that this message was sent is not recorded, but the ideas were discussed with Cochrane and Stocks before they left. Cochrane told Hallifax to load enough food in *E.7* for 10 days. The Admiralty received the message at 11:31am, but no reply was forthcoming.

The three boats headed out via the North Hinder route and made their way up the Dutch coast that afternoon. Tyrwhitt's force steamed past. *Firedrake* parted company with the submarines at 5pm off the Texel, but Waistell had been instructed to remain in touch until 8pm. He therefore took the opportunity to examine the papers of four Dutch trawlers in the area.

By 5:15pm the Admiralty had additional signal intelligence to hand, pointing to localised movements in the Bight, not a fleet sortie. Tyrwhitt was recalled. He queried whether the submarines should also return. Keyes intercepted the signals. He telephoned and asked a Staff Officer to find out what was going on, also requesting orders for the submarines at sea. He later received the obtuse reply that no more were to be sent out! He asked for orders again, but received nothing.

Back at the Admiralty, Oliver had begun to draft an order for the submarines to proceed to Heligoland. However, he had second thoughts. The original message was crossed out and re-drafted. Tyrwhitt was ordered to recall *Firedrake* and the submarines. It was eventually sent at 8:15pm, but it was now too late. *Firedrake* had got underway for Harwich and was moving beyond wireless range of the submarines. Waistell actually received the message at 9:46pm. There was no hope of passing it on and *Firedrake* reached Harwich at 9:40am next morning.

Meantime, despairing of a response, at 8:35pm Keyes signalled Tyrwhitt to tell the submarines to proceed and to recall *Firedrake*, unless Tyrwhitt heard otherwise from the Admiralty; which he did at almost the same time. Keyes eventually received a note by hand from Oliver at 11:45pm. The final twist was that the messenger had apparently initially gone to the wrong train station at Harwich.[1]

After *Firedrake* had turned back the two submarines soon lost touch in the darkness and proceeded independently to their billets, oblivious to their recall.

Stocks arrived in *E.2* nine miles north-northwest of Heligoland at 6:30am on the 23rd. He dived and headed towards the island. Visibility was good, but the only vessels in sight were two armed trawlers, working to the north and south of the island respectively. At 2:30pm Stocks headed back out to sea, surfacing to charge in the darkness at 6pm and reaching a position 12 miles from the island. There were no further sightings until 11pm when two merchant ships passed close by heading northwards.

At 7am next morning Stocks dived and headed back towards Heligoland. He soon spotted a submarine on raising the periscope. Stocks was not able to identify her. She dived 15 minutes later. *E.2* continued towards Heligoland, surfacing at 11:30am. It was very hazy and Stocks could not see the island. Shortly after noon a submarine was spotted to the south-southeast. *E.2* dived to attack, but Stocks again lost sight of her. He surfaced at 2pm, seven miles north-northwest of the island. The alarming sight of a German mine was spotted floating nearby! The trawler patrol was in sight, so he dived without trying to explode it. He ended the patrol at

---

1   TNA ADM137/2067: pp.590–4; TNA ADM186/621: pp. 219-22; TNA ADM137/81: pp.562, 640, 649, 695, 782, 795, 804, 836; TNA ADM53: *Firedrake*, *Lurcher* 21–22 December 1914; IWM: Documents.20134: 22 December 1914.

8TH FLOTILLA PATROL IN THE HELIGOLAND BIGHT
23-25 DECEMBER 1914

POSITIONS PER E.2 AND E.7 REPORTS AND LOG OF E.7

ALL POSITIONS OUT OF SIGHT OF LAND ARE APPROXIMATE AND SOME SIGHTING POSITIONS ARE ESTIMATED.

E.7 POSITIONS ON MORNING OF 23RD CANNOT BE RECONCILED. ALL E.7 POSITIONS ARE PRONE TO ERROR DUE TO COMPASS PROBLEMS

U.6 WAS PATROLLING BETWEEN AMRUM BANK AND HELIGOLAND ON 24TH

12TH TORPEDOBOOTS-HALBFLOTTILLE SEARCHED INNER BIGHT OUT OF THE JADE FROM 4.45AM TO 7AM ON 25TH

ZEPPELIN L.6 LEFT NORDHOLZ AT 6.31AM, FOLLOWED BY L.5 AT 7.40AM ON 25TH

AMRUM BANK

23RD-24TH   E.2

E.7
9.50AM 23RD
1.20PM 24TH →
3AM 23RD
2.10PM 24TH

OVERNIGHT
23RD-24TH
6.30AM 23RD
2PM 24TH

2 ↑
3
4   5
6

HELIGOLAND

EIDER

SIGHTINGS:
1 - 2 ARMED TRAWLERS FROM 11AM 23RD OVER NEXT 2 DAYS
2 - 2 STEAMERS BY E.2 11PM 23RD
3 - E.7 OR U.6 BY E.2 7.30AM 24TH
4 - U.6 BY E.7 8.45AM 24TH
5 - E.2 & U.6 BY EACH OTHER 12.20PM 24TH
6 - E.2 BY U.6 4PM 24TH
7 - DESTROYER BY E.7 6.20AM 25TH
8 - 2 ARMED TRAWLERS BY E.7 FROM 8.30AM 25TH
9 - L.6 BY E.7 FROM 8.50AM 25TH

1 →

E.7 25TH   7.30AM
4PM

7   9
8   ⚓E

⚓W
⚓J

ELBE

CUXHAVEN
NORDHOLZ

WANGEROOG   WESER

BREMER
-HAVEN

E.EMS
W.EMS
BORKUM

WILHELMSHAVEN
JADE

EMDEN

GERMANY

NETHERLANDS
GERMAN/DUTCH BORDER IN EMS AS CLAIMED BY GERMANY

● OWN REPORTED POSITIONS

NAUTICAL MILES

GERMAN PATROLS

◎ POSITION OF SIGHTINGS

10 5 0   10   20   30   40   50

MINEFIELD

••• 10 METRE LINE ⚓ JADE, WESER AND ELBE LIGHT VESSELS

4pm, arriving back in Harwich at 7pm on the 25th. According to Hallifax, *E.2* ran aground in the darkness on a Heligoland sandbank, but it is not mentioned in Stocks report. If so this was probably four miles north of the island.[2]

Cochrane's *E.7* arrived at what was reckoned to be 17 miles west-northwest of Heligoland at 3am on the 23rd. Lieutenant John R.A. Codrington had joined as an additional hand, having just returned to submarines after his compulsory ship service. He was one of three officers due to command D class in the near future. The aim was to better prepare them for an overseas command. The officers they relieved would graduate to new E class.

Cochrane adopted a cautious approach, diving as *E.7* approached the usual area of the destroyer patrol line and heading towards Heligoland at low speed. Only when it was fully light did he surface, proceeding for an hour before diving. It was beautifully clear, but bitterly cold on deck. Heligoland was glimpsed in the periscope 14 miles southeast at 9:50am. *E.7* surfaced at noon for a blow through and to take a sun sight. She proved to be north of her allocated position; Heligoland had not been sighted after all! Cochrane dived and headed south, taking a look round in the periscope every 15 minutes, but saw nothing all day. He surfaced to charge after dark, then spent most of the night on the bottom. The moon had set and the surface was 'too dark for possibility of attack.'

Cochrane surfaced again at 7am on the 24th. For Hallifax it was 'another splendid submarine day'; clear horizon, with a broken surface on the water to conceal the periscope. Heligoland was not in sight, so Cochrane headed southeast at low speed. At 8:40am a submarine was sighted ahead. It was thought to be *E.2*, but Cochrane nevertheless dived quickly. He raised the periscope. The other submarine was still on the surface. Cochrane suddenly told Hallifax to 'haul back the bow torpedo & put 5 ft [1½m] depth on.' All four torpedoes had been set for 10 feet (3m) during the night and had been rigged for surface firing during the dawn light. The crew worked as fast as possible. The torpedo was being returned to the tube when 'the order "Stand by" [to fire] came through & to report as soon as we were "ready";' Hallifax asked permission to flood the tube by opening the outer door. This would risk upsetting the boat's trim, but it would take four minutes to flood from the internal tank. Cochrane refused and to the frustration of all 'we could not get ready before the German (not E2) had dived; a sitting shot it would have been.' The target's periscope had been painted white, which had made Cochrane conclude that it was a German boat. *E.7* rested on the bottom for half an hour after the attack before taking a look through the periscope. Cochrane must have hoped that the target would return to the surface, but nothing more was seen of her.

E.7 resumed her course and briefly surfaced for Twyman to get another sun sight at noon. Heligoland was finally spotted nine miles southeast at 1:20pm. *E.7* had closed within six miles to the west of the island, when a ship was spotted approaching. Disappointingly it was just a patrolling trawler steering zig-zags. Soon another was sighted. Cochrane kept station in the area steering in circles, raising the periscope for a look every 15 minutes. At one point *E.7* broke surface for no apparent reason. A trawler was only a mile away but seemed not to notice. As darkness crept in at 3:50pm, Cochrane noticed a bright navigation light, apparently in the location of the Sellebrunnen Buoy north of the island. He wondered if this was an indication that

2   TNA ADM137/2067: p.598; TNA ADM53: *Adamant* 25 December 1914; IWM: Documents.1003: 27 December 1914.

the Germans had ships expected to leave or enter. *E.7* headed out to sea again, then surfaced to charge. At 9:15pm Cochrane turned round and headed for the Weser Lightship, having decided that anything coming in or out would be found there, but deviating from the Admiralty orders given him by Keyes.

By 11pm *E.7* was passing five miles off Heligoland. The moon was very bright, so Cochrane dived deep to pass by. However, since the battery was still only partially charged, he decided to try and sit it out on the bottom until the moon set, then make a surface run. Six attempts to find bottom failed after going down to 110 feet (34m), near the limit of the depth gauge. *E.7* surfaced again at 3am on Christmas morning. There was no moon, but it was a flat calm. A lot of phosphorescence in the water was being stirred up by *E.7* and was literally lighting her up. Cochrane had to submerge again. He surfaced at 5:50am and the conditions were better. *E.7* got underway on the surface charging the batteries. Suddenly, a destroyer was sighted 3,000 yards (2,750m) away, turning towards *E.7*. Cochrane crash dived. Soon afterwards he took her to the bottom to conserve the batteries until it was fully light. *E.7* was off the Elbe, 10 miles from the Weser entrance.

Cochrane came up to look through the periscope at 8:20am. Two trawlers were soon spotted patrolling in a northerly direction west of the Elbe entrance. After half an hour Cochrane surfaced for a better look round. He scanned the entire horizon from the bridge and saw nothing except for the trawlers. He then looked up to see a zeppelin almost directly overhead at about 600 feet (180m). Hallifax was 'on the ladder waiting for orders, when his [Cochrane's] face appeared, covered with a broad grin, & he sung out to dive.' Everyone had a look at the novelty of a nearby zeppelin through the periscope, then *E.7* was taken to the bottom. The zeppelin remained in sight most of the morning, occasionally going out of sight behind clouds. *E.7* spent over three hours on the bottom to conserve the batteries between occasional trips to periscope depth. She surfaced only once, for just five minutes. Several times during the morning Hallifax heard sounds that reminded him of the shells bursting during the Heligoland Battle, but Cochrane dismissed it as a loose boarding plank. Hallifax was despairing of ever getting their Christmas plum pudding in the oven, as they could not spare the drain on the charge![3] Mist started to gather in the afternoon. Cochrane headed west at low speed to close the Weser and get a position fix from Wangeroog. By 4pm a thick fog reduced visibility to just 100 yards (90m). Little could be seen through the periscope. Cochrane surfaced to sit stationary in a dead calm, running the port engine with the clutch out, charging the battery as quickly as possible. The anchor weight was later lowered to hold *E.7* in place. At 6:35pm a ship's siren suddenly bellowed through the boat. The alarms sounded for a crash dive and those on the bridge tumbled down the ladder. It had come from close astern and *E.7* was rapidly taken to the bottom. Everyone hoped that it was the German Fleet, which could be attacked when the fog lifted. Forty minutes later *E.7* surfaced and lifted her weight. The fog was as thick as ever. Nothing at all could be heard. The good news was that dinner had been cooked while they were charging. *E.7* returned to the bottom for a Christmas feast of soup, rabbit pie and the much anticipated plum pudding. That evening the four officers enjoyed a game of poker, all the while listening to new records on *E.7*'s gramophone, a present from the Navy League. The boat had been submerged for all but three hours that day. None of those on board could possibly have imagined five months earlier

3   Gifted to each submarine as part of a subscription appeal for troops at the front run by *The Daily News*.

that they would spend Christmas Day in this way, happily sitting at 17 fathoms (31m), just off the main German Fleet anchorage.

Cochrane surfaced at 1:35am on the 26th to find the fog gone and got underway on both engines towards the channel west of Heligoland for the trip home. The light from phosphorescence was once again lighting *E.7* up, so he dived whilst passing the island. Once clear Cochrane surfaced and headed for Harwich. At 10:55am a floating mine was spotted directly ahead by Hallifax, who was on watch. He immediately ordered the engine to stop, then manoeuvred *E.7* round. The mine looked British. That afternoon the weather took a turn for the worse and the sea became rough. After dark it began raining hard. Visibility got so bad that Cochrane cleared the bridge, closed the hatch and steered from below, as it was useless keeping a lookout. The gyrocompass and magnetic compass now started to give different readings! Hallifax was sent up with a lookout to keep an eye on the sea, to ensure that *E.7* was not steering into the Dutch coast. Cochrane followed the gyrocompass, as *E.7* had not been swung to adjust the magnetic compass recently. The gyrocompass now betrayed itself by beginning to go round and round in circles. Cochrane had been steering a false course! After a couple of hours the rain eased off but steering across the heavy sea had made Cochrane very sea sick. He decided to cut a corner across the edge of the danger area for the German minefield laid on the first day of the war, thought to be 'pretty safe'. Mines were apparently preferable to seasickness.

Codrington was on watch. To his surprise *E.7* suddenly made landfall near Orfordness via the North Hinder at 6:30am next morning, the 27th. Cochrane anchored until it was light. Knowing that he was overdue, *E.7* reported to Harwich using the recently completed wireless sending gear. With a gale threatening, Cochrane got underway and signalled the shore by lamp to ask for entry to what everyone had agreed was Felixstowe harbour. A puzzling reply was received: 'We haven't got one!' Whilst Hallifax was checking the signal book to make sure that they had not misunderstood, another signal revealed that they were off Aldeburgh, a town with no harbour, about 10 miles north of Felixstowe. *E.7* headed off into what was now a gale, finally reaching Harwich at 11:55am.

Meanwhile, on the morning of the 23rd Keyes had sent an exasperated note to Oliver, explaining how messages needed to be sent in order to guarantee timely receipt. He appealed that: 'when immediate action is necessary, coded or disguised messages should be sent direct to "MAIDSTONE", Harwich Exchange;' guaranteeing delivery within a few minutes, rather than hours.[4]

Oliver replied in a private letter later that day. He confirmed that he had already applied to have a secure telegraph line connected to *Maidstone*. He offers the rather poor excuse that: 'I hate tinkering with written plans or telegraphed orders by telephone and it is a very bad one to hear through.' Oliver reveals the reason for the change of orders with an alarming piece of news: 'I recalled the 2 submarines last night as I was disturbed about the new mines to the west of Heligoland and also because we have information that the Germans are making reconnaissances to the N.W. of Heligoland with aircraft & 2 Flotillas, evidently much disturbed at Naysmith's [*sic*] visit.' He also tells Keyes that the zeppelin *L.4* had reported that his two submarines were returning, so Keyes needed to ensure that his crews were more careful about

---

4   TNA ADM137/2067: pp.595-7, 551-2; TNA ADM173: *E.7* 22-27 December 1914; Douglas, *Maidstone Magazine*, p.69; IWM: Documents.1003: 22-27 December 1914.

being spotted by airships. All of the information was from decodes, of which German Fleet Command were oblivious.[5]

The zeppelin report and subsequent non-arrival of *E.7* had implied to Keyes that she had been lost. He was therefore relieved when Cochrane returned. Keyes had to report his regrets to Oliver that Cochrane had stayed an extra day without direct orders but had 'taken steps to ensure that such a misunderstanding can never happen again.' He also highlighted that Cochrane had ended up in a most fortuitous position and had believed that the discretion given on previous occasions had applied. Keyes highlighted that Cochrane had not encountered the new mines thought to have been laid in the channel to the west of Heligoland.

German Fleet command's fears about a British attack had been re-awakened by recent submarine sightings in the Bight, including Nasmith's attack on 1st Geschwader. Agent reports describing up to 200 ships being prepared in Britain to block the German estuaries had then been received. Plans were put in place to meet the possibility. The Fleet was initially to be held back in port, due to the fear that submarine ambushes would cover the attack. Only eight obsolete coast defence battleships would respond immediately. Greater reliance was to be placed on strengthening defensive minefields. The signals that had triggered the orders for a sortie by 8th Flotilla related to an operation on the night of the 21/22nd to extend the minefield off Heligoland. A new line of 516 mines was laid at a depth of 6m (20 feet), from the northern point of the existing minefield to a point 14 miles to the north, covered by a Flotilla of destroyers. The new mines were aimed at catching ships. A surfaced submarine would be able to pass over them, except at times of unusually low tides. Both *E.2* and *E.7* crossed the new line on the way in and out and probably at other points during their patrol. *E.7* may have crossed it submerged at least once. The mine spotted by *E.2* may have been one with a faulty sinker, but there were many existing drifting mines, including the one spotted by Hallifax.

The signals decoded on the 21st had made it obvious that a minelaying sortie was planned, but not its destination. Those on the 22nd confirmed that the minefield had already been laid in the Bight. Another of the regular night-time sweeps north of Heligoland was to be made that night to Horn's Reef by 1st and 9th Torpedoboots-Flottillen. *L.5* was to carry out a reconnaissance towards Yarmouth on the morning of the 23rd. This was all as described by Oliver to Keyes. He had received the reconnaissance report by *L.5* (not *L.4*) of supposed submerged British submarines spotted off the Texel within hours of it being sent. In reality there were none there!

Late on the 23rd the Germans received 'reliable information' that a blocking operation against their estuaries was imminent and went to increased readiness. The armoured cruiser *Prinz Heinrich*, on watch at the exit from the Jade, made plans to use the shallow channel off Wangeroog if it was necessary to sortie. It was assumed that the main exit would be blockaded by British submarines. From 2am on the 24th, two submarines were stationed to attack and report any ships approaching the minefield gaps; *U.20* off the Ems and *U.6* southwest of the Amrum Bank. *U.6* spotted submarines twice between noon and 4pm. *E.2*, *E.7* and *U.6* were all operating in the same area. The problems with *E.7*'s compasses make her reported positions particularly unreliable. It is impossible to determine whether *E.2* sighted *E.7* or *U.6* early that day. *E.7* then made her attack run, probably on *U.6*. Around noon *E.2* and *U.6* seem to have spotted each other. Finally, *U.6* later sighted *E.2* whilst leaving the area. It is never possible to

---

5   *Keyes Papers*, p.64, letter of Oliver to Keyes, 23 December 1914.

be fully confident about submarine sighting reports. Two days earlier the destroyer *S.16* reported a torpedo attack off the Jade; no British submarines were within a hundred miles at the time.

The increased state of readiness continued on the 25th. As a result of the sightings by *U.6*, a dawn submarine search of the Inner Bight was made by the 12th Torpedoboots-Halbflottille out of the Jade. The destroyer sighted by *E.7* was one of these boats. Two zeppelins were ordered out for a reconnaissance of the Bight at dawn. *E.7* saw *L.6* heading out. *L.5* also went up an hour later. Both would have been in sight at different times from *E.7's* position. With the exception of the two sightings by *U.6*, the British submarines seem to have gone unreported by aircraft, despite their close encounters.[6]

This operation demonstrates how hard it is to make use of even a rich source of intelligence data. Secret German signal traffic was being quickly decoded in Whitehall. Using it effectively meant building a picture of unfolding events, then leveraging it quickly whilst advantage could be gained. In this case it was impossible to exploit the movements without having submarines already in the forward area and in communication. Underlying issues of over-centralised control by Oliver and his staff, coupled with slow and incomplete communication, made things worse. The limitations of intelligence are also shown by Oliver's hesitation about the recall. There were new mines near Heligoland, but the signals referred to a written order that said exactly where they were. However, the crew of *E.7* did get an explanation for the mysterious pings heard on Christmas morning by Hallifax. Plan Y had gone ahead. They had been British bombs exploding in the Jade.

---

6   Groos, *Nordsee 3*, pp.125-8, Karte 14; BArch:RM92: *Nassau, Nautilus, Prinz Heinrich*, Kriegstagebuch 21–25 Dezember 1914, Befehl für S.M.S. "Pelikan" 22 Dezember 1914, Skizze zu G.B. 604 S.M.S. "Nautilus". Maps in Groos incorrectly show a gap between the minefields west of Heligoland. The cartographer employed mine charts made after subsequent sweeping.

27

Plan Y for Christmas

On 23 December, once it was clear that no German Fleet sortie was imminent, the Admiralty had notified Tyrwhitt and Keyes that Plan Y could proceed as soon as the weather was favourable. The forecast was good, so the raid was immediately scheduled for the earliest possible date, Christmas Day, with the submarines needing to begin leaving that very evening.[1]

Tyrwhitt would arrive at the launch point for the seaplanes, south of Amrum Bank, shortly before dawn. It was expected to take about an hour to get the nine aircraft ready to depart. Tyrwhitt would then leave by a 'circuitous route' out to sea, in order to conceal his destination. On arriving at a point north of Juist, he would spread out and head towards the Norderneyer Seegat to pick up the returning seaplanes. In the meantime these would have bombed the zeppelin sheds at Nordholz, flown over the High Sea Fleet anchorage in the Jade, along the islands off the north coast, then out to sea at the Norderneyer Seegat. A support force led by *Fearless* would hold position off the Ems and move in to join Tyrwhitt at 8am. The Grand Fleet would also be exercising in the northern part of the North Sea on the morning of the raid but would only advance south if the German Fleet came out.

The submarines would proceed to and from their allotted positions via the North Hinder route. They were to keep out of sight of the enemy as much as possible. Their primary function was to cover Tyrwhitt and the vulnerable carriers and secondly to assist pilots in difficulty. Their departure from Harwich was staggered in pairs. Those with the furthest journey were to leave first. *E.6* and *E.15* were to depart at 9pm on the 23rd, arriving just south of the take off point for the raid at 6am on the 25th. *E.6* would follow the seaplanes after take-off to look out for any that got into difficulties, then cruise off Heligoland for the rest of the day. *E.15* would cruise southwest past Heligoland to the pick-up point, keeping between Tyrwhitt and any force coming out to attack him. Next to leave would be *E.12* and *E.13*, at 12:15am on the 24th. They would take up positions just northwest of the original German minefield at 7am, then proceed at 8am to cover the pick-up point. *D.6* and *E.11* would be next at 1am, followed by *D.8* and *D.7* at 2am. These four would take up positions on a line on or just inside the 10 fathom (18m) line off Norderneyer Seegat. *S.1* and *E.10* would leave next at 3am and take up positions off the entrance to the Eastern Ems and Western Ems respectively. *D.8* and *D.6* were to remain in place on the surface from 9am to 9:30am unless they were in action, to give the seaplanes a

---

1   TNA ADM137/81 p.910.

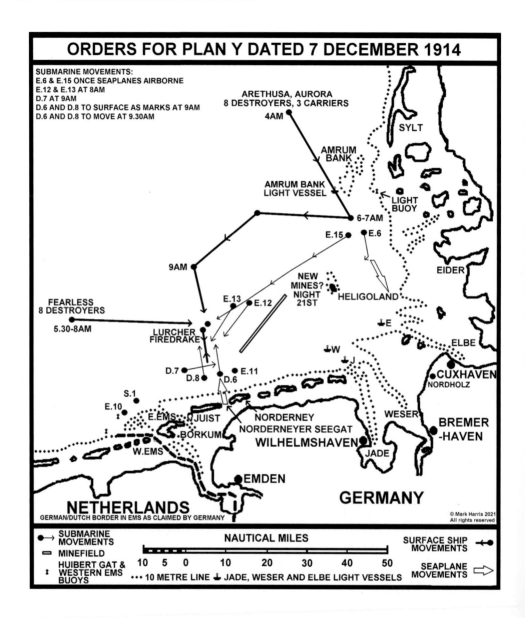

ORDERS FOR PLAN Y DATED 7 DECEMBER 1914

SUBMARINE MOVEMENTS:
E.6 & E.15 ONCE SEAPLANES AIRBORNE
E.12 & E.13 AT 8AM
D.7 AT 9AM
D.6 AND D.8 TO SURFACE AS MARKS AT 9AM
D.6 AND D.8 TO MOVE AT 9.30AM

ARETHUSA, AURORA
8 DESTROYERS, 3 CARRIERS
4AM

SYLT

AMRUM BANK

AMRUM BANK
LIGHT VESSEL

LIGHT BUOY

6-7AM

E.15   E.6

9AM

NEW MINES?
NIGHT 21ST   HELIGOLAND

EIDER

E.13   E.12

FEARLESS
8 DESTROYERS

5.30-8AM

LURCHER
FIREDRAKE

E

W

ELBE

D.7
D.8   D.6   E.11

J

CUXHAVEN
NORDHOLZ

S.1

E.10

E.EMS   JUIST   NORDERNEY   WESER
BORKUM   NORDERNEYER SEEGAT
WILHELMSHAVEN

BREMER
-HAVEN

W.EMS

JADE

EMDEN

NETHERLANDS
GERMAN/DUTCH BORDER IN EMS AS CLAIMED BY GERMANY

GERMANY

SUBMARINE
MOVEMENTS

NAUTICAL MILES

SURFACE SHIP
MOVEMENTS

MINEFIELD

HUIBERT GAT &
WESTERN EMS
BUOYS

10 5 0   10   20   30   40   50

••• 10 METRE LINE ⚓ JADE, WESER AND ELBE LIGHT VESSELS

SEAPLANE
MOVEMENTS

mark with their red and white checked conning towers, then retire along the seaplane route out to sea. *D.7* was to move east and patrol off Norderneyer Seegat at 9am, whilst *E.11* kept watch for anything coming along the coast from the Weser.

All submarines were to attack any targets that came long. Those directed to change position were ordered to do so at full speed on the surface, whilst being careful not to get in the path of Tyrwhitt's ships. When picking up pilots they were to take the seaplanes in tow back to the carriers. If this was not possible they were to try and save the engine, then sink the plane by bashing in the floats. This was wishful thinking. A note circulated from the RNAS squadron commander explained that saving the engine would take at least 45 minutes; he was more concerned that the bombsight was not left to fall into enemy hands. The submarine commanders were ordered to use 'any endeavour' to rescue pilots, as it might not be possible for the ships to pick them up. If they were driven away from a plane, they were to submerge nearby and endeavour to attack anything that tried to salve it. Submarines were ordered to wireless in sightings of hostile submarines, or surface forces which could interfere with the operation. They were to listen out by wireless for 20 minutes every hour until Midnight on the 24th and also for 10 minutes every hour on the return in the event of new orders. No wireless signals were to be made prior to the operation unless it was cancelled or a very urgent matter arose.

Keyes would leave Harwich in *Lurcher* with *Firedrake* at 6am. From dawn they would cruise on a line just west of the pick-up line, out of sight of land, both to give warning to Tyrwhitt of any force threatening him and assist any downed pilots. They would attempt to draw any enemy sighted toward the submarines off the Ems, away from Tyrwhitt. In a last minute change Keyes had agreed with the commander of the carrier *Engadine* that from 9am he would move onto the line between the pick-up point and Norderney to give an extra mark for the seaplanes to return along.

Once the surface forces began to withdraw any submarines that could see them were to spread out and cover their retirement, following along behind. If out of sight of the ships they were to remain looking out for pilots until noon, then all submarines were to return to Harwich. Confusingly, the orders also state that *E.6* was to remain off Heligoland until dusk.[2]

The position of the original German minefield was accurately known, but the new extension at the south-west end had not been identified. *E.11*, *D.6*, *Lurcher* and *Firedrake* would be near these mines. The large new minefield was known of, but was assumed to be in the channel between the old minefield and Heligoland.[3] As a result the plans had not been altered and it was fortunate that the launch point and route originally chosen for the ships on 2 December went around this minefield. *E.6* and *E.15* were unaware of the new danger on their billets, but its depth meant that it should not be a problem unless they submerged in it.

This time there were no more delays and the weather was ideal for flying. The force had an uneventful journey out to Heligoland. At just after dawn on Christmas Day, from slightly north of the planned position, seven seaplanes successfully got airborne and headed to their target in the first carrier launched air attack.

Talbot's *E.6* had the task of covering the seaplane take-off and the channel east of Heligoland. Talbot left Harwich at 9:30pm on the 23rd in heavy rain with *E.15*. Soon after passing the North Hinder there was a 'minor excitement'. A darkened steamer suddenly loomed out of the darkness. She switched her lights on and disappeared to the south. The 24th dawned sunny, but cold. A potential German patrol vessel was sighted ahead to port. Talbot dived for nearly an hour to avoid her, but eventually made her out to be a steamer. *E.6* later stopped twice to sink floating mines as she made her way up the Dutch coast. They were quickly sunk, as steel tipped bullets had now been issued for the rifles. Talbot closed the coast and got an accurate position fix from Vlieland Lighthouse before proceeding. In the afternoon there was patchy mist and rain as she headed for her billet, swinging out wide to the north.

---

2   TNA ADM137/2067: pp.519-23, 526-30.
3   The author of the naval monograph was unaware that Oliver and Keyes knew about the latest mines.

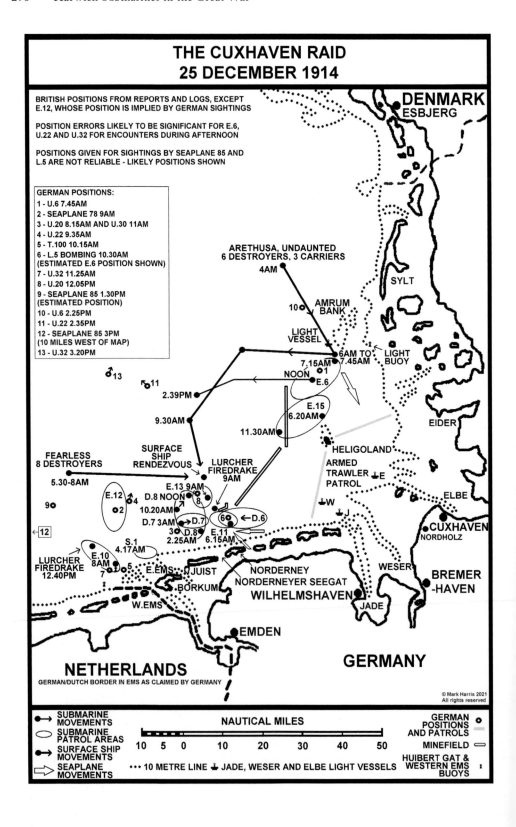

THE CUXHAVEN RAID
25 DECEMBER 1914

BRITISH POSITIONS FROM REPORTS AND LOGS, EXCEPT
E.12, WHOSE POSITION IS IMPLIED BY GERMAN SIGHTINGS

POSITION ERRORS LIKELY TO BE SIGNIFICANT FOR E.6,
U.22 AND U.32 FOR ENCOUNTERS DURING AFTERNOON

POSITIONS GIVEN FOR SIGHTINGS BY SEAPLANE 85 AND
L.5 ARE NOT RELIABLE - LIKELY POSITIONS SHOWN

GERMAN POSITIONS:
1 - U.6 7.45AM
2 - SEAPLANE 78 9AM
3 - U.20 8.15AM AND U.30 11AM
4 - U.22 9.35AM
5 - T.100 10.15AM
6 - L.5 BOMBING 10.30AM
(ESTIMATED E.6 POSITION SHOWN)
7 - U.32 11.25AM
8 - U.20 12.05PM
9 - SEAPLANE 85 1.30PM
(ESTIMATED POSITION)
10 - U.6 2.25PM
11 - U.22 2.35PM
12 - SEAPLANE 85 3PM
(10 MILES WEST OF MAP)
13 - U.32 3.20PM

DENMARK
ESBJERG

SYLT

ARETHUSA, UNDAUNTED
6 DESTROYERS, 3 CARRIERS
4AM

AMRUM
BANK

LIGHT
VESSEL

6AM TO   LIGHT
7.15AM 7.45AM   BUOY
NOON   1
E.6

2.39PM

9.30AM

E.15
6.20AM

11.30AM

EIDER

13

11

FEARLESS
8 DESTROYERS

5.30-8AM

9

SURFACE
SHIP
RENDEZVOUS

E.12
2

4

LURCHER
FIREDRAKE
9AM

E.13 9AM
D.8 NOON

10.20AM

D.7 3AM

S.1
4.17AM

3
D.8
2.25AM

D.7

6
E.11
6.15AM

D.6

HELIGOLAND

ARMED
TRAWLER   E
PATROL

W

J

ELBE

CUXHAVEN
NORDHOLZ

LURCHER
FIREDRAKE
12.40PM

E.10
8AM
7

5

12

E.EMS   JUIST

BORKUM

W.EMS

NORDERNEY
NORDERNEYER SEEGAT

WILHELMSHAVEN

JADE

WESER

BREMER
-HAVEN

EMDEN

GERMANY

NETHERLANDS
GERMAN/DUTCH BORDER IN EMS AS CLAIMED BY GERMANY

	SUBMARINE MOVEMENTS		**NAUTICAL MILES**			GERMAN POSITIONS AND PATROLS

SUBMARINE
MOVEMENTS

SUBMARINE
PATROL AREAS

SURFACE SHIP
MOVEMENTS

SEAPLANE
MOVEMENTS

NAUTICAL MILES

10 5 0   10   20   30   40   50

GERMAN
POSITIONS
AND PATROLS

MINEFIELD

HUIBERT GAT &
WESTERN EMS
BUOYS

••• 10 METRE LINE   JADE, WESER AND ELBE LIGHT VESSELS

By 1am on the 25th Talbot reckoned he was about 12 miles north of Heligoland. *E.6* was briefly lit up by a light. A few minutes later a light was trained on his stern. Talbot dived the boat. After 10 minutes nothing had happened. He came back to the surface and got underway. At 3am a light appeared close ahead out of a rain squall. Talbot quickly dived. To his surprise, *E.6* hit the bottom in only seven fathoms (13m). He turned northwest, but the water unexpectedly got even shallower. Talbot concluded that he was eight miles off course to the north and had reached the Amrum Bank. He had co-incidentally passed north of the new minefield. The lights had probably been first the Lightship and then the Vortrapptief Light Buoy. Talbot put this down to a combination of carelessness by the helmsman and putting his faith in a bad star sight made with an unclear horizon. He surfaced and headed southwest for half an hour to correct his position. *E.6* then went to the bottom and Talbot turned in for a sleep.

He was woken at 6:20am by the sound of several propellers passing overhead. Talbot came up to periscope depth, put a bag over his head to shut out the lights in the boat and took a look. He made out a British destroyer about 300 yards (275m) away. More destroyers and carriers came into sight and he realised that he was right in the middle of Tyrwhitt's force. Talbot went deep and headed southwards to get into position. By 7:45am he had seen all the seaplanes take off. Tyrwhitt cleared out to the west. *E.6* surfaced; it was a beautiful sunny day with excellent visibility and only a very light wind. Heligoland was in sight and smoke was rising there. This was presumed to be vessels raising steam for pursuit. Talbot dived and headed west to be in position to cut them off. A zeppelin was also coming out from the island. He writes that: 'I thought we were to have a busy day, but instead we were very bored;' the zeppelin was out of sight after ninety minutes and no ships came out! He surfaced at 9:23am for a look around. There was nothing in sight apart from the island to the south. He dived and briefly headed south to check that there were no stranded seaplanes. Talbot then chased some smoke to the northwest, but nothing came of it. He continued patrolling the area all morning, coming to the surface once an hour for a look round. Only a few patrol trawlers near the island and a lone merchant ship passing inshore were seen.

Talbot turned west at noon. He surfaced half an hour later to get underway for Harwich. At 2:40pm, about 20 miles west of Heligoland, Talbot: 'sighted a submarine right ahead, conning tower only and end on; five minutes later she dived. I was convinced she was British'. As a precaution he steamed straight over the position where she dived, then altered course sharply to frustrate any attack. After the patrol he realised it could not have been a British submarine and concluded that she must have been German. A strong south-westerly blew in that evening. The night was wintry, bitter cold and wet on the bridge after passing Terschelling at 10pm. No amount of clothing helped. *E.6* found herself dodging trawlers as she pressed on through the night. Talbot had to dive off the Dutch coast at 8:30am next morning, the 26th 'for what looked like a Cruiser looming up out of the mist, but what turned out to be a merchantman.' By the afternoon a full gale was blowing as he headed for the North Hinder: 'poisonous afternoon; pounding along at 13 knots in nasty beam sea, trying to save daylight.' Talbot had not realised that the wind had pushed him off course. He almost ran onto the Outer Gabbard sandbank but stopped just in time when he saw the marker buoys. *E.11* now came into sight, having the same trouble! Talbot finally reached Harwich at 6 pm.[4]

Brodie's *E.15* had the task of shadowing Tyrwhitt from the launch point off Heligoland to the pick-up point. She came to the surface at her billet at 6am on the 25th. Brodie soon sighted Heligoland five miles to the south, so *E.15* was further south than intended. Tyrwhitt arrived to the north. When he departed at 7:40am Brodie got underway to the west to shadow him, just as a zeppelin arrived over Heligoland. The smoke of two ships was almost immediately made out leaving the island. Brodie soon dived to intercept them. However, the smoke disappeared and so did the zeppelin. Brodie surfaced at 9:50am. He immediately spotted a German submarine ahead. The zeppelin was also returning from the west. Brodie dived and there are no further details of the submarine contact. An hour later the zeppelin finally headed south, so he surfaced and started the diesels. A 'German submarine periscope' was sighted off to port, aft of *E.15*. Since this was a poor position from which to fire, Brodie simply got underway again to the west. After 20 minutes it had disappeared. At 11:30am *E.15* was 14 miles WNW of Heligoland. Two large explosions were observed four miles to the northwest, crossing the unknown minefield, but nothing was heard. Brodie reached Harwich at 2:20pm on the 27th. *E.15* was the last boat back. Talbot says that she had trouble with both the weather and her engines, but this is not mentioned in Brodie's rather skimpy report.[5]

Kellett's *S.1* began sounding water depth north of the Eastern Ems at 3:10am on the 25th. *S.1* reached seven fathoms (13m) an hour later. Kellett turned south in the darkness to the exit from the Eastern Ems channel, where the depth should have been 10 fathoms (18m). He dived to periscope depth at slow speed. After checking the trim, one motor was shut off. Kellett ordered a bow down angle to glide to the bottom for the night. Only 30 seconds after giving the order *S.1* struck something with 21½ feet on the depth gauge (7m). The impact knocked off the forward drop keel. This weighed about 10 tons. *S.1* automatically shot to the surface as a result. This was supposed to happen if the keel was released in an emergency. Kellett flooded every tank with water, but nothing happened. Another 1½ tons of weight was probably needed to allow *S.1* to dive. Kellett considered flooding the diesel engines, but was doubtful this would be enough. Failure would mean it would take at least half an hour to drain the engines. It was now 4:50am with *S.1* stuck on the surface and daylight rapidly approaching. Kellett 'reluctantly abandoned the attempt.' He blew all the ballast tanks, headed back out to sea, then set course for Harwich, pushing both diesels at full power for 90 minutes to get clear of the Ems as fast as possible. Kellett was pleased with their performance, as they had previously been a source of trouble. Fortunately, *S.1* got a clear run and reached Harwich at 8am next day. It is assumed that *S.1* struck submerged wreckage, as the shallow water off the eastern Ems is flat and sandy; an unlucky start to the crew's first offensive patrol. *S.1* was docked on 1 January and spent the next six days having the drop keel replaced. Kellett suggested bolting the new one in place to avoid a repeat incident![6]

4   IWM: Documents.20134: 23–26 December; TNA ADM137/2067: p.547; TNA ADM173: *E.6* 23–26 December 1914.
5   TNA ADM137/2067: p.539; TNA ADM53: *Adamant* 27 December 1914; IWM: Documents.20134: 27 December
6   TNA ADM137/2067: p.531; TNA ADM173: *S.1* 24 December 1914-6 January 1915.

Lieutenant-Commander Brownlow V. Layard, aged 30, was on his first patrol in *D.7*. He had previously commanded *C.32* of the Dover Patrol. Layard had joined the Submarine Service in 1906. In 1911 Captain Napier had rated him an: 'Excellent S/M C[ommande]r. Good judgement.' The Admiralty disagreed in 1913. He was found at fault and incurred 'Their Lordship's displeasure' after a collision with the battle cruiser *Invincible* in *C.34*. A minor underwater collision with the Battleship *Prince of Wa*les soon followed in *C.32*, having got too close to her carrying out a torpedo attack on manoeuvres. He escaped with a caution and was advanced to Lieutenant-Commander days before war broke out.[7]

D.7 arrived at her billet at the western end of the offshore picket line at 3am on the 25th. Layard took her to the bottom until dawn. At 6:30am he came up to periscope depth to patrol the billet. Layard headed east to the Norderneyer Seegat, as planned, at 9am, passing a trawler heading south, the first thing seen. At 10:15am a seaplane was spotted and an airship was seen closing from the east through the periscope. Soon two small explosions were heard through the water. The airship remained in sight, preventing Layard from surfacing. It got quite close at mid-morning and was thought to be following *D.7*. Layard remained in the area until darkness 'on the chance that some destroyers might be called out by the airship.' This was last seen at 2pm. Nothing else arrived. At 4:50pm Layard surfaced with nothing in sight and headed back to Harwich. It appears that he had some trouble with the diesels, switching over to use the motors as he neared Harwich at 9:30pm next day. *D.7* was forced to anchor outside overnight at the Cork Light Vessel due to thick fog. Whatever the problem was, the ERAs got the diesels going again and she came in at 7am next morning, the 27th. A new exhaust valve had to be fitted to the starboard engine and a new piston on the port engine over the next two days. *D.7* was then put through her paces off Harwich on the 31st.[8]

Foster's *D.8* spotted a drifting German mine, shortly after passing the North Hinder on the morning of the 24th. It was sunk with a rifle. The billet off Juist was reached at 2:25am next morning. Foster dived to the bottom until 6:30am, then came up to periscope depth to patrol. At one point bubbles and oil were spotted coming up from an apparently sunken object. On her return to Harwich, this otherwise innocuous report caused anxiety that *S.1* might have hit and sunk the overdue *D.7*. Foster surfaced at 9am to head northwards, as planned. He remained on the surface south of the recovery point on varying courses at 10 knots. Only a seaplane passing to the west, some smoke on the horizon and later a zeppelin heading east were sighted. At noon Foster turned west to return to Harwich. That night off the Dutch coast a destroyer was spotted astern at 1,000 yards (900m). It was rapidly overtaking. Foster crash dived and stayed down for half an hour, losing a signal lamp in the process. *D.8* reached Harwich at 1pm on the 26th.[9]

Fraser's *E.10* was heading up the Dutch coast in company with *S.1* at 3:45pm on the 24th. Two destroyers were spotted closing at high speed. *E.10* dived, only to discover they were Tyrwhitt's. She surfaced half an hour later and got back underway with *S.1*. Kellett does not mention it, but Fraser was right to be cautious about unidentified warships. He lost touch with *S.1* after dark and stopped off the Western Ems at 1:15am on the 25th. Fraser surfaced at 7:10am, immediately sighting a trawler patrol to the south. *E.10* dived and headed east. The buoy at the entrance to the Western Ems was spotted a mile away an hour later. Two destroyers could be seen four

7   TNA ADM196/143/468: Brownlow Villiers Layard.
8   TNA ADM137/2067: pp.532-3; TNA ADM173: *D.7* 24-31 December 1914.
9   TNA ADM137/2067: p.534; TNA ADM173: *D.8* 25-26 December 1914.

miles to the south, going up the Huibert Gat channel. Fraser waited. Two hours later a: 'Large destroyer came out of Western Ems and turned towards me.' He commenced an attack run, but frustratingly the 'destroyer turned back when about 1½ miles off and proceeded up river.' Fraser thought the trawler patrolling at the entrance may have warned her after seeing his periscope, as the water was very calm. Another hour passed, when at 11:10am a German submarine came into sight. Fraser began an attack. Within five minutes two more enemy submarines came into sight, all on different courses and apparently zig-zagging on the surface. Ten minutes later Fraser had managed to line up for a bow shot to starboard of a submarine heading west from the entrance channel at 800 yards (750m). It was long range for a small target. Fraser took the shot. He fired both of the bow torpedoes. However, the submarine altered course away to port after the first torpedo left the tube. Fraser concluded that the water disturbance on firing had been spotted on the calm surface. Both torpedoes missed. Within 15 minutes all of the submarines had apparently disappeared back into the river to the southeast.

At noon *E.10* headed northwest out to sea to begin the journey back to Harwich. Forty minutes later two destroyers came into sight. Fraser manoeuvred into a good position to fire with his reloaded bow tubes. *E.10* was 600 yards (550m) off the bow of the leading boat. The periscope was raised for Fraser to make his final observation before firing. He now recognised *Lurcher* and *Firedrake*! Disaster had been narrowly avoided. Keyes reports that neither had been aware of the attack. *E.10* surfaced at 2pm, spotting *E.13* in the dusk to the south a couple of hours later. She reached Harwich at 10:30pm next day.[10]

Lieutenant-Commander Geoffrey 'Windy' Layton, aged 30, had taken command of *E.13* as she neared completion in early September. This would be their first mission. Layton was the son of a Liverpool solicitor and had joined the Submarine Service in 1905. He quickly lived down a shaky start after incurring the 'serious displeasure' of his Captain. An incident had resulted in damage to the engines of *B.3*. He had been in command of *C.23* in 7th Flotilla, based in the Forth, since 1912. His commander, Captain Haggard, rated him: 'Exceptional. Very fine Off[ice]r. Conscientious & thorough. Full of resource. Ideal temperament for S/M service.' Keyes concurred and Layton had been 'specially selected for c[omman]d of an "E" submarine.' He quickly received his own celebrity profile in *The Maidstone Magazine*. This recounts a number of exploits, including the mysterious overnight appearance of a bed of prize winning tulips in his garden.[11]

E.13 was assigned the billet screening the seaplane pick-up point, west of the original German minefield. Layton spotted an aeroplane off Terschelling at 7pm on the 24th, presumably scouting. At 4:30am next morning a destroyer suddenly came up at high speed from astern. It was showing only a dim white light. Layton dived for ninety minutes. After later surfacing and getting underway he spotted two destroyers and was forced to dive again. Finally, after nearly three hours playing cat and mouse he realised that the destroyers were British! It was *Lurcher* and *Firedrake*. Layton surfaced. The delays forced him to cut a corner and head at full speed direct to his second position covering the pick-up point. He reached it by 9am and observed *Lurcher* taking a seaplane in tow. He twice had to dive briefly when a zeppelin approached

10   TNA ADM137/2067: pp.535-6, 547-8.
11   TNA ADM196/143/364: Geoffrey Layton; Douglas, *Maidstone Magazine*, pp.110-2.

and had Tyrwhitt's force in sight to the north. Layton left for Harwich at noon and arrived at 3:50pm on the 26th.[12]

Bruce's *E.12* was assigned the billet just to the east of *E.13*. Bruce got underway after surfacing on the 25th and was soon forced to dive for a seaplane, presumed hostile, at 8:15am. He had only surfaced and been back underway for 20 minutes when another seaplane was sighted at 9am. Bruce decided to remain on the surface, but trimmed low in the water, in case it was British. He reports: 'Seaplane approached across bow of submarine about 100 yds [90m] ahead'. It was low in the air and was apparently intending to alight. He continues: 'both apparently discovered they were hostile craft at same time & seaplane went away full speed.' The number 78 was clearly seen on the tail; it was not one of the nine British seaplanes. An hour later a German submarine was sighted ahead to starboard, heading at about 14 knots in the direction of Heligoland. During the retirement to the west at 1:30pm another seaplane approached. It got to within 300 yards (275m) before Bruce spotted black crosses under the wings with red, white and black streamers on the wingtips; obvious German markings. He also made out the number 85. Bruce reports that it went away before rifle fire could be opened, which begs the question of why rifles were not already trained on it, especially after the first incident. *E.12* arrived back at Harwich at 5:10pm on the 26th.[13]

Nasmith's *E.11* had the easternmost inshore billet off Norderney. The island was sighted at 3:30am on the 25th. Nasmith dived and headed north to the 10 fathom line to rest on the bottom until dawn. Norderney Lighthouse was in sight when *E.11* surfaced at 6:15am. A bearing was taken and Nasmith corrected her position. He dived when a trawler was spotted ahead, but it disappeared to the northwest. Soon a gas light buoy was sighted. This was assumed to mark the southern limit of the German minefield. Nasmith returned to his position. When he surfaced at 9am he was quickly forced to dive again on spotting a vessel to the northwest, but could not find it in the periscope. He did spot a British seaplane heading out to sea half an hour later and immediately surfaced to give a guide mark. It proved to be '120', a Short Folder from the carrier *Engadine*. It circled, alighted and taxied over to *E.11*. The pilot, Flight Lieutenant Arnold J. Miley, could see no ships, but had spotted *E.11* surface and the band around the conning tower. He asked for the course and heading for the pick-up point; he only had five minutes of petrol left. This was not enough to reach the carriers, so Miley was taken aboard, together with his bombsight. The seaplane was secured for towing.

This had all taken 20 minutes. Nasmith got underway for the position of Tyrwhitt's squadron. An airship was now spotted closing from the northeast. Flight Commander Douglas A. Oliver and observer Chief Petty Officer (CPO) Budds had also spotted *E.11*. Their Short Type 74, '815', from the carrier *Empress*, was dangerously low on fuel. Oliver alighted and came alongside *E.11*. Meanwhile, another Type 74 from *Empress*, the '814', Flight Sub-Lieutenant Gaskell-Blackburn and observer CPO James Bell had passed by *E.11* a little earlier. They had been unable to find Tyrwhitt and were also virtually out of fuel. They returned to alight near *E.11*. One of the float supports had been badly damaged by anti-aircraft fire. It collapsed as '814' taxied over. The plane pitched nose first into the water, where it remained floating with the tail in the air. The airship was closing rapidly. As if that was not bad enough, a 'hostile submarine'

12   TNA ADM137/2067: pp.538, 549.
13   TNA ADM137/2067: p.537; TNA ADM53: *Adamant*, 26 December 1914.

was now observed, approaching end on, about two miles to the east. She had apparently been lying in wait off the gas buoy and minutes later dived. Nasmith now realised it was impossible to save the two intact planes. The '120' was cast off. Nasmith manoeuvred alongside '815'. The airship passed slowly, directly overhead at a height of 1,000 to 1,500 feet (300 to 450m) as Oliver and Budds stepped aboard. Nasmith defiantly waved his cap at her and to the surprise of everyone no bombs were dropped. *E.11*'s second officer, Lieutenant Guy D'Oyly-Hughes had been keeping his eye on the airship with his binoculars and could clearly see the crew in the aft gondola as she manoeuvred close, twisting, turning and at times standing up at an angle, before stopping her engines as she came directly overhead. *E.11* took another five minutes to manoeuvre alongside '814'. Gaskell-Blackburn and Bell jumped into the water from their up-ended plane and were fished out by *E.11*'s crew. The pilots were all very dazed from their ordeal as a result of the heavy fire they had experienced whilst over the land. It was now over 20 minutes since the submarine dived; Nasmith reported: 'Whilst this was happening several rounds from Automatic Pistols were being fired into the floats, petrol tanks, &c., of the two nearest machines, and as the hostile Submarine must by that time have been very close, directly the pilots could be got below I dived to 40 feet [12m].' As *E.11* levelled off two bombs exploded very loudly above, so much so that as the first went off Nasmith thought it was a torpedo from the submarine. He told Keyes that he 'remembered wondering for a moment why he was still alive so long after the torpedo had struck.' Nasmith made off to the northwest, observing the airship at intervals in the periscope. In doing so *E.11* must have passed close to the German anti-submarine minefield extension.

At noon, *E.11* went to the bottom at 20 fathoms [37m], the limit of the depth gauge. The crew now tucked in to a restorative Christmas meal of turkey and plum pudding, which was shared with their five guests. Nasmith surfaced at 1:25pm to return to Harwich. The wireless was used to report the rescue of the airmen. Keyes acknowledged the signal at 2:20pm. A seaplane was now sighted several miles away to the north. It disappeared, heading northeast. As the light failed at 5:15pm a periscope was spotted about half a mile away to port. Course was quickly altered, but no torpedo was seen. *E.11* arrived safely back at Harwich at 5pm on the 26th. Nasmith was praised by Keyes for his coolness in carrying out the rescue and received a commendation and a mention in despatches from the Admiralty. At last something had gone right for him and the rescue could have been a story straight out of *The Boy's Own Paper*.[14]

Halahan's *D.6* was assigned the billet west of *E.11*. She arrived off the coast at 1:15am on the 25th. Halahan headed inshore and dived to the bottom, but found it was only 40 feet (12m). He surfaced and dived in a somewhat deeper spot farther out to sea. Halahan came up to periscope depth at 6:45am. There was nothing to be seen and he was still unable to get a position fix due to haze inshore. *D.6* surfaced to act as a guide mark at 9am. Half an hour later a Schütte-Lanz type airship was sighted to the north. Halahan dived west to avoid being seen. He soon surfaced, then sighted the silhouette of *E.11* to the west, with three seaplanes around her. Either he or Nasmith was obviously badly out of position. Halahan: 'Approached Seaplanes at full speed to assist in rescuing Pilots, passing large light buoy en route.' Someone even took the time to sketch the distinctive shape of the buoy in the log. The airship was coming up fast astern. Halahan had

14   TNA ADM137/2067: pp.540–1, 549, 555, 560; IWM:Documents.1003: 27 December; Keyes, *Memoirs*, pp.154–6; BL:AddMS82459: Keyes Papers. Vol. IXXXVII. Reports on co-operation between seaplanes and submarines; 1914-1915, p.20, 23–27, 73.

E.11 crew, taken at Yarmouth aboard *E.12* in the same sitting as her crew: Nasmith is seated centre. To his left is Lieutenant D'Oyly-Hughes, then ERA Brooker. To his right are Sub-Lieutenant Robert Brown RNR, then PO Hodder. The Coxswain, CPO Dowell, is behind D'Oyly-Hughes. The original owner of the card, ERA Jupp, is behind Brown. Leading Seaman Chandler is nearest the Bridge in the row of four men on the platform. Stoker 1c Knotz is bottom row, extreme left. At the other end of the row *E.12*'s gramophone is just in shot beside the visiting Scout. (Darren Brown Collection)

to dive and went deep when he was about a mile from *E.11*, as it was almost overhead. Half an hour later *D.6* popped up to periscope depth. Halahan spotted the airship coming back from the west and 'dived to 60 feet [18m] just after losing sight of him in the periscope.' Minutes after levelling off a bomb exploded. *D.6* touched the bottom at 66 feet (20m) and could go no deeper. Three minutes had ticked by when there was: 'Another bomb, very heavy explosion.' Halahan turned south. He came up after 25 minutes and could see two seaplanes, one of which was standing on its nose. Halahan dived deep, then headed right alongside the undamaged seaplane. *D.6* rose until the conning tower poked out of the water. Halahan intended this to attract the attention of anyone still aboard, whilst he observed through the periscope. He reports that: 'at the same moment, the airship appeared about 100 yards [90m] the other side of it and 50 feet [15m] above the surface' The airship opened up with her Maxim machine guns on the seaplane, then directed fire at the conning tower. Halahan ordered *D.6* deep. She hit the bottom at just 52 feet [16m] and turned northwest for deeper water, passing close to the unknown mines. When Halahan took a look through the periscope the airship appeared to be following. Shortly afterwards *D.6* was taken to the bottom and stayed there for nearly two hours. His report does not mention going to the bottom and says he continued to use the periscope every half hour to check for the airship, which was still there. When the tanks were blown and *D.6* surfaced at 2:20pm, there was nothing in sight. *D.6* got underway on the diesels. Keyes reports that before leaving for Harwich, Halahan carried out a check to ensure that none of the seaplanes were still afloat, but they had actually drifted into the mined area. *Lurcher* was heard calling on the wireless at 7:30pm and Halahan reported in. *D.6* arrived back in Harwich at 6pm on the 26th.[15]

Lurcher and *Firedrake* encountered a particularly bad patch of drifting mines on their way up the Dutch coast on the afternoon of the 24th. Within the space of just half an hour, *Firedrake* stopped to sink three of them. Keyes had *Lurcher* examine the papers of a nearby Dutch trawler whilst she did so. As they neared their destination at 7am next morning *Lurcher* sighted a submarine and increased to full speed to close her. The submarine disappeared. Twenty minutes later *E.13* was recognised as British when she finally surfaced after recognising them. The destroyers resumed their course and arrived 10 miles north of the Norderneyer Seegat at 8:50am. Heavy intercepted wireless traffic suggested that the Germans were already aware of an attack. A zeppelin was spotted to the east. It remained in sight from northeast to east until 12:15pm, but never got closer than five miles. Keyes assumed that his two destroyers had been reported. Another zeppelin was sighted in the distance to the northeast and later another smaller airship in the haze to the southeast.

Just after 9am a seaplane came into sight flying very low. It closed and alighted alongside *Lurcher*. It was '119', a Short Folder from the *Engadine*. It was flown by Flight Commander Robert P. Ross. Keyes recognised him. He had been his pilot for an experiment before the war to see how well aeroplanes could detect submerged submarines. Ross was relieved, as he had been virtually running on fumes, having already had to alight once to fix a faulty fuel pump. He was taken aboard and '119' was taken in tow. Keyes now took the destroyers south. They quickly passed a large black buoy near which a mine could be clearly seen floating at the surface. The estimated position given was roughly at the southwest end of the extension to the German minefield! Another seaplane passed over flying high and fast; it steered towards *Lurcher*, then

---

15   TNA ADM137/2067: pp.542, 548-9, 558; TNA ADM173: *D.6*, 24-26 December 1914.

turned north. Keyes thought it was probably British, but could not make out any markings. *Firedrake* was ordered to break off and follow to note its course. It was soon lost sight of in the direction of Tyrwhitt's squadron and *Firedrake* re-joined astern. A British seaplane then passed on the correct course for the carriers.

At 9:45am Keyes reversed course to take '119' back to *Engadine*. It seemed implausible that German surface forces would not soon arrive, as he had been in sight of the zeppelin for an hour already. Another British seaplane passed by and smoke from Tyrwhitt's force was sighted soon afterwards. *Lurcher* closed the *Engadine* at 10:30am. The tow for '119' was slipped alongside for her to be hoisted back aboard. Keyes then headed back to the south. At 11:45am Tyrwhitt began withdrawing west. Keyes headed off independently at high speed with *Lurcher* and *Firedrake* towards the Ems, then along the coast to Terschelling. The objective given in his report was 'to prevent the enemy's trawlers and destroyers interfering with submarines returning on the surface' and to get into wireless contact with them. This rings a bit hollow and no doubt Keyes would have liked nothing better than to get into action with enemy destroyers and armed trawlers off the Ems. The news from *E.11* left only one seaplane and her pilot still unaccounted for, but there was no sign of the stray.[16] At 2:45pm a German seaplane was sighted by *Lurcher* coming up from astern. After a while it began to close. Neither *Lurcher* nor *Firedrake* had any anti-aircraft armament. However, the plane was low enough to allow the gunner on *Lurcher*'s aft 4-inch (10.2cm) gun to get his sights on target. Keyes had gone aft and was standing near the gunner. As an avid country sportsman, he now employed his experience shooting pheasant, which tend to fly up on being fired on! The gunner was told to give his gun a swing up as he fired, as it was able to elevate to another five degrees beyond the 15 degree limit of the sights. The shell seemed to have the desired effect. The plane veered off sharply and did not return. In the darkness at 9:55pm *Lurcher* suddenly swept past a submarine whilst doing 17 knots. She was apparently just 100 yards [90m] to port and the pendant number on the conning tower was recognised. It was *D.8* in the process of diving, explaining Foster's close encounter in the darkness at this time! The destroyers reached Harwich at 6:45am on the 26th.[17]

As chronicled in the previous chapter, the Germans were expecting an attack to block their harbours. *U.6* was still assigned to patrol north of Heligoland, with *U.20* covering the other gap in the minefield at the Norderneyer Seegat. The normal trawler outposts were off Heligoland and the Ems, with those in the Ems directly supported by a handful of old destroyers in the Local Defence Flotilla. Zeppelins *L.5* and *L.6* went up to scout from Nordholz.

The alarm was raised when Tyrwhitt's force was spotted from Heligoland at 7:30am in the excellent visibility. *U.6* could also see them, and dived to attack, but was unable to reach Tyrwhitt's force before it steamed away. She surfaced to make a wireless report and pursue. A conning tower then broke surface to starboard at about 7:45am. It disappeared before *U.6* could attack. This was almost certainly *E.6* and it is just as well that Talbot only remained at the surface for six minutes at this time. Zeppelin *L.6* was seen by both *E.6* and *E.15*, as she passed over Heligoland to attack *Empress*, then returned over the island. The *L.6* had a significant impact in keeping *E.6* and *E.15* submerged and was also seen by *Lurcher* and *Firedrake*. The submarine

---

16   The pilot got lost, landed next to a Dutch trawler and sank his seaplane. He was subsequently repatriated by the Dutch as a 'shipwrecked mariner'.

17   TNA ADM137/2067: pp.544-7; TNA ADM53: *Firedrake, Lurcher,* 24-26 December 1914; BL:AddMS82459: p.77-9; Keyes, *Memoirs*, pp.154, 157.

sightings north of Heligoland by *E.15* at 9:50am and 10:50am are difficult to identify, as her position is unclear. They could have been sightings of *E.6*, as the two were fairly close, but the supposed periscope could even have been some flotsam. *U.6* had been drawn away to the north at 9am by smoke from merchantmen, which also attracted the attention of *E.6*. Apparently no other German submarines came out from Heligoland.

Zeppelin *L.5*, commanded by Oberleutnant zur See Hirsch, headed west after taking off from Nordholz. Around 10:30am a submarine was sighted, surrounded by three smaller vessels, apparently 20 miles north of Norderney. As *L.5* got closer the small vessels were made out to be seaplanes, one of which was partially capsized. Hirsch reports: 'As we approached I saw the submarine was in great haste to get crews aboard and dive ahead of the airship.' Hirsch now also spotted Tyrwhitt's force and the sightings were reported by wireless. He continues: 'In order to prevent the aircraft from being picked up again by these forces and to possibly put the submarine out of action, two bombs were dropped, which fell between the planes; no particular effect from the bombs, which detonated about 20 to 30 meters [yards] from the aircraft, was observed.' There is no explanation why bombs were not dropped before *E.11* dived, but manoeuvring a zeppelin to get into exactly the right position to drop bombs on a small submarine that was still moving was not as simple as it sounds and was no doubt the cause of the gesticulations from the occupants observed by D'Oyly-Hughes. There is also no mention of a second submarine and it seems that *D.6* was either not sighted or not recognised as such. Keyes writes a good yarn explaining how Nasmith waving his cap must have convinced the airship that *E.11* was a German submarine attacking the seaplanes, causing *L.5* to bomb *D.6* in the belief that she had been attacking a supposedly German submarine. A nice story, but unfortunately, just that. *L.5* remained in the area observing Tyrwhitt's force to the west from a distance, heading back and forth and accounting for the numerous sightings by Keyes and the various submarines in the area. Hirsch continues: 'When *L.5* came close to the drifting aircraft again (followed by the enemy ships), it went down to a low altitude and took the aircraft under machine gun fire in order to make them useless to the pursuing enemy.' *D.6* was simply in precisely the wrong place at precisely the wrong time to get caught up in this! There is no evidence that her conning tower was spotted or deliberately fired on. Despite all the efforts to sink them, *L.5* reported all three of them still afloat, having drifted into the German minefield around 1pm when she finally left the area. Fog closed in shortly thereafter, preventing any recovery attempt by the Germans later that day. As is made clear in their reports, thanks to the excellent visibility, *L.5* had a huge impact on the British submarines. *E.11, D.7, D.6* and to a lesser extent *E.13*, were all forced to submerge and even go deep. Both Layard and Halahan both thought they could be seen and were being hunted, but this was only their first and second patrol respectively and they had perhaps not yet acclimatised to offensive patrolling. They were also mistaken in believing that their submarines might be visible underwater. The murky water of the Bight provided perfect cover. Whilst demonstrating just how effective airships could be in keeping submarines off the surface, they were not very effective in attacking moving targets.

Meanwhile, *U.20*, Kapitänleutnant Schweiger, had headed north at dawn after spending the night on the bottom off Borkum. At 8:15am he was about 12 miles north of the island when two British L Class destroyers were spotted four miles to the north, heading in an easterly direction. The leading boat later signalled to a submarine on the surface to the west, which dived. The destroyers then headed off to the northeast, going out of sight at 8:50am. There is no doubt that this was *Lurcher*, *Firedrake* and *E.13*, although *E.13* would simply have gone out of sight at her full speed of 15 knots, rather than diving. *U.20* surfaced long enough to report them. Schweiger then dived and headed north to investigate smoke. He spent the next three hours failing to get into position to attack Tyrwhitt's force. When the retirement west commenced, Schweiger once again spotted *Lurcher* and *Firedrake*, to the south of his position, now heading for the Ems. He also spotted a British submarine surface nearby south of his position. He commenced an attack but was foiled when his target dived on the approach of a second British submarine. Schweiger thought that she must have been spooked by the appearance of the second boat, believing it to be German. Both submarines were then seen rapidly leaving to the west. This was *D.8* and *E.13*. The former is the most likely candidate for the attack, but Schweiger was mistaken about the elaborate rationale for surfacing and diving. *D.8* was on the surface throughout. She was steering northwest coming into sight. He must have lost sight of her when she altered course to port at noon, turning her stern to him, then spotted her again as she headed west.

Despite the extremely clear weather, which removed the chance of a repetition of the disastrous short range encounters seen in August, the German Fleet Command adopted a passive response to the alarm. A reconnaissance sortie by 1st Torpedoboots-Flottille northwest from Heligoland was even cancelled. The key factor in not even allowing ships out of the estuaries was the fear of a submarine ambush at the exits. Ingenohl decided to wait for air reconnaissance before issuing orders.

Seaplanes were scrambled from Sylt, Heligoland and Borkum to help clarify the picture. Some carried small bombs, but as yet none carried machine guns. Some left their bombs behind to extend their scouting radius. At 7:45am Seaplane '78' from Borkum spotted an enemy submarine, 25 miles north of the entrance to the Western Ems.[18] This was the close encounter with *E.12*, after which '78' continued north to spot Tyrwhitt's force. Bruce was therefore about 30 miles west of his assigned position. His dead reckoning was badly out. This explains why he does not seem to have sighted anything other than German seaplanes. Seaplane '78' reported the sightings on returning to Borkum at 10:05am.

Seaplane '85' flew on a westerly heading from Borkum. *E.12*, as well as *Firedrake* and *Lurcher*, were separately encountered during the retirement in the afternoon. Seaplane '85' was undamaged by the shell from *Lurcher*.[19] At least 10 seaplanes went out, some of which made more than one sortie. They were potentially more dangerous than the airships, as they could quickly approach and were less obvious. There were four sightings whilst surfaced by British submarines of seaplanes that could only have been German. In two of these, both involving *E.12*, the seaplane got too close for the submarine to avoid attack by diving. Bruce was thus twice lucky not to have been bombed, whilst *E.12* dived without being seen on the first occasion. *E.11* ignored her sighting at 2:30pm and was not approached or seen. At 3:25pm Seaplane '53' from Sylt did drop two bombs on a suspected submerged submarine proceeding south off the island. Only *U.6* was in the area at the time, but does not appear to have been the target.

Korvettenkapitän Gayer, the commander of 3rd U-boots-Halbflottille in the Ems, had not waited for orders. *U.30* had been due to relieve *U.20* off Norderney later that morning. When the first sighting reports off Heligoland came in, he immediately despatched her, but she failed to get close to anything before returning. *U.22* was also sent at full speed to a position 55 miles

18   This time from Groos is possibly a transcription error; Bruce records the time as 9am
19   The time given for both sightings is 4pm GMT. Bruce gives 1:30pm and Keyes 2:45-3pm. The time
     quoted must be that of the report made by '85' on returning, not the time of the sighting.

to the north to attempt to intercept Tyrwhitt on his return. The only other submarine ready for sea, *U.32*, was ordered to stand by at the mouth of the Western Ems.

U.22, Kapitänleutnant Hoppe, headed north from the Ems. At 9:35am he spotted a submarine in the distance to the west steaming on a parallel course. At first Hoppe assumed this was *U.20*. After a while he realised it was a British submarine and the two continued on a parallel course for nearly an hour, when Hoppe spotted Tyrwhitt's force and dived to attack it. He had been shadowing *E.12*, as the position given is near her encounter with Seaplane '78' and ties up with Bruce's sighting of a submarine at 10am, the easterly direction being that taken when she headed to attack Tyrwhitt. Given the distance apart neither boat was in a position to attack the other.

Gayer now decided to leave the Ems to scout towards Norderney in his leader boat, the destroyer *T.100*. At 10:10am he received orders for additional patrols by wireless. He had just passed the exit and turned back into the Ems to pass on the orders to the only other submarine available, *U.32*. The course reversal saved *T.100* from attack by *E.10*, which had already begun her attack run. *U.32*, Oberleutnant zur See von Spiegel, closed *T.100* to pick up the new orders by signal lamp at 10:40am, then exited the Ems heading west. *E.10* magnified the comings and goings of both into three submarines. *T.100* was a small destroyer and could have easily been mistaken for a submarine at a distance. *E.10*'s periscope was spotted about 1,000m (1,100 yards) ahead as *U.32* left the Western Ems entrance at 11:05am. Around 1m (3 feet) had been showing above water. Spiegel altered course to avoid it and reported the sighting to *T.100*. About ten minutes later the periscope was sighted again about 1,200m (1,300 yards) to starboard, together with the swirl of water from torpedoes being fired. *U.32* immediately turned away, with her stern to the firing point. Three minutes later two torpedo tracks passed by on either side. Calm water and an alert watch had foiled Fraser's attack. Spiegel made off to the south, then worked round out of sight of the submerged *E.10* to head north for his assigned billet, 50 miles northwest of Heligoland. The outpost trawler *Julius Wieting* and *T.100* raised the alarm. The coast defence battleships *Frithjof* and *Hagen*, which were lying at readiness in the outer channel of the Ems, immediately retired behind the entrance barrier.

Their orders put *U.22* and *U.32* on converging courses to the north. Differences in dead reckoning mean that they may have crossed tracks in the late afternoon, but *E.6* was also crossing their path. *U.22* spotted a submarine at 2:35pm ahead of her heading roughly northwest. She was initially in a good attack position, but her torpedoes had been given depth settings for ship attack. Like the British submarines, the torpedoes had to be withdrawn from the tubes to adjust the depth setting. By the time this was done it was too late to attack. This was probably *E.6*, which evidently saw her at about the same time. At 3:20pm, some miles to the west, *U.32* sighted a submarine. Spiegel dived, but thought it could be *U.30* or *U.22* and chose not to fire. This may have been another interception of *E.6*, but it could have been *U.22*, which surfaced in the same area at this time.[20]

After all had returned to Harwich Nasmith and Halahan could compare notes. It was immediately obvious that Nasmith had abandoned the seaplanes to avoid *D.6*! Being end on to *E.11* made it virtually impossible to make out her type, but the conning tower markings ought to have given it away. It also seems odd that *L.5* never spotted her. Keyes reported that the

20   Groos, *Nordsee 3*, pp.126–39, Karte 14; BArch:RM92: *Frithjof, Nassau, Von der Tann*, Kriegstagebuch 25 Dezember 1914; BArch:RM97: *U.32*, Kriegstagebuch, 25 December 1914.

approach of *D.6* perhaps saved *E.11* by forcing her to dive. Nasmith was unimpressed by the danger posed by the lumbering airship and had been intending to try and save the two intact seaplanes. He had a point. *Empress* had dodged an airship bombing attack with relative ease that afternoon despite having no anti-aircraft armament, but Nasmith would have found it harder to manoeuvre towing the seaplanes. The metal of the conning tower and saddle tanks would also have been vulnerable to machine guns if the airship had come in low. *Empress* had used her low angle guns when her attackers did this, but *E.11* had no gun.

The submarine commanders read the modest claims of damage made by the airmen in their reports with interest in the days following the raid. As Talbot sums up: 'it is doubtful if they did any damage at all, ... but discovered a certain amount of information as regards where ships are lying, etc.' The Admiralty sent a note of appreciation for Keyes and those involved from 8th Flotilla, for the skilful manner in which the submarines were handled during the operation. In the days and months that followed overblown reports of rumours circulating about the damage caused by the seven seaplanes gained traction. These culminated in the British Official History incorrectly claiming that the battlecruiser *Von der Tann* had been rammed and put out of action as a result of panic caused by the raid.[21]

If the British had been planning an operation to block or mine in the German bases, the deliberate lack of response by the Fleet Command would have meant that its approach would have been essentially unopposed. The author of the German Official History concedes that unsupported light forces had sat for four hours in perfect visibility, within 30 miles of the German Coast, without any measures being taken to oppose them. What seems to have been widely overlooked is that the key factor in locking everything down in the estuaries was actually fear of submarine ambush. When the danger was confirmed by *E.10's* attack at the exit buoy off the Ems, the heavy vessels that could have engaged any blocking attempt were actually withdrawn right inside the estuary. It could be argued that Keyes submarines, through their relentless activity in the Bight, had already achieved their objective of protecting Tyrwhitt's force from surface attack by creating this strategic command paralysis. The fact that British submarines had no surface targets to attack masks this. Nothing changed as a result of the attack. The Fleet Command simply decided to station more submarines off the Ems when an attack was expected, to allow them to come into action more quickly.

The plan itself was not perfect. Keyes decision to place his destroyers in an exposed forward position on the return flight path and make a final dash at the Ems is questionable but is typical of his thirst for action. It did pay off with the rescue of '119' and her pilot, but the presence of surface forces off the Ems was reported by *U.20* significantly earlier than would otherwise have been the case. In the event the Germans made little use of the report. Keyes came within a hair's breadth of being attacked by *E.10*, another reminder that friendly submarines and warships did not mix well in a combat area. The lesson that German responses tended to be late in the day, or even on the following day had apparently still not been properly learned. It would have been better to have had all the submarines remain in position longer, but the complete lack of German response in this instance meant that it would have made no difference. The inevitable overlapping submarine billets as a result of navigational errors caused confusion. Whilst this was largely unavoidable with prevailing technology, there were perhaps too many submarines

21   TNA ADM137/2067, pp.553-560; TNA ADM186/621: pp.135-6; Corbett, *Naval Operations 2*, p.52

deployed off Norderney. Whilst not a flaw in the plan, the British were also inevitably still evolving their understanding of the placement of the German mine barriers. *Lurcher* and *Firedrake* certainly came within a whisker of mines. At least knowledge of the extension of the minefield off Norderney was gained without loss.

This action won renown as the first ever carrier borne air strike. It was just the kind of innovative project to use new technology to strike at the enemy so favoured by Churchill and enthusiastically executed by Tyrwhitt and Keyes. At this point aerial technology was not really up to the ambition. A less celebrated first was the use of submarines to rescue downed aircrew in enemy waters during an operation. They were ideally adapted to this role and Nasmith's rescue of five airmen who would otherwise have been drowned or captured proved its value on the first outing.

The crews made the best of delayed Christmas festivities after their return. On the afternoon of the 28th a Christmas party was held in one of the sheds on the Quay for children, complete with toys contributed by the wives and a Christmas tree. Stocks appeared as Father Christmas out of a mocked up submarine. Keyes wife, Eva, sent a gift of bull's-eyes (round humbugs) and a card to the crew of each boat. Every member of the Flotilla received a Christmas box from Princess Mary's Christmas Fund. At Harwich this contained either two boxes of acid drops, or a box of tobacco and a pipe, together with a photo and Christmas card from Princess Mary. Further gifts were received from a range of well-wishers as well as the builders of the Flotilla boats; Vickers for the submarine crews and Yarrow for *Firedrake* and *Lurcher*.

On the 28th *E.8* left for major work at Chatham replacing her motors and would not return until 14 January. Operations for the year at Harwich were appropriately enough brought to a close by the weather, with what Talbot described as 'a perfect hurricane' blowing up on the afternoon of the 28th. Hallifax went to a ship's concert in the sheds that evening, but the wind made so much noise that he could hear nothing and left. Next day, in true stiff upper lip style, Talbot managed to enjoy a game of golf with Fraser on a half-submerged golf course, despite the freezing cold and howling wind.[22]

22   IWM: Documents.20134: 28-29 December; *Keyes Papers*, p.66, letter to wife 26 December 1914; IWM:Documents.1003: 28 December and 14 January 1915; Douglas, *Maidstone Magazine*, p.69; TNA ADM173: *E.8*, 28 December 1914-14 January 1915.

28

Conclusion

When the Great War began no one knew whether submarines would be able to sustain operations in enemy waters. Keyes himself had reservations about their sustainability. Five months later the operations of 8th Flotilla had a profound impact on the German Navy's conduct of the war at sea.

Naval campaigns are won or lost by the side that dominates the sea space. The British Home fleets prevented the High Sea Fleet from leaving the North Sea in 1914. However, it was 8th Flotilla that effectively confined German surface forces in harbour. Their operations profoundly curtailed German surface unit operations in the Heligoland Bight. This major achievement has at best been badly overlooked, or even attributed solely to the activities of the surface fleet.

The impact that 8th Flotilla had was the result of hard work over the many patrols described previously. From September onwards German sources make it clear that fear of submarine ambush increasingly confined surface vessels to the estuaries. The German Fleet Command perceived a constant threat as a result of the sinking of *Hela* and *S.116*, together with the clear evidence of other near misses and submarine encounters. These real encounters were further amplified by false reports from over anxious lookouts. The Fleet was forced to move major tactical exercises to the safer waters of the Baltic, meaning that for much of the time at least one major fleet unit was absent from the North Sea. During daylight, patrol work largely became the province of armed trawlers. The impact on both morale and preparedness in the German surface fleet was corrosive. The degree to which the British were perceived to combine surface attack with submarine blockade in their offensive operations culminated in almost complete inertia in response to the Cuxhaven Raid. The almost perfect visibility would otherwise have enabled the German Fleet to come out and engage Tyrwhitt without hesitation.

A key enabler was of course the inability to counteract the threat posed by submarines in 1914. The regular night-time destroyer sweeps that the Germans tried were largely worthless, and *U.27*'s successful ambush of *E.3* proved to be a one-off.

The second key achievement of 8th Flotilla was the operational intelligence that identified German patrol patterns in the Bight and the position of the large minefield laid there in September. This intelligence was vital groundwork for the planning of the raid that led to the decisive First Battle of Heligoland. It was also an essential input to all of the subsequent operations in the Bight.

The achievements had come at great cost. The lives of 77 crew had been lost. Three submarines had been sunk, one by submarine torpedo, one by mine and one from a cause unknown to this day. The increase in activity by enemy submarines, prevalence of mines and dearth of suitable targets had combined to swing the pendulum of losses against the flotilla.

Maintaining operational effectiveness in the face of ongoing operational losses should not be taken for granted in a small force. Whilst some of their surface brethren went from one end of the war to the other without catching a glimpse of the enemy, every crew in the Flotilla faced regular patrols in enemy waters. The crews obviously faced constant danger of attack from enemy patrols. The reports are also rife with tales of near collision with other vessels and mines. The North Sea weather and sea conditions are famously fickle and dangerous for small vessels. It had not just played a part in restricting operations at times but had also claimed lives. These factors combined to create a high and unrelenting level of operational stress.

Considerable physical and mental resilience was needed to keep going. Some of the commanders and the men had inevitably not been equal to these challenges. The tales of Feilmann and Street are cases in point. Off patrol tensions were relieved as much as possible by blowing off steam in the wardroom, sport and occasional leave and perhaps less constructively with alcohol. It is a testament to the character, training and camaraderie of the officers and men who served that most of them were able to continue under the pressure, rather than being any reflection on those who fell by the wayside.

Leadership had been vital in creating the conditions for success. Keyes lived up to his nickname of the 'Arch Instigator', pushing the Flotilla to the fore and creating an effective partnership with Tyrwhitt to create and exploit operational opportunities. Churchill was a key ally in this and it is likely that Keyes would have been quickly swept away by Fisher without his patronage.

Like most leaders, Keyes had his flaws. His thirst for action could get in the way of the activities of the Flotilla and the surface operations it was supporting. The Heligoland Battle and to a lesser extent the Cuxhaven Raid are notable examples. His gregariousness, whilst creating loyalties and influence beyond his rank, lay at the root of many of his problems. This was especially true when he spoke his mind too freely, most notably in the simmering feud with Fisher. There was also a lack of rigorous analysis when things did not go as well as they should have done. Attack doctrine, for example, would have benefitted from an early systematic examination of torpedo misses.[1]

The overall direction of the campaign had inevitably gone down some blind alleys. Keyes initial dalliance with cruiser co-operation was an early example. The use of a patrol line off Terschelling, which Sturdee seems to have initially advocated, was a wasteful and largely ineffective use of resources. The exaggerated fears of a coastal raid kept the Flotilla on the defensive for much of the last two months of the year. Lack of patrolling in the Bight at this time had even emboldened the Germans to begin exercising there again. Fortunately Nasmith had returned and attacked on the very day that they had done so.

The intelligence led approach that was introduced from November onwards to replace standing patrols also bore little fruit. The North Sea was too big to allow for all the options and vagaries that could emerge from decoded signals. This tended to mean that the response was always one step behind the enemy, whether it was intercepting the Yorkshire Raid or ambushing submarines in transit to Zeebrugge. The Admiralty was inevitably on a steep learning curve in the use of

---

1   Later analysis in 1915-16 demonstrated that for a large number of attacks there was no available data to analyse.

intercepted signal intelligence. To be really effective the intelligence needed to be supplemented by real time tactical updates to assets in a position to exploit it. The communications technology was not really up to the job. The result was an over managed pre-placement of submarines, removing tactical initiative from commanders on the spot. Additionally, the type of submarine wireless set adopted had proved to be of limited use, preventing reporting of enemy movements, or receiving new orders once out on patrol.

The tactical results were modest, as the table shows. The flotilla had fired 21 torpedoes in all, including two at a neutral submarine. Two torpedoes had hit, both from Horton in *E.9*, sinking *Hela* and *S.116*. However, the results need to be viewed against the background of the fact that the targets were mostly small, alert and highly manoeuvrable. Most crews that escaped were conscious of how close they had come to being hit; this contributed to a pervasive fear of submarine attack.

EIGHTH FLOTILLA TORPEDO ANALYSIS – 1914			
	Torpedoes Fired	**Torpedo Hits**	**Percent Hits**
Target			
Battleship	1	-	-
Cruiser	4	1	25.0
Destroyer	8	1	12.5
Small warship	1	-	-
Submarine	6	-	-
Outpost Trawler	1	-	-
Firer			
Nasmith – *E.11*	5	-	-
Horton – *E.9*	4	2	50.0
Leir – *E.4*	3	-	-
Herbert – *D.5*	2	-	-
Fraser – *E.10*	2	-	-
Cochrane – *D.1*	1	-	-
Jameson – *D.2*	1	-	-
Benning – *E.5*	1	-	-
Talbot – *E.6*	1	-	-
Feilmann – *E.7*	1	-	-
TOTAL			
	21	2	9.5

Two lessons were emerging. Beam tubes had revealed their limitations in typical sea conditions. Horton had demonstrated how double shots in quick succession from bow tubes increased the chance of hitting an evading target.

Whilst there had been depth keeping problems identified with older torpedoes, these had actually been mitigated quickly. An analysis of the attacks indicates that four misses were probably 'unders'. However, none of these missed as a result of depth keeping problems: two were fired too close to the target; one at too great an angle from the horizontal and the last, on *Havmanden*, fortunately grazed the hull forward. It was running at about the correct depth. Of the remainder, four or five were simply misses for direction, nine or ten were evaded by the target and one was probably a misfire.

The number of evasions does point to a potential problem with the British doctrine of very close range attack. The amount of splash at the surface from British torpedo discharge was easily spotted at these ranges. The problem was caused by the discharge pressure being set too high.[2] It was also more difficult to respond to last minute changes of course. These lessons had not yet been learned.

The submarines had experienced problems, especially with the hydroplanes and engines. These had resulted in a significant level of down-time as the issues were rectified. However, the basic soundness of the overseas boat design pioneered in *D.1* had been demonstrated. Huge credit was due to the engineering branch for keeping the submarines going as there were no major breakdowns on patrol. The submarines had actually spent a creditable 27% of the days available to them on patrol. At least 23% of the time the boats had been unavailable as a result of major repairs or refits, the actual figure being a little higher as not all refits have been traced. The spell of bad wintry weather had given a useful breather to catch up on maintenance after the intense patrolling and wear and tear experienced earlier in the year.[3]

The need for accurate navigation became ever more pressing as mines proliferated. Gyrocompasses and Forbes Logs helped, but teething troubles with the technology were inevitable. Submarine armament had been enhanced, with the provision of faster, longer range heater torpedoes. However, there had so far been almost no mass targets to use them against. Better periscope optics and attack calculators were also needed to enable effective long range attacks. Talbot, whose relatively new boat had one of the best available British periscopes, still singles out the French periscopes on the *Archimède* as superior.

There was a massive leap forward in tactical capability over the period, with boats remaining submerged for most of their patrol and eking out their battery power with long spells sitting on the bottom. Diving depth had been safely pushed beyond design specifications to over 130 feet (40m). In August it had been considered remarkable that *E.4* had remained submerged for almost 24 hours. By December it was commonplace. The dangerous practice of sitting on the surface charging the diesels in daylight had been replaced by a much higher level of tactical awareness in the commanders. Crews had shown themselves capable of maintaining a sustained cycle of four to five day patrols and had even carried out extended patrols of up to 18 days. The need to ensure that submarines and friendly surface forces knew where each other was and that they should be kept apart had been understood, if not always adhered to. Submarines had

2   Compton-Hall, *Submarines 1914–18*, p.69.
3   See Appendix V.

demonstrated a new operational aspect to their capabilities in rescuing stranded personnel from enemy waters.

The success achieved by 8th Flotilla in 1914 can have no better illustration than the withdrawal of the surface forces in the Ems on Christmas Day as a result of the attack by *E.10*. It brings us full circle to Ingenohl's concerns with which the book opens. The entire German surface fleet had indeed been blockaded in its harbours on Christmas Day just as he feared, whilst the crew of *E.7* tucked into their plum pudding off the Weser.

At the end of 1914 the war was five months old and any hopes of a quick victory were gone. On New Year's Day 1915 Keyes sent a simple message to his wife sending his love and the hope that by the end of 1915 they would be together after 'a Glorious Peace'. For both Keyes and 8th Flotilla the war would go on, but 1915 would see them part ways. Weapon capabilities, tactics and strategy would evolve and pose new challenges in the years ahead.

Appendix I

8th Flotilla submarine specifications[1]

Classes in Flotilla during 1914	D Class*	E Class*	Later C Class	S Class	Archimède
Overall Length	164'7"(50.2m)	181' (55.2m)	142'2" (43.3m)	148'1" (45.1m)	60.9m (199'9")
Maximum Width	20'5" (6.2m)	22'9" (6.9m)	13'7" (4.1m)	14'5" (4.4m)	5.6m (18'6")
Mean Draught	11'5" (3.5m)	12'6" (3.8m)	11'6" (3.5m)	10'4" (3.2m)	4.4m (14'6")
Height of casing above waterline	6'3" (1.9m)	6'3" (1.9m)	3'10" (1.2m)	2'5" (0.7m)	About 1.2m (6'3")
Height of bridge above waterline	12' (3.6m)	12' (3.6m)	10' (3.0m)	6'9" (2.1m)	About 2.3m (7'6")
Surfaced Weight	495 tons (503t)	667 tons (677t)	290 tons (295t)	265 tons (269t)	580t (571 tons)
Submerged Weight	620 tons (630t)	807 tons (820t)	320 tons (325t)	324 tons (329t)	809t (796 tons)
Watertight Compartments	1	4 (3 for *E.1–E.8*)	1	10	7

1   TNA ADM186/15: pp.29-30; TNA ADM137/2067: p.679; Garier, *Sous–Marin 2*, pp.154–172; A.N. Harrison, *The Development of HM Submarines – BR3043* (MOD Ship Department, 1979) <http://rnsubs.co.uk/dits-bits/br-3043.html> (accessed 31 December 2020).

Classes in Flotilla during 1914	D Class*	E Class*	Later C Class	S Class	Archimède
Main Engines	2 x 6 cylinder Vickers diesels	2 x 8 cylinder Vickers diesels	1 x 12 cylinder Vickers petrol engine	2 x 6 cylinder Scott-FIAT diesels	2 x 3 cylinder steam engines; 2 x oil fired boilers
Main Engine Horsepower	1,200	1,600	600	650	1,700
Electric Motors	2	2	1	2	2
Electric Motor Horsepower	550	840	300	400	1,220
Propeller shafts	2	2	1	2	2
Maximum surface speed	14½ knots	15 knots	13 knots	13 knots	15 knots
Maximum underwater speed	9 knots	10¼ knots	8½ knots	8½ knots	10 knots
Surface cruising speed and radius	2,000 miles at 11½ knots	2,600 miles at 12½ knots	1,350 miles at 9½ knots	1,600 miles at 8½ knots	2,900 miles at 10 knots
Submerged endurance	65 miles at 5 knots	65 miles at 5 knots	55 miles at 5 knots	75 miles at 5 knots	99 miles at 5 knots
18-inch (45cm) bow tubes	2	2 (1 for E.1–E.8)	2	2	1
18-inch (45cm) stern tubes	1	1	None	None	None

Classes in Flotilla during 1914	D Class*	E Class*	Later C Class	S Class	Archimède
Other 18-inch (45cm) tubes	None	On each side internally: 1 beam tube firing at 90 degrees to bow	None	None	On each side externally: 2 torpedo frames; 1 Drzewiecki apparatus‡
Torpedoes carried	6	10 (8 for E.1–E.8)	4	4	8 (6 external, 2 internal)
Guns	None†	None	None	None	None
Crew	25	30	16	18	28
Cost	£89,000 (£10.2M 2020)	£105,500 (£12.3M 2020)	£50,500 (£5.8M 2020)	£70,000 (£8.0M 2020)	?
Notes					

* D.1, D.2 and E.1–E.8 had a slightly different hull shape to the rest of their class, with slightly different dimensions

† D.4 only was equipped with an experimental 12-pdr (76mm) gun mounting, which fired a 12lb (5.4kg) shell. This folded away into the deck casing and took a few minutes to fix into position. All boats carried some rifles and pistols

‡ French torpedoes in frames and Drzewiecki apparatus could only be fired if submerged. The Drzewiecki were turned to the desired angle from inside the boat prior to firing. Frames were fixed on a set bearing 6 & 10 degrees off the bow

Wireless installation in British boats was ongoing, with priority for overseas boats. All war built boats, including S.1, had it from completion. Based on log entries: D.3 equipped 1 August; D.7 fitted with wireless mast 6 August; D.6 equipped in refit prior to joining the Flotilla. Based on Hallifax and Talbot diary entries: D.2 fully equipped at outbreak of hostilities; E.5 not equipped and E.7 equipped only for receiving. On 13 October E.7 was still not fitted for sending, but D.4, D.8, E.2, E.4 and E.6 were. E.5 was equipped during a refit ended 27 December, but E.3 was lost before being fitted. Archimède had no wireless.

Appendix II

Submarine torpedo specifications[1]

Torpedoes in use in 1914	18-inch British RGF Mark IV	18-inch British RGF Mark V*	18-inch British RGF Mark VI	18-inch British RGF Mark VII**	45cm French Modèle 1906
Engine Type	Cold	Cold	Cold	Wet Heater	Cold
Length	16'7.4" (5.07m)	16'7.4" (5.07m)	16'7.4" (5.07m)	17'7.4" (5.37m)	5.07m (16'7.4")
Explosive	Wet Guncotton	Wet Guncotton	Wet Guncotton	Wet Guncotton	Wet Guncotton
Explosive Charge	209.5lb (95kg)	209.5lb (95kg)	200lb (90.7kg)	200lb (90.7kg)	86.8kg (191lb)
Settings	One speed only	Switch to Extreme Reducer setting with significant notice	Switch to Extreme Reducer setting with significant notice	Long or short range selected with sliding valve at short notice	One speed only
Side Lug Short Range Type (S.L.S.R.)	1,000yds (914m) at 27¼ knots	1,000yds (914m) at 32¼ knots; 4,000yds (3,658m) at 19 knots with extreme reducer*	1,000yds (914m) at 34 knots; 4,000yds (3,658m) at 21 knots with extreme reducer	None	1,000m (1,094yds) at 32½ knots

1   TNA ADM189/35: pp.31–2; Labayle–Couhat, *French Warships*, p.271.

Torpedoes in use in 1914	18-inch British RGF Mark IV	18-inch British RGF Mark V*	18-inch British RGF Mark VI	18-inch British RGF Mark VII**	45cm French Modèle 1906
Side Lug Long Range Type (S.L.L.R.)	2,000yds (1,829m) at 20¾ knots OR 1,750yds (1,600m) at 21¾ knots	3,000yds (2,743m) at 22 knots	2,000yds (1,829m) at 27½ knots; 4,000yds (3,658m) at 21 knots with extreme reducer	None	2,000m (2,187yds) at 24½ knots OR 1,500m (1,640yds) at 27 knots
Side Lug Type (S.L. selectable speed)	None	None	None	3,000yds (2,743m) at 41 knots, 7,000yds (6,401m) at 28¾ knots ‡	None
Guide Strip Type (G.S.)	1,000yds (914m) at 26¾ knots	1,000yds (914m) at 32 knots; 4,000yds (3,658m) at 18½ knots with extreme reducer*	1,000yds (914m) at 33½ knots; 4,000yds (3,658m) at 21 knots with extreme reducer	None	None
Usage	Older boats and reserve, not normally issued to overseas boats	Standard for overseas boats (S.L.S.R. & G.S. type) †	Some overseas boats, S.1 (S.L.S.R. & G.S. type) †	2 for bow tubes issued to each overseas boat: September to December 1914 §	Archimède

Notes
* Speed with extreme reducer setting for Mark V* considered unreliable.
† Logs indicate that the Mark V* was most commonly carried by overseas submarines, but *D.3*, *D.8* and *E.7* had newer Mark VI or VI*. The last two may have been entirely equipped with them and others probably had them. The Mark VI* was 1¼ knots faster at 1,000 yards and 1 knot faster at 4,000 yards.
‡ Short range was less in earlier variants: VII 5,500yds (5,029m); VII* 6,000yds (5,486m); VII*A 6,500yds (5,944m).
§ Apparently no submarines had heaters when war broke out. Log entries date the issue of the first two Mk VII torpedoes for the bow tubes: *D.3* 12 November; *D.6* 1 November; *D.7* 11 December; *E.4* 12 October; *E.5* 27 October; *E.6* 30 October; *E.7* 26 September; *E.8* 23 October. From *E.10* onwards E boats apparently had two from completion. New tools and training for torpedo hands required on issue. Virtually all Mark VIIs noted in logs were the latest Mark VII**, but one Mark VII* was issued to both *E.7* and *E.8*.
All British 18-inch torpedoes were actually 45cm (17.7-inch) calibre. For submarines they were fitted with either Side Lugs (S.L. type) for bow and stern tubes, or Guide Strips (G.S. type) for beam tubes. It was possible to refit one type to the other, or to change S.L.S.R to S.L.L.R., but not whilst in action.
For internal tubes only, depth settings could be altered and tubes rigged for either underwater or surface fire whilst at sea.

Appendix III

8th Flotilla vessels and commanders in 1914[1]

Vessel	Builder and Completion Date	Joining and leaving dates	Commanders in 1914	Fate
Submarine Depot Ships				
Maidstone	Scotts, Clydebank 15 October 1912		Captain (S) Arthur K. Waistell	Sold 31 August 1929
Adamant	Cammell Laird, Birkenhead 27 April 1912		Commander Frederick A. Sommerville	Sold 21 September 1932
SS Seti renamed *Pandora*	Raylton Dixon, Middlesbrough, 1902 Renamed 2 December 1914	After conversion to depot ship 23 November	Tender to *Maidstone*	Mined 23 November 1939
Attached Destroyers				
Lurcher	Yarrow, Scotstoun 5 November 1912		Commander Wilfred Tomkinson	Sold 9 August 1922

1 TNA ADM53; TNA ADM173; TNA ADM137/2067; F.J. Dittmar & J.J. Colledge, *British Warships 1914–1919* (London: Ian Allen, 1972) pp.62, 83-6, 294-5; Garier, *Sous-Marin 2*, p.155, 172; Aldo Fraccoroli, *Italian Warships of World War One* (London: Ian Allen, 1970), p.119.

Vessel	Builder and Completion Date	Joining and leaving dates	Commanders in 1914	Fate
Firedrake	Yarrow, Scotstoun 10 October 1912		Lieut.-Com. Alfred B. Watts	Sold 10 October 1921
Submarines				
D.2	Vickers, Barrow 29 March 1911		Lieut.-Com. Arthur G. Jameson to 23 November; Lieut.-Com. Clement G.W. Head from 23 November	Lost on or after 25 November 1914
D.3	Vickers, Barrow 30 August 1911		Lieut.-Com. Edward C. Boyle to 21 October; Lieut.-Com. Robert R. Turner from 22 October	Sunk 15 March 1918
D.4	Vickers, Barrow 29 November 1911	From refit 23 August	Lieut.-Com. Kenneth M. Bruce to 7 September; Lieut.-Com. John R.G. Moncreiffe from 7 September	Sold 19 December 1921
D.5	Vickers, Barrow 19 January 1912		Lieut.-Com. Godfrey Herbert	Mined 3 November 1914
D.6	Vickers, Barrow 19 April 1912	From refit 22 October	Lieut.-Com. Robert C. Halahan	Sunk 26 June 1918

Vessel	Builder and Completion Date	Joining and leaving dates	Commanders in 1914	Fate
D.7	Chatham Dockyard 14 December 1911		Lieut.-Com. George C. Street to 31 October; Lieut.-Com. Archibald D. Cochrane 31 October–20 November; Lieut.-Com. Brownlow V. Layard from 20 November	Sold 19 December 1921
D.8	Chatham Dockyard 23 March 1912		Lieut.-Com. Theodore S. Brodie to about 3 October; Lieut.-Com. William J. Foster from about 3 October	Sold 19 December 1921
E.1	Chatham Dockyard 6 May 1913	From refit 6 September, to Baltic 17 October	Lieut.-Com. Noel F. Laurence	Scuttled 8 April 1918
E.2	Chatham Dockyard 30 June 1913		Lieut.-Com. David de B. Stocks	Sold 7 March 1921
E.3	Vickers, Barrow 29 May 1914		Lieut.-Com. George F. Cholmley	Sunk 18 October 1914
E.4	Vickers, Barrow 4 January 1913		Lieut.-Com. Ernest W. Leir (promoted Commander 21 October)	Sold 21 February 1922
E.5	Vickers, Barrow 30 June 1913	From abandoned refit 5 August	Lieut.-Com. Charles S. Benning	Sunk 7 March 1916

Vessel	Builder and Completion Date	Joining and leaving dates	Commanders in 1914	Fate
E.6	Vickers, Barrow 15 October 1913		Lieut.-Com. Cecil P. Talbot (promoted Commander 21 October)	Mined 26 December 1915
E.7	Chatham Dockyard 14 March 1914		Lieut.-Com. Ferdinand E.B. Feilmann to 16 November; Lieut.-Com. Archibald D. Cochrane from 20 November	Sunk 5 September 1915
E.8	Chatham Dockyard 13 June 1914		Lieut.-Com. Francis H.H. Goodhart	Scuttled 4 April 1918
E.9	Vickers, Barrow 16 June 1914	To Baltic 18 October	Lieut.-Com. Max K. Horton	Scuttled 4 April 1918
Submarines allocated to the Flotilla after the commencement of hostilities				
D.1	Vickers, Barrow 1 September 1909	From Dover 4th Flotilla 23 August	Lieut.-Com. Archibald D. Cochrane to 31 October; Lieutenant Edward W.B. Ryan from 31 October	Expended as underwater target 23 October 1918
E.10	Vickers, Barrow 10 August 1914	After working up 27 August	Lieut.-Com. William St. J. Fraser	Lost, almost certainly mined 18 January 1915
E.11	Vickers, Barrow 19 September 1914	After working up 2 October	Lieut.-Com. Martin E. Nasmith	Sold 7 March 1921
E.12	Chatham Dockyard 14 October 1914	After working up 17 October	Lieut.-Com. Kenneth M. Bruce	Sold 7 March 1921

Vessel	Builder and Completion Date	Joining and leaving dates	Commanders in 1914	Fate
E.15	Vickers, Barrow 15 October 1914	After working up 5 November	Lieut.-Com. Theodore S. Brodie	Stranded, then destroyed 15 April 1915
C.34	Chatham Dockyard 17 September 1910	From Dover 4th Flotilla 17 November, to Yarmouth 3rd Flotilla 20 December	Lieutenant John F. Hutchings	Sunk 21 July 1917
S.1	Scotts, Clydebank 5 August 1914	From Dover 4th Flotilla 2 December	Lieut.-Com. Gilbert H. Kellett	Discarded by Italian Navy 23 January 1919
C.16	Vickers, Barrow 5 June 1908	From Dover 3rd Flotilla 2 December, to Dover 4th Flotilla 16 December	Lieut.-Com. Geoffrey N. Biggs	Sold 12 August 1922
Archimède (French)	Cherbourg Dockyard 27 September 1911	From French 3e Escadrille 3 December, returned 26 December	Lieutenant de Vaisseau Émile F.M. Deville	Sold 4 October 1921
E.13	Chatham Dockyard 10 December 1914	After working up 15 December	Lieut.-Com. Geoffrey Layton	Stranded 18 August 1915 wreck later sold 14 December 1921

Vessel	Builder and Completion Date	Joining and leaving dates	Commanders in 1914	Fate
C.31	Vickers, Barrow 19 November 1909	From Dover 4th Flotilla 16 December, to Yarmouth 3rd Flotilla 20 December	Lieutenant George Pilkington	Lost, almost certainly mined 4 January 1915
E.14	Vickers, Barrow 1 December 1914	After working up 16 January 1915	Lieut.-Com. Edward C. Boyle	Mined 27 January 1918

Appendix IV

The war patrols of 8th Flotilla in 1914[1]

Date and Objective	Vessels	Results
5–8 August Patrol off Heligoland Bight	*E.6, E.8*	Intelligence gathered on situation in Bight
5–6 August Patrol in Southern Bight and with 7th Cruiser Squadron	*Lurcher, Firedrake, D.3, D.5, E.4, E.9*	None, *D.3* recalled on 5th.
6–8 August Patrol in Southern Bight	*Lurcher, D.3, E.2*	None
9–15 August Covering passage of BEF to France	*Lurcher, Firedrake, D.2, D.3, D.5, D.7, D.8, E.2, E.3, E.4, E.5, E.6, E.7, E.8, E.9*	None

1   TNA ADM137/2067

Date and Objective	Vessels	Results
15–18 August Patrol in Heligoland Bight	D.2, D.3, E.5, E.7	E.5 fired one torpedo at unidentified target, presumed destroyer Intelligence gathered on defensive patrols E.5 and E.7 engaged on surface by light cruiser *Strassburg*
19–22 August Patrol in Heligoland Bight	D.5, E.4, E.9	Intelligence gathered on defensive patrols and cruiser sorties E.4 fired one torpedo at unidentified target, presumed submarine D.5 fired two torpedoes at light cruiser *Rostock*
20–21 August Patrol off Swarte Bank and Smiths Knoll	D.7, E.2, E.3	None
25–26 August Patrol north of the Ems	D.2, D.3, D.7, E.3	Intelligence gathering by D.2 frustrated by fog Other boats limited by fog to patrol between Yarmouth and Terschelling
26–29 August Participating in raid on Heligoland Bight patrols	Lurcher, Firedrake, D.2, D.8, E.4, E.5, E.6, E.7, E.8, E.9	E.7 fired one torpedo at destroyer G.194 E.6 engaged on surface by destroyer V.188 E.6 missed in ramming attack by British light cruiser *Southampton* E.4 rescued 10 crew of British destroyer *Defender* and took three survivors of destroyer V.187 prisoner D.2 fired one torpedo at destroyer G.169 Lurcher and Firedrake rescued and took prisoner 262 survivors from light cruiser *Mainz*
1–5 September Patrol off Heligoland Bight	D.3, D.4, D.5, E.3, E.5, E.8, E.9	Intelligence gathered on defensive patrols E.3 sank a capsized German seaplane and captured the two crewmen
5–8 September Patrol off Terschelling	D.1, D.7, E.10	Intelligence gathered on Ems patrol and Dutch neutrality watch

Date and Objective	Vessels	Results
9–12 September Covering surface attack on Heligoland Bight	Lurcher, Firedrake, D.2, D.8, E.4, E.6, E.7	Revised German defensive patrols in the Bight partially identified D.8 engaged on surface by destroyer G.111 E.4 fired one torpedo each at submarines U.23 and U.25
12–16 September Patrol in Heligoland Bight	D.3, D.5, E.1, E.8, E.9	Patrol arrangements and channels in vicinity of Heligoland identified E.9 sank the scout cruiser Hela with the loss of four crew, with one hit from two torpedoes fired E.8 returned early with defects, damaged by weather on return D.3 badly damaged by weather on return
16–20 September Patrol in Heligoland Bight	D.1, D.7, D.8, E.3, E.10	Intelligence gathered on revised patrol arrangements off the Ems and Heligoland D.7 returned early and damaged by severe gales
22 September–2 October Reconnaissance of the Kattegat	E.1, E.5	No signs of German activity detected E.1 return delayed by defects E.5 fired on off Flamborough Head by British Armed Trawler Ariadne.
22–27 September Patrol in Heligoland Bight	D.2, D.4, E.4, E.6	Intelligence gathered on defensive patrols off the Ems, Schleswig-Holstein coast and Heligoland E.6 fired one torpedo at destroyer G.193 German defensive minefield southwest of Heligoland identified by D.4 and E.6, which escaped from a fouled mine
27 September–1 October Patrol off Terschelling and the Ems	D.3, E.3, E.9	E.3 returned early and damaged by weather D.3 returned early and badly damaged by weather
29 September–5 October Patrol in northern Heligoland Bight	D.5, E.8, E.10	E.8 returned early and damaged by weather E.10 returned early due to weather

Date and Objective	Vessels	Results
30 September–5 October Patrol to Terschelling and southern Heligoland Bight	D.1, E.2, E.7	D.1 returned early due to weather E.7 confirmed extent of minefield between Heligoland and Norderney and destroyed one mine with rifle fire
3–7 October Patrol to Terschelling and southern Heligoland Bight	D.2, E.6, E.9	E.9 sank the destroyer S.116 with the loss of 14 crew, with one hit from two torpedoes fired
3–8 October Patrol in northern Heligoland Bight	D.4, D.8	D.4 returned early due to weather and chlorine gas in boat
6–9 October Defence of Flanders	Lurcher, E.4, E.11	None
6–10 October Patrol to Terschelling and Ems	D.4, E.10	Revised defensive patrols identified off Ems
8–14 October Patrol in northern Heligoland Bight	D.3, E.5	Intelligence gathered on defensive patrol arrangements off German and Danish coast north of Heligoland
9–14 October Patrol to the Ems	D.1, D.5	Intelligence gathered on defensive patrols off the Ems D.5 sighted a submarine heading out on patrol D.1 fired one torpedo at an outpost trawler
10–13 October Defence of Flanders	Firedrake, E.1, E.11	Firedrake sank a drifting mine
10–14 October Patrol to Terschelling	D.8, E.2, E.4	None, D.8 replaced E.4 after she aborted sortie with defects
13–24 October Transit out of theatre for extended patrol in the Baltic	E.1, E.9, E.11	E.1 and E.9 entered the Baltic E.11 fired two torpedoes at the Danish submarine Havmanden and returned to Harwich after considering The Sound impassable

Date and Objective	Vessels	Results
13–17 October Patrol to Terschelling and Ems	D.4, E.6, E.7	Each submarine observed an enemy submarine transit
16–20 October Patrol to Terschelling and Ems	E.3, E.8	E.8 sighted a number of aircraft and the hospital ship Ophelia, but misidentified a German destroyer sortie as Dutch E.3 sunk off the Ems with the loss of all 28 crew by a torpedo fired by U.27
18–23 October Patrol to Terschelling and Ems	D.1, D.3, D.4, D.5, D.8, E.7	D.1 aborted sortie and was replaced by D.4, reason unknown D.3 avoided ramming on the way to the patrol by the cruiser Arethusa D.4 and D.3 observed an enemy submarine in transit
21–25 October Patrol to Terschelling	D.2, E.5	D.2 observed an enemy submarine in transit
23–28 October Covering surface forces in Heligoland Bight	D.1, E.4, E.6	E.4 made four submarine sightings D.1 identified revised destroyer patrols off Heligoland
24–28 October Patrol to Terschelling	D.6	Observed one or two enemy submarines in transit
27–30 October Patrol to Terschelling	E.2	Patrol abandoned early due to heavy seas
29–30 October Abortive Patrol to the Ems	E.8	E.8 forced to return before reaching billet due to salt water in battery

Date and Objective	Vessels	Results
1–9 November Patrol to Terschelling and the Ems, impromptu defence of Gorleston	*D.3, D.5, D.8*	*D.3* and *D.5* held at Gorleston due to adverse weather *D.3* and *D.5* sortied on 3 November in response to German raid on Gorleston. *D.5* sunk with the loss of 21 crew after striking a mine, probably laid by Light Cruiser *Stralsund*. Five survivors rescued by drifters *Faithful* and *Homeland*. *D.3* returned to harbour due to damage and mine danger *D.3* sortied for patrol on the 5th, with *D.8* replacing *D.5*. *D.3* sighted enemy submarine in transit
1–16 November Patrol to the Kattegat, impromptu defence of Gorleston	*E.10*	Held at Gorleston due to adverse weather Sortied on 3 November in response to German raid on Gorleston, but returned to harbour due to mine danger Sortied for patrol on the 5th and confirmed Kattegat clear of German warships
3 November Defence of Gorleston, Harwich and the Thames	*Lurcher, D.2, D.4, D.6, D.8, E.5, E.11, E.12*	None
19–23 November Patrol to the Ems and Heligoland	*E.11, E.12*	*E.11* fired two torpedoes at destroyer *V.181*, identified use of channel west of Heligoland and pattern of patrols off the island *E.12* commenced patrol off Ems late and returned early due to adverse weather
20–22 November Patrol off Zeebrugge Harbour	*C.34*	Confirmed changes in navigation marks and absence of enemy vessels
22–25 November Covering surface forces in Heligoland Bight	*D.2, D.4, D.6, E.5, E.15*	Sortie by *D.2, E.5* and *E.15* abandoned in heavy seas off Yarmouth. Lieut.-Com. Jameson of *D.2* swept overboard and drowned *E.5* damaged by weather *D.4* and *D.6* reported low levels of patrol activity off the Ems

Date and Objective	Vessels	Results
24–26 November Patrol off Zeebrugge Harbour	C.34	Patrol abandoned early due to poor visibility and tide conditions
25 November–1 December Patrol to Heligoland	D.2, E.15	E.15 had one crew member swept overboard and drowned D.2 lost at some point on the patrol from unknown cause, with the loss of all 26 crew
11–13 December Patrol off Zeebrugge Harbour	C.34	None
11 December Patrol off Harwich	C.16, S.1	None
15–20 December Attempt to intercept German Fleet sortie	Lurcher, Firedrake, E.2, E.7, E.8, E.10, E.11, E.12, E.15, Archimède	E.11 fired one torpedo at battleship of 1st Geschwader, almost certainly Ostfriesland, and identified patrol patterns off the Weser Archimède badly damaged by weather
22–27 December Attempt to intercept potential German Fleet sortie	Firedrake, E.2, E.7	Sightings of defensive patrols
23–27 December Patrol in support of carrier launched raid in the Heligoland Bight	Lurcher, Firedrake, D.6, D.7, D.8, E.6, E.10, E.11, E.12, E.13, E.15, S.1	Six drifting mines sunk on the way to the patrol, three by Firedrake, two by E.6, one by D.8 S.1 forced to abandon patrol after losing drop keel in submerged collision on reaching billet Lurcher towed a stranded Short Folder seaplane back to her carrier E.11 rescued five airmen from three stranded British seaplanes, and had two bombs dropped on her position by Zeppelin L.5 whilst submerged E.10 fired two torpedoes at U.32 Lurcher fired 4-inch gun at German seaplane '85'

8th Flotilla submarine activity in 1914

Breakdown of all submarines in Flotilla

Week Commencing

■ Boats Patrolling ☐ Boats Repairing ■ Boats Available for Patrol

Some repairs and refits not identified for boats whose logs are missing

Bibliography

Archival Sources
The National Archives, Kew
ADM 53 Series: HM Ship Logs
ADM 137/51–82: Home Waters Telegrams, 1914
ADM137/818: War Plans and War Orders, Home Fleets and Detached Squadrons, October 1913 to July 1914
ADM 137/1926: Grand Fleet Secret Packs Vol. XLVI – Number 22, Part B – Submarine Committee
ADM 137/1943: Grand Fleet Secret Packs – Pack 0022 Operations – Section O – Miscellaneous Operations and Battles
ADM 137/2018: Grand Fleet Orders and Memoranda – Not for General Distribution
ADM 137/2067: Commodore (S) War Records, Vol. I. Reports of proceedings of submarines attached to HMS Maidstone, 1914
ADM 137/2068: Commodore (S) War Records, Vol. II. Reports of proceedings of submarines attached to HMS Maidstone, 1915
ADM 137/2081: Harwich Force: war records of the Rear Admiral commanding Harwich force (styled Commodore (T)) during the period 1914–1917, Vol. IV, packs 0029 to 0040
ADM 173 Series: HM Submarine Logs
ADM 186/12–46: War Vessels and Aircraft Monthly Returns 1915–1918
ADM 186/15: War Vessels and Aircraft (British and Foreign): Quarterly Return, Oct 1915
ADM 186/366: Addenda (1911) to Torpedo Manual, Vol. III, 1909
ADM 186/610/11: Naval Staff Monographs Vol. III: Monograph 11 – Battle of the Heligoland Bight, August 28th, 1914
ADM 186/610/6: Naval Staff Monographs Vol. III: Monograph 6 – Passage of the BEF, August 1914
ADM 186/619: Naval Staff Monographs Vol. X: Home Waters from the outbreak of War to 27 Aug 1914
ADM 186/620: Naval Staff Monographs Vol. XI: Home Waters – Part II September and October 1914
ADM 186/621: Naval Staff Monographs Vol. XII: Home Waters Part 3 – from November 1914 to the end of January 1915
ADM 188: Royal Navy Registers of Seamen's Services
ADM 189/31: Torpedo School Annual Report 1911
ADM 189/32: Torpedo School Annual Report 1912
ADM 189/33: Torpedo School Annual Report 1913

ADM 189/34: Torpedo School Annual Report 1914
ADM 189/35: Torpedo School Annual Report 1915
ADM 196: Officer's Service Records: Summaries of Confidential Reports
ADM 223/808: Admiralty Monthly Intelligence Reports – 1920

Imperial War Museum (IWM)
Documents.1003: Private Papers of Captain O E Hallifax, 1914 Daily Diary
Documents.2175: Private Papers of Commander F H H Goodhart
Documents.20134: Private Papers of Vice Admiral Sir Cecil Talbot, 1914 Daily Diary
Sound.721: Halter, William (Oral History)

Service Historique de l'État Major de la Marine
2ème Escadre Légère Carton 14: D.M. de l'année 1914
2ème Escadre Légère Carton 25: Correspondance Reçue - Sous-Marin
2ème Escadre Légère Carton 28: Correspondance Reçue - Autorités anglaises

Bundesarchiv, Freiburg
RM64/3: Kriegstagebuch des Ältesten Seebefehlshabers auf der Ems: Abhandlungen und
    Gefechtsberichte
RM92: Schwere und mittlere Kampfschiffe der Preußischen und Kaiserlichen Marine
RM97: Unterseeboote der Kaiserlichen Marine

British Library
AddMS82459: Keyes Papers. Vol. lxxxvii. Reports on co-operation between seaplanes and
    submarines; 1914-1915
AddMS82460: Keyes Papers. Vol. lxxxviii. War orders, disposition, and organisation; 1914-1915
AddMS82461: Keyes Papers. Vol. lxxxix. Submarines: reports by Commodore (S) 31 July–29
    October 1914
AddMS82462: Keyes Papers. Vol. xc. Submarines: reports by Commodore (S) 1 November
    1914–2 February 1915

Royal Navy Submarine Museum
Memoir of Commander Robert Ross Turner

Published Sources
Published Official Histories
Corbett, Julian, *History of the Great War based on official documents – Naval Operations – Vol. 1*
    (London: Longmans, Green and Co., 1920)
Corbett, Julian, *History of the Great War based on official documents – Naval Operations – Vol. 2*
    (London: Longmans, Green & Co., 1921)
Firle, Rudolph, *Der Krieg zur See 1914–1918 – Der Krieg in der Ostsee Band 1* (Berlin: Mittler &
    Sohn, 1921)
Groos, Otto, *Der Krieg zur See 1914–1918 – Der Krieg in der Nordsee Band 1* (Berlin: Mittler &
    Sohn, 1920)

Groos, Otto, *Der Krieg zur See 1914–1918 – Der Krieg in der Nordsee Band 2* (Berlin: Mittler & Sohn, 1922)

Groos, Otto, *Der Krieg zur See 1914–1918 – Der Krieg in der Nordsee Band 3* (Berlin: Mittler & Sohn, 1923)

Published Contemporary Sources

Anon., *Amtliche Kriegs-Depeschen nach Berichten des Wolff'schen Telegr.-Bureaus – Band 1* (Berlin: Nationaler Verlag, 1915)

Anon., *Department of State: Diplomatic Correspondence with Belligerent Governments Relating to Neutral Rights and Duties* (Washington: Government Printing Office, 1916)

Anon., *Geheime Marine Verlustliste* (Berlin: Kaiserliche Marine, published periodically 1914)

Anon., *Official Naval Despatches* (London: The Graphic, 1914)

Anon., *Third Supplement to the London Gazette of Tuesday, the 20th October, 1914* (London: HMSO, 1914)

Carr, William G., *By Guess and by God – The Story of the British Submarines in the Great War* (London: Hutchinson & Co., 1930)

Chatterton, E. Keble, *Amazing Adventure – A Thrilling Naval Biography* (London, Hurst & Blackett Ltd., 1935)

Churchill, Winston S., *The World Crisis 1911–1918 – Vol. 1* (London: Odhams Press, 1938)

Douglas, Stopford C. as Editor, *The Maidstone Magazine – Vol. 1 – 1915* (London: Strangeways and Sons, 1916)

Gilbert, Martin, *Winston S. Churchill: Companion Vol. III, Part 1, July 1914–April 1915* (Boston: Houghton Mifflin Company, 1973)

Jellicoe, John R., *The Grand Fleet 1914–1916: Its Creation, Development and Work* (London: Cassell & Company Ltd., 1919)

Keyes, Roger J. B., *The Naval Memoirs of Admiral of the Fleet Sir Roger Keyes – The Narrow Seas to the Dardanelles 1910–1915* (London: Thornton Butterworth, 1934)

Klaxon, J. G., *The Story of our Submarines* (Edinburgh and London: William Blackwood & Sons, 1919)

Navy Records Society, *The Keyes Papers – Vol. 1 – 1914–1918* (London: William Clowes & Sons Ltd., 1972)

Waldeyer-Hartz, Hugo von (Translated Holt, F.A.), *Admiral von Hipper* (London: Rich & Cowan, 1933)

Secondary Sources

Chalmers, W.S., *Max Horton and the Western Approaches* (London, Hodder & Stoughton, 1954)

Clemmesen, Michael H., 'E11s problemer – HAVMANDENS lykke', Tom Wismann (editor), *Marinehistorisk Tidsskrift, 50* årgang, *Nr. 3 – August 2017* (Marinehistorisk Selskab/ Orlogsmuseetsvenner, 2017)

Compton-Hall, Richard, *Submarines and the War at Sea 1914–18* (London: Macmillan, 1991)

Dittmar, F.J. & Colledge J.J., *British Warships 1914–1919* (London: Ian Allen, 1972)

Fraccoroli, Aldo, *Italian Warships of World War One* (London: Ian Allen, 1970)

Garier, Gérard, *Sous-Marin en France – Tome 2* (Nantes: Marines Edition, 1998)

Garier, Gérard, *Sous-Marin en France – Tome 3 – 2e partie – A l'épreuve de la Grande Guerre* (Nantes: Marines Editions, 2002)

Gröner, Erich, *German Warships 1815–1945 Vol. I: Major Surface Vessels* (London: Conway Maritime Press, 1990)

Labayle-Couhat, Jean, *French Warships of World War One* (London: Ian Allen Ltd., 1974)

Layman, R. D., *The Cuxhaven Raid* (London: Conway Maritime Press, 1985)

Le Nouvelliste du Morbihan, 20 Avril 1933

Marder, Arthur J., *From the Dreadnought to Scapa Flow: Vol. II – The War years to the Eve of Jutland 1914–1916* (London: Oxford University Press, 1965)

Patterson, A. Temple, *Tyrwhitt of the Harwich Force* (London: MacDonald, 1973)

Pavlovich, N. B. (Translated Rao, C. M.), *The Fleet in the First World War (Flot v Pervoi Mirovoi Voine) Vol. 1: Operations of the Russian Fleet* (New Delhi: Amerind Publishing Co. Pvt. Ltd., 1979)

Rayner, D.A., *Escort: the Battle of the Atlantic* (London, William Kimber & Sons Ltd., 1955)

Shankland, Peter & Hunter, Anthony, *Dardanelles Patrol* (London: Collins, 1964)

Wilson, Michael, *Baltic Assignment – British Submarines in Russia 1914–1919* (London: Leo Cooper, 1985)

Wilson, Michael, *Destination Dardanelles – The Story of HMS E 7* (London: Leo Cooper, 1988)

Electronic Sources

The Dreadnought Project <http://www.dreadnoughtproject.org>

Dulwich College <https://dulwichcollege1914-18.co.uk/fallen/halahan-rc/>

Famous Jamesons <http://www.famousjamesons.com>

Harrison, A.N., *The Development of HM Submarines – BR3043* (MOD Ship Department, 1979) from <http://rnsubs.co.uk/dits-bits/br-3043.html>

HMS D5 Off Lowestoft, Suffolk (Wessex Archaeology, 2016) <https://research.historicengland.org.uk>

Life of Cecil Talbot by his son <http://www.maritimequest.com/misc_pages/cecil_p_talbot/vadm_sir_cecil_p_talbot_his_life_above_and_below_the_waves.htm>

Index